Library of
Davidson College

The Newspaper Verse of Philip Freneau

The Newspaper Verse of Philip Freneau:
An Edition and Bibliographical Survey

by

Judith R. Hiltner

The Whitston Publishing Tompany
Troy, New York
1986

Copyright 1986
Judith R. Hiltner

Library of Congress Catalog Card Number 82-50409

ISBN 0-87875-248-X

Printed in the United States of America

CONTENTS

General Introduction
   I. Contents of the edition 1
  II. Format of the Edition 8
 III. Scope of the Research 12
 VI. Attribution 15

Poems and Variants   39

Introduction to the Appendixes 686

Appendix A: Probable Attributions 692

Appendix B: Possible Attributions 719

Appendix C: Unlikely or Erroneous Attributions 781

Bibliography of Newspapers Cited in the Edition and
    Appendixes 799

Bibliography of All Newspapers Examined 803

Index of Poems 813

GENERAL INTRODUCTION

I.
Contents of the edition

The majority of Freneau's known poems, which were collected in five volumes published between 1786 and 1815, first appeared in newspapers printed in the towns and cities where he lived, worked, and travelled. In his 1941 biography, *That Rascal Freneau,* Lewis Leary included a comprehensive bibliography, locating the earliest newspaper texts of many of Freneau's poems, as well as subsequent newspaper reprints. An examination of the earliest newspaper texts reveals that most of them vary substantively from all collected versions. Some of the newspaper texts were altered slightly, while others were rewritten almost completely, when Freneau first included them in a collection. Moreover, many newspaper reprints of his poems actually were authorial revisions, containing variants, some of which appeared later in his collected texts. With the publication of Freneau's original collections by Scholars' Facsimiles and Reprints, all variants among the collected texts of Freneau's poems are accessible to students of the poet. With this edition, supplying the original newspaper texts and subsequent newspaper variants of his poems, all texts of Freneau's poems, excluding separately published pieces, will for the first time be readily available to Freneau scholars.

The edition includes, in chronological order, the earliest newspaper texts of Freneau's collected poems, as well as lists of all subsequent newspaper variants, excluding variants appearing in texts that were merely reprinted by newspaper editors from one of Freneau's collections.[1] I am deeply indebted to, and have

---

[1] In the case of most poems included in this volume, almost all of

followed, Leary's bibliography in locating the earliest newspaper texts of Freneau's poems. This edition, however, supplements that bibliography: it includes newspaper texts of poems not included in Leary's list, earlier newspaper appearances for several poems, than those noted by Leary, and occasional corrections of dates and locations of newspaper texts.

In citing newspaper variants from the first published newspaper texts, I have noted substantive variants, that is, *word* changes, and I also have noted changes in stanza form, that is, changes in stanza division and line indentation. Accidental variants—changes in punctuation, spelling, capitalization, word emphasis (italics or large and small capitals), and the use of quotation marks—are not cited, because they could not be conveyed without duplicating every newspaper text of every Freneau poem. Given the variations in practices among printers of Freneau's day, it would be impossible to determine which accidental variants were authorized by Freneau. Some printers, for instance, never employed small capitals, and some italicized the title of every poem included in their columns. Although variations in stanza form technically might be considered "accidental" variants, authorial approval of major revisions in the layout of a poem is easier to document than other formal variants. Among the several collected texts of Freneau's poems,

---

which were first published in newspapers before Freneau collected them, I have not cited newspaper variants appearing in reprints merely extracted by editors, without alteration, from one of Freneau's collections, as these texts are available, and as the earlier newspaper text is provided here. I have, however, cited variants in newspaper texts appearing after the poem was first collected when there is evidence of authorial revision. Also, in order to indicate the full range of Freneau's poems that appeared in newspapers, I have noted the initial newspaper appearance of poems which *first* were published in one of his collections, or in separate pamphlet or broadside form, and *later* reprinted in papers. If the later newspaper text does not vary from the earlier collected or separately published version, I have noted only the title of the poem, the newspaper, and the date of the poem's appearance. If the later newspaper text does vary from the earlier collected or separately published version, a list of all variants from the earlier text is provided.

many demonstrate variants in stanza form, proving that Freneau habitually experimented with different layouts for his verses. Although newspaper editors may have changed the layout in reprinting a Freneau poem simply to fit the poem into their columns, when a change in stanza form occurs in a text demonstrating other substantive variants, we have grounds for assuming authorial approval for the change in stanza form. For the most part, then, I have noted changes in stanza form only in newspaper texts which demonstrate other substantive variants. A compelling reason for this policy was my discovery of variations in stanza form in otherwise unaltered texts reprinted in papers to which Freneau never was known to contribute, and probably would not or could not have contributed.

In addition to the original newspaper texts and subsequent newspaper variants of Freneau's poems, the main edition also annotates useful or interesting editorial comments appearing with the poems and information about the poems derived exclusively from my study of the newspapers themselves. The edition is not "annotated" in the sense of providing background material or explanatory comments with respect to allusions, content, theme or style of the poems. I note information about the poems derived solely from the newspapers in which they appeared or from other newspapers printed during the period. Several of Freneau's poems, for instance, were written in direct response to articles, editorials, or poems printed in rival newspapers. The substance of these "newspaper interchanges" is annotated, providing the newspaper background of several of Freneau's poems.

The edition includes only those poems that appeared in periodical publications; it excludes broadsides and other separately published pieces. Several of Freneau's news-carrier New Year poems, for instance, although addressed to the patrons of particular papers, never were published in the papers themselves but only as broadsides. These texts are not included in the edition.[2]

---

[2] In the attribution appendixes, however, several such poems are cited, as they actually did appear in a regular January issue of a newspaper.

Also excluded from the main volume and appendixes are the prose "epitaphs" that occasionally have been attributed to Freneau as poetry. These are really prose sentences, regarded as poems only because they were printed in a "tombstone stanza"—clauses typed in alternately long and short, indented lines as if engraved on a tombstone. Finally, also excluded from the edition is mention of unaltered reprints of Freneau's poems. Eighteenth century editors excerpted much of their material, especially poems, from other newspapers. During certain periods, Freneau's poems were very widely reprinted, particularly in Philadelphia, New York, and New Jersey papers. In his bibliography, Leary records hundreds of newspaper reprints. In the course of my research, I examined almost all of the reprints cited by Leary, checking for possible variants, and discovered scores of additional unaltered reprints as well. I have recorded all of these reprints, but have not listed them here because of their negligible usefulness to students of the poet.

Before concluding this description of the contents of the edition, a few words are in order respecting the authority of the newspaper variants that I have cited. How do we know that changes appearing in newspaper reprints of his poems were actually penned or authorized by Freneau? Obviously, an editor is most confident about those newspaper variants that reappear in later collected texts of the poems. However, as the appendixes to this volume indicate, Freneau probably contributed more poems to newspapers than he later collected, and, accordingly, probably made more "transitional" revisions in newspaper texts than ever appeared in later collected versions. For instance, occasionally we find a newspaper reprint containing revisions only some of which reappear in the later collected version, proving that he used newspapers, in part, as a "workshop" in revising particular texts, eventually rejecting some of the transitional revisions which he had made in earlier newspaper versions.

My policy, then, in citing newspaper variants of poems known to be Freneau's but lacking proof of authorial approval is admittedly looser than my general criteria for including the complete texts of poems. As my comments on attribution will indicate, I have excluded from the main volume poems never collected or signed by Freneau, however much evidence they may reveal of his authorship. But since, in the main volume, we are dealing with poems known to be Freneau's, and since the collected texts prove that he habitually revised his verses, we have some basis for assuming his approval of variants in poems which he acknowledged as his own, especially those appearing in papers to which he frequently contributed.

The authority of the variants is greatest, of course, for those revisions which later appeared in collected texts. Next in authoritativeness are those variants which never appeared in later collected texts but which appeared in newspaper texts containing variants which did, in fact, appear in later collected texts. Less authoritative than this type of variant are those that never appeared in later collected texts but that nonetheless appeared in texts printed in papers to which Freneau contributed original verses. Finally, last in degree of authority are those variants appearing in newspapers in a *context* that might imply authorial revision. For instance, in the *Port Folio's* extended review of Freneau's poems, October-November, 1807, several of the texts quoted contain variants from all previous newspaper or collected versions. For example, when it first was published in the *Freeman's Journal* on February 16, 1785, one line in the poem "To a Deceased Dog," read "That this kitchen of death is your place of repose." In the 1795 collected text, the line read, "That a mile from the church is your place of repose!" In the *Port Folio* excerpt, October 24, 1807, this line read, "That a mile from my cot is your place of repose!" Finally, in the 1808 collection, the line read, "That here you must take an eternal repose!" Although the *Port Folio* variant may have been invented by the editor of that paper, it seems possible that in preparing the review the editor requested the poet to authorize the texts to be quoted and that, in complying, Freneau made some revisions. The variant does not sound unlike Freneau, since in several of his poems he refers to his "cot." The newspaper context of the variant, then—in this case an extended review of his verses and a new revision in a line that Freneau repeatedly altered in other authorized texts—may provide a basis for assuming the probability of otherwise questionable variants.

Similarly, the newspaper context could bolster the probability of questionable variants when they appear in papers edited by personal acquaintances of the poet. Many of Freneau's poems reprinted in Matthew Carey's *American Museum,* for instance, contain grammatical revisions—most typically the relative pronoun "that" altered to "who" where appropriate. Although such changes may have been the result of editorial liberties taken with reprinted material, we know that on at least one occasion Freneau personally requested Carey to make a correction in reprinting an earlier text of his "Verses on General Washington's Arrival...", asking him to replace the objective with the nominative case of a pronoun.[3]

At least one other factor bears on the authoritativeness of the variants cited in this volume. Typically, newspaper reprints appearing shortly after the earliest newspaper texts of Freneau's poems do not contain variants, because editors merely extracted the poem from the paper in which it first appeared. However, in several cases, mostly after 1800, clearly authorized variants, later included in Freneau's collected texts of several poems, appeared in poems published in other papers only a few days after the earliest newspaper text and occasionally on the same day, proving that he sometimes contributed variant texts to two or more papers at the same time.

In general, then, I have listed all substantive variants appearing in newspaper reprints of Freneau's poems, excluding those merely reprinted from later collected texts and those reflecting obvious typesetting errors like deleted or nonsensical words. Hopefully, the lists include all the variants authorized by Freneau, although they may also include some he did not authorize. I advise the editor or critic using this edition to consider the following questions in assessing the authority of the variants cited: Do the variants appear in later collected tests? Do the variants occur in a text containing other variants that appear in later collected versions? Do the variants appear in a paper to which Freneau contributed first or revised versions of other poems? Does the newspaper context of the reprint make authorial revision probable? It should be noted that a close examination of the main volume reveals revised reprints recurring repeatedly in a small corpus of newspapers; ten or fifteen different papers are

---

[3] See C. T. Hallenbeck, "A Note for Future Editors of Freneau's Poems," *American Literature*, IV (1933), pp. 91-93.

cited again and again in my lists of variants, suggesting that Freneau occasionally did make revisions when his poems were reprinted in a number of papers he did not himself control. At the least, this edition locates the variant texts for the future editor or critic of the poet, who may uncover additional grounds for accepting or rejecting the authority of particular variants.

In concluding my description of the contents of the main volume, I acknowledge that this edition reverses the standard editorial practice of providing as copy text the last text authorized by a writer, and of annotating earlier variants. Later collected versions of Freneau's poems already are accessible to students of the poet, and no editor has yet provided a record of earlier newspaper variants. As a comparison of all newspaper texts provided here to the earliest collected versions indicates, the total amount of revision is so great that it necessarily would strain any feasible policy for annotating earlier newspaper variants in a complete edition of the poet. Consequently, a separate edition of newspaper texts and variants is necessary for complete access to Freneau's entire published work. This edition enables students of the poet to examine, in the earliest published texts, the "germ" of his later collected poetry and the entirety of his precollection revisions. Some texts included here, particularly those which first appeared in the *Freeman's Journal* from 1781 to 1784, were not altered at all in Freneau's first collection (1786). Even among these early poems, however, there are several that underwent major revisions in the 1786 collection, including "The Beauties of Santa Cruz" and "The House of Night." In the case of some later poems, where a longer time gap exists between the first newspaper and the first collected texts, the newspaper poem has been so completely revised that, in a complete edition of the poet, the earlier text might require separate editing in view of the fact that a majority of the lines never reappeared in any later published form. For instance, many poems published by Freneau between 1796 and 1800, but not collected until 1809 or 1815, were almost completely rewritten.

II.
Format of the Edition

The poems are arranged chronologically, by earliest newspaper appearance. At the outer margin appears the name of the paper and the date of the issue containing the earliest text of the poem. The title and full text are then provided. If revised reprints of the poem subsequently appeared in newspapers, excluding unaltered reprints of collected texts, the newspapers in which they appeared and the dates of their appearances are cited beneath the initial text. These newspaper titles and dates are indented to distinguish them from the citation provided for the initial text. A list of substantive variants in the revised reprint is included underneath each indented newspaper citation. Occasionally, the earliest text and the list and description of revised reprints covers several pages, but the reprint citations and lists of variants are all printed at the inner margin. Consequently, a citation for a revised reprint should not be mistaken for a citation for a first appearance, as it will not be printed at the *outer* margin, and it will not be followed by a complete text.

Freneau's notes to his poems appear at the end of the text in a single page text, or at the bottom of each page in a multi-page text. His notes appear at the *inner* margin, the margin of the text of the poem. I have not duplicated the original newspaper footnote symbols, but instead have employed only single and double asterisks or addition signs (+). My own notes are numbered and appear at the bottom of the page at the *outer* margin, with the earliest newspaper citation. I rarely have footnoted Freneau's texts with my own notes, so my notes cannot be mistaken for his. Generally, when I have supplied information about a particular poem, I have placed the footnote number directly after the newspaper citation at the top of the page. Those comments which appear in parentheses before the text or title of a poem are not taken directly from the original source. I have employed parentheses to set off my own summaries of and occasionally quotations from prose comments that appeared in a newspaper as an introduction to a poem. Everything that appears within brackets in this edition, either within the texts or titles of poems or around quoted portions of prose introductions, is duplicated from the original source.

In all cases, except for obvious typesetting errors, this edition duplicates the original newspaper spellings. However, the original distinctions in word emphasis—large and small capitals and italics—are not precisely duplicated. In comparing the first newspaper texts, reprints, and collected texts of Freneau's poems, I observed that although small capitals and italics often were employed interchangeably, large capitals tended to remain constant in all versions. Consequently, although large capitals are here duplicated, most words set in small capitals in the original newspaper texts are italicized in this edition. The only exception to this policy occurs when an original newspaper line or title contained *both* italics and small capitals. In such cases, the line appears in italics and *large* capitals respectively in order to duplicate the original emphasis. In few cases where an original newspaper line or title contained three distinctions in word emphasis—italics, small and large capitals—the line is here printed in italics, regular type, and large capitals respectively in order to duplicate the distinctions. In the rare instances where a single line or title contained four distinctions in word emphasis—regular type, italics, small and large capitals—this edition indicates only three distinctions, both the original italicized and small capital letters printed as italics. Also, in the few instances where an entire newspaper text appeared in italics, it here appears in regular type. Similarly, if the entire text, except for a few words in regular type, was set in italics, the entire text is printed here in regular type, except for the few words originally appearing in regular type, which are here italicized. In short, I have attempted to duplicate Freneau's distinctions in emphasis, though not always the original form of the distinction.

After each complete newspaper text, I have cited at the outer margin the location of the earliest collected text, in order to verify that the poem is Freneau's. If revised reprints appeared before the first collected text, the citation for the collected text appears after the descriptions of earlier reprints. I have not cited the location of the poems in later collections. The majority of poems in this edition are cited in Leary's bibliography in *That Rascal Freneau*, which supplies the locations of all collected texts of poems originally published in newspapers.

In many cases, the first collected version that I have cited constitutes a major revision of the newspaper text, but, so long as a majority of the original lines and the basic sense of the original poem remains intact in the later poem, the newspaper text is indisputably the forerunner of the later text. In a few cases, however, most or even *all* of the lines have been revised, yet I have still regarded the newspaper text as an earlier version of the collected poem cited for most or all of the following reasons: both poems have the same title; both develop the same idea in the same manner; both contain at least a few of the same lines, or lines so similar that the later are obviously a revision of the earlier by the same poet. In short, the poems are so similar that they could not have been penned by two different poets, the earlier poem merely the source of or an influence upon the later. In these few cases, however, where practically every line has been revised, or where almost all of the original newspaper lines have been completely discarded I have noted that the original newspaper text might require separate editing in a complete edition of the poet's work, simply because most of the lines never reappear in any later published form.

Readers should be advised of the method I have used for describing variant newspaper texts published after the original newspaper text provided here. In each case, the text being described is the *revised reprint;* unless I note otherwise, I am describing how this text *differs* from the earlier text, which has been provided.[4] All stanza numbers, or line numbers, cited at the left hand margin refer to stanzas or lines in the *reprint.* For instance, assume that an original text contained four stanzas and that a revised reprint of that text contained all four of those stanzas, two of which were slightly revised, plus a new stanza inserted between the original second and third stanzas. My description of the revised reprint would follow the entire text of the first newspaper appearance and would read as follows:

---

[4] In several instances, which I have noted, when describing a reprint published after a collected text, I describe variants from the collected text rather than from the original newspaper text given here.

Newspaper Title   Date of Revised Reprint
    New Title (if altered from the original)
Stanza 1:   First stanza of the original text, with the following variants:
          line 1: ....,
          line 2: ....!
Stanza 2:   Second stanza of the original text.
Stanza 3:   Entire text of the *new* stanza will be typed here.
Stanza 4:   Third stanza of the original text, with the following variants:
          line 2: ....?
Stanza 5:   Last stanza of the original text.

In cases where the revised reprint differs only slightly from the original text, containing the same stanzas in the same order with only a few variant lines, I have only cited thsoe stanzas containing the revised lines, as follows:

Newspaper Title   Date of Revised Reprint
Stanza 2, line 2: ....,

If a stanza of the original newspaper text has been entirely deleted from the revised reprint, no reference to it will appear in the description of the reprint, and I will note the deletion at the end of the description.

The same procedure has been employed when only *excerpts* of an original text were reprinted in a version containing variants from the excerpted portions of the original text. For instance, on July 3, 1797, Freneau reprinted, in the *Time-Piece,* only four stanzas from a much longer poem, "The Political Balance," first published in the *Freeman's Journal* on April 3, 1782. The four stanzas, which were originally stanzas 25-28 of the longer text, were altered slightly in the excerpt. I have presented the excerpt as follows:

Time-Piece   July 3, 1797
(Four stanza extract, stanzas 25-28 of the above text, including the following variants:)
Stanza 2, line 2: ....,
        line 4: ....
Stanza 3, line 1: ....,

Stanza 3, line 2: . . . . ,
Stanza 4, line 1: . . . . ,
line 2: . . . . ,

Again, the stanza numbers on the left refer to the order of stanzas in the reprinted extract.

As noted in the first section of this introduction, I have cited variations in stanza form when they occur in revised reprints. Unless I specifically mention a revision's stanza form, the reader may assume that the revised reprint was printed in the same stanza form as the original newspaper text.

III.
Scope of the Research

In searching for the first newspaper appearances and revised reprints of Freneau's poems I examined a wide range of late eighteenth and early nineteenth century American newspapers. As I was primarily attempting to locate the earliest newspaper texts of Freneau's known poems, rather than poems he may have written after 1815, the date of his last collection, I concentrated upon the years 1775-1815. I attempted to examine the complete files of all newspapers published during these years in cities and towns where Freneau is known to have lived, worked, or travelled, as well as every newspaper, wherever it was published, in which reprints of his poems have been cited by earlier bibliographers. My sources for identifying and locating the papers included *Charles S. Brigham's Bibliography of American Newspapers, 1690-1820, The Union List of Newspapers, Newspapers in Microform*, as well as the catalogues of the libraries at the institutions and historical societies which I visited. With few exceptions, my entire research was in American newspapers; the only magazines that I examined were those in which first appearances, revisions, extracts or reprints of Freneau's poems have been cited by earlier bibliographers.

I have included two bibliographies after the appendixes

Introduction: Scope of the Research 13

to this edition that describe which papers I examined and how extensively I examined them. The first bibliography, an alphabetical list of all papers cited in the edition and appendixes, is provided for anyone who wishes to see the original of any text that I have duplicated or cited. In this first bibliography, I have indicated the libraries in which I found the papers containing poems duplicated or cited in the edition and appendixes. Although the same papers may be found in other libraries as well, they can certainly be found either in the original or in microform or photostat at the location I cite. I provide the locations here because I found that every location guide I used was outdated in some way, as some libraries have sold or otherwise transferred some of their holdings. The second bibliography lists, by state and city of publication, all of the papers that I examined, as well as the years of publication for which I studied each.

As a survey of my two bibliographies will indicate, I attempted to examine all papers in the following classes, some of which overlap:

1. All papers in which previous bibliographers have located a first appearance or revised reprint of a Freneau poem.

2. Most papers in which previous bibliographers have noted a reprint of a Freneau poem.

3. All New York, New Jersey, and Philadelphia papers published between 1775 and 1815.

4. All papers published between 1784 and 1790 and between 1800 and 1809 in coastal cities or towns where Freneau was known to or may have docked during his years at sea.

5. All papers published in Charleston, South Carolina, between 1784 and 1809.

6. All papers published after 1815 in which a first appearance or a revised reprint of a Freneau poem appeared before 1815.

7. All papers published after 1815 in which a first appearance or reprint of any poem ever attributed to Freneau has been

cited.

8. All papers published in the Trenton-New Brunswick-Monmouth County area after 1815.

Although comprehensive, the scope of my research was not absolutely exhaustive. Over 150 poems collected by Freneau, about ninety of which were first published in the 1815 collection, never have been located in newspapers previous to the time of the collection. While it is possible that Freneau never contributed any of them to newspapers, the primary period still open for the discovery of possible newspaper texts would seem to be the years 1800-1815, when the majority of poems in the last collection first might have been published, particularly all of the poems pertaining to the War of 1812. Although I have examined almost all papers known to have been published in New York, New Jersey, Philadelphia, and other towns where Freneau travelled during the years 1775-1815, a paper may have been published in these areas which is unknown to me, and which carried some of his later poems. It is also possible that a more comprehensive study of papers published in other places than those towns and cities where we might expect to find a Freneau poem could reveal a Freneau text, perhaps reprinted from a more likely paper, the original of which has not survived. Such a study might also locate other interesting editorial comments appearing with reprints of his poems and, finally, might supply evidence supporting or weakening attributions of uncollected poems that have been ascribed to Freneau. An earlier appearance of the poem in a distant newspaper ascribed to another poet, for instance, would make the attribution unlikely. Further, a more comprehensive study than my own of New York, New Jersey and Philadelphia papers published between 1815 and 1832 might reveal other probable Freneau attributions—poems in his manner, on themes he pursued, signed with pseudonyms that have been identified with him. Such a study might also uncover evidence that would support or undermine attributions of post-1815 poems that already have been made. Finally, a study of magazines, other than those I have examined, for the entire period 1775-1832 might uncover other first appearances or revised reprints of poems known to be Freneau's or of probable attributions. However, although Leary apparently surveyed magazines as well as newspapers in compiling his bibliography, he records findings in only

Introduction: *Scope of the Research* 15

a handful of magazines, all of which I have examined.

To summarize this discussion of the scope of my research: I have examined the late eighteenth century (1775-1800) and early nineteenth century (1800-1815) holdings, as well as the partial 1815-1832 holdings previously described, either in original, photostat, or microform, in the libraries of the following institutions and societies:[5]

> American Antiquarian Society
> Charleston (S.C.) Library Society
> Harvard University
> Library Company of Philadelphia
> Library of Congress
> Maryland Historical Society
> Maryland University
> Monmouth County Historical Society
> New Jersey Historical Society
> New Jersey State Library
> New York Historical Society
> New York Public Library
> Pennsylvania Historical Society
> Rutgers University (New Brunswick)

IV.
Attribution[6]

The main volume of this edition includes the complete initial newspaper texts and all subsequent substantive news-

---

[5] Since many of these holdings overlap, it should be noted that approximately three-fourths of my research was done at the Library of Congress.

[6] The following comments on the problems involved in attributing uncollected, unsigned poems to Freneau are the product of a careful examina-

paper variants of all poems that can be indubitably ascribed to Freneau. Months of research in hundreds of newspapers of the period have persuaded me that the only indubitable basis of ascription is the poet's own acknowledgement of his original verse in the five collections compiled between 1786 and 1815, or in the few uncollected poems published under his full signature. This restricted basis of ascription is the product of my research; it was not established "a priori" and did not restrict the scope of my investigation. Because previous editors have collected verses uncollected by Freneau—Pattee in *The Poems of Philip Freneau,* Leary in *Last Poems of Philip Freneau,* and Marsh in *A Freneau Sampler*—I was prepared to consider for inclusion in this edition all verses that definitely or tentatively have been ascribed to Freneau by any previous Freneau scholar. But my investigation forced me to restrict the basis of attribution because I discovered evidence that proved a significant number of former attributions either erroneous or unlikely, because I discovered evidence that weakened the theories or basic assumptions under which uncollected texts have been attributed to Freneau, and because my observations of the manner in which pseudonyms or initials were employed in newspapers of the period persuaded me that they are not a reliable index to any poet's original work.

Poems have been attributed to Freneau primarily on the basis of some or all of the following criteria: 1) they are in his manner and pursue themes developed in his known poems; 2) they appeared in newspapers during a period when other poems later collected by Freneau were appearing; 3) they were signed with pseudonyms or initials which also appeared with the newspaper texts of other poems later collected by Freneau; 4) they were ascribed to him by his contemporaries. As my Appendix of Erroneous or Unlikely Attributions indicates, examples

---

tion of all such poems that have been ascribed to Freneau, as well as a large portion of all other poetry published in American newspapers from 1775-1832. Every poem that has been ascribed to Freneau by scholars of the poet is discussed, individually, in the attribution appendixes following the main volume. The appendixes provide the exact source of every attribution, including those mentioned in this discussion.

can be cited to prove each of these criteria fallible. My purpose here is to describe the general problems encountered in applying each of these four bases of attribution. The conclusions I have drawn are the sum of each particular instance of an erroneous or unlikely attribution. I encourage the reader to examine all three of my attribution appendixes, a careful survey of which will document more specifically and fully the general comments provided here.

(1)
Freneau's Manner and Themes

Most poems have been ascribed to Freneau primarily on the grounds that in style, subject and manner of treatment, they are similar to poems included in Freneau's collections. I believe, however, that in attributing poems to Freneau on the basis of style or manner, previous ascribers have not defined sufficiently what they mean, exactly, by the phrase "in his manner," which has been employed widely in the attribution lists and footnotes of several previous Freneau scholars, and which I also have employed repeatedly in my own appendixes.

In the most general sense, Freneau's "manner" is the manner of countless other poets publishing in American newspapers and magazines in the late eighteenth century, all influenced by the major traditions established by eighteenth century British poets in the first three-quarters of the century—Pope, Swift, Thomson, Gray, Collins and Goldsmith among the foremost. Like those of all other satirists publishing in American newspapers of the period, Freneau's satirical poems, generally on political subjects, are penned in couplets—either pentameter or tetrameter, usually end-stopped. In their general manner, they are distinguishable from the countless other satires published during the period only by their relative degree of competence, just as the work of any practiced poet can be distinguished from the occasional effusion of the amateur. Like those of all writers experienced in the couplet, Freneau's couplets do not scan evenly as, at his best, he demonstrates the mark of the skilled couplet writer—the ability to speak naturally, and in his case colloquially, within an artificial form, mixing iambs and anapests just as they are mixed in natural speech and dialogue. However, all satire that has survived from the period—verses penned by Trumbull, Brackenridge and Humphreys—at least in parts, demonstrates the marks of a practiced satirist. Moreover, in reading through the newspaper columns of the period, I have found specimens of remarkably good satire, often widely reprinted, which has never been attributed to any poet.

Similarly, in its general stylistic characteristics, Freneau's nonsatirical newspaper verses—his many poems on popular, topical subjects for popular audiences, as well as the reflective or philosophical pieces that he occasionally published—are structurally similar to the many other poems exploiting the stanza forms inherited from Pope, Gray, Collins and Goldsmith, frequently either in tetrameter couplets, or in four or six line stanzas with conventional rhyme schemes—AABB, ABAB, ABABCC, ABCABC, and AABCCB.

Obviously, then, when Freneau scholars who have examined a wide range of the newspaper poetry published during the period refer to "the manner of Freneau," they are alluding to a manner more characteristic than the stanza form, meter or rhyme scheme employed in his verses. The key question, then, respecting the phrase "in his manner," is—what distinguishes Freneau's newspaper poems from all other poems appearing in newspapers of the period? My study indicates that there are, in fact, identifiable and describable characteristics that seem to mark a Freneau poem, that probably have been the basis for the numerous attributions that have been made in the past on the general grounds that they are "in his manner," and that provide the basis for my use of the term in my appendixes of probable and possible attributions.

In general, Freneau's popular newspaper poetry is *more* colloquial, conversational, seemingly casual or "unforced," and self-assured, and *less* self-consciously "poetic" or artificial, less forced or stilted, than the majority of other verses appearing in newspapers of the period. His poetry employs a more sensual or physical vocabulary, and it is more *active,* demonstrating a far wider range of strong verbs than most other newspaper poetry. In sum, it is less fastidious or "polite" and more lively than most other newspaper poetry published in the last quarter of the eighteenth century. His poetry is uniquely conversational and colloquial in the extent to which it takes the form of monologues or one-sided conversations addressed to whatever person or object is the subject of the poem. One notes how many of his poems are titled "*To* someone or something," "*On* someone or something," and "*For* someone or something,"—and his purpose is always to talk to that person or thing, to tell them something in the most convincing manner, adapting the tone to the assumed listener and to the message being conveyed. In a sense, Freneau's lighter verses, in part, seem to have provided him with a means for communicating with people or things he could not literally talk to in life, be it an almanack maker, George Washington, a bee, a river, the keeper of the king's water-works, a fly, a young Quaker lady, young ladies who neglect the dentist, or his dead dog. Quotation marks appear in his poems more frequently than in the verses of other poets, as he talks and talks to his subjects or to his readers. Few other newspaper poets of the period demonstrate such natural conversational ease.

In many of his newspaper poems, when he is not addressing a person or thing in his own voice, Freneau demonstrates an ability unique among newspaper poets of the period to put himself in the place of others and to speak in their voices. From the *Freeman's Journal* to the *Time-Piece,* he published monologues, soliloquies, and dialogues where he speaks in the voices of the young and old, of men and women, of the celebrated and the obscure—George III, Lords Dunmore and Mansfield, Palemon and Lavinia, two housemaids, a landlord, a drunkard, a father of marriageable daughters, a debtor. He even speaks convincingly for inanimate objects like planets and moons. Again, this casual and confident imaginative flexibility is unique among poets publishing in American newspapers during the period. The manner I am describing, the ability to speak directly and naturally to and for other people and things, though most apparent in his lighter popular verses, also marks his most scathing satires as well as the poems on philosophical themes that he occasionally contributed to newspapers.

Like the general formal qualities of his poems, many of the popular subjects treated in Freneau's newspaper poetry also were exploited by other poets of the period. Obviously, all of the national and local political events that inspired much of

Freneau's newspaper verse also inspired other poets as well. A significant number of the unlikely or erroneous attributions listed in Appendix C are those on political subjects or themes typical among Freneau's known poems. It is easy, for instance, to attribute to Freneau any pro-French, pro-Jefferson, pro-Republican or anti-Federalist, anti-Hamilton poem appearing in the columns of the *National Gazette* or the *Time-Piece;* however, as even as cursory study of newspapers of the period indicates, there were entire "schools" of poets representing and defending each end of the political spectrum, and, given the sharply divided political commitments of newspaper editors of the period, each end attracted volumes of polemical political verses from poets who agreed with the editor. Further, editors of the same political bias reprinted much material, including political verses, from each other, as a close survey of the Philadelphia *General Advertiser,* Philadelphia *Aurora,* Greenleaf's *New York Journal,* and Freneau's *National Gazette* and *Time-Piece* during the 1790's will indicate. All of these were liberal, Republican papers and some of the political poems that have been attributed to Freneau on the basis of their appearing in the *National Gazette* actually were printed first in, and were extracted by Freneau from, one of these other papers. Even his contemporaries mistakenly attributed to him poems appearing in Freneau's papers on republican themes or poems attacking Federalists: the Probationary Odes in the *National Gazette,* penned by Virginia judge St. George Tucker in imitation of the British satirist John Wolcot ("Peter Pindar"), were widely attributed to Freneau on the basis of their themes as well as their manner.[7]

But even themes which might be thought more peculiar to Freneau were handled by other poets—sea voyages and hazards at sea were among the more popular themes of the period; and we can find other verses, for instance, on a village merchant, the labor of printers, the death of Captain Biddle, the death of blacksmiths, and a number of other specific subjects treated by Freaneau. In fact, as several of my notes to poems in this edition indicate, several of his poems on popular subjects appear to have

---

[7]Wolcot's influence on Freneau occasionally was cited by newspaper editors of the period when reprinting several of Freneau's known poems.

been directly inspired or influenced by earlier newspaper poems, apparently not his, on the same subjects. Again it is possible to detect, in some of Freneau's poems on subjects also handled by other poets, the same distinguishing characteristics previously described. In treating topical events, such as the removal of Congress from New York to Philadelphia, only Freneau, it seems, would think of discussing the issue from the perspective of two house maids; or in treating the bill to remove trees within the city limits of New York, to lament the loss in the voice of a landlord.

However, though it is possible to identify distinguishing characteristics in Freneau's handling of popular themes, two major considerations generate reservations respecting the attribution and editing of uncollected texts that seem indubitably "in Freneau's manner." The first is the ubiquitous practice of imitation among newspaper poets of the period, the second the extreme liberties assumed by editors with unsigned or pseudonymously signed materials extracted from other sources.

As even a brief survey of any American newspaper that published poetry in the last quarter of the eighteenth century reveals, a widely practiced technique was that of imitating the work of other poets. Because so many newspaper verses treated occasional and topical subjects, to be of interest they had to appear shortly after the event, a fact that did not allow much time for original composition. Casual imitations of other poets were easier to write than original verse: the meter, rhyme scheme and general pattern of development were already provided; the poet had only to insert the names and details of the contemporary situation. The appeal of such poems lay primarily in the cleverness or wittiness of their application of a recognized poet's manner to a situation he never could have addressed. The reader was expected to recognize the amusing disparity between the source and the application. Imitations also appealed to American readers because they enabled natives to hear the voice of beloved English poets addressing aspects of Yankee life, as if Goldsmith himself was describing the life of a Long Island village merchant. Imitations brought the admired traditions of eighteenth century English verse home to America. More serious imitations, of course, like Freneau's imitation of *Horace, Lib.* II. *Ode* 16, addressed to Governer Parr, aroused a different sort of interest.

They tried to persuade the reader that the judgments or criticisms of a poet of an earlier age retained a disturbing or telling application to contemporary life. By writing imitations, then, newspaper poets of the period knew they could provide immediate and easy pleasure for popular readers without much labor or risk of rebuke. The verses did not pretend to be original and were not taken as such. Anyone who liked the source of the poem probably would enjoy the imitation. Their popularity and broad application, plus the ease and speed with which they could be written, probably accounts for the frequency with which imitations appeared in American newspapers of the period.

Many of the poems that have been attributed to Freneau actually are imitations of the works of other identifiable poets. Others may also be imitations the originals of which have not survived, as we occasionally find newspaper poets of the period imitating one another as well as celebrated British poets. After Freneau's 1786 collection was published, for instance, several poems that appear to be direct imitations of Freneau's "The Power of Fancy" were printed in American newspapers. They are in the same stanza form and meter used by Freneau and consist of a similar listing of the various powers of fancy and the places it can take us. In Connecticut, Freneau's "The Retort" was paraphrased as "Advice to the Wits and Poets with variations for the latitudes and longitudes of Connecticut" by a poet addressing a local political contest. Several poems on blacksmiths followed the device, originated by Freneau in "Elegy on the Death of a Blacksmith," of punning on the tools of the blacksmith trade.

Among the newspaper poems Freneau later collected, many are imitations of pieces that were also imitated by other poets. Although ascribers might agree that Freneau's imitations appear to be "in his manner," his imitations read as much like the poet he is imitating as do other competent imitations of the same poet. Consequently, the phrase "in his manner" has little meaning when Freneau, along with other contributors of the period, habitually imitated the manner of other poets. For instance, Tucker's Probationary Odes for the *National Gazette*, imitating John Wolcot, read much like the verses of Freneau that demonstrate the influence of Wolcot. The following selected list includes poems which Freneau imitated in newspaper verses that were later collected, but which also were imitated by other poets of the period. In each case, it would be quite difficult to distinguish many of the other imitations of the same poem from that of Freneau:

> A popular poem on the death of General Wolfe
> (Freneau's "The Drunken Soldier")
>
> Watts' "Indian Philosopher"
> (Freneau's "Few Honest Cobblers"—mistakenly attributed to Dr. Ladd of Charleston when reprinted in the *Port Folio*)
>
> Sappho's Ode "Blest as the immortal gods is he"
> (Freneau's "Fair Shopkeeper")
>
> Psalm I (*Time-Piece* Book of Odes No. I—Probable Freneau attribution)
>
> Horace Lib II Ode 16
> (Freneau's "Addressed to Governor Parr")
>
> Burns' "Scots, Wha Hae"
> (Freneau's "The Volunteer's March")
>
> "God Save the King"
> (Freneau's "Ode")

All of Freneau's collected imitations are clearly distinguishable from the original source, because Freneau only duplicates the meter, the general developmental outline, and occasional echoes of the original lines to recall the source for his readers. But among the columns of the *National Gazette* and the *Time-Piece,* especially within editorials, are line by line paraphrases adapted from Pope and other satirists with contemporary names substituted for the original objects of attack. Sometimes these adaptations appear within quotations and sometimes they do not. It was conventional for editorial writers of the period to break into several stanzas of verse that summarized or reinforced points just developed in prose. Frequently in such cases, the writer borrowed appropriate stanzas from other poets, occasionally adapting the lines to his purposes. Because the practice of imitation was so widespread among newspaper contributors of the period, it seems to me to be hazardous to attribute poems to Freneau primarily on the grounds that they are "in his manner." Many poems sound like Freneau's because they are imitations or adaptations of poets who influenced Freneau and who he himself occasionally imitated.

The second major ground for caution respecting the attribution of poems "in Freneau's manner," was the license taken by newspaper printers of the period in extracting and reprinting unsigned or pseudonymously signed material from other papers. Many instances can be cited of unsigned poems extracted and reprinted by editors with title changes and deleted or added stanzas. Contributors similarly took liberties with verses they submitted for publication. Occasionally one finds a poem appearing with an introductory note from a contributor to the effect that he spotted the poem in another paper and is offering it to readers of this paper. In some cases the contributor acknowledged that he altered or adapted the poem in some way. As the attribution appendixes indicate, several of the poems attributed to Freneau on the grounds that they are in his manner and appeared in a paper which he edited actually were reprinted by him from other papers. In some cases, comparison of the Freneau reprint to the original, as well as to other reprints of the original, reveals variants only in the version printed by Freneau. Such an observation strongly suggests that he made "improvements" in poems he elected to include in his columns from other sources. The changes, of course, make the poems, which must have initially appealed to Freneau, seem even more "in his manner."

For example, "The Royalist and the Republican," a mock-heroic account of a battle between an lion and a terrapin, has been tentatively attributed to Freneau because it appeared in the *Time-Piece* and was "in his manner." Actually, the poem appeared in an earlier Freneau paper, the *National Gazette,* on July 17, 1793, but was probably reprinted from the *North Carolina Journal,* where it first appeared on July 3, 1793, signed "Columbus, Halifax, July 1793," and titled "The Lion and the Terrapin." This is the earliest appearance of the poem that I found, although it was widely reprinted under the original title and unaltered from the original text. But when it first appeared in a Freneau paper, the *National Gazette,* the title was altered to

"The Royalist and the Republican," giving the battle a political implication, several lines were added, and several of the original lines were revised, somewhat in the manner of Freneau's revisions of his own poems. Freneau later reprinted the revised text in his *Time-Piece*.

Other examples can be cited of uncollected Freneau attributions that were actually somewhat revised reprintings of poems from other newspapers in Freneau's own papers. Since many of these are political poems, expressing views voiced in his columns, their content, of course, "sounds like Freneau," as does their altered style. For instance, an untitled pro-French ode, tentatively attributed to Freneau on the basis of its appearance in the *Time-Piece* on April 26, 1797, first appeared in the *Virginia Chronicle* on September 21, 1793, titled simply "Ode." This eloquent poem was reprinted with minor revisions, including the rewriting of a repetitious refrain as a single, one-time stanza, in a number of Freneau papers. It first appeared, within quotations, at the end of a pro-French editorial in the *National Gazette* on October 2, 1793, shortly after the *Virginia Chronicle* appearance.[8] Similarly, "The History of Monarchy," a poem tentatively attributed to Freneau on the basis of its manner and its appearance in the *Jersey Chronicle* on August 15, 1795, actually first appeared in the *National Gazette* two years earlier under the signature "C.", which Freneau never used in that paper or, so far as we know, in any other. In the *Jersey Chroncile* version, the accidentals have been altered, reflecting Freneau-like patterns of word emphasis and stanza division.

A final example, among others that could be cited, is a poem, "Lines to the Memory of Charles Lee," which has been attributed to Freneau on the basis of its manner. Although the ascriber identifies the poem as first appearing in the *Time-Piece*, it in fact first appeared in the *Freeman's Journal* on July 23,

---

[8]This case and others like it suggest that occasionally poetry excerpted from other papers provided the source for prose essays and editorials in Freneau's papers. Often, as in this case, essays and editorials that have been attributed to Freneau were written as introduction to poems which were extracted from other papers.

1783, shortly after Lee died. Freneau contributed no verified poems of his own to the *Freeman's Journal* during the summer months of 1783, but he doubtless read the poem there. An introduction to the poem explains that it was extracted from the London *St. James's Chronicle,* and a later reprint in the *Massachusetts Centinel* also appears with a note indicating that it was taken from the London Press. Although I have not examined the *St. James's Chronicle* for this year, the introductory note "To the Memory of General Lee, who died in America, having served more nations than Britain," tends to confirm the British source, as does the fact that Lee was born and raised in England. The poem, apparently not Freneau's, appeared repeatedly with minor revisions in the title and several lines in almost all of the papers with which Freneau was associated. It last appeared in the New Brunswick *Fredonian,* on February 6, 1828, signed "F." This signature, according to Leary's theory of post-1815 ascriptions in the *Fredonian,* would make it an original Freneau poem, although it is not included in Leary's *Last Poems.* In the 1828 version, however, the original *Freeman's Journal* poem appeared as the second half of an expanded poem on Lee.

These examples, along with others that could be cited, prove that Freneau, as editor and contributor, felt free to revise poems borrowed from other sources. They have convinced me that he really meant what he said in his "Poetical Address" introducing the *Time-Piece* on March 13, 1797:

> If the best on the market can't always be had
> We'll mend what is middling, and better the bad.

Such evidence not only forces us to hesitate before attributing to Freneau unsigned poems that appeared in his own papers but also provides grounds for wondering what other editors may have done to unsigned or pseudonymously signed poems that he submitted to them, the texts of which he never authorized in any of his collections. How do we know what liberties other editors may have taken with all of the poems in his manner that have been attributed to him on the basis of their appearing, perhaps even under familiar pseudonyms, in papers other than those he personally edited, but to which he was known to contribute?

In one case a poem which has been discovered in Freneau's

autograph, "Winter," dated November 28, 1827, widely considered his last written but unpublished poem, did, in fact, appear in print—in the *Fredonian's* "Carrier's New Years Address," January 2, 1828. All twenty lines quoted in Leary's biography and twenty-seven of the thirty-two lines quoted in Philip Marsh's biography, appeared in the *Fredonian* poem. But Freneau's original stanzas were broken up and dispersed throughout the first third of the poem, and several new lines were added to fit the newsboy's occasion and the New Brunswick setting. Further, in the latter two-thirds of the poem, none of which appears in the autograph, the speaker addresses recent political events, specifically the presidential election to be conducted in the coming year. The writer's position is strongly anti-Jackson and pro-Adams, as was the *Fredonian's* editorial stance throughout 1828. Freneau wrote and collected several news carrier's addresses, and several later ones have been attributed to him. Because one-third of the poem appeared in Freneau's autograph, then, we might consider the attribution of this poem indubitable. But because of the manner in which the original text has been mutilated, because the rest of the poem bears no internal relationship to the original autograph lines, and because newspaper editors of the period were known to take liberties with original material contributed or excerpted for their columns, I would hesitate to include this entire text in an edition of Freneau's work.

In short, my observation of the numerous cases in which extracted material appears to have been revised or adapted by newspaper editors convinces me that editorial standards regarding the publication of unsigned or pseudonymously signed material were quite loose. By publishing pseudonymously or anonymously, poets may have been spared the risk of critical or hostile reaction in this volatile period of American newspaper history: but the price for this security, which many seemed willing to pay, was the loss of control over the use which future editors or readers might make of their verses. To contribute pseudonymously or anonymously was, in a sense, to resign one's claim to one's own verses. Freneau appears to have accepted these conditions from both sides of the fence—both as a poet-contributor and as an editor.

Accordingly, both the widespread practice of imitation and

the editorial liberty assumed with unsigned material have prevented me from including texts of poems ascribed to Freneau on the grounds that they were "in his manner."

(2)
Appearances in Papers During Periods When Freneau's Known Poems First Were Published

The primary locations where ascribers have spotted pre-1815 poems in the manner of Freneau are the newspapers which Freneau edited, or to which he frequently contributed, during periods when a majority of the poems he later collected first were published. The experience of closely studying only the papers which Freneau edited or to which he actively contributed tends to reinforce this basis of ascription. The New York *Daily Advertiser,* for instance, is thin in verse until 1790, when we know Freneau began to play an active editorial role. Many pre-1790 issues lack poems entirely, and the poems that do appear are conventional—epitaphs, retirement verse, moral/pious strains, imitations, and the like. With the spring of 1790, every issue contains poetry, and many more of the poems than those Freneau later collected sound like him. Towards the middle of 1791, the poetry section lapses into what it had been before. Similarly, in examining the columns of the *National Gazette* and the *Time-Piece,* the investigator is impressed by the number of poems that never appeared in Freneau's collections but read as if they could have been penned by him. It is from these poems that biographers, editors and critics have made either definite or tentative attributions to Freneau.

These attributions are supported by our knowledge of Freneau's periodical patterns of productivity throughout his career. As a survey of the dates of the first appearances of texts in this edition indicates, most of Freneau's pre-1815 poems were published in one of several "pockets" that correspond to his active association with or editorship of one of several papers. Freneau first published most of his verses, then, when he had a "guaranteed" and immediately accessible vehicle for doing so. Hence, one would expect also to find in such pockets poems that he wrote but did not later collect.

Again, doubts about poems ascribed on this basis arise not so much from examination of these key papers as from examination of other papers, to which he never was known to contribute original verse. In the columns of such papers, I found earlier appearances of several poems that have been attributed to Freneau on the basis of their assumed first appearance in papers to which Freneau was unquestionably contributing verse. Among the poems cited in my Appendix of Unlikely or Erroneous Attributions are many that I spotted in earlier papers to which Freneau never was known to contribute and at times when, or in places where, he probably would not or could not have been contributing. All of my observations above respecting the editorial practices of excerpting and occasionally revising material from other sources indicate the riskiness of attribution on the ground that a poem appeared in the columns of papers when Freneau was playing an active editorial role. Further, the fact that Freneau was himself a poet could account for the enlargement and improvement of the poetry sections in his columns. He appears to have culled a wide range of other papers for poems that appealed to him and probably attracted more verse contributions than other editors.

A final observation even suggests doubts about the authenticity of poems attributed to Freneau on the grounds that they appeared in prose pieces that have been attributed to him. Freneau, like other editors of the period, not only failed to acknowledge the sources of all material extracted for his columns but also occasionally obfuscated the sources of excerpted material to make the material seem to be the product of his own experience. Such obfuscations can fool the unwary reader, prompting him to attribute material to Freneau on the basis of the fabricated sources. For instance, a poem that has been collected as Freneau's under the title "The Lost Louisa," (Marsh, *Freneau Sampler,* 120-121) appeared September 15, 1797 in a *Time-Piece* editorial, also attributed to Freneau, condemning monasteries. The writer concludes the editorial by noting "the following stanzas were written some years ago, on a beautiful young woman. . .who was shut up in the monastery of Santa Clara, on the Island of Madeira, and affords a striking example of a convent." The poem that follows, however, actually first was published in a novel entitled *Vancenza,* printed in Dublin in 1792 (pp. 206-207) and written by Mrs. Mary Robinson, British novelist, poet, and actress. The poem, which appeared in a chapter of the novel set in Avignon, not Madeira, had been extracted and reprinted in several American papers before it appeared in the *Time-Piece* editorial. In borrowing the poem, which appeared without quotations, the author of the editorial, presumably Freneau, fabricated a context for the poem which could incline readers to attribute the poem to him.

(3)
Signatures

Another basis upon which previous editors have collected poems never acknowledged by Freneau is the signature over which the newspaper text was printed. Most of these ascriptions have been poems printed after 1815, since before that time, his known poems did not frequently appear under signatures, and those that were signed employed a wide range of signatures as opposed to a single, consistent one. Most of his known poems were published in the papers he personally edited or worked for, where they might be recognized as being his without his having to sign them. In a sense, then, he was able to enjoy the advantages of recognition even while retaining some degree of anonymity. The only time he used a signature consistently for his known poems was in the Charleston *Columbian Herald* in 1786. All of his contributions from January to July appeared under the signature "K.", which he had begun using occasionally at the end of 1784 for contributions to the *Freeman's Journal.* Although other verses can be found over signatures he occasionally used for verses later collected, his use of any single one, except for "K.", is too inconsistent before 1815 to guarantee that the signature in all or most cases is really his. As a survey of newspapers of the period indicates, many of the same signatures were attached to poems that are definitely not Freneau's. The practice of reprinting material from widely scattered papers tends to make it appear doubtful that any signature necessarily stands for a particular contributor.

The primary basis of post-1815 attributions is Leary's theory of initials. The discovery of autograph drafts of two poems, "Youth of the Mind," and "Stanzas on the Great Western

Canal," poems which appeared in the Trenton *True American* and the New Brunswick *Fredonian* under the initial ' F.", provides him with a tentative basis for attributing to Freneau all poems signed "F." in those papers between the years 1821 and 1824. Reprints of these two poems and of other poems signed "F." in these papers during these years under other letters in the poet's last name also have provided a tentative basis for attributing all other *Fredonian* and *True American* poems signed with any of these letters from the years 1821 to 1824 to Freneau. Finally, earlier (1816) appearances of some of these same poems in the New York *Weekly Museum* under the initials "F." and "P. F." have provided a tentative basis for attributing all poems under those signatures in that paper during that year to Freneau.

However, as any investigator will discover, Leary's post-1815 attributions are supported by more than Freneau's initials. Besides the general quality of being "in his manner," many of the poems in *Last Poems* demonstrate thematic affinity with Freneau's lighter collected verse. Furthermore, the pattern of reprinted revisions of these poems within a period of several months or, in some cases, several years, as well as the nature of the revisions, are much like those executed by Freneau in his known verse. We find no other newspaper poet of the period repeatedly resubmitting revised versions of poems already printed. Also strongly supportive of these attributions is the fact that they appear within two "pockets" of time—the first in 1816 and the second from 1821 to 1824. No "F." or "P. F." signatures appear in the *Weekly Museum* immediately prior to 1816, when a series of poems sounding much like Freneau and signed "F." and "P. F." do appear, several of which, in revised form, reappear five to eight years later in the *True American* and *Fredonian* under the initials "F," "R," "E," "N," "A," and "U." The fact that the initials do not appear in the New Jersey papers immediately preceding the years 1821 to 1824, the major years for Leary's attributions, likewise supports the idea that they were used by a single contributor. The existence of these two somewhat isolated pockets, the second including revised versions of poems that had appeared in the first, and the fact that both pockets contain poems in Freneau's manner, signed with initials from his name, make Leary's attributions seem highly probable.

It must also be noted that, unlike other pseudonyms that have been ascribed to Freneau, including "X." and "L.", those attributed to him by Leary in *Last Poems* are supported by external evidence. Several poems that were collected by Freneau first appeared or were reprinted with revisions in newspapers under the signatures "F." and "P. F." Also, drafts of several poems appearing under these signatures have been found in Freneau's autograph. Moreover, in printing revised reprints of several of these poems, the editor of the New York *Statesman* unmistakeably described the poet, without naming him, as Freneau. Finally, supporting the attribution at least of the signature "F." is my discovery of a later "pocket" of Freneau-like poems, appearing in the *Fredonian* in 1827 and 1828 and signed exclusively "F." Among this group are several revised reprints of verses that had appeared in the earlier groups, included in Leary's *Last Poems.*

It is true, however, that the letters of Freneau's last name were after 1815 attached to other poems, not distinctively in his manner, that appeared in other New York and New Jersey papers and, in some cases, in the same papers in which Leary's ascriptions appeared, though not during the specific periods during which the poems included in *Last Poems* were printed. Particularly after 1824, both in the *Fredonian* and *True American,* unlikely poems appear under the letters of Freneau's last name which, according to Leary's theory, ought to be ascribed to Freneau.[9] If, however, we were to conclude that these were not Freneau's poems, our grounds for attributing the poems published several years, or even several months earlier, under the

---

[9] Some of these poems are listed in the appendixes, as if they had been attributed, since, according to Leary's theory, all poems appearing under Freneau's initials in the *Fredonian* and *True American* after 1815 can be ascribed to him. Apparently Leary did not examine issues of the two papers after 1824; it is possible that, at the time of his research, no bibliography located these issues in the holdings of any library. I found them at the Library of Congress, but even there, they were not fully catalogued. The appearance of later, unlikely poems under some of Freneau's initials weakens Leary's theory, although it does not prove the earlier attributions are untenable.

same signature, primarily on the basis of the signatures, would obviously be weakened. Another major problem in attributing poems on the basis of pseudonyms is that we have no guarantee that a pseudonym was either intended by the contributor or assumed by readers of the period to be a masked identification of the person who actually wrote the poem. Throughout the period of my study, I came across many cases in which pseudonyms or initials appeared under poems the authors of which are identified after the title, the pseudonym or initial presumably referring only to the *contributor.* In the *True American* for 1825, for instance, several poems said to be reprinted from Baltimore and New York papers were offered for readers from contributors "F." and "E."

But the strongest grounds for excluding from this edition the full texts of poems appearing under Freneau's initials in the *True American, Fredonian,* and New York *Weekly Museum* after 1815 was my discovery of several instances in which lines definitely or probably not Freneau's were included in the texts of such poems, indicating that he personally did not regard the pseudonym as a claim to complete originality. For instance, the poem on Charles Lee, cited earlier, originally extracted by the *Freeman's Journal* from the London *St. James's Chronicle,* was included in a longer poem on Lee appearing in the *Fredonian* on February 6, 1828, signed "F." Although Freneau had reprinted the poem on Lee, with minor variants, in several of the papers he edited before 1815, he never collected it as his own. Accordingly, the appearance of the signature "F." with the *Fredonian* text provides conclusive evidence that he, like other contributors of the period, occasionally submitted derivative verses under a pseudonymous signature. Another poem, an imitation of Bion, which Freneau also had reprinted repeatedly, with occasional revisions, in papers that he edited before 1815, but which he never collected, also reappeared, like the Lee poem, in a longer text published in the *Fredonian* on November 28, 1822, under the signature "R." Although in this case I cannot prove that the poem was not originally his own, its newspaper history is so similar to that of the Lee poem—Freneau repeatedly revising and reprinting it, but never collecting it as his own, and finally reworking it into a longer text late in his career—that we have grounds for at least questioning the authenticity of the *Fredonian* text, despite the signature.

Finally, since Leary's signature theory was originally based on the discovery of autograph poems that appeared in print under Freneau's initials, a few words are in order respecting the authenticity even of verses discovered in Freneau's autograph. In at least one instance, a poem that has been attributed to Freneau on the basis of an autograph discovery contains what appear to be derivative stanzas. In "A Newly Discovered Poem by Philip Freneau on the Death of General Moreau," Charles Batten provides the text of a poem discovered in Freneau's autograph in the poet's copy of Brydone's *Tour Through Sicily and Malta*.[10] The poem is introduced with a note about the death of Moreau. Then, after the two stanza text, there is a note by a later owner of the book to the effect that the poem was evidently Freneau's because the book belonged to him. Batten tentatively dates the poem 1814, shortly after Moreau died, and notes that it never was published. However, at least one of the stanzas did appear in print several times. It first appeared, with another stanza, in the *National Gazette,* within quotation marks, at the end of an article on death that was also set in quotations and titled "Extract." It appeared again in the *Time-Piece,* where it is included in a poem attributed to the "Late King of Prussia." Translations of verse attributed to Frederick II were popular in American newspapers from 1780-1800, the earliest ones extracted from British papers. Most, like this stanza, deal with the theme of the vanity of ambition. Even though the stanza appears in Freneau's autograph, then, we have grounds beyond the fact that it never appeared in a collected poem for questioning its authenticity.[11] It seems possible that, upon learning of the death of General Moreau, killed in battle against Napoleon, his former ally who had banished him from Europe, Freneau recalled and was prompted to record the haunting stanza that had appeared twice before in the papers he had edited:

---

[10]*American Literature,* 44 (1972), pp. 457-459.

[11]The third stanza, however, of Freneau's "On the Tomb of Patriots" (*Poems,* 1815, II, pp. 31-37), almost directly paraphrases, in completely original lines, the above stanza and the other stanza that appeared with it in the original *National Gazette* extract, again suggesting that, although probably not his originally, the verses "stuck" with Freneau.

> How weak an Empress is the mind
> Whom wild Ambition's power can bind
>   And Captive to her altars lead;
> Weak reason yields to Frenzy's rage,
> And all the world is folly's stage
>   And all who act are fools indeed.

The ambiguous use of pseudonyms by newspaper poets of the period, the discovery of derivative verses in post-1815 texts signed with Freneau's initials, and the unreliability of autograph stanzas as a basis of attribution have discouraged me from including, in this edition, the full texts of uncollected poems on the grounds that they appeared with pseudonyms under which Freneau was known to contribute, or may have contributed, his verses. It must be noted that, in at least two instances after 1815, verses appeared in newspapers under Freneau's full signature, suggesting that the poet himself made a distinction, as contributor, between the use of pseudonyms and full of signatures.

(4)
Poems Ascribed to Him by His Contemporaries

Several poems have been collected or included in bibliographies of Freneau primarily on the grounds that they were ascribed to him by contemporaries, primarily by other editors in extracting and reprinting verses that appeared in papers edited by Freneau. This is probably the most unreliable of all bases for ascription, since several newspapers of the period, including the Boston *Independent Chronicle,* the New York *Diary,* and occasionally the Charleston *City Gazette,* indiscriminately attribute any poem reprinted from the *National Gazette* or *Time-Piece* to Freneau, whose name appeared at the top of the first page in both papers. Among these are poems that never were collected by Freneau and that never have been attributed to him by any Freneau scholar who has examined these papers. For instance, when it appeared in the Poughkeepsie *American Farmer* on March 28, 1799, a poem entitled "The Branch of Maple," which had appeared in the *Time-Piece* on May 7, 1798 under the heading "Selected Poetry," was said to be "By P. Freneau." However, the poem first appeared in the New Hampshire

Farmer's Weekly Museum on March 13, 1798, signed "Peter Pencil," a frequent contributor to the New Hampshire paper whose other effusions included unFreneau-like verses with local references. It probably was from this paper that Freneau reprinted the poem, two weeks later, in the *Time-Piece.*

Another poem attributed to Freneau by contemporary newspaper editors, "The American's Prayer for France," also appeared in Baltimore and Virginia papers before it was printed by Freneau. "The Death Song of a Cherokee Indian" was ascribed to Freneau by Pattee on the basis of the erroneous attribution of Matthew Carey, who reprinted it in his *American Museum.* Finally, among other examples of erroneous contemporary attributions are the Probationary Odes of the *National Gazette,* widely attributed to Freneau by contemporaries and even by some modern historians who, in discussing the *National Gazette,* have casually described the poems printed in its columns as if they all were written by Freneau. Due to the unreliability of contemporary ascriptions, then, I have not cited, even in the appendixes, any poem ascribed to Freneau *only* by contemporaries, if the contemporary ascription is the *only* basis for associating the poem with Freneau.

To repeat, I have not included the complete newspaper text of any poem that Freneau never fully signed or collected. My research has established, I believe, that even if we are sure that a poem was *contributed* by Freneau, we cannot be sure that the text was all or even partly Freneau's. On the other hand, in the entire course of my research, I found cause in only one case, of the several hundred texts included in the main volume, to doubt the complete authenticity of a poem he later collected.[12] The relative frequency of error in the attribution of uncollected poems has persuaded me that the only sound basis for attributing and fully editing Freneau texts must be

---

[12]This one case is Freneau's imitation of "God Save the King," which appeared only in the 1795 collection. Numerous parodies of this song appeared in papers during the early 1790's, and Freneau's version shares several lines in common with earlier texts probably not his. See Main Volume, *Federal Gazette,* July 3, 1793.

his acknowledgement of his verses in a collection or by his full signature. It must be noted that any reservations we have respecting pre-1815 attributions are supported by the fact that, although he had as many as five opportunities, the poet never chose to acknowledge the poems as his own by including them in a collection. Similarly, at least two post-1815 poems were contributed to papers over his full signature. Freneau's failure to acknowledge poems that seem to be his may have been based not simply on reservations about their substance or quality, but also on his awareness of the fact that their content was derivative.

However, I believe that Freneau did write many more poems than he collected, and that some of the uncollected poems that have been ascribed to him are completely original. I have examined all of them and believe some to be of notable interest to the student and biographer of Freneau. Many of the later attributions already have been published in Leary's *Last Poems.* Among those poems signed "F." appearing in the later issues of the *Fredonian,* uncollected by Leary, several express a muted but convincing vein of religious feeling, more personal than the versified tenets of deism we find in the 1809 and 1815 collections. If the newscarrier's address containing Freneau's autograph lines on "Winter" was entirely Freneau's, it suggests a significant departure from political biases expressed in his newspaper columns a generation earlier. In short, I believe that students of the poet should be aware of the existence and location of every uncollected newspaper poem probably or possibly penned by Freneau. To this end, I have supplied a series of descriptive appendixes in which all likely or possible attributions that have been found by others, and several additional poems that I have found, are listed, with a summary of the available evidence for ascribing them to Freneau. I have also included an Appendix of Unlikely or Erroneous Attributions, and the grounds for excluding them. (See the Introduction to the Appendixes for a complete account of the method employed for describing attributions.)

Constitutional Gazette   October 18, 1775

REFLECTIONS on GAGE's Letter to GENERAL WASHINGTON, of Aug. 13.

"REBELS you are," the hopeful Gen'ral cries,
Truth, stand thou forth and tell the wretch he lies.
Rebels—and see the high imperial lord
Already threats those rebels with a cord.
    The hour draws nigh, the glass is almost run,
When truth must shine, and Gage will be undone:
When this black monster shall forebear to sneer,
And curse his mocks and bitter insults here,
Nay wish himself, ere freedom sent to quel,
Had seen the lowest lurking place of hell.
    If to controul the cunning of a knave,
Our freedom love, and scorn the name of slave;
If to protest against a tyrant's laws,
And arm for battle in a righteous cause
Be deem'd rebellion—'tis a harmless thing.
This bug-bear name, like death, has lost its sting.
    Americans! at freedom's fane adore,
But trust Britannia's clemency no more,
The gen'rous genius of the isle has fled
And left a mere imposter in his stead:
If conquer'd—GAGE already let us know,
"Except no mercy from this viper foe"
Ay, even the grave, that sacred haunt of peace,
Where nature gives the toil of man to cease,
Shall ransack'd be, and mangled bodies there
Torn up to feast the armies of the air;
Spoil'd of their shrouds, and o'er Canadia's plains,
Be hung aloft to terrify in chains.
    To arms, to arms, and let the trusty sword,
Decide who best deserves the hangman's cord,
Nor think the hills of Canada too bleak,
When desperate freedom is the cause you seek.

> For that, the voice of honour bids you go,
> O'er frozen lakes, and mountains clad in snow,
> Let BAKER's head be snatch'd from infamy,
> And CARLETON's Popish scull be fixt on high,
> And all like him o'er St. John's castle swing,
> To shew that freedom is no trifling thing.

Poems (1786), 85-86.

New York *Public Advertiser*   July 14, 1812[1]

Last stanza only (twelve lines) reprinted under the title "PATRIOTIC APPEAL," including variants from later collected texts, as well as several post-1809 variants:

> lines 1-6   First six lines of the last stanza of the 1775 text, with the following variants:
> line 1:   not indented.
> line 4:   When Freedom's triumph is the prize you seek;
> line 5:   For *now* the voice of honour bids you go
> line 6:   O'er frozen lakes, and mountains wrap in snow;

line 7 to end of poem revised in collected versions, and slightly altered here:

> line 7:   No toils can daunt the warlike and the bold,
> line 8:   They scorn all heat, or wave congealing cold;
> line 9:   *Haste*, to your tents in iron fetters bring,
> line 10:   The menial slaves that serve a tyrant king,
> line 11:   So just, so virtuous, is your cause, I say,
> line 12:   HELL *must prevail if Britain wins the day.*"

Freneau, 1775

---

[1] The first newspaper texts of two poems later collected by Freneau were published in the *Public Adversiter;* see March 3 and November 11, 1809.

U. S. Magazine   February, 1779

(Untitled text follows an essay describing the island of Santa Cruz, which concludes, "I believe the best thing I can do with the rest of this paper is to transcribe a few dull heavy lines which I composed near two years ago on the spot.")

Sick of thy northern glooms, come shepherd seek
Less rigorous climes, and a more friendly sky:
Why shouldst thou toil amidst that frozen ground,
Where half year snows a barren prospect lie?

When thou mayst go where never frost was seen,
Or north-west winds with cutting fury blow;
Where never ice congeal'd the limpid stream,
Where never mountain crown'd its head with snow.

Two weeks, with prosperous gales, thy barque shall bear
To isles that flourish in perpetual green,
Where richest herbage glads each shady vale,
And ever-verdant plants on every hill are seen.

Nor dread the dangers of the billowy deep:
Autumnal gales shall safely waft thee o'er:
Put off the timid heart, or man unblest,
Ne'er shalt thou reach this gay enchanting shore.

So some dull minds, in spite of age and care,
Are grown so wedded to this globe below,
They never wish to cross death's dusky main
That parting them and happiness, doth flow.

Tho' reason's voice must whisper *to the soul*
That nobler climes for man the Gods design.
Come shepherd haste the rising breezes blow:
No more the slumbering winds thy barque confine.

From the vast caverns of *old* Ocean's bed,
St. Cruz arising laves her humed waist:
The threatening waters roar on every side;
For every side by ocean is embrac'd.

Sharp craggy rocks repell the surging brine,
Whose cavern'd sides by restless ocean wore,
Resemblance claim to that remoter isle,
Where once the prince of winds the sceptre bore.

Betwixt the Tropick and the Midway Line,
In happiest climate lies this envy'd isle;
Trees bloom throughout the year, flowers ever blow,
And fragment Flora wears a lasting smile.

No lowering skies are here; the neighbouring sun,
Clear and unveil'd his brilliant journey goes;
Each morn emerging from the azure main,
And sinking there each evening to repose.

In June's fair month, the spangled traveller gains
The utmost limits of his northern way,
And blesses with his beams cold lands remote,
Sad Greenland's coast and Hudson's frozen bay.

The shivering swains of those unhappy climes
Behold the mid-way monarch thro' the trees:
We feel his friendly heat, his zenith beams
Temper'd with cooling showers and trade-wind breeze.

No threatening tides upon our island rise:
Gay Cynthia scarce disturbs the ocean here:
No waves approach her orb, and she as kind
Attracts no water to her silver sphere.

The happy waters boast, of various kinds,
Unnumber'd myriads of the scaly race:
Sportive they play above the delug'd sand,
(Gay as their clime) in ocean's ample vase.

Some streak'd with burnish'd gold resplendent glare;
Some cleave the limpid deep all silver'd o'er;
Some clad in living green delight the eye;
Some red, some blue, of mingled colours more.

Here glides the spangled dolphin through the deep;
Here bulky, spouting whales more distant stray;

The huge green turtles wallow through the wave,
Well pleas'd alike with land or water they.

The rainbow cuts the deep of varied green;
The well fed grouper lurks remote below;
The swift bonetta swims and flies by turns;
The diamond coated angels kindle as they go.

Delicious to the taste, salubrious food,
Which might some frugal Samian sage allure,
To curse the fare of his abstemious school,
And turn for once a cheerful Epicure!

Hail, verdant isle! through thy dark woods I rove,
And learn the nature of each native tree—
The rustic hard, the poisonous manchineal,
Which for its fragrant apple pleaseth thee.

Enticing to the smell, fair to the eye,
But deadly poison in the taste is found:
O shun the dangerous fruit, nor taste, like Eve
This interdicted fruit in Eden's ground.

The lowly mangrove fond of wat'ry soil;
The white bark'd gregory rising high in air;
The mastic in the woods you may descry;
Tamarinds and lofty plumb trees flourish there.

Sweet orange groves in lonely vallies rise,
And drop their fruits unnotic'd and unknown:
The cooling acid limes in hedges grow;
The juicy lemons swell in shades their own.

Sweet spungy plumbs on trees wide spreading hang;
The happy flavour'd pine grows crested from the ground;
Plump grenadillo's and guava's small,
With melons in each wood and lawn abound.

The conic form'd cashew, of juicy kind,
Which bears at once an apple and a nut;
Whose poison coat indignant to the lips,
Doth in its cell a wholesome kernel shut.

The plaintain and banana flourish here,
Of hasty growth, and love to fix their root,
Where some soft stream of ambling water goes,
To give full moisture to their clustered fruit.

No other trees so vast a leaf can boast,
So broad, so long—through these refresh'd I stray;
And tho' fierce Sol his beams directly shed,
Those friendly leaves shall shade me all the way.

And tempt the cooling breeze to hasten there,
With its sweet odorous breath to charm the grove,
High shades and cooling air, while underneath,
A little stream by mossy banks doth rove.

Where once the indian dames inchanted slept,
Or fondly kiss'd the moon light eves away:
The lovers fled, the tearful stream remains,
And only I console it with my lay.

Pomegranates grace yon vale, and sweet-sops there
Ready to fall, require thy helping hand;
Nor yet neglect the papaw or mammee,
Whose slighted trees with fruit unheeded stand.

Those shaddocks juicy shall thy taste delight;
And yon high fruits that over-top the wood,
And cling in clusters to the mother tree—
The cocoa nut, rich milky healthful food.

Cassada shrubs abound, whose poison root,
Supplies the want of snow-white northern flour:
This grated fine, and steep'd in water fair,
Forsakes each particle of noxious power.

But the chief, the glory of these Indian isles,
Springs from the sweet uncloving sugar cane:
Hence comes the planter's wealth: Hence commerce sends
Such floating piles beyond the western main.

Who'er thou art, that leav'st thy native shore,
And shalt to fair West-India climates come,

Taste not the enchanting plant—to taste forbear,
If ever thou wouldst reach thy much-lov'd home.

Ne'er through the isle permit thy feet to rove,
Or if thou dost, let prudence lead the way;
Forbear to taste the magic sugar-cane;
Forebear to taste what will complete thy stay.

Whoever sips of this inchanting juice—
Delicious nectar, fit for Jove's own hall,
Returns no more from his lov'd Santa Cruz,
But quits his friends, his country, and his all.

And thinks no more of home----Ulysses so
Dragg'd off by force, his sailors from that shore,
Where Lotos grew; and had not force prevailed,
They never would have sought their country more.

No annual toil inters this juicy plant,
The stalks lopp'd off, the fresh'ning showers prolong,
To future years, unfading and secure,
The root so vig'rous, and the juice so strong.

On yonder peaked hill fresh harvests rise,
Where wretched he--the Ethiopian swain,
Oft o'er the ocean turns his wishful eyes,
To isles remote high luming o'er the main.

He pants a land of freedom and repose,
Where cruel slavery never sought to reign.
O quit thee them, my muse, and tell me why
Yon abject trees lie scatter'd o'er the plain?

These climes, lest nature should have been too kind,
And man have sought his happiest heaven below,
Are torn with mighty winds, fierce hurricanes,
Nature convuls'd in every form of woe.

Scorn not yon lonely vale of trees to rest:
There plaintain groves late grew of lovely green–
The orange flourish'd and the lemon bore--
The genius of the isle dwelt there unseen.

Wild were the skies, affrighted nature groan'd,
As though approach'd the last decisive day--
Skies blaz'd around, and bellowing winds had nigh
Dislodg'd those cliffs and tore those hills away.

And how, alas! could these fair trees withstand,
The killing fury of so fierce a blast,
That storm'd along the plain, seiz'd every grove,
And delug'd with a sea yon mournful waste?

But now the winds are past, the storm subsides,
All nature smiles again serenely gay,
The beauteuous groves renew'd--how shall I leave
My green retreat at Butler's verdant bay.

Fain would I view my native climes again,
But murder marks the cruel Briton there--
Contented here I rest, in spite of pain,
And quaff the enlivening juice in spite of care.

Winter and winter's gloom are far remov'd,
Eternal spring with smiling summer join'd.
Absence and death, or heart carroding care,
Why should they cloud the sunshine of the mind?

The drowsy pelican wings home his way,
The misty night sits heavy on the sea,
Yon lagging sail drags slowly o'er the main.
Night and its kindred glooms are nought to me.

To-morrow's sun new paints the faded scene;
Though deep in ocean sink his western beams,
His spangled chariot shall ascend more clear,
More radiant from the drowsy land of dreams.

Then shepherd haste, and leave behind thee far,
Thy bloody plains and iron glooms above,
Quit thy cold northern star, and here enjoy.
Beneath the smiling skies this land of love.

Soon shall the genius of the fertile soil,
A new creation to thy view unfold,

Admire the works of nature's liberal hand,
And scorn that vulgar bait, all-potent gold.

Yet if persuaded by no lay of mine,
You still admire your climes of frost and snow,
And pleas'd prefer above our southern groves,
The darksome forests that around thee grow,--

Still there remain--thy native air enjoy,
Repel the tyrant who thy peace invades,
While pleas'd I trace the vales of Santa Cruz,
And sing with rapture her inspiring shades.

Poems (1786), 133-50.

U. S. Magazine   May, 1779

King George *the* Third's SOLILOQUY.

O Damn this Congress, damn each *upstart* state,
On whose commands ten thousand warriors wait:
From various climes that dire assembly came,
True to their trust yet hostile to my fame;
'Tis these, ah these, have ruin'd half my sway,
Disgrac'd my arms, and led my realm astray.
    France aids them now, (I play a desperate game,)
And sun-burnt Spain, they say, will do the same.
My armies vanquish'd, and my heroes fled,
My people murmuring, and my commerce dead,
My shatter'd navy, pelted, bruis'd, and clubb'd,
My Dutchmen bully'd, and by Frenchmen drubb'd;
My name abhorr'd, my nation in disgrace,
What should I do in such a mournful case?
My hopes and joys are vanish'd with my coin,
My ruin'd army, and my lost Burgoyne!
What shall I do? confess my labours vain,
Or whet my tusks and to the charge again.
    But where's my force? my choicest troops are fled,

Some thousands crippled, and a myriad dead.
If I were own'd the stoutest of mankind,
And hell with all her rage inspir'd my mind,
Could I at once with France and Spain contend,
And fight the *rebels* on the world's green end.
　　Yet rogues and savage tribes I must employ,
And what I cannot conquer will destroy.
Is there a robber close in Newgate hem'd?
Is there a cut-throat fetter'd and condemn'd?
Haste loyal slaves to George's standard come,
Attend his lectures when you hear the drum,
Your chains I break, for better days prepare,
Come out my friends from prison and from care:
Far to the west I plan your desp'rate way,
There 'tis no sin to ravage, burn, and slay;
There without fear your bloody trade pursue,
And shew mankind what British rage can do.
　　Ye daring hosts that croud Columbia's shore,
Tremble ye traitors, and exult no more;
Flames I shall hurl with an unceasing hand,
Till fires eternal blaze throughout your land,
And every dome and every tower expires,
And traitors perish in the unfeeling fires;
But hold--though this be all my soul's desire,
Will my own towns be proof to *rebel* fire.
If in revenge my raging foes should come,
And burn my London-----it would strike me dumb,
To see my children and my queen in tears,
And these tall piles come tumbling round my ears,
Would to its inmost caverns fright my mind,
And stun *ourself,* the boldest of mankind.
　　Curs'd be the day when I first saw the sun,
Curs'd be the hour when I this war begun;
The fiends of darkness then inspir'd my mind,
And powers unfriendly to the human kind:
My future years I consecrate to woe,
For this great loss my soul in tears shall flow.
To wasting grief and sullen rage a prey,
To Scotland's utmost verge I take my way;
With nature's storms eternal concert keep,
And while her billows rage, as fiercely weep:
O let the earth my rugged fate bemoan,

And give at least one sympathizing groan.

Poems (1786), 171-74.

U. S. Magazine   June, 1779

The Dying Elm. An irregular Ode.

SWEET, lovely elm, who here dost grow,
    Companion of my musing care;
Lo, thy dejected branches die,
    Amid the burning air;
Smit by the sun or sickly moon,
Like fainting flow'rs that die at noon.

Thy withering leaves that drooping hang,
    Presage thy end approaching nigh,
And lo, thy amber tears distil,
    Attended with thy last remaining sigh.
O gentle tree no more decline,
But be thy shade and love-sick whispers mine.

Short is thy life if thou so soon must fade,
    Like angry Jonah's gourd at Nineveh,
That in a night its bloomy branches spread,
    And flourish'd for a day.
Come then revive, sweet shady elm, lest I,
Thro' vehemence of heat, like Jonah, wish to die.

Poems (1786), 38.

U. S. Magazine   June, 1779

Columbus to Ferdinand.

Columbus was a considerable time soliciting the court of Spain to fit him out on discovering a new continent to the westward; during his negotiation he is supposed to address king Ferdinand in the following stanzas.

Illustrious monarch of Iberia's soil,
Too long I wait permission to depart,
Sick of delays, I beg thy listning ear,
Shine forth the patron and the prince of art.

While yet Columbus breathes the vital air,
Grant his request to pass the western main,
Reserve this glory for thy native soil,
And what must please thee more, for thy own reign.

Of this huge globe how small a part we know?
Does heaven their lands to western suns deny?
How disproportion'd to the mighty deep,
The lands that yet in human prospect lie?

Does Cynthia, when to western skies arriv'd,
Spend her sweet beam upon the barren main,
And ne'er illume with midnight splendor, she,
The natives dancing on the lightsome green?

Should the vast circuit of the world contain
Such lengths of ocean and such scanty land?
'Tis reason's voice that bids me think not so,
I think more nobly of the Almighty hand.

Does yon fair lamp atchieve its daily round,
To light the waves and monsters of the seas?
No: be there must beyond the billowy waste,
Islands and men and animals and trees.

An unremitting flame my breast inspires,
To seek new lands amid the barren waves,
Where falling low the source of day descends,
And the blue sea his evening visage laves.

Even now I read in Plato's raptur'd page,
"The time shall come, when numerous years are past,
The ocean shall dissolve the bands of things,
And an extended region rise at last.

And Typhis shall disclose the mighty land,
Far far away, where none have rov'd before,
Nor shall the world's remotest region be,
The Hebride isles or Caledonia's shore."

Fir'd by the theme I languish to depart,
Supply the barque and bid Columbus sail;
He fears no storms across the pathless deep,
Reason shall steer and skill disarm the gale.

Think not that nature has unveil'd in vain,
The mystic magnet to the mortal eye;
So late have we the guiding needle plann'd,
Only to sail beneath our native sky?

Ere this was found the Ruling Power of all,
Form'd for our use an ocean in the land,
Its breadth so small we could not wander long,
Nor long be absent from the neighbouring strand.

Short was the course, and guided by the stars;
But stars no more shall point our daring way,
The bear shall sink and every guard be drown'd,
And great Orion scarce escape the sea,

When southward we shall steer----O grant my wish,
Supply the barque, and bid Columbus sail;
He fears no tempests on the faithless deep,
Reason shall steer, and skill disarm the gale.

Poems (1786), 39-41.

U. S. Magazine   July, 1779[1]

The LOYALISTS.

THAT Britain's rage should dye our plains with gore,
And desolation spread thro' every shore,
None ere could doubt that Britain's malice knew,
This was to rage and disappointment due;
But that those monsters, whom our soil maintain'd,
Who first drew breath in this devoted land,
Like famish'd wolves should on their country prey,
Assist its foes, and wrest our lives away:
This shocks belief: They are from Satan's den;
They must be devils in the form of men.
Retire, ye bloodhounds of some murderous line,
Nor thus disgrace the human form divine:
From these fair climes apostate spirits go;
Quick, seek your native coast the world below;
So vast your crimes, if longer you remain,
Earth must cry out, and hardest rocks complain:
The blushing moon to other worlds retire,
Or veil in long eclipse the solar fire,

---

[1] This poem in the above form, never was collected by Freneau, but lines 1-9 of the first stanza; lines 7-12 of the third stanza; and lines 1-8 of the last stanza appear in Canto II of the 1786 text of "The British Prison Ship"—stanza 3, lines 1-9; stanza 3, lines 11-16; and stanza 4, lines 1-8, respectively. Leary errs in noting that they appeared in the first (1781) text of the poem (*That Rascal Freneau,* pp. 77, 423). In the earlier text, after announcing his intention to describe the horrors of the prison ship, Freneau begins the second canto with a long attack on *native* Britains. In the 1786 text, the attack is focused upon loyalists in America, and these lines from the above poem are included, with slight revisions. There appears no reason to doubt that the rest of the poem, though uncollected, is Freneau's as well. The contributor is from "Shrewsbury, East-Jersey," and we know that during the year 1778-79, Freneau was sailing from Shrewsbury to Philadelphia for St. Eustacia. Also, his announcement of the necessity to turn from songs on "the pleasures of the plaintain shade," to those that "Expos'd the tyrant," and "aim'd the fatal dart," seems an apt description Freneau's poetical intentions at this point.

As if in dread his all-pervading eye
Should view your madness and forsake the sky.
    Ye Sylvan Bards who deal in flow'ry themes,
Who sing the meadows and the purling streams,
Who yet remote from blood and murder stray,
Blame not the toughness of the Muses lay:
Once, like yourselves, to quiet groves she stray'd,
And sun the pleasures of the plantain shade;
Sweet was the toil, and sweetly pass'd the time;
Soft was the verse, and easy was the rhyme;
But when she saw your blazing turrets fall,
Your slaughter'd friends in vain for mercy call,
Your captive sons with British poison die;
Your fields laid waste and total conquest nigh;
Griev'd at the view she rais'd a bolder strain,
Expos'd the tyrant and deny'd his reign;
At his mad bosom aim'd the fatal dart,
And if she reach'd not, meant it for his heart.
    Ye *Sages fam'd,* who sent from various climes,
Conduct our empire thro' these worst of times:
When Britain homeward calls her humbled train,
Say shall our traitors in these lands remain,
Who now, even now, assail yon roofs with fire,
And captive lead the children and the sire?
By *them* the widow mourns her partner dead;
Her sons perhaps to darksome prisons led
By them; and hence my keenest sorrows rise;
My friend, my guardian, my Orestes dies:
Still for that loss must wretched I complain,
And sad Ophelia weep her murder'd swain?
By them the mother her lost son deplores;
By them Cesarea weeps thro' half her shores;
Her plunder'd flocks to hostile cities go,
And help to feed the half dejected foe;
Yet here *their* children and their friends we find,
Hostile to us and traitors to mankind;
While we each mischief from her foes endure,
Safe are their flocks, and they from harm secure;
They dread no thieves by Clinton's mandate sent;
They fear no ruffians on destruction bent;
Leagu'd with the foe they join the friendly hand,
And teach him how to desolate the land:

On him who dares be known his country's friend,
On him these imps their hottest vengeance spend;
His blood they shed; but shall this bloody train,
Say, shall such traitors in these lands remain?
    Ah no, expel them from the ravag'd shore;
Far, far remove them to return no more.
To scorch'd Bahama let the traitors go,
With grief and rage and unremitting woe:
On burning sands to walk their painful round,
And sigh thro' all the solitary ground,
Where no gay flower their haggard eyes may see,
And find no shade but from the cypress tree.
Can crimes like theirs the power supreme approve,
Whose essence is benevolence and love,
While basely stabb'd yon murder'd victim dies,
Can he look on with unconcerned eyes?
Ah, wretches, no? some hidden vengence waits
Some sudden ruin from the angry fates:
Long do the skies their righteous rage suspend,
That hotter vengeance may from heaven descend,
Else why should fortune crown their deeds to-day?
Why harmless light'nings round their temples play?
Ah! but for this the skies would hostile grow,
And lightnings blast them to the shades below.

Shrewsbury, East-Jersey.

Poems (1786), 193-94.

U. S. Magazine   August, 1779[1]

The HOUSE *of* NIGHT; *Or, Six Hours Lodging with Death.*

A VISION.

Felis qui potuit rerum cognoscere causas,
Atque metus omnes et inexorabile Fatum
Subjecit pedibus, strepitumque Acherontis avari.
Virg. Georg. II. v. 490.

1.

LET others draw from smiling skies their theme,
    And tell of climes that boast eternal light;
I draw a deeper scene replete with gloom;
    I sing the horrors of the house of night.

2.

Stranger believe the truth experience tells;
    Poetic dreams are of a finer cast
Than those which oe'er the sober brain diffus'd
    Are but a repetition of some action past.

3.

By some sad means the mind cannot recal,
    Lonely I rov'd at midnight o'er a plain
Where Chesapeque's deep rivers upward flow
    Far to their springs, or seek the sea again.

---

[1] The poem is editorially introduced in the August *Notes to Correspondents* as follows:

The House of Night, a poem in the present number of the Magazine, is from a young gentleman who has favoured us with several original pieces in the course of this work; and readers of taste will no doubt be pleased with it, as perfectly original both in the design and manner of it.

4.

Though then the woods, in fairest vernal bloom,
    Flourish'd, yet nought of this could fancy see;
No wild pinks bless'd the meads, no green the fields,
    And naked seem'd to stand each childless tree.

5.

Dark was the sky, and not a friendly star
    Shone from the zenith or horizon clear:
Mist sat upon the woods, and darkness rode,
    In her black chariot, with a wild career.

6.

And from the woods the late resounding note
    Issued of the loquacious Whip-poor-will:
Hoarse roaring wolves, and nightly roving bears,
    Clamour'd from far-off clifts invisible.

7.

Fierce from the loudly sounding Chesapeke
    I heard the winds the dashing waves assail,
And saw from far, by picturing fancy form'd,
    The black ship travelling thro' the noisy gale.

8.

When to my view a pile of buildings stood,
    And near, a garden of autumnal hue,
Its lately pleasing flowers all drooping stood
    Amidst high weeds that in rank plenty grew.

9.

No pleasant fruit or blossom gaily smil'd;
    Nought but unhappy plants and trees were seen;
The yew, the willow, and the church-yard elm,
    The cypress with its melancholy green.

10.

Peace to those buildings; when at once I heard
    The voice of men in a remoter dome:
Much did they talk of death, and much of life;
    Of coffins, shrouds, and horrors of a tomb.

11.

Mean time from a superior chamber came
    Confused murmurs, scarce distinguish'd sounds;
And as I nearer drew disputes arose
    Of surgery, and remedies for wounds.

12.

Long were their feuds, for they design'd to talk
    Of anchylosis and the shoulder-blade;
Of femoris, trochanters, and whate'er
    Has been discuss'd by *Cheselden and *Mead.

13.

And often, each to prove his notion true,
    Brought proofs from Galen or Hippocrates.
But fancy led me hence and left them so,
    Firm at their points of hardy no and yes.

14.

Then up three winding stairs my feet were brought
    To a high chamber hung with mourning sad;
The unsnuff'd candles glar'd with visage dim;
    'Midst grief in exstacy of woe run mad.

** *Two famous Anatomists.*

15.

A wide leaf'd table stood on either side,
  Well fraught with phials, half their liquids spent;
And from a bed behind a curtain veil,
  I heart a hollow voice of loud lament.

16.

Turning to view from whence the murmur came,
  My frighted eyes a horrid form survey'd!
Death, dreary death, upon the gloomy couch,
  With flesh-less limbs in rueful form was laid.

17.

High o'er his head flew jealousies and cares:
  Ghosts, imps, and half the black Tartarian crew,
Arch-Angels damn'd, nor was their prince remote,
  Borne on the vaporous wings of Stygian dew.

18.

Sad was his aspect, if we so call,
  That aspect where but skin and bones were seen,
And eyes sunk in their sockets deep and low,
  And teeth that only shew'd themselves to grin.

19.

Reft was his scull of hair, and no fresh bloom
  Of chearful mirth sate on his visage hoar;
Sometimes he rais'd his head while deep-drawn groans
  Were mix'd with words that did his fate deplore.

20.

Then at my hand I saw a comely youth,
  Of port majestic, who began to tell
That this was Death, upon his dying bed,
  Sullen, morose, and peevish to be well.

21.

"Fixt is his doom: the miscreant reigns no more
    The monarch of the dying or the dead;
This night concludes his melancholy reign:
    Pour out, ye heavens, your vengeance on his head."

22.

But now the man of hell towards me turn'd,
    And straight with frightful tone began to speak:
Long held he sage discourse, but I forbore
    To answer, and much less his news to seek.

23.

He talk'd of tombstones and of monuments,
    Of equinoctial climes and India shores:
He talk'd of stars that shed their influence,
    Fevers and plagues, with all their sickly stores.

24.

He mention'd too the guilful calenture
    Tempting the sailor on the placid main,
That paints fine groves upon the ocean floor,
    Beckoning his footsteps to the faithless scene.

25.

Much spoke he of the myrtle and the yew;
    The summer winds, and of the church-yard hoar;
Of storms which on the wintry ocean blow,
    And dash the well-mann'd galley to the shore.

26.

Of broad-mouth'd cannon and the thunder-bolt;
    Of fevers and contagions, dearth and fire;
Of poisonous weeds; but seem'd to sneer at those
    Who by the laurel o'er him did aspire.

27.

Then with a hollow voice thus he went on:
    "Arise, make search, and bring, when found, to me
Some cordial potion or some pleasant draught;
    Sweet slumb'rous poppy, or the mild bohea.

28.

But hark, my pitying friend, and if you can
    Deceive the grim physician at the door,
Bring half the mountain springs; ah, hither bring
    The cold rock water from the shady bower.

29.

For till this night such thirst did ne'er invade,
    A thirst provok'd by heaven's avenging hand;
Hence bear me, friends, to quaff and quaff again
    The cool wave bubbling from the yellow sand."

30.

But now refresh'd, the phantom rais'd his head,
    And writhing, seem'd to aim once more to talk.
Quoth he, "Since remedies have small avail,
    Assist expiring death once more to walk."

31.

Then slowly rising from his loathsome bed,
    On wasted legs the monstrous spectre stood;
Gap'd wide, and foam'd, and hungry seem'd to ask,
    Tho' sick, an endless quantity of food.

32.

Now to the anxious youth his speech he turn'd,
    "Move quick, and bring from yonder black bureau,
The sacred book that may preserve my soul
    From long damnation and eternal woe.

33.

And with it bring, for you may find it there,
  The works of holy authors dead and gone:
The sacred tome of moving* Drelincourt,
  Or what more solemn Sherlock mus'd upon+."

34.

But he, unmindful of the vain command,
  Reason'd with Death, nor were his reasonings few:
"Quoth he, my lord, what phrenzy moves your brain;
  Pray what, my lord, can Sherlock be to you?

35.

Or all the sage divines that ever wrote,
  Grave Drelincourt, or heaven's inspired page;
These point their arrows at your harden'd breast,
  And raise new pains that time can ne'er assuage.

36.

Wicked old man, thy age has made thee dote;
  If peace, if sacred peace were found for you,
Hell would cry out, and all the damn'd arise,
  And more deserving ask for pity too.

37.

Bloody has been thy reign, O man of hell,
  Who sympathiz'd with no departing groan;
Cruel thou wast, nor dost thou now deserve
  To have "here lies" engrav'd upon thy stone.

Drelincourt on death.
+ *Sherlock on death.*

38.

He that could build his mansion o'er the tombs,
    Depending still on sickness and decay,
Might dwell unmov'd amidst November glooms,
    And laugh the dullest of his shades away.

39.

Even now, to glut thy savage rage, I see
    From eastern realms a bloody army rise*.
Else why those lights that tremble in the north;
    Why else yon comet blazing thro' the skies?

40.

Rejoice, O fiend, Britannia's tyrant sends
    From German plains his myriads to our shore;
The Caledonian with the Albion join'd;
    Bring them, ye winds, but waft them back no more!

41.

Why runs the stream dejected to the main,
    O Hudson, Hudson, dreary, dull and slow?
Seek me no more along that mountain stream,
    For on his banks is heard the sound of woe.

42.

Sword, famine, thirst, and pining sickness there,
    Shall people half the realms this monster owns;
He like the cruel foe, accursed be,
    Laughs at our pains, rejoices in our groans.

---

* British.

43.

How will you tremble if you hear your fate,
    Out of the dread Apocalypse your doom,
That death and hell must perish in the lake*
    Of fire, dispelling half hell's ancient gloom.

44.

He heard, and 'round with his black optics gaz'd,
    Full of despair, and curs'd, and rav'd and swore,
"And since this is my doom, said he, call up
    Your wood-mechanics+ to my chamber door.

45.

Blame not on me the havock to be made,
    Proclaim; even death abhors such woe to see:
I'll quit the world while decently I can,
    And leave the business to some deputy**."

46.

Now thus the drooping victim gave me charge,
    Pointing from the light window to the west:
"Go three miles o'er the plain and you shall see
    A burying-yard of sinners dead unblest.

47.

There, since 'tis dark, I'll plant a quivering light
    Just snatch'd from hell, by whose far glimmering beams
Thou shalt behold a tombstone, full eight feet,
    Hard by a grave, arrayed with ghosts and dreams.

---

* *Rev.* xx. *v.* 14.
+ *The Undertakers.*
** *George* III.

48.

And on that stone engrave this epitaph,
    Since death it seems must die like mortal men:
Yes, on that stone engrave this epitaph,
    Tho' all hell's furies snatch the engraving pen.

49.

"Death in this tomb his weary bones hath laid,
    Tir'd of his long continued victory:
What glory can there be to vanquish those
    Who all beneath his stroke are sure to die?

50.

Vast and unmatch'd throughout the world my fame
    Is born secure, and rides aloft in state:
No, by the stars, and by the heavens I sware
    Not Alexander's name is half so great.

51.

Six thousand years has sovereign sway been mine;
    None but myself can real glory claim;
Great regent of the earth I reign'd alone,
    And princes trembled when my mandate came.

52.

Traveller, wouldst thou his noblest trophies seek,
    Search in no narrow spot obscure for those;
The sea profound, the surface of all land,
    Is moulded with the myriads of his foes."

53.

Scarce had he spoke, when on the lofty dome
    Burst from the skies the fury of a blast;
Round the four eaves so loud and sad it play'd,
    As tho' all music were to breathe its last.

54.

Warm was the gale, and such as travellers say
    Sport with the sands on Zara's barren waste:
Black was the sky; a mourning carpet spread;
    Its azure blotted and its stars o'er cast.

55.

Lights through the air like blazing stars were hurl'd;
    Dogs howl'd, heaven mutter'd, and the tempest blew;
The red half moon peep'd from behind a cloud,
    As if afraid the fearful scene to view.

56.

The mournful trees that in the garden stood,
    Rend to the tempest as it rush'd along;
The elm, the myrtle, and the cypress sad,
    More melancholy tun'd its dreary song.

57.

Now from within the howls of Death I heard
    Cursing the dismal night that gave him birth;
Damning his ancient sire and mother sin,
    Who at the gates of hell accursed brought him forth*.

58.

Oft his pale breast with cruel hand he smote,
    And tearing from his limbs a winding sheet;
Roar'd like a devil; while the woods around,
    As wicked as himself, his words repeat.

---

* *See Paradise Lost, book II. v.* 780.

59.

Thrice toward the heaven his meagre arms he rear'd;
    Invok'd all hell and thunders on his head;
Bade light'nings fly, earth yawn, and tempests roar,
    And the sea wrap him in its ouzy bed.

60.

"My life for one cool draught: O fetch your springs:
    Haste, seize the wretch who my request denies.
Tophet receive him to thy lowest pit,
    Chain'd midst eternal oaths and blasphemies."

61.

Dim burnt the lamp, and now the phantom death
    Gave his last groans in horror and despair.
"All hell demands me hence," he said, and threw
    The red lamp hissing thro' the midnight air.

62.

Trembling across the plain my course I held,
    And found the cemetery in the gloom,
And in the midst a hell-red waving light
    Walking in horrid circles round the tomb.

63.

At distance far, approaching to the grave,
    By lamps and lanthorns guided thro' the shades,
A sable chariot drove with wild career,
    And following close a gloomy cavalcade;

64.

Whose spectre forms yet chill my soul with dread;
    Each wore a vest by Pluto's consort wove,
Death's kindred all; Death's horses they bestrode,
    And gallop'd fiercely as the chariot drove.

65.

Each horrid face a grisly mask conceal'd;
    Their busy eyes shot terror to my soul,
As now and then, by the pale lanthorn's beam,
    I saw them for their parted friend condole.

66.

Now deep was plac'd the carcase in the tomb,
    To dust and dull oblivion now resign'd;
Then turn'd the chariot to the house of night;
    The sable steeds went swifter than the wind:

67.

But as I stoop'd to write the appointed verse,
    Swifter than thought the airy scene decay'd;
Blooming the morn arose, and in the east
    Stalk'd gallantly in her sun-beam parade.

68.

Waking I found my weary night a dream;
    Dreams are perhaps forebodings of the soul;
Learn'd sages tell why all these whims arose,
    And from what source such mystic visions roll.

69.

Do they portend approaching death, which tells
    I soon must hence my darksome journey go?
Sweet Cherub Hope! Dispel the clouded dream
    Sweet Cherub Hope, man's guardian god below.

70.

Stranger, who'er thou art who this shall read,
    Say does thy nightly fancy rove like mine;
Transport thee o'er wide lands and wider seas
    Now underneath the pole and now the burning line?

71.

Poet, who thus dost rove, say, shall thou fear
    New Jordan's stream prefigured by the old?
It will but waft thee where they fathers are
    The bards with long eternity enroll'd.

72.

It will but waft thee where thy Homer shrouds
    His laurell'd head in some Elysian grove,
And on whose skirts perhaps in future years,
    At awful distance you and I may rove.

73.

Enough--when God and nature give the word,
    I'll tempt the dusky shore and narrow sea:
Content to die, just as it be decreed,
    At four score years, or now at twenty-three.

Poems (1786), 101-23.

U. S. Magazine   September, 1779

Psal. cxxxvii. *Imitated.*
By PHILIP FRENEAU*.

BY Babel's streams we sat and wept,
    When Sion bade our sorrows flow,
Our harps on lofty willows slept,
    That nigh the limpid waters grow.
The willows high, the waters clear
Behold our toils and sorrows there.

---

* *A young Gentleman to whom in the course of this work, we are greatly indebted.*

The cruel foe that captive led
    Our nation from their native soil,
The tyrant foe by whom we bled,
    Requir'd a song as well as toil.
Come with a song your sorrows cheer,
A song that Sion loves to hear.

How shall we, cruel tyrant, raise,
    A song on such a distant shore?
If I forget my Zion's praise,
    May my right hand be doom'd no more
To strike the silver-sounding string,
And thence the slumb'ring musick bring.

If I forget that happy home,
    My perjur'd tongue forbear to move,
My eyes go out in endless gloom,
    My joy, my rapture, and my love.
No rival grief my mind can share,
For thou shalt reign unrivall'd there.

Remember, Lord, that hated foe,
    When conquer'd Sion droop'd her head.
Who laughing at our deepest woe,
    Thus to our tears and sorrows said,
From its proud height debase her wall,
Destroy her towers, and ruin all.

Thou Babel's offspring, hated race,
    May some avenging monster seize,
And dash thy venom in thy face,
    For crimes and cruelties like these,
And proof to pity's melting tear,
With infant blood your walls besmear.

Monmouth, September 10, 1779

Poems (1786), 151-52.

U. S. Magazine   December, 1779

A DIALOGUE *between his Britannic Majesty and Mr. FOX.*

Supposed to have passed about the time of the approach of the combined Fleets of France and Spain to the British Coasts, August 1779.

King.

    GOOD Master Fox, your counsel I implore,
    Still George the Third, but potent George no more.
    By North conducted to the brink of fate,
    I mourn my folly and my pride too late:
5   The promises he made when once we met
    In Kew's gay shades*, I never shall forget,
    That at my feet the western world should fall,
    And bow to me the potent Lord of all
    Curse on his hopes, his councils and his schemes,
10   His plans of conquest and his golden dreams,
    These have allur'd me to the jaws of hell,
    By Satan tempted thus Iscariot fell:
    Divested of majestic pomp I come.
    My royal robes and airs I've left at home.
15   Speak freely, friend, whate'er you choose to say,
    Suppose me equal with yourself to day:
    How shall I shun the ruins that impend?
    How shall I make Columbia+ yet my friend?
    I dread the power of each revolted State,
20   The convex world hangs ballanc'd with their weight.
    How shall I dare the rage of France and Spain,
    And lost dominion o'er the waves regain?
    Advise me quick, for doubtful while we stand,
    Destruction gathers o'er this wretched land:
25   These hostile squadrons to my ruin led,
    These Gallic thunders fill my soul with dread,
    If these should conquer--Britain thou must fall

---

* *The royal gardens at Kew.*
+ *America, so called, by poetical liberty, from its discoverer.*

        And bend, a province, to the haughty Gaul,
        If this must be--thou earth expanding wide,
30   Unlucky George in thy dark entrails hide,
        Ye oceans, wrap me in your dark embrace,
        Ye mountains, shroud me to your lowest base.
        Fall on my head, ye everlasting rocks--
        But why so pensive, my good master Fox?

Fox.

35   While in the arms of power and peace you lay,
        Ambition led your restless soul astray
        Possest of lands extending far and wide,
        And more than Rome could boast in all her pride;
        Yet not contented with that mighty store,
40   Like a true miser, still you sought for more;
        And all in raptures for a tyrant's reign,
        You strove your subjects dearest rights to chain:
        Those ruffian hosts beyond the ocean sent
        By your commands on blood and murder bent,
45   With cruel hand the form of man defac'd,
        And laid the toils of art and nature waste.
        (For crimes like these imperial Britain bends,
        For crimes like these her ancient glory ends)
        These lands once truest to your name and race,
50   Whom the wide ocean's utmost waves embrace,
        Your just protection basely you deny'd,
        Their towns you plunder'd, and you burnt beside.
        Virginia's slaves without one blush of shame,
        Against their lords you arm'd with sword and flame,
55   At every port your ships of war you laid,
        And stove to ruin and distress their trade.
        Yet here, ev'n here, your mighty projects fail'd,
        For then from creeks their hardy seamen sail'd,
        In slender barques they cross'd a stormy main,
60   And traffick'd for the wealth of France and Spain,
        O'er either tropic and the line they pass'd,
        And deeply laden safe return'd at last:
        Nor think they had bow'd to Britain's sway,
        Though distant nations had not join'd the fray,
65   Alone they fought your armies and your fleet,
        And made your Clintons and your Howes retreat,

And yet while France stood doubting if to join,
Your ships they captur'd, and they took Burgoyne
How vain is Britain's strength, her armies now
70 Before Columbian's bolder veterans bow,
Her gallant veterans all our force despise,
Though late from ruin* we beheld them rise.
Before their arms our strongest bulwarks fall,
They storm the rampart and they scale the wall;
75 With equal dread, on either service sent,
They seize a fortress or they strike a tent.
  But should we bow beneath a foreign yoke,
And potent France atchieve the humbling stroke,
Yet every power and even ourselves must say,
80 "Just is the vengeance of the skies to day:"
For crimes like ours dire vengeance must atone,
Forbear your fasts, and let the skies alone,
By cruel kings in fierce Britannia bred,
Such seas of blood have first and last been shed,
85 That now distrest for each inhuman deed,
Our turn has come--our turn has come to bleed:
Forbear your groans; for war and death array,
March to the foe, and give the fates their way.
Can you behold without one hearty groan,
90 The fleets of France superior to your own?
Can you behold without one poignant pang,
The foreign conquests of the brave D'Estaing?
North is your friend, and now destruction knocks,
Still take his counsel, and regard not Fox.

King.

95 Ah! speak not thus--your words will break my heart,
Some softer counsel to my ears impart.
How can I march to meet the insulting foe,
Who never yet to hostile plains did go?
When was I vers'd in battles or in blood?
100 When have I fought upon the faithless flood?
Much better could I at my palace door

---

* *The Year* 1776.

Recline and hear the distant cannons roar.
Generals and admirals Britain yet can boast,
Some fight on land, and some defend the coast;
105 The fame of these throughout the globe resounds,
To these I leave the glory and the wounds;
But since this honour for no blood atones,
I must and will be careful of my bones.
    What pleasure to your monarch would it be,
110 If Lords and Commons could at last agree,
Could North with Fox in firm alliance stand,
And Burke and Sandwich shake the social hand,
Then should we bring the rebels to our feet,
And France and Spain ingloriously retreat,
115 Her ancient glories to this isle return,
And we no more for lost Columbia mourn.

Fox.

Alliance!--what,--Your Highness must be mad;
Say, what alliance can with these be had?
Can lambs and wolves in social bands ally?
120 When these prove friendly, then will North and I.
Alliance! no--I curse the horrid thought;
Ally with those their country's ruin sought?
Who to perdition sold their native land,
Leagu'd with the foe, a close connected band:
125 Ally with these?--I speak it to your face--
Alliance here is ruin and disgrace.
Angels and devils in such bonds unite,
So hell is ally'd to the realms of light:
Let North or Germaine still my prayers deride,
130 Let turncoat Johnston take the courtly side,
Even Pitt, if living, might with these agree;
But no alliance shall they have with me.
    But since no shame forbids your tongue to own,
A royal coward fills Britannia's throne;
135 Since our best chiefs must fight your mad campaigns,
And be disgrac'd at last by him who reigns.
No wonder, heaven! such ill success attends!
No wonder North and Mansfield are your friends!
Take my advice, with these to battle go,
140 These book-learned heroes may confront the foe.

Those first who led us tow'rds the brink of fate,
Should still be foremost when at Pluto's gate;
Let them, grown desperate by our ruin of woes,
Collect new fury from this host of foes,
145 And dally'd with themselves to ruin steer,
The just conclusion of their made career,

King.

No comfort in these cruel words I find–
Ungrateful words to my tormented mind!
With me alone both France and Spain contend,
150 And not one nation will be called my friend;
Unpitying now the Dutchman sees me fall,
The Russian leaves me to the haughty Gaul.
The German grown as Brutish as the Dane,
Consigns my carcase to the jaws of Spain.
155 Where are the hosts they promis'd me of yore,
When rich and great they herad my thunders roar,
While yet confess'd the master of the sea,
The Germans drain'd their wide domain for me;
And aiding Britain with a friendly hand,
160 Helpt to subdue the rebels and their land*?
Ah! rebels, rebels! insolent and mad,
My Scottish rebels were not half so bad+,
They soon submitted to superior sway**;
But these grow stronger as my hosts decay:
165 What hosts have perished on their hostile shore?
They went for conquest, but return'd no more.
Columbia, thou a friend in better times!
Lost are to me thy pleasurable climes.
You wish me buried in eternal night,
170 You curse the day when first I saw the light;
Thy commerce vanish'd, hostile nations share,
And thus you leave me naked, poor, and bare;
Despis'd by those who should my cause defend,

---

* *The Hessians, Waldeckers, Anspachers,* &c.
+ *The Year* 1745.
** *Culloden.*

       And helpless left without one pitying friend.
175 These dire afflictions shake my changeful throne,
       And turn my brain--a very idiot grown:
       Of all the isles, the realms with which I part,
       Columbia sits the heaviest at my heart,
       She, she provokes the deepest, heaviest sigh,
180 And makes me doubly wretched ere I die.
            Some dreary convents unfrequented gloom
       (Like Charles of Spain) had better be my doom:
       There while in absence from my crown I sigh,
       The Prince of Wales these ills may rectify.
185 A happier fortune may his crown await,
       He yet perhaps may save this state.
       I'll to my prayers, my bishops and my beads,
       And beg God's pardon for my heinous deeds;
       Those streams of blood, that spilt by my command,
190 Call out for vengeance on this guilty land.

              Fox.

       You ask for mercy--can you cry to God,
       Who had no mercy on a parson Dodd*?
       No inward image of the power divine,
       No gentle feelings warm that soul of thine,
195 Convents you have--no need to look for new,
       Your convents are the brothel and the stew.
       One horrid act+ disgrac'd old Jesse's son,
       And that one blemish have you hit upon:
       You seiz'd an English Quaker's tempting wife,
200 And push'd him off to lose his sneaking life;
       Even to that coast where freedom sent to quell,
       All in their pride the flower of Britain fell.
       But ruin'd was your scheme, the plan was vain,
       For when were Quakers in a battle slain?
205 As well might whales by closing waves expire,
       Or Salamander's perish in the fire.
            When France and Spain are thundering at your doors,

---

  * *Dr. William Dodd, whose history is well known.*
  + *In the case of Uriah.*

Is this a time for kings to lodge with whores?
In one short sentence take my whole advice.
210 (It is no time to flatter and be nice)
With all your soul for instant peace contend,
Thus shall you be your country's truest friend.
Peace, heavenly peace, may stay your tottering throne,
But wars and death and blood can profit none.
215 To Russia send, in humblest guise array'd,
And beg her intercession, not her aid:
Withdraw your armies from th'Americ' shore,
And vex Columbia with your fleets no more,
Vain are their conquests, past experience shews,
220 For what this hour they gain, the next they lose.
Implore the friendship of these injur'd states;
No longer strive against the stubborn fates.
Since heaven has doom'd Columbia to be free,
What is her commerce and her wealth to thee?
225 Since heav'n that land of promise has denied,
Regain by prudence what you lost by pride:
Immediate ruin each delay attends,
Imperial Britain scarce her coast defends;
Hibernia sees the threatening foes advance,
230 And feels an ague at the thoughts of France;
Jamaica mourns her half-protected state,
Barbadoes soon may share Grenada's fate,
And every isle that owns your reign to day,
May bow to-morrow to great Louis' sway.
235 Yes--while I speak, your empire, great before,
Contracts its limits, and is great no more.
Unhappy prince! what madness has possest,
What worse than madness seiz'd thy vengeful breast,
When white-rob'd peace before thy portal stood,
240 To drive her hence, and stain the world with blood?
For this destruction threatens from the skies;
See hostile navies to our ruin rise;
Our fleets inglorious shun the force of Spain,
And France triumphant stems the subject main.

NOTES

Line 117: *Alliance!--what,* &c] See his speech in the House of Commons, June 22, 1779, in answer to the Lord Nugent.

Line 130: *Let turncoat Johnston,* &c.] The worthy British Commissioner, of bribing memory, who, for the sake of a few guineas belyed his own conscience, and sided with the majority.

Line 136: *And be disgrac'd at last by him who reigns.*] As Gage, the Howe's, Burgoyen, &c. for not doing impossibilities.

Line 182: *Like Charles of Spain,* &c.] Charles V. who in 1556, resigning the crown to his son Philip II. shut himself up in the monastery of St. Just, in Spain, where he died two years after.

Line 187: *I'll to my prayers, my bishops, and my beads.*] This is not said without foundation, as he established the Roman Catholic religion in Canada, in 1775.

Line 199: *You seiz'd an English Quaker's tempting wife.*] "The connection between vice and meanness is a fit object for satire; but when the satire is a fact, it cuts with the irresistible power of a diamond. If a Quaker, in defence of his just rights, his property, and the chastity of his house, takes up a musket, he is expelled the meeting; but the present king of England, who seduced and took into keeping a sister of their society, is reverenced and supported with repeated testimonies, while the friendly noodle from whom she was taken, (and who is now in this city) continues a drudge in the service of his rival, as if proud of being cuckolded by a creature called a king."
American Crisis, No. 3. *Printed at Philadelphia,* 1777.

Poems (1786), 177-85.

Boston *Independent Ledger*   June 25, 1781

Copy of a late publication printed at Philadelphia, Entitled,
   The *British* PRISON-SHIP: A *poem,* in four Cantos.

This is a substantively unaltered reprint of the first published text of the poem, printed in Philadelphia by Francis Bailey.[1] Neither the complete poem nor excerpts reappeared in newspapers until November 14, 1807, when the New York *Port Folio* reprinted the major part of the 1786 Canto I as part of their extended review of Freneau's verse. The *Port Folio* excerpt, reflecting both 1786 and 1795 revisions in this portion of the poem, is introduced as follows:

> The following lines described the building, sailing, and capture of the Aurora with great beauty.

One full stanza and four additional lines, as well as canto divisions, were deleted in the excerpt.

Leary notes later excerpts of the poem in the New York *Public Advertiser,* May 24 and 25, 1809. However, I could not locate them in these or surrounding issues.

Poems (1786), 186-205.

---

[1] Several lines from the second canto of the 1786 text of poem, however, had appeared before Bailey's text, in which they were not included. See *U. S. Magazine,* July, 1779.

Freeman's Journal   August 8, 1781

A POEM on the memorable victory obtained by the gallant capt. Paul Jones, of the Good Man Richard, over the Seraphis, &c. under the command of capt. Pearson.

1. O'ER the rough main with flowing sheet
   The guardian of a numerous fleet,
      Seraphis from the Baltic came:
   A ship of less tremendous force
   Sail'd by her side the self same course,
      Countess of Scarbro' was her name.
2. And now their native coasts appear,
   Britannia's hills their summits rear
      Above the German main;
   Fond to suppose their dangers o'er,
   They southward coast along the shore,
      Thy waters, gentle Thames, to gain.
3. Full forty guns Seraphis bore,
   And Scarbro's Countess twenty-four;
      Mann'd with Old England's boldest tars--
   What flag that rides the Gallic seas
   Shall dare attack such piles as these,
      Design'd for tumults and for wars!
4. Now from the topmast's giddy height
   A seaman cry'd--"four sail in sight
      "Approach with favouring gales."
   Pearson, resolv'd to save the fleet,
   Stood off to sea these ships to meet,
      And closely brac'd his shivering sails.
5. With him advanc'd the Countess bold,
   Like a black tar in wars grown old:
      And now these floating piles drew nigh;
   But, muse, unfold what chief of fame
   In t'other warlike squadron came,
      Whose standards at his mast head fly.
6. 'Twas Jones, brave Jones, to battle led
   As bold a crew as ever bled
      Upon the sky-surrounded main;
   The standards of the Western World
   Were to the willing winds unfurl'd,
      Denying Britain's tyrant reign.

7. The *Good Man Richard* led the line;
   The *Alliance* next: With these combine
       The Gallic ship they *Pallas* call:
   The Vengeance, arm'd with sword and flame,
   These to attack the Britons came;
       But *two* accomplish'd all.
8. Now Phoebus sought his pearly bed:
   But who can tell the scenes of dread,
       The horrors of that fatal night!
   Close up these floating castles came;
   The Good Man Richard bursts in flame;
       Seraphis trembled at the sight.
9. She felt the fury of *her* ball;
   Down, prostrate down, the Britons fall;
       The decks were strew'd with slain;
   Jones to the foe his vessel lash'd;
   And, while the black artillery flash'd,
       Loud thunders shook the main.
10. Alas! that mortals should employ
    Such murdering engines, to destroy
        The frame by Heaven so nicely join'd;
    Alas! that e'er the god decreed
    That brother should by brother bleed,
        And pour'd such madness in the mind.
11. But thou, brave Jones, no blame shalt bear;
    The rights of men demand thy care:
        For *these* you dare the greedy waves;
    No tyrant on destruction bent
    Has plann'd thy conquests--thou art sent
        To hurtle tyrants and their slaves.
12. See!--dread Seraphis flames again--
    And art thou, Jones, among the slain,
        And sunk to Neptune's caves below--
    He lives--tho' crouds around him fall,
    Still he, unhurt, survives them all;
        Almost alone he fights the foe.
13. And can thy ship these strokes sustain?
    Behold thy brave companions slain,
        All clasp'd in ocean's dark embrace.
    Strike, or be sunk--the Briton cries--
    Sink, if you can--the chief replies,
        Fierce lightnings blazing in his face.

14. Then to the side three guns he drew,
    (Almost deserted by his crew)
        And charg'd them deep with woe:
    By *Pearson's* flash he aim'd the balls:
    His main-mast totters--down it falls--
        Tremendous was the blow.
15. Pearson as yet disdain'd to yield,
    But scarce his secret fears conceal'd,
        And thus was heard to cry--
    "With hell, not mortals, I contend;
    "What art thou--human, or a fiend,
        "That dost my force defy?
16. "Return, my lads, the fight renew."
    So call'd bold Pearson to his crew,
        But call'd, alas! in vain;
    Some on the decks lay maim'd and dead;
    Some to their deep recesses fled,
        And more were bury'd in the main.
17. Distress'd, forsaken and alone,
    He haul'd his tatter'd standard down,
        And yielded to his gallant foe;
    Bold Pallas soon the Countess took,
    Thus both their haughty colours struck,
        Confessing what the brave can do.
18. But, Jones, too dearly didst thou buy
    These ships possest so gloriously,
        Too many deaths disgrac'd the fray;
    Thy bark that bore the conquering flame,
    That the proud Briton overcame,
        Even she forsook thee on thy way.
19. For when the morn began to shine,
    Fatal to her, the ocean brine
        Pour'd thro' each spacious wound;
    Quick in the deep she disappear'd;--
    But Jones to friendly Belgia steer'd,
        With conquest and with glory crown'd.
20. Go on, great man, to daunt the foe,
    And bid the haughty Britons know,
        They to our Thirteen Stars shall bend;
    Those Stars that veil'd in dark attire,
    Long glimmer'd with a feeble fire,
        But radiant now ascend.

21. Bend to the Stars that flaming rise,
    In western not in eastern skies,
        Fair freedom's reign restor'd--
    So when the magi came from far,
    Beheld the God-attending Star,
        They trembled and ador'd.--

Poems (1786), 207-11.

Freeman's Journal   September 5, 1781

To his Excellency
GENERAL *WASHINGTON.*

ACCEPT, great chief, that share of honest praise
A greatful people to your merit pays:
Verse is too mean your virtues to display,
And words too weak our meaning to convey.
    When first proud Britain rais'd her heavy hand
With claims unjust to bind your native land,
Transported armies, and her millions spent
To enforce the mandates that a tyrant sent;
"Resist! Resist!" was heard through every state,
You heard the call and mourn'd your country's fate;
Then rising fierce her sons in arms array'd,
And taught to vanquish those who dar'd invade.
    Those *British chiefs* whom former wars had crown'd
With conquest--and in every clime renown'd;
Who forc'd new realms to own their monarch's law
And *whom* even George beheld with secret awe;
Those mighty chiefs, compell'd to fly or yield
Scarce dar'd to meet you on the embattl'd field:
To Boston's town you chas'd the trembling crew
Quick, even from thence the British ruffians flew
Through wintry waves they fled, and thought the sea
With all its storms less terrible than thee!
    What chief like you our armies could command
And bring us safely to the promis'd land?--

Not *Clinton-like,* with victory elate,--
'Tis in misfortune you are doubly great:
When *Howe* victorious thy weak army chas'd
And sure of conquest laid *Cesarea* waste
When prostrate bleeding at his feet she lay
And the proud victor tore her wreaths away,
You undismay'd put forth your warlike hand
And rais'd the drowning genius of the land,
Repell'd the foe, their choicest warriors slain,
And drove them howling to their ships again.

    While *others* kindle into martial rage
Whom fierce ambition urges to engage
An iron race by angry heaven design'd
To conquer first and then enslave mankind;
In *him* a hero more humane we see
He ventures life that others may be free.

    O! may you live to hail that glorious day
When Britain homeward shall pursue her way--
That race subdu'd, who fill'd the world with slain
And rode tyrannic o'er the subject main!--
What few presum'd, you boldly have atchiev'd
A tyrant humbled, and a world reliev'd.

    Rome's boasted chiefs, who, to their own disgrace
Prov'd the worst scourges of the human race,
Pierc'd by whose darts a thousand nations bled,
Who captive princes at their chariots led;
Born to enslave, to ravage and subdue--
Return to *nothing* when compar'd to you;
Throughout the world thy growing fame has spread,
In every country are thy virtues read;
Remotest *India* hears thy deeds of fame
The hardy Scythian stammers at thy name,
The haughty Turk, now longing to be free,
Neglects his *Sultan* to enquire of thee;
The barbarous Briton hails thee to his shores
And calls him *Rebel*--whom his heart adores!

    Still may the heavens prolong thy vital date
And still may conquest on thy banners wait;
Whether afar to ravag'd lands you go
Where wild *Patowmac's* rapid waters flow,
Or where *Saluda* laves the fertile plain
And swoln by torrents rushes to the main;

Or if again to Hudson you repair
To smite the cruel foe that lingers there--
Revenge *their* cause, whose virute was their crime,
The exil'd people of a southern clime--
  Late from the world in quiet may'st thou rise
And mourn'd by millions, reach thy native skies--
With patriot kings and generous chiefs to shine,
Whose virtues rais'd them to be deem'd divine:
May *Louis* only equal honors claim,
Alike in merits and alike in fame.

Poems (1786), 212-14.

American Museum   September, 1787

  Address to gen. Washington--By Philip Freneau.
     Written anno 1781.

This text reflects all of the substantive variants of the 1786 version, as well as the following additional revisions:

  Stanzas one and two combined into one stanza.

  Stanza 1, line 3: Verse is too mean your virtues to display,

  Stanza 4, line 5: In you a hero more humane we see,
        line 6: You venture life, that others may be free.

  Stanza 8, line 6: Alike in merit and alike in fame.

Freeman's Journal   September 5, 1781

Copy of an intercepted Letter from a New-York Tory, to his Friend in this city.

DEAR Sir I'm so anxious to hear of your health,
I beg you would send me a letter by stealth:
I hope a few months will quite alter the case
When the wars are concluded we'll meet and embrace;
For I'm led to believe from our brilliant success,
And what is as clear, your amazing distress,
That the cause of rebellion has met with a check
That will bring all its patrons to hang by the neck:
Cornwallis has manag'd so well in the South
That those rebels han't victuals to put in their mouth,
And Arnold has stript them, we hear, to the buff,--
Has burnt their tobacco and left them--the snuff.
Dear Thomas, I wish you would move from that town
Where meet all the rebels of fame and renown;
When our armies victorious shall clear that damn'd nest
You may chance, tho' a tory, to swing with the rest.
But again--on reflection--I beg you would stay--
You may serve us yet better than if mov'd away--
Give advice to Sir Harry of all that is passing,
What vessels are building, what cargoes amassing;
Inform to a day when those vessels will sail
That our cruisers may capture them all without fail--
By proceedings like these your peace shall be made
The rebellious shall swing, but be you ne'er afraid.
I cannot conceive how you do to subsist--
The rebels are starving, except those who list,
And as you reside in the land of Gomorrah,
You must fare as the rest do, I think, to your sorrow.
Poor souls! if ye knew what a doom is decreed
(I mean not for you but for rebels indeed)
You would tremble to think of the vengeance in store
The halters and gibbets--I mention no more.
The rebels must surely conclude they're undone,
Their navy is ruin'd, their armies have run
It is time they should now from delusion awaken--
The rebellion is done--for the Trumbull is taken!

                              TORY

Poems (1786), 214-16.

Freeman's Journal   September 19, 1781

DIALOGUE between the Lords DUNMORE and MANSFIELD.

Dunmore.

EVER since I return'd to my dear native shore,
No debtor in *Cheapside* was ever dunn'd more
I'm dunn'd by my barber, my taylor, my groom:
How can I do else than to fret and to fume?
They join to attack me with one good accord,
From morning 'till night 'tis, "my lord, and my lord."
And there comes the cobler, so often deny'd--
If I had him in private, I'd thresh his damn'd hide.

Mansfield.

Would you worry the man, that has found you in shoes?
Come, courage my lord, I can tell you good news--
Virginia is conquer'd, the rebels are bang'd,
You are now to go over and see them safe hang'd:
I hope it is not to your nature abhorrent
To sign for these wretches a legal death-warrant--
Were I but in your place, I'm sure it would suit
To sign their death-warrants and hang them to boot.

Dunmore.

My lord!--I'm amaz'd--have we routed the foe?--
I shall govern again then, if matters be so,--
And as to the hanging, in short, to be plain,--
I'll hang them so well they'll ne'er want it again.
With regard to the wretches who thump at my gates
I'll discharge all their dues with the rebel estates;
In less than three months I shall send a polacca
As deep as she'll swim, sir, with corn and tobacco.

Mansfield.

And send us some rebels--a dozen or so--
They'll serve here in London by way of a show;
And as to the tories, believe me, dear cousin,
We can spare you some hundreds to pay for the dozen.

Poems (1786), 217-18.

Freeman's Journal   October 8, 1781 (Postscript)

To Lord CORNWALLIS.

HAIL great destroyer (equall'd by none)
Of countries not thy master's nor thy own!
Hatch'd by some Demon on a stormy day,
Satan's best substitute to burn and slay
Confin'd at last,--hemm'd in by land and sea,
Burgoyne himself was but a type of thee!
Like his to freedom was thy deadly hate,
Like his thy baseness and be his thy fate.--
To you like him no prospect nature yields
But ruin'd wastes and desolated fields;
In vain you raise the interposing wall
And hoist those *standards* that like *you* must fall;
In vain you break old Charon's* sable boat
Lest you to hell with negro souls should float;
In *you* conclude the glories of your race;
Complete your monarch's and you own disgrace.
What has your Lordship's pilfering arms attaind?--
Vast hoards of *plunder* and no state regain'd--
That must return, tho' perhaps you may groan,
Resign it, Ruffian, for 'tis not your own;--
Then, *Lord* and *Soldier,* headlong to the brine
Rush down at once--the devil and the swine!--
Wouldst thou at once with *Washington* engage,
Sad object of his pity not his rage!
See, round thy posts how terribly advance
The chiefs, the soldiers and the fleets of France!
Fight while you can, for warlike *Rochambeau*
Aims at your head his last decisive blow;
A thousand ghosts from earth untimely sped
Can take no rest till you like them are dead;
Then die, my Lord--that only chance remains
To wash away dishonourable stains;
For small advantage would your *capture* bring,
The plundering servant of a bankrupt king.

Poems (1786), 216-17.

---

*He broke up the Charon man of war to serve in constructing redoubts.

Freeman's Journal   October 17, 1781

An EPISTLE from Lord CORNWALLIS to Sir HENRY CLINTON.

FROM clouds of smoke, and flames that round me glow,
To you dear Clinton I disclose my woe:
Here cannons flash, bombs glance, and bullets fly;
Not Satan's self endures such misery.
Was I foredoom'd like Korah to expire,
Hurl'd to perdition in a blaze of fire?
With these blue flames can mortal man contend,
What arms can aid me, or what walls defend?
Even to these gates last night a phantom strode,
And hail'd me trembling to his dark abode:
Aghast I stood, struck motionless and dumb,
Seiz'd with the horrors of the world to come.
    Were but my power as mighty as my rage,
Far different battles would Cornwallis wage;
Beneath his sword yon' threatning hosts should groan,
The earth should quake with thunders all his own.
O crocodile! had I thy flinty hide,
Swords to defy, and glance the balls aside,
By my own prowess would I rout the foe,
With my own javelin would I work their woe;
But fate's averse, and heaven's supreme decree
Nile's serpent form'd more excellent than me.
    Has heaven in secret for some crime decreed,
That I should suffer, and my soldiers bleed?
Or is it by the jealous skies conceal'd,
That I must bend, and they ignobly yield?
Ah! no--The thought o'erwelms my soul with grief.
Come, bold sir Harry, come to my relief;
Come thou brave man whom rebels Tombstone call,
But Britons, Graves,--come Digby, devil and all;
Come princely William with thy potent aid,
Can George's blood by Frenchmen be dismay'd?
From a king's *brother* once Scots rebels run,
And shall not these be routed by a *son*?
Come with your ships to this disastrous shore,
Come--or I sink--and sink to rise no more;
By every motive that can sway the brave

Haste and my feeble fainting army save;
Come and lost empire o'er the deep regain,
Chastise these upstarts that usurp the main:
I see their first rates to the charge advance,
I see lost Irish wear the flags of France;
There a strict rule the wakeful Frenchman keeps;
There undisturb'd by dogs lord Rawdon sleeps!
    Tir'd with long acting on this bloody stage,
Sick of the follies of a wrangling age–
Come with your fleet and help me to retire
To Britain's coast, the land of my desire–
For, me the foe their certain captive deem,
And every school boy takes me for his theme–
Long, much too long in this hard service try'd,
Bespatter'd still, be-devil'd and bely'd,
With the first chance that favoring fortune sends
I'll fly, converted, from this land of fiends;
Then, like Burgoyne, as fortunate at least,
Slip on the surplice, and be dubb'd a priest.

Poems (1786), 219-20.

Freeman's Journal   October 24, 1781

A MORAL THOUGHT.

IN youth gay scenes attract our eyes,
    And not suspecting their decay
Life's flow'ry fields before us rise,
    Regardless of its winter day;

But vain pursuits, and joys as vain,
    Convince us life is but a dream.
Death is to wake to rise again,
    To that true life I best esteem.

So nightly on the flowing tide,
    Oft have I seen a raree-show;

Reflected stars on either side,
    And glittering moons were seen below.

But when the tide had ebb'd away,
    The scene fantastic with it fled,
A bank of mud around me lay,
    And sea-weed on the river's bed.

Poems (1786), 221.

Freeman's Journal   November 7, 1781

On the fall of general earl CORNWALLIS, who, with above eight thousand men, surrendered themselves prisoners of war to the renowned and illustrious general GEORGE WASHINGTON, commander in chief of the allied armies of France and America, on the memorable 19th of October, 1781.

Give us the proudest prisoner of the Goths,
That we may hew his limbs, and on a pile
Ad manes fratum sacrifice his flesh,
Before this earthly prison of their bones:
That so the shadow be not unappeas'd,
Nor we distracted with prodigies on earth.
            Shakespear's Titus Andronicus, Act I. Scene II.

A DEVIL, ally'd to Howe, Burgoyne and Gage,
Once more, nor this the last, provokes my rage:--
Who saw these Nimrods first for conquest burn!
Who has not seen them to the dust return?
This ruffian next, who scour'd our ravag'd fields,
Foe to the human race, Cornwallis yields!--
None e'er before essay'd such desperate crimes,
Alone he stood, arch-butcher of the times,
Rov'd uncontroul'd this wasted country o'er,
Strew'd plains with dead, and bath'd his jaws with gore!
    'Twas thus the wolf, who fought by night his prey,

And plunder'd all he met with on his way,
Stole what he could, and murder'd as he pass'd,
Chanc'd on a trap, and lost his head at last.
      What pen can paint, what human tongue can tell
The endless murders of this man of hell!
Nature in him disgrac'd the form divine;
Nature mistook, she meant him for a--swine:
That eye his forehead to her shame adorns;
Blush! nature, blush!--bestow him tail and horns!--
By him the orphans mourn--the widow'd dame
Saw ruin spreading in the wasteful flame;
Gash'd o'er with wounds beheld with streaming eye
A son, a brother, or a consort, die!
Through ruin'd realms bones lie without a tomb,
And souls he sped to their eternal doom,
Who else had liv'd, and seen their toils again
Bless'd by the genius of the rural reign.
      But turn your eyes and see the murderer fall,
Then say--"Cornwallis has atchiev'd it all."--
Yet he preserves the honor and the fame
That vanquish'd heroes only ought to claim.--
Is he a hero?--Read, and you will find
Heroes are beings of a different kind:--
Compassion to the worst of men is due,
And mercy heaven's first attribute, 'tis true;
Yet most presume it was *too nobly* done
To grant mild terms *to Satan's firstborn son.*
      Convinc'd we are, no foreign spot of earth
But Britain only, gave this reptile birth.
That white-cliff'd isle, the vengeful dragon's den,
Has sent us monsters where we look'd for men.
When memory paints their horrid deeds anew,
And brings these murdering miscreants to your view,
Then ask the leaders of these bloody bands,
Can they expect compassion at our hands?--
      But may this year, the glorious eighty one,
Conclude successful, as it first begun;
This brilliant year their total downfall see,
And what Cornwallis *is*, may Clinton *be*.
      O come the time, nor distant be the day,
When our bold navy shall its wings display;
Mann'd by our sons, to seek that barbarous shore,

The wrongs revenging that their fathers bore:
As Samuel hew'd the tyrant Agag down,
So hew the wearer of the British crown;
Unpitying, next his hated offspring slay,
Or into foreign lands the fiends convey:
Give them their turn to pine and die in chains,
'Till not one monster of the race remains.
  Thou, who resid'st on those thrice happy shores,
Where white rob'd peace her envied blessings pours,
Stay, and enjoy the pleasures that she yields;
But come not, stranger, to our wasted fields,
For warlike hosts on every plain appear;
War damps the beauties of the rising year:
In vain the groves their bloomy sweets display;
War's clouded winter chills the charms of May;
Here human blood the trampled harvest stains;
Here bones of men yet whiten all the plains;
Seas teem with dead; and our unhappy shore
Forever blushes with its children's gore.
  But turn your eyes--behold the tyrant fall,
And think--Cornwallis has atchiev'd it all.--
  All mean revenge Americans disdain,
Oft have they prov'd it, and now prove again;
With nobler fires their generous bosoms glow;
Still in the captive they forget the foe--
But when a *nation* takes a wrongful cause,
And hostile turns to heaven's and nature's laws;
When sacrificing at ambition's shrine,
Kings slight the mandates of the power divine,
And devastation spread on every side,
To gratify their malice or their pride,
And send their slaves their projects to fulfill,
To wrest our freedom, or our blood to spill:--
Such to forgive, is virture too sublime;
For even compassion has been found a crime.
  A prophet once, for miracles renown'd,
Bade *Joash* smite the arrows on the ground--
Taking the mystic shafts, the prince obey'd,
Thrice smote the earth--and then he stay'd--
  Griev'd when he saw full victory deny'd
"Six times you should have smote," the prophet cried,
"Then had proud *Syria* sunk beneath thy power;"

"Now thrice you smite her—but shall smite no more."--
    Cornwallis! thou are rank'd among the great;
Such was the will of all-controuling fate.
As mighty men, who liv'd in days of yore,
Were figur'd out some centuries before:
So you with them in equal honour join,
Your great precursor's name was Jack Burgoyne!
Like you he was, a man in arms renown'd,
Who, hot for conquest, sail'd the ocean round;
This, this was he, who scour'd the woods for praise,
And burnt down cities* to describe the blaze!
    So, while on fire, his harp Rome's tyrant strung,
And as the buildings flam'd, old Nero sung.
    Who would have guess'd the purpose of the fates,
When that *proud boaster* bow'd to conquering Gates?--
Then sung the sisters+ as the wheel went round,
(Could he have heard the invigorating sound)
Thus surely did the fatal sisters sing—
"When just four years do this same season bring,
"And in his annual journey, when the sun
"Four times completely shall his circuit run,
"An *angel* then shall rid you of your fears,
"By binding *Satan* for a thousand years,
"Shall lash the serpent to the infernal shore,
"To waste the nations, and deceive no more,
"Make wars and blood, and tyranny to cease,
"And hush the fiends of Britain into peace."
    Joy to your lordship, and your high descent,
You are the Satan that the sisters meant.
Too soon you found your race of ruin run,
Your conquests ended, and your battles done!--
But that to live is better than to die,
And life you chose, tho' life with infamy
You should have climb'd your loftiest vessel's deck,
And hung a millstone round your halter'd neck--

---

*Charlestown, near Boston. See his letter on that occasion.
+*The Parcæ*, or *Fates*, who, according to the Heathen mythology, were three in number.

Then plung'd forever to the wat'ry bed,
Hell in your heart, and vengeance on your head.
    All must confess, that in regard to you,
'Twas wrong to rob the devil of his due:--
For Hayne, for Hayne! no death but thine atones;
For thee, Cornwallis, how the gallows groans!
That injur'd man's, and all the blood you've shed,
That blood shall rest on your devoted head;
Asham'd to live, and yet afraid to die,
Your courage slacken'd as the foe drew nigh.--
Ungrateful wretch, to yield your *favourite band*
To chains and prisons in a hostile land;
To the wide world your *Negro friends* to cast,
And leave your *Tories* to be hang'd at last!--
You should have fought with horror and amaze,
'Till scorch'd to cinders in the cannon blaze,
'Till all your host of Beezlebubs was slain,
Doom'd to disgrace no human shape again.--
As if from hell this horned host he drew,
Swift from the South the embodied ruffians flew;
Destruction follow'd at their cloven feet,
'Till you, Fayette, constrain'd them to retreat,
And held them close, 'till thy fam'd squadron came,
De Grasse, completing their eternal shame.
    When the loud cannon's unremitting glare,
And red hot balls compell'd *you* to despair,
How could you stand to meet your generous foe?
Did not the sight confound your heart with woe?--
In thy great soul what god-like virtues shine,
What inborn greatness, Washington, is thine!--
Else had no prisoner trod these lands to-day,
All, with his lordship, had been swept away,
All doom'd alike death's vermin to regale,
Nor one been left to tell the dreadful tale!--
But his own terms the anguish'd murderer nam'd--
He nobly gave the miscreant all he claim'd,
And bade Cornwallis, conquer'd and distress'd,
Bear all his torments in his tortur'd breast.
    Now curs'd with life, a *foe* to man and God,
Like *Cain*, I drove you to the land of *Nod*.
He with a brother's blood his hands did stain,
One brother he, you have a thousand slain.

And, O! may heaven affix some public *mark*
To know Cornwallis--may he howl and bark!--
On eagle's wings explore your downward flight
To the deep horrors of the darkest night,
Where, wrapt in shade on nature's utmost bound,
No longer sun, nor moon, nor stars, are found;
Where never light her kindling radiance shed
But the dark comets rove with all their *dead**,
Doom'd through the tracts of endless space to run
No more revolving to confound the sun.
    Such horrid deeds your spotted soul defame
We grieve to think your shape and ours the same!
Enjoy what comfort in this life you can,
The form you have, not feelings of a man:
Haste to the rocks thou curse to human kind,
There thou may'st wolves and brother tygers find,
Eternal exile be your righteous doom
And gnash your dragon's teeth in some sequester'd gloom--
Such be the end of each relentless foe
Who feels no pity for another's woe--
So may they fall--even you though much too late
Shall curse the day you languish'd to be great;
Haste from the torments of the present life
Quick, let the halter end thee or the knife;
So may destruction rush with speedy wing,
Low as yourself to drag your cruel king,
His head torn off, his hands, his feet and all,
Deep in the dust may Dagon's image fall;
His stump alone escape the vengeful steel
Sav'd but to grace the gibbet or the wheel.

Poems (1786), 222-28.

---

* See *Whiston's Hypothesis.*

To the memory of the brave Americans, under general Greene, who fell in the action of September 8, 1781.

AT Eutaw springs the valiant died;
    Their limbs with dust are cover'd o'er--
Weep on, ye springs, your tearful tide;
    How many heroes are no more!
If in this wreck of ruin, they
    Can yet be thought to claim a tear,
O smite thy gentle breast, and say
    The friends of freedom slumber here!
Thou, who shalt trace this bloody plain,
    If goodness rules thy generous breast,
Sigh for the wasted rural reign;
    Sigh for the shepherds sunk to rest!
Stranger, their humble graves adorn;
    You too may fall and ask a tear:
'Tis not the beauty of the morn
    That proves the evening shall be clear.--
They saw their injur'd country's woe;
    The flaming town, the wasted field;
They rush'd to meet the insulting foe;
    They took the spear--but left the shield.
Led by thy conquering standards, Greene,
    The Britons they compell'd to fly:
None distant view'd the fatal plain;
    None griev'd in such a cause to die.--
But, like the Parthian, fam'd of old,
    Who flying, still their arrows threw;
These routed Britons, full as bold,
    Retreated, and retreating slew.
Now rest in peace our patriot band;
    Tho' far from nature's limits thrown,
We trust they find a happier land,
    A brighter Phœbus of their own.

Poems (1786), 229-30.

Freeman's Journal   January 2, 1782

   PLATO the philosopher to his friend THEON.

Semel omnibus calcanda via Lethi.   Hor.

WHY Theon wouldst thou longer groan
    Beneath a weight of years and woe,
Thy youth is lost, thy pleasures flown
    And time proclaims, "Tis time to go."

To Willows sad and weeping yews
    With me a while, dear friend, repair,
Nor to the vault they steps refuse
    Thy constant home shall soon be there.

To summer suns and winter moons
    Prepare to bid a long adieu,
Autumnal seasons shall return
    And spring shall bloom, but not for you.

Why so perplext with cares and toil
    To rest upon this darksome road,
'Tis but a thin, a thirsty soil,
    A barren and a bleak abode.

Constrain'd to dwell with pain and care;
    These dregs of life are bought too dear,
'Tis better far to die than bear
    The torments of another year.

Subjected to perpetual ills
    A thousand deaths around us grow,
The frost the tender blossom kills
    And roses wither as they blow.

Cold nipping winds thy fruits assail,
    The infant apple seeks the ground
The peaches fall, the cherries fail
    The grape receives a fatal wound.

The breeze that gently ought to blow
    Swells to a storm and rends the main,
The sun that charm'd the grass to grow
    Turns hostile and consumes the plain:

The mountains waste, the shores decay,
    Once purling streams are dead and dry,
'Twas nature's work--'tis nature's play
    And nature says, that all must die.

Yon flaming lamp the source of light
    In chaos dark shall shroud his beam
And leave the world to mother night,
    A farce, a phantom or a dream.

What now is young must soon be old,
    Whate'er we love we soon must leave,
'Tis now too hot, 'tis now too cold--
    To live is nothing but to grieve.

How bright the morn her course begun
    No mists bedimm'd the solar sphere;--
The clouds arise--they shade the sun,
    For nothing can be constant here.

Now hope the longing soul employs
    In expectation we are blest;
But soon the airy phantom flies
    For lo, the treasure is possest.

Those monarchs proud that havoc spread
    (While pensive nature dropt a tear,)
Those monarchs have to darkness fled
    And ruin bounds their mad career.

The grandeur of this earthly round
    Where Theon would forever be
Is but a name, is but a sound--
    Mere emptiness and vanity.

Give me the stars, give me the skies,
    Give me the heaven's remotest sphere,

Above these gloomy scenes to rise
  Of desolation and despair.

Those native fires that warm'd the mind
  Now linguid grown too dimly glow,
Joy has to grief the heart resign'd
  And love itself is chang'd to woe.

The joys of wine are all you boast,
  These for a moment damp thy pain;
The gleam is o'er, the charm is lost--
  And darkness clouds the soul again.

Then seek no more for bliss below
  Where real bliss can ne'er be found,
Aspire where sweeter blossoms blow
  And fairer flowers bedeck the ground

Where plants of life the plains invest
  And green eternal crowns the year,
The little god within thy breast
  Is weary of his mansion here.

Like Phosphor clad in bright array
  His height meridian to regain
He can, nor will no longer stay
  To shiver on a frozen plain.

Life's journey past, for death prepare,
  'Tis but the freedom of the mind,
Jove made us mortal--his we are,
  To Jove dear Theon be resign'd.

Poems (1786), 230-234.

Freeman's Journal   January 9, 1782

(Untitled text appears after the following prose introduction:

On Wednesday evening the 2d instant, Alexander Quesnay esq. exhibited a most elegant entertainment at the playhouse, where were present his excellency general Washington, the minister of France, the president of the state, a number of the officers of the army and a brilliant assemblage of ladies and gentlemen of the city, who were invited.

After a prologue, suitable to the occasion, EUGENIE an elegant French comedy was first presented (written by the celebrated M. Beaumarchais) and in the opinion of several good judges was extremely well acted by the young gentlemen, students in that polite language. After the comedy, was acted the LYING VALET a farce, to this succeeded several curious dances, followed by a brilliant illumination, consisting of thirteen pyramidal pillars, representing the thirteen states--on the middle column was seen a Cupid, supporting a laurel crown over the motto--WASHINGTON--*the pride of the country and terror of Britain*. On the summit was the word--Virginia--on the right--Connecticut, with the names GREENE and la FAYETTE--on the left--the word Pennsylvania, with the names, WAYNE and STUBEN; and so on according to the birth place, and state proper to each general. The spectacle ended with an artificial illumination of the thirteen columns.

The prologue, written at the request of Mr. Quesnay, is as follows.--)

WARS, bloody wars and hostile Britain's rage
Have banish'd long the pleasures of the stage;
From the gay painted scene compell'd to part,
(Forgot the melting language of the heart)
Constrain'd to shun the bold theatric show,
To act long tragedies of real woe,
Heroes, once more attend the comic muse;
Forget our failings, and our faults excuse.
   In that fine language is a fable drest
Which still unrivall'd reigns o'er all the rest;
Of foreign courts the study and the pride,
Who to know *this* abandon all beside;

Bold, though polite, and ever sure to please;
Correct with grace, and elegant with ease;
Soft from the lips its easy accents roll,
Form'd to delight and captivate the soul:
In this Eugenia tells her easy lay,
The brilliant work of courtly Beaumarchais:
In this Racine, Voltaire and Boileau sung
The noblest poets in the noblest tongue.

    If the soft story in our play express'd
Can give a moment's pleasure to your breast,
To you, GREAT SIR*! we must be proud to say
That moment's pleasure shall our pains repay:
Return'd from conquest and from glorious toils,
From armies captur'd and unnumber'd spoils;
E'er yet again, with generous France ally'd,
You rush to battle, humbling British pride;
While arts of peace thy kind protection share,
O let the Muses claim an equal care.
You bade us first our future greatness see,
Inspir'd by you we languish'd to be free;
Even here where freedom lately sat distrest,
See, a new Athens rising in the west:
Fair science blooms where tyrants reign'd before,
Red war reluctant leaves our ravag'd shore--
Illustrious hero, may you live to see
These new republics powerful, great and free:
Peace, heaven born peace, o'er spacious regions spread,
While discord sinking veils her ghastly head.

Poems (1786), 234-35.

---

* *Addressed to his excellency general Washington.*

Freeman's Journal   January 23, 1782

STANZAS occasioned by the ruins of a country INN, unroofed and blown down in a storm.

WHERE now these mingled ruins ly
    A temple once to Bacchus rose,
Beneath whose roof, aspiring high,
    Full many a guest forgot his woes:

No more this dome by tempests torn
    Affords a social, safe retreat;
But ravens here with eye forlorn,
    And clustering batts henceforth shall meet.

The Priestess of this ruin'd shrine,
    Unable to survive the stroke,
Presents no more the ruddy wine,
    Her glasses gone, her china broke.

The friendly Host whose social hand
    Accosted strangers at the door,
Has left at length his wonted stand,
    And greets the weary guest no more.

Old creeping time that brings decay
    Might yet have spar'd these mouldering walls,
Alike beneath whose potent sway
    A temple or a tavern falls.

Is this the place where mirth and joy,
    Coy nymphs and sprightly lads were found?
Alas, no more the nymphs are coy,
    No more the flowing bowls go round.

Is this the place where festive song
    Deceiv'd the wintry hours away?
No more the swains the tune prolong,
    No more the maidens join the lay.

Is this the place where Chloe slept
    In downy beds of blue and green?

Dame Nature here no vigils kept,
    No cold unfeeling guards were seen.

'Tis gone!--and Chloe tempts no more,
    Deep, unrelenting silence reigns;
Of all that pleas'd, that charm'd before
    The tott'ring chimney scarce remains!

Ye tyrant winds! whose ruffian blast
    From locks and hinges rent the door,
And all the roof to ruin cast,
    The roof that shelter'd us before,

Your wrath appeas'd, I pray be kind
    If Mopsus should the dome renew;
That we again may quaff his wine,
    Again collect our jovial crew.

Poems (1786), 235-37.

Freeman's Journal   January 30, 1782

THE ROYAL ADVENTURER.

PRINCE William of the Brunswick race
To witness George's sad disgrace
    The royal lad came over
Rebels to kill by *Right Divine*;--
Deriv'd from that illustrious line,
    The beggars of Hanover.
So many chiefs got broken pates
In vanquishing the rebel states,
    So many nobles fell,
That George the third in passion cry'd,
"Our royal blood must now be try'd;
    'Tis that must break the spell:
To you (the fat pot-valiant SWINE
To Digby said) dear friend of mine,

To you I trust my boy.
The rebel tribes shall quake with fears,
Rebellion die when he appears;
  My tories leap with joy."
So said, so done--the boy was sent,
But never reach'd the continent,
  An island held him fast--
Yet there his friends danc'd rigadoons,
The hessians sung in high Dutch tunes
  "Prince William's come at last."
"Prince William comes!"--the Briton cry'd--
The glory of our empire wide
  Shall now be soon restor'd--
Our monarch is in William seen,
He is the image of our queen,
  Let William be ador'd!"
The tories came with long address,
With poems groan'd the *Royal Press*
  And all in William's praise--
The boy astonish'd look'd about
To find their *vast dominions* out,
  Then answer'd in amaze,
"Where all your *empire wide* can be,
Friends for my soul I cannot see:
  'Tis but an empty name;
Three wasted islands and a town
In rubbish bury'd--half burnt down,
  Is all that we can claim:
I am of royal birth, 'tis true,
But what alas, can princes do,
  No armies to command?
Cornwallis conquer'd and distresst--
Sir Henry Clinton grown a jest--
  I curse--and leave the land."

Poems (1786), 237-39.

New York Journal   August 16, 1787

1786 text reprinted at the request of a correspondent as a "proper reply to Prince William Henry, and a just comment on his conduct." The Prince had recently come to Nova Scotia to visit exiled Tories, and, according to this contributor, had cast "abusive, illiberal, and ungentlemanly" aspersions on the citizens of this continent.

New York Journal   March 4, 1795

Introduced as follows:

>(Old--*yet not out of date.*)

1786 text, with the following variants:

>No quotation marks.
>Stanza 2, line 5: Our royal blood shall now be tryd;
>Stanza 3:   First three lines of the third stanza of the 1786 text, plus all six lines of the fourth stanza of the 1786 text.
>   line 7: The British danc'd the rigadoons,
>Stanza 4:   Fifth stanza of the 1786 text.
>Stanza 5:   Lines 2, 3, 5, and 6 of the sixth stanza of the 1786 text, plus all six lines of stanza 7.
>Stanza 6:   Last stanza of the 1786 text.
>   line 6: I curse and quit the land.

Freeman's Journal   January 13, 1782

Lord DUNMORE's PETITION to the Legislature of Virginia.

>Humbly Sheweth,

THAT a silly old creature much noted of yore,
And known by the name of John, earl of Dunmore,
Has again ventur'd over to visit your shore;

The reason of this he begs leave to explain--
In England they said you were conquer'd and slain,
'But the devil take him that believes them again)--

So, hearing that most of your rebels were dead,
That some had submitted, and others had fled,
I muster'd my tories, myself at their head,

And over we scudded, our hearts full of glee,
As merry as ever poor devils could be,
Our ancient dominion Virginia to see;

Our shoe boys, and tars, and the very cook's mate
Already conceiv'd he possess'd an estate,
And the tories no longer were cursing their fate.

Myself, the don Quixote, and each of the crew,
Like Sancho, had empires and islands in view,--
They were captains and knights, and the devil knows who:

But, now to our sorrow, disgrace, and surprise,
No longer deceiv'd by the Father of Lies,*
We hear with our ears, and we see with our eyes:--

I have therefore to make you a modest request,
(And I'm sure in my mind it will be for the best,)
Admit Me again to your mansions of rest.

There are Eden, and Martin, and Franklin and Tryon,
All waiting to see you submit to the Lion,
And may wait till the devil is king of Mount Sion:--

Though a brute and a dunce, like the rest of the clan,
I can govern as well as most Englishmen can;
And if I'm a drunkard, I still am a man:

---

* The Printer of the Royal Gazette.

I miss'd it some how in comparing my notes,
Or six years ago, I had join'd with your votes;
Not aided the negroes in cutting your throats.

Altho' with so many hard names I was branded,
I hope you'll believe, (as you will if you're candid)
That I only perform'd what my Master commanded.

Give me lands, whores and dice, and you still may be free
Let who will be master, we shan't disagree;
If King or if Congress--no matter to me;--

I hope you will send me an answer straightway,
For 'tis plain that at Charleston we cannot long stay--
And your humble petitioner ever shall pray.

                                                    DUNMORE.

Charleston, January 6, 1782.

Poems (1786), 239-41.

Freeman's Journal   February 13, 1782

      EPIGRAM occasioned by the title of Rivington's
          Royal Gazette being scarcely legible.

SAYS Satan to Jemmy, I hold you a bet,
That you mean to abandon our Royal Gazette,
Or, between you and me, you wou'd manage things better,
Than the Title to print on so damned a Letter;

Now being connected so long in the art,
It would not be prudent at present to part;
And people perhaps would be frighten'd and fret
If the devil alone carry'd on the Gazette.

Says Jemmy to Satan (by way of a wipe)
Who gives me the matter should furnish the type:

And why you find fault I can scarcely divine,
For the types, like the Printer, are certainly thine.

'Tis yours to deceive with the semblance of truth,
Thou friend of my age, and thou guide of my youth!
But to prosper, pray send me some further supplies,
A sett of new Types, and a sett of new Lies.

                M.

Poems (1786), 241-42.

Freeman's Journal   February 20, 1782

[A SPEECH that should have been spoken by the king of the island of Britain to his parliament.

My lord, I can hardly from weeping refrain,
When I think of this year and its cursed campaign
But still it is folly to whine and to grieve,
For things will yet alter, I hope and believe.

Of the four southern States we again are bereav'd,
They were just in our grasp (or I'm sadly deceiv'd:)
There are wizzards and witches that dwell in those *lands*
For the moment we gain *them, they* slip from our hands

Our prospects at present most gloomy appear;
Cornwallis returns with a flea in his ear,
Sir Henry is sick of his station we know--
And Amherst, though press'd, is unwilling to go.

The *Hero* that steer'd for the cape of Good Hope
With Monsieur Suffrein was unable to cope.--
Many months are elaps'd, yet his task is to do--
To conquer the cape, and to conquer Peru:

When his squadron at Portsmouth he went to equip
He promis'd great things from his *fifty-gun-ship*;

But let him alone--while he knows which is which,
He'll not be so ready to *"die in the ditch."*

This session, I thought to have told you this much
"A treaty concluded, and Peace with the Dutch--"
But as stubborn as ever, they vapour and brag,
And sail by my nose with the Prussian flag.

The empress refuses to join on our side,
As yet with the indians we're only ally'd:
(Though such an alliance is rather improper
For we English are white, but their colour is copper.)

The Irish, I fear, have some mischief in view;
They ever have been a most troublesome crew--
If a truce or a treaty hereafter be made,
They shall pay very dear for their present free trade.

Dame Fortune I think has our standards forsaken,
For Tobago they say by Frenchmen is taken:
Minorca's beseig'd--and as to Gibralter,
By Jove if it's taken I'll take to the halter.

It makes me so wroth, I could scold like Xantippe
When I think of our losses along Mississippi--
And see in the Indies that horrible Hyder
His conquests extending still wider and wider.

'Twixt Washington, Hyder, Don Galvez, de Grasse,
By my soul we are brought to a very fine pass;--
When we've reason to hope new battles are won
A packet arrives--and an army's undone!--

In the midst of this scene of dismay and distress
What is best to be done, is not easy to guess,
For things may go wrong though we plan them aright,
And blows they must look for, whose trade is to fight.

In regard to the rebels it is my decree,
That dependent on Britain they every shall be;
Or I've captains and hosts that will fly at my nod
And slaughter them all--by the blessing of God--

But if they succeed, as they're likely to do,
Our neighbours must part with their colonies too:--
Let them laugh and be merry and make us their jest;
When La Plata revolts we shall laugh with the rest--

'Tis true that the journey to castle St. Juan
Was a project that brought the projectors to ruin;
But still, my dear lords, I would have you reflect,
Who nothing do venture can nothing expect--.

If the Commons agree to afford me new treasures,
My sentence once more is for vigorous measures
Accustom'd so long to head winds and bad weather
Let us conquer or go to the devil together.]

Poems (1786), 244-46.

Freeman's Journal   February 27, 1782

RIVINGTON'S LAST WILL AND TESTAMENT
(A true copy from the Records.)

Since life is uncertain, and no one can say,
How soon we may go, or how long we shall stay,
Methinks he is wisest who soonest prepares,
And settles in season his worldly affairs:

Some folks are so weak they can scarce avoid crying,
And think when they're making their wills they are dying;
'Tis surely a serious employment—but still,
Who e'er dy'd the sooner for making his Will?

Let others be sad when their lives they review,
But I know *whom* I've served— and *him* faithfully too;
And though it may seem a fanatical story,
He often has show'd me a glimpse of his glory.

Imprimis, my carcase I give and devise
To be made into cakes of a moderate size,
To nourish those tories whose spirits may droop
And serve the king's army with Portable Soup.

Unless I mistake, in the scriptures we read
That "worms on the dead shall deliciously feed;"
The scripture stands true--and that I am firm in,
For what are our tories and soldiers but vermin?--

This soup of all soups can't be call'd that of beef,
And this may to some be a matter of grief;
But I'm certain the bull would occasion a laugh,
That beef Portable Soup should be made of a *Calf*.

To the king, my dear master, I give a full sett
(In volumes bound up) of the Royal Gazette,
In which he will find the vast record contain'd
Of provinces conquer'd and victories gain'd.

As to Arnold the traitor and Satan his brother
I beg they will also accept of another;
And this shall be bound in Morocco red leather,
Provided they'll read it like brothers together.

But if Arnold should die, 'tis another affair,
Then Satan surviving shall be the sole heir;--
He often has told me he thought it quite clever;
So to him and his heirs I bequeath it forever.

I know there are some (that would fain be thought wise)
Who say my Gazette is the record of lies;
In answer to this, I shall only reply--
All the choice that I had was to starve or to lie.

My fiddles, my flutes, french horns and guittars
I leave to our heroes now weary of wars--
To the wars of the stage they more boldly advance,
The captains shall play and the soldiers shall dance.

To Sir Henry Clinton his use and behoof,
I shall leave my French brandy of very high proof;

It will give him fresh spirits for battle and slaughter
And make him feel bolder by land and by water:

Yet I caution the knight, for fear he do wrong,
'Tis *avant la viande et apres le poisson**--
It will strengthen his stomach, prevent it from turning,
And digest the affront of his effigy burning.

To Baron Knyphausen, his heirs and assigns,
I bequeath my *old bock*, and my Burgundy wines,
To a true Hessian drunkard no liquors are sweeter,
And I know the old man is no foe to the *creature*.

To a general my namesake+, I give and dispose
Of a purse full of clipp'd, light, sweated half joes;
I hereby desire him to take back his trash,
And return me my *Hannay's* infallible *wash***.

My chessmen and tables, and other such chattels
I give to Cornwallis renowned in battles;
By moving of these (not tracing the map)
He'll explain to the king how he got in a *trap*.

To good David Matthews (among other slops)
I give my whole cargo of Mareant's drops,
If they cannot do all, they may cure him in part,
And scatter the poison that cankers his heart:

Provided, however, and nevertheless,
That what other estate I enjoy and possess
At the time of my death (if it be not then sold)
Shall remain to the tories *to have and to hold*.

As I thus have bequeath'd them both carcass and fleece,
The least they can do is to wait my decease;

---

* Before flesh and after fish--See the Royal Gazette.
+ Gen. James Robertson.
** Used in the venereal disease.

But to give them what substance I have, e're I die;
And be eat up with vermin, while living--not I--.

In WITNESS whereof (though no ailment I feel)
Hereunto I set both my hand and my seal;
(As the law says) in presence of witnesses twain,
'Squire John Coghill Knapp*, and brother *Hugh Gaine.*
                    JAMES RIVINGTON. (LS.)

New York, February 20, 1782

Poems (1786), 247-50.

Freeman's Journal   March 13, 1782

LINES occasioned by Mr. Rivington's new titular Types to
   his Royal Gazette, of February 27.

[See an Epigram on the worn out Types of said Title,
   in No. XLIII. of this Journal.]

WELL--now (said the devil) it looks something better!
Your title is struck on a *charming* new *Letter*:
Last night in the dark, as I gave it a squint,
I saw my dear partner had taken the hint.
      I ever surmised (though 'twas doubted by some)
That the old types were shadows of substance to come;
But if the *new Letter* is pregnant with charms,
It grieves me to think of those cursed King's arms!
The *Dieu et mon droit* (his God and his right)
Is so dim that I hardly know what is meant by't;
The paws of the Lion can scarcely be seen,
And the Unicorn's guts are most shamefully lean!

---

* A notary public in New York.

The *Crown* is so worn of your master the Despot,
That I hardly know whether 'tis crown or a pispot:
When I rub up my day lights, and look very sharp,
I just can distinguish the Irishman's Harp:
Another device appears rather silly,
Alas! it is only the shade of the *Lilly*!
For the honour of George, and the fame of our nation,
Pray give his escutcheons a rectification--
Or I know what I know (and I'm a queer shaver)
Of *Him* and his Arms I'll be the *In*-grave-r.

Poems (1786), 242-43.

Freeman's Journal   March 27, 1782

On Mr. Rivington's engraved KING's ARMS to his ROYAL GAZETTE.

FROM the regions of night, with his head in a sack,
Ascended a person accoutred in black,
And upward directing his circular eye whites,
(Like the Jure-divino political Levites)
And leaning his elbow on Rivington's shelf,
While the printer was busy, thus mus'd with himself,

"My mandates are fully complied with at last,
"New *Arms* are engrav'd and new *Letters* are cast;
"I therefore determine, and freely accord,
"This servant of mine shall receive his reward."

Then turning about, to the printer he said,
"Who late was my *servant* shall now be my *Aid*;
Since under my banners so bravely you fight,
Kneel down!--for your merits I dubb you a *Knight*,
From passive subaltern I bid you to rise
The *Inventor* as well as the *Printer* of Lies."

Poems (1786), 243-44.

Freeman's Journal   March 27, 1782

(Untitled text follows this note, written in response to a reprint from the *Royal Gazette* of a prophecy concerning the failure of the American "insurrection":

> To shew that America has not been wholly destitute of oracular sages in past times, I send you the following *choice words*, or prophetical hints of an illiterate fisherman, who died about thirty years ago at his habitation a few miles above the mouth of the Susquehannah. I discovered the paper containing them by mere accident in tumbling over the leaves of an old book at an inn near that place. If you think the lines are worth inserting in your paper, they are at your service.)

"When a certain great king whose initial is G,
Shall force stamps upon paper, and folks to drink tea;
When these folks burn his tea, and stampt papers, like stubble,
You may guess that this king is then coming to trouble.
But when a petition he treads under his feet,
And sends over the ocean an army and fleet;
When that army half starved, and frantic with rage,
Shall be coop'd up with a leader whose name rhymes to cage,
When that leader goes home dejected and sad,
You then may be assur'd the king's prospects are bad:
But when B and C with their armies are taken,
This king will do well if he saves his own bacon.
In the year seventeen hundred and eighty and two,
A stroke he shall get that will make him look blue;
In the years eighty three, eighty four, eighty five,
You hardly shall know that the king is alive;
In the year eighty six the affair will be over,
And he shall eat turnips that grow in Hanover.
The face of the lion shall then become pale,
He shall yield fifteen teeth, and be sheer'd of his tail.
O king, my dear king, you shall be very sore,
The Stars and the Lilly shall run you on shore,
And your lion shall growl, but never bite more."

Poems (1786), 250-51.

Freeman's Journal   April 3, 1782

The POLITICAL BALANCE: or, The Fates of Britain and America compared. A Tale.

Deciding Fates, in Homer's stile, I shew,
And bring contending Gods once more to view.

As Jove the Olympian (who, both I and you know,
Was brother to Neptune, and husband to June)
Was lately reviewing his papers of state,
He happen'd to light on the records of Fate:

In Alphabet order this volume was written—
So he turn'd to B for the article Britain—
She struggles so well, said the god, I will see
What the Sisters in Pluto's dominions decree.

And first on the top of a column he read
"Of a king with a mighty soft place in his head,
Who should join in his temper the ass and the mule,
The third of his name, and by far the worst fool:

His reign shall be famous for multiplication,
The fire and the king of a *whelp* generation;
But such is the will and the purpose of fate,
For each child he begets he shall forfeit a state:

In the course of events he shall find to his cost,
That he cannot regain what he foolishly lost;
Of the nations around he shall be the derision,
And know by experience the Rule of Division."

So Jupiter read—a god of first rank—
And still he read on—but he came to a blank:
For the fates had neglected the rest to reveal—
They either fogot it or chose to conceal:—

When a leaf is torn out, or a blot on a page
That pleases our fancy, we fly in a rage—
So, curious to know what the fates would say next,
No wonder if Jove, disappointed, was vext.

But still as true genius not frequently fails,
He glanc'd at the *Virgin*, and thought of the *Scales*;
And said, "To determine the will of the fates,
"One scale shall weigh *Britain*, the other the *States*:

Then turning to Vulcan, his maker of thunder,
Said he, "My dear Vulcan, I pray you look yonder,
Those *creatures* are tearing each other to pieces,
And instead of abating, the carnage increases.

Now, as you are a blacksmith, and lusty south ham eater,
You must make me a globe of a shorter diameter;
The world in abridgement, and just as it stands,
With all its proportions of waters and lands;

But its various divisions must be so design'd,
That I can unhinge it whene'er I've a mind;--
How else should I know what the portions will weigh,
Or which of the combatants carry the day?"

Old Vulcan comply'd, (we've no reason to doubt it)
So he put on his apron and strait went about it--
Made center, and circles as round as a pancake,
And here the Pacific, and there the Atlantic.

An axis he hammer'd, whose ends were the poles,
(On which the whole body perpetually rolls;)
A brazen meridian he added to these,
On which were engraven twice ninety degress:

I am sure you had laugh'd to have seen his droll attitude,
When he bent round the surface the circles of latitude,
The zones and the tropics, meridians, equator,
And other fine things that are drawn on salt water.

Away to the southward (instructed by Pallas)
He plac'd in the ocean the Terra Australis,
New Holland, New Guinea, and so of the rest;--
America lay by herself in the west:

From the regions where winter eternally reigns,
To the climes of Peru he extended her plains;

Dark groves, and the zones did her bosom adorn,
And the *Crosiers**, new burnish'd, he hung at cape Horn.

The weight of two oceans she bore on her sides,
With all their convulsions of tempests and tides
Vast lakes on her surface did fearfully roll,
And the ice from her rivers surrounded the pole.

Then Europe and Asia he northward extended,
Where under the Arctic with Zembla they ended;
The length of these regions he took with his garters,
(Including Siberia, the land of the Tarters.)

In the African clime (where the cocoa nut tree grows)
He laid down the desarts, and even the negroes,
The shores by the waves of our oceans embrac'd,
And elephants strolling about in the waste.

In forming East India he had a wide scope,
Beginning his work at the cape of Good Hope;
Then eastward of that he continued his plan,
'Till he came to the empire and isles of Japan.

Adjacent to Europe he struck up an island,
(One part of it low, but the other was high land)
With many a comical creature upon it,
And one wore a hat, and another a bonnet:

Like emmits or ants in a fine summer's day,
They ever were marching in battle array,
Or skipping about on the face of the brine,
Like witches in egg shells (their ships of the line).

These poor little creatures were all in a flame,
To the lands of America urging their claim

---

* Stars in the form of a cross, which mark the south pole in Southern latitudes.

Still biting, or stinging, or spreading their sails;
(For Vulcan had form'd them with strings in their tails.)

So poor and so lean, you might count all their ribs*,
Yet were so enraptur'd with crackers and squibs,
That Vulcan with laughter almost split asunder,
"Because they imagin'd their crackers were thunder."

Due westward from these, with a channel between,
A servant to slaves Hibernia was seen,
Once crowded with monarchs, and high in renown,
But all she retain'd was the harp and the crown!

Her genius, a female, reclin'd in the shade,
And, merely for music, so mournfully play'd,
That Jove was uneasy to hear her complain,
And order'd his blacksmith to loosen her chain:

Then tipt her a wink, saying, "Now is your time!
(Though I do not assert that he said it in rhime)
When your fetters are off, if you will not be free
Be a slave if you will, but complain not to me."

But finding her timid, he cry'd in a rage--
"Tho' the doors are flung open, she stays in the cage!
Subservient to Britain then let her remain,
And her freedom shall be, *but the length of her chain*."

At length to discourage all stupid pretensions,
Jove look'd at the globe, and approv'd its dimensions,
And cry'd in a transport--"Why! what have we here!
Friend Vulcan, it is a most beautiful sphere!

Now while I am busy in taking apart,
This globe that is form'd with such exquisite art,
Go, Hermes, to Libra, (you're one of her gallants)
And ask, in my name, for the loan of her Balance."

---

* Their national debt being above 200,000,000 1. sterl.

Away posted Hermes as Swift as the gales,
And as swiftly return'd with the ponderous Scales,
And hung them aloft to a beam in the air,
So equally pois'd they had turn'd with a hair.

Now Jove to *Columbia* his shoulders apply'd,
But aiming to lift her, his strength she defy'd--
Then turning about to their godships, he says--
"A *body so vast* is not easy to raise;

But if you assist me, I still have a notion
Our *forces united* can put her in motion,
And swing her aloft, like a cat by a tail,
And place her, in spite of her bulk, in our scale;

If six years together the Congress have strove,
And more than* *divided the empire with Jove*+;
With a *Jove* like myself, who am ten times as great,
You can join, like these soldiers, to heave up this weight."

So to it they went, with handspikes and levers,
And upward she sprung, with her mountains and rivers!
Rocks, cities, and islands, deep waters and shallows,
Ships, armies, and forests, high heads, and fine fellows:

"Stick to it! cry'd Jove--now heave one and all!
"At least we are lifting "*one eighth of the ball*!"
If backward she tumbles--then trouble begins,
And then have a care, my dear boys, of your shins!"

When gods are determin'd what projects can fail?
So they gave a fresh shove and she mounted the scale;
Suspended aloft, Jove view'd her with awe--
And the *gods*** for their *pay*, had a hearty--huzza!

---

* "Divisum imperium cum Jove Cœsar habet.--Virg.
+ George III.
** American soldiers.

But Neptune* bawl'd out--"Why Jove you're a noddy,
"Is Britain sufficient to poise that vast body?
"Tis nonsense such castles to build in the air--
As well might an oyster with Britain compare."

"Away to your waters, you blustering bully,
Said Jove, or I'll make you repent of your folly,
Is Jupiter, sir, to be tutor'd by you?--
Get out of my sight, for I know what to do!--

Then searching about with his fingers for Britain,
Thought he, "This same island I cannot well hit on;
The devil take him who first call'd her the *Great*;
If she was--she is *vastly* diminish'd of late!"

Like a man that is searching his thigh for a flea,
He peep'd and he fumbled, but nothing could see:
At last he exclaim'd--I am surely upon it--
I think I have hold of a highlander's bonnet."

But finding his error he said with a sigh,
"This bonnet is only the island of Skie.+"
So, away to his *namesake* the PLANET he goes,
And borrow'd *two moons* to hang on his nose.

Through these, as thro' glasses, he saw her quite clear,
And in raptures cry'd out--"I have found her--she's here!
If this be not Britain, then call me an ass;
She looks like "a gem in an ocean of glass**."

But, faith, she's so small I must mind how I shake her;
In a box I'll inclose her, for fear I should break her;
Though a god, I might suffer for being aggressor,
Since scorpions and vipers and hornets possess her;

---

* Minority in Parliament.
+ An island on the north west of Scotland.
** Shakespeare.

The white cliffs of Albion are full in my view--
And the hills of Plinlimmon, I think I could shew--
But, Vulcan, inform me what creatures are these,
That smell so of onions and garlick and cheese?"

Old Vulcan reply'd--"Odd's splutter a nails!
Why these are the Welsh, and the country of Wales!
When Taffy is vext, no devil is ruder--
Take care of how you handle the offspring of *Tudor*!

On the crags of the mountains hur living hur seeks,
Hur country is planted with garlick and leeks;
So great is hur choler, beware how you teize hur,
For these are the Britons--unconquer'd--by Cesar."

Jove peep'd thro' his moons, & examin'd their features,
And said, "By my troth, they are wonderful creatures,
"The beards are so long that encircle their throats,
That (unless they are Welchmen) I swear they are *goats*:

But now, my dear Juno, pray give me my mittens,
(The insects I am going to handle are Britons)
I'll draw up their isle with a finger and thumb,
As the doctor extracts an old tooth from your gum."

Then he rais'd her aloft--but, to shorten our tale,
She look'd like a *clod* in the opposite scale--
Britannia so small, and Columbia so large--
A ship of first rate, and a ferryman's barge!

Cry'd Pallas to Vulcan, "Why, Jove's in a dream--
Observe how he watches the turn of the beam!
Was ever a mountain outweigh'd by a grain?
Or what is a drop when compar'd to a main?"

But Momus alleg'd--"In my humble opinion,
You should add to Great Britain her foreign dominion,
When this is appended, perhaps she will rise,
And equal her rival in weight and in size."

"Alas," said the monarch, your project is vain,
But little is left of her foreign domain;

And, scatter'd about in the liquid expanse,
That little is left to the mercy of France;

"However we'll lift them, and give her fair play"--
And soon in the scale with their mistress they lay;
But the gods were confounded and struck with surprise,
And Vulcan could hardly believe his own eyes!

For (such was the purpose and guidance of fate)
Her foreign dominions diminish'd her weight--
By which it appear'd to Britain's disaster,
Her foreign possessions were changing their master.

Then as he replac'd them, said Jove with a smile,--
"Columbia shall never be rul'd by an isle,--
But vapours and darkness around her shall rise,
And tempests conceal her a while from our eyes;

So locusts in Egypt their squadrons display,
And rising disfigure the face of the day:
So the moon at her full has a frequent eclipse,
And the sun in the ocean diurnally dips.

Then cease your endeavors, ye vermin of Britain--
(And here in derision their island he spit on)
'Tis madness to seek what you never can find,
Or think of uniting what nature disjoin'd:

But still you may flutter a while with your wings,
And spit out your venom, and brandish your stings;
Your hearts are as black, and as bitter as gall,
A curse to yourselves, and a blot on the *Ball*."

Poems (1786), 251-61.

Time-Piece   July 3, 1797

STANZAS *written on Ireland in the year* 1781; *extracted from a poem, Entitled,* The Political Balance.

(Four stanza extract, stanzas 25-58 of the above text, including the following variants:)

    Stanza 2, line 2: And sighing forever, so mournfully play'd
               line 4: And order'd old Vulcan to loosen her chain--
    Stanza 3, line 1: Then tipt her a wink, saying, "now is the time!
               line 2: To *rebel* is the sin--to *revolt* is no crime;
    Stanza 4, line 1: --So, finding her timid, he cry'd in a rage--
               line 2: "Though the doors are thrown open, she stays in the cage;

Freeman's Journal   April 17, 1782

SIR HARRY's CALL.

COME gentlemen Tories, firm loyal and true,
Here are axes and shovels and something to do!
    For the sake of our king,
    Come, labour and sing;
You left all you had for his honour and glory,
And he will remember the suffering tory:
    We have, it is true,
    Some small work to do;
    But here's for your pay
    Twelve coppers a day,
And never regard what the rebels may say
But throw off your jerkins and labour away.

To raise up the rampart, and pile up the wall,
To pull down old houses and dig the canal,
    To build and destroy;--
    Be this your employ,
In the day time to work at our fortifications
And steal in the night from the rebels your rations:

> The king wants your aid
> Not empty parade;
> Advance to your places
> Ye men of *long faces*
> Nor ponder too much on your former disgraces,
> This year, I presume, will quite alter your cases.
>
> Attend, at the call of the fifer and drummer,
> The French and the rebels are coming next summer,
> And forts we must build
> Though tories are kill'd--
> Then courage, my jockies, and work for your king,
> For if you are taken no doubt you will swing--
> If York we can hold
> I'll have you enroll'd;
> And after you're dead
> Your names shall be read,
> As who for their monarch both labour'd and bled,
> And ventur'd their necks for their *beef* and their *bread*.
>
> 'Tis an honour to serve the bravest of nations,
> And left to be hang'd in their capitulations--
> Then scour up your mortars
> And stand to your quarters,
> 'Tis nonsense for Tories in battle to run,
> They never need fear sword, halberd, or gun;
> Their hearts shall not fail 'em
> No balls will assail 'em,
> Forget your disgraces
> And *shorten* your *faces*,
> For 'tis true as the gospel, believe it or not,
> Who are born to be hang'd will never be shot.

Poems (1786), 261-62.

Freeman's Journal   April 24, 1782

A DIALOGUE at Hyde-Park Corner.

BURGOYNE.

LET those who will, be proud and sneer,
And call you an unwelcome peer,
But I am glad to see you here:

The prince that fills the British throne,
Unless successful, honours none;
Poor Jack Burgoyne!–you're not alone.

CORNWALLIS.

Thy ships, De Grasse, have caus'd my grief–
To rebel shores and their relief
There never came a happier chief:

In fame's *black* page it shall be read,
By Gallic arms *my* soldiers bled–
The rebels *thine* in triumph led.

BURGOYNE.

Our fortunes various forms assume,
Had I been blest with *elbow room*,
I might have found a different doom;

But you, that conquer'd far and wide,
In little York thought fit to hide,
The *subject ocean* at your side.

CORNWALLIS.

And yet no force had gain'd the post–
Not Washington, his country's boast,
Nor Rochambeau with all his host,

Nor all the Gallic fleet's parade--
Had Clinton struggled in my aid,
And Sammy Graves been not afraid.

BURGOYNE.

For head knock'd off, or broken bones,
Or mangled corpse, no price atones;
    Nor all that prattling rumour says,
    Nor all the piles that art can raise,
    The poet's or the parson's praise.

CORNWALLIS.

Tho' I am brave, as well as you,
Yet still I think your notion true:
    Dear brother Jack, our toils are o'er;--
    With foreign conquests plagu'd no more,
    We'll stay and watch our native shore.

Poems (1786), 263-64.

Freeman's Journal   April 24, 1782

On the late royal sloop of war Gen. Monk (formerly the Washington) mounting six quarter deck wooden guns.

WHEN the Washington ship by the English was beat,
They sent her to England to shew their great feat,
And Sandwich straightway, as proof of his spunk,
Dash'd out her old name, and call'd her the Monk.

"This Monk hated rebels, said Sandy--'od rot 'em--
So heave her down quickly, and copper her bottom;
With the sloops of our navy we'll have her enroll'd,
And mann'd with pick'd sailors to make her feel bold:

> To show that our king is both valiant and good
> Some guns shall be iron and others be wood,
> And in truth (tho' I wish not the secret to spread)
> Her guns should be wooden, as well as his head."

Poems (1786), 264-65.

Freeman's Journal   May 8, 1782

(Untitled text preceded by the following note to the editor:

> Mr. Bailey,
>
> READING capt. Barney's late gallant exploit in your and other newspapers, I could not restrain myself from scribbling the few following stanzas relative to that affair; and descriptive not of what was really said or done in the more minute particulars, but of what might be supposed to have passed in similar circumstances.
>
>   Yours, RUSTICUS.

Dover, April 26, 1782.)

To the tune of The Tempest; *or,* Hosier's Ghost.

O'ER the waste of waters cruising,
    Long the General Monk had reign'd;
All subduing, all reducing,
    None her lawless rage restrain'd:
Many a brave and hearty fellow
    Yielding to this warlike foe
When her guns began to bellow,
    Struck his humbled colours low.

But grown bold with long successes,
    Leaving the wide watry way,
She, a stranger to distresses,
    Came to cruise within Cape May:
"Now we soon (said captain Rogers)
    Shall their men of commerce meet;
In our hold we'll have them lodgers,
    We shall capture half their fleet.

Lo! I see their van appearing--
    Back our topsails to the mast--
They toward us full are steering
    With a gentle western blast;
I've a list of all their cargoes,
    All their guns, and all their men,
I am sure these modern Argo's
    Can't escape us one in ten:

Yonder comes the Charming Sally,
    Sailing with the General Greene,--
First we'll fight the HYDER ALI,
    Taking her is taking them;
She intends to give us battle,
    Bearing down with all her sail;--
Now, boys, let our cannon rattle!
    To take her we cannot fail.

Our eighteen guns, each a nine pounder,
    Soon shall terrify this foe;
We shall maul her, we shall wound her,
    Bringing rebel colours low."--
While he thus anticipated
    Conquests that he could not gain,
He in the Cape May channel waited
    For the ship that caus'd his pain.

Captain Barney then preparing,
    Thus address'd his gallant crew,--
"Now, brave lads! be bold and daring,
    Let your hearts be firm and true;

This is a proud English cruiser,
    Roving up and down the main,
We must fight her--must reduce her,
    Tho' our decks be strew'd with slain.

Let who will be the survivor,
    We must conquer or must die,
We must take her up the river,
    Whate'er comes of you or I:
Tho' she shows most formidable
    With her eighteen pointed nines,
And her quarters clad in sable,
    Let us baulk her proud designs.

With four nine pounders, and twelve sixes
    We will face that daring band;
Let no dangers damp your courage,
    Nothing can the brave withstand.
Fighting for your country's honour,
    Now to gallant deeds aspire;
Helmsman, bear us down upon her,
    Gunner, give the word to fire!"

Then yard arm and yard arm meeting,
    Strait began the dismal fray,
Cannon mouths, each other greeting,
    Belch'd their smoky flames away:
Soon the language, grape and chain shot
    That from Barney's cannons flew,
Swept the Monk, and clear'd each round top,
    Kill'd and wounded half her crew.

Captain Rogers strove to rally
    His men, from their quarters fled,
While the roaring Hyder Ali
    Cover'd o'er his decks with dead.
When from their tops their dead men tumbled
    And the streams of blood did flow,
Then their proudest hopes were humbled
    By their brave inferior foe.

All aghast, and all confounded,
    They beheld their champions fall,
And their captain, sorely wounded,
    Bade them quick for quarters call.
Then the Monk's proud flag descended,
    And her cannon ceas'd to roar;
By her crew no more defended,
    She confess'd the contest o'er.--

Come, brave boys, and fill your glasses,
    You have humbled one proud foe,
No brave action, this surpasses,
    Fame shall tell the nations so.--
Thus be Britain's woes completed,
    Thus abridg'd her cruel reign,
Till she ever, thus defeated,
    Yields the sceptre of the main.

Poems (1786), 271-74.

Freeman's Journal   May 22, 1782

On Sir Henry Clinton's recall.

THE *dog that is beat has a right to complain,*--
Sir Harry returns a disconsolate swain
To the face of his master, the Devil's anointed,
To the country provided for thieves disappointed.

Our *freedom*, he thought, to a tyrant must fall,
He concluded the weakest must go to the wall:
The more he was flatter'd the bolder he grew;--
He quitted the old world to conquer the new.

But in spite of the deeds he has done in his garrison,
(And they have been curious beyond all comparison,)
He must now go home, at the call of his king,
To answer the charges that Arnold may bring.

But what are the acts that this chief atchiev'd?--
If good, it is hard he should now be aggriev'd,
And the more, as he fought for his national glory,
Nor valued a farthing the *right* of the story.

This famous great man and two birds* of his feather,
In the Cereberus frigate came over together;
But of all the bold chiefs that remeasure the trip,
Not two have been known to return in one ship.

Like children that wrestle and scuffle in sport,
They are very well pleas'd as long as unhurt,
But a thump on the nose, or a blow in the eye,
Ends the fray—and they go to their *daddy* and cry.

Sir Clinton, thy deeds have been mighty and many,
You said all our paper was not worth a penny,
('Tis nothing but rags,+ quoth honest Will Tryon,
Are *rags* to discourage the *Sons of the Lion?*)

But Clinton thought this—"It is folly to fight,
When things may by easier methods come right,
There is such an art as counterfeit-action,--
And I'll do my utmost to honour our nation;

I'll shew this damn'd country that I can enslave her,
And that by the help of a skilful engraver,
And then let the rebels take care of their bacon,
We'll play 'em a trick, or I'm vastly mistaken."

But the project succeeded not quite to your liking,
So you paid off your *artist* and gave up BILL STRIKING;
But 'tis an affair I am glad you are quit on,
You had surely been hang'd had you try'd it in Britain.

---

* Gen. Howe and Burgoyne.
+ See his letter to gen. Parsons.

At the taking of Charleston you cut a great figure.
The terms you propounded were terms full of rigour,
Yet could not foresee poor *Charley's** disgrace,
Nor how soon your own *colours* would go to the *case*;

When the town had surrendered, the more to disgrace ye,
(Like another *true Briton* that did it at 'Statia,)
You broke all the terms yourself had extended,
Because you suppos'd the rebellion was ended:

Whoever the tories mark'd out as a whig,
If gentle, or simple, or little, or big,
No matter to you—to kill 'em and spite 'em,
You soon had 'em up where the dogs couldn't bite 'em.

Then thinking these rebels were snug and secure,
You left them to Rawdon and Nesbit Balfour:
(The face of the latter no mask need be draw'd on,
And to fish for the Devil my bait should be *Rawdon*.)

Returning to York with your ships and your plunder,
And boasting that rebels must shortly knock under,
The first thing that struck you as soon as you landed
Was the fortress at West Point, where Arnold commanded.

Thought you, "If friend Arnold this fort will deliver,
We then shall be masters of all Hudson's river,
The *east* and the *south* losing communication,
The Yankees will die by the act of *starvation*."

So off you sent Andre (not guided by Pallas)
Who soon purchas'd Arnold, and gave him the gallows;
Your *loss* I conceive than your *gain* was far greater,
You lost a good fellow and got a damn'd traitor.

---

* Cornwallis.

Now Carleton comes over to give you reflief,
A knight like yourself, and commander in *chief*,
But the *chief* he will get, you may tell the *dear honey*
Will be a black eye, hard knocks, and *no* money.

Now with—"Britons, strike home!" your sorrows dispel,
Away to your master, and honestly tell,
That his *arms* and his *artists* can nothing avail,
His men are too few, and his tricks are too stale;

Advise him at length to be just and sincere;
Of which not a symptom as yet doth appear,
As we plainly perceive from his sending Sir Guy,
Commission'd to steal, and commission'd to lie.

Poems (1786), 275-78.

Freeman's Journal   June 5, 1782

Sir Guy Carleton's ADDRESS to the Americans

FROM Britain's fam'd island once more I come over,
(No island on earth is in prowess above her)
With powers and commisssions your hearts to recover!

Our king, I must tell you, is plagu'd with a phantom,
(Independence they call it) that hourly doth haunt him,
And relief, my dear rebels, you only can grant him.

Tom Gage and Sir Harry, Sir William (our boast)
Lord Howe, and the rest that have scouted the coast,
All fail'd in their projects of laying this ghost:

So unless the damn'd spectre myself can expel
It will yet kill our monarch, I know very well,
And gallop him off on his Lion to hell.

But I heartily wish, that instead of Sir Guy,
They had sent out a seer from the island of Skie,
Who rebels and devils and ghosts may defy:

So great is our prospect of sailing at last,
When I look at the present, and think of the past
I wish with our heroes I had not been class'd;

For though, to a man, we are bullies and bruisers,
And cover'd with laurels, we still are the losers,
Till each is recall'd with his tory accusers:

But the war now is alter'd, and on a new plan;
By negociation we'll do what we can--
And I am an honest, well-meaning old man:

Too proud to retreat, and too weak to advance,
We must stay where we are at the mercy of chance
'Till Fortune shall help us to lead you a dance.

Then lay down your arms, dear rebels--O hone!
Our king is the best man that ever was known,
And the greatest that ever was stuck on a throne:

His love and affection by all ranks are sought;
Here take him, my honies, and each pay a groat--
Was ever a monarch more easily bought?

In pretty good case and very well found
By night and by day we carry him round;
He must go for a groat, if we can't get a pound.

Break the treaties you made with *Louis Bourbon*;
Abandon the Congress, no matter how soon,
And then, all together, we'll play a new tune.

'Tis strange that they always would manage the roast,
And force you their healths and the Dauphin's to toast;
Repent, my dear fellows, and each get a *post*;

Or if you object that *one post* is too few,
We generous Britons will help you to *two*,
With a beam laid across--that will certainly do.

The folks that rebell'd in the year forty five,
We us'd them so well, that we left few alive,
But sent them to heaven in swarms from their hive.

Your noble resistance we cannot forget,
'Tis nothing but right we should honour you yet;
If you are not rewarded, we die in your debt.

So, quickly submit and our mercy implore,
Be as loyal to George as you once were before,
Or I'll slaughter you all--and probably more.

What puzzled Sir Harry, Sir Will, and his brother,
Perhaps may be done by the son of my mother,
With the *Sword* in one hand & the *Branch* in the other.

My bold predecessors, (as fitting their station)
At their first coming out all spoke *Proclamation*;
'Tis the custom with us, and the way of our nation.

Then Lil-la-la-loo!--Shelaly, I say;--
If we cannot all fight, we can all run away--
And further at present I choose not to say.

May 30, 1782   G.C.

Poems (1786), 278-81.

Freeman's Journal   June 19, 1782

(Untitled text appears as part of a prose essay, "The Pilgrim, No. 15," on the subject of war. ". . . Is it possible that a being illuminated with the rays of that spiritual sun could write the following lines;--they were composed (with a great deal more) by one of the warrior chiefs of the Scandinavians, more than 800 years ago, a few hours before he expired:")

Balderi patris scamna
Parata scio in aula;
Bibemus cerevisiam
Ex concavis crateribus craniorum.
Non gemit vir fortis contra mortem
Magnifici in Odini* domibus, &c.

Brave deeds atchiev'd, at death's approach I smile,
In Balder's hall I see the table spread;
The enlivening beer shall now reward my toil,
Quaff'd from their sculls that by my faulchion bled.
The brave no more at death's approach shall groan;
In lofty Odin's dome all sighs forbear,
Conscious of bloody deeds my fearless soul,
Mounts to great Odin's hall, and revels there!

Miscellaneous Works (1788), 375-80 (entire essay); *Poems* (1795), 268 (text of poem only).

Freeman's Journal   June 26, 1782

The English Quixote of 1778; or, Modern Idolatory.

My native shades delight me no more,
I haste to meet the ocean's roar,
I seek a wild rebellious shore
    Beyond the Atlantic main:

'Tis honour calls!–I must away!--
Nor east nor pleasure tempts my stay,
Nor all that Love himself can say,
    A moment shall detain.

---

    *Odin or Woden, the Scythian god of war, whose image they worshipped.

To meet these hosts that dare disown
Allegiance to Britannia's throne
I draw the sword that pities none,
    I draw their rebel blood;

Amazement shall their troops confound
When gasping, prostrate on the ground,
My sword shall drink from every wound
    A life destroying flood!

The swarthy Indian, yet unbroke,
Shall bend his neck to Britain's yoke,
Or flee from her avenging stroke
    To desarts all unknown;

The Atlantic isles shall own her sway,
Peru and Mexico obey,
And those* who yet to Satan pray
    Beyond the southern zone.

For George the third I dare to go
Through Etna's fire and Greenland's snow,
Where'er our kindred waters flow,
    The vast unbounded main;

In him true glory shines complete,
In him a thousand virtues meet--
'Twere Heaven to die at George's feet,
    Could I that blessing gain!

For George the third I dare to fall,
Since he to me is all in all,
May he subdue this earthly ball,
    And nations tribute bring--

Yon' rebel States shall wear his chain
Where traitors now with tyrants reign,--
And subject shall be all the main
    To George our potent king.

---

* The inhabitants of New Holland in the south seas.

When honour calls to guard his throne
My life I dare not call my own—
My life I yield without a groan
    For him whom I adore:

In endless glory he shall reign
'Tis he shall conquer France and Spain—
Though I perhaps may ne'er again
    Behold my native shore!

['Tis so well known 'tis hardly worth relating
That men have worship'd gods, tho' of their own creating;
Art's handy work they thought they might adore,
And bow'd to gods that were but logs before.

Idols, of old, were made of clay or wood
And in themselves did neither harm nor good,
Acted as though they knew the good old rule
"Friend, hold thy peace and you'll be thought no fool."

Britons! their case is yours—and link'd in fate
You like your Indian allies—good and great—
Bow to the frowning block yourselves did rear,
And worship *Satan's image*—out of fear—.]

Poems (1786), 281-83.

The PROJECTORS.

BEFORE the brazen age began,
And things were yet on Saturn's plan,
None knew what sovereign bliss there lay,
In ruling, were it but a day.
    Each with spontaneous food content,
His life in simple affluence spent:
The sun was mild, serene and clear,
And walk'd in Libra all the year,
No tempests did the heaven deform,
'Twas not too cold, nor yet too warm;
People were then at small expence,
They dug no ditch, and made no fence,
No patentees by slight or chance
For Indian lands got ample grants
Not for their wants, but just to say,
"If you come here, expect to pay."
    Base grasping souls, your pride repress;
Beyond your wants must you possess?
If ten poor acres will supply
A rustic and his family,
Why, grumblers, would you have ten score,
Ten thousand and ten thousand more?
    It is a truth well understood,
"All would be tyrants if they cou'd."
The love of sway has been confess'd
The ruling passion of the breast:
Those who aspire to govern states,
If baulk'd by disapproving fates,
Resolve their purpose to fulfill,
And scheme for *tenants at their will.*
    "Ten thousand acres, fit for toil,
In Indiana's fertile soil--
Ten thousand acres! let's agree--
Let me become the patentee,
And while the longing stomach craves,
I'll honour fools and flatter knaves."
    If Rome of old to greatness rose
Triumphant over all her foes,
None need believe that people then
Were more in strength than modern men;

If o'er the world her eagles wav'd,
'Twas policy the world enslav'd;
From lands not shar'd amongst the few,
An independent spirit grew;
Each on a small and scanty spot,
With much ado his living got,
Great as a monarch on the throne
By having something of his own.

CASSIBILAN.

Poems (1786), 284-85.

Freeman's Journal   July 3, 1782

On a Lady's Singing Bird, a native of the Canary islands, confined in a very small cage: Written in Bermuda, 1778.

HAPPY in my native grove,
I from spray to spray did rove,
Full of music, full of love.

Drest as fine as bird could be,
Every thing that I did see,
Every thing was mirth to me.

There had I been happy still,
With my mate to coo and bill
In the vale or on the hill;

But the cruel tyrant man,
Tyrant since the world began,
Soon abridg'd my little span:

How shall I the wrong forget!--
Over me he threw a net,
And I am his captive yet.

To this rough and rocky shore,
Ocean I was wafted o'er,
Ne'er to see my country more.

To a narrow cage confin'd
I, who once so gaily shin'd
Sing to please the human kind.

I so fond, so full of play,
I so innocently gay,
Sing my little life away.

Thus to pine and flutter here,
Thus to grieve from year to year,
This is usage too severe;

Gentle shepherds of the plain,
Who so fondly hear my strain,
Help me to be free again;

'Tis a blessing to be free,
Fair Belinda, pity me,
Pity that which sings for thee:

But if cruel, you deny
That your captive bird should fly
Here detain'd so wrongfully,

Full of anguish, full of woe,
I must with my music go
To the cypress groves below.

Poems (1786), 285-87.

Freeman's Journal   July 10, 1782

Untitled poem follows a reprint of the text of General Robertson's proclamation of June 22, 1782, commanding the citizens of New York to militia duty, in defence of "his majesty's interests there.")

[OLD Judas the traitor, (nor need we much wonder)
Falling down from the gallows his paunch split asunder
Affording, 'tis likely, a horrible scent
Rather worse than the sulphur of hell, where he went.

So now this bra' chieftain, who long has suspended
And kept out of view what his master intended,
Bursts out all at once, and an inside discloses
Disgusting the tories, who stop up their noses.

The short of the matter is thus, as I take it--
New-York of true Britons is plainly left naked,
And their conduct amounts to an honest confession
That they cannot depend on the run-a-way Hessian:

In such a dilemma pray what should they do?--
Hearts loyal, to whom should they look but to you?--
You know pretty well how to handle the spade,
To dig their canals and to make a parade;

The city is left to your valiant defence,
And of course it will be but of little expence,
Since there is an old fellow that looks somewhat sooty
Who *gratis* will help you in doing your duty--

"In doing our duty!--'tis duty indeed
(Says a tory) if this be the way that we speed:
We never lov'd fighting: the matter is clear,--
If we had, I am sure we had never come here.

George we own'd for our king, as his true loyal sons,
But why will he force us to manage his guns?--
Who 'list in the army or cruise on the wave,
Let them do as they will--'tis their trade to be brave.

Gun bullets in boxes we easily face,
But when they're in motion--it alters the case,
To skirmish with *Huddies* is all our desire--
For though we can murder we cannot stand fire.

To the standards of Britain we fled for protection
And here we are gather'd, a goodly collection;
And most of us think it is rather too hard
For refusing to arm to be put under guard:

Who knows *under guard* what ills we may feel?--
It is an expression that means a great deal--
'Mongst the rebels they fine 'em who will not turn out,
But here we are left in a sorrowful doubt----

These Britons were always so sharp and so shifty--
The rebels excuse you from serving when fifty,
But here we are counted such wonderful men
We are kept in the ranks, tho' we're five score and ten.

Provided the Clergy but preach *non resistance*,
And *passive obedience*-- they wave their assistance:
But we--tho' we're sick and have death in our faces,
Must purchase a proxy to serve in our places.

If matters go thus it is easy to see
That as blockheads we've been, so slaves we shall be;
And what will become of that peaceable train
Whose tenets enjoin them from war to abstain?

Our city commandant must be an odd shaver
Not a single exception to make in their favour!--
Come let us turn round and *rebelliously* sing,
Huzza for the Congress!--the De'el take the king!"]

Poems (1786), 287-89.

Freeman's Journal   July 10, 1782

The Tenth Ode of Horace's Book of Epodes, imitated.

Written in December 1781, upon the departure of gen. Arnold from New York.

With evil omens from the harbour sails
The ill fated ship that hated Arnold bears,
God of the southern wind, call up thy gales
And whistle in rude fury round his ears.

With horrid waves insult his vessel's sides,
And may the east wind on a leeward shore
Her cables snap, while she in tumult rides
And shatter into fragments every oar;

And let the north wind to her ruin haste
With such a rage as when from mountains high,
He rends the tall oak with his mighty blast
And ruin spreads where'er his forces fly.

May not one friendly star that night be seen
Where sad Orion darts his parting ray,
Nor may she ride on oceans more serene
Than Greece triumphant found that stormy day.

When angry Pallas spent her rage no more
On vanquish'd Ilium then in ashes laid,
But turn'd it on the barque that Ajax bore*,
Avenging thus her temple and the maid.

When tost upon the vast Atlantic main
Your groaning ship the southern gales shall tear
How will your sailors sweat, and you complain
And meanly howl to Jove that will not hear.

---

*Ajax the younger, son of Oileus, king of the Locrians. He debauched Cassandra in the temple of Pallas, which was the cause of his misfortune on his return from the siege of Troy.

But if at last upon some winding shore
A prey to hungry cormorants you lie,
A wanton goat to every stormy power*,
And a fat lamb in sacrifice shall die.

Poems (1786), 290-92.

Freeman's Journal   July 17, 1782

PHILOSOPHICAL REFLECTIONS.

STILL round the world triumphant discord flies,
Still angry kings to bloody contest rise;
Hosts bright with steel in dreadful order plac'd,
And ships contending on the watry waste;
Distracting demons every breast engage,
Unwearied nations glow with mutual rage,
Still to the charge the routed Briton turns,
The war still rages and the battle burns;
See, man with man in deadly combat join,
See, the black navy from the flaming line;
Death smiles alike at battles lost or won—
Art does for him what nature would have done.
    Can scenes like these delight the human breast?—
Who sees with joy humanity distrest?
Such tragic scenes fierce passions might prolong,
But slighted Reason says, they must be wrong.
    Curs'd be the day how bright soe'er it shin'd,
That first made kings the masters of mankind;
And curs'd the wretch who first with regal pride
Their equal rights to equal men deny'd;
But curs'd o'er all, who first to slav'ry broke
Submissive bow'd and own'd a monarch's yoke,

---

* The *Tempests* were goddesses amongst the Romans.

Their servile souls his arrogance ador'd
And basely own'd a brother for a lord;
Hence wrath and blood, and feuds and war began,
And man turn'd monster to his fellow man.
    Not so that age of innocence and ease
When men, yet social, knew no ills like these;
Then dormant yet, ambition (half unknown)
No rival murder'd to possess a throne;
No seas to guard, no empires to defend--
Of some small tribe the father and the friend.
The hoary sage beneath his sylvan shade,
Impos'd no laws but those which reason made;
On peace not war, on good not ill intent,
He judg'd his brethren by their own consent;
Untaught to spurn those brethren to the dust;
In virture firm, and obstinately just,
For him no navies rov'd from shore to shore,
No slaves were doom'd to dig the glittering ore;
Remote from all the vain parade of state,
No slaves in diamonds saunter'd at his gate,
Nor did his breast the guilty passions tear,
He knew no murder and he felt no fear.
    Was this the patriarch sage?--Then turn thine eyes,
And view the contrast that our age supplies;
Touch'd from the life, I trace no ages fled,
I draw no curtain that conceals the dead;
To distant Britain let thy view be cast,
And say the present far exceeds the past;
Of all the plauges that e'er the world have curs'd,
Name George the tyrant, and you name the worst!
    What demon hostile to the human kind,
Planted these fierce disorders in the mind?
All urg'd alike one phantom we pursue
But what has war with *happiness* to do?
In death's black shroud this gem can ne'er be found;
Who deals for that the life destroying wound,
Or pines with grief to see a brother live,
That life dissolving which he cannot give?
    'Tis thine, Ambition!--Thee these horrors suit:
Lost to the human, she assumes the brute;
She proudly vain or insolently bold
Her heart revenge, her eye intent on gold,

Sway'd by the madness of the present hour
Mistakes for happiness *extent of power*;
That shining bait which dropt in folly's way
Tempts the weak mind, and leads the heart astray!
      Thou happiness! still sought but never found,
We, in a circle, chase thy shadow round;
Meant all mankind in different forms to bless
Which yet possessing, we no more possess:--
Thus far remov'd and painted on the eye
Smooth verdant fields seem blended with the sky,
But where they both in fancied contact join
In vain we trace the visionary line;
Still as we chase, the empty circle flies,
Emerge new mountains or new oceans rise.

                                           PHILOMEIDES.

Poems (1786), 291-94.

Freeman's Journal   July 24, 1782

Prince WILLIAM HENRY's SOLILOQUY.

PEOPLE are mad thus to adore the Dauphin--
Heaven grant the brat may soon be in his coffin--
The honours here to this Frenchman shown,
Of right should be Prince George's, or my own;
And all those wreathes that bloom on Louis now,
Should hang, unfading, on my father's brow.
      To these far shores with longing hopes I came,
(By birth a Briton, not unknown to fame)
Pleasures to share that loyalty imparts,
Subdue the rebels, and regain their hearts.
      Weak, stupid expectation--all is done!
Few are the prayers that rise for George's son;
Nought through the waste of these wide realms I trace,
But rage, contempt, and curses on our race,
Hosts with their chiefs by bold usurpers won,

And not a blessing left for George's son!
    Here on these isles (my terrors not a few)
I walk attended by the tory crew:
These from the first have done their best to please,
But who would herd with sychophants like these?
This exil'd race, who their lost shores bemoan,
Would bow to Satan, if he held our throne,--
Rul'd by their fears--and what is meaner far,
Have worshipp'd William only for his *Star!*
To touch my hand their thronging thousands strove,
And tir'd my patience with unceasing love--
In fame's fair annals told me I should live,
But they, poor creatures, had no fame to give:
Must Digby's royal pupil walk the streets,
And smile on every ruffian that he meets;
Or teach them, as he has done--he knows when--
That kings and princes are no more than men?
    Must I alas disclose, to our disgrace,
That Britain is too small for George's race?
Here in the west, where all did once obey,
Three islands only, now, confess our sway;
And in the east we have not much to boast,
For Hyder Ali drives us from the coast:
Yield, rebels, yield--or I must go once more
Back to the white cliffs of my native shore;
(Where in the process of time shall go sir Guy,
And where sir Harry has return'd to sigh,
Whose hands grew weak when things began to cross,
Nor made one effort to retrieve our loss)
Oatmeal and Scottish kale pots round me rise,
And Hanoverian turnips greet mine eyes;--
Welch goats and naked rocks by bosom swell,
And Teague! dear Teague!--to thee I bid farewell.--
Curse on the dauphin and his friends, I say,
He steals our honours and our rights away.
Digby--our anchors!--weight them to the bow,
And eastward through the wild waves let us plough.

Such dire resentments in my bosom burn,
That to these shores I never will return,
Till fruits and flowers on Zembla's coast are known,
And seas congeal beneath the torrid zone.

Poems (1786), 294-96.

New York Journal   August 23, 1787

1786 text reprinted, as the request of a contributor, on the occasion of the prince's trip to Nova Scotia to visit exiled tories. The correspondent asked that the poem be reprinted from Freneau's *Poems* without comment, as "ample opportunity is offered, by that pragmatic tar, for the Severest Satire and Retort."

Freeman's Journal   July 31, 1782

The FLAGELLATORS.

"The exemplary punishment of the grand pensionary, Van Berkel, must be the preliminary article of any treaty of pacification entered into with Holland."

English Ministry.

FULL three long years has haughty Britain try'd
By Dutchmen's hands to thresh Van Berkel's hide,
'Till this should be she gave no hopes of peace,
For only *this* could make her anger cease.

What rais'd the droll conceit is hard to say,
"That poor Van Berkel's back for peace should pay,"
Long, very long, our heads were kept in doubt
Yet fail'd to find the stubborn secret out.

But lately reading of la Mancha's knight
And Sancho Panza, that ill-fated wight,
Sudden the clouds from my rack'd brains withdrew
And all the mighty secret rose to view.

Enchanted long fair Dulcinea lay
In a dark cave secluded from the day,
Chang'd to a country wench with haggard face;--
Lost her imperial charms and every winning grace,
While sad don Quixote through the wide world stray'd
And mourn'd the hard fate of the peerless maid.

At length from Hell's dark chambers Merlin came
And told him how he might release the dame
And get her up from her dull situation
By Sancho's hide enduring flagellation.

"He on his back (said Merlin) tho' he grieve
Three thousand stinging lashes must receive,
(Even his own hand the scourging must inflict
Or else my lady will at last be trick'd)
And when to these he adds just fifteen score
Then Dulcinea comes and not before,"

"De'el take her, said the squire, and all her crew!
"What has her freedom with my back to do?--
"Ere my back-basting shall her beauty save
"Faith she may go enchanted to the grave."

Britain, 'tis plain, has took the hint from hence
And peace, Van Berkel, seeks at thy expence:
Convince her now that you can hold your place
And arm'd with scorpions lash her bull dog race.

Don QUEVEDO.

Poems (1786), 296-97.

Freeman's Journal   August 7, 1782[1]

SATAN's REMONSTRANCE.
(Occasioned by Mr. *Rivington's* late apology for *lying*.-- See the *Royal Gazette* of the 10th ult. and our last.)

YOUR golden dreams, your flattering schemes,
    Alas! where are they fled, Sir?
Your plans derang'd, your prospects chang'd,
    You now may go to bed, Sir.--

How could you thus, my partner dear,
Give up the hopes of many a year--?
Your fame retriev'd and soaring high
In *Truth's* resemblance seem'd to fly:
But now you grow so wondrous wise,
You turn, and own that all is lies.

A fabric that from hell we rais'd,
On which astonish'd rebels gaz'd,
And which the world shall ne'er forget,
No less than *Rivington's Gazette*,
Demolish'd at a single stroke--
The angel Gabriel might provoke.

---

[1] This poem was composed in response to an editorial apology in Rivington's *Royal Gazette*, July 10, 1782:

To the PUBLIC.

The publisher of this paper, sensible that his zeal for the success of his Majesty's arms, and his sanguine wishes for the good of his country, and his friendship for individuals, have at times led him to credit and circulate paragraphs, without investigating the facts so closely as his duty to the public demanded; trusting to their feelings, and depending to their generosity, he begs them to look over past errors, and depend on future correctness; for henceforth he will neither desire nor expect nor solicit their favours longer than his endeavours shall stamp the same degree of authenticity and credit upon the Royal Gazette (of New-York) as well as all Europe allow to the Royal Gazette of London.

"That all was lies" might well be true,
But why must this be told by you?
Great master of the wooden head,
Where is thy wonted cunning fled?
It was a folly to engage
That truth henceforth should fill your page,
When you must know, as well as I,
Your only mission is to *lie*.

Such are the plans which folly draws—
We now, like bears, may suck our paws;—
Brought up in lying from our youth,
You should have dy'd a foe to truth,
Since none but fools in this accord,
That *Virtue is its own reward.*

Your fortune was as good as made,
Great artist in the lying trade!
But now I see with grief and pain
Your credit cannot rise again:
No more the favourite of my heart,
No more will I my gifts impart.

Yet something shall you gain at last
For lies contriv'd in seasons past:—
When pressing to the "narrow gate"
I'll show the portal mark'd by Fate,
Where all mankind (as parsons say)
Are apt to take the wider way,
And, though the *Royal* Printer swear,
Will bolt him in and keep him there!

Poems (1786), 298-99.

Freeman's Journal   August 28, 1782

The REFUGEES PETITION to Sir Guy Carleton.

    Humbly sheweth,
THAT your honour's petitioners, tories by trade,
From the first of the war have lent Britain their aid
And done all they could both in country and town
In support of the king and the rights of his crown;
But now to their grief and confusion they find
"The De'el may take them who are farthest behind."

In the rear of all rascals they still have been plac'd
And halter and gibbets full often have fac'd,
Have been in the midst of distresses and doubt
Whene'er they came in or whene'er they went out;
Have supported the king and defended *his church*
And now in the end--must be left in the lurch.

Though often, too often, his arms were disgrac'd
We still were in hopes he would conquer at last
And restore us again to our sweethearts and wives
The pride of our hearts and the joy of our lives,
But he promis'd *too far* and we trusted *too much*,
And who could have look'd for a war with the Dutch?

Our *board* broken up and discharg'd from our stations,
Sir Guy, it is cruel to cut off our *rations*;
Of a project like that whoe'er was the mover
It is, we must tell you, a cursed manœvre,
A plan to destroy us--the basest of tricks
To get us away to the shallows of Styx.

If a peace be intended as people surmise,
(Though we hope from our souls it is nothing but lies)
Inform us at once what we have to expect,
Nor treat us, as usual with a surly neglect;
Or else by the *mass* and the will of the *Fates*,
We'll to to *the rebels*--and get our estates--

Poems (1786), 303-04.

Freeman's Journal   August 28, 1782

SIR GUY's ANSWER.

WE have reason to think there will soon be a peace,
And that war with the rebels will certainly cease
But, be that as it will, I would have you to know
That as matters are changing we soon may change too;
In short I would say, (since I have it at heart)
Though the war should continue, yet *we* may depart.

Four offers in season I therefore propose,
(As much as I can do in reason God knows)
In which, though there be not too plentiful carving,
There still is sufficient to keep you from starving;

And, first of the first, it would mightily charm me
To see you, my children, *enlist in the army*,
Or *enter the navy* and get for your pay
A *farthing* an hour, which is *sixpence* per day--
There's Hector M'Lean and Arthur O'Gregor
And Donald M'Donald shall rule you with vigour:
If these do not suit you, then take your new plan,
Make your peace with the rebels (that is, if you can)
There rank and distinction perhaps you may find
And rise into offices fit to your mind--
But if still you object--to be all on a level,
Burn up your red coats and go off to the Devil.

Poems (1786), 304-05.

Freeman's Journal   August 28, 1782

The following lines are addressed to the *Foe* to *Tyrants*, in the Independent Gazetteer of Saturday last, by
A *Foe* to *Malice.*

WHEN round the *barque* the howling tempest raves,
Toss'd in the conflict of a thousand waves,
The lubber landsmen weep, complain and sigh,
And on the pilot's skill, or heaven rely,
Lurk in their holds, astonish'd and aghast.,
Dreading the moment that must be their last--
The tempest o'er--their terror also ceases,
And up they come to show their shameless faces,
At once grow brave, and tell the pilot too,
"He did no more than they themselves could do."

"A FOE TO TYRANTS--*One* thy heart restores--
There is a *Tyrant* that thy soul adores,
And every stupid line too plainly shows
Your heart is hostile to that tyrant's foes.

What mighty malice urg'd this Genius dull
With *Churchill's* wreathes to shade his barren scull?
So utter darkness union claims with light,
So oil and water in one mass unite:
No more thy rage in borrow'd rhimes repeat;
Sneak into prose--the dunce's last retreat!
Reed's patriot fame to distant climes shall last
When these base reptiles to the dogs are cast,
Or, when Oblivion spreads her dreary wings,
Lost in the lumber of forgotten things,
And none shall ask, nor wish to know, or care
Who--what their names--or when they liv'd, or where.

Poems (1786), 299-300.

Freeman's Journal   September 4, 1782

To the *Foe* to *Tyrants*.

VILE as they are, this lukewarm tory crew
Seem viler still, when they are prais'd by you;
By you adorn'd, in *yellow* robes they shine,
Sweat through your verse, and stink in every line.
    True child of Dullness—eldest of their tribe—
How couldst thou dream that thou wast worth a bribe?
Ill fated scribbler, with thy clumsy quill,
Retract the *threat* you dare not to fulfil,
And round your neck the *withe* or halter twine,
And be the office of the hangman thine.
Have I from you purloin'd one shred of wit,
Or did I imitate one line you writ?
Peace to your works—'twere base to rob the dead,
The clay cold offspring of your empty head.
    Scribbler retire—what madness would it be
To point a cannon at a mite like thee!
Such noxious vermin crawling from the shell,
By squibs and crackers might be kill'd as well.
    But if you must torment the world with rhimes,
(Since thou wert sent to scourge us for our crimes)
In stupid odes indulge thy smoky wit,
Dull lyrics would thy happy genius fit;
With thy coarse *white wash* daub some scoundrel's face,
Blockheads in power, or traitors in disgrace:
To gain immortal praise I leave you free;
Go—scratch and scribble unchastis'd by me.
Haste to the realms of nonsense and despair,
The ghosts of murder'd rhimes shall meet you there,
Like rattling chains provoke incessant fears,
And with eternal jinglings stun your ears.

A *Foe* to *Malice*.

Poems (1786), 300-01.

Freeman's Journal   September 11, 1782

To the FOE to TYRANTS on his FAREWELL, in the Independent Gazeteer of the 7th inst.

SINCE ink, thank heaven, is all the blood you spill,
Health to the driver of the true *goose* quill;
Such war shall leave no widow in despair,
Nor curse one orphan with the public care.
'Tis the worst wound the heart of man can feel,
Thus to be wounded by an ass's heel:
With generous satire give me all my due,
Nay, give me more, and call me scoundrel too,
Make me as black as hell's remotest gloom,
But still to genius let me owe my doom:
By Jove's red lightnings 'tis no shame to bleed,
But by a grovelling swine--is death indeed.
    Now, by the laurels of your *yellow* crew,
I felt no shame 'till I engag'd with you;
But such an odour scented from your song,
I stopt my nose, and quickly pass'd along,
Blush'd for the wretch that could such filth display,
His guts disgorging in the public way.
    Arm'd as I stand, unusual tumults rise,
And all my soul comes swelling through my eyes,
To think that in the skirmish of a day
This bard must perish, and his fame decay,
So quick retire to black oblivion's clime,
Turn'd, chas'd, and routed by the power of rhime!
    I *wish'd* him still *unhandled* and unhurt,
I wish'd no evils to this man of dirt;
I thought to leave him swelt'ring in his den,
Not with such rotten trash to stain my pen,
But his base labours wrought his utter woe,
And his own efforts now shall lay him low:--
Before his eyes the sexton's spade appears,
And bells unceasing ring within his ears,
Already is his span of being fled,
Sense, wit, and reason--all proclaim him *dead*;
In his own lines he toll'd his funeral knell,
And when he could not *sing* he *stunk* FAREWELL.

Poems (1786), 302-03.

Freeman's Journal   September 25, 1782

To those whom it may Concern.

THE sage that took the wrong sow by the ears
And independence claim'd for Vermonteers
Who from twelve numbers down to eight decreas'd,
Is now your scribbler and may serve for priest,
To him apply, dear Oswald, in distress,
From him ask favours and to him *confess*,
He'll pardon all your sins--ay, more than once,
And will forgive you, e'en for being a dunce.

When first that slave of slaves began to write
Truth curs'd his pen and reason took her flight,
Dullness on him her choicest opiates shed
Black as his heart and empty as his head:
Him on her soil Hibernia could not bear,
The viper sicken'd in his native air,
Then rush'd abroad, a Jesuit in disguise,
Borne on the wings of malice, rage, and lies,
To this new world a nuisance and a pest
To curse his betters and abuse the best.

Thou base born lump of impudence and dirt,
With all the *will* but not the *pow'r* to hurt;
Whose barren soul each empty line reveals
Come, let me tie thee to my chariot wheels,
And o'er the surface of this prickly ground
Drag thy vile carrion carcase round and round.
Or like a FELON, hang'd to after time,
Be one more victim to the power of rhyme!

Bear me ye gods to some sequester'd place
Where never rascal show'd his brazen face;
Remove me far from all the rascal kind
(Dullness with insolence forever join'd)
To some retreat of solitude and rest--
Not let another pang disturb thy breast,
When I have wept to think the world shall know
I had to combat with so mean a foe.
                         VIRGINIUS.

Poems (1786), 305-06.

Freeman's Journal   December 4, 1782

RIVINGTON's REFLEXIONS.

Inclusus pœnam expectat.   *Virg.*

THE more I reflect, the more plain it appears,
If I stay, I must stay at the risque of my ears,
I have so be-pepper'd the foes of *our* throne,
Be-rebel'd, be-devil'd, and told them their own,
That if we give up to these rebels at last,
'Tis a chance if my ears will atone for the past.
    'Tis always the best to provide for the worst--
So evacuation I'll mention the first:
If Carleton should sail for our dear native shore
(As Clinton, Cornwallis, and Howe did before)
And take off the soldiers that serve for our guard
(A step that the Tories would think rather hard)
Yet still I surmise, for aught I can see,
No Congress or *Senates* would meddle with me.
    "For what have I done, when we come to consider,
But sold my commodities to the best bidder?
If I offer'd to lie for the sake of a post
Was I to be blam'd if the king offer'd most?
The King's Royal Printer!--Five hundred a year!
Between you and me 'twas a handsome affair:
Who would not for *that* give matters a stretch
And lie back and forward, and carry and fetch,
May have some pretensions to *honour* and *fame;*
But what are they both but the sound of a name,
Mere words to deceive us, as I have found long since,
Live on them a week, and you'll find they're but nonsense.
    The late news from Charleston my mind has perplext
If that is abandon'd, I know what goes next:
This city of York is a place of great note,
And that we should hold it I now give my vote;
But what are your voices against Shelburne's decrees?
These people at helm steer us just where they please,
So often they've had us all hands on the brink.
They'll steer us at last to the devil, I think;
And though in the danger themselves have a share,
It will do us small good that they also go there.

It is true that the Tories, their children and wives
Have offer'd to stay at the risque of their lives,
And gain to themselves an immortal renown
By ALL turning soldiers, and keeping the town:
Whoe'er was the laddie that struck out the plan,
In my humble conceit, was a very good man;
But our words on this subject need be very few--
Already I see that it never will do:
For suppose a few ships should be left us by Britain,
With tories to man them, and other things fitting,
In truth we should be in a very fine box,
As well they might guard us with ships on the stocks,
And when I beheld them abroad and afloat
I am sure I should think of *the bear in the boat**.

    On the faith of a Printer, things look very black--
And what shall we do, alas! and alack!
Shall we quit our young princes and full blooded peers,
And bow down to Viscounts and French Chevaliers?
Perhaps you will say, "As the very last shift
"We'll go to New Scotland, and take the king's gift:"

    Good folks, do your will—but I vow and I swear,
I'll be boil'd into soup before I'll live there:
Is it thus that our monarch his subjects degrades?--
Let him go and be d--'d with his axes and spades!
Of all the vile countries that ever were known
In the frigid or torrid or temperate zone,
(From accounts that I've had) there is not such another;
It neither belongs to this world or the other:
A favour they think it to send us there gratis
To sing like the Jews at the River Euphrates,
And after surmounting the rage of the billows,
Hang ourselves up at last with our harps on the willows:
Ere I sail for that shore may I take my last nap--
Why, it gives me the palsy to look on its map!
And he that goes there (tho' I mean to be civil)
May fairly be said to have gone to the Devil.

    Shall I push for old England, and whine at the throne?

---

* See Gay's Fables.

Alas, they have *Jemmies* enough of their own!
Besides, such a name I have got from my trade,
They would think I was lying, whatever I said;--
Thus scheme as I will, or contrive as I may,
Continual difficulties rise in the way:
In short, if they let me remain in this realm,
What is it to Jemmy who stands at the helm?
I'll petition the rebels (if York is forsaken)
For a place in their Zion which ne'er shall be shaken;
I am sure they'll be clever: it seems their whole study;
They have not young *Asgill* for old captain *Huddy*,
And it must be a truth that admits no denying,
If they spare us for *murder* they'll spare us for *lying*.

                G.

Royal Gazette   December 14, 1782

Above text reprinted, and introduced as follows:

> *Mr.* Rivington having been applied to by many Gentlemen for a pleasant Public dish respecting himself, exhibited in the Philadelphia Freeman's Journal, of December 4, takes leave to copy it into this Day's Gazette, and assures the Author that a Column should at any time be most cheerfully reserved to convey that Gentleman's *lively* Lucubrations to the public.

Poems (1786), 310-13.

Freeman's Journal   December 11, 1782

The PROPHECY of King TAMMANY.

THE Indian chief who, fam'd of yore,
Saw Europe's sons advent'ring here,
  Look'd sorrowing to the crowded shore,
   And sighing dropt a tear:
He saw them half his world explore,
He saw them draw the shining blade,

He saw their hostile ranks display'd,
And cannons blazing thro' that shade
    Where only peace was known before.

"Ah, what unequal arms!" he cry'd,
How art thou fall'n, my country's pride,
    The rural, sylvan reign!
Far from our pleasing shores to go
To western rivers, winding slow,--
Is this the boon the gods bestow?
What have we done, great patrons, say,
That strangers seize our woods away,
    And drive us naked from our native plain!

Rage and revenge inspire my soul,
And passion burns without controul;
    Hence, strangers, to your native shore!
Far from our Indian shades retire,
Remove these *gods* that vomit fire,
    And stain with blood these ravag'd glades no more.

In vain I weep, in vain I sigh,
These strangers all our arms defy,
As they advance our chieftains die!--
    What can their hosts oppose?
The bow has left its wonted spring,
The arrow faulters on the wing,
Nor carries ruin from the string
    To end their being and our woes:

Yes, yes,--I see our nation bends;
The gods no longer are our friends,
    But why these weak complaints and sighs?
Are there not gardens in the west,
Where all our far fam'd Sachems rest?--
I'll go, an unexpected guest,
    And the dark horrors of the way despise.

Ev'n now the thundering peals draw nigh,
'Tis theirs to triumph, ours to die!
But mark me, Christian, ere I go--
Thou too shalt have thy share of woe,
The time rolls on, not moving slow,
When hostile squadrons for your blood shall come,
    And ravage all your shore!
Your warriors and your children slay,
And some in dismal dungeons lay,
Or lead them captive far away
    To climes unknown, thro' seas untry'd before.

When struggling long, at last with pain
You break a cruel tyrant's chain,
That never shall be join'd again,
    When half your foes are homeward fled,
    And hosts on hosts in triumph led,
    And hundreds maim'd and thousands dead,
    A timid race shall then succeed,
Shall slight the virtues of the firmer race,
That brought your tyrant to disgrace,
Shall give your honours to an odious train,
Who shun'd all conflicts on the main
And dar'd no battles on the bloody plain,
    Whose little souls sunk in the gloomy day
    When *virtue only* could support the fray
And sunshine friends kept off--or ran away."

So spoke the chief, and rais'd his funeral pyre--
    Around him soon the crackling flames ascend;
He smil'd amid the fervours of the fire
    To think his troubles were so near their end,
Till the freed soul, her debt to nature paid,
Rose from the ashes that her prison made,
And sought the world unknown, and dark oblivion's shade.

Poems (1786), 308-10.

Columbian Centinel   December 15, 1802

The above text is reprinted as part of the following letter from a correspondent, who offers a novel interpretation of the poem as evidence to prove Freneau's "prophetic" distrust of Jefferson:

> Mr. Russell,
>
> I THINK your correspondent Honorius[1] has proved, beyond denial, that *Freneau*, the Poet, was originally a patriot, a federal republican, and an active friend to the government which *Washington* and *Adams* advocated and administered; and which *Jefferson* and *Paine* have calumniated, and are now endeavoring to destroy. But to demonstrate farther that he held Mr. J. in contempt, *before he became his pensioner*, I send you, for insertion, the inclosed *Prophecy;* desiring you would particularly notice the lines I have underscored; and in which *Freneau* appears to have had a *second sight*, that he who now holds the reigns of government, would in time, as a punishment of the country for the injuries it has done the aborigines, succeed to the chair. Besides being beautifully poetical, the parts underscored are too plain to be misunderstood, and have been too often acknowledged to be now denied.   Yours &c.
>   PHILO-MUSE.

December 9, 1802.

Text substantively identical to the 1782 version, except for the following variants:

The last eight lines of stanza 7 are underscored.

---

[1] See reference to the letter from Honorius in *Columbian Centinel* (December 8, 1802) reprint of "Verses occasioned by General Washington's arrival . . ." *Freeman's Journal,* December 10, 1783.

The last line of stanza 7 is footnoted as follows, to explain the application of the phrase "or ran away" to this interpretation of the poem:

> * *To the* Allegheny *ridges, when Col. TARLETON attempted to "pay the homage of his high respect and consideration" to the Governor and Legislature of* Virginia!

Freeman's Journal   December 11, 1782

> (Untitled Latin text and verse translation introduces an essay on city burying places.)

Simon Petrus, vir pius et probus,
Qui vivus omnibus profuerat
Sub dio sepeliri voluit,
Ne mortuus cuiquam nocerat.
                    Epit. Monachi.

A certain man nam'd Simon Peter,
Honest by principle and nature,
Who as he aim'd, while yet alive,
To help his fellow men to thrive,
So in his will took special care
To give due orders to his heir
To place no piles of church yard stones,
Or church floor pavement o'er his bones,
Lest he who living was well bred
Should people stink to death when dead.

Miscellaneous Works (1788), 403.

(Untitled.)

SHOULD Oswald's scribblers call you all that's base,
Abuse your stature and blaspheme your face,
Make you the worst and vilest of your kind,
With not one spark of reason in your mind,
Who would to Oswald's rancorous page reply,
So fam'd for scandal, and so prone to lie?
  Still may those bagpipes of sedition play,
For fools must prate, and dogs must have their day;
Still from that page let hoarse mouth'd whelps defame,
And madness rave and malice take her aim,
May scribes on scribes in verse and prose combine,
And one dark chaos gloom through every line!
Long may they write unquestion'd and unhurt,
And all their age discharge, and all their dirt:
Night owls must screech by heaven's severe decree,
And wolves must howl, or wolves they would not be.
  From empty froth these scribbling insects rose;
What honest man but counts them for his foes?
When they are lash'd, may dunce with dunce condole,
And bellow nonsense from the tortur'd soul!
When they are dead, and in some dungeon cramm'd,
(For die they will, and all their works be damn'd)
When they shall belch their last departing groans,
May dogs and doctors barbeque their bones,
And the last horrors of their souls to calm,
Fallon, the priest, console them with a psalm!

Poems (1786), 307.

Freeman's Journal   December 25, 1782

RIVINGTON's REFLEXIONS.
[Continued.]

Incertus quo fata ferant, quo sistere detur.   *Virg.*

FOLKS may think as they please, but to me it would seem
That our great men at home have done nothing but dream.
Such trimming and twisting and shifting about,
And some getting in, and others turn'd out;
And yet, with their bragging and looking so big,
All they did was to dance a theatrical jig;
Seven years now, and more, we have try'd ev'ry plan,
And are just as near conquering as when we began,
Great things were expected from Clinton and Howe
But what have they done, or where are they now?
Sir Guy was sent over to kick up a dust,
Who already prepares to return in disgust--
The object delusive we wish to attain
Has been in our reach, and may be so again,--
But so oddly does heaven its bounties dispense,
And has granted our king such a small share of sense
That, let Fortune favour or smile as she will,
We are doom'd to drive on like a horse in a mill,
And tho' we may seem to advance on our rout,
'Tis but to return to where we sat out.
    From hence I infer (by way of improvement)
That nothing is got by this circular movement;
And I plainly perceive, from this fatal delay,
We are going to ruin the round-about way:
Some nations, like ships, give up to the gale,
And hurry'd ashore with a full flowing sail;
So Sweden submitted to absolute power,
And freemen were chang'd to be slaves in an hour;
Thus Theodore soon from his grandeur came down,
Forsaking his subjects and Corsican crown;
But we--'tis our fate, without ally or friend,
To go to perdition close haul'd to the wind.
    The case is too plain, that if I stay here
I have something to hope and somewhat to fear:
In regard to my carcase I shouldn' mind that--

I can say "I have liv'd," and have grown very fat;
Have been in my day remarkably shifty,
And soon, very soon, will be verging on fifty.
'Tis time for the state of the dead to prepare,
'Tis time to consider how things will go there;
Some few are admitted to Jupiter's hall,
But the kitchen of Pluto is open to all--
The day is approaching as fast as it can
When Jemmy shall be a mere moderate man,
Shall sleep underground both summer and winter,
The husk of a man, and the shell of a printer,
And care not a farthing for George, or his line,
What empires start up or what kingdoms decline.
    Our parson last Sunday brought tears from my eyes
When he told us of heaven, I thought of my lies--
To his flock he describ'd it, and laid it before 'em
(As if he had been in its *Sanctum sanctorum*)
Recounted its beauties that never shall fade,
And quoted John Bunyan to prove what he said,
Debarr'd from the gate who the truth should deny,
Or "whosoe'er loveth or maketh a lie"
    Thro' the course of my life it has still been my lot
In spite of myself to say "things that are not,"
And therefore suspect that upon my decease
Not a poet will leave me to slumber in peace,
But at least once a week bescribble the stone
Where Jemmy, poor Jemmy, lies sleeping alone!
    Howe'er in the long run these matters may be,
If the scripture is true it has bad news for me--
And yet when I come to examine the text,
And the learn'd annotations that *Poole* has annex'd,
Throughout the black list of the people that sin
I cannot once find that I'm mention'd therein;
Whoremongers, idolators, all are left out,
And wizzards and dogs (which is proper, no doubt,)
But he who says I'm there, mistakes or forgets--
It mentions no *Printers of Royal Gazettes*!
    In truth, I have need of a mansion of rest,
And *here* to remain might suit me the best--
Philadelphia in some things wou'd answer as well,
(Some tories are there, and my papers might sell)
But then I should live amongst wrangling and strife,

And be forc'd to say *credo* the rest of my life:
For their sudden conversion I'm much at a loss--
I am told that they bow to the wood of the cross,
And worship the *reliques* transported from Rome,
St. Peter's toe-nails and St. Anthony's comb.--
If thus the true faith they no longer defend
I scarcely can think where the madness will end--
If the greatest among them submit to the Pope,
What reason have I for indulgence to hope?
If the Congress themselves to the *Chapel* did pass*,
Ye may swear that poor *Jemmy* would have to sing mass.

Poems (1786), 313-16.

---

* On the 4th of November last, the clergy and select men of Boston paraded through the streets after a crucifix, and joined in a procession in praying for a departed soul out of Purgatory; and for this they gave the example of Congress, and other American leaders on a former occasion at Philadelphia, some of whom it is said even went so far as to sprinkle themselves with what they call holy water.

Royal Gazette of December 11. inst.

Freeman's Journal   January 8, 1783

TO the Senate of York, with all due submission,
Of honest HUGH GAINE *the humble Petition;*
An Account of his Life he will also prefix,
At least what was previous to Seventy-Six;
He hopes that your honours will take no offence,
If he sends you some groans of contrition from hence,
And further to prove that he's truly sincere,
He wishes you all a HAPPY NEW YEAR.

AND first he informs in his representation,
That he once was a printer of some reputation,
And dwelt in the street call'd Hanover Square,
(You'll know where it is if you ever was there)
Next door to the drug shop of doctor Brownejohn
(Who now to the dog house of Pluto is gone)
But what do I talk--who e'er came to town,
And knew not HUGH GAINE at the *Bible* & *Crown?*
    Now, if I were ever so given to lie,
My dear native country I wouldn't deny;
(I know you love Teagues) and I shall not conceal,
That I came from a kingdom where Phelim O'Neale
And other brave worthies ate butter and cheese,
And walk'd in the clover fields up to their knees:
Full early in youth without basket or burden,
With a staff in my hand I pass'd over Jordan,
(I remember my comrade was doctor Magaw,
And many strange things on the waters we saw,
Sharks, dolphins, and sea-dogs, bonettas, and whales,
And birds at the tropic with quills in their tails)
And came to your city and government seat,
And found it was true you had something to eat;
When thus I wrote home--"The country is good,
"They have plenty of victuals and plenty of wood;
"The people are kind, and, whate'er they may think,
"I shall make it appear I can swim where they'll sink,
"And yet they're so brisk, and so full of good cheer,
"By my soul I suspect they have always new year,
"And therefore conceive "it is good to be here."

So said, and so acted--I put up a press,
And printed away with amazing success;
Neglected my person, and look'd like a fright,
Was bother'd all day, and was busy all night,
Saw money come in as the papers went out,
While Parker and Weyman* were driving about,
And cursing, and swearing, and chewing their cuds,
And wishing Hugh Gaine and his press in the suds,
(Old Weyman was printer, you know, to the king,
And thought he had got all the world in a string,
Tho' riches not always attend on a throne)
For he swore I had found the philosopher's stone,
And call'd me a rogue and a son of a bitch,
Because I knew better than him to get rich!
    To malice like that 'twas invain to reply--
You had known by his looks he was telling a lie.
    Thus life ran away, so smooth and serene--
Ah, these were the happiest days I had seen!
But the saying of Jacob I know to be true,
"The days of thy servant are evil and few!"--
The days that to me were joyous and glad,
Are nothing to those which are dreary and sad!
    The feuds of the *Stamp-Act* foreboded foul weather,
And war and vexation all coming together;
Those days were the days of riots and mobs,
Tar, feathers, and tories, and troublesome jobbs--
Priests preaching up war for *the good of our souls*,
And libels, and lying, and Liberty-Poles,
From which, when some whimsical *colours* you wav'd,
We had nothing to do, but look up and be sav'd--
(You thought, by *resolving*, to terrify Britain--
Indeed, if you did you were damnably *bitten*)
I knew it would bring an eternal reproach,
When I saw you a burning Cadwallader's+ coach;
I knew you would suffer for what you had done,
When I saw you lampooning poor Sawny his son,

---

  * New York Printers.
  + Lieutenant Governor Cadwallader Colden.

And bringing him down to so wretched a level,
As to ride him about in a cart with the devil.
    Well, as I predicted that matters would be--
To the stamp act succeeded a tax upon *Tea*:
What chest fulls were scatter'd, & trampl'd, & drown'd,
And yet the whole tax was but threepence per pound!
May the hammer of Death on my noddle descend,
And Satan torment me to time without end,
If this was a reason to fly into quarrels,
And feuds that have ruin'd *our* manners and morals;
A parson himself might have sworn round the compass,
That folks for a trifle should make such a *rumpus*,
Such a rout as to set half the world in a rage,
Make France, Spain, and Holland with Britain engage,
While the Emperor, the Swede, the Russ, and the Dane
All pity *John Bull*--and run off with his gain.
    But this was the season that I must lament--
I first was a whig with an honest intent;
Not a fellow among them talk'd louder or bolder,
With his sword by his side, or his gun on his shoulder;
Yes, I was a whig, and a whig from my heart,
But still was unwilling with Britain to part--
I knew to oppose her was foolish and vain,
I knew she would turn and embrace us again,
And make us as happy as happy could be,
By renewing the œra of mild SIXTY-THREE:
And yet, like a cruel undutiful son,
Who evil returns for the good *to be done*,
To gain a mere trifle, a shilling or so,
I printed some treason for Philip F--neau,
Some damnable poems reflecting on *Gage*,
The *King* and his *Council*, and writ with such rage,
So full of invective, and loaded with spleen,
So pointedly sharp, and so hellishly keen,
That, at least in the judgement of half our wise men,
Alecto herself made the nib to his pen.
                                 (to be continued.)

Poems (1786), 317-20.

Freeman's Journal   January 29, 1783

HUGH GAINE's LIFE, continued from No. 90.

AT this time arose a certain king *Sears*,
Who made it his study to banish our fears:
He was, without doubt, a person of merit,
Great knowledge, some wit, and abundance of spirit;
Could talk like a lawyer, and that without fee,
And threaten'd perdition to all that drank *Tea*.
Ah! don't you remember what a vigorous hand he put
To drag off the great guns, and plague captain Vandeput.*
That *night* when the HERO (his patience worn out)
Put fire to his cannons and folks to the rout,
And drew up his ship with *a spring on her cable*,
And gave us a second confusion of *Babel*,
And (what is more *solid* than *scurrilous language*)
Pour'd on us a tempest of *round shot* and *langrage*:
Scarce a broadside was ended 'till another began again–
By Jove! it was nothing but *Fire away Flannagan*
At first we suppos'd it was only a sham,
'Till he drove a *round ball* thro' the roof of *black Sam***;
The town by their flashes was fairly enlighten'd,
The women miscarry'd, the beaus were all frighten'd;–
For my part, I hid in a cellar (as sages
And Christians were wont to in the *primitive ages*:
Thus the *Prophet of old that was rapt to the sky*,
Lay snug in a cave 'till the tempest went by,
But, as soon as the comforting spirit had spoke,
He rose and came out with his mystical cloak)
Yet I hardly could boast of a moment of *rest*,
The dogs were a howling, the town was distrest!--
But our terrors soon vanish'd, for suddenly *Sears*
Renew'd our lost courage and dry'd up our tears.

---

* *Captain of the Asia man of war.*
+ *A cant phrase among privateers men.*
** *A noted tavern keeper in New York.*

    Our memories, indeed, must have strangely decay'd
If we cannot remember what *speeches* he made,
What handsome *harangues* upon every occasion,
How he laugh'd at the whim of a *British Invasion*!
    "P-x take 'em (said he) do ye think they will come?
If they shou'd--we have only to beat on *our drum*,
And *run up the flag of American freedom*,
And people will *muster* by millions to *bleed 'em*!
What *freeman* need value such blackguards as these?--
Let us sink in our channel some *Chevaux de frise*--
And then let 'em come--and we'll show 'em fair play--
But they are not madmen--I tell you--not they!"
    From this very day 'till the *British* came in
We liv'd, I may say, in the *Desart of Sin*;--
Such beating and bruising and *scratching and tearing*,
Such kicking and cussing and *cursing* and *swearing*!
But when *they* advanc'd with *their numerous* fleet,
And WASHINGTON made his *nocturnal retreat*,
(And which *they permitted*, I say, to *their* shame,
Or else *your* NEW EMPIRE had been but a name)
We townsmen, like women, of *Britons* in *dread*,
Mistrusted their meaning, and foolishly fled;
Like the *rest* of the dunces I mounted my steed,
And gallop'd away with *incredible* speed,
To NEWARK I hastened--but *trouble* and *care*
Got up on the crupper, and follow'd me there!
There I scarcly got fuel to keep myself warm,
And scarcely found spirits to *weather the storm*;
And was quickly convinc'd I had little to do,
(The *Whigs* were in arms, and my *readers* were few,)
So after remaining one cold winter season,
And stuffing my *papers* with something like treason,
And meeting misfortunes and endless disasters,
And forc'd to submit to a hundred *new masters*,
I thought it more prudent to hold to the *one*--
And (after repenting for what I had done,
And cursing my folly and idle pursuits)
Return'd to the city, and hung up my boots.
    As matters have gone, it was plainly a blunder,
But *then* I expected the Whigs must knock under,
And I always adhere to the sword that is longest,
And stick to the party that's like to be strongest:

That you have succeeded is merely a chance,
I never once dreamt of the conduct of France!--
If alliance with her you were promis'd--at least
You ought to have show'd me your STAR *in the* EAST,
Not let me go uniform'd as a beast.
When your army I saw without stockings or shoes
Or victuals--or *money* to pay them their dues,
(Excepting your wretched Congressional *paper*,
That stunk in my nose like the snuff of a taper,
A cart load of which for a dram might be spent all
That damnable bubble the *old continental*,
That *took* people *in* at this wonderful crisis,
With its *mottos* and *emblems*, and cunning *devices*;
Which, bad as it was, you were forc'd to admire,
And which was, in fact, the *pillar of fire*,
To which you directed your wandering noses,
(Like the Jews in the desart conducted by *Moses*,)
When I saw them attended with *famine* and *fear*,
Distress in their front and *Howe* in their rear;
When I saw them for debt incessantly dunn'd,
Nor a shilling to pay them laid up in your fund;
Your ploughs at a stand, and your ships run ashore;--
When this was apparent, (and need I say more?)
I *handled* my cane, and I *look'd* at my hat,
And cry'd--"G-d have mercy on armies like that)"
I took up the bottle, disdaining to stay,
And said--"Here's a health to the *Vicar* of *Bray*,"
And cock'd up my beaver, and--strutted away.

(The remainder, if we have room, shall be in our next.)

Poems (1786), 320-23.

Freeman's Journal   February 12, 1783

HUGH GAINE's LIFE, continued from No. 93.

ASHAM'D of my conduct, I sneak'd into town,
(Six hours and a quarter the sun had been down)
It was, I remember, a cold frosty night,
And the stars in the firmament glitter'd as bright
As if (to assume a poetical stile)
Old Vulcan had lent them a rub with his file.
    Till this cursed night, I can honestly say,
I ne'er before dreaded the dawn of the day;
Not a wolf or a fox that is caught in a trap
E'er was so asham'd of his nightly mis-hap—
I couldn't help thinking what ills might befal me,
What rebels and rascals the British would call me;
And how I might suffer in credit and purse,
If not in my person, which still had been worse:
At length I resolv'd (as was surely my duty)
To go for advice to parson *Auchmuty*:
(The parson, who now I hope is in glory,
Was then upon earth, and a moderate Tory,
Not *Cooper* himself, of ideas perplext,
So nicely could handle and torture a text,
When bloated with lies thro' his trumpet he sounded
(The damnable sin of resisting a crown'd head.)
Like a penitent sinner, and dreading my fate
In the grey of the morning I knocked at his gate;
(No doubt he was vext that I rous'd him so soon,
For his worship was often in blankets till noon.)
    At length he approach'd in his *vestments of black*--
(Alas my poor heart! it was then on the rack,
Like a man in an ague, or one to be *try'd*;
I shook--and recanted, and snivell'd, and sigh'd:)
His gown of itself was amazingly big,
Besides, he had on his canonical wig
And frown'd at a distance; but when he came near
Look'd pleasant and said--*What, Hugh are you here!*
    Your heart, I am certain, is horribly harden'd,
But if you confess--your sin will be pardon'd:
In spite of my preachments, and all I cou'd say,
Like the prodigal son you wander'd away,

Now tell me, dear penitent, which is the best,
To be with the rebels, pursu'd and distrest,
Devoid of all comfort, all hopes of relief,
Or else to be here, and eat the king's beef?
  More people resemble the snake than the dove,
And more are converted by terror than love:
Like a sheep on the mountains, or rather a swine,
You wander'd away from the ninety and nine:
Awhile at the offers of mercy you spurn'd,
But your error you saw, and at length have return'd!
Our Master will therefore consider your case,
And restore you again to favour and grace,
Great light shall arise from utter confusion,
And rebels shall live to lament their delusion.
"Ah, rebels! (said I) they are *rebels* indeed–
Chastisement, I hope, by the king is decreed:
They have hung up his subjects with bed-cords and halters,
And banish'd his *prophets*, and thrown down his *altars,*
And I--even I--while I ventur'd to stay,
They fought for my life--to take it away!
I therefore propose to come under your wing,
A foe to *rebellion*--a slave to the *king.*"
  Such pitiful whining in scriptural style
Work'd out my salvation, at least for awhile;
The parson pronounc'd me deserving of grace,
And so *they* restor'd me to *profit* and *place.*
  But days such as these were too happy to last:
The sand of felicity settled too fast!
When I swore and protested I honour'd the throne
The least they could do was to let me alone;
Tho' *George* I compar'd to an angel above,
They wanted some solider proofs of my love;
And so they oblig'd me each morning to come
And turn in the ranks at the beat of the drum,
While often too often (I tell it with pain)
They menac'd my head with a hickory cane,
While others my betters as much were oprest--
But shame and confusion shall cover the rest.
  You doubtless will think I am dealing in fable
When I tell you I *guard an officer's stable*–
With usage like this my feelings are stung;
The next thing will be, I must heave out the dung!

Six hours in the day is duty too hard,
And Rivington sneers when'er I mount guard,
And laughs till his sides are ready to split
With his jests, and his satires and sayings of wit:
Because he's excus'd on account of his post
He cannot go by without making his boast,
As if I was all that is servile and mean--
But Fortune perhaps may alter the scene,
And give him his turn to stand in the street,
Burnt brandy supporting his radical heat--
    With his paunch of a hog, and his brains of an oyster,
Whence the mischief came he with his radical moisture,
Or what for the king or the cause has he done
That we must be toiling while he can look on?
    From hence you may guess I do nothing but grieve,
And where we are going I cannot conceive--
The wisest among us a change are expecting;
It is not for nothing these ships are collecting,
It is not for nothing that *Matthews* the may'r
And legions of tories for sailing prepare;
It is not for nothing that *John Coghill Knap*
Is filing his papers and plugging his tap;
See *Skinner* himself, the fighting attorney
Is boiling potatoes to serve a long journey;
But where they are going or meaning to travel
Would puzzle John Faustus himself to unravel,
Perhaps to penobscot to starve in the barrens,
Perhaps to St. John, in the gulph of St. Lawrence;
Perhaps to New Scotland to perish with cold,
Perhaps to Jamaica, like slaves to be sold,
Where scorch'd by the summer all nature repines,
Where Phœbus, great Phœbus, too glaringly shines,
And fierce from the zenith diverging his ray
Distresses the isle with a torrent of day.
    Since matters are thus, with proper submission
Permit me to offer my humble *petition*;
(Tho' the *form* is uncommon, and lawyers may sneer,
With truth I can tell you the scribe is sincere.)

THAT, since it is plain we are going away,
You will suffer *Hugh Gaine* unmolested to stay,

His sand is near run (life itself is a span)
So leave him to manage as well as he can:
Whoe'er are his masters, or monarchs, or regents,
For the future he'll promise to swear them allegiance;
If the Turk with his turban should set up at last here
While he gives him protection he'll own him his master
And yield due obedience (when Britain is gone)
Tho' rul'd by the sceptre of *Presbyter John.*

 My press that has call'd you (as tyranny drove her)
Rogues, rebels and rascals, a thousand times over,
Shall be at your service by day and by night,
To publish whate'er you think proper to write:
Those *types* which have rais'd George the third to a level
With angels--shall prove him as black as the devil,
To him that contriv'd him a shame and disgrace,
Nor blest with one virtue to honour his race!

 Who knows but, in time, I may rise to be great,
And have the good fortune to *manage* a state?
Great noise among people great changes denotes,
And I shall have *money* to purchase their votes--
The time is approaching, I'll venture to say,
When folks of my stamp shall come into play,
When the false hearted tory shall give himself airs,
And rise to take hold of the helm of affairs,
While the honest bold soldier that sought your renown,
Like a dog in the dirt shall be crush'd and held down.

 Of honours and profits allow me a share!
I frequently dream of a president's chair!
If folks would prefer me to Oliver Delancey,
Ah! then it would be--Hugh Gaine, your excellency!

 Blest seasons advance, when *Tories* shall find
That they can be happy, and *Whigs* can be kind,
When Rebels no longer at Traitors shall spurn,
When *Arnold* himself shall in triumph return!

 But my *paper* informs me it's time to conclude;
I fear my address has been rather too rude--
If it has--for my boldness your pardon I pray,
And further, at present, presume not to say,
Except that, (for form's sake) in *haste* I remain
Your humble Petitioner--honest--HUGH GAINE.

Poems (1786), 323-28.

Port Folio   October 24, 1807

As part of its extended review of Freneau's verse, the *Port Folio* cites the first two lines of the seventh stanza of the third segment above:

> And, again, with a happy allusion to one of the emblems of Time:
>> But days such as these were too happy to last;
>> The *sand of felicity settled too fast!*

Port Folio   November 28, 1807

In the final segment of the review, the major part of the poem is reprinted:

> As a proof of that kind of satire, which can
>> "Tickle, while it gently probes the wound"
> we select the following lines from the Life of Hugh Gaine, which we are disposed to mention with much encomium.

Reprint includes the better part of the first and second segments above, and a small part of the third, reflecting 1795 substantive variants, but not 1795 section and stanza divisions.

Freeman's Journal   February 19, 1783

> STANZAS, occasion'd by the departure of the British from
>   CHARLESTON, December 14, 1782.

HIS triumphs of a moment done,
His race of desolation run,
The Briton, yielding to his fears,
To other shores with sorrow steers:

To other shores--and coarser climes
He goes, reflecting on his crimes,
His broken oaths, a murder'd *Hayne*,
And blood of thousands, spilt invain.

To *Cooper's* stream, advancing slow,
Ashley no longer tells his woe,
No longer mourns his limpid flood
Discolour'd deep with human blood.

Lo! where those social streams combine
Again the friends of Freedom join;
And, while they point where once they bled,
Rejoice to find their tyrants fled.

Since Memory paints that dismal day
When British squadrons held the sway,
And circling close on every side,
By sea and land retreat deny'd--

Shall she recall that mournful scene,
And not the virtues of a *Greene*,
Who great in war--in danger try'd,
Has won the day, and crush'd their pride.

Thro' barren wastes and ravag'd lands
He led his bold undaunted bands,
Thro' sickly climes his standard bore
Where never army march'd before:

By fortitude, with patience join'd,
(The virtues of a noble mind)
He spread, where'er our wars were known,
His country's honour and his own.

Like Hercules, his generous plan
Was to redress the wrongs of men;
Like him, accustom'd to subdue,
He freed the world from *monsters* too.

Thro' every want and every ill
We saw him persevering still,
Thro' Autumn's damps and Summer's heat,
'Till his great purpose was complete.

Like the bold eagle, from the skies
That stoops to seize his trembling prize,
He darted on the slaves of kings
At Camden plains and Eutaw Springs.

Ah! had our friends that led the fray
Surviv'd the ruins of that day,
We should not damp our joy with pain,
Nor sympathising now complain.

Strange! that of those who nobly dare
Death always claims so large a share,
That those of feelings most refin'd
Are soonest to the grave consign'd.

But fame is theirs--and future days
On pillar'd brass shall tell their praise;
Shall tell--when cold neglect is dead--
"*These* for their country fought and bled."

Poems (1786), 392-30.

Port Folio October 24, 1807

Three stanzas reprinted, as part of the extended review of Freneau's verse, introduced as follows:

> Speaking of the battle of Eutaw springs, his language is both pathetick and forcible, and the epitaph on those who were slain in the action, is, at once, beautifully simple and comprehensive:

Extract includes the last three stanzas of the poem, reflecting 1795 variants, as well as the following new variant:

> Stanza 1, line 3: We should not mix our joy with pain,

Freeman's Journal   March 12, 1783

(Untitled.)

GROWN sick of war, and war's alarms,
Good *George* has chang'd his note at last--
Conquest and Death have lost their charms;
        He and his nation stand aghast
    To see what horrid lengths they've gone,
    And what a brink they stand upon.

Old *Bute* and *North*! twin sons of hell,
If you advis'd him to retreat
Before our humbled thousands fell
        And lay submissive at his feet,
    Awake once more his latent fire,
    And feed with hope his heart's desire:

The Macedonian wept and sigh'd
Because no other world was found
Where he might glut his rage and pride
        And by its ruin be renown'd;
    The *world* that *Sawny* wish'd to view
    George fairly had and lost it too!

Let jarring powers make war or peace,
Monster!--no peace shall greet thy breast:
Our murder'd friends shall never cease
        To hover round and break thy rest:
    The Furies shall thy bosom tear;
    Remorse, distraction and despair
    And hell with all its fiends be there!

Curs'd be the ship that e'er sets sail
Hence freighted for thy odious shore;
May tempests o'er her strength prevail,
        Destruction round her roar!
May Nature all her *aids* deny,
The sun refuse his light,
The needle from its object fly,
No star appear by night;
      Till the base pilot conscious of his crime,
      Directs the prow to some more grateful clime.

Genius! that first our race design'd,
To other kings impart
The finer feelings of the mind,
The virtues of the heart:
When'er the honours of a throne
Fall to the bloody and the base
Like Britain's monster pull them down,
Like his be their disgrace!

Hibernia, seize each native right!
Neptune, exclude him from the main;
Like *her* that sunk with all her freight,
The Royal George, take all his fleet,
      And never let them rise again:
Confine him to his gloomy isle,
Let Scotland rule her half,
Spare him to curse his fate awhile,
And *Whitehead*,* Thou to write his Epitaph.

Poems (1786), 331-32.

Freeman's Journal   May 7, 1783

    A New York Tory's EPISTLE to one of his Friends in PENNSYLVANIA.--Written previous to his departure for NOVA SCOTIA.

DARK glooms the day that sees me leave this shore
To which fate whispers I must come no more:
From civil broils what dire disasters flow--
Those broils condemn me to a land of woe

---

    *William Whitehead, Poet laureat to his majesty—author of the execrable Birth-day odes.

Where barren pine trees shade the dreary steep,
Frown o'er the soil or murmur to the deep,
Where sullen fogs their heavy wings expand,
And nine months winter chills the dismal land!
Could no kind stars have mark'd a different way,
Stars that presided on my natal day?--
Why is not man endued with power to know
The ends and upshots of events below?
Why did not heaven (some other gift deny'd)
Teach me to take the true-born *Buckskin* side,
Show me the balance of the wavering fates
And fortune smiling on these new born *States*!

      Friend of my heart!--my refuge and relief
Who help'd me on thro' seven long years of grief,
Whose better genius taught you to remain
Who still despis'd the *Rebels* and their cause
And while you paid the taxes, damn'd their laws,
And wisely stood spectator of the fray
Nor trusted *George*, whate'er he chose to say;
Thrice happy thou, who wore a double face
And as the balance turn'd could *each* embrace;
Too happy *Janus*! had I shar'd thy art
To speak a language foreign to my heart
And stoop'd from pomp and dreams of regal state
To court the friendship of the *men* I hate,
These strains of woe had not been penn'd to day,
Nor I to foreign climes been forc'd away:
Ah! *George*--that name provokes my keenest rage,
Did he not swear, and promise, and engage
His loyal sons to nurture and defend,
To be their God, their father and their friend,--
Yet basely quits us on a hostile coast
And leaves us wretched where we need him most:
His is the part to promise and deceive
By him we wander and by him we grieve;
Since the first day that these dissentions grew,
When Gage to Boston brought his blackguard crew,
From place to place we urge our vagrant flight
To follow still this vapour of the night,
From town to town have run our various race,
And acted all that's mean and all that's base--

Yes--from that day until this hour we roam,
Vagrants forever from our native home!
  And yet, perhaps, fate sees the golden hour
When happier hands shall crush rebellious power,
When hostile tribes their plighted faith shall own
And swear subjection to the British throne,
When George the fourth shall their petitions spurn,
And banish'd tories to their fields return.
  From dreams of conquest, worlds and empires won
Britain awaking, mourns her setting sun,
No rays of joy her evening hour illume,
'Tis one sad chaos, one unmingled gloom!
Too soon she sinks unheeded to the grave
No eye to pity and no hand to save:
What are her crimes that she alone must bend;
Where are her hosts to conquer and defend--
Must she alone with these new regions part,
These realms that lay the nearest to her heart,
But soar'd at once to independent power,
Not sunk like Scotland in the trying hour--
See slothful Spaniards golden empires keep;
And rule vast realms beyond the Atlantic deep;
Must *we* alone surrender half *our* reign,
And they their empires and their worlds retain?
Britannia rise--send *Johnstone* to Peru,
Seize thy bold thunders and the war renew,
Conquest or *ruin*--one must be thy doom,
Strike--and secure a triumph or a tomb!
  But we, sad outcasts from our native reign
Driven from these shores, a poor deluded train,
In distant wilds, conducted by despair,
Seek, vainly seek, a hiding place from care!
Even now yon tribes, the foremost of the band,
Croud to the ships and cover all the strand:
Forc'd from their friends their country and their god
I see the unhappy miscreants leave the sod!
Matrons and men walk sorrowing side by side
And virgin grief, and poverty, and pride,
All, all with aching hearts prepare to sail
And late repentence that has no avail!
While yet I stand on this forbidden ground
I hear the death bell of destruction sound,

And threat'ning hosts with vengeance on their brow
Cry—"where are Britain's base adherents now?"
These, hot for vengeance, by resentment led,
Blame on our hearts the failings of the head;
To us no peace, no favours they extend,
Their rage no bounds, their hatred knows no end;
In one firm league I see them all combin'd,
We, like the damn'd, can no forgiveness find--
As soon might Satan from perdition rise,
And the lost angels gain their vanish'd skies
As malice cease in their dark souls to burn,
Or we, once fled, be suffer'd to return.
      Curs'd be the union that was form'd with France,
I see their *lillies* and the *stars* advance!
Did they not turn our triumphs to retreats,
And prove our conquests nothing but defeats?--
My heart misgives me as their chiefs draw near,
I feel the influence of all potent fear,
Henceforth must I, abandon'd and distrest,
Knock at the door of pride, a beggar guest,
And learn from years of misery and pain
Not to oppose fair Virtue's cause again!--
One truth is clear from changes such as these,
Kings cannot always conquer when they please,
Nor are they *rebels* who mere *freedom* claim,
Conquest alone can ratify the name--
But great the task, their efforts to controul
When genuine virtue fires the stubborn soul;
The warlike beast in Lybian desarts plac'd
To reign the master of the sun burnt waste
Not tamely yields to bear a servile chain,
Force may attempt it, and attempt in vain,
Nervous and bold, by native valour led,
His prowess strikes the proud invader dead,
By force nor fraud from freedom's charms beguil'd
He reigns secure the monarch of the wild.

                                              TANTALUS.

Poems (1786), 333-37.

Freeman's Journal   September 10, 1783

NEW-YORK.

THOU mistress of a warlike state,
What crime of thine deserves this fate;
While other towns to freedom rise,
In thee that flame of honour dies.

With wars and horrors overspread,
Seven years and more, we fought and bled,
Seiz'd British hosts and Hessian bands,
And all--to leave thee in their hands.

While Tory tribes forsake our plains,
In you a motley crew remains--
Must vipers through thy streets repair,
Must poison taint thy purer air?

Ah! what a scene afflicts mine eye,
In thee what putrid monsters lie!
What dirt and mud, and mouldering walls,
Burnt domes, dead dogs, and funerals:

Those grassy banks where oft I stood,
And fondly view'd the passing flood,
There owls obscene, that day light shun,
Pollute the waters as they run.

Thus in the east--once Asia's queen,
Palmyra's tottering towers are seen;
While through her streets the serpent feeds,
Thus she puts on her mourning weeds.

Lo! Skinner there collects a crew,
(Their temples brush'd with Stygian dew)
While to receive the ghastly freight,
A thousand sable gallies wait.

Had he been born in days of old,
When men with gods their beasts enroll'd,
Like Nero's horse, he had been made
A consul for some Nero's aid:

O chief, that wrangled at the bar,
Grown old in less successful war,
What crouds of miscreants round thee stand,
What vagrants bow to thy command!

Long, much too long, in York reside,
A race that mortifies our pride,--
A race that all the world defames,
And Nova Scotia only claims.

When Jove from darkness smote the sun,
And nature *earth* from *chaos* won,
One part to polish she forgot,
And Nova Scotia was the spot.

Jove saw her vile neglect, and cry'd,
"What madness did thy fancy guide!
"Why hast thou left so large a space
"With winter brooding o'er its face!

"No trees of stately growth ascend,
"Eternal fogs their wings expand–
"My favourite, *Man*, I place not here,
"But phantoms of a darker sphere:

"If Nature's self forgets her trade,
"What strange confusion will be made--
"Such scenes as *this* had been no crime,
"In Saturn's cold, unsocial clime;

"But such a blemish *here* to see,
"What can it else but anger me?
"Where chilling winds forever freeze,
" "What fool will fix in climes like these?"

Nature, half timorous, dar'd reply,
"When earth I form'd, I don't deny
"Some parts I portion'd out for care,
"And Nova Scotia has her share;

"Mankind are form'd of different souls,
"Some will be suited near the poles,
"Some pleas'd beneath the burning line,
"And some, New Scotland, will be thine:

"Yet in due time, my plastic hand,
"Shall mould it o'er, if you command;
"By you I act--if you stand still,
"The world comes tumbling down the hill."

"Untouch'd, said Jove, remain the place;--
"In days to come, I'll form a race
"Born to commit the basest crime,
"With souls congenial to the clime.

"When traitors to their country die,
"To realms like this their phantoms fly,
"But when the brave by death decay,
"The soul finds out a diff'rent way:

"Then nature cease at my command--
"As matters are, let matters stand,
"While this degenerate work of thine,
"To Thieves and Traitors I resign."

Poems (1786), 341-44.

Freeman's Journal   December 10, 1783

   VERSES occasioned by General WASHINGTON's arrival in this city, on his way to his Seat in Virginia.

THE great unequal conflict past,
The Briton banish'd from our shore,
Peace, heaven descended, comes at last,
And hostile nations rage no more;
    From fields of death the weary swain
    Returns to rural toils again.

In every vale she smiles serene,
Freedom's bright stars more radiant rise,
New charms she adds to every scene,
Her brighter sun illumes our skies;
    Remotest realms, admiring, stand,
    And hail the *Hero* of our land.

He comes!--the Genius of these Lands,
Fame's thousand tongues his worth confess,
Who conquered with his suffering bands,
And grew immortal by distress:
    Thus calms succeed the stormy blast,
    And virtue is repaid at last.

O *Washington!*--thrice glorious name,
What due rewards can man decree--
Empires are far below thy aim,
And sceptres are no charms for thee;
    Virtue alone has thy regard,
    And she must be thy great reward.

Encircled by extorted power
Monarchs must envy thy *retreat*,
Who cast, in some ill fated hour,
Their country's freedom at their feet;
    'Twas thine to act a nobler part--
    For injur'd *Freedom* had thy heart.

For ravag'd realms and conquer'd seas,
Rome gave the great imperial prize,
And, swell'd with pride, for seats like these
Transferr'd her heroes to the skies--
    A brighter scene your deeds display
    You gain those heights a different way.

When faction rear'd her snaky head
And join'd with tyrants to destroy
Where'er you march'd the monster fled,
Timorous her arrows to employ.
    Hosts catch'd from you a bolder flame
    And despots trembled at your name.

Now hurrying from the busy scene--
Where thy Potowmack's waters flow,
May'st thou enjoy thy rural reign,
And every earthly blessing know:
    Thus HE* whom Rome's proud legions sway'd,
    Return'd and sought his native shade.

Not less in wisdom than in war,
Freedom shall still employ your mind,
Slavery shall vanish, wide and far,
'Till not a trace is left behind;
    Reflexion in thy rural shade,
    Shall still be busy for our aid.

So when the bright all-cheering sun,
From our contracted view retires,
Tho' fools may think his race is run,
On other worlds he lights his fires,
    Cold climes beneath his influence grow,
    And frozen rivers learn to flow.

For states redeem'd, our western reign
Restored by these to milder sway,
Thy conscious glory shall remain
When this great globe is swept away,
    And all is lost that pride admires,
    And all the pageant scene expires.

O say, thou great exalted name!
What muse can boast of equal lays,
Thy worth disdains all vulgar fame,
Transcends the noblest poet's praise,
    Art soars unequal to the flight,
    And genius sickens at the height.

---

* Cincinnatus.

Though thou must meet the general doom,
While gratitude in man is found
Honour shall guard thy future tomb,
And laurels deck that hallow'd ground:
    Late times shall see, and own in you,
    The *Patriot* and the *Statesman* too.

Bailey's Pocket Almanack for 1784

Lines, written by *Mr. Freneau,* as one of the handsomest compliments paid to this great man, on his retiring from the theatre of public action.

Stanzas are numbered, to the left of the first line of each.

Stanza 1:   First stanza of the *Freeman's Journal* text, with the following variants:
line 6: Returning, seeks his native plain.

Stanzas 2-7:   Second to seventh stanzas of the *Freeman's Journal* text, with the following variants:
Stanza 3, line 6: And valour is repaid at last.

Stanza 8:   Ere war's dread horrors ceas'd to reign
What leader could your place supply--?
Chiefs crowded to the embattled plain,
Prepar'd to conquer or to die--
    Heroes arose--but none like you,
    Could save our lives and freedom too.

Stanza 9:   In swelling verse let kings be read,
And princes shine in polish'd prose;
Without such aid your triumphs spread
Where'er the convex ocean flows,
    To Indian worlds by seas embrac'd
    And Tartar, tyrant of the waste.

Stanza 10:   Throughout the east you gain applause,
And soon the *Old World*, taught by you,
Shall blush to own her barbarous laws,
Shall learn instruction from the *New*:
  Monarchs shall hear the humble plea,
  Nor urge too far the proud decree.

Stanza 11:   Depising pomp and vain parade,
At home you stay, while France and Spain
The secret, ardent wish convey'd,
And hail'd you to their shores in vain:
  In *Vernon's* groves you shun the throne,
  Admir'd by kings, but seen by none.

Stanza 12:   Your fame, thus spread to distant lands,
May envy's fiercest blasts endure,
Like Egypt's pyramids it stands,
Built on a basis more secure;
  Time's latest age shall own in you
  The patriot and the statesman too.

Stanza 13:   Stanza 8 of the *Freeman's Journal* text, with the following variants:
Line 6: Return'd and sought his sylvan shade.

Stanza 14:   Stanza 9 of the *Freeman's Journal* text, with the following variants:
line 5: Your counsels not bestow'd in vain
line 6: Shall still protect this infant reign.

Stanza 15:   Stanza 10 of the *Freeman's Journal* text.

Stanza 16:   Stanza 12 of the *Freeman's Journal* text.

Stanza 17:   Stanza 11 of the *Freeman's Journal* text.

(Stanza 13 of the *Freeman's Journal* text deleted.)

Poems (1786), 356-59.

American Museum   August, 1787

　　Verses on the arrival of general Washington in Philadelphia, December *1783*, on his way to his seat at Mount Vernon.--By Philip Freneau.

Substantively identical to the 1786 text, except for the following variants:

Stanzas unnumbered.
Stanza 7, line 5: Hosts catch'd from you a nobler flame:
Stanza 13, line 5: Footnote deleted.

Massachusetts Centinel   August 1, 1789

Extract of the poem included in the following tribute to Freneau:

　　(In the preceding paper we had occasion to mention Mr. FRENEAU--who is considered the Pindar of the United States--and perhaps as nearly related to the Poet of Thebes, as his English relation Peter. To those who have seen his pleasantries during the war, the versification of the British king's speeches--Rivington's and H. Gaine's confessions, petitions, wills &c. nothing need be said of his satirical, humourous, and yet chaste abilities--That he can also deal in the sublime of song, his Farm House, Poems written at sea, the American Hero &c. will amply demonstrate:--From the latter we have extracted the following lines as another specimen.)

ADDRESSED TO HIS EXCELLENCY GENERAL WASHINGTON, in 1784.

Extract includes stanzas 7-17 of the 1786 text, to which it is substantively identical, except for the following variants:

Stanzas unnumbered.
Lines 2 and 4 of each stanza indented, all others begin at margin.
Stanza 1, line 4: Fearful her arrows to employ;

Columbian Centinal   December 8, 1802

An excerpt of the poem is included in a letter to the editor signed "Honorius, Boston, Dec. 6, 1802." He quotes the poem as evidence of Freneau's true feelings about Washington, which, as a poor poet, he was forced to betray under the "patronage" of Jefferson. But, in his earlier verse, he still was free to "follow nature, and sang the unbiased feelings of his heart," before he was forced to calumniate the president in the *National Gazette*. "In a Poem written in 1783, occasioned by General *Washington's* arrival in *Philadelphia*, on his way to his residence in *Virginia*, are the following stanzas:"

Extract includes stanzas 4, 5, 6, 7, 8, 12, 14, 16, and 17 of the 1795 text.

Freeman's Journal   December 21, 1783

RIVINGTON's CONFESSIONS.
Addressed to the Whigs of New-York.

LONG life and low spirits were never my choice,
As long as I live I intend to rejoice;
When life is worn out, and no wine's to be had
'Tis time enough then to be serious and sad.

'Tis time enough then to reflect and repent
When is liquor is gone, and our money is spent,
But I cannot endure what is practis'd by some
This anticipating of evils to come:

A debt must be paid, I am sorry to say,
Alike, in their turns, by the grave and the gay,
And due to a despot that none can deceive
Who grants us no respite and signs no reprieve.

Thrice happy is he that from care can retreat,
And its plagues and vexations put under his feet;
Blow the storm as it may he is always in trim,
And the sun's in the zenith forever to him.

Since the world then in earnest is nothing but care,
(And the world will allow I have also my share)
Yet, tos'd as I am in the stormy expanse,
The best way, I find, is to leave it to chance.

Look round, if you please and survey the wide ball
And chance, you will find, has direction of all:
'Twas owing to *chance* that I first saw the light
And chance may destroy me before it is night!

'Twas a chance, a mere chance, that your arms gain'd the day,
'Twas a chance that the Britons so soon went away,
To chance by their leaders the nation is cast
And chance to perdition will send them at last.

Now because I remain when the puppies are gone
You would willingly see me hang'd quarter'd & drawn,
Though I think I have logic sufficient to prove
That the *chance* of my stay--is proof of my love.

For the deeds of destruction some hundreds are ripe,
But the worst of my foes are your lads of the type:
Because they have nothing to put on their shelves
They are striving to make me as poor as themselves.

There's a *Loudon* and *Kollock*, those strong bulls of Bashan,
Are striving to *book* me away from my station,
And *Holt*, all at once, is as wonderful great
As if none but himself was to print for the *State*,

Ye all are convinc'd I'd a right to expect
That a sinner returning you would not reject--
Quite sick of the scarlet and slaves of the throne,
'Tis now at your option to make me your own.

Suppose I had gone with the tories and rabble
To starve, or be drown'd on the shoals of Cape Sable
I had suffer'd, 'tis true--but I'll have you to note
My woes would have helpt you to dinner nor coat.

You say that with grief and dejection of heart
I packt up my awls with a view to depart,
That my shelves were dismantled, my cellars unstor'd,
My boxes afloat and my hampers on board:

And hence you infer (I am sure without reason)
That a right you possess to entangle my weazon--
But who ever argued, where blood was not spilt,
That terror of heart is conviction of guilt?

The charge may be true--for I found it in vain
To lean on a staff that was broken in twain,
And ere I had gone at Port Roseway to fix,
I had chose to sell drams on the margin of Styx.

I confess, that with shame and contrition opprest,
I sign'd an agreement to go with the rest,
But ere they weigh'd anchor to sail their last trip,
I saw they were vermin, and gave them the slip.

Now, why should you call me the worst man alive,
On the word of a convert, I cannot contrive,
Though turn'd a plain honest republican, still
You own me no proselyte, do what I will.

My paper is alter'd--good people, don't fret;
I call it no longer the *Royal Gazette*:
To me a great monarch has lost all his charms,
I have pull'd down his *lion*, and trampled his *arms*.

While fate was propitious, I thought they might stand,
You know I was zealous for George's command,
But since he disgrac'd it, and left us behind,
If I thought him an angel--I've alter'd my mind.

On the very same day that his army went hence
I ceas'd to tell lies for the sake of his pence;
And what was the reason--the true one is best,--
I worship no suns when they decline to the west:

In this I resemble a Turk or a Moor,
The day-star ascending, I prostrate adore;
And, therefore, excuse me for printing some lays,
An ode or a sonnet in Washington's praise.

His prudence alone has preserv'd your dominions,
The bravest and boldest of all the Virginians!
And when he is gone--I pronounce it with pain--
We scarcely shall meet with his equal again.

Old Plato asserted that life is a dream
And man but a shadow (whate'er he may seem)
By which it is plain he intended to say
That man, like a shadow must vanish away:

If this be the fact, in relation to man,
And if each one is striving to get what he can,
I hope, while I live, you will all think it best,
To allow me to bustle along with the rest.

A view of my life, though some parts might be solemn,
Would make, on the whole, a ridiculous volume:
In the life that's hereafter (to speak with submission)
I hope I shall publish a better edition:

Even swine you permit to subsist in the street;--
You pity a dog that lies down to be beat--
Then forget what is past--for the year's at a close--
And men of my age have some need of repose.

Poems (1786), 337-41.

Freeman's Journal   January 7, 1784

RIVINGTON's CONFESSIONS. Part II.
Addressed to the Whigs of New-York.
(Continued from our last.)

BUT as to the tories that yet may remain
They scarcely need give you a moment of pain;
What dare they attempt when their masters are fled;--
When the soul is departed who wars with the dead?

Poor souls! for the love of the king and his nation
They have had their full quota of mortification;
Wherever they fought, or whatever they won,
The dream's at an end--the delusion is done.

The TEMPLE you rais'd was so wonderful large
Not one of them thought you could answer the charge,
It seem'd a mere castle constructed of vapour,
Surrounded with gibbets and founded on *paper*.

On the basis of freedom you built it too strong:
And *Clinton* confess'd, when you held it so long,
That if anything human the fabric could shatter--
The *Royal Gazette* must accomplish the matter*.

An engine like that, in such hands as my own
Had shaken king *Cudjoe*+ himself from the throne,
In another rebellion had ruin'd the Scot,
While the pope and pretender had both gone to pot.

If you stood my attacks, I have nothing to say--
I fought, like the Swiss, for the sake of my pay;
But while I was proving your fabric unsound
Our vessel *miss'd stay*, and we all went aground.

---

*Si Pergama dextra
Defendi possent, etiam hac defensa fuissent.   Virg.
+The Negro King in Jamaica, whom the English declared independent in 1739.--See our Journal, No. 37, for the Treaty.

Thus ended in ruin what madness begun
And thus was our nation disgrac'd and undone,
Renown'd as we were, and the lords of the deep,
If our outset was folly, our exit was sleep.

A dominion like *this*, that some millions had cost!--
The king might have wept when he saw it was lost;--
This Jewel--whose value I cannot describe;
This pearl--that was richer than all his Dutch tribe.

When the war came upon us, you very well knew
My income was small and my riches were few--
If your money was scarce, and your prospects were bad,
Why hinder me printing for people that had?

'Twould have pleas'd you, no doubt, had I gone with a few setts
Of books, to exist in your cold Massachusetts;
Or to wander at *Newark*, like ill fated *Hugh*,
Not a shirt to my back, nor a soal to my shoe.

Now, if we mistook (as we did, it is plain)
Our error was owing to wicked *Hugh Gaine*,
For he gave us such scenes of your starving and strife
As prov'd that his pictures were drawn from the life.

On the waves of the Styx had he rode quarantine,
He could not have look'd more infernally lean
Than the day, when returning dismay'd and distrest,
Like the doves to their windows, he flew to his nest.

The part that he acted, by some men of sense
Was wrongfully held to be malice propense,
When to all the world it was perfectly plain,
One principle rul'd him--a passion for gain,

You pretend I have suffer'd no loss in the cause,
And have, therefore, no right to partake of your laws:
Some people love talking--I find to my cost,
I too am a loser--my character's lost!

Nay, did not your printers repeatedly stoop
To descant and reflect on my *portable soup*?
At me have your porcupines darted the quill,
You have plunder'd my Office*, and publish'd my *will*+.

Resolv'd upon mischief, you held it no crime
To steal my *Reflexions***, and print them in rhyme,
When all the world knew, or at least they might guess,
That the time to reflect is the time to confess,

You never consider'd my children and wife,
That my lot was to toil and to struggle thro' life;
My windows you broke–they are all on a jar,
And my house you have made a mere old *man of war*.

And still you insist I've no right to complain!--
Indeed if I do, I'm afraid it's in vain--
Yet am willing to hope you're too learnedly read
To hang up a printer for being misled.

If this be your aim, I must think of a flight--
In less than a month I must bid you good night,
And hurry away to the *whelp* ridden shore
Where *Clinton* and *Carleton* retreated before.

From signs in the sky, and from tokens on land
I'm inclined to suspect my departure's at hand:
The man in the moon is unusually big,
And *Inglis* they tell me, has got a new wig.

For many days past, as the town can attest,
The tail of the weather-cock hung to the west--
My shop, the last evening, seem'd all in a blaze,
And a hen crow'd at midnight, my waiting man says;

---

* November 1775.
+ See our Journal No. 45.
** See Freeman's Journal, No. 85, and No. 88.

Even then, as I lay with strange whims in my head,
A ghost hove in sight, not a yard from my bed,
It seem'd GENERAL ROBERTSON, *brawly* array'd,
But I grasp'd at the substance, and found him a shade!

He appear'd as of old, when, head of the throng,
And loaded with laurels, he waddled along--
He seem'd at the foot of my bedstead to stand
And cry'd--"Jemmy Rivington, reach me your hand;

"And Jemmy (said he) I am sorry to find
"Some demon advis'd you to loiter behind;
"The country is hostile--you had better get off it,
"Here's nothing but squabbles, all plague, and no profit!

"Since the day that Sir William came here with his throng
"He manag'd things so that they always went wrong,
"And tho', for his knighthood, he kept *Meschianza*,
"I think he was nothing but mere Sancho Panza.

"Other luck we had once in the battle of Boyne!
"But here they have ruin'd Earl *Charles* and *Burgoyne*,
"Here brave col'nel *Monckton* was thrown on his back,
"And here lies poor *Andre!* the best of the pack."

So saying he flitted away in a trice,
Just adding, "he hop'd I would take his advice--"
Which I surely shall do if you push me too hard,--
And so I remain with eternal regard

JAMES RIVINGTON printer, of late, to the king,
But now a republican--under your wing--
Let him stand where he is--and don't push him down hill
And he'll turn a true Blue-Skin, or just what you will.

Poems (1786), 345-49.

Freeman's Journal   March 17, 1784

The DYING INDIAN; or, Last Words of SHALUM.

Debemur morti nos, nostraque.

"On yonder lake I spread the sail no more!
Vigour, and youth, and active days are past--
Relentless demons urge me to that shore,
On whose bleak forests all the dead are cast:
Ye solemn train, prepare the funeral song,
For I must go to shades below,
Companion to the airy throng,
      What solitary streams,
      In dull and dreary dreams,
   All melancholy, must I rove along!

To what strange lands must Shalum take his way!
Groves of the dead departed mortals trace;
No deer along these gloomy forests stray,
No huntsmen there take pleasure in the chace,
But all are empty unsubstantial shades,
That ramble through those visionary glades;
    No spongy fruits from verdant trees depend,
      But sickly orchards there,
      Do fruits as sickly bear,
And apples a consumptive visage shew,
And wither'd hangs the hurtle-berry blue,
Ah me! what mischiefs on the dead attend.

Wandering a stranger to the shores below,
Where shall I brook, or real fountain find!
Lazy and sad deluding waters flow--
Such is the picture in by boding mind!
      Fine tales, indeed, they tell
      Of shades and purling rills,
      Where our dead fathers dwell
      Beyond the western hills,
But when did ghost return his state to shew;
Or who can shew that half the tale is true?

I, too, must be a fleeting ghost—no more—
None, none but shadows to those mansions go;
I leave my woods, I leave the Huron shore.
       For emptier groves below!
       Ye charming solitudes,
       Ye tall ascending woods,
    Ye glassy lakes and prattling streams,
       Whose aspect still was sweet,
       Whether the sun did greet,
Or the pale moon embrac'd you with his beams—
       Adieu to all!

To all, that charm'd me where I stray'd,
The winding stream, the dark sequester'd shade;
       Adieu all triumphs here!
    Adieu the mountain's lofty swell.
       Adieu, thou little verdant hill,
    And seas, and stars, and skies—farewell,
       For some remoter sphere!

Perplext with doubts, and tortur'd with despair,
Why so dejected at this hopeless sleep?
Nature at least these ruins may repair,
When death's long dream is o'er, & she forgets to weep;
Some real world once more may be assign'd,
Some new born mansion for the immortal mind!—
Farewell, sweet lake, farewell surrounding woods,
To other groves through midnight glooms I stray,
Beyond the mountains, and beyond the floods,
       Beyond the Huron bay!
Prepare the hollow tomb, and place me low,
My trusty bow, and arrows by my side,
The cheerful bottle, and the ven'son store;
For long the journey is that I must go,
Without a partner, and without a guide."

He spoke, and bid the attending mourners weep;
Then clos'd his eyes, and sunk to endless sleep.

Poems (1786), 350-52.

American Museum   February, 1788

The dying Indian, or the last words of Shalum.
  By mr. Philip Freneau.

(No Latin subtitle.)

Stanza 1:   Substantively identical to the 1784 text, except for the following variants:
  lines 1, 3, 5, 8, and 11 begin at margin.
  lines 2, 4, 6, and 7 indented three spaces.
  lines 9 and 10 indented seven spaces.
  line 4:   On whose black forests all the dead are cast.

Stanza 2:   Substantively identical to the 1784 text, but layout of lines varies:
  lines 1, 3, 5, 6, 10, and 11 begin at margin.
  lines 2, 4, 7, and 12 indented three spaces.
  lines 8 and 9 indented seven spaces.

Stanza 3:   Substantively identical to the 1784 text, except for the following variants:
  lines 1, 3, 9, and 10 begin at margin.
  lines 2 and 4 indented three spaces.
  lines 5 and 7 indented seven spaces.
  lines 6 and 8 indented ten spaces.
  line 10:   Or who can promise half the tale is true?

Stanza 4:   Substantively identical to the 1784 text, but layout of lines varies:
  lines 1, 3, 7, 10, 12, 13, 15, 16, and 17 begin at margin.
  lines 2, 4, 14 and 18 indented three spaces.
  lines 5, 6, 8, 9, and 11 indented ten spaces.

Stanza 5:   Substantively identical to the 1784 text, except for the following variants:
  line 3: Nature at last these ruins may repair,
  lines 1, 3, 5, 6, 7, 9, 11, 13, and 14 begin at margin.
  lines 2, 4, 8, 12, and 15 indented three spaces.
  line 10 indented seven spaces.

Stanza 6:   (last two lines) Identical to the 1784 text.

Independent Chronicle   December 14, 1801

Reprint of the *American Museum* text, included in a tribute to Freneau's verse, penned in response to a hostile attack, reprinted from the *New England Palladium* of December 11:

> (Who published a volume of poems? Mr. Philip Freneau.
> Where did he get his rhymes? Out of the dictionary:
> Where the spirit and originality? There isn't any.
>
> *Palladium.*)
>
> (The following Poem, by Mr. FRENEAU, had he written nothing more, would entitle him to rank among our first poets. Pope, never in his happiest moments, produced a piece which has a stronger claim to elegance, ease, strength or simplicity. The ideas are truly appropriate to Indian mythology, and expressed in a manner, which takes immediate possession of the heart.)

Text, including stanza form, identical to the *American Museum* text.

Freeman's Journal   May 19, 1784

Lines intended for Mr. Peale's Exhibition, May 10, 1784.

1.

TOWARD the skies
What columns rise
In Roman style, profusely great!
What lamps ascend,
What arches bend,
And swell with more than Roman state!

2.

High o'er the central arch display'd
Old Janus shuts his temple door,
And shackles war in darkest shade;--
Saturnian times in view once more.

3.

Pride of the human race, behold
In Gallia's king the virtues glow,
Whose conduct prov'd, whose goodness told,
That kings can feel for human woe.
Thrice happy France in Louis blest,
Thy genius droops her head no more;
In the calm virtues of the mind
Equal to him no Titus shin'd--
No Trajan--whom mankind adore.

4.

Another scene too soon displays!
Griefs have their share, and claim their part,
They monuments to ruin raise,
And shed keen anguish o'er the heart:
Those heroes that in battle fell
Demand a sympathetic tear,
Who fought, our tyrants to repell--
Memory preserves their laurels here.
       In vernal skies
       Thus tempests rise,
And clouds obscure the brightest sun--
       Few wreathes are gain'd
       With blood unstain'd--
No honours without ruin won.

5.

The arms of France three lillies mark--
In honour's dome with these enroll'd
The plough, the sheaf, the gliding barque
The riches of our state unfold.

6.

Ally'd in Heav'n, a sun and stars
Friendship and peace with France declare--
The *branch* succeeds the spear of Mars,
Commerce repairs the wastes of war:
In ties of *concord* ancient foes engage
Proving the day-spring of a brighter age.

7.

These *States* defended by the brave,
Their military trophies, see!
The virtue that of old did save
Shall still maintain them *great* and *free*:
And shall pervade the western wild,
And savage hearts become more mild.

8.

Of science proud, the source of sway,
Lo! emblematic figures shine;
The arts their kindred forms display,
Manners to soften and refine:
A stately tree to heaven its summit sends
And cluster'd fruit from thirteen boughs depends.

9.

With laurel crown'd
A chief renown'd
(His country sav'd) his faulchion sheaths;
Neglects his spoils
For rural toils
And crowns his plough with laurel wreaths:
While we this Roman chief survey,
What apt resemblance strikes the eye!
Those features to the soul convey
A *Washington* in fame as high,
Whose prudent, perserving mind
Patience with manly courage join'd,
And when disgrace and death were near,
Look'd through the black distressing shade,
Struck hostile Britons with unwonted fear
And blasted their best hopes, and pride in ruin laid!

10.

Victorious virtue! aid me to pursue
The tributary verse to triumphs due--
Behold the peasant leave his lowly shed,
Where tufted forests round him grow;--
Tho' clouds the dark sky overspread,
War's dreadful art his arm essays,
He meets the hostile cannon's blaze,
And pours redoubled vengeance on the foe.

11.

Born to protect and guard our native land,
Victorious virtue! still preserve us free;
Plenty–gay child of peace, thy horn expand,
And, *Concord*, teach us to agree!
May every virtue that adorns the soul
Be here advanc'd to heights unknown before;
Pacific ages in succession roll,
    'Till nature blots the scene,
    Chaos resumes her reign
And heaven with pleasure views its works no more.

Poems (1786), 352-55.

Freeman's Journal   December 8, 1784

HUMANITY *and* INGRATITUDE;
A Common Case.
[Translated from the Mercure de France.]

I.

BY the side of the sea in a cottage obscure,
There liv'd an old fellow nam'd Charlot Boncœur,
Who was free to his neighbor and good to the poor,

Catching the fish was his trade,
And all people said,
That mischief to nothing but fish he design'd,
To all people else he was candid and kind.

II.

One day as he went to the brink of the lake,
Persuading the fishes their dinner to take,
(The last he intended they ever should make)
While his hooks he employ'd, to their sorrow and woe,
A grunting he heard in the waters below,
And casting his eye to the bottom (for here
We'll suppose that the water was perfectly clear)
He saw on the bed of the liquid profound
An unfortunate wight who was drowning, or drown'd.

III.

That the man to the surface once more might ascend,
He took up his pole, with a hook at the end,
And to it he fell,
And manag'd so well,
That soon to the margin the carcase was drawn,
And who should it be but his old neighbour John!

IV.

Now, somehow or other, it popp'd in his head
That in spite of this drowning the man was not dead,
And while he was thinking what means to devise
That his friend might recover and open his eyes,
He saw, with vexation and sorrow, no doubt,
That in lugging him up he had put one eye out.--
However, convinc'd from what he had heard,
That John might be living for aught that appear'd;
To his cottage he took him, and there had him bled,
Rubb'd, roll'd on a barrel, and then put to bed.
So in less than a week (to his praise be it said)
In less than a week the man was as sound
(Excepting the loss of his eye and the wound)
As if in his life he had never been drown'd.

V.

But when John had begun to travel about,
He was sadly chagrin'd that his eye was put out,
And forgetting what service his neighbour had done him,
Went off to a lawyer, and clapt a writ on him,
Talk'd much of the value of what he had lost,
That Charlot must pay all the damage and cost,
And if with such sentence he would not comply,
He swore he would have his identical eye.

VI.

That Charlot was vex'd, we hardly need say,
Yet he urg'd what he could in a moderate way,
"Declar'd to the Judges, by way of defence,
That the action was wrought without malice propense
That his conscience excus'd him for what he had done,
That fortune was only to blame--and that John
Might have thought himself happy (when death was so nigh)
To purchase his life with the loss of an eye–
That the loss of an eye was a serious affair
Was certain–and yet he'd be bold to declare
That the man who can shew but one eye in his head,
Is better by far than a man that is dead."

VII.

In answer to all the defendant's fine pleading,
John said, "He had never yet found in his reading
A people, or nation, or senator sage,
Or a law, or a custom in whatever age,
Permitting (unpunish'd) by force of surprize,
One neighbour to put out his next neighbour's eyes."

VIII.

The lawyers and judges were all at a stand,
Which way to conclude on the matter in hand.
Till a half-witted fellow who chanc'd to be there,
Undertook to decide on this weighty affair,
And cry'd, "Can you doubt in a case that's so plain?
Be guided by me, and you'll ne'er doubt again:

The plea of the plaintiff rests wholly on this:
In fishing him up he takes it amiss,
That Charlot manœvred with so little skill,
So aukwardly fumbled and manag'd so ill
As thus with his bungling to ruin John's look,
And put out an eye with the point of his hook--
Well, now, my lord judges, attend my decree,
Straitway let the plaintiff be thrown in the sea,
And after reposing a while on the bottom,
If he get out alone from where Charlot got him,
Safe, sound, and undamag'd--why, then 'tis my sentence
That Charlot be punish'd and brought to repentence;
But if, after gasping and flouncing about
He drowns in the water, and never gets out,
Why then it is justice, it must be confest,
That Charlot forthwith be discharg'd from arrest,
Absolv'd from all punishment due to the wound,
And paid in the bargain, 'cause John was not drown'd."

IX.

The audience were struck with a world of surprize,
To find that a fool could give counsel so wise.
The judges themselves the sentence espous'd
And freely consented that John should be sous'd.--
    John finding that matters had took a wrong turn,
Nor waiting to see if the court would adjourn,
Sneak'd out of the house, with a hiss of disgrace
In dread, lest the sentence should quickly take place--
Grown pliant at last, his cause he withdrew--
His plea was so bad, and his friends were so few,
It was needless he thought on the cast of a die
To venture his life for the sake of an eye,
And concluded 'twas better to give up the suit,
Than risk the one left, and be drowned to boot.
                                             K.

Poems (1786), 360-63.

Freeman's Journal   December 15, 1978

Sketches of American History.

THE American world, as our histories say,
Secluded from Europe long centuries lay,
But peopled by beings whom white men detest,
The sons of the Tartars that came from the west.

These Indians, 'tis certain, were here long before ye all,
And dwelt in their wigwams from time immemorial;
In a mere state of nature, untutor'd, untaught,
They did as they pleas'd, and they spoke as they thought--

No Priests they had then for the *cure* of their souls,
No lawyers, recorders, nor keepers of rolls;
No learned physician vile *nostrums* conceal'd–
Their druggist was nature--her shop was the field.

In the midst of their forests how happy and blest,
In the skin of a bear or a buffaloe drest!
No care to perplex, and no luxury seen
But the feast, and the song, and the dance on the green.

Some bow'd to the moon, and some worshipp'd the sun,
And the king and the captain were center'd in one;
In a cabbin they met on their councils of state,
Where *age* and *experience* alone might debate:

With quibbles they never essay'd to beguile,
And nature had taught them the orator's stile;
No pomp they affected, nor quaintly refin'd
The nervous idea that glanc'd on the mind.

When hunting or battle invited to arms,
The women they left to take care of their farms--
The toils of summer did winter repay,
While snug in their cabbins they snor'd it away.

If death came among them his dues to demand,
They still had some prospect of comfort at hand,--
The dead man they sent to the regions of bliss,
With his bottle and dog, and his fair maids to kiss.

Thus happy they dwelt in a rural domain
Uninstructed in commerce, unpractic'd in gain,
Till, taught by the loadstone to traverse the seas,
Columbus came over, that bold Genoese.

From records authentic, the date we can shew,
One thousand, four hundred, and ninety and two
Years, borne by the seasons, and vanish'd away,
Since the *Babe* in the manger at *Bethlehem* lay.

What an aera was this, above all that had pass'd,
To yield such a treasure, discover'd at last--
A new world, in value exceeding the old,
Such mountains of silver, such torrents of gold!

Yet the schemes of Columbus, however well plann'd
Were scarcely sufficient to find the main land;
On the *islands* alone with the natives he spoke,
Except when he enter'd the great *Oronoque*:

In this he resembled old Moses, the Jew,
Who, roving about with his wrongheaded crew,
When at length the *reward* was no longer deny'd
From the top of Mount Pisgah he saw *it* and dy'd.

These islands and worlds in the wat'ry expanse,
Like most mighty things, were the offspring of chance,
Since steering for Asia, Columbus, they say,
Was astonish'd to find such a world in his way!

No Wonder, indeed, he was smit with surprize--
This empire of nature was new to their eyes--
Cut short in their course by so splendid a scene,
Such a region of wonders intruding between!

Yet great as he was, and deserving, no doubt,
We have only to thank him for finding the rout;
These climes to the northward, more stormy and cold,
Were reserv'd for the efforts of *Cabot* the bold.

Where the sun in December appears to decline
Far off to the southward, and south of the line,
A merchant* of Florence, more fortunate still,
Explor'd a new track, and discover'd Brazil:

Good Fortune, *Vespucius,* pronounc'd thee her own,
Or else to mankind thou hadst scarcely been known–
By giving thy name, thou art ever renown'd–
Thy *name* to a world that another had found!

Columbia the name was that merit decreed,
But Fortune and Merit have never agreed–
Yet the poets, alone, with commendable care
Are vainly attempting the wrong to repair.

The bounds I prescribe to my verse are too narrow
To tell of the conquests of *Francis Pizarro*;
And *Cortez* 'tis needless to bring into view,
One Mexico conquer'd, the other Peru.

Montezuma with credit in verse might be read
But Dryden has told you the monarch+ is dead!
And the woes of his subjects–what torments they bore,
De Casas, good bishop, has mention'd before:

Let others be fond of their stanzas of grief–
I hate to discant on the fall of the leaf–
Two scenes are so gloomy, I view them with pain,
The annals of Death, and the triumphs of Spain.

---

* Americus Vespucius.
+Indian Emperor, a Tragedy.

Poor *Ata-bualpa* I cannot forget--
He gave them his utmost--yet died in their debt,
His wealth was a crime that they could not forgive,
And when they possess'd it--forbade him to live.

Foredoom'd to misfortunes (that come not alone)
He was the twelth Inca that sat on the throne,
Who fleecing his brother* of half his domains,
At the palace of *Cusco* confin'd him in chains.

But what am I talking--or where do I roam?--
'Tis time that our story was brought nearer home--
From Florida's cape did *Cabot* explore
To the fast frozen region of cold *Labradore*.

In the year fourteen hundred and ninety and eight
He came, as the annals of England relate,
But finding no gold in the lengthy domain,
And coasting the country, he left it again.

Next Davis,--then *Hudson* adventur'd, they say,
One found out a *streight*, and the other a *bay*,
Whose desolate region, or turbulent wave
One present bestow'd *him*--and that was a grave.

In the reign of a virgin (whom some call a whore)
Drake, Hawkins, and Raleigh in squadrons came o'er--
While Barlow and Grenville succeeded to these
Who all brought their colonies over the seas.

These, left in a wilderness teeming with woes,
The native, suspicious, concluded them foes,
And murder'd them all without notice or warning,
Ralph Lane, with his vagabonds, scarcely returning.

---

* Huascar, who was legal heir to the throne.

In the reign of king James (and the first of the name)
George Summers with *Hacluit* to Chesapeake came,
Where far in the forests, not doom'd to renown,
On the river Powhatan* they built the first town.+

Twelve years after this, some scores of Dissenters
To the northernmost district came, seeking adventures;
Outdone by the bishops, those great faggot fighters,
They left them to heel, with their cassocks and nitres.

Thus banish'd forever and leaving the sod,
The first land they saw was the pitch of Cape Cod,
Where famish'd with hunger and quaking with cold
They plann'd their new Plymouth--so call'd from the old.

They were, without doubt a delightful collection;--
Some came to be rid of a Stuart's direction,
Some sail'd with a view to dominion and riches,
Some to pray without books--and a few to hang witches.

Some came, on the Indians to shed a new light,
Convinc'd long before that their own must be right,
And that all who had died in the centuries past
On the Devil's lee-shore were eternally cast.
K.

Poems (1786), 398-402.

---

* James River, Virginia.
+ James Town.

Freeman's Journal   December 22, 1784

The Progress of Balloons.

Perdomita tellus, tumida cesserunt freta,
Inferna nostros regna sensere impetus;
Immune cœlum est, dignus Alcidœ labor,
In alta mundi spatia sublimes feremur.
                          Senec. Herc. Furens.

ASSIST me, ye muses (whose harps are in tune)
To tell of the flight of the gallant balloon!
As high as my subject permit me to soar
To heights unattempted, unthought of before.

Ye grave learned Doctors, whose trade is to sigh,
Who labour to chalk out a road to the sky,
Improve on your plans--or I'll venture to say,
A chymist, of Paris, will show us the way.

The earth, on its surface, has all been survey'd,
The sea has been travell'd--and deep in the shade
The kingdom of Pluto has heard us at work
When we dig for his metals, wherever they lurk.

But who would have thought that invention could rise
To find out a method to soar to the skies,
And pierce the bright regions, which ages assign'd
To spirits unbodied, and flights of the mind.

Let the gods of Olympus their revels prepare--
By the aid of some pounds of inflammable air
We'll visit them soon--and forsake this dull ball
With coat, shoes and stockings, fat carcase and all.

How France is distinguish'd in Louis's reign!
What cannot her genius and courage attain?
Throughout the wide world have her *arms* found the way,
And *art* to the stars is extending her sway.

At sea let the British their neighbours defy--
The French shall have frigates to traverse the sky,
In this navigation more fortunate prove,
And cruise at their ease in the climates above.

If the English should venture to sea with their fleet,
A host of balloons in a trice they shall meet.
The French from the zenith their wings shall display,
And souse on these sea dogs and bear them away.

Ye sages who travel on mighty designs,
To measure meridians and parallel lines--
The task being tedious--take heed if you please--
Construct a balloon--and you'll do it with ease.

And ye who the heav'n's broad concave survey,
And, aided by glasses, its secrets betray,
Who gaze, the night through, at the wonderful scene
Yet still are complaining of vapours between,

Ah, seize the conveyance, and fearlessly rise
To peep at the *lanthorns* that light up the skies
And floating above, on our ocean of air,
Inform us, by letter, what people are *there*.

In Saturn, advise us if snow ever melts,--
And what are the uses of Jupiter's belts;
And (Mars being willing) pray send us word, greeting,
If his people are fonder of fighting than eating.

That Venus has horns we've no reason to doubt
(I forget what they call him who first found it out)
And you'll find, I'm afraid, if you venture too near,
That the spirits of cuckolds inhabit her sphere.

Our folks of good morals it wofully grieves
That Mercury's people are villains and thieves,
You'll see how it is,--but I'll venture to show
For a dozen among them, twelve dozens below.

From long observation one proof may be had
That the men in the moon are incurably mad;
However, compare us, and if they exceed
They must be surprisingly crazy indeed.

But now to have done with our planets and moons--
Come, grant me a patent for making balloons--
For I find that the time is approaching--the day
When horses shall fail, and the horsemen decay.

Post riders, at present (call'd centaurs of old)
Who brave all the seasons, hot weather and cold,
In future shall leave their dull *poneys* behind
And travel, like ghosts, on the wings of the wind.

The Stagemen, whose gallopers scarce have the power
Through the dirt to convey you ten miles in an hour,
When advanc'd to balloons shall so furiously drive
You'll hardly know whether you're dead or alive.

The man who at Boston sets out with the sun,
If the wind should be fair, may be with us at one,
At Gunpowder Ferry drink whiskey at three
And at six be in Edenton, ready for tea.

(The machine shall be order'd, we hardly need say,
To travel in darkness as well as by day)
At Charleston by ten he for sleep shall prepare,
And by twelve the next day be the Devil knows where.

When the ladies grow sick of the city in June
What a jaunt they shall have in the flying balloon!
Whole mornings shall see them at toilets preparing,
And forty miles high be their afternoon's airing.

Yet more with its fitness for commerce I'm struck--
What loads of tobacco shall fly from Kentuck,
What packs of best beaver--bar-iron and pig,
What budgets of leather from Conococheague!

If Britain should ever disturb us again,
(As they threaten to do in the next George's reign)
No doubt they will play us a set of new tunes,
And pepper us well from their fighting balloons.

To market the farmers shall shortly repair
With their hogs and potatoes, wholesale, thro' the air,
Skim over the water as light as a feather,
Themselves, and their turkies conversing together.

Such wonders as these from balloons shall arise--
And the giants of old that assaulted the skies
With their Ossa on Pelion, shall freely confess
That all they attempted was nothing to this.

            K.

Poems (1786), 300-03.

National Gazette   January 2, 1793

ON BALLOONS.

Stanza 1: One sixteen line stanza, which begins with the third stanza and concludes with the sixth stanza of the 1784 text, and contains the following variants:
line 1: Indented.
line 6: To contrive a machine that would soar to the skies
line 10: By the help of a breeze of inflammable air
line 12: With a streamer display'd--and no fear of a fall.
line 13: How France* is distinguish'd in *liberty's reign*!

Stanza 2: Seventh stanza of the 1784 text, with the following variants:
line 1: Indented.

Note added to stanza 1, line 13:
* *Balloons are wholly of French invention.*

> line 3: In this navigation invincible prove,
> line 4: And cudgel your *Fredericks* and *Brunswicks* above.

Stanza 3: Eighth stanza of the 1784 text.
> line 1: Indented.

Stanza 4: (last stanza of this text): One twelve line stanza which begins with stanza nine and ends with stanza eleven of the 1784 text, including the following variants:
> line 1: Indented.
> line 2: To measure equators and tropical lines--
> line 3: Instead of a vessel, to traverse the seas
> line 4: Engage a balloon and you'll do it with ease.

Freeman's Journal   December 29, 1784

Sketches from American History.
[Continued from Number 191.]

Sit Mihi fas audita loqui----------------

Virgil.

THESE exiles were cast in a whimsical mould,
And were aw'd by their priests, like the Hebrews of old;
Disclaim'd all pretenses to jesting and laughter,
And sigh'd their lives through, to be happy hereafter.

On a crown immaterial their hearts were intent,
They look'd toward *Zion*, wherever they went,
Did all things in hopes of a future reward,
And worry'd mankind--for the sake of the Lord.

With rigour excessive they strengthen'd their reign,
Their laws were conceiv'd in the ill-natur'd strain
With mystical meanings the saint was perplext,
And the flesh, and the devil were slain by a text.

The body was scourg'd for the good of the soul,
All folly discourag'd by peevish controul,
A knot on the head was the sign of no grace,
And the Pope and his *comrade* were pictur'd in lace.

A stove in their churches, or pews lin'd with green
Were horrid to think of, much less to be seen--
Their bodies were warm'd with the linings of *love*,
And the *fire* was sufficient that flash'd from above.

'Twas a crime to assert that the moon was opaque,
To say the earth mov'd, was to merit the stake;
And he that could tell an eclipse was to be,
In the college of *Satan* had took his degree.

On Sundays their faces were dark as a cloud--
The road to the meeting was only allow'd,
And those they caught rambling, on bus'ness, or pleasure,
Were sent to the stocks, to repent at their leisure.

This day was the mournfullest day in the week--
Except on religion, none ventur'd to speak--
This day was the day to examine their lives,
To clear off old scores, and to preach to their wives.

In the school of *oppression* tho' woefully taught,
'Twas only to be the *oppressors* they sought;
All, all but themselves were be-devil'd and blind,
And their narrow-soul'd creed was to serve all mankind.

This beautiful system of nature below
They neither consider'd, nor wanted to know,
And call'd it a dog-house wherein they were pent,
Unworthy themselves, and their mighty descent.

They never perceiv'd that in nature's wide plan
There must be that whimsical creature, call'd *Man*,
Far short of the rank he affects to attain,
Yet a link in its place, in creations vast chain.

Whatever is foreign to us and our kind
Can never be lasting, tho' seemingly join'd–
The hive swarm'd at length, and a tribe that was teaz'd
Set out for *Rhode Island*, to think as they pleas'd.

Some hundreds to Britain ran murmuring home–
While others went off in the forests to roam,
When they found they had miss'd what they look'd for at first,
The downfall of sin, and the reign of the just.

Hence, dry controversial reflections were thrown,
And the old dons were vext in the way they had shown;
So those that are held in the work-house all night
Throw dirt the next day at the doors, out of spite.

Ah, pity the wretches that liv'd in those *days*,
(Ye modern admirers of novels and plays)
When nothing was suffer'd but musty, dull rules,
And nonsense from *Mather*, and stuff from old schools!

No story, like Rachel's, could tempt them to sigh,
Susanna and *Judith* employ'd the bright eye–
No fine spun adventures tormented the breast,
Like our modern Clarissa, Tom Jones, and the rest.

Those tyrants had chosen the books for your shelves,
(And, trust me, no other than suited themselves,
For always by *this* may a bigot be known,
He speaks well of nothing but what is his own.)

From *indwelling evil* these souls to release
The Quakers arriv'd with their kingdom of peace–
But some were transported and some bore the lash,
And *four* they hang'd fairly for preaching up trash.

The lands of New England (of which we now treat)
Were famous, ere that, for producing of wheat;
But the soil (or tradition says strangely amiss)
Has been pester'd with *pumpkins* from that day to this.

Thus, feuds and vexations distracted their reign,
(And perhaps a few vestiges still may remain)
But time has presented an offspring as bold,
Less free to believe, and more wise than the old.

Their phantoms, their wizzards, their witches, are fled--
Matthew Paris's* story with horror is read--
His daughters, and all the enchantments they bore,--
And the demon, that pinch'd them, is heard of no more.

Their taste for the fine arts is strangely increas'd,
And Latin's no longer a mark of the *Beast*:
Mathematics, at present, a farmer may know,
Without being hang'd for connexions below.

Proud, rough, *independent*, undaunted and free,
And patient of hardships, their task is the sea,
Their country too barren their *wish* to attain,
They make up the loss by exploring the main.

Wherever bright Phœbus awakens the gales,
I see the bold *Yankees* expanding their sails,
Throughout the wide ocean pursuing their schemes,
And chasing the whales on its uttermost streams.

No climate, for them, is too cold or too warm,
They reef the broad canvas, and fight with the storm;
In war with the foremost their standards display,
Or glut the loud cannon with death, for the fray.

No valour in fable their valour exceeds,
Their spirits are fitted for desperate deeds;
No rivals have they in *our* annals of fame,
Or if they are rivall'd, 'tis *York* has the claim.

---

* See Neal's History of New England.

Inspir'd at the sound, while the *name* she repeats,
Bold Fancy conveys me to Hudson's retreats--
Ah, sweet recollections of juvenile dreams
In the groves, and the forests that skirted his streams!

How often, with rapture, those streams were survey'd
When, sick of the city, I flew to the shade--
How often the bard, and the peasant shall mourn
Ere those groves shall revive, and those shades shall return!

Not a hill, but some fortress disfigures it round!
And ramparts are rais'd where the cottage was found;
The plains and the vallies with ruin are spread,
With graves in abundance, and bones of the dead.--

The first that attempted to enter this *streight*
(In *anno* one thousand, six hundred, and eight)
Was *Hudson* (the same that was mention'd before,
Who was lost in the gulph that he went to explore.)

For a sum that they paid him (we know not how much)
This captain transferr'd all his right to the Dutch;
For the *time* has been here, to the world be it known,
When all a man sail'd by, or saw, was his own.

The Dutch on their purchase sat quietly down,
And fix'd on an *island* to lay out a town;
They modell'd their streets from the horns of a ram,
And the name that best pleas'd them was, *New Amsterdam*.

They purchas'd large tracts from the Indians, for beads,
And sadly tormented some runaway Swedes,
Who, none knows for what, from their country had flown
To live here in peace, undisturb'd and alone.

New Belgia, the Dutch call'd their province, be sure,
But names never yet made possession secure,
For *Charly* (the second that honour'd the name)
Sent over a squadron, asserting his claim.

(Had his *sword* and his *title* been equally slender,
In vain they had summon'd Mynheer to surrender)
The soil they demanded, or threaten'd their worst,
Insisting that *Cabot had look'd at it first.*

The want of a squadron to fall on their rear
Made the argument perfectly plain to Mynheer--
Force ended the contest--the right was a sham,
And the Dutch were sent packing to hot *Surinam.*

'Twas hard to be thus of their labours depriv'd,
But the age of republics had not yet arriv'd--
Fate saw--tho' no wizzard could tell them as much--
That the crown, in due time, was to fare like the Dutch.

FINIS.

Poems (1786), 403-07.

Port Folio October 24, 1807 (Part of extended review)

Two stanzas from this section of the poem are excerpted and introduced as follows:

> In many passages he evinces a capacity for the pathetick; but in general passes rapidly to other sensations. The following lines are not unlike some written by Cowper on seeing a fafourite grove of trees cut down.

Excerpt includes stanzas 27 and 28 of this section, with the following variants (not in the 1786 or 1795 texts):

Stanza 1, line 2: Wild fancy conveys me to Hudson's retreats--

Bailey's Pocket Almanack for 1785

Stanzas on the Emmigration to America, and peopling the Western Country.

To western woods, and lonely plains,
Palemon from the crowd departs,
Where nature's wildest genius reigns,
To tame the soil, and plant the arts--
    What wonders there shall freedom show,
    What mighty *States* successive grow!
From Europe's proud, despotic shores
Hither the stranger takes his way,
And in our new found world explores
A happier soil, a milder sway,
    Where no proud despot holds him down,
    No slaves insult him with a crown.
What charming scenes attract the eye,
On wild Ohio's savage stream!
Here nature reigns, whose works outvie
The boldest pattern art can frame;
    Here ages past have roll'd away,
    And forests bloom'd--but to decay.
From these fair plains, these rural seats,
So long conceal'd, so lately known,
The unsocial Indian far retreats,
To make some other clime his own,
    Where other streams, less pleasing, flow,
    And darker forests round him grow.
Great Sire of floods*! whose varied wave
Through climes and countries takes its way
To whom creating nature gave
Ten thousand streams to swell thy sway!
    No longer shall *they* useless prove,
    Nor idly through the forests rove;
Nor longer shall thy princely flood,
From distant lakes be swell'd in vain,

---

* *Mississippi.*

Nor longer through a darksome wood
Advance, unnotic'd to the main,
> Far other ends the fates decree--
> And commerce plans new freights for thee.

While virtue warms the generous breast,
Here heaven-born freedom shall reside,
Nor shall the voice of war molest,
Nor Europe's all aspiring pride--
> Here reason shall new lands devise,
> And order from confusion rise.

Forsaking kings and regal state,
(A debt that reason deems amiss)
The traveller owns, convinc'd tho' late,
No realm so free, so blest as this--
> The *east* is half to slaves consign'd,
> And half to slavery more refin'd.

O come the time, and haste the day,
When man shall man no longer crush,
When reason shall enforce her sway,
Nor these fair regions raise our blush,
> Where still the African complains,
> And mourns his yet unbroken chains.

Far brighter scenes, a future age,
The muse predicts, these states shall hail,
Whose genius shall the world engage
> And happier systems bring to view,
> Than all the eastern sages knew.

                                        K.

Pennsylvania Packet   May 24, 1785

Substantively identical to the *Almanac* text, but stanzas laid our differently:

lines 1 and 3 begin at margin.
lines 2 and 4 indented three spaces.
lines 5 and 6 indented 5 spaces.

Poems (1786), 378-80.

Pennsylvania Packet   June 23, 1786

Stanzas laid out as in the 1785 *Pennsylvania Packet* text. Substantively identical to the *Almanac* text, except for the following variants:

Stanza 4, line 2: In parentheses.
Stanza 10, line 6: *Than ever eastern sages knew.*

American Museum   February, 1787

In each stanza, lines 1, 3, 5, and 6 begin at margin; lines 2 and 4 indented.
Demonstrates the 1786 *Pennsylvania Packet* variants from the *Almanac* text, and the following additional variants:

Stanza 5, line 1: Great sire of floods!* whose rapid wave
        line 2: Thro' various countries take its way,
        line 3: To which creating Nature gave
        line 4: Unnumber'd streams to swell thy sway:
        line 6: Nor idly through the forest rove.
Stanza 8, line 2: With all their pomp and fancied bliss,
Stanza 9, line 4: Nor those fair regions raise our blush,
Stanza 10, line 6: Than ever eastern sages knew.

Bailey's Pocket Almanack for 1785

The
SEASONS MORALIZED.

THEY who to warmer regions run,
May bless the favour of the sun,
But seek in vain what charms us here,
Life's picture varying with the year.

Spring and her wanton train advance
Like *Youth* to lead the festive dance,
All, all her scenes are mirth and play,
And blushing blossoms own her sway.

The *Summer* next (those blossoms blown)
Brings on the fruits that spring had sown,
Thus men advance, impell'd by time,
And nature triumphs in her prime.

Then *Autumn* crowns the beauteous year,
The groves a sicklier aspect wear,
And mournful she (*the lot of all*)
Matures her fruits to make them fall.

Clad in the vestments of a tomb,
Old age is only winter's bloom--
Winter, alas! shall spring restore,
But youth returns to man no more.

Poems (1786), 380-81.

Freeman's Journal   January 19, 1785

THE LITERARY PLUNDERERS.

THE head, whose toiling concave teems
With millions of unfinish'd schemes,
Plans that in shapeless embrio ly,
Or projects form'd, the lord knows why,
Had better far those whims resign,
And aid this humble theme of mine;
Contrive some means to crush the power
Of *Mice,* that every art devour,
Check, with success, their hostile rage,
And slay these Vandals of the age.
     Fame says that Wales did first contrive
To seize the unwary mice alive,

And they who scorn'd all locks and keys,
Were caught by means of toasted cheese--
Vain scheme! for still these fiends annoy,
And dare my favourite books destroy--
No cares of mine their rage defeat,
The Welchman's trap is incomplete!--
See Homer there, the bard renown'd,
His Iliad one perpetual wound--
Each chief by their infernal teeth
Once more was doom'd to suffer death;
Even Helen's charms they dar'd to gnaw,
Great Ajax' carcase fill'd their maw,
And half the gods that crowd his strain
In mangled morsels scarce remain.
    But, wretch, who taught thee to engage
A poet of a later age?
Alas! thy cruel weapons tore
The only genius I adore--
Is *Shakespeare* thus disgrac'd by you
Who look'd the world of nature through,
Who soaring high, where others fail'd,
Invention's brightest heav'n assail'd
And saw beyond the dark disguise
What lay too deep for vulgar eyes.
    Is this the end of human wit,
Must mice untouch'd such spoils commit!
Must all these fine ideas die
That warm'd the heart, or fill'd the eye--
Must reptiles thus our shelves molest,
Insects that nature made in jest,
Who, when their learned feast is o'er,
Shrink from the light--to rise no more.
    Yes--fates like these, our toils attend,
And Goths have serv'd no other end.
    Vex't tho' I am, 'tis vain to frown,
I sigh--and lay my cudgel down:
'Tis worse than mad to arm for fight
When not a mouse appears in sight--
Yet, here they stood in dark array,
Their tragic footsteps I survey!
Here--for no cat the plunderers chac'd--
They laid the lands of learning waste,

Made war with wit, such havock there
As scarce three ages can repair!--
Like British hosts, where'er they go
They leave their vestiges of woe,
Towns half destroy'd, polluted shades,
Fields robb'd of fence, and ruin'd maids.

    Why, Susan, couldst not thou defend
These shelves that did with learning bend?
One *mew* of thine had put to flight
These children of congenial night.
Where wast thou when these cruel teeth
Spread through my leaves untimely death?--
See! how my *Montesquieu* is torn--
See! *Rabelais*, the mices scorn.
See, how they tore the *Mantuan swain*,
Who wrote in so divine a strain--
Milton, whose fancy soar'd so high,
No more delights my tearful eye,
And *Swift*, so late a fund of wit,
No longer prompts the laughing fit.

    Ah, Susan, such neglect was hard--
I fear you kept a careless guard,
Or gadded o'er the neighbouring plain,
To seek some favourite bright-ey'd swain--
Had but those eyes fail'd in their art,
To tell their language to your heart,
I should not thus have lost repose,
Nor sigh'd in vain to crush my foes.

    My Mezzotinos--ah behold--
The beauties fam'd in days of old!
She, who for Tarquin's lawless love,
In her own breast the dagger drove
These fiends of night have made their prey,
And gnaw'd her charming face away.

    And here in ragged robes is seen,
Bright Cleopatra, Egypt's queen;
With cruel fangs those eyes they tore
That warm'd a gazing world of yore,
With hostile tooth they gnaw'd that breast,
Which robb'd a Roman prince of rest,
He who for crowns and conquest strove
Till *honour* was disgrac'd by *love*.

   And here in vile condition lies,
What once had charm'd a hermit's eyes--
This picture, art can ne'er restore,
This *Venus*, that shall bloom no more;
Art form'd her such as angels are,
Beyond all mortal beauty fair,--
But time can every charm displace,
And *Mice* have spoil'd the finest face!
   But must that soft, bewitching eye
With meaner shreds neglected ly,
Must all those lovely colours fade,
By nicest art so lavish laid
On her fair face--to sooth my pain,
I sigh, and look, and sigh again.
   Yes--miscreant, though thy venom tore
The painting, art can ne'er restore,
Still in the dreams of fancy blest,
I steal her image to my breast,
By fancy's aid that form repair,
And, miser like, retain it there.
   Good captain Mouse, what mov'd thine ire,
To mangle what I most admire?--
Could not this chief have led his band
Where yonder brainless authors stand--
To those that deal in forms and modes,
To laureat Whitehead's new year odes,
To verses wrote on puppies dead,
To elegies that ne'er were read,
To *Whaycum's* tale, that brings repose,
To Wesley's hymns, or Whitefield's prose,--
Why didst thou not attack the train
Who teize us with their frothy strain,
The tribe who female honour blast,
In sniveling rhimes, at random cast,
Or those who fly to domes of state,
At folly's door submissive wait,
And servile still, where wealth appears
Their works inscribe to financiers?
   To arms, to arms! ye chosen few
Who science love, and arts pursue;
Or, if your arms should nought avail
(Since mice may over men prevail)
Put on some wise, inventive cap,
And find us a completer Trap.
           K.

Poems (1786), 393-97.

Freeman's Journal   February 16, 1785

ELEGAIC VERSES *on the* DEATH *of a favourite* DOG.

IF all the world mourn for the loss of a friend,
And even in stanza their virtues commend,
Why, *Jolly,* shouldst thou by the green turf be prest,
And not have a stanza along with the rest.

The miser, that ne'er gave a farthing away,
Xantippe, that scolded throughout the long day,
The drunken young Quixote that died in his prime,
In their graves never fail to be flatter'd with rhyme.

There is an old adage that poets have read,
That *nothing but good should be spoke of the dead,*
Hence even your critics of *truth,* we defy,
When we write of the dead—they allow us to lie.

But I, my dear dog, will a poem compose,
That shall break half the hearts of the belles and the beaus;
To the view of each reader your virtues shall shine
In verses, that *Hannah* shall fancy divine.

The Stoics of old were forbid to complain
At losses and crosses, vexation and pain—
When the day I recal that depriv'd me of you,
I find, my dear Jolly, I'm not of *their* crew.

How oft in the year shall I visit your grave
Amid the long forest that darkens the wave;
How often lament, when the day's at a close,
That this kitchen of death is your place of repose.

Ah here! (I will say) was the path where he run;—
My dog with his smellers, and I with my gun—
And here, in this spot, where the willow trees grow,
He brought out a rabbit that lurk'd in the snow!

If absent a while on the ocean I stray'd,
I still had in view to revisit this shade--
But alas! you consider'd the prospect as vain,
Or how could you die till I saw you again.

A country there is, 'tis invain to deny,
Where monkies and puppies are sent when they die,
But you----and old *Minos* shall grant you his pass--
Must rank with the dogs of the gentleman class.

The boatman of Styx shall a passage prepare,
And the Dog at the portal shall welcome you there,
With the Cynics of hell you shall walk a *grave* pace,
For *dogs* among *doctors* are no such disgrace.

On the bark of this *maple,* that shadows your bones,
I am proud to engrave these poetical groans,
If a *tombstone* of *wood* serves a soldier--'tis clear,
This tree may preserve all your fame for a year.

For the squirrel you tree'd, and the duck from the lake,
These stanzas are all the return I can make;
But these, unaffected, my friendship will shew--
And the world shall allow that I give you your due.

Poems (1786), 366-68.

Port Folio   October 24, 1807   (Part of extended review)

Stanzas 6 and 7 extracted and introduced as follows:

> The lines to his dog are an affectionate recollection of that faithful animal, and all who read them will remember the days of their boyhood.

Excerpt includes 1795 variants, as well as new variants:

How oft in the year shall I visit your grave,
Amid the lone forest that shadows the wave!
How often lament, when the day's at its close,
That a mile from my cot is your place of repose!

Ah here (I will say) in this path he has run;
And there stands a tree where a squirrel he won;
And here, in this spot where the willow trees grow,
Here dragg'd out a rabbit that lurk'd in the snow.

Freeman's Journal   February 23, 1785

PEWTER PLATTER ALLEY: *A Poem.*

FROM Christ Church graves, across the way,
A dismal, horrid place is found,
Where rushing winds exert their sway,
And Greenland winter chills the ground:
  No blossoms there are seen to bloom,
  No sun pervades the dreary gloom!
The people of that stormy place
In penance for some ancient crime
Are held in a too narrow space,
Like those beyond the bounds of time.
  Who darken'd still, perceive no day,
  While seasons waste, and moons decay.
Cold as the shade that wraps them round,
This icy region prompts our fear;
And he who treads this frozen ground
Shall curse the chance that brought him here;--
  The slippery mass predicts his fate,
  A broken arm, a wounded pate.
When August sheds his sultry beam
May Celia never find this place,
Nor see upon the muddy stream,
And mourn the wrinkles on her face!
  And may I ne'er discover there
  The grey that mingles with my hair.
The watchman sad, whose drowsy call
Proclaims the hour forever fled,
Avoids this path to Pluto's hall;
For who wou'd wish to wake the dead?--

   Still let them sleep—it is no crime—
   They pay no tax to know the time.
No coaches, hence, in glittering pride,
Convey their freight to take the air,
No gods nor heroes here reside,
Nor powder'd beau, nor lady fair—
   All, all to warmer regions flee,
   And leave these glooms to *Towne* and me!

Poems (1786), 363-64.

Freemans Journal   March 9, 1785

(Untitled text introduced as follows:)

   On Saturday morning last departed this life, in the 43d year of his age, General JOSEPH REED, esq. formerly president of this state; and on Sunday his remains were interred in the Presbyterian burying ground in Arch-Street. His funeral was attended by his excellency the President and the supreme executive council, the honorable the Speaker, and the general assembly, the militia officers, and a greater number of citizens than were ever seen here on any similar occasion.

   Swift to the dust descends each honour'd name,
That rais'd their country to these heights of fame,
Sages that plann'd, and chiefs that led the way
To freedom's temple—all too soon decay;
Alike submit to one unalter'd doom,
Their glories closing in perpetual gloom,
Like the dim splendours of the evening, fade,
While night advances to complete the shade!
   Reed! 'tis for thee we shed the unpurchas'd tear,
Bend o'er thy tomb and plant our laurels here,
Thy own brave deeds the noblest pile transcend,
And virtue, patriot virtue, mourns her friend,
Gone to those realms where worth may claim regard,
And gone where virtue meets her best reward.

No single art engag'd his manly mind,
In every scene his active genius shin'd,
Nature in him, in honour to our age,
At once compos'd the soldier and the sage;--
Firm to his purpose, vigilant, and bold,
Detesting traitors, and despising gold,
He scorn'd all bribes from Britain's hostile throne--
For all his country's wrongs were *thrice* his own.
   Reed, rest in peace, for time's impartial page,
Shall blast the wrongs of this ungrateful age:
Long in these climes thy name shall flourish fair,
The statesman's pattern, and the poet's care;
Long on these plains thy memory shall remain,
And still new tributes from new ages gain,
Fair to the eye that injur'd honour rise--
Nor traitors triumph while the patriot dies.

Poems (1786), 372-73.

Freeman's Journal   March 23, 1785

The Five Ages.

THE reign of old Saturn is highly renown'd,
For many fine things that no longer are found,
Trees always in blossom, men free from all pains,
And shepherds as mild as the sheep on their plains.

In the midland Equator, dispensing his sway,
The Sun, they pretended, pursu'd his bright way,
Not rambled, unsteady, to regions remote,
To talk, once a year, with the *crab* and the *goat*.

From a motion like this, have the sages explain'd,
How summer for ever her empire maintain'd;
While the turf of the field, by the plough was unbroke,
And a house for the shepherd, the shade of the oak.

Yet some say there never was seen on this stage,
What poets affirm of that innocent *age*,
When the brutal creation from bondage was free,
And men were exactly what mankind should be.

But why should they labour to prove *it* a dream--
The poets of old were in love with the theme,
And leaving to others, mere truth to repeat,
In the regions of fancy, they found it complete.

Three ages have been on this globe, they pretend;
And the fourth, some have thought, is to be without end:
The first was of Gold--But a fifth, *we* will say,
Has already begun, and is now on its way.

Since the days of Arcadia, if ever there shin'd,
A ray of the first, on the heads of mankind,
Let the critics dispute--but with us it is clear,
That the œra of PAPER was realiz'd *here*.

Four ages, however, at least, have been told,
The first is compar'd to the purest of *Gold*--
But, as bad luck would have it, its circles were few,
And the next was of *Silver*--if Ovid says true.

But this, like the former, did rapidly pass--
While that which came after was nothing but *Brass*--
An age of mere tinkers--and when it was lost,
Old *Iron* succeeded-we know to our cost.

And hence you may fairly infer, if you please,
That we're nothing but blacksmiths, of various degrees,
Since each has a weapon, of one sort or other,
To stir up the coals, and to shake at this brother.

Should the Author of nature reverse his decree,
And bring back the age we're so anxious to see,
Agreement, alas!--you would look for, in vain,
The *stuff* might be chang'd, but the *staff* would remain.

The lawyer would still find a client to fleece,
The doctor, a patient to pack off in peace,
The parson, some hundreds of hearers prepar'd
To measure his grace, by the length of his beard.

Old Momus would still have some cattle to lead,
Who would hug his opinions, and swallow his creed--
So, it's best, I believe, that things are as they are.
If iron's the meanest--we've nothing to fear.

Poems (1786), 373-74.

Freeman's Journal   March 30, 1785

[To the Great--the Warlike--the United--the Independent Americans!

WE tories, who lately were frighten'd away,
When you march'd into York, all in battle array,
Dear Whigs, in our exile have something to say.

From the clime of New Scotland we wish you to know
We still are in being--mere spectres of woe,
Our dignity high, but our spirits are low.

Great people we are, and are call'd the king's friends--
But on friendships, like these, what advantage attends?
We may starve and be damn'd when we've answer'd his ends.

The Indians themselves, whom no treaties can bind,
We have reason to think are perversely inclin'd--
And where we have friends is not easy to find.

From the day we arriv'd on this desolate shore
We still have been wishing to see you once more,
And your freedom enjoy, now the danger is o'er.

Although we be-rebel'd you up hill and down,
It was all for your good--and to honour a crown
Whose splendors have spoil'd better eyes than our own.

That villains we are, is no more than our due,
And so may remain for a century through,
Unless we return, and be doctor'd by you.

Although with the dregs of the world we are class'd,
We hope your resentment will soften at last,
Now your toils are repaid, and our triumphs are past,

When a matter is done, 'tis a folly to fret--
But your market-day mornings we cannot forget,
With your coaches to lend, and your horses to let.

Your dinners of beef, and your breakfast of toast!
But we have no longer such blessings to boast,
No cattle to steal, and no turkies to roast.

Such enjoyments as these, we must tell you with pain,
'Tis odds we shall only be wishing in vain
Unless we return, and be brothers again.

We burnt up your mills and your meetings, 'tis true,
And many bold fellows we crippled and slew--
(Ay! we were the boys that had something to do!)

Old Huddy we hung on the Neversink shore--
But, sirs, had we hung up a thousand men more,
They had all been aveng'd in the torments we bore

When Asgill to Jersey you foolishly fetch'd,
When each of us fear'd that his neck would be stretch'd,
When you were be-rebel'd, and we were be-wretch'd.

  In the book of destruction it seems to be written,
That tories must still be dependent on Britain--
The worst of dependence that ever was hit on.

Now their work is concluded--that pitiful jobb--
They send over convicts to strengthen our mob--
And so we do nothing but snivel and sob.

The worst of all countries has fell to our share,
Where winter and famine provoke our despair,
And fogs are forever obscuring the air.

Although there be nothing but sea-dogs to feed on
Our friend Jemmy Rivington made it an Eden--
But, alas! he had nothing but lies to proceed on.

Deceiv'd we were all by his damnable schemes--
When he colour'd it over with gardens and streams,
And grottoes and groves, and the rest of his dreams.

Our heads were so turn'd by that conjuror's spell,
We swallow'd the lies he was tutor'd to tell--
But his "happy retreats" were the visions of hell.

We feel so enrag'd we could rip up his weazon
When we think of the soil he describ'd with its trees on,
And the plenty that reign'd, and the charms of each season.

Like a parson that tells of the joys of the blest
To a man to be hang'd--he himself thought it best
To remain where he was, in his haven of rest.

Since he help'd us away by the means of his types,
His precepts should only have lighted our pipes,
His example was rather to honour your stripes.

Now if we return, as we're bone of your bone,
We'll renounce all allegiance to George and his throne
And be the best subjects that ever were known.

In a ship, you have seen (where the duty is hard)
The cook and his scullion may claim some regard,
But it takes a good fellow to brace the main yard.

Howe'er you despise us because you are free,
The world's at as loss for such fellows as we,
Who can pillage on land, and can plunder at sea.

So long for our rations they keep us in waiting--
The Lords and the Commons, perhaps, are debating
If tories can live without drinking and eating

So we think it is better to see you, by far--
And have hinted our meaning to governor Parr--
The worst that can happen is--feather and tar.]

Poems (1786), 375-78.

Freeman's Journal   April 13, 1785

VERSES, made at *Sea*, in a *Heavy Gale*.

HAPPY the man who, safe on shore,
Now trims, at home, his evening fire;
Unmov'd he hears the tempests roar,
That on the tufted groves expire:
    Alas! on us they doubly fall,
    Our feeble barque must bear them all.

Now to their haunts, the birds retreat,
The squirrel seeks his hollow tree,
Wolves in their shaded caverns meet,
All, all are blest but wretched we—
    Foredoom'd a stranger to repose,
    No rest the unsettled ocean knows,

While o'er the dark abyss we roam,
Perhaps, whate'er the pilots say,
We saw the Sun descend in gloom,
No more to see his rising ray,
    But hury'd low, by far too deep,
    On coral beds, unpitied, sleep!

But what a strange, uncoasted strand,
Is that, where death permits no day--
No charts have we to mark that land,
No compass to direct that way--
    What pilot shall explore that realm,
    What new Columbus take the helm!

While death and darkness both surround,
And tempests rage with lawless power,
Of friendship's voice, I hear no sound,
No comfort in this dreadful hour--
    What friendship can in tempests be,
    What comfort on this angry sea?

The barque, accustom'd to obey,
No more the trembling pilots guide,
Alone she gropes her trackless way,
While mountains burst on either side--
    Thus, skill and science both must fall,
    And ruin is the lot of all.

Poems (1786), 365-66.

American Museum   August, 1787

    Verses written at Sea, in a heavy gale.
                By Philip Freneau.

Stanza 3, line 2:   Perhaps (whate'er the pilots say)

Pennsylvania Packet   January 12, 1788

In each stanza, lines 1 and 3 begin at margin; lines 2 and 4 indented three spaces; lines 5 and 6 indented seven spaces.

Stanza 2, line 5:   For, doom'd a stranger to repose,
Stanza 3, line 3:   We saw the sun's descending gloom,
Stanza 5, line 6:   What comforts on this angry sea?
Stanza 6, line 4:   While mountains burst on every side;

Freeman's Journal   August 20, 1788

1785 text introduced as follows;

> In that violent hurricane at Jamaica, on the night of the 30th of July, 1784, in which, no more than eight, out of 150 vessels, in the ports of Kingston and Port-Royal, were saved, capt. Freneau was at sea, and arrived at Kingston next morning, a mere wreck. On that occasion, the following beautiful lines, extracted from the first volume of his writings, were penned.

City Gazette   June 9, 1792

Text includes all of the *Pennsylvania Packet* variants, including the stanza form, as well as the following additional variants:

Stanza 1, line 3:   Unmov'd, he hears the tempest roar,
Stanza 5, line 3:   Of friendship's voice I heard no sound.

Freeman's Journal   May 18, 1785

Epitaph intended for the Tombstone of Patrick Bay, an Irish Soldier and Inn-holder, killed by an ignorant Physician.

NOT Death or Fate,--but Doctor Rowe
Advanced to give the deadly blow
That smote me to the shades below.

Had death alone approach'd too nigh,
Had Fate or Nature bid me die
I must have borne it patiently.

But to be robb'd of life and ease
By such infernal quacks as these,
And pay, besides, their *modest* fees,

And leave a world of joys behind!--
Doctor, if I may speak my mind,
It was not fair, it was not kind.

Now folks that travel by this way
Pointing toward my tomb, shall say,
"There lie the bones of *Patrick Bay*,

"Who ne'er a cheerful glass deny'd,--
"All force of arms and grog defy'd--
"Yet by a vile Jack Pudding died!"

Pennsylvania Packet   May 30, 1785

Printed as one 18 line stanza.

Line 17:   "All force of cares and grog defy'd--

Columbian Herald   July 6, 1785

Freeman's Journal text, with the following variants:

Stanza 1, line 1:   NOT death nor fate--but Doctor Rowe
Stanza 6, line 2:   "All force of cares and grog defy'd--

Poems (1786), 35.

Freeman's Journal   May 18, 1785 [1]

The Deserted Farm-House.

THIS antique dome the unmouldering tooth of Time
Now level with the dust has almost laid;
Yet ere 'tis gone, I fix my humble rhyme
On these low ruins, that his years have made.

Behold the unsocial hearth! where once the fires
Blaz'd high, and check'd the wint'ry travellers woes,
See the weak roof, that abler props requires,
Admits the chilling winds, and swift descending snows.

Here, to forget the labours of the day,
No more the swains at evening hours repair,
But wandering flocks assume the well known way,
To shun the rigours of the midnight air.

In yonder chamber, half to ruin gone,
Once stood the ancient housewife's curtain'd bed--
Timely the prudent matron has withdrawn,
And each domestic comfort with her fled.

The trees, the flowers, that her own hands had rear'd,
The plants, the vines that were so verdant seen,
The trees, the flowers, the vines have disappeared,
And every plant has vanish'd from the green.

So sits in tears on wide Campania's plain,
The ancient mistress of a world enslav'd
That triumph'd o'er the land, subdu'd the main,
And Time himself in her wild transports brav'd.

---

[1] This poem is a revision of "Upon a very ancient Dutch House on Long-Island," first published in Freneau's *American Village* volume, 1772, pp. 26-27.

So sits in tears on Palestina's shore
The Hebrew town, of splendor once divine,--
Her kings, her lords, her triumphs are no more,
Slain are her priests, and ruin'd every shrine.

Once in the bounds of this sequester'd room
Perhaps some swain nocturnal courtship made,
Perhaps some Sherlock mus'd amid the gloom,
Since love and death for ever seek the shade.

Perhaps some miser, doom'd to discontent,
Here counted o'er the heaps acquir'd with pain;
He to the dust--his gold on traffick sent,
Shall ne'er disgrace these mouldering walls again.

Nor shall the glow-worm fopling, sunshine bred,
Seek, at the evening hour, this wonted dome--
Time has reduc'd the fabrick to a shed,
Scarce fit to be the wandering beggar's home.

And none but I, its piteous fate lament--
None, none but I o'er its cold ashes mourn
Sent by the muse, (the time perhaps misspent)
To shed her latest tears upon its silent urn.

            K.

Poems (1786), 30-31.

Independent Gazetteer   November 5, 1787

Poem reprinted from an English paper, and introduced as follows:

> (The following is copied from the *London Morning Herald*, of July 12.)
>
> THE DESERTED FARM-HOUSE.
> *Written in* America, *by* Mr. FRENEAU, *whose poetical productions* tended considerably to keep alive the spirit of INDEPENDENCE, *during the late civil war.*

In each stanza, lines 2 and 4 are indented.
Stanza 1, line 3: Yet ere 'tis gone, I trace my humble rhyme
         line 4: From the low ruins that his years have made.

Stanza 2, line 2: Blaz'd high, while yonder wandering current froze;

Stanza 3, line 2: No more the swains of evening hours repair,
         line 4: To shun the rigours of the *inclement* air.

Stanza 8, line 1: Once in the bounds of this half ruin'd room
         line 3: Perhaps some Sherlock mus'd amidst the gloom,

Stanza 11, line 2: None, none but I o'er its sad ashes mourn.

Freeman's Journal   November 14, 1787

(Introductory note claims that the text is reprinted from the *Independent Gazetteer*, and includes the text of the *Morning Herald* introduction, but this version includes some new variants, and lacks some of those in the *Gazetteer* text. Variants from the 1785 text:

Stanza 1, line 2: Now level with the dust is almost laid;
         line 3: Yet ere 'tis gone, I trace my humble rhyme
         line 4: From these low ruins that his years have made.

Stanza 2, line 2: Blaz'd high, while yonder wandering current froze;

Stanza 3, line 4: To shun the rigours of the *inclement* air.

Stanza 8, line 3: Perhaps some Sherlock mus'd amidst the gloom,

Stanza 10, line 2: Seek at the close of eve this wonted dome;

Stanza 11, line 4: To write dull stanzas on a dome forlorn.

In each stanza, lines 2 and 4 are indented.

Freeman's Journal   May 25, 1785

The *Monument* of *Phaon*.

> Phaon, the admirer of Sappho, both of the isle of Lesbos, privately forsook this first object of his affections, and set out to visit foreign countries. Sappho, after having long mourned his absence (which is the subject of one of Ovid's finest epistles) is here supposed to fall accidentally into the company of Ismenius, a traveller, who informs her, that he saw the tomb of a certain Phaon in Sicily, erected to his memory by a lady of the island, and gives her the inscription, hinting to her that, in all probability it belonged to the same person she bemoans. She thereupon, in a fit of rage and despair, throws herself from the famous Leucadian rock, and perishes in the gulph below.

Sappho.

NO more I sing by yonder shaded stream,
Where once intranc'd I fondly pass'd the day,
Supremely blest, when Phaon was my theme,
But wretched now, when Phaon is away!

Of all the youths that grac'd our Lesbian isle
He, only he, my heart propitious found,
So soft his language, and so sweet his smile,
Heaven was my own when Phaon clasp'd me round!

But soon, too soon, the faithless lover fled
To wander on some distant barbarous shore--
Who knows if Phaon is alive or dead,
Or wretched Sappho shall behold him more.

Ismenius.

As late in fair Sicilia's groves I stray'd,
Charm'd with the beauties of the vernal scene
I sate me down amid the yew tree's shade,
Flowers blooming round, with herbage fresh and green.

Not distant far a monument arose
Among the trees and form'd of Parian stone,
And, as if there some stranger did repose,
It stood neglected, and it stood alone.

Along its sides dependent ivy crept,
The cypress bough, Plutonian green, was near,
A sculptur'd Venus on the summit wept,
A pensive Cupid dropt the parting tear.

Strains deep engrav'd on every side I read,
How Phaon died upon that foreign shore--
Sappho, I think your Phaon must be dead,
Then hear the strains that do his fate deplore:

Thou swain that lov'st the morning air,
To those embowering trees repair,
Forsake thy sleep at early dawn,
And of this landscape to grow fonder,
Still, O still, persist to wander
Up and down the flowery lawn;
And as you there enraptur'd rove
From hill to hill, from grove to grove,
Pensive now and quite alone,
Cast thine eye upon this stone,
Read its melancholy moan;
And if you can refuse a tear
To the youth that slumbers here,
Whom the Lesbians held so dear,
Nature calls thee not her own.
    Echo, hasten to my aid!
Tell the woods and tell the waves,
Tell the far off mountain caves
(Wrapt in solitary shade);
Tell them in high tragic numbers,
That beneath this marble tomb,
Shrouded in unceasing gloom
Phaon, youthful Phaon, slumbers,
By Sicilian swains deplor'd–
That a narrow urn restrains
Him who charm'd our pleasing plains,
Him, whom every nymph ador'd.

  Tell the woods and tell the waves,
Tell the mossy mountain caves,
Tell them, if none will hear beside,
How our lovely Phaon died.
  In that season when the sun
Bids his glowing charioteer
Phœbus, native of the sphere,
High the burning zenith run;
Then our much lamented swain,
O'er the sunny, scorched plain
Hunting with a chosen train,
Slew the monsters of the waste
From those gloomy caverns chas'd
Round stupendous *Etna* plac'd.--
Conquer'd by the solar beam
At last he came to yonder stream;
Panting, thirsting there he lay
On this fatal summer's day,
While his locks of raven jett,
Were on his temples dripping wet;
The gentle stream ran purling by
O'er the pebbles, pleasantly,
Tempting him to drink and die.
He drank indeed--but never thought
Death was in the gelid draught!--
Soon it chill'd his boiling veins,
Soon this glory of the plains
Left the nymphs and left the swains,
And has fled with all his charms
Where the Stygian monarch reigns,
Where no sun the climate warms!--
Dread Pluto then, as once before,
Pass'd *Avernus'* waters o'er;
Left the dark and dismal shore,
And strait enamour'd, as he gloomy stood,
Seiz'd Phaon by the waters of the wood.
  Now o'er the silent plain
We for our much lov'd Phaon call again,
And Phaon! Phaon! ring the woods amain--
From beneath this myrtle tree,
Musidora, wretched maid,
How shall Phaon answer thee,

Deep in vaulted caverns laid!--
Thrice the myrtle tree hath bloom'd
Since our Phaon was intomb'd,
I, who had his heart, below,
I have rais'd this turret high,
A monument of love and woe
That Phaon's name may never die--
With deepest grief, O muse divine,
Around his tomb thy laurels twine
And shed thy sorrow, for to morrow
Thou, perhaps, shalt cease to glow--
My hopes are crost, my lover lost,
And I must weeping o'er the mountains go!

Sappho.

Ah faithless Phaon, thus from me to rove,
And bless my rival in a foreign grove!
Could Sicily more charming forests show
Than those that in my native Lesbos grow--
Did fairer fruits adorn the bending tree
Than those that Lesbos did present to thee,
Or didst thou find through all the changing fair
One beauty that with Sappho could compare!
So soft, so sweet, so charming and so kind,
A face so fair, such beauties of the mind--
Not Musidora can be rank'd with me
Who sings so well the funeral song for thee!--
I'll go--and from the high Leucadian steep
Take my last farewell in the lover's leap,
I charge thee, Phaon, by this deed of woe
To meet me in the Elysian shades below,
No rival beauty shall pretend a share,
Sappho alone shall walk with Phaon there.
    She spoke, and downward from the mountains height
Plung'd in the plashy wave to everlasting night.

Poems (1786), 18-22.

Columbian Herald January 12, 1786

The POETASTER.

OF all the fools that haunt your coast
The scribbling tribe I pity most;
Their's is a standing scene of woes,
And their's no prospect of repose.

A garret high (say upper room)
Or lonely cell is still their doom--
Hopes rais'd to heaven must be their lot,
Yet bear the curse--to be forgot.

Boldly they tell of things above,
And trace their tribe from father Jove,
Yet stand abash'd, with all their fire
When brought to face some country squire.

The wight that keeps a tippling inn,
The red-nos'd boy that deals out gin,
If aided by some paltry skill
May both be statesmen, if they will.

The man that mends the beggar's shoes,
The quack that heals your negro's bruise,
The wretch that turns a cutler's stone--
Have something they can call their own.

The head that plods in trade's domains
Gets something to reward its pains--
But *wit*, that does the world beguile,
With pain attracts an empty smile.

Yet each presumes his verse shall rise
And gain a place beyond the skies,
When every age that passes by
Beholds that verse unpitied die.

  Poor Sappho's fate shall Milton know;
His scenes of grief, and tales of woe
Time scarce shall save from ruin's sway,
When *Goths*, once more, shall have their day.

  Be chearful, then, my scribbling friends,
One common fate on both attends,
The bards that please the monarch's ear,
And them, who rhyme on bread and beer.

  To all that write, and all that read,
Death shall with hasty step succeed;—
Even *Shakespeare's* scenes of mirth and tears
Shall sink beneath this flood of years.

  Ned Spenser's doom, shall *Pope*, be thine!
The music of each moving line
Shall bribe an age or two to stay,
Admire thy strain, and flit away.

  The people of old *Chaucer's* times
Were once in raptures with his rhymes;
But time that over verse prevails
To other ears tells other tales.

  Mere structures form'd of common earth
Not these from Jove derive their birth,
But like successive baubles pass
To mingle with the wasting mass.

  Great Robert,* of mercantile skill,
(Without whose aid *our world* stands still,
And by whose financiering play
Our rights are fixt, his flatterers say.)

---

  *"America had produced nothing yet like a poet." *Mr. Morris's late speech in the Pennsylvania Assembly.*

Great Robert has *in house* declar'd
These states as yet have borne no bard,
And all the sing-song of our clime
Is only nonsense--tagg'd with rhyme.

With such a bold, conceited air
When such assume the critic's chair,
Low in the dust is genius laid,
The Muses with the man in trade.

Then scribbler, come--let you and I
Retreat in time to garret high--
These are the flights the muses mean,
And here *Parnassus* shuts the scene.

K.

Miscellaneous Works (1788), 38-41.

Columbian Herald   January 19, 1786

LITERARY IMPORTATION.

HOWEVER we wrangled with Britain awhile,
We think of her now in a different stile,
And many fine things we receive from her isle;
    Among all the rest,
    Some demon possess'd
Our dealers in morals and sellers of sense,
To have a good *bishop* imported from thence.

The words of Sam. Chandler* we thought to be vain,
When he argued so often, and prov'd it so plain,
That Satan must flourish till bishops should reign;

---

*Dr. Samuel Bradbury Chandler, of New-Jersey, a once strennuous advocate for American Episcopacy.

> Though he went to the wall,
> With his project and all,
> A second bold *Sammy**, in bishop's array,
> Has got something more than his *pains* for his *pay*.
>
> It seems we had courage to humble the throne,
> Have genius for science inferior to none,
> But rarely encourage a plant of our own;
> If a college be plann'd,
> 'Tis all at a stand
> Till to Scotland we send, at a pretty expence,
> To bring us a pedant to teach us some sense.
>
> Can we never be found to have learning or grace,
> Unless it be sent from that damnable place,
> Where poverty reigns, with her pitiful face,
> And wizzards and witches,
> And men without breeches
> Have ever been hostile to science and wit,
> And are led by their priests, who will conquer them yet.
>
> 'Tis a folly to fret at the picture I draw;
> But I say what was said by a *Doctor Magraw*,+
> "If they give us our learning, they'll give us their law;"
> How that will agree,
> With such people as we,
> I leave to the learn'd to reflect on a while,
> And say what they think in a handsomer stile.
>   K.

Miscellaneous Works (1788), 145-46.

---

*Dr. Seabury, the Connecticut Bishop.
+A cynical Doctor of Physic, formerly of New-York; a man, in his day, of considerable note in the political world.

Columbian Herald   February 2, 1786

LINES *written at the* Pallisades, *near Port-Royal, in the Island of Jamaica--September,* 1784.

HERE, by the margin of the murmuring main,
While her proud remnants I explore in vain,
Though abject now, *Port Royal* claims a sigh,
Nor shall the muse the unenvied gift deny.

    Of all the towns that grac'd Jamaica's isle,
This was her glory, and the proudest pile;
Where toils on toils bade wealth's gay structures rise,
And commerce swell'd that glory to the skies:
St. Jago seated on a distant plain,
Ne'er saw the tall ship entering from the main;
Unnotic'd streams her *Cobre's* margin lave
Where yon' tall plaintains cool her glowing wave,
And burning sands, or rock-surrounded hill
Confess its founder's fears--or want of skill.

    While o'er these wastes with pensive step I go,
Past scenes of death return with all their woe;--
Here opening gulphs confess'd the Almighty hand,*
Here, the dark ocean roll'd across the land;
Here, domes on domes a moment tore away--
Here, crowds on crowds in mingled ruin lay,
Whom fate scarce gave to end their noon-day feast,
Or time to call the sexton or the priest.

    Where yon proud barque, with all her ponderous load,
Commits her anchor to its dark abode;
Eight fathoms down, where unseen waters flow
To quench the sulphur of the caves below;
There, midnight sounds torment the sailor's ear,
And drums and fifes play drowsy concerts there;
Dull songs of woe prevent the hours of sleep,
While fancy hears the fiddlers of the deep.

---

* June 7, 1692.

What now is left of all thy boasted pride;
Lost are thy splendours that were spread so wide;
A spit of sand is thine, by fate's decree,
And mouldering mounds that scarce oppose the sea;
No sprightly lads, or gay, bewitching maids
Walk on these wastes, or wander in these shades;
To other shores past time beheld them go,
And some are fiddling in the groves below:--
A negro tribe but ill their place supply,
With bending back, short hair, and downcast eye;--
A feeble rampart guards the wretched town
Where banish'd *Tories* come to seek renown,--
Where worn-out slaves their drams of gin retail,
And hungry Scotsmen watch the distant sail.
    To these dull scenes with eager haste I came
To find some reliques in this sink of fame--
Not worth the search, what domes are left to fall,
Guns, fires, and earthquakes shall destroy them all.
Where shall I go, what *Lethe'* shall I find,
To drink these dark ideas from my mind!--
A tatter'd roof o'er every hut appears,
And mouldering brick-work prompts the stranger's fears:
A church without a priest I grieve to see,
Grass round its door, and rust upon its key;
One only inn, with weary search I found,
Where parson *Lovegrog* deal'd the porter round,
And gay *Quadroons* their *killing* glances stole,
Watch'd at the bar, or drain'd the passing bowl.
                                                   K.

Miscellaneous Works (1788), 176-79.

Columbian Herald   February 16, 1786

The PRISONER.

TO fields of green and tufted pines,
Where nature forms her bold designs,
Where little souls for pleasure stray,
I find content an easier way.

Once, like the rest in folly's train,
A gaol I deem'd the worst of pain;
But reason says, and say we can
'Tis wisdom's walk, the school for man.

Your men of sense take half an age
To moralize from Plato's page--
But truth, that guides my pen, can tell
A sheriff's writ will do as well.

Of debts and duns no more afraid,
I now enjoy a happier shade--
And more secure retreats from pain
Than fancy paints or poets feign.

When friends forsake and riches fail,
The last resource is still a gaol--
Here busy fools from toil repair,
And find an end of all their care.

While others pay for learning sense,
We here are taught at no expence--
With doubts and fears the world is curs's,
But we are blest--who know the worst.

When at my window, dark and high,
I stand to see the crowd go by;
My fate with theirs I scorn to share,
For all betray the marks of care.

>   Of all the woes they feel or fear,
> How few have gain'd admittance here
> No scolding wives disturb our rest--
> No storms at sea our sleep molest.
>
>   If sickness comes, so blest are we
> That doctors scarce expect a fee--
> What station can with ours compare,
> Who, with our keys, thus lock out care!--
>   K.

American Museum   January, 1787 (1)[1]

THE PRISONER.
by Philip Freneau.

Stanza 2, line 2: A jail I deem'd the greatest pain:
Stanza 8, line 4: No storms at sea our peace molest.

American Museum   January, 1787 (2)[1]

The prisoner.--By Philip Freneau.

Same variants as *American Museum* (1), plus an additional variant:

Stanza 8, line 2: How few can find admittance here!

Miscellaneous Works (1788), 72-73.

---

[1] Volume I of Carey's *American Museum* (January-July, 1787) appears to have been bound on at least two different occasions, the later volume differing slightly from the earlier both in content and pagination. The first (*American Museum* 1) I found on a microprint of the Library of Congress original, and the second (*American Museum* 2) I found on a microfilm of the A.A.S. original. In both texts, the preface to the subscribers is dated June 30, 1787.

Columbian Herald   February 20, 1786

The NEWSMONGER.

Moritur ignotus sibi.----
                Seneca.

AN insect lives among mankind
For what wise ends by fate design'd
I never yet could clearly find.

In pain for all and thank'd by none,
And most perplext when most alone,
No *state* regards him or the throne.

The flowers that deck the summer field,
The vernal bloom that frost conceal'd,
To him no spark of pleasure yield.

He life supports on self esteem;
He plans, contrives, and deals in scheme,
And spoils good paper, many a ream.

Distrest for those he never saw,
Of kings and princes not in awe,
He scorns their mandates, and the law.

Now Europe's feuds disturb his brains,
Now Asia's news his head contains--
But still his labour for his pains.

The river *Scheldt* he opens wide,
And *Joseph's* ships in triumph ride,--
The Dutchmen are not on his side.

He hopes the French will study soon
To build new dock-yards at *Toulon*,
"The old ones sir are out of tune."

Our western posts (that Britons keep
In spite of treaties) break his sleep;--
He plans their conquest at one sweep.

Relief he finds for others woes;
The wants of all the world he knows--
His boots are only out at toes.

He grumbles at the price of flour,
Then mourns and mutters many an hour,
That *Congress* has so little power.

Although he keeps no ships to lose,
The *Algerines* he must abuse,
And longs to hear some better news.

He doubts, and frets, and seems afraid
That folk will lose by *Canton* trade--
Unless the public lend their aid.

He hopes that by the month of June
Lunardi, in his new balloon,
Will take a journey to the moon.

He prophesies the time will come,
When few will drink West-India rum--
For this will save a mighty sum.

The Tories on New Scotland's coast,
He deems may all their freedom boast
In half a century at most.

Then shakes his head, and shifts the scene;
Talks much about the Empress queen,
And wonders what the Germans mean.--

Thus all the business of mankind,
And every folly we might find,
Are huddled in his crazy mind:

'Till, doom'd to think of *new affairs,*
At last with death he walks down stairs,
And leaves--the wide world to his heirs.

K.

American Museum   February, 1787 (1)[1]

THE NEWSMONGER.
By Philip Freneau.

Substantively identical to the *Columbian Herald* text, except for the following variants:

First line of each stanza not indented.
Stanza 2, line 3:   Nor state regards him, nor the throne.
Stanza 6, line 3:   But still his labour's for his pains.
Stanza 9, line 1:   Our western posts (which Britons keep
Stanza 15, line 3: And this will save a mighty sum.

At the end of the poetry section appears the following note:

> After the poetical piece, "the Newsmonger," in page 179, had been put to press, the writer republished it, with some alterations and additions. The added and altered stanzas are as follows.

Included are the texts of six stanzas which were added or altered in the following *Freeman's Journal* version of the poem.

Freeman's Journal   February 21, 1787

The NEWSMONGER.

The following are the variants from the *Columbian Herald* text:

Introductory quotation: "*Nimium notus omnibus*
                         "*Moritur ignotus sibi.*"   Seneca.

First line of each stanza not indented.

---

[1] For an explanation of the two texts of Carey's *American Museum*, Volume I, see footnote to the *American Museum* reprint of "The Prisoner," *Columbian Herald*, February 16, 1786.

Stanza 5, line 3: He scorns their mandates, and their law.

Stanza 6: Tenth stanza of the *Columbian Herald* text.

Stanza 7: Sixth stanza of the *Columbian Herald* text, with the following variants:
line 1: Now Europe's feuds employ his brains,

Stanza 8: Seventh stanza of the *Columbian Herald* text.

Stanza 9: On great affairs condemn'd to fret
The interest on our foreign debt
He hopes good *Louis* may forget.

Stanza 10: He fears the Bank will hurt our trade,
And fall it must without his aid--
And yet his barber goes unpaid.

Stanza 11: Ninth stanza of the *Columbian Herald* text.

Stanza 12: Eleventh stanza of the *Columbian Herald* text, with the following variants:
line 3: That Congress have so little power.

Stanza 13: Twelth stanza of the *Columbian Herald* text, with the following variants:
line 1: Although he has no ships to lose,
line 2: The *Algerines* he *dares* abuse,

Stanza 14: The French, he thinks will soon prepare
To undertake some grand affair--
"So 'tis but war, we need not care."

Stanza 15: Where *Mississippi* laves the plain,
He hopes the bold *Kentucky* swain
Will seize her forts and plague *Old Spain*.

Stanza 16: Such morning thoughts, such evening dreams
Thro' long dull nights he plans odd schemes
To dispossess her of those streams.

Stanza 17: Stanza 15 of the *Columbian Herald* text, with the following variants:
line 2: When few shall drink *West-India* rum,--
line 3: Our *spirits* will be *proof* at home.

Stanza 18: Stanza 16 of the *Columbian Herald* text.

Stanza 19: Stanza 17 of the *Columbian Herald* text.

Stanza 20: Stanza 13 of the *Columbian Herald* text, with the following variants:
line 2: The *States* will lose by *China* trade,
line 3: Since dollars for their tea are paid;

Stanza 21: Stanza 14 of the *Columbian Herald* text, with the following variants:
line 1: Then hopes that by the month of June
line 3: Will make a passage to the moon.

Stanza 22: Stanza 18 of the *Columbian Herald* text, with the following variants:
line 2: And all the follies we might find

Stanza 23: Stanza 19 of the *Columbian Herald* text.

American Museum   February, 1787 (2)

Substantively identical to the *Freeman's Journal* text, except for the following variants:

Stanza 11, line 1: Our western posts (which Britons keep
Stanza 21, line 1: He hopes that by the month of June

Massachusetts Centinel   March 10, 1787

Substantively identical to the *Freeman's Journal* text, except for the following variants:

Stanza 8:   One moment Government he'll flatter--
            The next 'bout duties make a clatter--

The third at *Shays*, he'll wing his satire.

Stanzas 10-16: Stanzas 11-17 of the *Freeman's Journal* text.
(Stanza 10 of the *Freeman's Journal* text deleted.)

Stanza 17: Our glorious prospect is display'd,
Our wealthy mines are open laid--
Poor soul--his barber is not paid.

Stanzas 18-23: Last six stanzas of the *Freeman's Journal* text.

Miscellaneous Works (1788), 147-79.

Columbian Herald   March 6, 1786

The LOST ADVENTURER.

TRUE to his trade, the slave of fortune still,
In a sweet isle, where never winter reigns,
I found him at the foot of a tall hill
Mending old sails, and chewing sugar canes:
'But what (said *Ralph*) have I, that sails the seas,
Ah! what have I to do with scenes like these!

'With masts so trim, and sails as white as snow,
'The painted barque allur'd me from the land,
'Pleas'd, on her sea-boat decks I wish'd to go
'Mingling my labours with her hardy band;
'The Captain bade me for the voyage prepare
'And said, *by Jasus, 'tis a grand affair!*

'To combat with the winds who first essay'd,
'Had these gay groves his lightsome heart beguil'd,
'His heart attracted by the charming shade
'Had chang'd the deep sea for the woody wild,
'And slighted all the gain that Neptune yields
'For Damon's cottage, or Plaemon's fields.

'His barque, the bearer of a feeble crew,
'How could he trust, when none had been to prove her--
'Courage might sink when lands and shores withdrew.
'And sickly whelps might spoil the best manœvre;
'But fortitude--though woes and death await,
'Still views *bright* skies and leaves the *dark* to fate.

'From monkey climes, where limes and lemons grow,
'And the sweet orange swells her fruit so fair,
'To wintry worlds, with heavy heart, I go
'To face the cold glance of the northern bear--
'Where lonely waves, far distant from the sun,
'And gulphs of mighty strength, their circuits run.

'But how disheartning is the wanderer's fate!--
'When conquer'd by the loud, tempestuous main,
'On him no mourners in procession wait,
'Nor do the sisters of the grove complain;--
'Nor can I think on coral beds they sleep
'Who sink in storms, and mingle with the deep.

'Tis folly all!--for who can truly tell
'What streams disturb the bosom of that main;
'What ugly fish in those dark climates dwell
'That feast on men--then stay my gentle swain,
'Bred in yon' happy shades--be happy there,
'And be these quiet groves thy only care.'

So spoke poor *Ralph*, and with a smooth sea gale
Fled from the magic of the inchanting shore;
But, whether winds or waters did prevail,
I saw the black ship ne'er returning more;
    Though long I walk'd the margin of the main,
    And long have look'd, and still must look in vain.

K.

Miscellaneous Works (1788), 74-75.

New York Gazetteer   *April 18, 1786*

The STUDENT's Complaint.

WELL, surely, it was a most sorrowful thing
That we must commence, and no Ladies would sing!--
So long at our studies, and poring on Greek,
And Logic, and Latin, and learning to speak;
And not, in return of our manifold pains,
Not a quaver to have of their holiday strains!
Was hard in extreme--and I'm sorry to find,
No reason as yet for their malice assign'd:
Tho' tutor'd by LAW, who is music's delight,
They have not a single idea of the right;
Or else, I presume, they had freely bestow'd,
Some elegants notes on the elegant *Ode*:--
The poet, poor fellow, no doubt had his share
Of trouble and thinking, his lines to prepare;
And they to neglect them, and fall in a pet,
Was such an affront as he'll never forget.
    Hereafter, commencing, to punish the sex,
With Latin and Logic their brains we will vex;
In dark metaphysics we'll rattle away,
Nor shall they be wiser for all we may say;
No witty orations shall tempt them to smile;
But after haranguing on *nothing* a while,
We'll send them away just as dull as they came;
And year after year shall still be the same,
'Till each cruel creature in concert agrees,
And cry out--*Dear Fellows, we'll sing what you please*!

                              ORESTES.

New-York, 17th April.

Miscellaneous Works (1788), 153.

Columbian Herald   July 6, 1786

The wild HONEY—SUCKLE.

FAIR flower, that dost so comely grow,
Hid in this dreary dark retreat,
Untouch'd thy honey'd blossoms blow,
Unseen thy little branches meet;
    No roving foot shall find thee here,
    No busy hand provoke a tear.

By Nature's self, in white array'd,
She bade thee shun the vulgar eye,
And planted here the guardian shade,
And sent soft waters murmuring by--
    Thus quietly thy summer goes,
    Thy life declining to repose.

Smit with those charms that must decay,
I grieve to see thy future doom--
(They died--nor were those flowers less gay,
The flowers that did in Eden bloom)
    Unpitying frosts, and autumn's power,
    Shall leave no vestige of this flower!

From morning suns and evening dews
At first thy little being came--
If nothing once--you nothing lose,
For when you die you are the same--
    The space between is but an hour,
    The empty image of a flower.

                          K.

Miscellaneous Works (1788), 152.

Columbian Herald   July 10, 1786

The DRUNKEN SOLDIER.
"In a mouldering cave where the wretched retreat, &c."

IN a cottage forlorn, with a sigh and a pout,
Poor *Trim* sat distracted with care;
He look'd at his bottle and saw it was out,
And gave himself up to despair:
The walls of his cell were bespatter'd around
With the grog he had vomited up;
And even the dirt and the grass on the ground
Were bedew'd with the dregs of his cup.

The house-wife beheld through a hole in the wall
Him weeping, (his whiskey half spent)
She curs'd him, his liquor, his bottle and all,
And these were the blessings she sent:
"O *Trim*, do forebear—not a grunt, not a swear
"For your grog so deservedly lost,
"Your bones shall be broke—I will put up my prayer,
"And the answer shall be to your cost.

"The boys of the barracks, those soldiers so bold,
"Of gaming have finished their task,
"And such is the news, it is currently told,
"They are coming to drink out your flask:
"A council was held ere your eyes were awake,
"And this was the captain's decree,
"That when it is emptied the bottle shall break,
"And the charge they have trusted to me."

To the broomstick straightway, like a fury she flew--
But he with his bottle began,
And said, shut the door—let me touch it once more,
And then—they may drink if they can—
With a circle of black she encompass'd his eyes;
At last into slumbers he sunk,
Then she laid him down snug, lest the sight of his jug,
Should tempt him again to get drunk.

                                                K.

Miscellaneous Works (1788), 154-55.

Columbian Herald   July 13, 1786

THE
ROGUISH SHOEMAKER.
In Imitation of Watt's
INDIAN PHILOSOPHER.

"Why should our joys be turn'd to pain,
"Why gentle Hymen's silken chain," &c.

WHY should our shoes so soon grow old,
So soon the hide, with which they're soal'd
    Be worn and out of date?--
Crispin, 'tis strange the thread that sews
Millions of coats, should leave our shoes
    In such a ragged state!--

In vain I sought the secret cause,
Search'd in the leather for its flaws,
    The tanner curs'd in vain;
Stept into shops where shoes are made,
Saw artists hourly ply their trade,
    But none would this explain.

Then tow'rd the west, and cross the street,
Where folks at tall *St. Michael's* meet
    I hurry'd, vext in mind;
'Till near the banks of Ashley's flood,
On soil of marsh, I sighing stood,
    For tanners use design'd.

Not far from thence, a cobler's son
Stood by his hides, and thus begun,
    With aspect dull and sad:
(Twice he came o'er the lazy stream,
The faults of shoes was all his theme,
    And why they were so bad.)

He said, "The spacious ample hide
"That does for all our hoofs provide,
    "Should still be free from blame,

"For shap'd into so many soals,
"Some would have flaws, and some have holes,
    "Just as by chance it came.

"The artist wise that form'd the shoe,
"One hide from every creature drew,
    "And scrap'd that hide with care:
"This is an honest skin, he said,
"Then down he sat to try his trade,
    "And knew no cheating there.

"But when these hides had left the vat,
"Lodg'd in our shop, a hungry rat
    "Attacks them with his jaws--
"Ah! cruel chance, and ragged fate!
"He knaw'd them early, gnaw'd them late,
    "For hunger has no laws.

"Happy the man that finds a shoe
"That's to his expectation true,
    "One real good below--
"But, O! the crowds of wretched wights,
"That travel barefoot these dull nights,
    "And wound the bleeding toe!"--

Thus sang the cobler's hopeful son--
I found, at length, his song was done--
    He said he was no Jew--
Sure then, cry'd I, ere I'll agree
For these damn'd shoes you mean for men,
    I will go barefoot too.

Some happier Crispin, tell me where,
What other shop affords a pair,
    Where better shoes are found--
Swift as Don Quixote's steed of old
I'd run to get my boots new soal'd,
    And wear them--tight and sound.

                                        K.

Miscellaneous Works (1788), 79-80.

South Carolina State Gazette   March 24, 1794

PARODY on Dr. WATT'S INDIAN PHILOSOPHER, or
few honest COBLERS.

Substantively identical to the *1788* text, except for the following variants:

Stanza 1, line 2: Why should the hide with which they're soal'd,

Stanza 2, line 5: Saw artists hourly ply the trade,

Stanza 3, line 4: Till on the banks of Ashley's flood,
line 6: For tanning use design'd.

Stanza 4, line 4: Thrice he came o'er the lazy stream,

Stanza 5, line 3: No thinking man could blame;

Stanza 6, line 1: The artist wise who shap'd the shoe
line 5: Then he resolv'd to try his trade,

Stanza 7, line 1: Soon as the hide had left the vat,
line 2: And lodg'd aloft, a hungry rat
line 3: Attack'd it teeth and claws;
line 4: He gnaw'd it early, gnaw'd it late,

Stanza 8, line 1: Happy the man who finds a shoe,
line 4: But, oh, the croud of wretched wights,

Stanza 9, line 4: Sure then, cry'd I, ere I agree

Stanza 10, line 4: Swift as on Quixote's steed of old
line 5: I'd fly to get my boots new soal'd,

Columbian Centinel   April 23, 1794

PARODY, *On Dr.* WATTS' *INDIAN PHILOSOPHER, or, Few Honest COBLERS.*
(Written in *Charleston,* S.C.)

Substantively identical to the *State Gazette* text.

Port Folio   May 14, 1803

Text is introduced and erroneously attributed as follows:

> (The following exquisite Parody of one of the finest lyrics in our language we believe is the production of Dr. *Ladd,* late of Charleston, S.C. In this species of ludicrous composition, the poetical mimic is generally too servile, in aping the original. But this remark is inapplicable to the poem before us. It displays a very humourous vein of invention, and is of a character superior to the mass of ephemeral productions.)

Text reflects all of the *South Carolina State Gazette* variants, as well as the following additional variants:

Stanza 2, line 2: Look'd in the leather for its flaws--
Stanza 5, line 2: That doth for all our hoofs provide,
Stanza 6, line 3: And shap'd that hide with care:
Stanza 9, line 3: And thought his reasoning true.
         line 5: For those cur'd shoes you mean for me,
Stanza 10, line 3: Where better work is found.
          line 4: Swift as Quixote's steel of old,
          line 5: I'll fly to get my boots new sol'd,

Freeman's Journal   October 4, 1786

On the Honorable Emanuel Swedenburg's
UNIVERSAL THEOLOGY.

IN this choice work the curious eye may find
The noblest system to reform mankind,
Old truths confirm'd, that sceptics have deny'd,
By most perverted, and which some deride.
     Here truths divine in heavenly visions grow
From the vast *influx* on our world below,
Here, like the blaze of our material *sun,*
Enlighten'd reason proves, that *God is one;*--

As *that,* concenter'd in itself, a sphere,
Illumes all nature with its radiance here,
Bids tow'rd itself all trees and plants aspire,
Awakes the winds, impells the seeds of fire,
And, still subservient to the almighty plan,
Warms into life the changeful life of man,
So, like the sun, in heaven's bright realms we trace
One power of *Love,* that fills unbounded space,
Existing always by no borrow'd aid,
Before all worlds, eternal, and not made;--
To that indebted, stars and comets burn,
Owe their first movement, and to that return:
Prime source of wisdom, all contriving mind,
First springs of reason, that this globe design'd,
Parent of *order,* whose unwearied hand
Upholds the fabric that his wisdom plann'd,
And, its due course assign'd to every sphere,
Revolves the seasons, and sustains the year;
Pure light of *Truth!* where'er thy rays combine
Thou art the substance of the power divine!
Nought else on earth that full resemblance bears,
No sun, that lights us through our circling years,
No stars, that through yon' heavenly mansions stray,
No moon, that glads us with her evening ray,
No seas, that o'er their gloomy mansions flow,
No forms beyond us, and no shapes below.
  Then slight, ah, slight not this instructive page
For the low follies of the thoughtless age,
Here, to the truth by reason's aid aspire,
Here, the gay visions of the blest admire,
Behold that heaven, in these neglected lines,
In whose vast space perpetual day light shines,
Where streams of joy through plains of pleasure run,
And night is banish'd from so bright a sun.
  Plung'd in that gulph, whose dark unfathom'd wave
All tongues and nations to destruction gave,--
Here, man no more disgrac'd by death appears,
Lost in dull slumbers through the waste of years--
No empty dream, or still more empty shade;--
Remains the substance, but the form decay'd;
Sees what he saw, knows what before was known,
The same ideas, but more perfect grown.

Where parted souls with kindred spirits meet,
Rapt to the bloom of beauty, all complete,
In that celestial, vast, unbounded sphere,
Nought there exists but has its image here!
All there is *mind*!--that intellectual flame,
From whose vast depth Platonic visions came,
In which creation ended and began--
Flows to this abject world, and beams on man.

K.

Philadelphia October 2.

Miscellaneous Works (1788), 76-77.

Freeman's Journal   October 11, 1786

On prohibiting the sale of Dr. *David Ramsay's* History of the Revolution of South-Carolina, in London.

SOME bold bully *Dawson*, expert in abusing,
Having pass'd all his life in the practice of bruising;
When at last he is drove to reform and repent,
And wishes his life and been soberly spent,
Tho' a course of contrition in earnest begins
He cannot endure to be told of his sins.

So, the British worn out with their wars in the west
(Where burning and murder their prowess confest)
When at last they agreed 'twas invain to contend,
(For the days of their thieving were come to an end)
They got their historians to scribble and flatter
And foolishly thought they could hush up the matter.

But *Ramsay* arose, and with truth on his side
Has told to the world what they labour'd to hide--
With his pen of *dissection*, and pointed with steel,
If they ne'er before felt--he has taught them to feel;
Themselves and their projects has truly defin'd,
And drag'd them to blush at the bar of mankind,

As the *author* himself, and the world might expect,
They have treated his work with a surly neglect,
In reply to his reason they splutter and rail,
And, prompted by *Rawdon*, prohibit the sale.

   But, alas! their chastisement is only begun--
Thirteen are the *states*--and the tale is of *one*;
When the *twelve* yet remaining their stories have told,
The King will run mad--*and the book will be sold.*

Philadelphia October 9.

Massachusetts Centinel   October 25, 1786

   The following lines were wrote, on seeing an English paragraph mentioning the prohibiting the sale of Dr. DAVID Ramsey's *History of the Revolution of South-Carolina, in London.*

Text identical to that in the *Freeman's Journal.*

Miscellaneous Works (1788), 144-45.

Freeman's Journal   October 11, 1786

The AUTHOR *and the* CRITIC.

SIX sheets compos'd--struck off and dry--
The work may please the world, thought I,
If some, impell'd by spleen or spite
Refuse to read--then let them write--
I too with them shall have my turn,
And give advice to tear or burn.

Now from the binder's, hurry'd home
In neat array, my leaves are come—
Alas, alas! is this my all!
The volume is so light and small
That, aim to save it as I can,
'Twill fly before *Flirtilla's* fan!
Did I for this so often rise
Before the sun bedeck'd the skies,
And near your Schuykill's wandering stream
Invoke the Muse's morning dream,
And scorn the winds that blew so cool?—
I did—and I was more the fool.

Yet slender tho' the book, and small,
And harmless, (take it all in all)
I see a dreadful *form* appear,
A quill suspended at his ear—
Its fate depends on his decree,
And what he writes must sacred be.

A *brute* of such a horrid mien
At wild *Sanduski* ne'er was seen,
And in the dark *Kentucky* groves
No beast, like this, for plunder roves,
Nor dwells in *Scotia's* horrid waste
A reptile of so vile a taste!—

The monster comes—severe and slow—
His eyes with forked lightnings glow—
Takes up the book—surveys it o'er—
Cries out—*damn'd stuff*!—but says no more!—
The book is *damn'd* by his decree,
And what he says must sacred be!

Give me a *cane* of mighty length,
A *staff* proportion'd to my strength,
Like *that,* by whose prodigious aid
The *man of Gath* his motions made—
Like *that,* which once on *Etna's* shore,
The giant of the cavern bore.—

For wit traduc'd at such a rate
To other worlds I'll send him strait,
Where all the past shall nothing seem,
Or just be imag'd like a dream,
Where new vexations are design'd,
No dull *quietus*, for the mind.

Arm'd with a staff of such a size,
I strike--he groans--the *critic* dies!
Here, watchman, help me--seize his pen
With which he kills all rhyming men;
This *goose*-quill must not with him go
To persecute the *scribes* below.

How vast a change an hour may bring!
How abject lies this snarling thing!
No longer wit to him shall bow,
To him the world is nothing now!
And all he writ, and all he read
Is, like himself, to *Tophet* fled.
Dead though he be, (and sent to rest)
No keen remorse torments my breast--
Yet something in me seems to tell
I might have let him live, as well--
*'Twas his to snarl and growl and grin,
And life had else a burden been.*

Miscellaneous Works (1788), 140-42.

Daily Advertiser   October 26, 1786

The DESOLATE ACADEMY.

Text reprinted from the 1786 collection, with the following variants:

Stanza 2, line 7: Some writ their themes, whilst others read,
Final line: *The cobler shall conclude my song.*

Poems (1786), 82.

American Museum   June, 1787

Stanza 2, line 7: Some wrote their themes, while others read.

Bailey's Pocket Almanack for 1787

(Untitled poem follows prose account of the West Indies.)

1.

THESE Indian isles, so green and gay,
In summer seas by nature plac'd--
Art hardly told us where they lay
Till tyranny their charms defac'd;
 Ambition there her conquests made,
 And av'rice rifled every shade.

2.

The *Genius* wept his sons to see
By foreign arms untimely fall,
And some to other climates flee
Where later ruin met them all--
 He saw his sylvan offspring bleed
 That fiercer natures might succeed.

3.

No more to Indian coasts confin'd,
Aw'd by some proud victorious chief,
While he to tears his heart resign'd,
With pain he saw the falling leaf;
    "And thus (he cry'd) our reign must end,
"We, like the leaves, must now descend.

4.

"Ah, what a change! the ambient deep
"No longer hears the lover's sigh--
"But wretches meet to wail and weep
"The loss of their dear liberty,
    "Unfeeling hearts possess these isles,
    "Man frowns, and only nature smiles."

5.

Proud of these vast extended shores
The haughty Spaniard calls his own,
No other world may share those stores
To other worlds so little known--
    His CUBA shall this truth confess
    Where *slavery* digs what *slaves* possess.

6.

JAMAICA's sweet romantic vales
Invain with golden plenty teem;
Her endless spring, her balmy gales
Did more to me than magic seem--
    Yet, what the God profusely gave
    Is here denied the toiling slave.

7.

Fantastic joy and fond belief
Through life support the galling chain,
Hope's airy scenes dishearten grief
And bring his native climes again--
    His native groves his heaven display,
    The funeral is the happy day.--

8.

For man reduc'd to such disgrace
Invain from Jove fair virtue fell--
Distress compells him to be base,
He has no motive to excell--
    In death alone his prospects end,
    The world's worst foe is his best friend!

9.

How great their praise, let truth declare,
Who, smit with honour's sacred flame,
Bade freedom to these coasts repair,
Assum'd the slaves neglected claim,
    And scorning interest's sordid plan
    Prov'd to mankind the rights of man.

10.

Ascending here, may this warm sun
With freedom's beams, divinely clear,
Throughout the world his circuit run
Till these dark scenes shall disappear,
    And a new race, not bought or sold,
    Springs from the ashes of the old.

                      K.

Miscellaneous Works (1788), 155-57.

Freeman's Journal   February 7, 1787

STANZAS *on a Young Lady in a Consumption.*

On the lost charms of *Cynthia's* eyes,
And wasted bloom, when I would gaze,
Strange feelings in my bosom rise,
And passion all my reason sways;
  Worlds I would banish from my view,
  And leave the gods, to talk with you.

The smile that decks your fading cheek
To me a heavy heart declares,
When you are silent I would speak,
But cowardice alarms my fears;
  All must be *heaven* that you do prize,
  As all is *death* that you despise.

When, wandering in the evening shade,
I shar'd her pains and felt her grief,
Though many a tender thing I said,
No words of mine could bring relief;
  When from her hair I brush'd the dew
  She sigh'd, and said--*'tis not for you.*

When drooping, dull, and almost dead
With fevers brought from sultry climes,
She would not hold my fainting head,
But recommended me some rhymes
  On patience, and on fortitude,
  And other things, less understood.

When aiming to engage her heart
With verses from the muse's stock,
She sate, regardless of my art,
And counted seconds by the clock;
  And thus, she cry'd, shall verse decay,
  And thus the world shall pass away!

When languishing upon her bed
(No longer fond of *India* gowns)
I came—and while the parson read
Of chrystal skies and coral crowns,
    She bade me at a distance stand,
    And lean'd her head upon her hand.

So, drooping hangs the fading rose
When *August* sends the driving shower,
So in the grave my *Cynthia* goes--
Her whole duration--but an hour;
    Yet who would think she aught did ail.
    So beautiful--and yet so pale!

Such virtue in her spirit dwells,
Such triumphs crown her bed of pain,
That now with pride my bosom swells
To think I have not liv'd invain,
    Since, slighting all the sages knew,
    I learn philosophy from you.   T.

        B

January 26th, 1787

Miscellaneous Works (1788), 259-60.

    National Gazette   October 13, 1792

        Marcella in a Consumption.

Substantively identical to the *1788* text, except for the following variants:

All six lines of each stanza begin at the margin.

Stanza 1, line 1: SMIT by the glance of thy bright eyes

Stanza 2, line 5: All must be sense, that you do prize,
         line 6: All that I say, be grave and wise.

Stanza 8, line 1: Such virtue in that spirit dwells,
line 2: Such fortitude amid such pain--
line 3: That now with pride my bosom swells

Freeman's Journal   February 14, 1787

The ALMANACK-MAKER.

WHILE others dwell on mean affairs,
Their kings, their councils, and their wars,
Philaster roves among the stars.

Not one of all the learned train,
Like him, can manage *Charles' wain,*
Or motion of the moon explain.

He tells us when the sun will rise,
Points out fair days, or clouded skies--
No matter if he sometimes lies.

An annual almanack to frame
And publish with pretended name
Is all his labour, all his aim.

He every month has something new,
Yet mostly deals in what is true,
Obliging all and cheating few.

Our sister moon, the stars, the sun
In measur'd circles round him run,
He knows their motions--every one.

The solar system at his will,
To mortify such daring skill,
The comets--they are rebels still.

Advancing in its daily race
He calculates the planets place
Nor can the moon elude his chace.

In dark eclipse when she would hide
And be a while the modest bride,
He pulls her veil of crape aside,

Each passing age must have its taste,
The sun is in the centre plac'd,
And *fuel* must supply his waste,

But how to find it he despairs--
Nor will he leave his idle cares,
Or Jove to mind his own affairs.

He prophesies the sun's decay--
And while he would his fate delay
New sorrows on his spirits prey.

So much upon his shoulders laid,
He reads what Aristotle said,
Then--calls the comets to his aid.

The people of the lunar sphere
As he can plainly make appear
Are coming nearer year by year.

Though others often gaze invain
Not one among the starry train
Could ever puzzle his firm brain.

The ram, the twins, the shining goat,
And Argo, in the skies afloat,
To him are things of little note;

And *that* which now adorns the bear,
(I heard him say) the sailor's star,
Will be, in time, the lord knows where.

Thus nature waiting at his call,
His book in vogue with great and small,
Is sought, admir'd, and read by all.

How happy thus on earth to stay,
The planets keeping him in pay,--
And when 'tis time to post away

Old *Saturn* will a bait prepare,
And hook him up from toil and care
To make new calculations *there.*

Philadelphia February 12.

Miscellaneous Works (1788), 150-52.

Freeman's Journal   February 28, 1787

THOMAS and SUSAN,
An Irish-town dialogue.--(*Suitable to the times.*)

Thomas.

I WISH I was over the water again;
'Tis a pity we cannot agree,
When I try to be merry, it's labour invain,
You always are scolding at me--
    Then what shall I do
    With this termagant *Sue*;
    Tho' I hug her and squeeze her
    I never can please her----
Was there ever a devil like you?

Susan.

If I was a maid, as I now am a wife,
With a sot and a brat to maintain,
I think it should be the first care of my life
To shun such a drunkard again--
    Not one of the crew
    Is so hated by Sue--
    Though they always are bawling,
    And pulling, and hauling,
Not one is a lounger like you.

Thomas.

Dear Susan, I'm sorry that you should complain,
There is nothing indeed to be done—
If war should break out, I would venture again
To live by the trade of the gun;
    Arriving from sea
    I would kneel on one knee,
    And plunder presenting
    To Susan, relenting—
Who then would be honour'd like me!

Susan.

To day as I came by the sign of the ship
A mighty brisk captain was there,
He was asking for sailors to take a small trip
But I cannot remember well where;—
    He was hearty and free,
    And if you can agree
    To leave me, dear honey,
    To bring me some money!
How happy indeed I shall be.—

Thomas.

The man that you saw not a sailor can get,
We all are afraid of the *Dey;*
Algiers and *Morocco* are both in a fret,
And their cruisers are coming this way;
    So to whine and complain
    Is but labour invain—
    For an *Englishman's* pass
    He must purchase—alas!—
Or the devil may take him for me.

Philadelphia February 26.

Miscellaneous Works (1788), 16-17.

Massachusetts Centinel   March 24, 1790

1788 text reprinted, and introduced as follows:

> (*Freneau*, in his "*Pictures of Columbus*"--after shewing the variety of obstacles thrown in the way of that intrepid adventurer in search of new worlds, from the want of faith in his King--the superstition of the Clergy--and the ignorance of his countrymen in general--in the following lines, shews that prejudice against him had even affected the lowest orders of the community.--They are natural and lively, and as such we present them to our readers.)

Freeman's Journal   February 28, 1787

(Untitled text included in the following note to the editor:)

> Mr. Bailey,
>
> > The following lines were occasioned by the death of Mr. ROBERT BELL, the celebrated humorist, and truly philanthropic bookseller, of this city:--they were written more than two years ago, and are now sent for insertion in your Journal.)

BY Schools untaught, from nature's source he drew
That flow of wit which wits with toil pursue:--
Above dependence, bent to virtue's side;
Beyond the folly of the pedants pride--
Born to no power, he took no splendid part,
Yet warm for freedom glow'd his honest heart:
Foe to all meanness; not afraid to hate
The fop in scarlet, or the knave in state.--
Bound to no sect, to blame them or defend,
He lov'd his glass, a female, and his friend--
The ready jest, to each occasion fit,
In him was nature, and that nature, wit;
Alike to pride and mad ambition dumb,

He saw no terrors in the world to come—
In chace of fortune half his life was whim
Yet fortune saw no sychophant in him:
Too social *Bell!* in *others* so refin'd,
One sneaking *virtue* ne'er possess'd your mind;
Had *prudence* only held her share of sway
Still had thy glass been full, thy self been gay!
But while we laugh'd, and while the jest went round,
The lamp was darken'd—and no help was found—
On distant shores you died, where none shall tell,
Here rest the virtues and the wit of BELL!

Miscellaneous Works (1788), 187-88.

Freeman's Journal   April 11, 1787

The INSOLVENT's RELEASE, or, *Miseries of a country Jail.*

1.   "NOT from those dismal dreary coasts I come
     Where wizzard *Faustus* chews his brimstone rolls,
     Nor have I been to wrangle with the men
     Of that sad country, where, for want of rum,
     Dead putrid water from the stagnant fen
     Is drank unmingled by departed souls;
     Nor from that dog house do I bring you news
     Where Macedonian Philip* mends old shoes—
          But from that dreadful place, arriv'd,
               Where men in debt, at cribbage play,
          And I most cunningly contriv'd
               To fatten on two groats a day—
     Full on my back they turn the key,
     The 'squire himself is not so free.

---

* See Lucian's Dialogues.

2. When to these rugged walls, a fathom thick,
    I came, directed by the sheriff's stick;
    Alas! said I, what can they mean to do!
    I am not conscious of one roguish trick!
    I am no thief--I took no Christian's life,
    Nor have I meddled with the parson's wife,
    (Which would have been a dreadful thing, you know)
    Then, by these gloomy walls, this iron grate,
    Appointed by the wisdom of your State
    To shut in *little* rogues, and keep out *great;*
    Tell me, ye pretty lads that deal in law,
    Ye men of mighty wigs, ye judges, say,--
    Say! by the Jailor's speckled face,
    That never beam'd one blush of grace;
          How long must I
          In prison lie
    For just nine shillings, that I--cannot pay!

3. Return, ye happy times, when all were free--
    No jails on land, no nets at sea;
    When mountain beasts unfetter'd ran,
    And man refus'd to shut up man
    As men of modern days have shut up me!--
    This is the dreary dark abode
    Of poverty and solitude;
    Such was the gloomy cell where Bunyan lay,
    While his dear *Pilgrim* help'd the time away--
    Such was the place where Wakefield's vicar drew
    Fine morals from the imprison'd crew.
    And found both time to preach and pray.

4. In bed of straw and broken chair
        What consolation could be found!
    No gay companions ventur'd there
        To push the ruddy liquor round!
          From jug of stone
          I drank, alone,
    A beverage neither clear nor strong,
        No table laid,
        No village maid
    Came there to cheer me with her song:
    My days were dull, my nights were long!

My evening dreams,
My morning schemes
Were how to break that cruel chain,
And, Jenny, be with you again."

Philadelphia April 10, 1787

Miscellaneous Works (1788), 157-59.

Freeman's Journal   April 11, 1787

St. PREUX *to* ELOISA.

(In *J. J. Rousseau's* letters, *St. Preux* is supposed to make a voyage round the world in *Lord Anson's* squadron, with a view of forgetting his passion for *Eloisa.* He is here supposed to write the following lines to her, during the passage round *Cape Horn*.)

As there is pleasure in being mad,
Which none but madmen know,
So, I a secret pleasure had
In rambling to and fro',
Which they that always stay at home,
Like lazy plants, untaught to roam--
Which they shall never know.

But leaving France last New-Year's day,
I bade a long adieu!
Had I not minded what the sailors say,
I had been still with you;
And, from these frosts and chilling snows,
On your fond bosom found repose.

Now, while through barbarous climes we sail,
Should Neptune force our ship on shore
On some rude isle, by some rough gale--
I to your arms return no more,
But for some swarthy dame shall bring
Cool waters from the Indian spring.

Yet love, with undiminish'd joy,
Shall trace your form in fancy's glass,
While I more fond, and you, less coy,
O'er swelling seas together pass--
No rocks nor seas can love divide,
Where heart with heart is thus ally'd.

Philadelphia *April* 9.

Miscellaneous Works (1788), 159-60.

Freeman's Journal   April 18, 1787

The DEPARTURE.
[Written at leaving Sandy-Hook on a voyage to the West-Indies.]

1. FROM Hudson's cold, congealing streams
   As winter comes, I take my way
   Where other suns prompt other dreams,
   And shades less willing to decay
   Beget new raptures in the heart,
   Bid spleen's dejective crew depart,
   And wake the sprightly lay.

2. Good-natur'd Neptune, now so mild–
   Like rage asleep, or madness chain'd–
   By dreams amus'd, or love beguil'd,
   Sleep on–'till we our port have gain'd.
   The gentle breeze, that curls the deep,
   Shall paint a finer dream on sleep!--
   Ye nymphs, that haunt his grottoes low,
   Where sea-green trees on coral grow–
      No tumults make
      Lest he should wake;
   And, thus, the passing shade betray
   And sails that o'er his waters stray.

3. Sunk is the sun from yonder hill:
   The busy day is past;
   The breeze decays, and all is still,
   As all shall be at last;
   The murmuring on the distant shore,
   The dying wave is all I hear;
   The yellow fields now disappear,
   No painted butterflies are near,
   And laughing folly plagues no more.

4. The woods that deck yon' fading waste,
   That every wanton gale embrac'd,
       Ere summer yet made haste to fly;
   How smit with frost the pride of June!
   How lost to me! how very soon
       The fairy prospects die!
   Condemn'd to bend to winter's stroke
   Low in the dust the embowering oak
   Has bid the fading leaf descend;
   Their short-liv'd verdure at an end
   How desolate the forests seem,
       Beneath whose shade
       The enamour'd maid
   Was once so fond to dream!

5. What now is left of all that won
   The eye of mirth, while summer stay'd—
   The birds that sported in the sun—!
   The sport is past, the song is done;
   And nature's naked forms declare
   (The rifled groves, the valley bare)
   Persuasively, tho' silent, tell
       That, at the best,
       They were but drest
   Sad mourners for the funeral bell.

6. Now, while I spread the vent'rous sail
   To catch the breeze from yonder hill,
   Say, what does all this folly mean--?
   Why grieve to pass the wat'ry scene--?
   Is happiness to *place* confin'd--?

No–planted also in the mind,
She makes an *Eden* where she will

7. But man must groan: what ills must try,
What malice dark and calumny,
Indifference, with her careless eye,
    And Slander with her tale begun;
Bold Ignorance, and forward air,
And Cowardice, that has no share
    In honours gain'd, or trophies won.

8. To these succeed (and these are few
Of nature's dark, unseemly crew)
Unsocial pride, and cold disgust;
Servility, that licks the dust;
Those harpies that disgrace the mind;
Unknown to haunt the human breast
When pleasure her first garden dress'd;
But vanish'd is the shade so gay,
And lost in gloom the summer day
    That hush'd the soul to rest.

9. What season shall restore that scene
When all was calm, and all serene,
And *Happiness* no empty sound,
The golden age that pleas'd so well--?
The mind that made it shall not tell
To those on life's uncertain road;
Where, lost in folly's idle round,
And seeking what shall ne'er be found,
We press to one abode.

November 26, 1785.

Miscellaneous Works (1788), 163-65.

Freeman's Journal   April 18, 1787

MAY to APRIL.

"WITHOUT your showers
I breed no flowers,
Each field a barren waste appears;
If you don't weep
My blossoms sleep,
They take such pleasure in your tears.

As your decay
Made room for May,
So I must part with all that's mine;
My balmy breeze,
My blooming trees
To torrid suns their sweets resign.

For April dead
My shades I spread;
To her I owe my dress so gay;
Of daughters *three*
It falls on me
To close the triumphs on one day.

Thus, to repose
All nature goes;
Month after month must find its doom--
Time on the wing,
May ends the spring
And *summer--* triumphs o'er her tomb!

Philadelphia *April* 16, 1787.

Miscellaneous Works (1788), 78.

New York *Weekly Museum*   May 7, 1796

Reprint of the *Freeman's Journal* text.
Signature: BLANDITUS.

Pennsylvania Packet   June 9, 1787

The INDIAN STUDENT,
Or *FORCE OF NATURE.*

FROM Susquehanna's utmost springs
Where savage tribes pursue their game;
His blanket tied with yellow strings,
A shepherd of the forest came.

From long debate the council rose,
And viewing *Shalum's* tricks with joy,
To *Harvard** Hall, o'er wastes of snows
They sent the tawny-coloured boy.

A while he writ, a while he read,
A while he learn'd their grammar rules;
An Indian savage, so well bred,
Great credit promis'd to the schools.

Some thought he would in law excel,
Same said, in physic he would shine;
And one that knew him passing well,
Beheld in him a sound divine.

But those of more discerning eye
Even then could other prospects show,
And saw him lay his Virgil by
To wander with his dearer bow.

The tedious hours of study spent,
The heavy moulded lecture done,
He to the woods a hunting went,
But sigh'd to see the setting sun!

The shady bank, the purling stream,
The woody wild his heart possess'd—
The dewy lawn, his morning dream,
In Fancy's finest colours drest:

---

* HARVARD COLLEGE, *at Cambridge, in Massachusetts.*

'And why (he cried) did I forsake
'My native wood for gloomy walls;
'The silver stream, the limpid lake,
'For musty books and college halls!

'A little could my wants supply--
'Can wealth and honour give me more?
'Or, will the Sylvan God deny
'The humble treat he gave before?

'Where Nature's ancient forests grow,
'And mingled laurel never fades,
'My heart is fixt, and I must go
'To die among my native shades.'

He spoke, and to the western springs,
(His gown discharg'd, his money spent)
His blanket tied with yellow strings,
The shepherd of the forest went.

Returning to the rural reign,
The Indians welcom'd him with joy--
The council took him home again,
And bless'd the tawny-colour'd boy.

American Museum   October, 1787

The Indian student: or the force of nature.

Substantively identical to the *Packet* text, except for the following variants:

Lines 2 and 4 in each stanza indented.

Stanza 3, line 1:   A while he wrote, a while he read,

Miscellaneous Works (1788), 69-71.

Columbian Centinel   January 26, 1803

Reprint of the 1795 text is introduced with an anecdote that may have been the source of the poem. According to the story, in 1786 Lafayette took an American Indian, Peter Otsequot, to France to be educated, but upon returning, the Indian retreated to the forest and to his Indian ways, forgetting most of his education. "The principal object, in the recital of the above anecdote, is to introduce the following poetical production:"

Port Folio   October 24, 1807   (Part of extended review)

Poem introduced as follows:

> The following little poem very beautifully describes what may be supposed to have been the feelings of an Indian lad, who, separated from his companions, had been some time immured in a New-England College.

The Indian Student.

Substantively identical to the 1795 text, except for the following variants:

Lines 2 and 4 of each stanza indented.

Stanza 1, line 3:   A native of the forest came.
Stanza 5, line 2:   This gave a sheaf, and that a skin;
Stanza 9, line 3:   And one, who knew him, passing well,
Stanza 11, line 4: Through lonely wastes he'd walk, he'd run.
Stanza 14, line 3: "The silver brook, the limpid lake
Stanza 20, line 4: The native of the forest went.

Freeman's Journal   July 18, 1787

Address to MISFORTUNE.

DIRE *Goddess* of the haggard brow,
Misfortune, at thy shrine I bow,
Where forms uncouth betray thee still,
A leaky ship, a doctor's bill,
A poem damn'd, a beggar's prayer,
An empty purse, a load of care,
The critic's growl, the pedant's sneer,
The urgent dun, the law severe,
A smokey house, rejected love,
And friends that void of friendship prove.

 Foe to the pride of scheming man,
Whose power confounds the deepest plan;
To thy decree we still submit
Our views of gain, our works of wit.

Untaught by *thee,* the feeble mind
A dull repose, indeed, might find;
But life unvext by such controul
Can breed no vigour in the soul.

The calm that smooths the summer seas
Is a soft scene of rest and ease,
But skies that fret, and storms that rave,
Alone can teach us to be brave.

If half the woes for which we groan,
In reason's view, are all our own,
Why should we paint fine shadows here,
Then sigh, to find them disappear.

On *Hatteras'* cliffs who hopes to see
The maiden fair, or orange tree,
Awhile on hope may fondly lean
Till sad experience blots the scene.

For ruin'd States or trade perplext
'Tis almost folly to be vext;

The world at last will have its way,
'Tis ours no longer than to-day.

On other shores, a happier guest,
The mind must fix her heav'n of rest,
Where milder skies, and softer climes
Shall please the men of other times.

M.

Philadelphia *July* 16.

Miscellaneous Works (1788), 160-61.

Freeman's Journal   August 29, 1787

The SCORNFUL LADY.

DRESS'D out in all her gay attire,
Who sees but, seeing, must admire
The nymph with all her cruel arts
Bound on a cruise to capture hearts.

Aloft her silken streamers play,
The ensigns of unbounded sway:
For her the wretched victim burns,
Yet she no love for love returns.

Young Jockey from the woods of Kent
In chasing her a year had spent,
And own'd at last no privateer
Could ever yet compare with her.

Proud of the artillery of her eyes
She would not own so poor a prize,
But disregarding force or prayer
She struck him dumb, and left him there.

Thus huntsmen of their prowess boast
Who hunting on the Spanish coast
No deer at once by them is slain
But left to languish on the plain.

When first this heav'nly form I pass'd,
She back'd her topsails to the mast—
I saw there was no chance to fly,
At once she bade me yield or die.

Amaz'd at such a strange attack
I chang'd my course and hurried back,
But such a fatal arrow met
As pierc'd me deep, and pains me yet.

Ah, Celia, what a strange mistake
To *ruin* just for *ruin's* sake;
Thus to delude us in distress
And quit the prize you should possess.

Years may advance with silent pace
And rob that form of every grace,
And all your conquests be repaid—
With Teague O'Murphy, and his spade.

T.B.

August 26, 1787.

Miscellaneous Works (1788), 66-67.

Port Folio   October 24, 1807   (Part of extended review.)

Last two stanzas of the original text excerpted and introduced as follows:

> Freneau very seldom attuned his lyre to love, and in his works we find none of those "fabled tortures, quaint and tame," so common in the writings of the amatory poets. The following stanzas conclude an address, in a seaman's phrase, to a "scornful lady;" and although the threat of Time punishing the fair one for her cruelty is very common, yet the introduction of this personage in the last line is certainly very uncommon:

In each stanza, lines 2 and 4 indented.

Freeman's Journal   September 5, 1787

> HORACE, Lib. II. Ode 16. Imitated,
> and addressed to Governor *Parr.*

> *Otium divos rogat in patenti*, &c.

THE sailor toss'd on stormy seas
Implores his patron god for ease,
When Luna hides her paler blaze
And stars obscurely dart their rays.

For ease the Yankee, fierce in war,
His stores of vengeance points afar;
For ease the toiling Dutchman sighs
Which gold, nor gems, nor purple buys.

No treasur'd heaps from India trade,
No doctor's or the lawyer's aid
Can ease the tumults of the mind,
Or cares to gilded roofs assign'd.

The lot of man he best completes
Whose board is crown'd with frugal treats,
Whose sleep, no fears nor thirst of gain,
Beneath his homely roof, restrain.

Why, then, with wasting cares engage,
Weak reptiles of so frail an age;
Why thus to distant climates run
And lands beneath another sun?

For, though to *China's* coasts we roam,
Ourselves we ne'er can leave at home;
Care, swift as deer, as tempests strong,
Ascends the prow, and sails along.

The mind that feels an even state,
And all the future leaves to fate;
In every ill shall pleasure share,
As every pleasure has its care.

> Death early seal'd *Montgomery's* doom,
> In youth brave *Laurens* found a tomb,
> While *Arnold* spends in peace and pride
> The years that heaven to them deny'd.
>
> An hundred *slaves* before you fall,
> A coach and six is at your call,
> And vestments, ting'd with Tyrian dye,
> Where'er you go, attracts the eye;
>
> On me a poor and small domain
> With something of the rhyming vein
> The Muse bestow'd--and share of pride
> To spurn a *traitor* from my side.

Philad. *September* 3, 1787.

Massachusetts Centinel September 19, 1787

    HORACE, Lib. II. Ode 16. imitated. Addressed to Gov. *Parr*--on reading in the papers the paragraphs which mentioned, that Gen. Arnold proposed to reside under his auspices in Nova-Scotia.

Reprint of the *Freeman's Journal* text, dated September 3, 1787, but without "Philad."

Miscellaneous Works (1788), 67-68.

National Gazette October 24, 1792

The sixteenth Ode of the second book of Horace's Odes, imitated.
Otium divos rogat in patenti, &c.
To Pomposius Atticus.

Substantively identical to the *Freeman's Journal* text, except for the following variants:

Stanza 9, line 1:   A host of votes are at your call,

Stanza 9, line 2: A seat--perhaps--in Congress-hall;
         line 3: And vestments dipt in Stygian dye

Stanza 10, line 4: To spurn a scoundrel from my side.

Port Folio   October 24, 1804   (Part of extended review)

Last stanza only quoted in the following paragraph:

> Freneau has given several translations and imitations from the Latin and French. The conclusion of the sixteenth ode of the second book of Horace,
>
>> On me a poor and small domain,
>> With something of a poet's vein,
>> Kind fate bestow'd--and *share of pride*
>> *To spurn a scoundrel from my side,*
>
> is extremely indignant, and expresses the very sensations of the Prince of lyrick poets:

Freeman's Journal   October 17, 1787

(Poem included in following note to the editor:

Mr. *Bailey,*

THE subsequent lines were written two or three years after the event that occasioned them, but have never been printed. If you think them in any degree worthy of the memory of the patriotic young officer they attempt to celebrate (and whose death has been so deeply regretted throughout America) I must request of you to insert them in your journal.
                                                                A.B.)

To the Memory of the brave, accomplished and patriotic Col. JOHN LAURENS, *who, in the 27th year of his age, was killed in an engagement with a detachment of the British from Charleston, near the river* CAMBAHEE, *in South Carolina, August,* 1782.

SINCE on her plains this generous chief expir'd,
Whom sages honour'd, and whom France admir'd;
Does Fame no statues to his memory raise,
Nor swells one column to record his praise
Where her palmetto shades the adjacent deeps,
Affection sighs, and Carolina weeps!
    Thou, who shalt stray where death this chief confines
Approach, and read the patriot in these lines:
Not from the dust the muse transcribes his name,
And more than marble shall declare his fame
Where scenes more glorious his great soul engage,
Confest thrice worthy in that closing page
When conquering Time to dark oblivion calls,
The marble totters, and the column falls.
    Laurens! thy tomb while kindred hands adorn
Let northern muses, too, inscribe thy urn.--
Of all, whose names on death's black list appear,
No chief, that perish'd, claim'd more grief sincere,
Not one, Columbia, that thy bosom bore,
More tears commanded, or deserv'd them more!--
Grief at his tomb shall heave the unwearied sigh,

And honour lift the mantle to her eye:
Fame thro' the world his patriot name shall spread
By heroes envied and by monarchs read:
Just, generous, brave--to each true heart allied,
The Briton's terror, and his country's pride;
For him the tears of war-worn soldiers ran,
The friend of freedom, and the friend of man.
    Then what is death, compar'd with such a tomb,
Where honour fades not, and fair virtues bloom,
Ah, what is death, when fame like *this* endears,
The brave man's favourite, and his country's tears.

Miscellaneous Works (1788), 289-90.

Aurora   July 19, 1799

Excerpt from the original text appears in an article entitled "Extract From An Oration, Delivered by Mr. Elias B. Caldwell, At the city of Burlington, on the Anniversary of American Independence, July Fourth, 1799.

Part of the excerpt provides an account of Laurens and then quotes the third stanza of Freneau's poem.

American Museum   November, 1787

Lines occasioned by a visit to an old Indian burying ground.
                              --By Philip Freneau.

IN spite of all the learn'd have said,
    I still my old opinion keep;
The posture that we give the dead
    Points out the soul's eternal sleep.

Not so the ancients of these lands--
    The Indian, when from life releas'd,
Again is seated with his friends,
    And shares again the joyous feast.

His imag'd birds, and painted bowl,
    And ven'son, for a journey drest,
Bespeak the nature of the soul,
    Activity that wants no rest.

His bow for action ready bent,
    And arrows, with a head of bone,
Can only mean that life is spent,
    And not the finer essence gone,

Thou, stranger, that shalt come this way,
    No fraud upon the dead commit,
Yet, mark the swelling turf and say,
    They do not lie, but here they sit.

Here, still, a lofty rock remains,
    On which the curious eye may trace
(Now wasted half by wearing rains)
    The fancies of a ruder race.

Here, still an aged elm aspires;
    Beneath whose far projecting shade,
(And which the shepherd still admires)
    The children of the forest play'd.

There, oft' a restless India queen,
    (Pale Marian, with her braided hair)
And many a barb'rous form is seen,
    To chide the man that lingers there.

By midnight moons, o'er moist'ning dews,
    In vestments for the chace array'd,
The hunter still the deep pursues,
    The hunter, and the deer--a shade.

And long shall tim'rous fancy see
    The painted chief, and pointed spear,
And reason's self shall bow the knee
    To shadows and delusions here.

Miscellaneous Works (1788), 188-89.

Massachusetts Centinel   January 27, 1790

LINES, *Occasioned by a* VISIT *to an* old *Indian burying Ground.*   By Capt. *Philip Freneau**

Reprint of the 1788 text, with the following note respecting the poet:

NOTE.

*Who, we are told, from a long succession of calamities and misfortunes at sea, has determined once more to try the powers of his pen in his native city of New-York.--That the future success of this American bard--this genuine son of *Neptune* and *Clio*--whose writings both in verse and prose have rendered such excellent services to his country--may be greater than he has heretofore experienced, must be the wish of every friend to genius and merit.

New Hampshire Journal   September 13, 1796

Reprint of the 1795 text, introduced as follows:

Whatever the sober federalists may think of the politicks of Capt. Freneau every critick must admire the beautiful simplicity of such poetry as the following.

Port Folio   August 17, 1805

Reprint of the 1788 text, introduced as follows:

Every political enthusiast has perused, and been pleased with *Collins's* Pensive Ode, on the death of the poet Thomson. The following stanzas, from the pen of Philip Freneau, resemble the tone and manner of
        "In yonder grave a Druid lies."
They may be read with complacency by those who detest and deride the *politics* of the author. Criticism, sitting in judgement on the *poetry* or *learning* of a *democrat,* will dismiss political prejudices and credit genius of any party, for the successful exercise of the noble energies of the soul.

Port Folio   October 17, 1807   (Part of extended review)

Poem introduced as follows:

> Freneau's habits of life lead to an acquaintance with Nature, and he did not pass by her with a regardless eye. The measures of his poetry, like the subjects of his Muse, are various and desultory. The following lines, on an Indian burying-ground, are extremely beautiful: the last stanzas are in the sweetest style of Collins:

1795 text with the following variants:

Stanza 7, line 3:   (And which the ploughman still admires)

City Gazette   January 28, 1788

A PARODY on SAPPHO's ODE:
Blest as the immortal Gods is he, &c.
Addressed to OLD ENGLAND.

CURS'D as a Beggar's dog is he,
The unlucky wight that deals with thee;
Who still our hearts in bondage hold,
Fairly bought and poorly sold.

'Twas this that robb'd our ships of freight,
And caus'd such grumblings in the state;
For ere we well could count the cost,
Our cash was gone, our credit lost.

My girls grew vain—their dress and show,
Alas! soon brought my pockets low:
With English silks their shoes were bound,
The news went all the country round,

With constant duns my ears were vext,
My house with sherriffs was perplext,
My barber's bill I could not pay,
I blunder'd–broke–and ran away.

Daily Advertiser   March 4, 1790

A TRADESMAN's REFLECTION.
(A Parody) addressed to Old England.

Stanza 1, line 2: The unlucky wight that trades with thee,
          line 4: Slyly bought and poorly sold.
Stanza 3, line 3: With foreign silks their shoes were bound;
Stanza 4, line 1: With constant duns my doors were vext,

National Gazette   August 22, 1792

RINALDO'S COMPLAINT:
To the fair Shopkeeper.
(Imitated from Sappho's Ode)

Stanza 1, line 2: The unlucky man that deals with thee
          line 3: Who still behind the counter sit,
          line 4: Steal our cash, and show your wit.

Stanza 2:   Whate'er you prais'd, with sly design,
                  Whate'er you touch'd I wish'd it, mine–
                  And homespun trash from Nabby's paws
                  In your fair hands was Irish gauze.

Stanza 3:   'Twas this that made me look so sad
                  At times; and almost ran me mad,
                  For, ere I well could count the cost
                  My cash was gone, my credit lost.

Stanza 4:   Third stanza of the *City Gazette* text.

Stanza 5:   Fourth stanza of the *City Gazette* text, with the following variants:
                  line 1:   With constant duns my doors were vext,

Poems (1795), 364-65.

Port Folio   October 31, 1807   (Part of extended review)

Poem introduced as follows:

> We cannot refrain from copying the humourous effusion, a parody of Phillip's harmonious translation from Sappho.

1795 text, with the following variants:

> *TO A HANDSOME MILLENER.*
> "Blest as the immortal gods is he."

Stanza 1, line 2:   The unlucky wight who deals with thee,
Stanza 3, line 1:   Twas this that drove Rinaldo mad

City Gazette   January 30, 1788

(Untitled.)

THUS safe arriv'd, she greets the strand
And leaves her pilot for the land–
But Lydia, why to desarts roam,
And thus neglect your floating home.

To what fond swain shall I resign
The bosom–that shall ne'er be mine–
Those eyes, like diamonds, finely set
In ivory--how shall I forget!

As o'er the seas with you I stray'd
The hostile winds our course delay'd--
But, proud to waft a charge so fair,
To me were kind–and held you there.

I could not grieve when you complain'd
That adverse gales our barque detain'd
Where foaming seas to mountains grow
On gulphs of death conceal'd below.

When travelling o'er that lonely wave
To me your feverish hand you gave,
And sighing, bade me tell you true
What lands again would rise to view.

When night came on with blust'ring gale,
You fear'd the tempest would prevail,
And anxious ask'd, if I was sure
That on this globe we sail'd secure?

Delighted with a face so fair
I half forgot my weight of care,
And saw, unmov'd, the whirlwind rise,
Encircled moons, and threatening skies,

Then now, at length, arriv'd from sea
Consent, kind girl, to stay with me--
The barque, still faithful to her freight,
Should still on your direction wait.

To all your questions--*when* or *why*--?
I still will make a kind reply--
Give all you ask--each whim allow,
And change my style to *thee* and *thou*.

Then, Lydia, why our barque forsake?
The road to western forests take?--
That lip, on which hung half my bliss,
Some savage now will bend to kiss.

Some rustic soon, with fierce attack,
Shall force his arms about that neck--
And you, perhaps, will weeping come
To seek--in vain--your floating home!

Daily Advertiser   August 26, 1788

Poem introduced as follows:

>Mr. *Printer,*

>The following copy of *Verses* came accidentally into my hands:

–I am told it was written by Captain *Freneau,* and addressed to a young *Quaker Lady,* that went passenger in his Vessel to Georgia, to reside in the Western parts of that state.   A.B.

Stanzas 1-4:   First four stanzas of the *City Gazette* text, with the following variants:
Stanza 1, line 4: And thus forsake your floating home.

Stanza 5:   With timorous heart and wat'ry eyes,
You saw the vast Atlantic rise—
Saw wintry seas their storms prepare,
And wept to find no safety there.

Stanza 6:   Throughout the long December's night,
(While still your lamp was burning bright)
To dawn of day, from evening's close,
My pensive girl found no repose.

Stanzas 7-11:   Fifth to ninth stanzas of the *City Gazette* text, with the following variants:
Stanza 8, line 4: That on those depths we sail'd secure.
Stanza 10, line 4: Shall still on your direction wait.

Stanza 12:   If verse can life to beauty give,
For ages I can make you live;
Beyond the stars, triumphant rise,
While *Chloe's* tomb neglected lies.

Stanzas 13-14:   Last two stanzas of the *City Gazette* text, with the following variants:
Stanza 13, line 2: The road to western deserts take?

Poems (1795), 297-99.

American Museum   February, 1788

   The sea-faring bachelor--By mr. Philip Freneau.

Text reprinted from the 1786 collection.

Gazette of the United States   October 3, 1789

Substantively identical to the 1786 text, except for the following variants:

First line of each stanza indented.
Stanza 5, line 4: May safely keep one nymph on shore.
Stanza 6, line 2: That, on her lips, the meanest fly

Poems (1786), 84-85.

City Gazette   February 2, 1788

The EXILE.
[*Several of the thoughts in the following stanzas are taken from lord Bolingbroke's* Reflections on Exile, *written about the time of his banishment to France in 1715.*]

SINCE man may every region claim,
And nature's works are still the same
And we a part of her wide plan,
Tell me, what makes a banish'd man?

The favorite spot that gave us birth
We fondly call our mother earth;
And, hence, our vain distinction grow,
And man to man becomes a foe.

The Grecian sage,* as stories say,
When question'd where his country lay–
By reason taught, made no reply,
But rais'd his finger to the sky.

No region has on earth been known
But some of choice have made their own–
Your tears are not from reason's source
If *choice* can take the path of *force*.

"Alas (you cry) that is not all!
"My former friendships I recall;
"My house, my farm, my days, my nights,
"Scenes vanish'd now, and past delights!..–

Distance for *absence* you mistake–
Here days and nights their circuits make,
Still nature walks her beauteous round,
And friendship may, perhaps, be found.

If times grow dark, or wealth retires,
Let reason check your proud desires–
Misers had never gold to spare,
And loss of wealth is loss of care.

Thus, half unwilling, half resign'd,
Desponding why the noble mind–?
Think right–nor be the hour delay'd
That flies the sun to seek the shade.

Tho' injur'd, exil'd and alone
Boldly presume the world your own,
And then–deny it, if you can–
Death only makes the banish'd man.

---

* *Anaxagoras*

Daily Advertiser   September 1, 1790

The BANISHED MAN.

[A little before Lord Bolingbroke *was banished into France, he wrote an Essay upon* Exile.--*Some of his thoughts on that occasion are expressed in the following Stanzas.]*

Stanzas 1-2:   First two stanzas of the *City Gazette* text, with the following variants:
Stanza 1, line 2:   And nature is in all, the same,
Stanza 2, line 3:   And hence our vain distinctions grow

Stanza 3:   That friendship to all nations due,
And taught by reason to pursue,
That love, which should the world combine,
To country, why do we confine?

Stanzas 4-10:   Stanzas 3-9 of the *City Gazette* text, with the following variants:
Stanza 4, line 1: The Grecian Sage,* old Stories say,
     line 4: Inspir'd by heaven, made no reply
Stanza 7, line 3: Here nature walks her beauteous round,
Stanza 9, line 2: Desponding why the generous mind!
Stanza 10, line 2: Nobly presume the world your own,
     line 3: Convinc'd that, since the world began,

National Gazette   December 1, 1791

The BANISHED MAN.
[The following is founded upon some ideas of Lord Bolingbroke's, written a little before his sentence of exile into France.--see his Works.]

Substantively identical to the 1790 text, except for the following variants:

Stanza 4, line 1: Note deleted.
Stanza 7, line 4: And friendship may, perhaps, be found.

Poems (1795), 23-24.

City Gazette   February 9, 1788

The INVALID.
Written in 1785.

O'ER barren hills and desart plains
Lysander made a swift retreat,
Rode day and night through winds and rains
To fly the doom he fear'd to meet;
    Resolv'd, he left our cool sea-breeze
    In Pyrmont's springs to drown disease.

"And Oh! (he cry'd) in prime of days
"Must I with death my lodging keep,
"On yonder sun no longer gaze?
"Is nature blind, or fate asleep?
    "What have I done—what shall I say?--
    "To yonder springs let's haste away!"

Tho' death pursu'd with all his might—
The sickly youth, when he got there,
Drank grog all day, play'd cards all night,
Hoping the waters would repair
    His wasted carcase, doom'd to bring
    Destruction from this mineral spring.--

Ye sons of Bacchus, brisk and gay,
Blame not the health-restoring wave—
How can these streams prevent decay,
Or better streams from ruin save,
    When you mistake that tempting thing
    The *landlord's cask* for *Pyrmont's springs!*

Daily Advertiser   May 26, 1791

The INVALID.
[*Written at Charleston*, (South Carolina.)]

Stanza 1, line 2: Mambrino made a swift retreat,
         line 6: In Pacolet* Springs, to drown disease.

Stanza 2, line 6: To Pacolet Springs I'll haste away!"

Stanza 4, line 6: The *Landlord's casks*, for Pacolet Springs!

NOTE.

*Pacolet Springs, in the interior parts of South Carolina, to which, great numbers resort from Charleston, and other places, for the recovery of their health.

(First line of each stanza not indented.)

Poems (1795), 317.

Norfolk and Portsmouth Journal   May 28, 1788

The *Prayer* of *Orpheus*.
(By Mr. *Freneau*, of Philadelphia.)

Reprint of the 1786 text of the poem.

Poems (1786), 28-29.

City Gazette   June 23, 1788

MODERN DEVOTION.

TO church I went,
With good intent,
To hear Membrino preach and pray;
But objects there,
Too heavenly fair,
Turn'd eyes and hearts a different way.

Miss Patty's fan,
Miss Molly's man,
With powder'd hair and dimpled cheek;
Miss Delia's eyes,
That once made prize
Of Tomkin, with his hair so sleek.

Embroider'd gowns,
And play house tunes,
Estrang'd their hearts from heaven too wide;
I felt most odd,
This *House of God,*
Should be all flutter, pomp, and pride.

Now, pray be wise–
No prayers will rise
To heaven, where hearts are not sincere–
Leave pride at home,
Whene'er you come,
To pay to heaven your offerings *there*.

National Gazette   December 5, 1791

In each stanza, lines 3 and 6 begin at the margin, and lines 1, 2, 4, and 5 are indented.

Stanza 1, line 3: To hear *Sangrado* preach and pray;
line 5: Black, brown, and fair,
line 6: Turn'd eyes and heart a different way.

Stanza 2, line 6: Of *Fopling*, with his hair so sleek.

Stanza 3, line 3: Estrang'd all hearts from heav'n too wide:

Stanza 4, line 4: No church was made
        line 5: For Cupid's trade,
        line 6: Then why these arts of ogling here?

Stanza 5:
          Since time draws nigh
          When you and I
  At church must claim the sexton's care;
          Leave pride at home
          When'er you come
  To pay to Heaven your offerings--there.

Poems (1795), 100.

City Gazette   June 25, 1788

The virtue of Tobacco.

THIS Indian weed that once did grow
    On fair Virginia's fertile plain,
From whence it came again may go,
    To please the shepherd swain:
Of all the plants that Nature yields,
This, only this, shall shun my fields;

For while I smok'd, in thought profound,
    And wreath'd the spiral circle high,
My heart grew sick, my head flew round,
    And what can all this mean--said I--
Tobacco surely is design'd,
To poison and destroy mankind!

Unhappy they, whom choice or chance
    Incline to prize this bitter weed,
Of all our native western plants
    The least supportable indeed,
Which chills my heart & turns my head,
And sends me reeling home to bed.

Maryland Journal   January 2, 1789

On TOBACCO.

In each stanza, lines 1-4 begin at the margin, and lines 5 and 6 are indented.

Stanza 1, line 4:   To please some happier swain:--

Stanza 2:   In evil hour I first essay'd
              To smoke this vile forbidden leaf,
              When half asham'd, and half afraid,
              I touch'd and tasted--to my grief:
                 ADAM was hardly of my mind--
                 He took some plant of nobler kind:

Stanza 3:   Second stanza of the 1788 text, with the following variants:
    line 5:   Tobacco, surely was design'd

Stanza 4:   Third stanza of the 1788 text.

Baltimore, December 29, 1788

Daily Advertiser   July 31, 1790

Substantively identical to the *Maryland Journal* text, except for the following variants:

Stanza 1:   lines 1,2,3,5, and 6 begin at margin; line 4 indented. (Remainder of poem laid out as in the *Maryland Journal*.)

Stanza 2, line 2:   To chew this vile forbidden leaf,
         line 5:   Ah me! the more it was forbid,
         line 6:   The more I wish'd to take a quid.

Stanza 3, line 1:   But when I smoak'd, in thought profound,
         line 2:   And rais'd the spiral circle high,

Stanza 5, line 4:   The most contemptible indeed,
         line 5:   That chills my heart & turns my head,

National Gazette   November 7, 1791

Lines written on a paper of TOBACCO.

Substantively identical to the *Daily Advertiser* text, except for the following variants:

Stanza 1, lines 1-4 begin at margin; lines 5 and 6 indented.
       line 6:   This, least belov'd, shall shun my fields.

Stanza 2, line 5:   Ah me! the more I was forbid

Stanza 3, line 4:   My heart grew sick, my head turn'd round–

Stanza 4, line 1:   Unhappy they, whom choice, or fate
       line 3:   Perpetual source of female hate--
       line 4:   On which no beast, but man, will feed--

Poems (1795), 125.

City Gazette   March 28, 1739

Reflections on Credit.

Allur'd by *trust*, from shop to shop I ran,
Gaz'd at the windows deck'd with gaudy geer;
Muslins and lawns and laces, papers, books,
Too tempting to the eye! Much did I talk
With that thrice happy wight, who daily stands
Musing behind the counter–all his aim
To catch the pence of lady or of squire.
Most things I bought, but always sigh'd for more;
I bought indeed! but not one ounce of wit;
Mark that, and mark it down to my confusion!
O credit, credit–what a cheat art thou!
I paid no cash–'twas noted for a crime
By that recording hand, which *waste book* keeps;
Nor that alone, but cruelly transfers

To *journal, ledger,* and the Lord knows what.
    Away I went, my buyings safely stow'd,
Whether on negro's head, or dray, no matter.
Sweet pass'd the joyous months that interven'd,
While yet the days of grace ran smoothly on,
While yet no 'prentice boys approach'd my door,
With lectures short—but serious as the grave,
Preaching up mournful truths from beardless chin.
    But *Pay-day* came at last, and with it brought
Unnumber'd plagues, and cares, and doubts, and fears,
And grunts, and growls, and grumblings without end,
And quirks, and quibbles, lies & subterfuges,
Billets and notes with compliments cut short;
Ay, such as scarcely said—*your humble servant.*
    In short, (to end my melancholy story)
If there be men on earth that should be lov'd,
(And such there are, who doubts or dares deny)
They must be such as take delight in *trusting,*
But never look for pay or retribution.

Massachusetts Centinel   April 18, 1789

Stanza 2, line 2: Whether on children's head, or wife, no matter.

Daily Advertiser   May 27, 1789

Substantively identical to the *City Gazette* text, but stanza division is altered:

Stanza 1:   First 7 lines of the *City Gazette* text.
Stanza 2:   Lines 8-15 of the *City Gazette* text; first line indented.
Stanza 3:   Second stanza of the *City Gazette* text.
Stanza 4:   Third stanza of the *City Gazette* text.
Stanza 5:   Fourth stanza of the *City Gazette* text.
(Double space between stanzas.)

Poems and Variants 329

Daily Advertiser August 23, 1790

Orator SKIP's *Apology.*

Stanza 1: First stanza of the 1789 *Daily Advertiser* text, with the following variants:
line 3: Muslins, and lawns, and broadcloths; paper, books,
line 4: Silk hose, the finest from Britannia's looms,
line 5: line 4 of the 1789 text.
line 6: With that thrice happy wight who constant stands
lines 7 and 8: lines 6 and 7 of the 1789 text.

Stanza 2: Second stanza of the 1789 *Daily Advertiser* text.

Stanza 3: Third stanza of the 1789 *Daily Advertiser* text, with the following variants:
line 4: While yet the busy hours ran smoothly on,

Stanza 4: Fourth stanza of the 1789 *Daily Advertiser* text. (Single space between stanzas 3 and 4, although first line of stanza 4 is indented.)

Stanza 5: Whene'er I walk'd the streets I found no rest,
And rather would have met (horn'd, tail'd, and hooff'd)
Old Satan's self than fac'd one creditor!
The knocker had no interval of pause,
And every man that came--came with a dun,
And saucy looks, and stiff impertinence,
And heavy lowering eye that spoke no good!
What could I more--?--I bundled up my duds,
Pull'd to the door, that stood upon a jar,
Beneath the threshold lodg'd the landlord's key,
And, at the hour when ghosts are said to walk,
March'd off--and left even Master Snip unpaid!

Stanza 6: Blame me, ye men of dull philosophy,
That fear not sheriffs, constables, or writs--
Blame me who will--I relish not a jail,
And be my trotters in what plight they may,
Even tho' my gallygaskins were unsoal'd
Still should they save me from those damn'd retreats,

> Where *want of spirit* keeps the prisoner fast,
> And wretches pine, and harpies turn the key.

Signature: ARISTOPHANES.
Aug. 21.

National Gazette   December 8, 1791

The DEBTOR's SOLILOQUY.

Stanza 1:   First stanza of the 1790 version, with the following variants:
line 3: Muslins, and lawns, and laces; papers, books,
line 4: And cloths, the finest from Britannia's looms

Stanza 2:   Second stanza of the 1790 version.

Stanza 3:   Third stanza of the 1790 version, with the following variants:
line 4: While yet the busy hours ran sweetly on,

Stanza 4:   Fourth stanza of the 1790 text. (Double space between stanzas 3 and 4.)

Stanza 5:   Fifth stanza of the 1790 version, with the following variants:
line 7: And heavy lowering brow, that spoke no good!
line 10: Beneath the threshold laid the landlord's key.

Stanza 6:   Sixth stanza of the 1790 version, with the following variants:
line 1: Blame me, ye men of cold philosophy,
line 5: (Even tho' my *galley-gaskins* were unsoal'd)
line 7: Still should they bear me from those dull retreats

Philadelphia, December 6, 1791.

Poems (1795), 27-28.

City Gazette   April 10, 1789

To John Dickinson, Esquire.

Thus, while new laws our stubborn states reclaim,
And most for pensions, some for honors aim;
You, who first aim'd a shaft at George's crown,
And mark'd the path to conquest and renown,
While from the vain, the lofty, and the proud,
Retiring to your groves, you shun the croud,
Can toils like yours in dull oblivion end,
Columbia's patriot and her earliest friend?

Blest--doubly blest--from public toils retir'd,
Where public virtue all your bosom fir'd;
Your life's best days in studious labors pass'd
Your own *reflections* are your crown at last:
When all things fail, the soul must rest on these!--
May heaven restore you to your favorite trees;
And calm content, best lot to man assign'd,
Be heaven's reward to your superior mind.

Since her base projects you beheld with pain,
And early doom'd an end to Britain's reign;
When rising nobly in a generous cause
You prov'd the poison to imported laws.
O *Dickinson!* what genuine glory shines
From each bright page of your immortal lines;*--
Those lines, the check of tyrants and of knaves,
Gave birth to *heroes,* who had else been slaves;
Who, taught by you, denied a monarch's sway,
And if they brought him low--you plann'd the way.

Tho in this glare of day you take no part,
Still must your conduct warm each grateful heart;
What tho' you shun the patriot vain and loud,
While hosts neglect, that once to merit bow'd;

---

* *Farmer's Letters.*

Shun those gay scenes where *recent* laurels grow,
The mad procession and the painted show;
In days to come, when pomp and pride resign,
Who would not change his name and fate for thine.
In fame's fair fields such well-earn'd honors share,
But Dickinson confess unrivall'd there.

Poems (1795), 324.

Daily Advertiser   April 15, 1789

LINES written at SEA.
Addressed to Miss------, New Jersey.

DRIVEN from my course by cold December's gale,
As near your shores I spread my weary sail,
From bar to bar, from cape to cape I stray,
From you still absent, still too far away:
What shall repay me for those nights of pain,
And weeks of absence on this restless main;
Where every dream recalls that desart shade,
Where once, dear Margery, once with you I stray'd,
And fondly talk'd, and counted every tree,
And minutes, ages, when remov'd from thee?

    Blest be the man, who fear beneath him cast,
From his broad decks first rear'd the tapering mast,
And catching life and motion from the breeze,
Stretch'd his white canvass o'er a waste of seas,
And taught some Swain whom distance doom'd to mourn,
His absent charmer–taught a quick return;
He, homeward borne by favoring gales, might find,
Remembrance welcome to his anxious mind,
And grateful vows, and generous thanks might pay,
To *Him*, that fill'd the sail, and smooth'd the way.

>   To me, alas! the heaven's less favoring prove,
> Each day more distant from the nymph I love--
> Whose sun-burn't skin, and brightly beaming eyes,
> More than molasses--more than life I prize--
> Here wint'ry sun's their scanty light restrain,
> Here stars obscur'd, shoot glimmering o'er the main,
> Here boisterous gales the rapid gulph controul,
> Here bursting breakers near my *Argo* roll,
> And cloudy, sullen *Hatteras,* restless raves,
> Scorns all repose, and swells his weight of waves.
>
>   Now, while the winds their wonted aid deny,
> For other shores and other streams I try,
> Where nature still her magic scenes may shew--
> Alas!--not welcome, since not known by you--
> Yet dreams of thee shall sweeten my repose,
> Thy full, broad face, and long projecting nose;
> That nose, by which such numbers are undone,
> Such hearts are lost, and I myself was won--
> That nose, for which a thousand lovers sigh,
> That nose, which while it lives, shall never die:--
>
> One dream of *that* shall all my woes repay,
> Turn storms to calms, and night transform to day.

December 10th, 1788.

City Gazette   April 16, 1789

A YANKEE EPISTLE.
Written at sea, December, 1788.
Addressed to Miss ------.

Substantively identical to the *Daily Advertiser* text, except for the following variants:

Printed as one 42-line stanza--no lines indented.

line 2:	When near your shores, I reef'd my wearied sail;
line 3:	From bar to bar, from cape to cape I roam,
line 4:	From you still absent, still detain'd from home

line 5:   What shall repay me for these nights of pain
line 7:   Where every dream recalls that long lost shade
line 38: Such hearts are lost, and I--even I--was won--
line 40: That nose, which, whilst it lives, shall never die--
Date deleted.

Daily Advertiser   February 10, 1791

POLYDORE to AMANDA.
[Written at Sea.]

Stanza 1:
LAMP of the Pilot's hope, the wanderer's dream,
Far glimmering o'er the wave, we saw thy beam!
Forc'd from your aid by cold December's gale,
As near those coasts I reef'd the wearied sail,
From bar to bar, from cape to cape I roam,
From you still absent, still too far from home:
What shall repay me for these nights of pain
And weeks of absence on this restless main,
Where every dream recalls that charming shade,
Where once *Amanda,* once with you I stray'd,
And fondly talk'd, and counted every tree,
And minutes, ages, when remov'd from thee.

Stanza 2:
What sad mistake this wandering fancy drew
To quit my native shores, this woods, and you,
When safely anchor'd on that winding stream,
When you were all my care, and all my theme,
There, pensive, loitering still from day to day,
The pilot wonder'd at my strange delay,
Musing, beheld the western winds prevail,
Nor once surmis'd that love detain'd the sail.

Stanza 3: Second stanza of the 1789 version with the following variants:
line 5: And taught some swain, whom absence doom'd to mourn
line 6: His distant Fair One, taught a quick return,

Stanza 4:
To me, alas! the heavens less favouring prove,
Each day returning, finds a new remove;

Sorrowing I reef the sail, while slowly creeps
The dull Columbia o'er a length of deeps,
Her northern course no favoring breeze befriends,
Hail, storm, and lightning on her path attends;
Here wint'ry suns their scanty light restrain,
Stars dimly glow, and boding birds complain,
Here boisterous gales, the rapid *gulph* controul,
Unpitying breakers near my Argo roll,
Here cloudy, sullen Hatteras, restless, raves,
Scorns all repose and swells his weight of waves;
Here drown'd so late (sad cause of many a tear)
Amyntor floats upon his wat'ry bier,
By bursting seas to horrid distance toss'd,
Thou *Palinurus,* in these depths wer't lost,
When torn by waves, and conquer'd by the blast,
Art strove in vain—and ruin siez'd the mast!

Stanza 5:   Now, while the winds their wonted aid deny,
For other ports, from day to day we try;
Strive all I can to gain th'unwilling shore,
Dream still of you—the faithful chart explore,
Seek other groves in happier climates plac'd,
Untouch'd their bloom, and not one flower defac'd:

Stanza 6:   Did Nature there a heaven of pleasures shew,
Could they be welcome, if not shar'd with you?
Lost are my toils, my longing hopes are vain,
Yet midst these ills permit me to complain,
And half regret, that finding fortune fail,
I left the Muses to direct the sail;
Unmov'd amidst this elemental fray
Let me once more the Muse's art essay,
Once more amidst these scenes of Neptune's strife,
Catch at her forms, and mould them into life,
By Fancy's aid to unseen coasts repair,
And fondly dwell on past transactions there.

February 9.

Poems (1795), 181-82.

Daily Advertiser   November 14, 1789

The Pilot of Hatteras
By Capt. P. FRENEAU.

I.

IN fathoms four the anchor gone,
    While here we furl the sail,
No longer vainly labo'ring on
    Against the western gale;
Whilst here thy bare and barren cliffs,
    O *Hatteras*, I survey,
And shallow grounds and broken reefs,
    What shall provoke my lay?

II.

The PILOT comes--from yonder sands,
    He shoves his barque so frail,
And, hurrying on, with busy hands,
    Employs both oar and sail.
Beneath this rude unsettled sky
    Content to pass his years,
No other shores delight his eye
    No prowling foe he fears.

III.

For nature here, to make him blest
    No quiet harbor plann'd,
And penury, his constant guest,
    Restrains the pirate band:
His hopes are all in yonder flock
    And some few hives of Bees,
Except when bound for *O Cracock*
    The gliding barque he sees.

IV.

His *Marian* then he leaves with grief
    And spreads his tottering sails,
While waving high her hankerchief
    Her Commodore she hails--
She grieves and fears to see no more
    The sail that now forsakes,
From Hatteras sands to banks of *Core*
    Such tedious journeys makes!

V.

Sad Nymph, thy sighs are half in vain,
    Restrain those idle fears--
Can you, that should relieve his pain,
    Thus kill him with your tears!
Can absence thus beget regard,
    Or does it only seem?--
He comes to see a wandering Bard
    That aims for *Ashley's* stream.

VI.

'Till eastern gales once more awake
    No danger shall be near;
On yonder shoals the billows break,
    But leave us quiet here--
With gills of rum and pints of gin,
    Again your lad shall land,
And drink--'till he and all his kin
    Can neither sit nor stand.

Massachusetts Centinel   November 25, 1789

[*Daily Advertiser* text appears with the following note:

> This celebrated Genius, the Peter Pindar of America, is now a Master of a Packet, which runs between New-York, Philadelphia and Charleston. His tuneful numbers, during the war, did much to soften the disagreeable sensations which

a state of warfare so generally occasions.)

City Gazette   December 1, 1789

Substantively identical to the *Daily Advertiser* text, except for the following variants:

The PILOT of HATTERAS.
Written at the Cape, in June, 1788.

All lines begin at margin, and stanzas are unnumbered.

Stanza 1, line 1: IN fathoms five, the anchor gone,
line 2: While here thy bare and barren cliffs,
line 8: What shall inspire my lay!

Stanza 2, line 5: Beneath this wild, unsettled sky,
line 7: No other shores allure his eye,
line 8: No plundering foe he fears.

Stanza 3, line 3: And poverty his constant guest,
line 7: Unless when bound for Ocracock,
line 8: Some gliding barque he sees:

Stanza 4, line 1: His Marian then he quits with grief,

Stanza 5, line 1: Fond nymph, your sighs are half invain,
line 2: Forgo those idle fears;
line 7: He comes to meet a wandering bard,

National Gazette   January 16, 1792

Substantively identical to the *Daily Advertiser* text, except for the following variants:

The PILOT of HATTERAS.*

All lines begin at margin, and stanzas are unnumbered.

Stanza 1: First stanza of the *Daily Advertiser* text, with the fol-

	lowing variants: line 1: IN fathoms five, the anchor gone, line 5: While here thy bare and barren cliffs, line 8: What shall amuse my stay!
Stanza 2:	Second stanza of the *Daily Advertiser* text, with the following variants: line 6: Condemn'd to pass his years, line 8: No foe alarms his fears.
Stanza 3:	In depths of woods his hut he builds Where ocean round him flows, And blooming in the barren wilds His simple garden grows. His wedded nymph, of sallow hue, No mingled colours grace-- For her he toils, to her is true, The captive of her face.
Stanza 4:	Third stanza of the *Daily Advertiser* text, with the following variants: line 1: Kind nature here, to make him blest line 3: And poverty--his constant guest, line 6: Or some few hives of bees line 7: Except, when bound for *Ocracock*+ line 8: Some gliding barque he sees;
Stanza 5:	Fourth stanza of the *Daily Advertiser* text, with the following variants: line 1: His *Marian* then he quits with grief line 8: Such tedious journies takes!
Stanza 6:	Fifth stanza of the *Daily Advertiser* text, with the following variants: line 1: Fond nymph! your sighs are breath'd in vain; line 7: He comes to meet a wandering bard, line 8: That seeks fair *Ashley's* stream.
Stanza 7:	Tho' disappointed in his views, Not joyless will we part; Nor shall the god of mirth refuse The balsam of the heart:

No niggard key shall lock up *joy*;
I'll give him half my store,
Will he but half his skill employ
To guard us from your shore.

Stanza 8: Sixth stanza of the *Daily Advertiser* text, with the following variants:
  line 1: When eastern gales once more awake
  line 2: What dangers will be near!--
  line 3: Alas! I see the billows break,
  line 4: Alas! why came I here--
  line 5: With quarts of rum and pints of gin
  line 6: Go, pilot, seek the land,
  line 7: And drink, till you and all your kin,
Signature:: SINBAT.

* Written off the Cape, July, *1789*, on a voyage to South-Carolina, being detained sixteen days with strong gales a-head.

+ All vessels from the northward that pass within the Hatteras shoals, bound for Newbern, and other places on Pamlico sound, commonly, in favourable weather, take a Hatteras pilot, to conduct them over the dangerous bar of Ocracock, 11 leagues W.S.W. of the Cape.

City Gazette   November 28, 1789

A view of COLUMBIA.

FROM Charleston's gay abode,
O'er many a tiresome road,
Lysander, musing, takes his way,
Through dark and dismal groves,
Where the sad turtle loves
To spend the night and kill the day.

In an obscure retreat,
I see Lysander greet,
The barren soil and dreary town,

Whose streets and buildings gay
Shall long in embrio lay,
Columbia, barren of renown.

What shall amuse him there?--
Not even a house of prayer,
With gilded spire, attempts to rise;
No nymphs in gaudy trim
Shall there be seen by him--
No music, sermons, balls, or oyster-pies.

Dull melancholy streams,
Dutch politics and schemes,
Owls screeching in the empty street,
Wolves howling at their doors,
Bears breaking into stores--
These make the picture of the town complete.

Daily Advertiser   December 30, 1789

This poem, and the "Procession to Columbia" (*City Gazette*, December 14, 1789) are reprinted, with the following introduction:

> The Seat of Government in South-Carolina, is removed by Act of Assembly, from Charleston to Columbia, a dismal place in the center of that state, consisting of only town houses. This removal is by many in Carolina, considered as premature, and amongst other animadversions, has occasioned the two following poetical pieces, which, from several circumstances, we conclude to have been written by Mr. *Freneau*.

Text identical to that in the *City Gazette*, except date appears under the final line:

Charleston, Nov. 28

Poems (1795), 320.

City Gazette   November 30, 1789

To HARRIOT.

The hermit's wish, a cell, be mine,
In sylvan shades to find repose:
To please the eye--that task be thine--
And hourly kill a thousand beaus,
    Whose easy charms, so like your own,
    With jealousy you gaze upon.

You ask'd me, Harriot, how I came
To shun the wild tempestuous deep,
And disappointing Neptune's aim,
On his cold bosom shun long sleep;--
    'Twas chance, 'twas luck--I scarce can tell
    What genius play'd my cards so well--

Yes! Neptune frown'd, so heaven decreed,
Yet life might be preserv'd at least,
Since cruel must he be, indeed,
Who robs a church and kills the priest:--
    Then, Harriot, now some pity shew,
    Nor be the seas more kind than you.

Daily Advertiser   January 5, 1789

To HARRIOT.
By Capt. P. Freneau.

Identical to the *City Gazette* text.

Poems (1795), 365.

City Gazette   December 8, 1789

Lines formerly written in a tavern at *Log Town*, in the pine-barrens of New-Jersey.

THROUGH sandy wastes and floods of rain
    To this dejected place I came,
Where swarthy nymphs, in ragged gowns,
    From pine-knots catch their evening flame.

Thou town of logs, (so justly call'd)
    In thee who halts at evening's close,
Not dreams from Jove, but hosts of fleas
    Shall join to *sweeten* his repose.

Since here I pac'd on weary steed,
    Ah, blame me not, should I repine
That sprightly girl, nor social bed,
    Nor jovial glass this night is mine!

Jamaica, that inspires the mind,
    In these abodes no time has seen
To dart its genial influence found,
    To kindle wit and kill the spleen.

The squire of this disheartening inn
    Affords to none the generous bowl,
Displays no Bacchus on the sign
    To warm the heart and cheer the soul.

Dead cyder drawn from tilted cask,
    Lean poultry on his board display'd--
A *grace* that Indians scarce would ask,
    Was all he *sung* and all he said.

A snivelling hag with snuffy rose
    Screech'd out a song to cheer my grief,
Her sons their dull adventures told,
    A shepherd each, and each a thief.

The horse that bore me on my way
    Around him cast a rueful eye
He look'd--and saw no manger near
    And hung his head, and seem to sigh.

At stump of pine, for want of stall,
    All night beneath a dripping tree
Not fed with oats, but swoln with wind
    And buckwheat straw) alone stood he--

May never weary pilgrim here
    (Unless for penance he's equipt)
Be forc'd to take his dull repast,
    Or doom'd to sleep where I have slept.

Daily Advertiser   February 19, 1790

LINES descriptive of a Tavern at *Log-Town*, a small Place in the Pine Barrens of *North-Carolina*.

Substantively identical to the *City Gazette* text, except for the following variants:

All lines begin at the margin.

Stanza 1:   First stanza of the *City Gazette* text, with the following variants:
    line 3:   Where swarthy nymphs in tatter'd gowns,
    line 4:   From pine-knots light their evening flame,

Stanza 2:   Where barren Pines, in close array,
    In mournful melody condole,
    Where no gay fabric meets the view,
    Nor painted board, nor Barber's pole!

Stanza 3:   The Landlord (goug'd in either eye)
    Here drains his bottle to the dregs,
    Or borrows Susan's pipe, while she
    Prepares the bacon and the eggs.

Stanza 4:   Second stanza of the *City Gazette* text.

Stanza 5: Third stanza of the *City Gazette* text.

Stanza 6: Fourth stanza of the *City Gazette* text, with the following variants:
line 1: Jamaica (foe to grief and care)

Stanza 7: Fifth stanza of the *City Gazette* text.

Stanza 8: Sixth stanza of the *City Gazette* text.

Stanza 9: Seventh stanza of the *City Gazette* text, with the following variants:
line 1: A scolding wife, with snuffy nose,
line 2: Screech'd out a song to ease my grief,
line 3: Her boys their dull adventures told--

Stanza 10: Eighth stanza of the *City Gazette* text, with the following variants:
line 4: And hung his head and seem'd to sigh.

Stanza 11: Ninth stanza of the *City Gazette* text, with the following variants:
line 3: (Not fed with oats, but fill'd with wind,

Stanza 12: Last stanza of the *City Gazette* text.
Signature: M.

Maryland Gazette   April 16, 1790

LINES *Descriptive of a Tavern at LOGTOWN,*
NORTH-CAROLINA.

Substantively identical to the *Daily Advertiser* text, except for the following variants:

Printed as one 48-line stanza.

Line 39: He look'd--and saw no manger nigh.

Massachusetts Centinel   April 7, 1790

Substantively identical to the *Daily Advertiser* text, except for the following variants:

Stanza 8, line 3:   A grace, that Indians scarce could ask--
Stanza 12, line 2: (Unless for penitence he's equipt)
          line 3: Be forc'd to take this vile repast,

Freeman's Journal   May 26, 1790

Substantively identical to the *Daily Advertiser* text, except for the following variants:

Lines descriptive of a Tavern in Logtown North-Carolina

In each stanza, lines 2 and 4 indented.
Stanza 2, line 3: Where no gay fabric meet the view,
Stanza 10, line 3: He look'd--and saw no manger nigh,

City Gazette   September 9, 1790

Lines on a *Tavern* in *Logtown,* (North Carolina)
By Captain *Freneau.*

Substantively identical to the *Daily Advertiser* text, except for the following variants:

In each stanza, lines 2 and 4 indented.
Stanzas 1-9: First nine stanzas of the *Daily Advertiser* text, with the following variants:
Stanza 3, line 3: Or borrows Susan's pipe, whilst she
Stanza 4, line 3: Not dreams of Jove, but hosts of fleas
Stanza 7, line 3: Displays no Bacchus on his sign,

Stanza 10: With scraps of songs and smutty words
              Each lodger here adorns the walls:
           The bawdy muse no pencil gives,
              The *coal* her mean idea scrawls.

Stanza 11: In murmuring streams no chrystal wave
              To cheer the wretched hamlet flows,
      But frowning to the distant bog
              Rosanna with the pitcher goes.

Stanza 12: At dusk of eve the scanty treat
              Was plac'd on board of rugged pine,
      Each gaping, gaz'd to see me eat
             While round me lay the grunting swine.

Stanzas 13-15:   Stanzas 10-12 of the *Daily Advertiser* text.

New York Journal   September 17, 1791

Substantively identical to the 1790 *City Gazette* text, except for the following variants:

STANZAS,
Written at leaving an Inn, in North-Carolina--
By PHILIP FRENEAU.

All lines begin at the margin.

Stanzas 1-9: First nine stanzas of the *City Gazette* text, with the following variants:
Stanza 1, line 3: Where swarthy nymphs, in ragged gowns,
        line 4: From pine-knots catch their evening flame.

Stanza 2, line 1: Where barren oaks, in close array,
        line 3: Where no gay fabric meets the eye,

Stanza 3, line 3: Or borrows *Susan's* pipe, while she

Stanza 4, line 1: Thou town of hags (so justly call'd)
        line 3: Not dreams from Jove, but hosts of fleas

Stanza 5, line 4: Nor jovial fleas, this night is mine!

Stanza 6, line 1: *Jamaica*, that inspires the soul;

Stanza 8:   Dead cyder, drawn from tilted cask,
            Here lends to care no generous aid--
            Our salt box is a broken flask,
            Our table but a stone decay'd.

Stanza 9, line 1:   A snivelling hag, with snuffy nose,
         line 2:   Draws out a song, to ease my grief;
         line 3:   Two lads, their dull adventures tell,

Stanza 10: Dame justice here in rigour reigns;
            All have on all a griping paw--
            Who'er with them a bargain makes,
            Scheme as he will--it ends in *law*.

Stanzas 11-16: Tenth to fifteenth stanzas of the *City Gazette* text,
            with the following variants:
Stanza 11, line 2: Each ledger here adorns the walls:
         line 4: A *coal* her mean idea scrawls.

Stanza 12, line 2: To cheer the wretched hamlet, flow,
         line 4: *Hosanna* with the pitcher goes.

Stanza 13, line 1: At close of eve, the scanty treat,

Stanza 16, line 4: Be forc'd to take his dull repast,

Boston *Argus*   September 30, 1791

Substantively identical to the *New York Journal* text, except for the following variants:

Stanza 11, line 2: Each lodger here adorns the walls:
         line 3: The *coal* her main idea scrawls.

Stanza 13, line 1: At close of eve, the scanty treat,

Stanza 15, line 2: A night beneath a dripping tree

Stanza 16, line 1: May never weary pilgrims here

National Gazette   November 7, 1791[1]

LOG TOWN TAVERN.

[The following poem was composed some years ago at a small Inn, situated in a remote and desart part of Carolina. A very incorrect copy having appeared in a Northern Newspaper, the subsequent Stanzas are now published as written by the Author.]

THROUGH sandy wastes and floods of rain
To this dejected place I came,
Where swarthy nymphs, in tatter'd gowns
From pine-knots light their evening flame.

Where barren oaks in close array,
With mournful melody, condole,
Where no gay fabric meets the eye,
No painted board, no barbers pole.

Thou town of Logs!--so justly call'd
In thee who halts at evening's close
Not dreams from Jove, but hosts of fleas
Shall join, to sweeten his repose.

Since here I pac'd on weary steed,
Ah! blame me not, should I repine
That sprightly girl, nor social bed,
Nor jovial glass, this night is mine.

---

[1] The "incorrect copy" referred to in the introductory note to this text is probably the *New York Journal* text, with its apparent corruptions, (i.e. "town of hags," "jovial fleas"). The New York text was reprinted in papers from New Jersey to Boston, and, however corrupt, does contain the first appearance of a stanza later included in the text collected by Freneau, indicating that the poet himself contributed the *New York Journal* text. Most of the earlier texts cited above also contain variants that are incorporated into the first collected text. Since the *National Gazette* text contains variants from several earlier texts, as well as new variants, the entire text is duplicated here.

The Landlord, goug'd in *either* eye
Here drains his bottle to the dregs,
Or borrows Susan's pipe, while she
Prepares the bacon, and the eggs.

JAMAICA, that inspires the soul
In these abodes no time has seen
To dart its general influence round,
To kindle wit, and kill the spleen.

The squire of this disheartening inn
Affords to none the generous bowl,
Displays no BACCHUS on the sign,
To warm the heart and cheer the soul.

To cider drawn from tilted cask,
While *some* their fond attention paid,
He griev'd to see the empty flask,
Its substance gone, its strength decay'd.

A wandering hag, in dismal notes
Screech'd out a song, to ease my grief;
Two boors their dull adventures told,
A shepherd each, and each a thief.

Dame justice here in rigour reigns,
All have on all the griping paw;
Who'er with them a bargain makes,
Scheme as he will, it ends in *law*.

With scraps of songs and smutty words,
Each lodger here adorns the walls--
The wanton muse no pencil gives,
The coal her mean idea scrawls.

In murmuring streams no chrystal wave
To cheer the wretched hamlet flows,
But frowning to the distant bog
Susanna, with the pitcher, goes.

At dusk of eve, the tardy treat
Was plac'd on board of knotty pine;
Each gaping, gaz'd to see me eat,
While round me lay the snoring swine.

Unblest be she, whose heavy hand
Before me plac'd the mouldy *pone*;*
May she ne'er meet the joyous kiss,
Condemn'd to fret and sleep alone.--

The horse, that bore me on my way
Around him cast a rueful eye,
He look'd--and saw no manger near,
And hung his head, and seem'd to sigh.

At stump of pine, for want of stall,
All night beneath a dripping tree,
Not fed with oats, but fill'd with wind,
And husks, and blades, alone stood he.

Discourag'd at so vile a treat,
Yet pleas'd to see the early dawn
In haste we left this dismal place
Nor stay'd to drink their dear YOPPON.+

May never weary pilgrim here,
Unless for penance he's equipt,
Be forc'd to pass his tedious night,
Or, doom'd to sleep where I have slept.

* A composition of Indian meal and water, baked before the fire.

+ A shrub leaf frequently used in some parts of Carolina, as a substitute for tea.

Daily Advertiser   November 12, 1791

National Gazette text, with the following variants:

Stanza 3, line 3: Not dreams from Jove, but hosts of flies
Stanza 13, line 4: While round me lay the snoring swine.

Poems (1795), 301-03.

City Gazette   December 10, 1789

(Untitled.)

As far from home to southern isles
Thro' lonely seas I held my way
A songster of the feather'd kind
Approach'd with golden plumage gay.

To see the bird forlorn and lost
What bosom but must heave a sigh,
Thus wandering from her native coast
Condemn'd in foreign climes to die.

"Weak traveller o'er a stormy deep,
"What cruel tempest has compell'd
"To leave so far the shady grove
"And wander on a watry field.

"Ah why amidst some flowery mead
"Could you not stay, where late you play'd,
"But thus forsake the sylvan scene,
"Such fragrant flowers, so fine a shade?

"In vain you spread your weary wings
"To shun the dismal gulph below;
"Our barque must be your only hope
"But *man* you justly deem your foe.--

"Now hovering near, you stoop to lodge
"Where yonder lofty canvas swells;
"Again you fly--you scorn our aid,
"And rather trust the ruffian gales.

"But nature tires--your toils are vain!
"Could you on bolder pinions rise
"Than eagles have, for days to come
"Your prospects are but sea and skies."--

Again she comes--again she lights
And casts a pensive eye below:
"Sweet creature, trust the traitor *man*
"And take the help that I bestow."

Down to my side with circling flight
She flew, and perch'd, and linger'd there;
But, worn with toil, she droop'd her wings,
And life dissolv'd in empty air.

Daily Advertiser   February 22, 1790

The BIRD *at* SEA.

Substantively identical to the *City Gazette* text, except for the following variants:

Stanza 1, line 1:   As southward bound to southern isles
          line 2:   O'er lonely seas I held my way,

Stanza 2:   Second stanza of the *City Gazette* text.

Stanza 3, line 1:   "Sad pilgrim on a savage waste
          line 4:   And wander o'er a watry field.

Stanza 4:   Not such a dismal swelling scene,
            (Dread Neptune's wild unsocial sea,)
            But gentler streams and groves of green,
            Dear wandering bird, were made for thee.

Stanza 5:   Fourth stanza of the *City Gazette* text, with the following variants:
            line 3:   But thus forsake the sylvan haunt,

Stanza 6:   Fifth stanza of the *City Gazette* text, with the following variants:
            line 2:   To shun the gaping gulph below,

Stanza 7:   Sixth stanza of the *City Gazette* text, with the following variants:
            line 3:   Again you fly--refuse our aid,

Stanzas 8-10: Seventh to ninth stanzas of the *City Gazette* text.
February 20.
Signature: E.

Poems (1795), 354-55.

City Gazette　　December 14, 1789

The *Procession* to COLUMBIA.

In life's dull round how often folks are cross'd,
Their projects spoil'd, their sayings misapplied,
Some friends in *woods,* and some in oceans lost;
Some doom'd to walk on foot, while others ride?

But now—let parsons moralize in verse,
While I to yonder caravan attend
Which creeping on, like some slow moving herse
With tardy footsteps seeks its journey's end,

Bound for Columbia!--sad, disheart'ning town!
When thou art nam'd, how many a nymph will sigh—
Sigh, lest her lover should return a clown
With grizzly homespun coat, long beard and pumpkin pye.

This caravan with wondrous geer is stow'd—
All sorts of furniture, excepting cradles;
Old records--salted fish--make up their load,
With kegs of brandy, frying pans, and ladles.

A pensive printer in a one horse-chair,
(Dragg'd slowly on by sullen, sleepy steed)
With some ill fated 'squires, brings up the rear
Contriving future news--for folks to read.

To guard the whole, a trusty knight appears,
With chosen men, to keep the wolves in awe—
Ram home the cartridge, boys--and scorn all fears
Of ruffian's club, bear's hug, or panther's claw.

Daily Advertiser   December 30, 1789

(Appears under the same introductory note as "A View of Columbia;" See *City Gazette,* November 28, 1789.)

Substantively identical to the *City Gazette* text, except for the following variants:

Stanza 2:   Eight line stanza, composed of stanzas 2 and 3 of the *City Gazette* text.

Stanzas 3-5:   Stanzas 4-6 of the *City Gazette* text, with the following variants:

Stanza 3, line 2:   All sorts of moveables, excepting cradles;

Poems (1795), 321.

Daily Advertiser   January 2, 1790

STANZAS
Written at St. Catharine's, an Island
upon the coast of GEORGIA, Nov. 1789.
By Capt. FRENEAU.

HE that would wish to sport awhile;
In forests green and gay,
From Charleston bar to Catharine's isle
Might sigh to find the way;
What scenes on every side appear,
What pleasure strikes the mind,
From folly's train thus wandering far
To leave the world behind.

The music of these savage groves
In simple accents swells,
And freely here their sylvan loves
The feather'd nation tells;

The panting deer thro' mingled shades
Of oak for ever green,
The vegetable world invades
That skirts the wat'ry scene.

Thou sailor, now exploring far
The broad atlantic wave,
Crown all your canvas, gallant tar,
Since Neptune never gave
On barren seas so fine a view
As here allures the eye;
Gay verdant scenes that nature drew
In colors from the sky.

Ye western winds, awhile delay
To swell th'expecting sail,
Who would not here a hermit stray
In yonder fragrant vale,
Could he engage what few can find,
That coy unwilling guest--
(All avarice banish'd from the mind)
Contentment in the breast.

National Gazette   February 16, 1792

Lines written at St. Catharine's Island, on the coast of Georgia, Nov. 1789

No stanza divisions--poem appears as one 32-line stanza.
Line 1: HE that would wish to rove a while
line 6: What rapture strikes the mind,
line 22: As here delights the eye,
Signature: SINBAT.

Poems (1795), 358-59.

City Gazette   January 8, 1790

On the present situation of the theatre in Charleston.

HEALTH to the muse!--and fill the glass--
Heaven grant her soon some better place
Than earthen floor and fabric mean,
Where disappointment shades the scene.

There as I came, by rumour led,
I sigh'd, and almost wish'd her dead,
Her visage shin'd with many a tear,
No *Hallam* and no *Harry* here!

But what could all their art attain?--
When pointed laws the stage restrain
The prudent muse obedience pays
To rural 'squires that damn all plays.

Like thieves they hang beyond the town
They shove her off, to please the gown,
Tho' Rome and Athens own'd it true
The stage might mend our morals too.

See, Mopsus all the evening sits
O'er bottled beer that drowns his wits:
Were plays allow'd, he might at least
Blush, and forget to act the beast.

See Marcia (now from guardian free)
Retailing scandal o'er her tea:--
Might she not come, nor danger fear
From *Hamlet's* sigh or *Juliet's* tear?

The world but acts the player's part, *
(So says the motto of their art)
That world in vice great lengths is gone
That dreads to see its picture drawn.

---

* *Totus mundus agit Histrionem.*

Mere vulgar actors ne'er can please,
(The streets afford enough of these)
And what can wit or beauty gain
When sleepy dullness joins their train?

A *state* betrays a homely taste.
By which the stage is thus disgrac'd,
Where, dress'd in all the flowers of speech,
True honour might her precepts teach.

Let but a dancing bear arrive,
A pig that counts you *four* or *five*,
And Cato, with his moral strain
Shall strive to mend the town in vain.

Daily Advertiser   January 8, 1790

The following STANZAS were lately written in Charleston, (S.C.) on the situation of their Theatre--all diversions of the Stage being prohibited by law, within the bounds of the city.

Substantively identical to the *City Gazette* text, except for the following variants:

First line of each stanza idented:

Stanza 1, line 1: HEALTH to the Muse!--she wants it much--
         line 2: Sickly, lame, and limping on a crutch
         line 3: From earthen floor, in fabric mean,
         line 4: She meets us with a shocking Scene.

Stanza 2, line 1: There as I came, with caution tread,
         line 3: Her visage bath'd with many a tear--

Stanza 3, line 1: But what could all their art attain
         line 3: Wisely the Muse obedience pays
         line 4: To rigid laws that damn all plays

Stanza 4, line 2: They pack her off, to please the gown,

Stanza 5: Seventh stanza of the *City Gazette* text, with the following variants:
line 3: That world in vice, great lengths has gone,

Stanza 6: Eighth stanza of the *City Gazette* text, with the following variants:
line 2: Not in parentheses.
line 3: And what can *wit* and *beauty* gain

Stanza 7: Ninth stanza of the *City Gazette* text, with the following variants:
line 3: Where dress'd in all the charms of speech,
line 4: True virtue might her precepts teach.

Stanza 8: Last stanza of the *City Gazette* text, with the following variants:
line 4: Shall strive to mend the world--IN VAIN.

(Stanzas 5 and 6 of the *City Gazette* text deleted.)

National Gazette   November 21, 1791

The DISTREST THEATRE.

[The amusements of the Theatre were some time since prohibited within the limits of the city of Charleston, by act of the legislature of the state of South-Carolina. In obedience to this act, all subsequent Dramatic exhibitions were removed to an obscure building in the city Liberties, called *Harmony Hall*. The following stanzas owe their origin to the above edict.]

Substantively identical to the *City Gazette* text, except for the following variants:

Stanza 2, line 3: Her visage stain'd with many a tear,
line 4: No *Hallam* and no *Wignell* here!

Stanza 3, line 4: To sleepy 'squires, that damn all plays.

Stanza 5, line 4: Blush--and no longer act the beast.

Stanza 7, line 4: That fears to see its picture drawn.

Stanza 8, line 2; The streets supply enough of these;

Stanza 9, line 4: True virtue might her precepts teach.

Poems (1795), 351-52.

City Gazette   January 15, 1790

Farmer DOBBIN's *Complaint*

THREE daughters I have, and as prettily made,
As handsome as any you'll see,
And lovers they count, but I still am afraid
They always will hang upon me.

In writing of letters and talking of love
They are foolishly spending their time,
One gives them a ribbon, and one a new glove;
And thus they are passing their prime.

These bucks of the town--with their elegant coats
I'm sick of their horses and chairs:
They plunder my hay, and they pilfer my oats--
Am I keeping a tavern my dears?

This courting and courting, and never concluding,
Is nonsense, (I'm sorry to say)
Your kissing and playing is rather intruding
Unless you will-take them away.

Daily Advertiser   February 6, 1790

Farmer DOBBIN's *Complaint.*
By Capt. *Freneau.*

Substantively identical to the *City Gazette* text, except

for the following variants:

Stanza 1, line 3: And lovers they count, but still I'm afraid

National Gazette   August 25, 1792

Farmer DOBBINS to the *Buck-Suitors.*

Substantively identical to the *City Gazette* text, except for the following variants:

Stanza 1, line 3: And lovers they count, but still I'm afraid

Stanza 2, line 3: One sends them a ribbon, and one a new glove--

Stanza 3:   With idle Romances my book-case is stor'd
            That teach them to praise nor to pray,
            And the *Bible* itself is discharg'd from the board
            Where once with *John Bunyan* it lay.

Stanza 4:   These suitors and lovers, that never can love,
            [Content with a squeeze of the hand]
            Though often the subject of *Hymen* I move,
            The subject they can't understand.

Stanza 5:   Third stanza of the *City Gazette* text.
Aug. 22.
Signature: DOBBINS.

Freeman's Journal   January 20, 1790[1]

Stanzas written at Baltimore, in Maryland, January, 1789, *By* Capt. P. FRENEAU

THROUGH Monmouth's groves, a wandering stream
That still its wonted music keeps,
Inspires no more my evening dream
Where Cynthia on her sofa sleeps.

Sweet murmuring stream! how blest art thou
To kiss the bank where she resides,
Where nature decks the budding bough
That trembles o'er thy shallow tides.

The shepherd's moon, that beam'd so bright
No longer casts her varying shade;
The bird that cheer'd the lonely night,
I scarce remember what she said.

To me, alas! too long remov'd,
What rapture, once, that music gave
Ere wandering yet from all I lov'd,
I sought a deeper, drearier wave.

Your absent charms my soul employ–
I sigh to think how sweet you sung
And still adore the painted toy
Which near my careless heart you hung.

Now fetter'd fast in icy fields
Invain I loose the sleeping sail
The frozen wave no longer yields
And useless blows the favouring gale:

---

[1] Leary and Pattee both note that this poem first appeared in the *Freeman's Journal* on January 29, 1789. However, there was no issue on that day; the paper which appears with that date in the files of the A.A.S. is actually the January 20, 1790 number.

Yet still in hopes of April showers
And breezes moist with morning dew
I pass the lingering, lazy hours
Reflecting on the spring–and *you*.

Daily Advertiser   August 25, 1790

STANZAS
Written at Baltimore, January, 1789.

Stanza 1, line 1: THROUGH Morven's vale the wandering stream
Stanza 3, line 1: The shepherd's moon, that gleam'd so bright,
Stanza 4, line 1: To me, alas! so far remov'd,
Stanza 5, line 1: Your absent charms my dreams employ,
         line 3: And half adore the painted toy
         line 4: That near my careless heart you hung.

Poems (1795), 378-79.

City Gazette   February 2, 1790

A characteristic sketch of the LONG ISLAND *Dutch.*
[From the *Rising Empire*, a poem]

STILL on these plains their numerous race survive,
And, born to labour, still are found to thrive;
Thro' rain and sunshine toiling for their heirs
They hold no nation on this earth like theirs.
Fond of themselves, no generous motives bind,
To those that speak their gibberish, only kind:--
Yet still some virtues candour must confess,
And truth shall own, some virtues they possess.
Where'er they fix, all nature smiles around,
Groves bend with fruit and plenty cloathes the ground;
No barren trees to shade their domes are seen,
Trees must be fertile and their dwellings clean,
No idle fancy dares its whims apply,

Or hope attention from the master's eye,
All tends to something that must self produce,
All for some end, and every thing its use:
Eternal scowerings keep their floors afloat,
Neat as the outside of the Sunday coat;
The wheel, the loom, the female band employ,
These all their pleasure, these their darling joy;--
The strong-ribb'd lass no idle passions move,
No nice ideas of romantic love;
He to her heart the readiest path can find
Who comes with gold, and courts her to be kind,
She heeds not valour, learning, wit, or birth,
Minds not the swain--but asks him what he's worth.
No female fears in her firm breast prevail,
The helm she governs, and she trims the sail,
In some small barque the way to market finds,
Hauls aft the sheet or veers it to the winds,
While, plac'd a-head, subservient to her will,
Hans smokes his pipe, and wonders at her skill.
Health to their toils--thus may they still go on--
Curse on my pen!--What virtues have I drawn!
Is this the general taste?--No truth replies--
If fond of beauty, guiltless of disguise,
See--(where, the social circle meant to grace)
The handsome Yorker shades her lovely face,
She, early led to happier tasks at home,
Prefers the labours that her sex become,
Remote from view, directs some favourite art
And leaves to hardier man the ruder part.

Daily Advertiser   March 4, 1790

A characteristic sketch of the LONG ISLAND Dutch.

Stanza 1: First 32 lines of the *City Gazette* text, with the following variants:
  line 1: Still on those plains their numerous race survive,

Stanza 2: Last 10 lines of the *City Gazette* text. (line 1: indented.)

American Museum   June, 1790

Characteristic sketch of the Long Island Dutch.

Substantively identical to the *Daily Advertiser* text, except for the following variants:
Stanza 1: lines 5-8 of the *Daily Advertiser* text deleted.

Poems (1795), 18-19.

Daily Advertiser   February 5, 1790[1]

A COLUMBIAN DIALOGUE.
Supposed to have been written by Capt. Freneau.

TIR'D of his journey o'er a sandy waste
Sangrado to Columbia came at last;
A bear-skin coat was round his carcase roll'd
Shivering with Hobcaw winds, that blew so cold!
Dark was the night--much for his shins he fear'd,
For not one lamp in all the town appear'd;
Twelve was the hour--the citizens in bed
Slept sound--of bears and wolves no more in dread;
No city guards, no watchmen hove in sight,
No chyming clock sung out the time of night;
But foggy blasts their wintry music blew
Thro' shabby trees that round the State House grew:
At length alighting at one scurvy dome
He knock'd--and hop'd the people were at home.
Ho! (cried the man within) Ho!--who are you!
What! heigh!--from Charleston?--have you nothing new?

---

[1] Leary notes an earlier appearance of this poem in the *City Gazette*, on January 16, 1790. However, this issue is missing from the files of the Charleston Library Society, and I could not locate it in any other library.

Sangrado.

Nothing at all--the times are *shameful* bad
Discount at ten per cent--hard to be had;
With apples and potatoes our dear cousins,
The northern-men, are pouring by the dozens;
The French, 'tis said, are going to kill their king,
This, friend, is all I have, and all I bring.

Citizen.

What!--not some oysters, gather'd near the coast,
Such as in days of old we lov'd to roast?

Sangrado.

Not an oyster!--faith you're in a dream
To think I'd load my little nag with them;
We both are weary--let me in, I pray,
Even tho' you turn us out at break of day.

Citizen.

'Tis midnight now--return from whence you *come;*
High time all honest people were at home.

Sangrado.

Brother, methink my toes are rather cold,
Unbar your door, if I may be so bold;
Wet to the skin, and travelling all the day,
I want some rest--open the door, I say!

Citizen.

Open the door, forsooth--the man is mad
Lodging is not so easy to be had:
It is an article we do not trade in,
Nor shall my bed by all the world be laid in,
Our very garret is as full as can be,
Push off, I say, and try your luck at *Granby*!

Poems (1795), 321-22.

Massachusetts Centinel   March 3, 1790

    The MAN *of* NINETY: *or, a* VISIT *to the* OAK.
             From Freneau's Poems.

Text reprinted from *Miscellaneous Works* (1788), 64-66.

Daily Advertiser   March 6, 1790

    On the American and French Revolutions.

   BORNE on the wings of time, another year
   Sprung from the past, assumes its proud career;
   From that bright spark which first illum'd these lands,
   See Europe kindling, as the blaze expands,
   Each gloomy tyrant, sworn to chain the mind,
   Presumes no more to trample on mankind:
   Even potent LOUIS trembles on his throne
   The generous Prince that made our cause his own,
   More *equal rights* his injur'd subjects claim
   No more a country's strength–that country's shame;
   Fame starts, astonish'd at such prizes won,
   And rashness wonders how the work was done.

       Flush'd with new life, and brightening at the view
   Science, triumphant, moulds the world a new;
   To these far climes in swift succession moves
   Each art that reason owns and Sense approves.
   What tho' this age is bounded to a span
   Time sheds a nobler dignity on man,
   Some happier breath his rising passion swells,
   Some kinder genius his bold arm impels,
   Dull superstition from the world retires
   Dishearten'd zealots haste to quench their fires;
   One equal rule o'er twelve vast *states* extends,
   Europe and Asia join to be our friends,
   Our active flag in every clime display'd
   Counts stars on colours that shall never fade;

A far fam'd chief o'er this vast whole presides
Whose motto *honor* is--whom *virtue* guides;
His walks forsaken in Virginia's groves
Applauding thousands bow where'er *he* moves,
Who laid the basis of this *empire* sure
Where public faith should public peace secure.
    Still may she rise, exalted in her aims,
And boast to every age her patriot names,
To distant climes extend her gentle sway
While choice--not force--bids every heart obey:
Ne'er may she fail when liberty implores
Nor want true valour to defend her shores,
'Til Europe, humbled, greets our western wave
And owns an equal--whom she wish'd a slave.

American Museum   June, 1790

Substantively identical to the *Daily Advertiser* text, except for the following variants:

Stanza 1, line 8:   The gen'rous prince, who made our cause his own,

Stanza 2:   Contains second and third stanzas of the *Daily Advertiser* text.
           line 21: not indented.

Poems (1795), 323.

Columbian Centinel   December 8, 1802[1]

Last six lines of the second stanza of the *Daily Advertiser* text are extracted, and introduced as follows:

---

[1] This extract appears in a letter to the editor, penned by "Honorius," documenting Freneau's high regard for Washington, before the poet was influenced by Jefferson. See *Columbian Centinel* extract of "Verses occasioned by General WASHINGTON'S arrival. . . ," *Freeman's Journal*, December 10, 1783.

In another Poem, written in 1788, on the prospect of a *Revolution in France*, speaking of *President* WASHINGTON, he says:

Extract includes one variant from the *Daily Advertiser* text:

line 6:   Where public faith should public peace restore.

Daily Advertiser   March 9, 1790

On the proposed demolition of FORT GEORGE, *in this City.*

AS giants once, in hopes to rise,
Heap'd up their mountains to the skies;
With Pelion plac'd on Ossa, strove
To reach the immortal throne of Jove;

So here the hands of former days,
Their fortress from the earth did raise,
On whose proud heights, proud men to please
They mounted guns and planted trees.

Those trees to lofty stature grown--
All is not right--they must come down,
No longer waste their wonted shade
Where Colden* slept, or Tryon* stray'd.

Let *him* be sad that plac'd them there,
We shall a youthful race prepare;
Another set shall bloom, we trust,
When these are prostrate in the dust.

---

* * British governors before the Revolution.

Where Dutchmen once, in ages past,
Huge walls and ramparts round them cast,
New fabrics rais'd, on new design,
Gay *streets* and *palaces*, shall shine.

Another GEORGE shall here reside,
While Hudson's fierce majestic tide,
Well pleas'd to see this chief so nigh,
With livelier aspect passes by.

Along his margin, fresh and clean
Ere long shall belles and beaus be seen,
Through moon light walks, delighted stray
To view the islands and the bay.

Of evening dews no more afraid,
Reclining in some favourite shade,
Each nymph, in rapture with her trees,
Shall sigh to quit the western breeze.

To barren hills far southward shov'd,
These blackguard guns shall be remov'd,
No longer here a vain expense,
Since time has prov'd them no defence.--

Advance, bright days! make haste to crown
With such fair scenes this honour'd town,
Where Freedom finds the charter clear,
And plants her seat of Empire here.

National Gazette   June 21, 1792

(Untitled text concludes an article describing the view of New York City from the southwest, enhanced by the removal of Fort George. "The following stanzas on this subject, were written when the demolition of Fort George was first in contemplation by the legislature.")

Stanza 1:   First stanza of the 1790 version.

Stanza 2:   Second stanza of the 1790 version with the following

	variants:
	line 1: So here the hands of ancient days
Stanza 3:	Third stanza of the 1790 version.
Stanza 4:	Fourth stanza of the 1790 version with the following variants: line 3: Another grove shall bloom, we trust,
Stanza 5:	Fifth stanza of the 1790 version.
Stanza 6:	To foreign kings no more a slave (Disgrace to Freedom's passing wave) No flags we rear, we feign no mirth, Nor prize the day that gave them birth.
Stanza 7:	While time degrades Palmyra low, Augusta lifts her lofty brow-- While Europe falls to wars a prey Her monarchs *here*, assume no sway.
Stanza 8:	Sixth stanza of the 1790 version with the following variants: line 1: Another GEORGE+ shall here reside, line 2: While *Hudson's* bold, unfetter'd tide
Stanza 9:	Seventh stanza of the 1790 version.
Stanza 10:	Eighth stanza of the 1790 version.
Stanza 11:	Ninth stanza of the 1790 version with the following variants: line 4: Where time has prov'd them no defense.--
Stanza 12:	Tenth stanza of the 1790 version with the following variants: line 4: *And plants her seat of Commerce here.*

Additional note: + His excellency *George Clinton*.

(Stanzas are numbered and the stanza number appears to the left of the first line of each stanza.)

Poems (1795), 412-13.

Daily Advertiser   March 10, 1790

A Descriptive Sketch of Maryland.

TORN from herself, where depths her soil divide
And Chesapeake intrudes her angry tide,
Gay Maryland attracts the wandering eye,
A fertile region with a temperate sky:
In years elaps'd, her heroes of renown
From British *Anna* nam'd her favourite town*
But lost her commerce, tho' she guards their laws
Proud *Baltimore* that envied commerce draws;
Few are the years since there, at random plac'd
Some wretched huts her happy port disgrac'd;
Safe from all winds, and cover'd from the bay
There, at his ease the lazy native lay,--
Now rich and great, no more a slave to sloth
She claims importance from her hasty growth,
High in renown, her streets and domes arrang'd
A group of cabbins to a city chang'd.
   Tho' rich at home, to foreign lands they stray,
For foreign trappings trade their wealth away.
Politest manners thro' their towns prevail
And pleasure revels, tho' her funds should fail;
In each gay dome soft music charms its lord,
Where female beauty strikes the trembling chord,
On the fine air with nicest touches dwells
While from the heart the bright idea swells;
Proud to be seen, 'tis theirs to place delight
In dances measur'd by the winter's night,
The evening feast that wine and mirth prolong,
The lamp of splendor, and the midnight song.
Religion here no gloomy garb assumes
But sells her tears for patches and for plumes:
The blooming belle (some favorite swain to win)
Talks not of angels but the world she's in,

---

* Annapolis.

Attach'd to earth, here born and to decay,
She leaves to better worlds all finer clay.
    In those whom choice or different fortunes place
On rural scenes, a different mind we trace;
There solitude that still to dullness tends
To rustic forms no sprightly action lends,
Heeds not the garb, mopes o'er the evening fire,
And bids the maiden from the man retire--
On winding floods the lofty mansion stands
That casts a mournful view o'er neighbouring lands,
There the sad master strays amidst his grounds
Directs his negroes, or reviews his hounds,
Then home returning plies his past-board play,
Or dreams o'er wine that hardly makes him gay:
If, chance, some guest arrives in weary plight
He more than bids him welcome for the night.
Kind to profusion, spares no pains to please,
Gives him the product of his fields and trees,
On his rich boards shines plenty from her source
The meanest dish of all--his own discourse.

American Museum   September, 1790

Poem has four stanzas, beginning with lines 1, 9, 17, and 35.

Stanza 4, line 13: If some chance guest arrive in weary plight.

Poems (1795), 355-56.

Daily Advertiser   March 12, 1790

FEDERAL HALL.

WITH eager step and wrinkled brow,
    The busy sons of care
Disgusted with less splendid scenes
    To Federal Hall repair.

In order plac'd, they patient wait
    To sieze each word that flies,
From what they hear they sigh or smile,
    Look cheerful, grave, or wise.

Within these walls the doctrines taught
    Are of such vast concern,
That all the world with one consent
    Here strives to live—and learn.

The timorous heart that cautious shuns
    All churches, but its own,
No more observes its wonted rules,
    But ventures here alone.

Four hours a day each rank alike,
    (They that can walk or crawl)
Leave children, business, shop and wife,
    And steer for Federal Hall.

From morning tasks of mending soals
    The cobbler hastes away;
At *three* returns and tells to Kate
    The business of the day.

The debtor, vext with early duns,
    Avoids his hated home
And here and there at random roves
    Till hours of Congress come.

The barber at the well-known time
    Forgets his lather'd man,
And leaves him, grac'd with half a beard,
    To shave it--as he can.

The taylor, plagu'd with *suits* on *suits*
    Neglects Sir Fopling's call,
Forsakes his goose, disdains his board,
    And flies to Federal Hall.

American Museum   May, 1790

Federal-hall--by captain Philip Freneau.

Stanza 5, line 2: (Those who can walk or crawl)
Stanza 6, line 1: From morning task, of mending soals,
Stanza 7, line 4: Till hour of congress come.

Poems (1795), 384-85.

Daily Advertiser   March 13, 1790

Philosophical Sketch of America.

AMERICA, to every climate known,
Spreads her broad bosom to the burning zone,
To either pole extends her vast domain
Where different summers different realms attain.
Wide wandering streams, vast plains, and pathless woods,
Bold shores confin'd by circumscribing floods
Denote this land—whose fertile, flowery breast
Teems with all life; and man, its nobler guest.
In days of old from oceans deepest bed
Gulphs unexplor'd and countries of the dead
Rous'd by some voice that shook all Nature's frame
From the vast depth this new creation came:
Perpetual change its varying nature feels,
The wave once flow'd that now with frost congeals,
Suns on its breast have shed a feebler fire,
Oceans have roll'd where mountains now aspire;
The soil's proud lord a changeful temper knows,
From differing earths his various nature grows;
And long before the time that Sophists plan
Subsisted in these woods the race of man,
That, like the rest, from empty nothing came
Warm'd into life by some creating flame:
Not from the west their swarthy tribes they brought
As Europe's pride and Asia's folly taught;

With the same ease the great disposing power
Produc'd a man, a reptile, or a flower:
See the swift deer, in lonely groves that strays,
See the tall elk, that in the valley plays,
See the fierce tiger's raging, ravenous band,
And wolves (their race as ancient as the land)--
Did these of old from Asia's desert come
Or traverse seas, to find a happier home?
No--from this dust, this common dust, they drew
Their varying forms, proud man, that moulded you.
    At first half beasts, untaught to till the land
Careless they fed from Nature's fostering hand,
In depths of deserts dream'd their lives away,
Sought no new worlds nor look'd beyond to day:
The splendid power that cheers the earth and sky
Beheld this offspring with a pitying eye,
Early to them did reasoning souls impart
(Mere sons of nature, undisguis'd by art)
Then left them here, with sense enough to win,
Or cheat the bear, or leopard of his skin,
Mean tents to build, regardless of their form,
Completely blest if sheltered from the storm,
To see the seasons change, day turn to night
Bow to the works of Heaven--and own them right.

Poems (1795), 17-18.

Daily Advertiser   March 16, 1790

(Untitled poem introduced as follows:

[In several parts of New-England it is customary not to suffer the travellers to proceed on a journey on the Sabbath day. If a person is obstinate on these occasions, he is either forcibly (and commonly to the ridicule of the whole Congregation) conducted to the Church door, led through the principal ile, and placed in a conspicuous seat by the wardens, or must be detained till next day under guard, and submit to pay a fine, or be committed. The following lines commemorate an event of this sort, which some years ago really befel Mr. P. the noted performer in the feats of horsemanship. The author, however, seems to have left his poem incomplete.])

On a fine Sunday morning I mounted my steed
And southward from Hartford had meant to proceed;
My baggage was stow'd in a cart very snug,
Which *Ranger*, the gelding was fated to lug;
With his harness and buckles he loom'd very grand
And was drove by young *Darby*, a lad of the land--
On land, or on water, most handy was he,
A jockey on shore and a sailor at sea,
He knew all the roads, he was so very keen,
And the Bible by heart at the age of fifteen.

   As thus I jogg'd on, to my saddle confin'd,
With *Ranger* and Darby a distance behind,
At last in full view of a steeple we came
With a cock on the spire (I suppose he was game;
A dove in the pulpit may suit your grave people,
But always remember--a cock on the steeple)
Cries Darby--"dear master, I beg you to stay
Believe me, there's danger in driving this way;
Our Deacons on Sundays have pow'r to arrest
And lead us to Church--if your honour thinks best--
Tho' still I must do them the justice to tell
They would choose you should pay them the fine--full as well."

The fine (said I) Darby! pray, what may it be--
A shilling or sixpence?--why now let me see
Three shillings are all the small pence that remain,
And to change a half joe would be rather profane.
Is it more than three shillings, the fine that you speak on;
What say you, good Darby--will that serve the Deacon?

"Three shillings (cried Darby) why master you're jesting!--
Let us luff while we can and make sure of our westing--
Forty shillings, excuse me, is too much to pay
It would take my month's wages--that's all I've to say!--
By taking this road that inclines to the *right*
The squire and the sexton may bid us good night,
If once to old Ranger I give up the rein
The parson himself may pursue us in vain."

"Not I, my good Darby (I answer'd the lad)
Leave the Church on the left!--they would think we were mad;
I would sooner rely on the heels of my steed,
And pass by them all like a *Jehu* indeed:--
As long as I'm able to lead in the race
Old Ranger, the gelding, will go a good pace,
As the Deacon pursues he will fly like a swallow,
And you in the cart must, of consequence, follow."

Then approaching the Church, as we passed by the door
The sexton peep'd out, with a saint or two more,
A Deacon came forward and wav'd us his hat,
A signal to drop him some money--mind that
--Now, Darby (I whisper'd) be ready to skip,
Ease off the curb bridle--give Ranger the whip;
While you have the rear, and myself leads the way,
No Doctor or Deacon shall catch us to day.

By this time the Deacon had mounted his poney
And chac'd for the sake of our souls and our money--
The saint, as he follow'd, cried--"stop them, halloo!"
As swift as he follow'd as swiftly we flew--
Ah master! (said Darby) I very much fear
We must drop him some money to check his career,
He is gaining upon us, and waves with his hat
There's nothing, dear master, will stop him, but that--

Remember the Beaver (you well know the fable)
Who, flying the hunters as long as he's able
When he finds that his efforts can nothing avail
But death and the puppies are close at his tail,
Instead of desponding at such a dead lift
He bites off *their object*, and makes a free gift--
Since fortune all hope of escaping denies
Better give them a little than lose the whole prize."

But scarce had he spoke, when we came to a place
Whose muddy condition concluded the chace,
Down settled the cart--and old Ranger stuck fast
Aha! said the Deacon--I've catch'd ye at last!

Cœtera desunt.

American Museum　　　September, 1790

The adventures of a New England sabbath. *

Stanza 1, line 2:　And southward from Hartford I meant to proceed;

Stanza 3, line 1:　"The fine," said I, "Darby:--pray how much may it be--

Stanza 8, line 1:　But scarce had he spoke, when he came to a place,
　　　　　line 4:　"Aha!" said the deacon, "have I caught you at last!"

* (Note under poem substantively identical to the *Daily Advertiser* introduction.)

Poems (1795), 28-29.

Daily Advertiser   March 17, 1790

A Description of Pennsylvania.

SPREAD with stupendous hills, far from the main
Fair Pennsylvania holds her golden reign,
In fertile fields her wheaten harvest grows,
Charg'd with its freights her favorite Delaware flows;
From *Erie's* Lake her soil with plenty teems
To where the Schuylkill rolls his limpid streams--
Sweet stream! what pencil can thy beauties tell-
Not gay *Cadorus* charms me half so well,
Nor yet *Swetara* could your loss supply,
Nor *Juaniata* thus delight the eye.--
Where'er those floods through groves or mountains stray
The God of nature still directs the way,
With fondest care has trac'd each river's bed
And mighty streams thro' mighty forests led,
Bade agriculture thus export her freight,
The strength and glory of this favour'd State.

    She, fam'd for science, arts, and polish'd men
Admires her *Franklin,* but adores her *Penn,*
Who, wandering here, made barren forests bloom
And the new soil a happier robe assume.
He plann'd no schemes that honor disapproves,
He robb'd no Indian of his savage groves,
But, just to all, beheld his tribes increase,
Did what he could to bind the world in peace,
And, far retreating from a brutal band,
Bade virtue flourish in this foreign land.

    Thy followers, Fox, pacific in each aim,
In this far climate still revere your name;
To them long practice prudent foresight gave,
Proof to the projects of the keenest knave.
On things to come they fix an anxious eye
Fond to be thought the favourites of the sky,
Paths of their own they clear to future bliss,
Praise *other* worlds but keep their hold on *this*
Nor mean I, hence, to censure or condemn,
Perhaps 'twere best the world should think like them;--

What tho' on visions they may place their trust,
I hold their general principles are just,
Good will to all, themselves their first great care,
Precise in dealing, foes to blood and war;
Let kings invade, or potentates assault,
No aid they lend, for passive to a fault,
They still are found, all complaisant to power
To bow to ruffians in the trying hour.

March 16.

Poems (1795), 376.

    Philadelphia *Daily Advertiser*   February 21, 1797

Substantively identical to the 1790 text, except for the following variants:

Stanza 2, line 5: He plann'd no schemes, which honour disapproves;

Stanza 3, line 13: *Good will to all--themselves their first care--*

Date: New-York, February 16.

Daily Advertiser   March 20, 1790

On the SLEEP *of* PLANTS.
(*A Curious novel Discovery.*)

WHEN suns are set, and stars in view,
    Not only *Man* to slumber yields;
But nature gives this blessing too
    To yonder plants, in yonder fields.

The summer heats and lengthening days
    (To them the same as toil and care)
Thrice welcome make the evening breeze
    That kindly does their strength repair.

At early dawn each plant survey
    And see, reviv'd by nature's hand,
With youthful vigour fresh and gay
    The blossoms blow, their leaves expand.

Yon garden plant, with weeds o'er run
    Not void of thought, perceives its hour,
And, watchful of the parting sun,
    Throughout the night conceals her flower.

Like us, the slave of cold and heat
    She too enjoys her little span,
A structure only less complete
    Than that which makes the boast of man.

Thus, moulded from one common clay,
    A varied life adorns the plain;
By nature subject to decay,
    By nature meant to bloom again.

National Gazette   November 14, 1791

ON THE SLEEP OF PLANTS.
(*A curious new discovery.*)

All lines begin at margin.
Stanza 5, line 3: With *reason* something less complete

Poems (1795), 84.

Daily Advertiser   March 22, 1790

[On December the 31st last, the old College at Dartmouth in New-Hampshire, was entirely demolished by the Students, notwithstanding every endeavour of the Rev. President to persuade them to desist from their unwarranted undertaking. It stood the shock of their united efforts about 20 minutes, and then fell to the ground.]

ON the DEMOLITION of DARTMOUTH COLLEGE.

ON New-Year's eve, the year was eighty-nine,
All clad in *black,* a Dartmouth college crew
With crow-bar, sledge, and pick ax did combine
To level with the dust their antique hall,
In hopes the President would build a new:
Yes, yes, they said, the ancient pile should fall
And laugh no longer at yon cobler's stall.

The clock struck seven--in social compact join'd,
They pledg'd their sacred honors to proceed:
The number seventy-five this feat design'd,
But first some oaths they swore by candle light
On Euclid's Elements--no bible did they heed
One must be true, they said, the other might--
Besides, no bible could be found that night.

Now darkness o'er the plain her pinions spread
Then rung the bell an unaccustom'd peal:
Out rush'd the brave, the cowards went to bed
And left the attempt to those that felt full bold
To pull down halls, where years had seen them kneel,
Where *Wheelock* oft at rakes was wont to scold
Or sung them many a psalm in days of old.

Advancing then towards the tottering hall
That now at least one hundred years had stood
They gave due notice that it soon should fall--
Lest there some godly wight might gaping stand;
(For well they knew the world wants all its good
To awe the sturdy sinners of the land,
And shame old Satan, with his sooty band.)

The reverand man that Dartmouth college awes
Hearing the bell at this unhallow'd hour,
Vext at the infringement of the college laws
With lengthy stride out-sally'd from his den,
And made a speech (as being a man in power)
Alas! it was not heard by one in ten—
No time to heed his speeches, or his pen.

"Ah, rogues, said he, ah whither do ye run,
"Bent on the ruin of that harmless pile
"That, all the war, has brav'd both sword and gun?--
"Reflect, dear boys, some reverand rats are there
"That now will have to scamper many a mile
"For whom past time old Latin books did spare,
"And Attic greek, and manuscripts most rare.

"Relent, relent! to accomplish such designs
"Our Dartmouth college fare is much too weak--
"For such attempts folks drink your high-proof wines,
"Not wretched switchel* and vile *bogo* drams
"Hardly sufficient to digest your Greek--
"Come, let the fabric stand, my dear black lambs--
"Besides--I think we have no battering rams."

Thus he--but all his signs and tears were lost
To work they went with pick-ax, spade and hammer,
One smote a wall, and one dislodg'd a post,
Tugg'd at a beam, or aim'd at pigeon holes,
Where Indian boys were wont to study grammar:
Indeed, they took great pains, and dug like moles,
And work'd--as if they work'd to save their souls.

Now to its deep foundation shook the dome
Farewell to all its learning, fame, and honor!
So fell the capitol of heathen Rome
By Goths and Vandals level'd with the dust--
And so shall die the works of *John O'Connor,*
Which he himself will even outlive, we trust
But now our story's coming to the worst:

---

* A mixture of molasses and water.

Down fell the Pile!--aghast these rebels stood
And wonder'd at the mischiefs they had done
To such a pile, compos'd of stone and wood,
To such a pile, so antique and renown'd,
Which many a prayer had heard and many a pun--
So, three huzzas they gave, and fir'd a round,
Then homeward trudg'd--half drunk--but safe and sound

March 20.

Poems (1795), 374-75.

Daily Advertiser   March 29, 1790

A View of Massachusetts.

THERE, in vast stocks, the wooly nation strays,
There endless herds the beauteous meadow graze,
There smiling plenty crowns the labourer's pain
And blooming beauty weds the industrious swain.--
Were this thy *all*, what happier State could be!--
But avarice drives the native to the sea,
Ficticious wants all thoughts of ease controul,
Proud independence sways the aspiring soul.
Midst foreign waves, a stranger to repose
Thro' the moist world the keen adventurer goes:
Not India's seas restrain his daring sail,
Far to the south he seeks the polar whale:
From those vast *banks* where frequent tempests rave
And fogs eternal brood upon the wave,
There (furl'd his sail) his daring hold he keeps,
Drags from their depths the natives of those deeps;
Then to some distant clime explores his way,
Bold avarice spurs him on--he must obey.

Yet, from such aims one great effect we trace
That holds in happier bonds our restless race;
Like some deep lake, by circling shores compress'd,
All nature tends to universal rest:
Unfed by springs, that find some secret pass
To mix their current with the mightier mass,
Unmov'd by moons, that some strange impulse guides
To move its waters, and propel its tides,
Soon would that lake (a putrid nuisance grown,)
Lose all its vigour, prais'd or priz'd by none:
Thus, even base avarice helps to make us blest
Not vainly planted in the human breast;--
With her, *ambition* join'd; they proudly drive,
Rule all our race, and keep the world alive.

Here first, to quench her once lov'd freedom's flame,
With their proud fleets, Britannia's warriors came;
Here, sure to conquer, she began her fires,
Here, sent her lords, her lordlings, and her squires:
All, all too weak to effect the vast design
That swell'd, poor *Gage,* that puny heart of thine,
That urg'd *Burgoyne* to slight his *Celia's* charms,
The brother *Howes* to furbish up their arms
And modern *Percies* lose their wonted sleep
To conquer countries, that they could–not keep.

Long, long on *Boston's* hills shall strangers gaze
On those vast mounds that magic seem'd to raise;
Stupendous piles that hasten'd Britain's flight,
Extended hills, the offspring of a night.--
In that devoted town they hop'd to stay
And, fed by rapine, doze their years away:
Vain hopes, vain schemes–the unconquer'd spirit rose
That still surviv'd thro' all succeeding woes;
Imprison'd crowds, in cruel durance held,
Disarm'd, restrain'd from honor's earliest field;
Imprison'd thousands, worn with wasting grief,
Now half adoring, met their guardian chief
Whose conquering army bade the foe retreat;
Disgrace their portion, and their route complete.

March 27.

Poems (1795), 383-84.

Daily Advertiser   April 28, 1790

STANZAS,
Occasioned by the Death of Dr. FRANKLIN.

THUS, some tall tree that long has stood
The glory of its native wood,
By storms destroy'd, or length of years
Demands the tribute of our tears.

The pile that took long time to raise
Will sink, 'tis true, by slow decays;
But when it's destin'd years are o'er,
We must regret the loss the more.

So long befriended by your art,
Philosopher, we must not part!--
When Monarchs tumble to the ground
Successors easily are found;

But matchless *Franklin,* what a few
Can hope to equal such as *you,*
Who seiz'd from Kings their sceptr'd pride,
And turn'd the lightning's darts aside!

Poems (1795), 417.

Daily Advertiser   May 1, 1790

(Untitled.)

SICK of the world, in prime of days
Constantia took a serious fit--
Resolv'd to shun all balls and plays,
And only read what saints had writ--
    To *Bethlehem's* walls she would repair,
    And be a pensive sister there.

A sailor, loitering from his crew,
As chance would have it pass'd along,
She told him what she had in view,
And he reply'd—My dear you're wrong,
    Let wither'd hags to Bethlehem go
    Where kisses freeze, and love is snow.

With such a dull and drowsy train
Who, but a hermit, could agree—
Ah, rather stay to grace the plain
Or wander on the wave with me:
    For you the painted barque shall wait,
    And I would die for such a freight.

No wandering seaman (she replied)
Can tempt me to forgo my plan,
No barque that wafts him o'er the tide,
Nor many a better looking man:
    Go, wanderer, plough your gloomy sea,
    Constantia must a sister be.

To gain so fair a flower as you
(The tar return'd) who would not plead?
Nor shall you, nymph, to Bethlehem go,
While love can write what you must read:
    Come, to yon' meadow let us stray,
    I have some handsome things to say.

    Love has its wish when reason fails—
In vain he sigh'd, in vain he strove;
Forsake (said she) those swelling sails
If you would have me think of love:
    Great merit has your sailing art—
    But absence would distract my heart.

Where else was said we secret keep—
The tar, grown fonder of the shore,
Neglects his prospects on the deep,
And she of Bethlehem talks no more;
    He slyly quits the coasting trade—
    She pities her—that dies a maid.

National Gazette   August 8, 1792

CONSTANTIA.

Text contains eight stanzas.

Stanza 1:   First stanza of the 1790 version.

Stanza 2:   Second stanza of the 1790 version with the following variants:
line 4:   And he reply'd–"Fair maid, you're wrong,
line 5:   "Let faded nymphs to Bethlehem go
line 6:   "Where kisses freeze and love is snow.

Stanza 3:   "The barren oak and cluster'd pine
"Afford a gloomy, sad delight;
"But why that bloom of health resign,
"The mingled tint of red and white:
    "In cloister'd cells the flowers expire
    "That on the plain all eyes admire.

Stanza 4:   Third stanza of the 1790 version with the following variants:
Quotation marks begin each line and conclude last line.
line 1:   "With such a pensive, pious train

Stanza 5:   Fourth stanza of the 1790 version.

Stanza 6:   Fifth stanza of the 1790 version.
Quotation marks begin the first line and conclude the last line.

Stanza 7:   Sixth stanza of the 1790 version.
Quotation marks being the third line and conclude the last line.

Stanza 8:   Seventh stanza of the 1790 version.
July 30.

Poems (1795), 381-82.

Daily Advertiser   May 10, 1790

Description of Connecticut.

HERE, fond remembrance stampt her much lov'd names,
Here boasts the soil its *London* and its *Thames;*
Throughout her shores commodious ports abound,
Clear flow the waters of the varying ground;
Cold nipping winds a lengthen'd winter bring,
Late rise the products of the tardy spring.
The broken soil a labouring race requires,
Each barren hill its generous crops admires,
Where nature meanly did her gifts impart,
Yet, smiling, owns how much she owes to art.

    But keen as winds that guide the wintry reign,
All bow to lucre, all are bent on gain;
As chance decreed, their various lots are thrown;
Its house each acre, every mile its town;
With gilded spire the frequent church is seen
Sacred to him, that taught them to be keen;
Eternal squabblings grease the lawyer's paw,
All have their suits, and all have studied law;
With tongue that art and nature taught to speak
Some rave in Latin, some dispute in Greek;
Proud of their books, in ancient lore they shine,
And one month's study makes a learn'd divine;
Fond to converse, with deep designing views,
They pump the travelling stranger of his news;
Fond of his wit, but fonder to be paid,
Each house a tavern, claims a tavern's trade,
While he that comes, as surely hears them praise
The hospitality of modern days.

Yet brave in arms, of enterprising soul,
They tempt old Neptune to the farthest pole,
In learning's walks explore the mazy way
(For genius there has shed his golden ray)
In wars bold arts thro' various contests try'd,
True to themselves, they took their country's side,
And, party feuds dismiss'd, join'd to agree
That scepter only just--that left them free.

Poems (1795), 307-08.

New York *Public Advertiser*   February 8, 1808

DESCRIPTION OF CONNECTICUT.

Substantively identical to the 1790 text, except for the following variants:

Stanza 1, line 8: Each barren hill its gen'rous crop admires,
Stanza 2, line 9: With tongues that art and nature taught to speak,
Stanza 3, line 1: Indented.
         line 2: They tempted old Neptune to the farthest pole;
         line 4: (For learning here has shed his golden ray)
         line 7: And party feuds dismiss'd, join to agree

Daily Advertiser   May 24, 1790

VERSES
From the other World, by Dr. Fr--k--n.

DEAR Poets, why so full of pain,
Why so much grief for Dr. Ben?
Love for your tribe I never had;
Nor wrote three stanzas, good or bad.

At funerals sometimes grief appears,
Where legacies have purchas'd tears--
'Tis nonsense to be sad for nought,--
From me you never gain'd a groat.

To better trades I turn'd my views,
And never meddled with the Muse:
Great things I did for rising States,
And kept the lightning from some pates:

This grand discovery, you adore it,
But ne'er will be the better for it;--
You still are subject to those fires,
For poets' houses have no spires.

Philosophers are fam'd for pride,
But pray be modest--when I died
No sighs disturb'd old ocean's bed,
Nor Nature wept--for Franklin dead.

That day on which I left the coast,
A beggar man was also lost;
If Nature wept, you must agree
She wept for him--as well as me.

There's reason even in telling lies--
In such profusion of her sighs
She was too sparing of a tear--
In Carolina, all was clear.

And if there fell some snow and sleet,
Why must it be her winding sheet?
Snows long have cloath'd the vernal plain,
Have melted--and will melt again.

Poets, I pray you go to school--
Dame Nature is not quite a fool:
When to the dust great men she brings,
Make her do some--uncommon things.

New-York. May 22.

Massachusetts Centinel June 12, 1790

Text introduced as follows:

> (The following did not, we conceive, originate in disrespect for the late illustrious Philosopher of America, but was intended merely as a satire of the extravagant effusions of some of the poetical writers in the southern papers.)

VERSES *from the other world, by Dr. F.*

Stanza 4, line 3: But still are subject to those fires,

Poems (1795), 417-18.

Daily Advertiser   June 11, 1790

A Descriptive Sketch of Virginia.

FULL of her ancient claims, where all is *new*,
Vast in her bounds, Virginia swells to view:
First in imagin'd rank she long has stood,
Built the first town, and first explor'd the wood:
Vain boast!--for what can age or arts avail
When years, succeeding, see her efforts fail;
On northern plains more vigorous acts display
Where pleasure holds no such a general sway;
Slaves scarce are found (that scandal to the land)
From the rough plough to save the fopling's hand,
Where fiercer wants the daily pittance ask,
Compel to labour, and complete the task.

    Yet shall not malice rob them of their due,
Not all their wealth is center'd in a few;
On Fame's bright lists their sages they enroll,
Theirs is the brave, and high aspiring soul,
Heroes and chiefs, the firm unconquer'd mind
That rul'd in councils, or in battles shin'd,
Sent *traitorous* bands new regions to explore
And drove their titled miscreant* from the shore.

    A race of slaves, throughout their country spread,
From fertile fields extorts the owner's bread;
Rais'd by their care, *tobacco* spreads its leaf,
The master's pleasure, and the labourer's grief;
Hence comes the lofty port, the haughty air,
The proud demeanor, and the brow severe:
Averse to toil, the natives still rely
On the sad negro for the year's supply;
While the keen lash some little tyrant wields,
Foe to the free-born genius of the fields,

---

* Lord Dunmore.

He patient, early, quits his poor abode,
Toils at the hoe, or bears some ponderous load
Silent beholds (proud object of reproach)
His whole year's labour lost on Mammon's coach!
Sweats at the ax, or, pensive and forlorn,
Sighs for the noon, to parch his stinted corn,
With watchful eye maintains his much lov'd fire,
Nor even in summer lets its spark expire;
At night returns, his evening toils to share,
Lament his rags, or sleep away his care,
Bind up the recent wound, with many a groan,
And thank his gods--that Sunday is his own!

To these mild climes the waspish Scotchman runs,
Leaves his cold hills to bask in warmer suns,
Eyes well the native--marks his weaker side,
And heaps up wealth from luxury and pride,
Exports the produce of exhausted plains,
Nor fears a rival to divide his gain.

Deep in their beds, as distant to their source
Here many a river winds its wandering course:
Proud of her bulky freight, thro' plains and woods
Moves the tall ship majestic o'er the floods,
Where *James's* strength the salter brine repells
Or, like a sea, the deep *Potowmack* swells--
Yet here the sailor views with wandering eye
Impoverish'd fields that near their margins lie,
Mercantile towns where dullness holds her reign
And boors, too lazy to manure the plain:--
There, where two creeks divide the sickly lands,
Mis-shapen pile, the gloomy college stands,
With mingled *chefs,* the sophs their vigils keep[1]

---

[1] In citing the original newspaper variants from the 1795 version of this poem, Pattee quotes this line, "With mingled *chess,* the sophs their vigils keep" (III, 19). It is difficult to distinguish the "f" from the "s" in this line, and I also initially had read the word "chess." But on closer examination, I determined the word to be "*chefs,*" which, meaning "masters" in French, clearly seems the word indicated by the context of this line.

And *William* nods to *Mary*--half asleep;
The mopish muse no lively theme essays
But toils in *law*, that best her toil repays,
With modern Latin, ancient trash explains,
Or deals in Logic--for the want of brains.

    Attach'd to other times, I cast my view
To former days, where all was fresh & new,
When *Pocahunta*, in her bearskin clad,
Sigh'd to be happy with her English lad:
Queen of those woods, embarking on the main,
(With *Tomo como* following in her train)
First of her race, she reach'd the British shore
But doom'd to perish, saw her own no more!
Chang'd is the scene--where once her gardens smil'd
A negro race now wander through the wild
And with base gabbling, vex that injur'd shade
Where Freedom flourish'd and *Powhatan* stray'd.

Poems (1795), 380-81.

Daily Advertiser   June 17, 1790

LINES
Occasioned by the Skeletons dug up in FORT GEORGE.

TO sleep in peace when life is fled,
Where shall our mouldering bones be laid--
What art can shun this *source of fears,*
These shovels of succeeding years.

Alas! what griefs must man endure!
Not even in Forts he rests secure:
Time wastes the splendors of a crown,
And brings the loftiest rampart down.

The breath once gone--no art recalls--
Away we haste to mouldering walls:
Some future whim inverts the plain,
And suns behold our bones again.

Those teeth dear girls (so much your care)
That such a fine enamel wear,
Tho' still unhurt, all in their prime,--
'Tis best to have them drawn in time:

Example take from yonder scull,
And, ere the flames of life grow dull,
Leave not a tooth to grace the jaw,
Since dentists steal--and fear no law.

He that expects a sound repose
To barren hills and deserts goes,
Where busy hands admit--no sun,
Where he may sleep till all is done.

But still--tho' shrouded in the shade,
'Tis folly to defy the spade;
Posterity pulls down the hill,
And plants our relicks where she will.

Times cloathes us all in wooden coats,
And men deceas'd can have no votes,
So let them slumber--free from pain--
Till Life shall vegetate again

June 16.

Poems (1795), 409-10.

Daily Advertiser   June 29, 1790

The ORATOR of the WOODS.
[Occasioned by hearing a very elegant Discourse preached in a mean Building, by the Parson of an obscure Parish.]

PHILANDER asks with fond surprize,
Why Damon wastes the fleeting year,
Where no gay steeple meets the eyes,
And only rustics come to hear--
    His case is hard (he seems to say)
    Such talents in so poor a way!

While you lament his barren trade,
Tell me--in yonder vale,
Why droops those plants beneath the shade,
So feeble and so pale!--
    Why were they not in gardens plac'd
    To blush--and please your men of taste.

In lonely wilds, these flowers so fair,
No curious step allure,
And chance--not choice--has fix'd them there,
More charming as obscure,
    Where heedless of such sweets so nigh
    The lazy Hind goes loitering by.

But see!--on such retreats as these
Ambition turns her view!
Still hopes some future hour to seize,
And, Damon, live like you:
    Alas, no joys on age await,
    Retirement comes a day too late.

June 28.

National Gazette   November 10, 1791

THE ORATOR OF THE WOODS.

Stanza 1: First stanza of the 1790 version, with the following variants:
line 1: EACH stranger asks, with fond surprize,
line 3: Where Indian forests round him rise
line 5: "His case is hard (they seem to say)

Stanza 2: To those that courts and titles please,
How dismal is his lot,
Beyond the hills, beneath some trees--
To live and be forgot
    In dull retreats where Nature binds
    Her mass of clay to vulgar minds.--

Stanza 3: Second stanza of the 1790 version, with the following variants:
line 3: Why grows that flower beneath the shade
line 5: Why was she not in gardens plac'd
line 6: To blush, and please the man of taste?

Stanza 4: Third stanza of the 1790 version, with the following variants:
line 3: And chance, not choice, has plac'd them there,
line 4: Still charming, though obscure,

Philadelphia, November 8.
(Fourth stanza of the 1790 version deleted.)

Poems (1795), 82-83.

Daily Advertiser   July 1, 1790

NANNY, *the Philadelphia House Maid, to* NABBY, *her friend in New-York.*

SIX WEEKS my dear mistress has been in a fret
And nothing but *Congress* will do for her yet,
She says they must come, or her senses she'll lose,
From morning till night she is reading the news,
And loves the dear fellows that vote for *our town*
(Since no one can relish *New York* but a clown,
Where your beef is so lean, it would make people laugh,
And folks are too haughty to worship--a *calf*:)
She tells us how she has read in her books
That God gives them meat but the devil sends cooks;
And *Grumbleton* told us (who often shoots flying)
That fish you have plenty, but spoil them in frying;
That your streets are as crooked as crooked can be
Right forward three perches he never could see
Till his view was cut short with a house or a shop
That stood in the way--and compel'd him to stop.

    Those speakers that wish for New-York to decide,
Tis a pity that talents are so misapplied;
My mistress declares she is vext to the heart
That genius should take such a pitiful part,
For *the question*, indeed, she is daily distrest,
And *G----*, I think, she will ever detest,
Who did all he could, with his tongue and his pen
To keep the dear Congress shut up in your den.

    She insists, the expence of removing is small,
And that *two* or *three thousands* will answer it all,
If that is too much, and we're so very poor--
The passage by water is cheaper, be sure;
If people object the expence of a team,
Here's *Fitch*, with his wherry, will bring them *by steam*;
And Nabby!--if once he should take them on board,
The *honour* will be a sufficient reward.

But, as for myself, I vow and declare
I wish it would suit them to stay where they are;
I plainly foresee, that if once they remove
From morning to night we shall drive and be drove,
My madam's red rag will ring like a bell
And the hall and the parlour will never look well;
Such scowering will be as has never been seen,
We shall always be cleaning, and never be clean

And threats in abundance will work on my fears
Of blows on the back and of flaps on the ears--
Two trifles, at present, discourage her paw,
The fear of the Lord and the fear of the law--
But if *Congress* arrive, she will have such a sway
That gospel and law will be both done away;--
For the sake of a place I must bear all her din,
And if ever so angry, do nothing but grin;
So Congress, I hope in your town will remain
And Nanny will thank them again and again.

June 29.

Poems (1795), 414-15.

Daily Advertiser   July 12, 1790

THE BERGEN PLANTER.

ATTACH'D to lands that ne'er deceiv'd his hopes
This rustic sees the harvests come and go;
His autumn's toil returns in summer crops,
While limpid streams, to cool his herbage, flow;
    And if some cares intrude upon his mind
    They are such cares as heaven for man design'd.

He on no party hangs his hopes or fears,
Nor seeks the vote that *baseness* must procure,
No *Stall fed Mammon* for his gold reveres,

No splendid offers from his chests allure:--
    While showers descend, and suns their beams display,
    The same to him if Congress go or stay.

Where wandering brooks from mountain sources roll
He seeks at noon the waters of the shade,
Drinks deep--and fears no poison in the bowl
That nature for her happiest children made,
    And from whose clear and gently passing wave,
    All drink alike--the master and the slave.

The scheming statesman shuns his homely door,
Who, on the miseries of his country fed,
Ne'er glanc'd his eye from that base pilfer'd store
To view the sword, suspended by a thread,
    Nor that hand-writing, grav'd upon the wall
    That tells him--but in vain--the sword must fall

He ne'er was made a holiday machine
Wheel'd here and there by 'squires in livery clad,
Nor dreads the sons of legislation keen,
Hard hearted laws, and penalties most sad;
    In humble hope his little fields were sown,
    A trifle in your eye--but all his own.

July 10.

American Museum   October, 1791

THE BERGEN PLANTER.
By Philip Freneau.

Stanza 1, line 2: The rustic sees the harvest come and go;
        line 3: His autumn's toil return in summer's crops,

National Gazette   October 3, 1792

THE PENNSYLVANIA PLANTER.

Stanza 1:   First stanza of the 1790 text, with the following variants:

line 3: His autumn's toil returns in summer's crops,
lines 5 and 6 begin at margin.

Stanza 2: He to no pompous domes comes, cap in hand,
Where new-made-squires affect the courtly smile,
Nor where Alcander, midst his foreign band,
Extols *the rule of kings* in swelling style,
A tongue that babbled, when it should have hush'd,
A head that never thought--a face that never blush'd.

Stanza 3: Second stanza of the 1790 version.
(lines 5 and 6 indented.)

Stanza 4: Third stanza of the 1790 version.
(lines 5 and 6 indented.)

Stanza 5: Fourth stanza of the 1790 version.
(lines 5 and 6 indented.)

Stanza 6: Fifth stanza of the 1790 version.
(lines 5 and 6 indented.)

September 29.

Poems (1795), 418-19.

Daily Advertiser   July 15, 1790

NABBY, the New York House Maid, to NANNY, her friend in Philadelphia.

WELL, Nanny, I am sorry to say, since you writ us
That Congress at last has determin'd to quit us:
You now may begin with your brushes and brooms
To be scowering your knockers and scrubbing your rooms;
As for us, my dear Nanny, we're much in a pet,
And hundreds of houses will be to be let;
Our streets, that were just in a way to look clever,

Will now be neglected and nasty as ever;
Again we must fret at the Dutchify'd gutters
And pebble-stone pavements, that wear out our trotters.--
My master looks dull, and his spirits are sinking,
From morning till night he is smoking and thinking;
Laments the expence of destroying the fort,
And says, your great people are all of a sort--
He hopes and he prays they may die in a stall
If they leave us in debt--for *Federal Hall*--
And *Strap* had declar'd, he has such regards,
He will go, if they go, *for the sake of their beards.*
Miss *Letty,* poor lady, is so in the pouts,
She values no longer our dances and routs,
And sits in a corner, dejected and pale
As dull as a cat, and as lean as a rail!--
Poor thing, I am certain she's in a decay,
And all--because Congress resolve not to stay!--
The Congress unsettled is, sure, a sad thing,
Seven years, my dear Nanny, they've been on the wing;
My master would rather saw timber, or dig,
Than see them removing to Conneqocheague,
Where the houses and kitchens are yet to be fram'd,
The trees to be fell'd, and the streets to be nam'd;
Of the two, we had rather your town should receive 'em--
So here, my dear Nanny, in haste I must leave 'em,
I'm a dunce at inditing--and as I'm a sinner,
The beef is half raw--and the bell rings for dinner!

July 14.

Poems (1795), 415.

New York Daily Gazette   August 10, 1790

THE REMOVAL.

FROM Hudson's Bank, in proud array,
(Too mean to claim a longer stay)
Their *new ideas* to improve,
Behold the great *Sanhedrim* move!

Such thankless usage much we fear'd
When Robert's coach stood ready geer'd,
And he, the foremost on the floor,
Sat pointing to the Quaker shore.

So long confin'd to little things,
They now shall meet where *Bavius* sings;
Where *Mammon* guilds his walls in style,
And *B-b-'s bawdy* seasons smile.

The Yorker asks, but asks in vain,
"What Demon bids them move again!"
The house that moves must suffer loss,
And rolling stones attract no moss.

Have we not to our utmost strove,
For fear the Congress should remove?
At dull debates no silence broke,
And walk'd on tiptoe while they spoke?

Have we not paid for Chaplain's prayers,
That Heav'n might smile on state affairs?
Put some things up, pull'd others down,
And rais'd our streets through half the town?

Have we not toil'd through cold and heat,
To make the *Fed'ral Hall* complete?
Thrown down our fort to give them air.
And mov'd our guns, the Lord knows where?

Times change! but memory still recalls
The day when ruffians scal'd their walls,
When sovereigns bow'd to black guard men,
Mere *prisoners in the town of PENN*!

Can they forget, when, half afraid,
The timorous *Council* lent no aid;
But left them to the rogues that rob--
The tender mercies of the mob?

Why, if they can, their lot is cast--
One hundred miles shall soon be pass'd.
This day the *Federal Hall* is clear'd,
To *Powles Hook* their barge is steer'd,
Where Robert's coach stands ready geer'd.

City Gazette September 11, 1790

On the removal of Congress from NEW-YORK
to PHILADELPHIA.
Supposed to have been written by Captain FRENEAU

Substantively identical to the *Daily Gazette* text, except for the following variants:

Stanza 3, line 4: And Bingham's bawdy *seasons* smile.

Stanza 4: New chaplains now shall stretch their jaws,
 New pensions grease their sacred paws,
 Some reverend dunce, that turtle carves
 Shall fatten--while the soldier starves,

Stanza 5: Fourth stanza of the *Daily Gazette* text.

Stanzas 6-10: Sixth to tenth stanzas of the *Daily Gazette* text, with the following variants:
 Stanza 9, line 4: The gentle mercies of the mob!--
 Stanza 10, line 4: To Jersey shores the barge is steer'd

(Fifth stanza of the *Daily Gazette* text deleted.)

Poems (1795), 419-20.

Daily Advertiser   September 7, 1790

TORMENTINA's Complaint.
Written at Cape Hatteras, June 1789.

IN shades we live, in shades we die,
Cool Zephyrs breathe to our repose,
In shallow streams we love to play,
Yet, cruel, you that praise deny
Which you might give, and nothing lose,
And then pursue your destin'd way.

Ungrateful man! when anchoring here,
On shore you came to beg relief,
I show'd you where the fig-trees grow,
And wandering with you, void of fear,
To hear the story of your grief,
I pointed where sweet waters flow.

A ram, the favorite of the flock,
To your unpitying crew I gave,
To roast or boil on yonder deep:
My heart could scarce endure the shock,
When, on the margin of the wave,
You slew the father of my sheep!

Along these vast extended shores,
From isle to isle where'er we stray,
Of all the nymphs that please the eye,
They scarce can be excell'd by ours,
Altho' in cooler shades they play,
And summer suns come not so nigh.

Confess your fault, mistaken swain,
And own, at least, our equal charms--
Have you no flowers of *yellow* hue
That please your fancy on the plain;
Would you not guard those flowers from harms,
If Nature's self each picture drew?

Vain are your sighs, in vain your tears
Your barque must still at anchor lay,
And you remain a slave to care,
A thousand doubts, a thousand fears,
Till what you said you shall unsay,
That Hatteras Maidens are not fair.

National Gazette   March 19, 1792

Tormentina's Complaint.

Stanza 1:   First stanza of the 1790 text, with the following variants:
line 4:   But, cruel, you that praise deny,

Stanza 2:   Second stanza of the 1790 text.

Stanza 3:   The men that scorn'd your ragged crew,
(So long the sport of Neptune's rage--)
I told them what your sufferings were;
Told them, that landsmen never knew
The trade, that hastens frozen age,
The life, that brings the brow of care!

Stanza 4:   Third stanza of the 1790 version.

Stanza 5:   Fourth stanza of the 1790 version, with the following variants:
line 1:   Along your native northern shores
line 3:   Of all the nymphs, that catch the eye,

Stanza 6:   Fifth stanza of the 1790 version.

Stanza 7:   Sixth stanza of the 1790 version, with the following variants:
line 6:   Bermudian Lasses are not fair!

Signature: SINBAT.

Castle Island, Bermuda, January 20, 1789.

Poems (1795), 179-80.

General Advertiser   November 9, 1790

Published by a particular desire.
To the LADIES.

SINCE time too soon the life of man impairs
And brings on age, with all its pains and cares;
Why then, by nature subject to decay,
Ah, why invite what *art* might long delay?
Foes to the race of man, neglect and sloth
Corrodes the ivory of the loveliest tooth;
And that rank breath where every sweet might dwell
Tempts the nice beau to slight his careless belle,
And thinks no longer 'tis his heaven to sip
Love's draught of pleasure from the damask lip.
The Dentist's care, bright maids, can shield from harms
And to your kisses add a thousand charms.
Safe from the ills of torture and decay,
Love there would fix, and half his flames display--
Low at their shrine more constant lovers fall
Who leave not nature to accomplish all--
Revere *that* art which thus prevents your pain,
Which ages past have sought, but sought in vain;
So shall your lovers to their oaths be true
And, years elaps'd, each beauty still be new;
While those who proudly would our skill despise
And trust alone the conquests of the eyes,
In loves bright circle why should they be seen
Who toothless age succeeds to gay fifteen!

National Gazette   September 29, 1792

ADVICE to the LADIES,
Not to neglect the Dentist.

Stanza 1:   First ten lines of the 1790 version, with the following variants:
           line 1:   SINCE time too soon the race of man impairs
           line 2:   And age comes on with all its pains & cares,
           line 5:   Foe to the bloom of health, neglect and sloth

line 7: And that coarse breath, where every sweet might dwell,
line 9: And think no longer 'tis his heaven to sip
line 10: Love's draft of pleasure from the damask lip.

Stanza 2: Revision of the remainder of the 1790 text--double space between stanzas:

> The *Dentist's* care, bright maids, can shield from harms
> And to your kisses lend a thousand charms,
> Safe from the ills of torture and decay
> Love there would perch, and all his flames display--
> Low at *their* shrine more constant lovers fall
> Who leave not *nature* to accomplish all--
> Revere that art which thus prevents your pain,
> Which ages past have sought, but sought in vain;
> So shall your lovers to their oaths be true,
> And, years elaps'd, each beauty still be new;
> While *she*, who proudly would all art despise,
> And trust alone the conquests of her eyes,
> Too soon beholds her wonted influence lost,
> Neglected wit, and love congeal'd to frost;
> In vain her *rouge* the mask of health restores,
> No more the lover sighs, the slave adores;
> Insulting prudes no more a rival fear,
> But cruel whispers thus insult her ear:
> *In Love's bright circle, why should they be seen*
> *Whose toothless charms encroach on gay sixteen?*

September 24.

Poems (1795), 52-53.

Daily Advertiser   November 17, 1790

(Untitled text introduced as follows:

About thirty years ago, O'Reilly, the Spanish governor of West Florida, having by some means discovered a conspiracy that had been very secretly concerted by a number of the inhabitants of New Orleans, to deliver up the province to the French, invited one day the principal gentlemen of the town to a public dinner. They had no sooner finished their repast (which was very sumptuous) and were sitting down to a cheerful glass of wine, than, their entertainer disappeared: they were surrounded by a strong guard of armed soldiers, a gibbet (that had been previously prepared) was instantly erected, and those unfortunate gentlemen were hanged in the sight of the whole town, without being allowed to take a last farewell of their families and friends. The following stanzas are supposed to have been founded on this tragical event, and written by a person nearly connected in family and friendship with one of the unfortunate sufferers.])

Amidst these shades and heart depressing glooms
What comfort can I give, what shall I say?
Come here and sit with me—let's talk of tombs,
For this, my Catharine, is a cloudy day.

The pensive priest accosts me with a sigh:
With movement slow, in sable robes he came—
But why so sad—philosopher—ah why?
Since from the tomb alone, all bliss we claim.

Alcander!—ah—what tears for thee shall flow—
What doom awaits the wretch that murder'd thee?
May never flower in his curs'd garden blow,
May never fruit adorn his hated tree.

May that fine spark which nature lent to man,
Reason! be thou extinguish'd in his brain;
Sudden his doom, contracted be his span,
Ne'er to exist, or rise from dust again.

May no kind genius save his step from harms,
Where'er he sails may tempests rend the sea,
May never maiden yield to him her charms,
Nor prattling infant hang upon his knee.

Retire, retire from this disastrous shore,
Dark is the sun, when woes like these dismay--
I quit my groves, and view with joy no more
The fragrant orange, and the floweret gay.

National Gazette   January 26, 1792

PALEMON *to* LAVINIA+.

Stanza 1: First stanza of the 1790 version, with the following variants:
line 2: What comfort shall I give--what can I say?
line 4: For this, Lavinia, is a cloudy day.

Stanza 2: Say, do I wake?--or are my woes a dream;
If so--dread vision! waft me far away;
Remove me quick from this sky glancing stream
That glides, unconscious, to the Indian bay.

Stanza 3: Third stanza of the 1790 version, with the following variants:
line 1: Alcander!--ah--what tears for thee must flow--

Stanza 4: Fourth stanza of the 1790 version.

Stanza 5: Fifth stanza of the 1790 version.

Stanza 6: Second stanza of the 1790 version.

Stanza 7: Sixth stanza of the 1790 version.

+ Occasioned by a melancholy event mentioned in the history of Louisiana. O'Reilly, governor of the Spanish territories in those parts, discovering a number of citizens engaged in a conspiracy to deliver up the province to the French, invited forty of them to dinner; who having dined, were instantly ordered to be hanged in sight of the whole town of New Orleans. The above lines are founded on this tragical event, and may be supposed to have been written by a person nearly connected in family and friendship with one of the unfortunate sufferers.

G.D.

Poems (1795), 83-84.

Daily Advertiser   November 18, 1790

The BLESSINGS of the POPPY,

----*Opiser per Orlem dicor.*   Ovid.

WHEN the first men to this world's climate came
Smit by the winter's rude, unsocial blast,
Unskill'd to raise the wall, or wake the fire
Badly in narrow huts their days they pass'd.

Conscious of pains they knew not how to cure
In vain they sigh'd and sighing, begg'd relief,
No druggist came, by art or reason taught
With strength of potent herbs to calm their grief.

Fierce tortures to allay, some reverend sage
Preach'd *Patience* to the pangs, that could not hear,
For restless anguish doom'd her victim still
To groan through life, and sigh from year to year.

At length from Jove, and Heaven's œtherial dome
Sky-walking Hermes came to view these plains,
He look'd--and saw what fate or gods had done,
And formed the Poppy, to relieve all pains.

Then to the sons of grief his speech address'd,
"Through this dull flower is shed such potent dew,
When pain distracts--drink this--and drown in sleep
Your present ills, and all the future too.

From other worlds, by other Beings trod,
To these bleak climes this plunder'd plant I bore;
Receive a gift, thrice worthy of a god,
Since pain, when hush'd to sleep,--is pain no more."

New York. November 16.

Poems (1795), 104.

Daily Advertiser   November 24, 1790[1]

The following Lines were addressed to a gay young Lady that was courted by a grave religious Lover, and far advanced in years.

To musty books, and cob-web halls,
Must Cynthia now retire,
Where pictur'd on the darken'd walls,
Old Whitehead to devotion calls,
Or Bunyan tunes the lyre.

Your lover's sigh, your lover's tear,
Is spent for joys above;
When such a worthy saint is near
How can you with indifference hear
So fine a tale of love?

---

[1] Except for the phrase "to a gay young lady that was" in the title, this text has no lines in common with the first collected version, and in a complete edition of the poet would have to appear as a separate poem. However, the titles are similar, the basic idea developed in both four-stanza texts is the same, and the first two lines of stanza 3 of the collected text are a condensed paraphrase of stanzas 2 and 3 of the *Daily Advertiser* text; the time between the two texts simply has altered the perspective of the poet's cautionary stance. In 1790, the poet warns the "gay young lady" who is *courted* by a "grave religious lover" that life with such a lover will be austere rather than amusing. In 1795, he advises this "gay young lady," who is now *married* to a "doting old deacon," to give up her efforts to find any signs of life in him. The similarity of titles and ideas convinces me that this is the earlier version of the completely revised poem. Other evidence includes the similarity between several lines here and the first newspaper version of "Constantia," (*Daily Advertiser*, May 1, 1790), as well as the verbal parallels between the last two lines of stanza 1 here, and several lines of "On the crew of a certain vessel . . ." (*Daily Advertiser*, May 20, 1791), i.e. "Old Erskine swabs the decks . . .
    And Bunyan heaves the log."

Dear Cynthia, things beyond the moon
Are all that he desires:
Where he would have you go so soon,
No fiddler plays a merry tune,
No beau your face admires,

No painted scene, no stage have they,
No lively strokes of wit,
But praise alone, and folks that pray,
And deacons dress'd in parson's grey--
Can these your fancy hit?

Poems (1795), 334-35. (EPISTLE to a gay *Young Lady* that was married to a doating old *Deacon.*)

Daily Advertiser   January 24, 1791

The AMERICAN SOLDIER.
(*A Picture from the Life,*)

DEEP in a vale, a stranger now to arms,
Too poor to shine in courts, too proud to beg,
He, who once warr'd on *Saratoga's* plains
Sits musing o'er his scars, and wooden leg.

Remembering still the toils of former days
To other hands he sees his earnings paid;
They share the due reward--*he* feeds on praise,
Lost in the abyss of want, misfortune's shade.

Far, far from domes where splendid tapers glare,
'Tis his from dear-bought *Peace* no wealth to win,
Remov'd alike from courtly-cringing squires,
The great man's levee, and the proud man's grin.

Sold are those arms that once on Britons blaz'd,
When flush'd with conquest to the charge they came,
That power repell'd, and *Freedom's* fabric rais'd
She leaves her soldier--*Famine,* and a *name*!

January 22.

Poems (1795), 479.

Daily Advertiser   January 27, 1791

BEDLOW ISLAND.

Messrs. *Printers,*

There is an Island in the neighbourhood of this city, of which the Citizens in general, have a very imperfect knowledge. As I cannot find a description of it in Mr. Morse's, or any other system of geography, I send you the following sketch, taken on the spot.

IN *Hudson's* waves, three miles from town
(Its baby Light-House tumbled down)
Extends an Island full in view,
Beheld by all, but known to few.

Surrounded by the watry waste
No haven here has Nature plac'd,
But those, who wish to walk it o'er
Must land upon the open shore.

Here as I came, to view the ground,
No blooming goddesses I found,
But lasses skill'd in mixing grog,
In milking cows, or making *nog.*

Ten stately trees adorn the Isle--
The house,* a crazy tottering pile,
Where once the Doctor ply'd his trade
On feverish wights, and rakes decay'd.

Six hogs about the Island feed
(Sweet *mudlarks* of the Georgia breed)
Who, while the house-wife deals out drams
Can oysters catch, and open clams.

Upon its surface, smooth and clean,
The world in miniature is seen;
Tho' scarce a journey for a snail
We meet the mountain, hill, and vale.

To those that guard this stormy place
Two cities stare them in the face;
There York her spiry summits rears:
And here--COMMUNIPAW appears.

The tenant, *now* but ill at ease,
Derives no fuel from his trees,
And Jersey boats, tho' begg'd to land,
All leave him--on the larboard hand.

Some monied man, grown sick of care,
To this neglected spot repair;
What Nature sketch'd, let art complete,
And your's shall be this *Country Seat.*

January 25.

Poems (1795), 126-27.

---

*Formerly occupied as a Hospital.

Daily Advertiser   January 26, 1791

STANZAS,
Written on the Hills of NEVERSINK, near Sandy Hook, 1790.

THESE heights, the pride of all the coast,
What happy genius plann'd;
Aspiring o'er the distant wave
That sinks the neighboring land:
These hills for solitude design'd,
This bold and broken shore,
These haunts, impervious to the wind,
Tall oaks, that to the tempest bend,
Half Druid, I adore.

The lapse of time, and change of lords
Beholds you still the same;
You saw the angry Briton come,
You saw his blasted fame.
With towering crest, you first are doom'd
The news of *Land* to tell;
To him that comes, fresh joys impart,
To him that goes, a heavy heart,
The lover's long farewell!

In early days, and vanish'd years
To rougher toils resign'd,
You saw me rove, in search of care,
And leave true bliss behind;
You saw me rig the barque, so trim,
To trace a tiresome road;
By wintry seas and tempests chas'd
You saw me o'er the ocean haste,
A comfortless abode!

Your shaded springs of azure blue
What luxury to sip,
As from the mountain's breast they flow
To moisten Celia's lip!
In rude retirements herd the deer,
Where forests round them rise,

Dark groves--their tops in œther lost,
Which, haunted still by *Huddy's* ghost,
The trembling rustic flies.

Proud heights! with pain so often seen,
I quit your view no more,
And see, unmov'd the passing sail,
Tenacious of the shore:
Let those who pant for wealth or fame
Pursue the watry road,
Soft sleep and ease, blest days and nights,
And health, attend these favorite heights,
Retirement's safe abode!

January 25.

Freeman's Journal   February 2, 1791

Stanza 1:   First stanza of the *Daily Advertiser* text, with lines 2, 4, 6, and 9 indented.

Stanza 2:   Second stanza of the *Daily Advertiser* text, with lines 2, 5, and 8 indented and line 4 deleted.

Stanza 3:   Third stanza of the *Daily Advertiser* text, with lines 2, 4, 6, and 9 indented.

Stanza 4:   Fourth stanza of the *Daily Advertiser* text, with lines 2, 4, 6, and 9 indented.

Stanza 5:   Fifth stanza of the *Daily Advertiser* text, with lines 2, 4, 6, and 9 indented.

National Gazette   November 28, 1791

Written on the Hills of the NEVERSINK, *near Sandy--Hook, July,* 1791.

Substantively identical to the *Daily Advertiser* text, with the following variants:

First line of the first three stanzas indented.
Stanza 5, line 9: Retirement's blest abode.
Signature: SINBAT.

Poems (1795), 386-87.

Daily Advertiser   January 28, 1791

The MARKET MAID.

AT dawn of day, from short repose,
At hours that might all townsmen shame,
To catch our money, round or square,
In coarse attire, and low heel'd shoes,
She from the heights of *Guanos* came,
With kail and cabbage, fresh and fair.

At Brooklyn wharf, in cherry trim,
Arrived an hour before the Sun,
Young Charon's bark receives her store;
Across the briny wave they skim,
And thus they laughing, come to town,
She at the helm, and he the oar.

Full early taught the arts of gain,
No sharping knave that walks the street,
Though vers'd in all the tricks of trade,
No city nymph, nor powder'd swain,
With all their art, can hope to cheat
A *bargain* from this country maid.

The Market done, her cash secur'd,
She homeward takes her wonted way,
The painted chest behind the door,
With many a trusty guinea stor'd,
Receives the earnings of the day,
Laid up–to see the sun no more!

> Sweet nymph! why all this useless pain,
> Such early toil and evening care,
> This hoarding for the age to come?
> Say, is there not one city swain
> That strikes your fancy--for an heir?
> Relent, relent,--and take him home.

January 26

National Gazette   May 28, 1792

The MARKET GIRL.
[*a real character*]

First line of each stanza begins at the margin.

Stanza 1:   First stanza of the 1791 version, with the following variants:
    line 4:   In plain attire, and low-heel'd shoes,
    line 5:   She from the groves of Glouc'ster came

Stanza 2:   Second stanza of the 1791 version, with the following variants:
    line 1:   At *Cooper's* wharf, in travelling trim,
    line 4:   Across the wavy waste they skim,

Stanza 3:   Third stanza of the 1791 version.

Stanza 4:   Fourth stanza of the 1791 version, with the following variants:
    line 4:   (With many a rusty dollar stor'd)
    line 5:   Receives the gainings of the day--

Stanza 5:   Fifth stanza of the 1791 version, with the following variants:
    line 1:   Sweet nymph! why all this ceaseless pain,
    line 4:   If he that courts you, courts in vain,
    line 5:   And you, regardless of an heir,
    line 6:   Refuse--alas!--to take him home!

May 24.

Poems (1795), 58-59.

Daily Advertiser   February 1, 1791

The ISLAND FIELD NEGRO.
[*Written some years ago, on a Sugar Plantation in Jamaica.*]

IF there exists a Hell, (the case is clear,)
Sir *Toby's* slaves enjoy that portion here:
Here are no burning brimstone lakes, 'tis true,
But kindled rum, full often burns as blue;
In which some fiend, half serious, half in jest,
Steeps *Toby's* name, and brands poor Cudjoe's breast.

    Here whips on whips excite a thousand fears,
And mingled howlings vibrate through my ears;
Here Nature's plagues abound, of all degrees,
Snakes, scorpions, despots, lizards, centipedes--
No art, no care escapes the busy lash,
All have their dues, and paid in ready cash:
The lengthy cart-whip guards this tyrant's reign,
And cracks, like pistols from the fields of cane.
Ye powers that form'd these wretched tribes relate,
What have they done to merit such a fate!--
Why were they brought from Eboe's sultry waste
To see the plenty that they must not taste?
Food which they cannot buy, and dare not steal;
Yams and potatoes--many a scanty meal!
    One with a gibbet wakes his negroe's fears,
One to the wind-mill nails him by the ears;
One keeps his slave in dismal dens unfed,
One puts the wretch in pickle, ere he's dead;
This, to a tree suspends him by the thumbs,
That, from his table grudges even crumbs!

    O'er yon rough hills a tribe of females go,
Each with her gourd, her infant, and her hoe,
Scorch'd by a sun, that has no mercy here,
Driven by a devil, that men call *Overseer:*
In chains twelve wretches to their labor haste,
Thrice twelve I see with iron collars grac'd--
Are these the joys that flow from vast domains,
Is gold thus got, Sir Toby, worth your pains;

Who would your wealth on terms like these possess,
Where all we see is pregnant with distress?--

Talk not of blossoms, and your endless spring,
No joy to me these scenes of misery bring,
Hell's Picture, I this rich plantation call;
And you the Beezlebub—that rule it all,

January 31.

Freeman's Journal   March 2, 1791

Stanza 4, line 2: No joy to me these scenes of miseries bring,

New York Weekly Museum   June 16, 1792

The ISLAND FIELD NEGRO
Written on a Sugar Plantation in Jamaica

Stanza 1, line 2: Sir Toby's slaves receive their portion here:

Stanza 2, line 9: Ye pow'rs who form these wretched tribes relate,
         line 19: This to the tree suspends him by the thumbs,

Stanza 3, line 3: Scorch'd by a sun which has no mercy here,
         line 4: Driven by a devil called an Overseer:

Stanza 4, line 2: No joy to me these scenes of pleasure bring;

National Gazette   July 21, 1792

Stanza 1:   First stanza of the 1791 version.

Stanza 2:   Second stanza of the 1791 version, with the following variants:
line 2:   And mingled howlings vibrate on my ears;
line 6:   All have their dues, and all are paid in cash:
Stanza concludes with line 8.

Stanza 3: Begins with line 9 of the second stanza of the 1791 version, and ends with the last line of the second stanza of the 1791 version.
(line 1 indented, line 7 begins at margin)

Stanza 4: Third stanza of the 1791 version, with two additional lines:
line 11: Angola's natives flogg'd by hireling hands,
line 12: And toil's hard product shipp'd to foreign lands?

Stanza 5: Talk not of blossoms, and your endless spring,
No joy to me these scenes of mis'ry bring
Where Stygian pictures half their shades renew,
Pictures of woe that Virgil's pencil drew:
Where black-guard Charons make their yearly trip,
And souls arrive on every Guinea ship--
Where they who pine, and languish to be free
Must climb the tall cliffs of the *Liganee;*
Beyond the clouds in skulking haste repair,
And hardly safe from brother butchers there.

Poems (1795), 301-92.

Daily Advertiser   February 2, 1791

Messrs. *Printers,*

Please to insert the following lines on the failure of Mr. Churchman's scheme of going to BAFFIN's BAY, to ascertain the truth of his Variation Chart.

I. CHURCHMAN, methinks your scheme is rather wild
Of travelling to the pole
Where icy mountains roll,
And pork and pease
Are said to freeze
Even at the instant they are boil'd.

II. Rejected now your humble ardent prayer
   For *cash,* to speed your way,
   To Baffin's frozen bay,
  'Tis your own fault, if you repine;
  You should have mentioned some rich silver mine,
  Not variation stuff, that claims no care.

III. *Avarice* alone would sooner bid you go
  Than all the allurements art can show:
  The men, whom you petition for some dollars
  Tho' willing to be thought prodigious scholars,
  Yet care no more for variation charts
  Than ace of spades or king of hearts.

IV. Churchman, 'tis best to quit this vain pursuit
  This *variation* is a slighted thing;
  Rather attach yourself to Cesar's wing
  You'll find it better--better, Sir, by half
  To tell him Yankee jokes, and make him laugh:
  Then shall you, mounted in a coach and six
  Ride envoy to the country of the Creeks;
  Then shall you visit Europe's gaudy courts
  And see the polish'd world at public charge,
  Come back, and spend your life in sports,
  Be air'd in coach, and sail'd in barge.--
  Pursue this track, thou man of curious soul,
  Nor, like a whale, go puffing to the pole.

Columbian Centinel February 23, 1791

Of much of *Peter Pindar's fire,* and some of his *sauciness,* the following taken from a New York paper partakes.

To *mr.* CHURCHMAN,
On the failure of his SCHEME *of sailing to Baffin's Bay,*
To ascertain the truth of his VARIATION CHART.

Text of the poem is identical to the *Daily Advertiser* version, but the stanza pattern is altered and the stanzas are unnumbered:

Stanzas 1 and 2: Lines 2-5 indented, 1 and 5 at margin.

Stanza 3: All lines indented.

Stanza 4: Lines 2, 3, 4, 5, 6, 7, 9, and 11 indented; lines 1, 8, 10, 12, and 13 at margin.

Poems (1795), 428-29.

Daily Advertiser   February 5, 1791

The Tea-Drinker.

I.

LET some in Grog place their delight,
O'er bottled Porter waste the night,
    Or sip the rosy Wine;
    A dish of Tea
    More pleases me;
    Yields softer joys,
    Provokes less noise,
And breeds no bad design.

II.

If learned men the truth would speak,
They prize it far beyond their Greek,
    More fond attention pay:
    No Hebrew *root*,
    So well can suit;
    More quickly taught,
    Less dearly bought,
And *studied* twice a day.

III.

When worn with toil, or vext with care,
Let Susan but this draught prepare
    And I forget my pain:
    This magic bowl
    Revives the soul,
    With gentle sway,
    Bids care be gay,
Nor mounts to cloud the brain.

IV.

From China's clime this present brought,
Enlivens every power of thought,
    Rigs many a ship for sea;
    Old maids it warms,
    Young widow's charms,
    And ladies men
    Not one in ten,
But courts them--for their *Tea*.

V.

This shrub from distant regions sprung,
Puts life into the female tongue,
    And aids the cause of LOVE.--
    Such power has TEA,
    O'er bond and free--
    Which Priests admire--
    Delights the 'Squire,
And GALEN's sons approve!

February 4.

National Gazette   July 7, 1792

THE DISH OF TEA.

In each stanza, lines 1 and 2 are at the margin; lines 3 and 8 are indented three spaces, and lines 4, 5, 6, and 7 are indented five spaces.

Poems and Variants

The stanzas are not numbered.

Stanza 1: First stanza of the 1791 text, with the following variants:
line 8: And breeds no base design.

Stanza 2: Fourth stanza of the 1791 version, with the following variants:
line 6: And misses' men

Stanza 3: When throbbing pains assail my head
And dullness o'er my brain is spread,
   The muse no longer kind,
     A single sip
     Dispels the hyp:
     To chase the gloom
     Fresh spirits come
The flood-tide of the mind.--

Stanza 4: Third stanza of the 1791 version.

Stanza 5: Second stanza of the 1791 version.

Stanza 6: Fifth stanza of the 1791 version, with the following variants:
line 1: This leaf from distant regions sprung

Poems (1795), 99.

Weekly Visitor   July 29, 1820

1795 text of the poem, introduced as follows:

Mr. Ming;

Many a pen has been engaged in praise of the intoxicating drinks, which might have been better employed–it is to be regretted that talents should be so prostituted. Among the very few poetical attempts to detract from that accursed poison, I have selected the following; I know not who is the writer, it has the merit of morality to make amends for the want of sublimity. Perhaps you may tender a service to society by publishing it.
                                                        R.

Daily Advertiser   February 8, 1791

The SHELBURNE THREAT.

[A True Story.]

From Shelburne's boasted town, o'er Fundy's bay,
To put himself in Madam Fortune's way,
A Scotite came, 'tis worthy of remark,
Master and owner of a ragged barque;
Fish made the whole, T--totum of his load,
With fish was every hole and cranny stow'd,
Even in the cabbin where he made his bed,
Bundles of fish were for his pillow spread.
In every corner, heaps on heaps lay slain,
'Twas fish, and fish--and cut and come again.

    At length to Boston's haughty town arriv'd,
There many a scheme to run them, he contriv'd
Vain were his schemes, the unlucky sequel shews,
Striving to cheat the Yankees of their dues,
Ere he was able to complete his wish,
The Port-collector seiz'd them--every fish!

"S'blood, death and wounds, (The angry captain cry'd)
"What vile, ungrateful wretches here reside'
'May I be d----d, (this dreadful oath he swore,
And stamp'd indignant on his cabbin floor)
"May I be d----d, if at some future day,
"When *Famine* marks these Yankees, for her prey,
"When pinching wants their growling guts assail--
"If prayers or tears shall o'er my wrath prevail,
"Starve and be d----d shall be the word, that's plain,
"Shelburne, nor I, shall aid your wants again!"

February 7.

National Gazette   April 5, 1792

The SHELBURNE THREAT.

[A story founded on fact.--The captain of a Nova-Scotia

Bank vessel, in attempting to land his fish at Boston, without paying the foreign duty, had his vessel and cargo seized. The captain, in a fit if irritation, swore, that if the Bostonians were reduced to a starving condition, he would never again bring a fish to their port!]

Stanza 1: First stanza of the 1791 version, with the following variants:
line 4: Master and owner of a painted barque;
line 5: 'Twas fish on fish--and cut--and come again!

Stanza 2:
At length to Boston's haughty port arrivd,
There, many a scheme to *run them* he contriv'd;
For *here*, by law (we scarcely need to say)
All foreign fish a heavy impost pay.
To save this *duty* was the captain's wish
And land, unseen, his long imprison'd fish:
Vain were his plans!--no scheme could he devise
To cheat old *Argus*, with his hundred eyes,
(That wight who, ceaseless, *waits* the coming *tides*,
Peeps in the hold, or through the cabbin glides)--
Vain were his plans, the unlucky sequel shews,
Striving to cheat the customs of their dues,
Ere he was able to complete his wish,
The Port-collector seiz'd them--every fish!

Stanza 3: Third stanza of the 1791 version, with the following variants:
line 10: "*Shelburne,* nor I--will aid your wants again!

April 3.

Poems (1795), 352.

Daily Advertiser   February 11, 1791

THE JUG OF RUM.

WITHIN these earthen walls confin'd
The ruin lurks of human kind,
More mischiefs here united, dwell,
And more diseases haunt this cell
Than ever plagu'd the Egyptian flocks,
Or ever curs'd Pandora's box.

Within these Prison-walls repose
The seeds of many a bloody nose,
The chattering tongue, the horrid oath,
The fist for fighting nothing loth,
The nose with diamonds glowing red,
The bloated eye, the broken head!

Forever fasten'd be this door--
Confin'd within, a thousand more
Destructive fiends of hateful shape
Even now are planning an escape.

Here, only by a cork controul'd
And slender walls of earthen mould,
In all their pomp of death reside
Revenge, that ne'er was satisfied,
The *tree* that bears the deadly fruit
Of maiming, murder, and dispute,
Assault, that innocence assails,
The images of gloomy Jails--
All these within this jug appear,
And--Jack, the hangman, in the rear!

Thrice happy he, who early taught
By Nature--ne'er this poison sought;
He, with the purling stream content
The beverage quaffs that Nature meant;
In reason's scale his actions weigh'd
His spirits want no foreign aid--
Long life is his, in vigour pass'd,
Existence welcome to the last--
A spring that never yet grew stale;
Such virtue lies in *Adam's ale.*

February 10.

National Gazette   January 23, 1792

(Poem introduced by the following paragraphs:

ON COUNTRY TAVERNS.

A COUNTRY tavern is generally a place of rendezvous for all the choice spirits of a neighborhood. Here petty law suits are decided at least once a fortnight, and he must be an indifferent justice of peace, who presides at such trials (as they are called) who will not drink both with plaintiff and defendant, after the suit is decided: with the first to congratulate him on his success; with the latter to to console him for being *cast*, and having costs to pay.

Happy would it be for every community if ardent spirits could be banished from amongst them. The consequences of too free a use of these are too well known to be recapitulated.--It is observable, at those country taverns where liquors of that description are kept, the traveller is frequently induced to delay his journey, the neighboring ploughman to misspend his time, and the once industrious tradesman to neglect and beggar his family.

I shall conclude these observations with some lines written last winter at a country tavern, where from the introduction of a single *jug of rum*, conviviality and good humour were changed into madness and brutality, and numbers of the guests, who came, perhaps, only to pass a social hour, went away maimed, muttering, and lastingly embittered against each other.)

The JUG *of* RUM.

Stanza 4:   Two lines have been inserted after line 8.
        line 9:   The *giddy thought*, on mischief bent,
        line 10: The *evening hour* in folly spent,--
        line 11: All these within this jug appear,
        line 12: And--Jack, the hangman, in the rear!

Philadelphia, January 21.

American Museum   August, 1792

THE JUG OF RUM.
By Philip Freneau.

Substantively identical to the *National Gazette* text, except for the following variants:

Stanza 1, line 1: not indented.
Stanza 5, line 7: Lifelong is his, in vigour pass'd,

General Advertiser   October 9, 1792

THE JUG OF WHISKEY

(Text substantively identical to the *National Gazette* version.)

Poems (1795), 61.

Port Folio   October 24, 1807

(An abbreviated text that never appeared in any of Freneau's collections but was widely reprinted in newspapers. It is included in the *Port Folio's* extended review of Freneau, and is introduced as follows:

> The Address to a Jug of Rum is very much in the manner of Swift, who, with all his power of condensing his expression, could not afford us a better example of the *multum in parvo* than the following:)

Here only by a cork controul'd,
And slender walls of earthen mould,
In all the pomp of death repose
The seeds of many a bloody nose;
The chattering tongue, the horrid oath,
The fist for fighting nothing loth,
The passion which no words can tame,
That bursts, like sulphur, into flame;

The nose carbuncled, glowing red,
The bloated eye, the broken head;
The tree that bears the deadly fruit
Of murder, maiming, in dispute;
Assault that Innocence assails,
The images of gloomy jails,
The giddy thought, on mischief bent,
The midnight hour in riot spent;
All within this Jug appear,
With Jack, the hangman, in the rear!

New York Weekly Museum   September 10, 1808

ON A JUG OF RUM.

Identical to the *Port Folio* text, except for the following variants:
line 7:   The passions, which no words can tame,
line 8:   That burst, like sulphur, into flame;
line 9:   The nose carbuncled, growing red

Centinel of Freedom   May 14, 1811

Reprint of the 1795 text, with the following variants:

Stanza 1, line 6: Or issued from Pandora's box.

Stanza 2, line 3: The abusive tongue, the horrid oath,
          line 4: The fist of fighting nothing loth;
          line 7: The face with furnace flowing red,

Stanza 3: Includes both the third and fourth stanza of the 1795 text, with the following variants:
           line 1: Forever fastened by that door,
           line 3: Destructive fiends of horrid shape,
           line 7: In all the pomp of death reside,

Stanza 4: Fifth stanza of the 1795 text, with the following variants:
           line 6: The beverage quaffs which nature meant,
           line 9: Not swell'd too high nor sunk too low,

line 13: A spring that never yet grows stale,
line 14: Such virtue grows in Adam's Ale.

New York Weekly Museum   November 20, 1813

ADDRESS TO A JUG OF RUM.

Identical to the *Port Folio* text, with the following variants:
line 9:   The nose carbuncled, growing red.

Daily Advertiser   February 18, 1791

On the *proposed taxation* of NEWS-PAPERS.

'Tis time to tax the news (*old Gripus cries*)
Subjects were never good that were too wise:
In every hamlet, every trifling town,
Some vain ambitious fellow sits him down,
On spacious folio prints his weekly mess,
And spreads around the poison of the Press.
Hence to the *world* the streams of scandal flow,
To tell them secrets that they should not know,
Hence courtiers strut with libels on the backs;
And shalt not news be humbled by a tax.

Once ('tis most true) these papers did some good,
When British chiefs came bouncing o'er the flood
By these enkindled, every heart grew warm,
By these excited, all were taught to arm,
When I retiring to Britannia's clime,
Sat brooding o'er the vast events of time;
Doubtful which side to take, or what to say,
Or who would win, or who would lose the day.

Those times are past; (my sentiment excuse,)
The well-born sort alone, should read the news,
No common herds intrude behind the scene,

To view the movements of the state machine:
One paper only, fill'd with pompous stuff,
One paper, for this country is enough,
That fill'd with gifts, from chaplains, 'squires, and quacks,
Shall have the merit to escape a tax."

February 17.

Poems (1795), 377.

Daily Advertiser   February 26, 1791

The USEFUL *only in Vogue at COURT.*

WHOE'ER at court would hope to cut a dash,
He must go loaded with some *useful* trash;
Something, sage *dullness,* to assist your reign;
All fancy–stuff, all ornament is vain.

    Happy the man who plans, by force of steam,
To drive his boat twelve knots against the stream;
Still happier *he,* who born to build a bridge,
Schemes mighty matters on some river's edge:
Such to the world the noblest light impart,
The first in genius, and the first in art.

    Hence then, ye Bards, from our wise court refrain;
Wiseacres have forstall'd the present reign;
"No empty scribblings we endure at court,
(Cries Memmius, poring o'er a dull *report,*)
"Nothing but *useful* projects we require,
(Cries a new-fangled, self-imported squire,)
For Lisbon's court has sail'd our man of song,
And trust me, Bards, the *Muses* went along:
Since that bright morn he stepp'd on board his brig,
No Muses here–no Muses are with pig,
Nor, till his barque shall heave in sight once more,
Can one true Muse grow pregnant on this shore."

Now, had not wayward fortune fix'd me fast,
Firm to a point that never shall be pass'd,
Did I the smiles of fortune still pursue,
And Memmius, wish to rise in fame like you--
Were this my scheme, I'd quit at once the mob,
And haste to court with pendulum and bob,
Quit all the gains the finer arts bestow,
The fiends of fancy, and the flowers that blow;
Indulge this potent *something* in the skull,
That makes us famous while it makes us dull,
To the best place prefers its steady claim--
The road to fortune, and the road to fame.

February 25.

Poems (1795), 385-86.

Daily Advertiser   March 4, 1791[1]

(Untitled.)

CAN love of fame the gentle muse inspire
Where he that hoards the most has all the praise;
Where avarice and her fiends each bosom fire,
All heap enormous store for rainy days,
    Owning by such perpetual round of toil
    That man was made to grovel on the soil.

Suspended in my view, quick flows the sand,
The *good man Richard* has no time to lose--
What's yet to come, record with nimble hand,
Time may, perhaps, another glass refuse;
    By time is many an honest fellow jew'd,
    And who is sure to see his glass renew'd?

None ever yet in rhyming wrought so well
But he, himself or else the world would tire;
With endless music odious grows the shell,
With frequent absence brighter glows love's fire;
    When e'er this current stops, advise me then
    To finish with the sand--and quit the pen.

---

[1] This text has only one stanza, the first, in common with the first collected version; the other three stanzas were totally rewritten. As such, a complete edition of the poet might edit this text separately. The idea developed has altered significantly by 1795. In this text, the poet's persuasion to quit the muse is motivated, in part, by a suspicion that his verses will be appreciated more if they appear less frequently (stanza 3), and in part by a feeling that time is too precious to waste on what is likely to prove an unrewarding career in verse (stanza 2). In the 1795 text, the only reason suggested for quitting the muse is the one also suggested in the earlier text (stanza 1 and the first two lines of stanza 4): that truly worthy verse is not rewarded in these times, only that of ambitious bootlickers, and, consequently, any self respecting poet would "quit the stage."

Yet while it walks the page, let no one say
It flatter'd knaves or help'd to puff the vain--
Sick of the wasted hours, some toil, some play,
Half pleas'd, I seek my barren fields again,
> Look back on years, that can return no more,
> And fools at sea, that might have stay'd on shore.

March 3.

Poems (1795), 433-34.

Daily Advertiser   March 11, 1791

THE ISLAND SAVAGE.

WHEN first to feel love's fire this Lout begins
He combs his hair, and cocks his hat with pins,
Views in some stream, his face, with fond regard,
Plucks from his upper lip the bristly beard,
With soap and sand his homely visage scowers
Rough from the joint attack of sun and showers;
The sheepskin breeches stretch'd upon his thighs
Next on his back the homespun coat he tries;
Round his broad breast he wraps the jerkin blue
And sews a mighty soal on either shoe;
Thus, all prepar'd, the fond impatient swain
Cuts from his groves of pine a ponderous cane;
In thought a Beau, a savage to the eye
Forth from his mighty nostrils heaves the sigh;
Tobacco is the present for his fair,
This he admires, and this best pleases her--
The bargain struck--few cares his bosom move
How to maintain, or how to lodge his love;
Close at his hand the piny forest grows,
Thence for his hut a slender frame he hues,
His art, not copied from Palladio's rules,
A hammer and an ax, his only tools,
By nature taught, a hasty hut he forms

Safe in the woods, to lodge them from the storms,
Here sees the Summer pass and Winter come,
Nor envies Britain's King his loftier home.

March 10.

Poems (1795), 377-78.

Daily Advertiser   March 22, 1791

Marriage A la-Mode.

BORN in the woods, in neighbouring cabbins bred,
Two lovers long a mutual passion sway'd,
When vex'd with lice, she fondly comb'd his head;
He often help'd her with the hoe and spade.

Her spinning wheel if accidents befel,
He strait with joy repair'd the rough machine,
And once a week (not led by sound of bell)
At country church was each fond Lover seen.

Amidst these joys ambition had no share,
No hopes of splendid domes, no wealth had they;
Amidst these joys, this loving, lounging pair
What could have tempted to have run away?

To gossip Joan's she hardly knew the road,
He to the market and the mill had been;
Their names unknown beyond the adjacent wood,
He had no towns, and she no cities seen.

At midnight hour, when troubled ghosts patrol
He, silent, to her bed-room-window came;
She from her nest of straw to meet him stole;
He, mounted on his nag, bore off the dame.

A straggling Parson tied the sacred knot--
A quick pursuit the trembling couple fear'd,
Then mov'd again, and forc'd the steed a-trot,
Her father's voice in every breath she heard.

By break of day be-devil'd and be-swampt,
Deep in the mire, this couple and their nag
Were fix'd--she snuffled, while he swore and a stampt,
Horse-whip'd the horse, and call'd his bride a hag.

Slow and on foot, with shame returning home,
Both from their angry friends forgiveness pray,
Then to her wheel she turns, and he his loom;
And when they're ask'd the reason of their flight
He answers strait (as many others might)
"Sirs, tis the fashion now to run away!"

March 21.

National Gazette   February 6, 1792

MARRIAGE A-LA-MODE.

[Occasioned by a quarrel between a weaver and a ditcher; the latter having supposed his family consequence disgraced by the clandestine marriage of his son with the weaver's daughter.]

Stanza 2, line 2:   He strait with joy repair'd the rude machine,

Stanza 8, line 3:   Then to his spade he turns, and she her loom;

           line 6:   "Zurs, 'tis the fashion, now, to run-a-way!"

February 2.

Poems (1795), 102.

Daily Advertiser   March 24, 1791

On putting a DOG *ashore at the island of* SAPOLA,
for stealing: written 1788.

SINCE Nature taught you, *Tray,* to be a thief,
What blame have you for working at your trade?
What, if you stole a handsome round of beef,
Theft, in your code of laws, no crime was made.

The ten commandments you have never read,
Nor did it ever enter in your head:
But art and nature, careful to conceal,
Disclos'd not even the eighth--*Thou shalt not steal.*

>Then to the green wood, caitiff, haste away.
>There take your chance to live: for Truth must say,
>We have no right, for theft, to hang up *Tray.*

March 23.

National Gazette   November 3, 1791

LINES
Occasioned by the putting a Dog on shore at the Island of Sapola, for theft.--1788.

Text identical to the *Daily Advertiser* version, but, in each stanza, lines 1 and 3 are indented; all other lines begin at the margin.

Daily Advertiser   April 13, 1791

On the prohibition of
SPIRITOUS LIQUORS
In the New-York and Albany Jails.

"GIVE to the wretched, drink that's strong,"
(Said David's Son) but we, more wise
With *Cyder,* from the cistern, rough,
Molasses-Beer, and such dull stuff
The miseries of the imprison'd heart prolong.

"Shut up in jail from day to day
(Methinks I hear a debtor say)
Victims to public rage and private spite,
All that we had to keep our spirits up
Was glowing *grog* that fill'd the chearing cup,
This banish'd care, and check'd the rising sigh
Chac'd grief from every heart, gave joy to every eye.

"And will ye not this only comfort leave,
Ye men that frame the public laws?--
Parted from children, friends and wives
How heavily the moments roll;
What comfort have we of our lives
If you deny this cordial of the soul!
'Tis this that kills the tedious hour
Puts misery out of fortune's power,
Tis this that to the dial's hand lends wings
Gives to the Beggar all the pride of Kings,
Sheds joy throughout our gloomy cage
And bids us scorn the little Tyrant's rage.

"They that are unconfin'd drink what they will--
Who gave the right to limit men in jail?
Because misfortune sent us here
Must we for that be drench'd with "table beer,"
Or, in its stead, with Adam's ale?--
Relent--relent! contrive some other plan;
Rum is the dearest, choicest friend of man--
They that are *out* of jail, of all degrees,
Can spend their leisure as they please,
We, that are *in,* must pass it as we can."

April 12.
Poems (1795), 416.

Daily Advertiser   April 15, 1791

KAY-GROVE.

WITH eastern winds and shorten'd sail
To these delightful haunts we came
Where budding trees and gentle streams
Adorn the sweetly winding vale;
Where from the breezy grove we claim
The tribute of poetic dreams.

These simple woods delight me more
Than all the busy town can show,
More pleasure here Menalcas took
And more he priz'd this barren shore
Than groves that near Poughkeepsie grow,
Than all the charms of Kinderhook.

Here still remains a hermit's cell
Who, doom'd the haunts of men to fly
Enjoy'd his heaven beneath this shade--
In mouldering caves well pleas'd to dwell
He sought not from the flowers that die
A verdure that shall never fade.

The native of this happy spot
No cares of vain ambition haunt;
Pleas'd with the partner of his nest
Life flows--and when the dream is out
The earth, that once supply'd each want,
Receives him, fainting, to her breast.

April 10.

Poems (1795), 248-49.

New York Journal   April 16, 1791

Charity-A-La-Mode.

FROM southern climes a wandering vessel came
That from her looks or size small note could claim:
Her freight discharg'd, compell'd in port to stay,
Long by the walls this empty schooner lay;
In vain the Capt. scratch'd his sapient skull,
And flush'd her masts, and painted up her hull,
No sails to trim, no work but mixing grog,
Pensive he sate, and long'd to heave the log;
In vain he search'd, and stopt up every leak,
And advertised his barque from week to week.
All would not do!--the dock was still her fate
Idle the Master, unemployed the Mate;
While, with the tide she lay to rise and fall,
The wharfinger, 'twas thought, would take her all.

  At length a man, who had much gold in stock,
One morning fair, came waddling to the dock,
Address'd the Capt. as he pensive sate,
And cry'd *"what say you, friend, wilt take a freight?"*
  "Take it! (said Jonas) take it!--that I will
Take it as quick as patient takes a pill;
This idle life's the very worst disease:--
But, let me know your terms, Sir, if you please."
  "My terms are so and so" the merchant cry'd,
  "What! sixpence less than all the world beside?
What reason can be given, I humbly ask,
That *six-pence* should be clipt from every cask--
Five shillings, trust me, is the usual freight,
And given by every shipper in the state."
  "That may be so--the miser said (most cool)
And yet there's *one* exception to the rule.
If you're averse, there's hundreds will agree,
This sixpence sav'd is *meant for charity*;
My terms are good-you can't be angry, sure,
Each six-pence squeez'd from you, *shall bless the poor!*"

              April 13.

General Advertiser   April 25, 1791

Stanza 1, line 5: In vain the Capt. search'd his sapient skull.

National Gazette   February 20, 1792

CHARITY A-LA-MODE,
(*A TRUE STORY*)

Text contains six stanzas, with space between each.

Stanza 1:   First two lines of the 1791 text, with the following variants, followed by four new lines:
line 2:   That from her size, or looks small note could claim,
line 3:   Yet sound throughout, she many a gale had try'd,
line 4:   And still had Neptune, and his waves, defied;
line 5:   Not fam'd to be the foremost in the chase,
line 6:   Nor yet the rear-most in the watry race.

Stanza 2:   Last twelve lines of the first stanza of the 1791 text, with two additional lines inserted, and the following variants:
line 1:   indented.
line 4:   And scrap'd her masts, and furbish'd up her hull--
line 5:   (inserted) Hung on the rich, or flatter'd up the great--
line 6:   (inserted) Not one would trust a poet with his freight:
line 7:   No sails to trim; no work but mixing grog,
line 8:   Pensive he stood, and sigh'd to heave the log;
lines 9-14: last six lines of stanza 1 of the 1791 text.

Stanza 3:   Second stanza of the 1791 text, with the following variants:
line 4:   And ask'd, *What say you, friend; wilt' take a freight?*

Stanza 4:   Third stanza of the 1791 text.

Stanza 5:   Fourth stanza of the 1791 text, with the following

variants:
line 1:   *My terms are so and so* [the man replied] --
line 2:   not indented.

Stanza 6:   Fifth stanza of the 1791 text.
February 14.
Signature: SINBAT.

Poems (1795), 312-13.

Daily Advertiser   April 20, 1791

To the Keeper of the King's WATER-WORKS, *near Rock-Fort, in Jamaica; on being refused to fill a Puncheon of Fresh Water.*
Written, August 1784.

CAN *he*, that o'er two Indias holds the sway,
Where e're the ocean flows, whose fleets patrol,
Who bids Hibernia's rugged sons obey,
And at whose nod (you say) shakes either pole;

Can he, whose crown a thousand jewells grace,
Of worth untold--can he, so rich, deny
One simple puncheon from his ample vase,
Begg'd of his *quondam* subject--water dry?

Keeper! must I with empty cask return,
Just *see* the limpid stream, that runs to waste--
Deny'd the wave that flows from nature's urn,
By locks and keys secur'd from vulgar taste?

Yes! if I must--inform the royal ear,
Poor are some Kings that still in Britain live;
Tell him, that nature is no niggard here,
Tell him--that he with-holds what Beggars give.

April 19.

National Gazette   January 12, 1792

[The following lines were written some years ago (Sept. 1784) on board the brig Dromilly, in Kingston harbour, Jamaica; and sent to the keeper of the King's water-works, near Rock fort; who had refused the writer a puncheon of water from a reservoir that was, by royal order, appropriated to the use of the royal navy.]

Stanza 1:   First stanza of the 1791 text, with the following variants:
line 1:   CAN *he,* that o'er two Indies holds the sway,

Stanza 2:   Second stanza of the 1791 text.

Stanza 3:   Vast are the springs in yonder cloud-capt hill:
Why then confine the free-born chrystal wave?
Where *hogs* and *dogs* and *keepers* drink their fill,
May I not something from your bounty crave?

Stanza 4:   Third stanza of the 1791 text.

Stanza 5:   Fourth stanza of the 1791 text.

Signature: *SINBAT.*

Poems (1795), 380.

Daily Advertiser   April 29, 1791

Written on a BEAU drowned in a *Mill Pond.*

LOST in the suds, the rouge upon his cheek,
And matted in the wave, his hair so sleek;
His India vest, and coat of bottle green
No more at Church, or play-house shall be seen
No more shall Ladies that complexion praise,
No more the buckle shine, the button blaze!

How will Belinda, when this news she hears
Mourn her *Adonis*, in a sea of tears,
Drown'd in a pool, one fathom only deep,
(A shallow grave) how will Belinda weep!

"Had this but hap'd (the pensive maiden cries)
"Far on the Atlantic main, where billows rise
"And stormy gales the foundering vessel chace,
"I might have borne it with a better face;
"But to be drown'd where only cat fish play
"Or slippery eels pursue their grovelling way,
"Where shepherd Damon scours his lousy goats,
"And truant school-boys sail their baby boats,
"This breaks my heart--this prompts the heavy sigh:
"Was ever wretched girl so plagu'd as I
"Condemn'd to pass *three days* in grief and pain--
"Go--Jackey--go--dear Boy--and haul the sain!"

June, 1788.

National Gazette   November 24, 1791

Lines sacred to the Memory of
FOPLING FLUTTER,
[*Unfortunately drowned in a Mill-pond, about a week before his intended marriage, April, 1787.*]

Text appears as one 22-line stanza.

line 9:   Drown'd in a pool, and scarce a fathom deep,

Poems (1795), 88.

Daily Advertiser   May 2, 1791

Lines written some years ago, on the death of a *Fiddler.*
Addressed to Mrs. _____.

In life's fair morn a *Fiddle,* was his choice,
This he preferr'd to reason's sober voice;
Some scores of tunes, on cat gut taught to play,
Sweetly he scrap'd the dream of life away:
From house to house (the joy of all) he ran,
Welcome to all, this music-making man;
Where'er he went, he bade all *discord* cease
And howling brats by him were hush'd to peace:
Where'er he went, to play for beau or belle,
Much they admir'd the *god* within the shell;
Each grey-hair'd dame for *this,* postpon'd all care
And own'd, this fiddle was a sweet affair.--
No foe had he (tis worthy of remark)
Except perhaps, the preacher and his clerk,
Some deacon grave, who liv'd by looking sad,
Some rival wight, who no such fiddle had:
These were, indeed, disgusted with its tone;
Because--the world preferr'd it to their own.

    But, mark the event--with all his fiddling skill,
This man of tunes was verging down the hill:
From endless mirth, an idle habit sprung,
And years advanc'd, in spite of all he sung!--
Despising home, and absent day from day,
Perplext with weeds his little garden lay;--
Hence plagues came on, and hence, too soon, arose
From midnight drams the diamonds on his nose;
Hence, saucy cares, that would no longer wait,
Seiz'd all the man, and pictured out his fate,
New artists rose; that each became his foe,
Play'd livelier tunes (or people thought them so);
Soon out of date the grey-hair'd scraper grew,
(The truth was this, they wanted something *new*)
Surpriz'd he saw full seventy years were past--
"And do I wake!--(the fiddler cry'd) at last?
"While others toil'd, *to bless the rainy day,*
"Ye Gods! have I done nothing else but *play?*"--

Surpriz'd he saw the patches on his coat,
Himself--his fiddle--on the world afloat;
His hat, a slouch that Beggars might abuse,
And toes uncouth, that peep'd from both his shoes--
Then curs'd his strings, his rosin, and his art,
And said--" 'Tis so!--Your fiddler must depart!"

  Now he is dead!--Ye few that prize him still,
That once admir'd--nay, once ador'd his skill;
And *thou,* to whom I dedicate my lay,
Ah!--for the joys he gave, this tribute pay!
You--at whose wedding he so finely play'd,
That night, when *Celia* ceas'd to be a maid,
Whose charms, *that night,* bade every bosom glow,
Charms, that were toasted fifty years ago!--
To *him*--that once you deem'd out-done by none,
For *him,* provide the monumental stone!
From other worlds he had not much to hope,
No slave to Luther, Calvin, or the Pope.
(Perhaps some better work employs him there--
Perhaps on Pluto's coast no fiddles are!--
Howe'er that be, allow me to remark--
(Since things to come are sadly in the dark)
A *Newark stone,* companion of repose,
Should tell the inscription that the muse bestows:
And ere that STONE his mouldering dust confines,
You, give me but the *hint*--I'll write the lines!

April 30.

Columbian Centinal   June 4, 1791

 (Much easy humour, may be found in the following.)

     To Mrs. _____.
   On the *death* of a FIDDLER.

Text identical to the *Daily Advertiser's.*

Poems (1795), 15-16.

Daily Advertiser   May 13, 1791

THE RURAL BACHELOR.
A real Character.

I.

QUITTING the town, and gay abodes of men
Chance led my footsteps to a lonely den
Around whose walls no lively floweret grew,
Dull was its aspect, and its doors were few,
The crowing cock was all its morning bell
Mix'd with no pleasant voice of Nan or Nell;
No blooming trees, no flowering shrubs were nigh
Nothing to cheer the heart or please the eye:
One weeping-willow rais'd its baleful head,
Ivy and mint were through his garden spread–
Disgusted with the scene, when drawn more near
I smote my breast, and ask'd–"What beast lives here?"–

II.

No milk-maid here the selfish Wight allows
But forth he walks himself to milk his cows;
(In hand a staff, on either arm a pail
Pity he had no dish-clout at his tail)
Cows, that have given him many a hearty kick
And only fear him for his walnut stick:
Humbled they stand, a pensive, pining crew
And see their calves defrauded of their due.

    None but himself the juicy curd may squeeze
None like himself can change the milk to cheese
Cheese that appears at every slender treat,
And fate foredoom'd that he alone must eat;
The refuse of his store, the very cheese
That, if to market sent, the clerk would seize.

III.

Tir'd as I am with travelling this long road,
Much as I want, this night, some snug abode,

Something whereon to rest my weary head,
Something, at least that bears the name of bed,
Tho' many a mile, perhaps, may intervene
Ere yet again the haunt of man is seen,
Onward I jog--till Sol the light restores,
Rather than lodge with him, lodge out of doors.

May 11.

Poems (1795), 366-67.

Daily Advertiser   May 17, 1791

Stanzas to the memory of Mrs. GERTRUDE BURNET, *who died at Newark, in Essex county, New-Jersey, on the 4th of May,* 1791.

To the dark grave, where silence reigns,
And death his shadowy host detains,
Of life bereft, and quench'd its fires,
Gertruda in her turn retires.

Inclos'd in that obscure abode,
The bosom cold, with life that glow'd,
No more we trace its wonted charms,
No more the gentle spirit warms.

Blest form! tho' mouldering into dust,
This is not all thy doom, we trust;
To other worlds the active mind
Some new perfection goes to find:

From height to height advancing still,
To HIM that doth creation fill,
The power that measured out our span,
And planted reason, first in man.

Compos'd of nature's finest clay,
To *nature* she her debt did pay,
Who sympathizing, mingles here,
The rising sigh, the melting tear.

In her, whose memory ne'er shall fade,
Each milder virtue was display'd,
The breast of sentiment refin'd,
And beauties, native to the mind.

To make her image all complete,
How many of her sex must meet!
Virtues in them but thinly sown,
In her conjoin'd, were all her own.

She (doom'd to shine in honour's page,
A model to the rising age)
Was grac'd with all that could impart
Affection to the coldest heart.

Remov'd from hence so far away,
What shall your pensive poet say?
By friendship led, and grief sincere,
He drops his pen--and sheds a tear!

New-Ark, May 10, 1790.

Poems (1795), 363-64.

Daily Advertiser   May 20, 1791

On the Crew of a certain Vessel, several of whom happened to be of the same name with celebrated Clergymen.

In life's unsettled, odd career
What changes everyday appear
    To please or plague the eye;
A goodly brotherhood of priests
Are here transform'd to swearing beasts
    That Heaven and Hell defy.

Here *Bonner*, bruis'd with many a knock,
Has chang'd his surplice for a frock,
    Old *Erskine* swabs the decks:
And *Watts*, that once such pleasure took
In writing hymns, here grown a cook,
    Sinners no longer vex.

Here *Burnet*, *Tillotson* and *Blair*,
With *Jemmy Hervey*, curse and swear,
    Here *Cudworth* mixes grog;
Pearson the crew to dinner hails,
A graceless *Sherlock* trims the sails,
    And *Bunyan* heaves the log.

May 17.

American Museum   September 1971

VERSES *on the crew of a certain vessel, several of whom happened to be of the same name with celebrated clergymen. Supposed to be written by Philip Freneau.*

Stanza 2, line 3:   Old Erskine swabs the deck:

American Appollo   September 27, 1793

Stanza 1, line 6:   *Who heaven and hell defy.*

Columbian Centinel   August 23, 1794

Wrote on a Crew of an English vessell, their names happening to be the same as the following clergymen, viz. *Bonner, Erskine, Watts, Burnet, Tillotson, Blair, Hervey, Cudworth, Pearson, Sherlock* and *Bunyan.*

Stanza 1, line 1: In life's unsettled, sad career,
    line 4   Men bearing names of pious priests,
    line 5: Here in this ship are swearing beasts,

Stanza 2, line 2: Has chang'd the surplice for a frock;
    line 4: And *Watts,* a name that pleasure took
    line 5: In writing Hymns is here a Cook,
    line 6: Sinners he does not vex.

Stanza 3, line 2: With *Hervey,* who all curse and swear

Poems (1795), 161.

Columbian Museum   February 3, 1797

On the crew of an English vessel, whose names were Bonner, Erskin, Watts, Burnett, Tillotson, Blair, Hervey, Cudworth, Pearson, Sherlock, and Bunyan.

Text demonstrates the *Columbian Centinel* variants, with an additional variation in stanza lay-out. In each stanza, lines 1 and 4 are indented, and lines 2, 3, 5, and 6 begin at the margin.

Port Folio   November 14, 1807

Text included in the extended review of Freneau, October 17 to November 14, 1807, and introduced as follows:

> He, in too many places, shows a disrespect for the pulpit, which deserves to be highly censured; but although we touch, with much reverence, in whatever is connected with that guardian of our happiness both here and hereafter, we

cannot avoid smiling at the odd association in the stanzas on the crew of a certain vessel several of who happened to be of the same name with celebrated clergymen.

Identical to the 1791 text, except for the following variants:

Stanza 2, line 5: In writing hymns, here turn'd a cook,
    line 6: No more shall sinners vex.

Daily Advertiser   May 27, 1791

Lines occasioned by reading Mr. Paine's RIGHTS of MAN.

THUS briefly sketch'd the sacred Rights of Man,
How inconsistent with the regal plan,
Which for itself exclusive honour craves,
Where some are masters born, and some are slaves;
With what contempt must every eye look down,
On that base childish bauble, call'd a crown;
Yet, source of half the mischiefs men endure,
The quack that kills them, while it seems to cure.

Rous'd by the *reason* of his manly page,
Once more shall *Paine* a listening world engage;
From reason's source, a bold reform he brings,
By raising up mankind he pulls down kings,
Who, source of discord, patrons of all wrong,
On blood and murder, have been fed too long:
Hid from the world, and tutor'd to be base,
The curse, the scourge, the ruin of our race--
Their's was the task, a dull designing crew,
To govern beings that they scarcely knew,
Who deem'd this world a settlement of slaves,
And form'd their sway on systems built by knaves--
Advance, bright years, to work their final fall,
And haste the period, that shall crush them all.

Who that has read and scann'd the Historic page,
But glows at every line with kindling rage,
To see *by them*, the rights of men aspers'd;
Freedom restrain'd, and Nature's law revers'd;
Men, ranked with beasts, *by them* bequeath'd away,
And bound, even *fools* or *madmen* to obey,
Now driv'n to fight, and now oppress'd at home,
Compell'd in crowds, o'er distant seas to roam,
From Indian climes, the plunder'd prize to bring,
To glad the strumpet, or to glut the king,
Who, sworn to please her vain capricious mind,
Was forc'd new diamonds, at her call to find;
Or thus, like *Nero*, his proud dame address'd,
Who made this modest offer (not in jest)
"Let but these fingers o'er your bosom stray,
And conquer'd nations at your feet shall lay!"

Columbia, hail!–immortal be thy reign;
Without a king we till the fertile plain;
Without a king we trace the encircling sea,
And travel round the globe in each degree,
Each distant clime, our gallant flag reveres,
Nor asks a monarch to support the *stars;*
Without a king the laws maintain their sway,
While honour bids each loyal heart obey.
Be ours the task, the ambitious to restrain,
And this great lesson teach, That kings are vain,
That warring realms to certain ruin haste,
That kings subsist on war, and wars are waste;
So shall our nation, form'd on Reason's plan,
Remain the guardian of the Rights of Man,
A vast republic, fam'd thro' every clime,
Without a king, to see the end of time!

Poems (1795), 396-97.

Daily Advertiser   May 31, 1791

THE LANDLORD's SOLILOQUY.

A MAN that own'd some trees in town,
(And much averse to cut them down)
Finding the *Law* was full and plain,
No trees should in the streets remain,
One evening seated at his door
Thus gravely talk'd the matter o'er.

"The fatal *day,* dear trees, draws nigh
When you must, like your betters, die.
Must die!--And every leaf shall fade
That many a season lent its shade,
To drive from hence the summer's heat
And make my *stoop* a favorite seat.

"Thrice happy age, when all was new
And trees untouch'd, unenvied grew,
While yet regardless of the axe,
They own'd no law, and paid no tax;
The shepherd then at ease was laid
Or, walk'd beneath their cooling shade--
Alas! those times are now forgot
An iron age is all our lot,
Trees now to grow, is held a crime;--
And *these* must perish in their prime!

"The trees that once our fathers rear'd
And even the plundering Briton spar'd
When shivering here full oft he stood
Or kept his bed for want of wood--
These trees, whose gently bending boughs
Have witness'd many a lover's vows
When half afraid, in whining strain
He only *here* could tell his pain
And coaxing here his nymph by night
Forsook the parlour and the light,
In talking love his greatest bliss
To squeeze her hand or steal a kiss--
These trees that thus have lent their shade

And many a happy couple made,
These old companions, thus endear'd
Who never tattled what they heard,
Must these, indeed, be kill'd so soon--
Be murder'd by the tenth of June!

"But if my harmless trees must fall
(A fortune that awaits us all,
And in my line I cannot trace
A single shade of Levi's race)
Are *those* that round the Churches grow
In this decree included too--?
Must these, like common trees, be bled?
Is it a crime to shade the dead?
Review the *law,* I pray, at least
And have some mercy on the priest
Who every Sunday sweats in black
To make us steer the God-ward track:
The Church has lost enough, God knows,
Plunder'd alike by friends and foes--
I hate such amean attempts as these--
Come--let the Parsons keep their trees!

"Yet things, perhaps, are not so bad--
Perhaps a *respite* may be had:
The vilest rogues that cut our throats,
Or knaves that counterfeit our *notes,*
When, by the judge their sentence pass'd,
The gallows proves their doom at last,
Villains and pests of every kind,
For weeks and months a *respite* find;
And shall such nuisances as they
Who make all honest men their prey,
Shall they for months avoid their doom
And you, my trees, in all your bloom,
Who never injur'd small or great--
Be murder'd at so short a date!

"Ye men of law, the occasion seize
And name a counsel for the trees--
Arrest of judgement, Sirs, I pray;
Excuse them till some future day:
These trees that such a nuisance are
Next *New Year* we can better spare,
To warm our shins, or boil the pot--
The law, by then, will be forgot."

National Gazette   March 8, 1792

(Text introduced by a prose piece "ON TREES IN CITIES," which discusses the therapeutic value of at least some natural vegetation within the confines of the "artificial" and "tedious" city. Noting that a year previous, the legislature had ordered the universal extirpation of trees in New York, until the public interfered to save them, the author includes the following verses that had been written on the occasion.)

Stanza 1:   Substantively identical to the 1791 text.

Stanza 2, line 6:   And make my porch a favorite seat.

Stanza 3:   Two lines inserted after line 6 of the 1791 text:
From slender twigs a garland wove,
Or trac'd his god within the grove;

Four lines inserted after line 8 of the 1791 text:
Men are not now what once they were,
To hoard up gold is all their care:
The busy tribe old Plutus calls
To pebbled streets and painted walls;

Stanza 4, line 7:   When half afraid, and half in jest,
line 8:   With nature busy in his breast,

Two lines inserted after line 8 of the 1791 text:
With many a sigh, bestow'd in vain,
Beneath these boughs he told his pain,

line 11: Or coaxing here his nymph by night

Stanza 5, line 2:   A fortune that awaits us all,
line 3:   (All, all must yield to Nature's stroke,
line 4:   And now a man, and now an oak)
line 12: To make us steer the skyward track:
line 16: Come–let the parson keep his trees!

Stanzas 6 and 7 substantively identical to the 1791 text.

Poems (1795), 410-12.

Daily Advertiser   July 9, 1791

The DRUNKARD's *Apology.*

YOU blame the blushes on my nose,
And yet admire the blushing rose;
On Celia's cheek the bloom you prize,
And yet on mine, that bloom despise.

The world of Spirits you admire,
To which all holy men aspire;
Yet me with curses you requite,
Because in *Spirits* I delight.

When'er I fall, and crack my crown,
You blame me much for falling down,
Yet to the god that you adore,
You, too, fall prostrate on the floor.

You call me fool for drinking hard,
And yet Old Hudson you regard,
Who fills his jug from yonder bay,
And drinks his guts full--every day.

New York, July 8.

National Gazette   December 15, 1791

The DRUNKARD's APOLOGY.
[*Written at an Entertainment on Governor's Island, near New-York.*]

Stanza 2, line 1: indented.

Stanza 3, line 1: indented.
         line 3: Yet to some god that you adore

Stanza 4, line 1: indented.

Poems (1795), 100.

Carey's Daily Advertiser   July 29, 1797

1971 text with the following variants:

Stanza 3, line 1: Whenever I fall, and crack my crown,
Stanza 4, line 2: And yet old Del'ware you regard,
Signature: BIBO.

New York Journal   July 16, 1791

Pomposo *and his* PRINTER.

I.

AS at his country-house *Pomposo* sat
(Volumes on volumes round him pil'd
Stephen Boetius, and the Lord knows what,
Enough to make a man look wild)
A *Wight* approach'd his door with ink and pen,
One of your snug, complying men,
Titles to whom, and wealth, are every thing,
Subject to all their dreams, of every deed the spring.

II.

Pomposo look'd, with insolent disdain,
With silly face, and transatlantic grin,
And wonder'd what the stranger-man would mean;
Whether he thought some *twenty pence* to win,
Or, like some fool, he only came to stare--
(For well he knew, that none but foes came there,
That fondly hop'd, by sneaking arts, to rise;
Dunces of every rank, puppies of every size.)

III.

"What want you, friend? Pomposo loudly cri'd,
"What is your errand--tell me *whence you sprung;*

"Are you *well born*? If so, come to my side,
"If not, keep off, thou simple man of dung;
"No vulgar creatures shall my door disgrace,
"I'll have you know I am of *Crispin's* race.

IV.

The man, abash'd, stepp'd back a yard, or so,
And gave the porter something neatly penn'd,
Then slyly bade him to Pomposo go,
Present the book, and say, "he was his friend,
"A man that much had wrote, and much had read,
"And had some *noble notions* in his head."

V.

Now, reader, to to keep you in the dark,
This book was written in Pomposo's praise,
Praising him high beyond the common mark,
By far the "greatest man" of modern days--
    [One who had read ten thousand books,
      Sold, long ago, to pastry cooks;
      Had written, too, a dull *defence*,
      Contriv'd at Montesquieu's expence,
      In which so much on "Balances" was said
      It scented of the *grocer's* trade--]
In short, the flattery had been laid so thick,
It would have made even *Doctor Fallon* sick.

VI.

"Billy (said he) who's this that writes so well,
"That so sublimely praises "our *defence*!"--
"Some handsome things have from his goose quill fell,
"He is, no doubt, a fellow of good sense.
"Reward from us such real merits claim;
"Go, porter, go, and quickly bring his name,
"We'll give him something, if he'll venture near,
"A *quarter dollar,* or a quart of beer!"

VII.

"Nay (says the Wight) approaching with a smile,
"Your honor's slave expects some better boon,
"Something, at least, that may appear *in style,*
"Something to put my *squeaking pipes* in tune:
"*Such* panegyric claims a *nobler* fate--
"*Come, let me wriggle into something great.*"

VIII.

Have you a Printing press--Pomposo cri'd--
"I have not now"--the gaping Wight repli'd--
"But if *you'll* promise work, I can, with ease,
"Provide a press, *and play what tune you please.*"

IX.

Here, *Billy,* take this key (Pomposo said)
"You'll find, among my manuscripts, are laid
Ten volumes of enchanting stuff,
Comments on Davila--surely that's *enough;*
Print these, and when you've worried thro' the task,
Ten more are at your service--if you ask..

Anti Hypocrite.

Poems (1795), 408-09.

Daily Advertiser   August 4, 1791

MINERVA's ADVICE.
Fortia pœtora opponite rebus---------

Virg.

AS from the port in airy trim,
Old *Argo* first was seen to glide,
With sails so white and masts so slim,
The moving wonder of the tide;

As down the stream she made her way,
With all so new and all so gay,
Thus Neptune whisper'd in my ear,
"*Who know not danger, know not fear.*

"Bred up to sail on Meles' stream,
"These wights at length would grow more wise;
"The ocean has such waves, they deem,
"As on that gentle river rise;
"For songs and dances they prepare,
"But *fortune is the child of care.*"

    Arriv'd upon the vast domain,
Where tempests rave and monsters play,
Strange feelings seiz'd each gallant swain,
As stretch'd upon the decks they lay.
The gale grew high, the barque was toss'd,
The pilot cry'd, the ship is lost!
The chaplain left his cards and cup,
The boatswain spew'd his entrails up;
When forth Minerva shone confest,
And thus the trembling chief address'd:

    "Ah Jason, why those sighs and tears,
Why is that nervous arm unstrung,
To honour, best, true courage steers,
When thickest dangers round her throng,
Sighs ne'er will hush the waves to peace,
Nor gain for you, the *Golden Fleece.*"

"Would you the gentle nymph review,
That hopes and sighs for your return,
To labour drive the skulking crew,
That now their speedy ruin mourn:
Jove hates the wretch that's in the dumps,
But smiles on him that jogs the pumps.

"Would you surmount old Neptune's snares,
Unfathom'd seas that gape to drown,
Send not to Jove those sneaking prayers,
But bring the yards and topmasts down;
When storms blow high such folks as you,
Should learn to set their canvas low."

Rous'd by the voice that seem'd divine,
No more the chief dejected lay,
Convinc'd 'twas idle to repine,
He boldly fac'd the stormy day,
Through lurking dangers steer'd his barque,
And, landing, made this grave remark;
 Danger the ruffian never meets,
 As he grows saucy, she retreats!

New York, August 1.

Poems (1795), 104-05.

Freeman's Journal   August 24, 1791

On a Painter, who was endeavoring to recover, from memory, the features and portrait of a Lady *who died at Sea.*
Written—1788.

WHILE Health supplies the swelling veins,
And Youth's warm blush the face retains,
A second life the pencil gives,
Whose form upon the canvas lives.

 The Artist views with fond surprise,
From nature stol'n the glossy eyes,
The blushing cheek, the forehead fair,
The damask lip, the auburne hair.

 The Nymph, by nature meant to please,
Her second self on canvas sees,
Her face, that now so frail appears,
Renew'd to last a thousand years.--

 All this was gain'd from Flemish schools,
From Raphael's plans or Titian's rules;
Man did to man his gift import,
And age to age transferr'd the art.

On schemes deriv'd from Reason's law,
They copy'd well whate'er *they* saw,
Of active Life the semblance drew;
To Nature's form each picture true.--

But, oh--the cheek that lives no more
On canvas how can *you* restore!
Where death his frozen hand hath laid
No art recalls the charms decay'd.

By memory's help, from ocean's urn,
Can you this gentle nymph return;
Can you again my bosom warm,
Nor cheat me with a meaner form?

Here, only here, within this breast
(Not wrong'd by art) her beauties rest,
Not for the vulgar view design'd,
And imag'd only--on the Mind.

Philadelphia August 22.

Poems (1795), 101.

Daily Advertiser   September 17, 1791

The PARTING GLASS.
Written at an Inn.

THE man that joins in life's career,
And hopes to find some comfort here,
To rise above this earthly mass,
The only way's to drink his glass.

But still on this uncertain stage,
Where hopes and fears the soul engage;
And while amid the joyous band,
Unheeded flows the measur'd sand,
Forget not, as the moments pass,
That time shall bring the parting glass.

In spite of all the mirth I heard,
This was the glass I always fear'd--
The glass that would the rest destroy,
The farewell cup, the close of joy.

With you, whom reason taught to think,
I could for ages sit and drink;
But with the fool, the sot, the ass,
I haste to take the farewell glass.

The luckless wight that still delays
His drink of joy to future days--
Delays too long: for then, alas!
Old age steps in and breaks the glass.

The girl whose modest beauty fires;
Whose sprightly language never tires;
What tho' she keeps this country Inn,
And mixes grog, or deals out gin,
With such a kind obliging lass,
I sigh to drink the parting glass.

With him who always plods on Scrip,
Nor throws off care to steal a sip;
With people of the sordid class,
The first is still my parting glass.

The man whose friendship is sincere,
Who feels no guilt, and knows no fear:
It would require a heart of brass,
With him to take the parting glass.

With those who drink before they dine,
With him that preaches o'er his wine--
Lamenting much *all flesh is grass,*
Boy, give me quick the parting glass.

With him who loves a pot of ale,
And vows to drink no beer that's stale--
With him content my days to pass,
May Heaven forbid the parting glass.

September 16.

National Gazette   May 10, 1792

Stanzas 1-5:   Substantively identical to the 1791 text.

Stanza 6, line 1: The nymph, who boasts no borrow'd charms,
         line 2: Whose sprightly wit my bosom warms,
         line 6: I sigh to take the parting glass.

Stanza 7:   With him who always plods on scrip,
            Nor throws off care to take a sip,
            The wretch who thrives by others woes
            And scatters grief where'er he goes;--
            With people of this knavish class
            The first is still my parting glass.

Stanza 8:   With those that drink before they dine--
            With him that acts the grunting swine,
            Who fills his page with low abuse
            And strives to act the gabbling goose
            Turn'd out by fate, to feed on grass--
            Boy, give me quick the parting glass.

Stanza 9:   Stanza 8 of the 1791 text.

Stanza 10: With him, who loves a pot of ale;
            Who holds to all an even scale,
            Who hates a knave, in each disguise,
            And fears him not--what'er his size--
            With him, well pleas'd my days to pass,
            May Heaven forbid the *parting glass*.

May 2.

Poems (1795), 85-86.

National Gazette   October 31, 1791

Poetical ADDRESS *to the* PUBLIC *of the* UNITED STATES.

>THIS age is so fertile of mighty events
That people complain, with some reason, no doubt;
Besides the time lost, and besides the expence,
With reading the papers they're fairly worn out;
>>The *past* is no longer an object of care,
>>The *present* consumes all the time they can spare.--

Thus reasons the reader, but still he reads on,
With his pence and his paper unwilling to part,
He sees the world passing, men going and gone,
Some riding in coaches, and some in a cart:
>For a peep at the farce a *subscription* he'll give;
>Revolutions must happen--that Printers may live.

For a share of your favour we aim with the rest--
To enliven the scene we'll exert all our skill;
What we have to impart shall be some of the best,
And *Multum in Parvo* our text--if you will:
>Since we never admitted a clause in our Creed
>That the greatest employment of life is--to read.

The King of the French, and the Queen of the North
At the head of the play for the season we find:
From the spark that we kindled a flame has gone forth
To expand thro' the world and enlighten mankind:
>With a code of new doctrines the universe rings,
>And *Thomas* is preaching strange sermons to kings.

Thus launch'd as we are on the ocean of *news*,
In hopes that your pleasure our pains will repay,
All honest endeavors the author will use
To furnish a feast for the grave and the gay;
>At least he'll essay such a track to pursue
>That the world shall approve--and his news shall be true.

Poems (1795), 395-96.

Columbian Repository   September 30, 1803[1]

1795 text reprinted, in a condensed form, in this, the first issue of the paper, as an introduction to the public. Substantively identical to the 1795 text except for the following variants:

Stanza 1, line 1: The people complain (with reason no doubt)
         line 6: The *present* consumes all the time we can spare.

Stanza 3, line 6: That the greatest employment in life is--to read.

Stanza 4: Fifth stanza of the 1795 text, with the following variants:
     line 1: Launch'd as we shall be on such an ocean of news,
     line 3: All honest endeavours the authors will use
     line 5: At least we'll essay such a track to pursue
     line 6: That the world shall approve--and our news shall be true.

(Stanza four of the 1795 text deleted.)

National Gazette   November 14, 1791

A MISTAKE RECTIFIED.
By Sinbat, *the Sailor.*

YOUR men of the land, from the King to Jack Ketch,
All join in supposing the sailor a wretch;
That his life is a scene of vexation and woe,
With always too much or too little to do.
In the dead of the night, when other men sleep,
He, starboard, and larboard his watches must keep;
Imprison'd by Neptune, he lives like a dog;
To know where he is, must depend on a *log*;
Must fret in a calm, and must sigh in a storm;
In winter, much trouble to keep himself warm;
Through the heat of the summer he follows his trade,

---

[1] I found this "modified" text, never atrributed to Freneau, used by several later editors to introduce their first number.

Not a tree, but his top-mast to yield him a shade!
Then add to the list of the mariner's evils,
The water corrupted, the bread full of weevils;
Salt-Junk* to be eat, be it better or worse,
And often *Bull*-beef of an Irishman's horse--
Whosoever is free, *he* must still be a slave,
Despotic is always the rule on the wave:
Not relish'd on water, your lads of the main
Abhor the republican doctrines of *Paine,*
And each, like the Despot+ of Prussia, may say,
That his crew has no right--but the *Right to obey.*

    Thus argue the landsmen: but *Sinbat* well knows
Things are not so bad as these lubbers suppose.
There ne'er was a task but afforded some ease,
Nor employment in life, but had something to please.
If the sea has its storms, it has also its calms,
A time to sing songs, and a time to sing psalms!

    Yes--give me a vessel well timber'd and sound,
Her bottom well plank'd, and in rigging well found;
If her sails are but good, and her oakum swell'd tight,
From yon damnable waves I'll extract some delight.

    You'll say, it's a prison, (by way of abusing)
But, if it's a prison--'tis of my own choosing--
At sea I would rather have Neptune my jailor,
Than a lubber on shore, who despises a sailor,
Do you ask me what pleasure I find on the sea?
Why *absence from land* is a pleasure to me--

A hamper of porter, and plenty of grog,
A friend, on occasion, to give me a jog,
A coop that will always some poultry afford,
Some bottles of gin--and no parson on board--
A crew that are brisk when it happens to blow,

---

* *The sea-faring term for very old, or lean beef.*
+ Frederick 2d.

A compass on deck, and a compass below,
A girl with more sense than the *girl at the head,*
To read me a novel--or, make up my bed--
The man that has these, has a treasure in store,
That millions possess not--who live upon shore!
But--if it should happen that commerce grew dull,
Or Neptune, grown crusty, should batter my hull,
Should damage my cargoes, or get me aground,
Or pay me with farthings instead of a pound--
Should I always be left in the rear of the race,
And *this* be forever--forever--the case,
Why, then--if the honest plain truth I may tell
I'd clew up my top-sails, and bid him farewell.

SINBAT.

Philadelphia, October 12.

Poems (1795), 355-56.

National Gazette   November 17, 1791

The PRUDENT PHILOSOPHER.
[Occasioned by the conduct of some gentlemen, at the conflagration of a certain southern Court-House, during the sessions.]

WHEN from a dome where lawyers *spoke,*
Issued the mingled flame and smoke,
Marcella at her window sate,
Gazing towards the *Dome* of *State*--
That cost the laborer many a tear--
That ne'er would be rebuilt--that's clear;
And thrice she sigh'd, and smote her breast
To see their squire-ships so distrest;
To see in such a little while
To ashes turn'd so fine a pile!

Meanwhile avoiding pump and pail,
(For what could one man's help avail?)
Fearing to hurt his tender hand,
Should be amongst the vulgar stand,
Where buckets fly and engines play,
Where slaves *must* work, and masters may;
Philander to her chamber came,
Thus comforting the tearful dame:

"Behold, (said he) my lady fair
How vain these mortal buildings are!
'Tis madness--madness--all things show
To set our hearts on things below;
(Thank heaven for all its stores of grace,
Our TREASURE's in a *safer place*:)
But thus the pride of man shall bend;
The gods such fabrics only *lend*;
Whether contriv'd of brick and stone,
They hardly can be call'd our own:
What time might spare the flame destroys,
To heaven such fabrics are but toys;
Life is a spark from Vulcan stole,
The Indian summer of the soul:
And we ourselves, with years oppress'd,
In time, shall sink among the rest.

Ah! lovely nymph--no longer sigh--
'Tis true the flames are mounting high--
But oh!--forbear that trickling tear,
For thus the world shall disappear;
And temples of stupendous size,
In empty vapor thus shall rise,
When nature droops her weary wings
To give a sad account of things;
When time has run his idle round,
And you and I are--under ground.

In such a view, Marcella fair,
How beautiful these blazes are!
From such a view of human things
Philosophy her comfort brings,
Instructing us when mischiefs come,

When folks are burnt from house and home;
When public buildings burn, or fall,
To bear it with--no grief at all!"

    Kind moralist (the nymph replied)
Your doctrines shall not be denied;
And tho' you make things mighty clear,
I'm almost vex'd, to see you here:
A fate like this impends o'er all--
(Even high-heel'd shoes at last must fall!)
But, whether preach'd in prose or rhyme,
'Twould better suit another time.

    How can we justly blame the fire
That gives us so much to admire!
If people skulk when temples burn,
How can they but to ashes turn--?
Such fire as this *some water* claims--
These are, indeed, no common flames--
So leave me, Love, to sigh and pout--
You--run--and help to put them out!

Poems (1795), 353-54.

National Gazette   November 17, 1791[1]

[The following lines convey the substance of a satirical French Epitaph upon *Frederick the second,* King of Prussia. The sting principally lies in glancing at the well known aversion of that monarch to the female sex; and his having died without leaving an immediate heir to the throne.]

HERE rests a King--his mortal journey done;
Through life, a tyrant to his fellow man,
Who bloody wreaths in bloody battles won,
Nature's worst savage since the world began.

---

[1] The reader will see the freedom of Freneau's version by comparing this text to what is probably the original, printed in the *Pennsylvania Packet* August 15, 1786, where it is followed by a strictly accurate translation:

The following French lines were wrote by an anonimous author under a fine portraiture of his present Prussian Majesty; they were generally ascribed to Monsieur *Voltaire.*

CE mortel profana tous les talens divers;
Il charma les humains, qui tuerent ses victimes.
Barbare en action, Philosophe en vers;
Il chanta les virtues, et commit tous les crimes.
Hai de dieu d'amour, cher au dieu de combats;
Il plonga dans le sang, l'Europe & sa patrie,
Cent mille hommes par lui, recurent le trepas,
Et pas un n'en recut la vie.

TRANSLATION

This mortal ev'ry talent wrong display'd,
Mankind he charm'd, and men his victims made;
Cruel in deed, humane alone in rhyme,
Virtue he sung, committing ev'ry crime.
Despis'd by Cupid, dear to Mars he stood:
He Europe and his Country plung'd in blood.
    An *hundred thousand* met by him their death;
From him, not *one* receiv'd his vital breath.

Millions were doom'd beneath his sword to die:
No art, no care his blasting breath could shun—
Did he one man for all his waste supply--?
No!--tell the world--*He never gave it one*!

Poems (1795), 362.

National Gazette   December 19, 1791

The COUNTRY PRINTER.
[*Description of his Village.*]

BESIDE a stream that never yet ran dry,
There stands a *Town,* not high advanced in fame;
Tho' few its buildings, rais'd to please the eye,
Still this proud title it may fairly claim;
A *Tavern* (its first requisite) is there,
A *mill, a black-smith's shop, a house of prayer.*

Nay, more--a little market-house is seen
And iron hooks, where beef was never hung,
Nor pork, nor bacon, poultry fat or lean,
Pig's head, or sausage link, or bullock's tongue:
Look when you will, you see the vacant bench
No butcher seated there, no country wench.

Great aims were his, who first contriv'd this town;
A market he would have--but, humbled now,
Sighing we see its fabric mouldering down,
That only serves, at night, to pen the cow:
And hence, by way of jesting, may be said
That beef is there, tho' never beef that's dead.

Abreast the inn--a tree before the door,
A Printing-Office lifts its humble head
Where master *Type* old journals doth explore
For news that is all thro' the village read;
Who, year from year, (so cruel is his lot)
Is author, pressman, devil--and what not?

Fame says he is an odd and curious wight,
Fond to distraction of this native place
In sense not very dull nor very bright,
Yet shows some marks of humour in his face,
One who can pen an anecdote, complete,
Or plague the parson with the mackled sheet.

Three times a week, by nimble geldings drawn
A stage arrives; but scarcely deigns to stop,
Unless the driver, far in liquor gone,
Has made some business for the black-smith-shop;
Then comes this printer's harvest-time of news,
Welcome alike from Christians, Turks, or Jews.

[*To be continued.*]

Poems (1795), 421.

National Gazette   December 22, 1791

The COUNTRY PRINTER.
[*Continued.*]

ALL is not *Truth* ('tis said) that travellers tell--
So much the better for this man of news:
For hence, the country round that know him well,
Will, if he prints some lies, his lies excuse.
Earthquakes, and battles, shipwrecks, myriads slain--
If false or true--alike to him are gain.

But if this motley tribe say nothing new,
Then many a lazy, lounging look is cast
To watch the weary post-boy travelling through,
On horse's rump, his budget buckled fast;
With letters safe in leathern prison pent
And, wet from press, full many a packet sent.

Not Argus with his fifty pair of eyes
Look'd sharper for his prey than honest *Type*
Explores each package, of alluring size,
Prepar'd to seize them with a nimble gripe
Did not the post-boy watch his goods, and swear
That village *Type* shall only have his share.

Ask you what *matter* fills his various page?
A mere farrago 'tis of mingled things;
Whate'er is done on madam *Terra's* stage
He to the knowledge of his townsmen brings:
One while, he tells of Monarchs run away;
And now, of witches drown'd in Buzzard's bay.

Some miracles he makes, and some he steals;
Half nature's works are giants in his eyes:
Much, very much, in wonderment he deals,--
New-Hampshire apples grown to pompkin size,
Pompkins almost as large as country inns,
And ladies bearing each,--three lovely twins!

He, births and deaths with cold indifference views;
A paragraph from him is all they claim:
And here the rural 'squire, amongst the news
Sees the fair record of his father's fame;
All that was good, minutely brought to light,
All that was ill,--conceal'd from vulgar sight!

[*To be continued.*]

Poems (1795), 422.

National Gazette   December 29, 1791

The COUNTRY PRINTER.
[*Continued.*]

THE OFFICE.

SOURCE of the wisdom of the country round,
Again I turn to that poor lonely *shed*
Where many an author all his fame has found,
And wretched proofs by candle-light are read,
Inverted letters, left the page to grace,
Colons derang'd, and commas out of place.

Beneath this roof the Muses chose their home;--
Sad was their choice, less bookish ladies say,
Since from the blessed hour they deign'd to come
One single cob-web was not brush'd away:--
Fate early had pronounc'd this building's doom
Ne'er to be plagu'd with boonder, brush, or broom.

Here, full in view, the ink-bespangled press
Gives to the world its children, with a groan,
Some born to live a month--a day--some less.
Some, why they live at all, not clearly known.
All that are born must die--TYPE well knows that--
The *almanack's* his longest living brat.

Here lie the types, in curious order rang'd
Ready alike to imprint your prose or verse;
Ready to speak [their order only chang'd]
Creek-Indian Lingo, Dutch, or Highland erse;
These Types have printed Erskine's *Gospel Treat,*
Tom Durfey's songs, and Bunyan's works complete.

But faded are their charms--their beauty fled!
No more their work your nicer eyes admire;
Hence, from this press no courtly stuff is read
But almanacks and ballads for the Squire,
Dull paragraphs in homely language dress'd
The pedlar's bill, and sermons by request.

Here doom'd the fortune of the press to try
From year to year poor TYPE his trade pursues--
With anxious care and circumspective eye
He dresses out his little sheet of news;
Now laughing at the world, now looking grave,
At once the Muse's midwife--and her slave.

[*To be continued.*]

Poems (1795), 423.

National Gazette   January 5, 1792

The COUNTRY PRINTER.
[*Concluded.*]

    THOU, who are plac'd in some more favor'd spot,
Where spires ascend, and ships from every clime
Discharge their freights--despise not thou the lot
Of master *Type*, who here has pass'd his prime
At case and press has labour'd many a day
But now, with years, is verging to decay.

    He, in his time the patriot of his town
With Press and Pen attack'd the royal side,
Did what he could to pull their Lion down,
Clipp'd at his tail, and twitch'd his *sacred* hide,
Mimick'd his roarings, trod upon his toes,
Pelted young whelps, and tweak'd the old one's nose.

    Rous'd by his page, at church or Court-House read,
From depths of woods the willing rustics ran,
Now by a priest, and now some deacon led
With clubs and spits to guard the rights of man;
Lads from the spade, the pick-ax, or the plough
Marching afar, to fight *Burgoyne* or *Howe.*

Where are they now?--the Village asks with grief,
What were their toils, their conquests, or their gains?--
Perhaps, they near some State-House beg relief,
Perhaps they sleep on Saratoga's plains;
Doom'd not to live, their country to reproach
For seven-years pay transferr'd to Mammon's coach.

  Ye *Guardians* of your country and her laws!
Since to the pen and press so much we owe
Still bid them favour freedom's sacred cause,
From this pure source, let streams unsullied flow;
Hence, a new order grows from reason's plan,
And turns the fierce barbarian into--man.

  Child of the earth, of rude materials fram'd,
Man, always found a tyrant or a slave,
Fond to be honour'd, valued, rich, or fam'd
Roves o'er the earth, and subjugates the wave:
Despots and kings this restless race may share,--
But knowledge only makes them worth *your* care!

Poems (1795), 424.

National Gazette   February 23, 1792

On the present state of Rivers.

  WHILE hid from day, the wandering *Lehigh* weeps
Deep on his bed the gentle *Schuylkill* creeps;
While ruffian *Hudson* takes a long repose
The frozen *Delaware* wraps his breast in snows:
His wave, that bore the pile of mighty freight
Now wafts the new-form'd sailor on the skait:
Where once the pilot spread the shivering sail
Or haul'd his bowlines, to embrace the gale,
There, now he walks, repining at his lot,
Nor cares a farthing if it blows, or not.--
Here, where whole fleets, safe moor'd at anchor lay

Now Jersey nymphs and gentle ladies stray;
Where lofty ships with streamers cut a dash
They show their ribbons, and the gay calash;
Some, by themselves, some convoy'd by a beau,
All wander, heedless of the the gulph below,
Devoid of fear, on Nature's bridge they float,
And scorn the aid of Charon, and his boat.

Poems (1795), 103.

National Gazette   April 2, 1792

ODE *to the* ECHO *Writer.*

IN ECHO's caves, with shrill-voic'd conchs hung round,
   And pumpkin shells, responding all they hear,
A Bard, call'd *Whaacum,* catches every sound,
   Governs their tone, pricks up his lengthy ear;
In putrid ink then dips his pen of lead
And scribbles down what prattling Echo said.

Bard of the lengthy ode! whose knavish paw
   Ne'er grasp'd the helm, *besprent* with odious pitch,
'Twas better far, (you know) to *practice* law,
   Whine at the church or in the court-house screech;
No heart had you to face the wintry blast
Fight with the storm, or climb the tottering mast.

Then why so wroth, thou bard of narrow soul,
   If *Sinbat,* tir'd of puppies, sought the brine?--
He drank no swichell from your white-oak bowl,
   Nor from your poems *filch'd a single line:--*
     When he does this--then echo from your caves,
     "Who robs a beggar, is the worst of knaves."

March 31.

American Mercury   April 30, 1792

The above text is reprinted, followed by a letter to the editor from the "Echo." The writer states his apprehensions that "Captain Sinbat," was affronted by his poem that had appeared in the March 12, 1792 number and that had prompted Freneau's response in the above ode. A parody of Brackenridge's "Further and concluding thoughts on the Indian War," the poem includes a direct attack on Freneau, ridiculing his attachment to Jefferson, his verses, and his career at sea. The "Echo" wishes to assure "Sinbat" that his intentions were not to ridicule, but to immortalize him. Then, playing on the line (deleted from the 1795 text) "If *Sinbat,* tir'd of puppies, sought the brine?--", the "Echo" offers a novel, if spurious, interpretation of the poet's motives for going to sea, and concludes with a fantastical account of his throwing a fit and being driven permanently insane upon reading the "Echo."

Poems (1795), 404-05.

National Gazette   May 17, 1792[1]

The VILLAGE MERCHANT.

SPRUNG from a race that long had till'd the soil
And first dis-rob'd it of its native trees,
He chose to heir their lands, but not their toil,
And thought the ploughman's life no life of ease--
" 'Tis wrong (thought he) these pretty hands to wound
"With felling oaks, or delving in the ground:
"I who, at least, have forty pounds in cash
"And in a country store might cut a dash,
"Why should I till these barren fields (he said)
("I who have learnt to cypher, write, and read)
"These fields that shrubs, and weeds, and brambles bear,
"That pay me not, and only bring me care!"

Some thoughts had he, long while, to quit the sod
In sea-port towns to try his luck in trade,
But then their way of living seem'd most odd--
For dusty streets to leave his native shade,
From grassy plats to pebbled walks remov'd--
The more he thought of them the less he lov'd:

---

[1] A shorter poem, entitled "Description of a Village Merchant: in Imitation of Goldsmith's style," was reprinted in several papers between 1788 and 1792, and may have been the source of Freneau's "Village Merchant." The shorter poem briefly develops the same character type. The earliest appearance of that poem was in the Boston *American Mercury,* November 17, 1788. It was reprinted later in the *Pennsylvania Packet* on August 13, 1789, in the Charleston *City Gazette* on September 19, 1789, where Freneau might have seen it, and, among other papers, in the *New York Journal,* on May 16, 1792, entitled "Description of a Long-Island J------a Merchant, in Imitation of Goldsmith's Style." Although in the 1809 collection, Freneau notes that he wrote the poem in 1768, I believe that this poem, so similar in concept, probably inspired his own treatment of the subject. It is unlikely that the shorter poem was, in fact, Freneau's, because it first appeared in papers to which he was not known to contribute, and because the style and diction, closely modelled on Goldsmith's, are unlike that of Freneau's poem.

The city-springs he could not drink; and still
Preferr'd the fountain, underneath the hill.--

And yet no splendid objects there were seen
No distant scenes in gaudy colours clad,
Look where you wou'd the prospect still was mean,
Scrub-oaks, and scatter'd pines, and aspins sad--
Banks of a shallow river stain'd with mud;
A stream where never swell'd the tide of flood,
No lofty ship her topsails did unloose,
Nor sailor sail'd--except in log-canoes.

It would have puzzled Faustus to have told,
What did attach him to this paltry spot
Where even the house he heir'd was very old,
And half his fences hardly worth a groat:
Yet so it was, the fancy took his brain
A country shop might here some custom gain:--
Whiskey, he knew, would always be in vogue
While there are country 'squires to take a cogue,
Laces and lawns would draw each rural maid,
And one must have her *shawl,* and one her *shade.*

(To be continued.)

Poems (1795), 9.

National Gazette   May 24, 1792

The VILLAGE MERCHANT.
[Continued from No. 58]

HARD by the road a pigmy building stood,
Thatch'd was its roof, and earthen were its floors:
So small its size, that (in a jesting mood)
It might be call'd a house turn'd out of doors--
Yet here, adjacent to an aged oak,
Full fifty years *old dad* his hams did smoke,

Nor ceas'd the trade, till worn with years, and spent,
To Pluto's smoke-house he himself was sent.

Hither our merchant turn'd his curious eye
And mus'd awhile upon this sable shell--
Here father smoak'd his hogs (he said) *and why,
In truth, may not our garret do as well?*--
So down he took his ham and bacon flitches,
Resolv'd to fill the place with other riches:
From every hole and cranny brush'd the soot,
And fix'd up shells throughout the crazy hut:
A counter, too, most cunningly was plann'd
Behind whose breast-work none but he might stand,
Excepting now and then (by special grace)
Some brother merchant from some other place.--

Now, muster'd up his cash, and said his prayers,
In Sunday suit he rigs himself for town.
Two raw-bon'd steeds (design'd for great affairs)
Are to the waggon hitch'd, old Bay and Brown;
Who ne'er had been, before, a league from home,
But now are doom'd full many a mile to roam,
Like merchant ships, a various freight to bring
Of ribbons, lawns, and many a tawdry thing.

Molasses too (blest sweet) was not forgot,
And island *rum*, that every taste delights--
And *teas*, for maid and matron, must be bought,
Rosin and cat-gut strings for fiddling wights--
But why should I his invoice here repeat?
'Twould be like counting grains in pecks of wheat;
Half Europe's list was on his invoice found,
And all was to be bought with--*forty pound!*

Soon as the early dawn proclaim'd the day
He cock'd his hat with pins, and comb'd his hair:
Curious it was, and laughable, to see
The *village-merchant* mounted in his chair:
The shelves pil'd with lawns and linens, in his head,
Coatings, and stuffs, and cloths, and scarlets *red*--
All that would suit man, woman, girl, or boy,
Muslins, and muslinets, jeans, grograms, corduroy.

Alack! said I—he little, little dreams
That all the cash he guards with mickle care—
His cash!—the mother of a thousand schemes,
Will hardly buy—a load of earthen ware!
But why should I excite the hidden tear
By whispering truths, ungrateful to his ear?
Still let him travel on, with heart elate,
As Disappointment never comes too late.

[To be continued.]

May 21.

Poems (1795), 9-10.

National Gazette   May 31, 1792

The VILLAGE MERCHANT.
(Continued from No. 60.)

THROUGH woods obscure and dull perplexing way
Slow and alone he urg'd the clumsy wheel;
Now stopping short, to let his horses graze,
Now treating them with straw and Indian meal;
At length a lofty steeple caught his eye,
"Higher (thought he) than ever kite did fly:—
"But so it is, these churchmen are so proud
"They ever will be tip-toe with a cloud:
"Bound on a sky-blue cruise, they always rig
"The longest steeple and the largest wig."

Now safe arriv'd upon the pebbled way
Where well-born steeds the rattling coaches trail,
Where shops on shops are seen—and ladies gay
Walk, with their *curtains* some, and some, their veil;
And one cries, *fish!* and one cries *muslins, ho!*
Amaz'd alike, the merchant and his pair
Of scare-crow steeds, did nothing else but stare;

So new was all the scene, that, smit with awe,
They grinn'd, and gaz'd, and gap'd at all they saw,
And often stopp'd, to ask at every door,
"*Sirs, can you tell us where's the cheapest store?*"

"The cheapest store! (a sly retailer said)
"Cheaper than cheap, *guid faith*, I have to sell;
"Here are some colour'd cloths that never fade:
"No other shop can serve you half so well.
"Wanting some money, now, to pay my rent,
"I'll sell them at a loss of *one per cent*.--
"*Hum-bugs* are here, and muslins--what you please--
"Bandanas, bastas, *pull-cats*,--India teas
"Improv'd by age, and now grown very old,
"And given away--you may depend--not sold!"

Lur'd by the bait the wiley trader laid,
He gave his steeds their mess of straw and meal,
Then gazing round the shop, thus, cautious, said,
"Well, if you sell so cheap, I think we'll deal,
"But pray remember, 'tis for *goods* I'm come,
"For, as to *pole-cats*, we've enough at home:--
"Full *forty pounds* I'm worth--and that in gold,
"(Enough to make a trading man look bold)
"Unrig your shelves, and let me take a peep;
" 'Tis odds I leave them bare--you sell so cheap."

The city-merchant stood, with lengthen'd jaws,
And star'd awhile--then made this short reply---
"You clear my shelves! (he said)--This shelf of gauze
"Is more than all your *forty pounds* can buy--
"On yonder board, whose burthen seems so small
"That one man's pocket might contain it all,
"More value lies, than you, and all your race
"From Adam down, did purchase or possess."

Convinc'd, he turn'd him to another street
Where humbler shop-men from the croud retreat:
Here, caught his eye coarse collicoes and crape,
Pipes and tobacco, ticklenbergs, and tape,
Pitchers and pots--of value not so high
But he might sell,--and *Forty Pounds* would buy.

[*To be continued.*]

May 26.

National Gazette   June 4, 1792

The FAIR BUCKLE-THIEF.
[A true Story.]

A Country girl, from Flushing's coast,
Of three miles round the pride and boast,
To market came with early fruit,
Apples that might the townsmen suit,
With cabbage-head, and parsnip root.

With hat of straw and homespun gown,
(Her Sunday suit) she came to town
Too see, and walk the city through,
With leather strings in leather shoe,
But sighing much for buckles new.

Six hours, and more, she patient stood
And traded off whate'er she cou'd;
Her apples met with small regard,
She did not get her due reward.

Her cash receiv'd--alas! how small--
With pensive heart she left the stall--
Look'd at her shoes, and curs'd the strings,
Like mother Eve (as Milton sings)
Impatient for forbidden things.

Arriv'd at length, before a shop,
Some glittering gew-gaws made her stop--
There buckles hung, of various size,
The diamonds dazzled on her eyes;
And, pray, why mayn't she seize the prize?

The shopman absent from his door,
She seiz'd the *buckles* from his store,
And off she walk'd, an easy gait,
With lightsome step, and look sedate,
Things purchas'd at so cheap a rate!--

But *Argus,* with his hundred eyes,
Missing his buckles, in surprize,
The fair retreating nymph attack'd,
The buckles from the bag unpack'd,
And quickly made her own the fact.

"Now (cry'd the merchant) honest *Joe,*
"Come, take a kiss and let her go."
--"*Not I*--(the surly shopman said)--
"To jail shall go this country jade--
"The debt to justice must be paid."

"How can you have so hard a heart?
"Come, let this country girl depart--
"Like *Adam's wife,* she went astray;
"*Her* daughters all will have their way;
"Men must not steal, but women may.

Lost was this logic on his ears,
And vain were Blouzelinda's tears--
And go she must--and go she must!
But, if 'twas said the laws were just,
Their *mercy* she was loth to trust.

Conducted to a junior 'squire
(Whom all the neighboring girls admire)
He ask'd her, "what she had to say
"Why justice should not have its way
"On nymphs by buckles led astray?"

"Alack (she cry'd) I cannot utter
"A word--my soul's in such a flutter--
"While you my *mittimus* prepare
"Pray, let me take a moment's air;
"These summer heats require some shade,
"And nature, sir, must be obey'd"--
So, stealing back, as fairies do,
(The 'squire too modest to pursue)
  Without a fall,
   She scal'd the wall,
And left his worship reading *Law!*

May 30.

Poems (1795), 35-36.

National Gazette   June 7, 1792

The VILLAGE MERCHANT.
[Continued from No. 62]

SOME jugs, some pots, some fifty ells of tape,
A keg of wine, a cask of low-proof rum
Bung'd close--for fear the *spirit* should escape
That many a sot was waiting for at home;
A gross of pipes, a case of home-made gin;
Tea, powder, shot--small parcels he laid in:
Molasses too, for *swichell*-loving wights,
(Swichell, that wings dull *Whaacum's* boldest flights
When *Echoed* forth, the wild ideas roll,
Flash'd from that farthing candle, call'd his soul:)
All these he bought, and would have purchas'd more
To furnish out his Lilliputian store;
But cash fell short--and *they* who smil'd while yet
The cash remain'd--now took a serious fit--
No more the shop-girl could his talk endure
But, like her cat, sat sullen and demure--
The dull retailer found no more to say,
But bow'd his head, and wish'd to sneak away;
Leaving his house-dog *now,* to make reply,
And watch the counter with a lynx's eye--
    Our merchant took the hint; and off he went,
Resolv'd to sell at--*twenty-five per cent.*

Returning far o'er many a hill and stone
And much in dread his earthen-ware would break
Thoughtful he rode, and uttering many a groan
Lest at some worm-hole vent his cask should leak--
His cask, that held the joys of rural squire,
Which even ('twas said) the parson did admire,
And valued more than all the dusty pages
That Calvin writ, and fifty other sages;--
Once highly priz'd--be-prais'd in verse and prose,
But now unthumb'd, *enjoy a safe repose.*

At dusk of eve he reach'd his old abode
Around him quick his anxious townsmen came
One ask'd what luck had happ'd him on the road,

And one ungeer'd the mud-bespatter'd team:
While on his casks each glanc'd a loving eye,
Patient, to all he gave a brisk reply--
Told all that had befall'n him on the way,
What wonders in the town detain'd his stay,--
"Houses as high as yonder whiteoak tree,
"And boats of monstrous size, that go to sea:
"Streets throng'd with busy folk, like swarming hive,
"The lord knows how they all contrive to live--
"No ploughs I saw; no hoes; no care; no charge,
"In fact they all are gentlemen at large;
"And *goods* so thick on every window lie,
"They all seem born to sell--and none to buy."

[To be continued.]

Poems (1795), 12-13.

National Gazette   June 14, 1792

The VILLAGE MERCHANT.
[*Continued from No. 64.*]

ALACK-a-day! on life's uncertain road
How many plagues, what evils must befal;
Jove has on none unmingled bliss bestow'd,
But disappointment is the lot of all:
Thieves rob our stores, in spite of locks and keys;
Cats steal our cream, and rats infest our cheese,
The finest coat a grease spot may assail,
Or Susan pin a dish-clout to its tail!

Our Village-Merchant (trust me) had his share
Of vile mis-haps--for now, the *goods*, unpack'd
Discover'd, what might make a deacon swear,
Jugs, cream-pots, pipes, and grog-bowls sadly crackt.--
A general groan through all the crowd was heard
Most pitied him, and some his ruin fear'd:

Poor wight! 'twas sad to see him fret and chase,
While each enquir'd--*Sir, is the rum-case safe?*

Alas! even *that* some mischief had endur'd--
One rascal hoop had started, near the chine!--
Then curiously the bung-hole they explor'd
With stem of pipe, the leakage to define--
"*Five gallons must be charg'd to loss and gain!*"
"--*Five gallons!*" (said the merchant) writh'd with pain--
"Now may the cooper never see full flask
"But still be driving at an empty cask--
"Five gallons might have mellow'd down the 'squire,
"And made the captain strut a full inch higher:
"Five gallons might have prompted many a song,
"And made a frolic more than five days long--
"Five gallons now are lost--and, sad to think,
"That when they leak'd, no soul was there to drink!"

Now slightly treated with a proof-glass dram,
Each neighbour took his leave, and mov'd to bed,
All but our merchant!--he, with grief o'ercome,
Resolv'd strange notions in his scheming head--
"For losses such as these (thought he) 'tis meant
"That *goods* are sold at twenty-five per cent--
"(No doubt, your trading men know what is just)
" *'Tis twenty-five times what they cost at first.*"

So rigging off his shelves by light of candle,
The ancient smoke-house walls begin to shine:
Here stood his tea-pots (some without a handle)--
A broken jar--and there his keg of wine,--
Pipes, many a dozen (ordered in a row)--
Jugs--mugs--and grog-bowls--less for *sale* than *show*--
The leaky cask--replenish'd from the well,
Roll'd to its birth--but we no tales will tell--
    Catching the eye in elegant display,
All was arrang'd, and snug, by break of day:
The blue *dram-bottle* on the counter plac'd,
Stood, all prepar'd for *him that buys* to taste--
Sure bait! by which the man of cash is taken,
As rats are caught by cheese, or scraps of bacon.

[*To be continued.*]

Poems (1795), 13-14.

National Gazette   June 28, 1792

The VILLAGE MERCHANT.
[*Continued from No. 66.*]

WELL--strange it is that fools will still apply
Things to themselves, that authors never meant;
Each country shop-man asks me, "Is it I
On whom your rhiming ridicule is spent?
Friends, hold your tongues--Such myriads of your race
A man might rove seven years from place to place
Ere he would find the *subject* of my rhymes--
Perhaps in Georgia is the creature known,
Perhaps Rhode-Island claims him for her own:
And if from fancy's world this wight I drew,
What is the imagin'd character to you?

NOW, from all parts the rural people ran,
With ready cash to buy what might be bought;
One went to choose a pot, and one a pan,
And they that had no cash their *produce* brought,
A hog, a calf, safe halter'd by the neck,
Potatoes (Ireland's glory) many a peck;
Bacon and cheese, of real value more
Than India's gems, or all Potosi's ore.

Some questions ask'd, the folks began to stare--
No soul wou'd purchase pipe, nor pot, nor pan;
Each shook his head--hung back--*your goods so dear!*
In fact (said they) *the devil's in the man"*
"Rum ne'er shall meet my lips (said honest Sam)
"In shape of toddy, punch, grog, sling, or dram,"
"No cash of mine you'll get (said pouting Kate)
"While gauze is valued at so dear a rate."--

Thus things dragg'd on for many a tedious day,
No custom came, and nought but discontent
Gloom'd through the shop--"*Well let them have their way,*
(The merchant said) *I'll sell at cent per cent;*
By which 'tis plain I scarce myself shall save,
For cent per cent *is just the price I gave.*"

"Aye (said the 'squire, who still had kept his pence)
"Now, sir, you reason like a man of sense!--
"*Custom* will now from every quarter come;
"In ceaseless streams shall flow the inspiring rum,
"Till every soul in pleasing dreams is sunk--
"And even *Socrates*--himself--is drunk!"

Soon were the shelves disburthen'd of their load;
In three short hours the keg of wine ran dry--
Swift from its source even dull molasses flow'd--
Each saw the rum-cask wasting with a sigh:--
"*Here lies a worthy corpse* (Sangrado said)
"Its debt *to drunkards* now, no doubt, is paid--
"Well--'twas a vile disease that kill'd it, sure;
"A quick *consumption,* that no art could cure!
"Thus shall we all, when life's vain dream is out,
"Be lodg'd in corners dark, or kick'd about!
"Time is the tapster of our race below,
"That turns the key, and bids the juices flow--
"Quitting my books, henceforth be mine the task
"To moralize upon this *empty cask*----
"Thank heaven, we've had the taste--so far 'twas well--
"And still, thro' mercy, may enjoy the smell!"

* * * * * * * * *

[Cœtera desunt.]

Poems (1795), 14-15.

National Gazette   July 4, 1792

INDEPENDENCE.

REmov'd from Europe's feuds, a hateful scene
(Thank heaven, such wastes of ocean roll between)
Where tyrant kings in bloody streams combine,
And each forebodes in tears, *Man is no longer mine;*
Glad we recal the *day* that bade us first
Spurn at their power, and shun their wars accurst;
Pitted and gaff'd no more for England's glory
Nor made the tag-rag-bob-tail of their story.

Something still wrong in every system lurks.
Something imperfect haunts all human works--
Wars must be hatch'd unthinking men to fleece,
Or we, *this day*, had been in perfect peace,
With double bolts our Janus temple shut,
Nor terror reign'd through each back-woodsman's hut,
No rattling drums assail'd the peasants ear
Nor Indian yells disturb'd our sad frontier,
Not gallant chiefs, 'gainst Indian hosts combin'd
Scap'd from the trap--to leave their tails behind.

Peace to all feuds!--and come the happier day
When Reason's sun shall light us on our way;
When erring man shall all his RIGHTS retrieve,
No despots rule them, and no priests deceive;
'Till then, Columbia!--watch each stretch of power
Nor sleep too soundly at the sleeping hour,
By flattery won, and lull'd by soothing strains
Silenus took his nap--and wak'd in chains--
In a soft dream of smooth delusion led
Unthinking Gallia bow'd her drooping head
To tyrant's yokes--and met such bruises there
As now must take three ages to repair.
Then keep the paths of dear-bought freedom clear,
Nor slavish systems, grant admission here--

July 3.

Poems (1795), 430-31.

National Gazette   July 14, 1792

ODES ON VARIOUS SUBJECTS.

He who does not read in the book of Odes is like a man standing with his face flat against a wall: he can neither move forward, nor stir an inch backward.--   Hau Kiou Choaan.

ODE I.
On the Fourteenth of July.

BRIGHT DAY, that did to France restore
What priests and kings had seiz'd away,
That bade her generous sons disdain
The fetters that their fathers wore,
The titled slave, a tyrant's sway,
That ne'er shall curse her soil again:

Bright day! a partner in thy joy,
COLUMBIA hails the rising sun,
She feels her toils, her blood repaid,
When fiercely frantic to destroy
(Proud of the laurels he had won)
The Briton, here, unsheath'd his blade.

By traitors driv'n to ruin's brink
Fair freedom dreads united knaves,
The world must fall if she must bleed;
And yet, by heaven! I'm proud to think
The world was ne'er subdued by slaves--
Nor shall the hireling herd succeed.

Boy! fill the generous goblet high;
Success to France, shall be the toast:
The fall of kings, the fates foredoom,
The crown decays, its splendours die;
And they, who were a nation's boast
Sink, and expire in endless gloom.

Thou, stranger, from a different shore,
Where fetter'd men their rights avow,
Why on this joyous day so sad?
Louis insults with chains no more,--

Then why thus wear a clouded brow,
When every manly heart is glad?

Some passing days and rolling years
May see the *wrath of kings* display'd,
Their wars to prop the tarnish'd crown;
But orphans' groans, and widows' tears,
And justice lifts her shining blade
To bring the tottering bauble down.

July 12.

Poems (1795), 431-32.

Time-Piece   September 25, 1797

ON THE FOURTEENTH OF JULY,
A Day ever memorable to regenerated France.

Substantively identical to the 1795 text, but stanza layout has been altered:

Stanzas 1-5:   lines 1 and 4 at margin; lines 2 and 5 indented five spaces; lines 3 and 6 indented three spaces.

Stanza 6:   lines 1 and 4 at margin; lines 2 and 6 indented five spaces; lines 3 and 5 indented three spaces.

National Gazette   July 18, 1792

ODE II.
Addressed to *Crispin O'Connor*, Esq. a backwoods Planter.

  WISE was your plan when forty years ago
From *Patrick's Isle* you first resolv'd to stray,
  Where lords and knights as thick as rushes grow,
And vulgar folks are in each other's way;

  Where mother-country acts the step-dame's part,
Cuts off, by aid of hemp, each pretty sinner,
  And twice or thrice in every score of years
Hatches sad wars to make her brood the thinner.

  How few aspire to quit the ungrateful soil
That starves the plant it had the strength to bear;
  How many stay, to grieve, and fret, and toil,
And view the plenty that they must not share.

  This you beheld--and westward set your nose,
Like some bold prow, that ploughs the Atlantic foam--
  And left less vent'rous wights, like famish'd crows,
To feed on hog-peas, hips and haws at home.

  Safe landed here, not long the coast detain'd
Your wary steps--but, wand'ring on, you found
  Far in the west, a paltry spot of land,
That no man envied, and that no man own'd.

  A woody hill beside a dismal bog--
This was your choice; nor were you much to blame:
  And here, responsive to the croaking frog,
You grubb'd, and stubb'd, and fear'd no landlord's claim.

  An axe, an adze, a hammer, and a saw;
These were the tools that build your humble shed:
  A cock, a hen, a mastiff, and a cow;
These were your *subjects,* to this desert led.

Now times are chang'd--and Labour's nervous hand
Bids harvests rise where clustering bushes grew;
   The dismal bog by lengthy sluices drain'd,
Supports no more the hoarse captain Bull Frog's crew.--

Prosper your toil!--but, friend, had you remain'd
In lands, where starr'd and garter'd nobles shine,
   When you had thus, to sixty years attain'd,
What different fate, 'Squire Crispin, had been thine!

Nine pence a day, coarse fare, a bed of boards,
The midnight loom, high rents, and excis'd beer;
   Slave to dull squires, kings' brats, and huffish lords,
(Thanks be to Heaven) not yet in fashion here!

July 16.

Poems (1795), 159-60.

Federal Gazette   July 24, 1792[1]

Poem introduced as follows:

FOR THE FEDERAL GAZETTE.

THE subsequent short, though melancholy narrative cannot fail of exciting the sympathy of the brave and good wherever it may be read, and whenever the fate of the three amiable youths shall be disclosed to the heart and eye of sensibility.

Robert Sevier and *William Sevier* were twin brothers,

---

[1] Leary notes an earlier appearance of this poem in the New York *Diary,* June 27, 1792. However, the poem actually appeared in the *Diary* on July 27, and was identical to the *Federal Gazette* text.

in the seventeenth year of their age, "lovely and pleasant in their lives, and in their deaths they were not divided." They, with *Valentine Sevier,* their brother, were sons of Col. *Valentine Sevier,* of North Carolina.

On the fifteenth day of January last, influenced by motives of humanity, they lent their voluntary aid to Capt. *Rice,* whilst endeavouring to stem the current of the Cumberland river, with all his numerous family and the small remains of an humble property, in order to escape the unrelenting barbarity of savage foes, whose insidious plans were too successful in lopping off from human existence, at *one fire,* and at the same instant, the above-nam'd amiable twin-youths and fraternal friends. *Valentine Sevier* their brother, fell by the fire of the savages the next day, whose anxiety had impelled to go in search of those unfortunate youths, from a knowledge of their temerity, originating in generosity, honour, and humanity.

Ye men of sympathy, what must be your feelings for the keen distress of a father, in a few hours deprived of three promising sons not yet arrived to the age of manhood, and who promised to be his stay and support in the decline of life.--Notwithstanding the provocation, however, it is hoped the friends of the deceased will manifest such a share of generous magnanimity as not to take vengeance on the innocent for the ferocious act of the guilty, and what may, possibly, be reckoned justifiable in their mode of warfare.--The following stanzas were occasioned by this melancholy event, and may be considered as an inadequate tribute to the memory of deceased virture.

IN the same hour two lovely youths were born,
    Nature with care had moulded either clay;
In the same hour from this world's limits torn
    The murderous Indian seized their lives away.

Distress to aid, impell'd each gen'rous breast,
    With nervous arm they stemm'd the adverse tide,
In friendship's act encounter'd death's arrest,
    Blameless they liv'd, in honour's path they died.

But ah! what art shall dry a father's tears--
    Lost, early lost! no art relieves his pain,

Clouds shade his sun, and griefs advance with years;
  Nature gave joys, to take those joys again.

Thou, who shalt stray to these sequestered streams
  When times to come their story shall relate--
Let the fond heart, that native worth esteems,
  Revere their virtues, and lament their fate.

(After the text appears the following editorial note:

   The worthy character who pays tribute to the memory of the deceased, is in one point mistaken. *Valentine Sevier* the elder brother to the twins, went not in quest of them, but by a different route, to render an equally humane and generous service.)

National Gazette   July 28, 1792

Introductory note revised slightly:

Paragraph 2:   "in the seventeenth year of their age" deleted.
Paragraph 3:   "Whose insidious plans, while skulking in the woods along the river, were too successful . . ."
"*Valentine Sevier*, their brother, fell by the fire of the savages the next day; who had gone upon a different route, to render a service equally humane and generous."
Includes the fourth paragraph of the *Federal Gazette* note.
"promising sons not yet arrived to the prime of manhood . . ."
"What may possibly be held justifiable . . ."
"The following stanzas were occasioned by the foregoing melancholy event, and may be considered as a small, inadequate tribute to the memory of deceased worth and virtue:"
Stanza 3, line 2:   Lost, early lost!--no art beguiles his pain,
Stanza 4, line 1:   Thou, that shalt stray to these sequestered streams,
         line 4:   Revere their virtues and bemoan their fate.

Poems (1795), 103.

National Gazette   July 28, 1792

ODE III.
[*Note well--the following is to be sung or said as occasion may require.*]

SINCE the day we attempted the NATION'S GAZETTE
Pomposo's dull printer does nothing but fret;
      Now preaching
      And screeching,
      Then nibbling
      And scribbling,
      Remarking
      And barking,
      Repining
      And whining,
      And still in a pet
From morning till night with the Nation's Gazette.

Instead of whole columns, our page to abuse,
Your readers would rather be treated with news;
      While wars are a-brewing
      And kingdoms undoing,
      While monarchs are falling
      And princesses squalling,
      While France is reforming
      And Irishmen storming--
In a glare of such splendour, what nonsense to fret
At so humble a thing as--the Nation's Gazette!

No *favours* we asked from *your friends* in the east;
On your wretched soup-meagre I left them to feast--
So many base lies you have sent them in print
That scarcely a man at your paper will squint:
      And now you begin
      With a grunt and a grin,
      With the bray of an ass,
      And a visage of brass,
With a quill in your hand and a lie in your mouth
To play the same trick on the men of the south.

One National Paper, you think, is enough
To flatter and lie, to pallaver and puff;
To preach up in favour of monarchs and titles,
And garters, and ribbons, to prey on our vitals;
Who knows but our Congress will give it in fee
And make Mr. Fenno the grand patentee!
    Then take to your scrapers
    Other national papers--
    No rogue shall go snacks,
    And the NEWSPAPER-TAX
    Shall be puff'd to the skies
    As a measure most wise--
So a spaniel, when master is angry and kicks it
Sneaks up to his shoe, and submissively licks it.

July 26.

Poems (1795), 397-98.

National Gazette   August 4, 1792

ODE IV.
To the National Gazette.

NINE months are now elaps'd, dear rambling paper,
Since first on this world's stage you cut your caper
With spirit still of democratic proof,
And still despising *Whaacum's* canker'd hoof--
What soon the fates decree, is hard to say,
Whether to live to some far distant day,
    Or sickening in your prime
    In this news-taxing clime,
Take pet, make wings, say prayers, and flit away.

AIR.

"*Virtue, Order,* and *Religion,**
Haste, and seek some other region:
Your plan is fix'd, to hunt them down;
Destroy the mitre, rend the gown,"
And that vile b tc-h--Philosophy--restore--
Did ever paper plan so much before!

For nine months past, a host of busy foes
Have buzz'd about your nose
White, black, and grey,
By night and day;
Garbling, lying,
Singing, sighing:--
These eastern gales a cloud of insects bring
That fluttering, snivelling, whimpering on the wing,
And wafted still as Discord's demon guides,
Flock around the flame, and yet must scorch their hides.

Well--let the fates decree whate'er they please,
Whether you're doom'd to drink Oblivion's cup,
Or *Praise-God-Bare-Bones* eats you up,
This we can say, you've spread your wings afar
Hostile to garter, ribbon, crown and star;
Still on the people's, still on freedom's side,
With full determin'd aim
To battle every claim
Of well-born wights, that aim to mount & ride.

August 2.

Poems (1795), 394-95.

---

* "The National Gazette is--the vehicle of party spleen and opposition to the great principles of order, virtue, and religion.
Gaz. U. States.

National Gazette   August 11, 1792

A CURIOUS DIALOGUE.
[Occasioned by Emblematic Devices on a certain Travelling-Coach.]

ONE Sabbath-day-morning, said *Samuel* to *Sue*,
"I've thought--and I've thought--that a Title would do--
Believe me, my dear it is sweeter than syrup
To taste of a Title, as cook'd up in Europe--
"Your ladyship" here, and "your ladyship," there,
"Sir knight," and "your grace," and "your lordship, the Mayor"--
"But *here* we are nothing but vulgar all over
And the wife of a cobler scarce thinks you above her:
     What a country is this
     Where madam and miss
Is the highest salute by each low-minded cur
And I--even I--am but *Mister* and *Sir*!

"Your equal-right-gentry, I ne'er could abide--
That all are born equal, by me is denied,
     And Barlow and Paine
     Shall preach it in vain:
Look even at brutes, and you'll see it confest
That some are intended to *manage* the rest--
Yon' dog of the manger, how stately he struts,
You may know he is great by the loom of his guts,
Not a better-born whelp ever snapp'd at his foes,
All he wants, is a glass to be stuck on his nose,
     And then, my dear Sue
     Betwixt "me and you"
He would look like the ge'mman, whose name I forget,
Who lives in a castle, and never pays debt."

"My dear [answer'd Susan] 'tis said, in reproach,
That you climb like a bear, when you get in a coach;
Now, your nobles that sprung from the nobles of old,
Your knights, and your earls, and your barons so bold
From nature inherit so handsome an air
They are noblemen born, at first glance we may swear,--
But you, that have cobbled, and I that have spun,
'Tis wrong for our noddles on titles to run:

Moreover, you know
That to make a fine show
Your people of note
Of arms get a coat--
A boot, or a shoe,
Wou'd but sneakingly do,
And would certainly prove our nobility new."

"No matter--(said Samuel) a coach shall be brought--
Tho' puppies may chatter, I care not a groat--
Around it a score of devices shall shine
And mottoes, and emblems--to prove it is mine:
Fair Liberty's cap
And a star and a strap,
A *dagger* that somewhat resembles an *awl,*
A pumpkin-fac'd goddess, turn'd out from a stall;
All these shall be there--
How people will stare!
And Envy herself, that our *Title* would blast,
Shall smile at the motto--*The first shall be LAST.*"*

**Primus qui fuit, nunc ultimus.*   August 8.

Poems (1795), 401-02

National Gazette   August 29, 1792

AN OLD HEATHEN STORY.
Adapted to Modern Times.

AS Aristippus once, with weary feet
Pursued his way through polished *Athens* street,
Minding no business but his own;
Out flew a set of whelps
With sun-burnt scalps,
Black, red, and brown,
That nipt his heel and nibbled at his gown--

While with his staff he kept them all at bay
Some yelp'd aloud, some howl'd in dismal strain,
Some ask'd the sage to bark again--
    Even little *Snapnose* seem'd to say,
    "Answer us, sir, in your best way;--
    "We are, 'tis true
    "A paltry crew
    "But with our jaws
    "Have gain'd applause
    "And Sir--can worry such as you."

The sage beheld their spite with steady eye,
And only stop'd to make this short reply:
    "Hark ye, my dogs--I have not learn'd to yelp,
    "Nor spend my breath on every lousy whelp,
    "Much less to write, or stain my wholesome page
    "With puppies lingo--answering to their rage--
    "Home to your straw!--such contest I disdain,--
        Learn this,
        ('Tis not amiss)
        For men
        I keep an *pen*,
        For dogs--a cane."

August 27.

Poems (1795), 393.

National Gazette   September 19, 1792

THE SPECULATOR.

EGG'd on by hope, from town to town he flew,
The soldier's curse pursued him on his way,
Care in his eye, and anguish on his brow,
He seem'd a sea-hawk watching for his prey.

With soothing words the widows mite he gain'd,
With piercing glance watch'd misery's dark abode,
Filch'd paper scraps while yet a scrap remain'd
Bought where he must, and cheated where he cou'd.

Vast loads amas'd of scrip, and god knows what,
Potosi's wealth seem'd lodg'd within his clutch--
But wealth has wings (he knew) and instant bought
The prancing steed, gay harness, and gilt coach.

One Sunday morn, to church I saw him ride
In glittering state--alack! and who but he--
The following week, with Madam at his side,
To routs they drove--and drank Imperial tea.

In cards and fun the live-long day they spent,
With songs and smut prolong'd the midnight feast,
If plays were had, to plays they constant went
Where Madam's top-knot rose a foot at least.

Three weeks, and more, thus pass'd in airs of state,
The fourth beheld the mighty bubble fail--
And he, who countless millions *own'd* so late
Stopt short--and clos'd his triumphs on a *Jail.*

September 17.

Poems (1795), 429-30.

National Gazette   September 26, 1792

(Untitled text introduced as follows:

It is asserted in Mr. Russel's (Boston) *Columbian Centinel* of September 12 (and copied in Mr. Fenno's *Gazette of the United States* of last Saturday) that "the Clergy of this country are constantly vilified, and *Religion* ridiculed through the medium of the *National Gazette*." The aughor of the assertion is requested to produce one or more passages from the National Gazette to support his charge, otherwise, we shall conclude it only a *dirty attempt to prevent the circulation of the National Gazette in the Eastern States:*–But further,)

IF of Religion I have made a sport
Then why not cite me to the Bishops court?--
Fair to the world let every page be set
And prove your charge from *National Gazette*.
What if this heart no narrow notions bind,
Its pure good will extends to all mankind–
Suppose I ask no portion from your feast
Nor ride to heaven behind *your* parish priest,
Because I wear not Fenno's Sunday face,
Must I for that be loaded with disgrace?

The time has been–the time, I fear, is now
When holy phrenzy would erect her brow,
Round some poor wight with *painted* devils meet,
And worse than *Smithfield* blaze thro' every street;
But wholesome laws prevent such horrid scenes:
No more afraid of deacons and of deans
In this new world our joyful hymn we sing
That even a Bishop is a harmless thing.

September 25.

Poems (1795), 390.

National Gazette   December 8, 1792[1]

[The following Stanzas are addressed to the Americans of the United States, by the French patriotic society of Charleston, S.C.]

(Text of a three-stanza poem in French.)

[Some of the ideas in the foregoing are transfused into the subsequent lines.]

THESE Jacobins, that some so much despise
Did not, like mushrooms, spring up in a night:
By them instructed, France again shall rise,
And every Frenchman learn his native right.
American! when in your country's cause
You march'd, and dar'd the English lion's jaws,
Crush'd Hessian slaves, and made their hosts retreat,
Say, were you not a Jacobin--complete?

Forever banish'd now, be prince and king,
To Nations and to Laws our reverence due:
And let not language to my memory bring,
A word that might recall the infernal crew.
Monarch!--henceforth I blot it from my page,
Monarchs and slaves too long disgrace this age;
But Jacobin!--the race that some disclaim,
Shall save a world, and damn a tyrant's fame.

Friends to republics, cross the Atlantic brine,
Low in the dust see regal splendour laid:
Hopeless forever, sleeps the Bourbon line
Long practis'd adepts in the murdering trade!
With patriot care the nation's will expressing

---

[1] Comparison with the original text reveals that Freneau's version of the poem is not a literal translation; although it includes every idea expressed in the original, each statement has been rhetorically and emotively intensified.

These Jacobins shall prove all Europe's blessing,
Pull from his height each blustering noble down
And chace these modern Tarquins from the throne.

Poems (1795), 430, 31.

National Gazette   December 15, 1792[1]

[*Translation of the Latin Verses in our last.*]

NO more let barbarous Memphis boast
Base structures, rear'd by slavish hands--
A nation on the Atlantic coast
(Fetter'd no more in foreign bands)
A nobler *Pyramid* displays
Than Egypt's *marble* e'er could raise.

Columbia's sons, to extend a proof
Of their bold deeds to future years,
Disdain to use such vulgar stuff;
But, soaring to the starry spheres,
Materials seek in Jove's blue sky
T'endure when brass and marble die.

---

[1] The original fourteen-line poem, which, in translating, Freneau revised and lengthened, was sent in by a contributor, along with the following note, and the sketch of an emblem, containing fifteen stars arranged in the shape of a pyramid:

"Mr. *Freneau,*
THE state of Kentucky having encreased the number of emblematic stars, and afforded the opportunity of arranging them in a new form,--I send you the following trifle on the subject. The National Motto, which I wished to include, will furnish a sufficient apology for writing in Latin.   Yours, &c.
                                                                                A.B."

Arriv'd among the shining host,
Fearless, the proud invaders spoil
From countless gems, in œther lost,
Some stars, to crown their mighty toil:
To heaven a *pyrimid* they rear,
And point the fabric with a star.

Old wasted *time*! tho' still you gain
Dominion o'er the brazen tower,
On *this* your teeth shall gnaw in vain,
Finding its strength beyond their power--
While kindred stars in heaven shall glow,
This pyramid will shine below!

Poems (1795), 435-36.

National Gazette December 19, 1792

Present View of FRANCE *and her Combined Enemies.*

FROM *Bourbon's* brow the crown remov'd
Low in the dust is laid,
And parted, now, from all she lov'd
Maria's beauties fade:
What shall relieve her sad distress,
What power recall that former state,
When drinking deep the drafts of bliss
She smil'd--and look'd so sweet*!--
With aching heart and haggard eye
She views the palace,+ towering high,
Where once were pass'd her joyous days,
And nations stood, in wild amaze,
Louis! to see you eat!

---

* *See Mr. Burke's book on the French Revolution.*
+ *Thuilleries.*

The gaudy vision to restore
Shall fate its laws repeal,
And cruel despots rise once more
To plan a new Bastille?
Shall "from their sheathes ten thousand blades
In glittering vengeance start,"
To *cut up beef,* and slice off heads,
Taking their monarch's part?--
Ah no!--the fates this hope refuse,
Louis, they send you no such news--
Nor *Conde* fierce, nor *Frederick* stout,
Nor *Catherine* brings this work about,
Nor *Brunswick's* warlike art.

Valour, at length, by freedom led
The rights of man restores,
And Gallia, now from tyrants freed,
Her *Jacobin* adores!
On *equal rights* their fabric plann'd,
Storms idly round it rave,
Nor longer breathes in Gallic land
A monarch or a slave.
At distance far, and self-remov'd
From all he own'd, and all he lov'd,
See--turn'd his back on freedom's blaze--
In foreign lands the apostate strays,
Th'aristocratic knave.

Enroll'd with these, but close immur'd,
The gallant chief* is found,
Whom once admiring crowds ador'd,
Thro' *either* world renown'd:
Here, bold in arms and firm in heart
He help'd to win our cause;
Yet could not from a tyrant part,

---

* M. de la Fayette, now confined in the castle of Spandau, in Prussia--His estates lay in the rich country of Auvergne, and now are confiscated to the nation.

But turn'd to embrace his laws.--
Ah! hadst thou stay'd in fair *Auvergne*
And *truth* from *Paine** vouchsaf'd to learn,
There happy, honour'd, and retir'd,
Both hemispheres had still admir'd,
Still crown'd you with applause!

See, doom'd to feast on famish'd steeds,
The rude Hungarians fly;
Brunswick with drooping courage leads
Death's dismal family:
In horrid groups, o'er hosts of dead,
Their madness they bemoan,
No friendly hand to give them bread,
No *Thionville* their own;
The Gaul enrag'd as they retire
Aims at each head his stream of fire--
What hosts of Frederick's *reeking* crew
Dying, must bid the world adieu,
To dogs their flesh been thrown!

Escap'd from death, a mangled train
In scatter'd bands retreat
Where bounding on Silesia's plain
The despot holds his seat--
With feeble step I see them go
The heavy news to tell
Where *Oder's* lazy waters flow
Or glides the swift *Moselle:*
Where *Rhine* his various journey moves
Thro settled lands or savage groves,
Or where the vast Danubian flood
(So often ting'd by Austrian blood)
Foams with th'autumnal swell.

---

* See Mr. Paine's dedication of his second Part of the Rights of Man, to M. de la Fayette.

But shall they not some tidings bear
Of freedom's sacred flame,
And shall not fetter'd millions hear
The long abandon'd name?--
Thro' ages past, their spirits broke,
I see them spurn old laws,
Indignant burst the Austrian yoke
And clip the *Eagle's* claws:
From shore to shore, from sea to sea
They aim to set the wretched free,
And driving from the servile court
Each royal knave--they help support
The democratic cause.

O France! the world to thee must owe
A debt they ne'er can pay:
The rights of man you bid them know,
And kindle reason's day.
Columbia, in your friendship blest,
Your gallant deeds shall hail,
On the same ground our fortunes rest,
Must flourish or must fail:
But should all *Europe's* slaves combine
Against a cause so fair as thine,
And *Asia* aid a league so base,
Defeat would every plan disgrace;
And Liberty prevail!

December 18.

Poems (1795), 453-55.

National Gazette   December 22, 1792

On the ROYAL PORTRAITS, *in the Senate Chamber.*

DISCHARD'D by France, no more the royal pair
Claim from a nation's love a nation's care:
Their splendid race no more a palace holds,--
While *Louis* frets, *Antoinetta* scolds;
Folly's sad victims, fortune's bitter sport,
They take their stand among the "common sort,"
Doom'd through the world, in sad reverse, to roam
Perhaps--without a shelter or a home!

    To shew our pity for their short liv'd reign
What shall we do, or how express our pain?
Since for their *persons* no relief is found
But cruel mobs degrade them to the ground,
To shew how deeply we regret their fall
We hang their portraits in our *Senate Hall.*

Poems (1795), 433.

National Gazette   January 12, 1793

(Poem concludes the following reflections:

> One cannot help admiring at the weakness, or effrontery, of certain writers who would, if possible, persuade the public that no happiness, nor temporal benefit of any kind, is at present enjoyed in this country but thro' the operative influence of the federal government. Candour should induce them to confess, that no visible alteration for the better is wrought thereby on the circumstances of the generality of the people. Poverty still reigns triumphant over her thousands; and thousands after every effort of œconomy and industry, still shrink into the cheerless hut of want and misery, as before. Speculators and ministerial favorites may, indeed, boast of the vast blessings ensured to them from the change, and it is from these, chiefly, that certain animated eulogiums proceed. At the same time let it be remembered that this class of citizens do by no means speak the sense of the people at large--)

Since federal-sway hath been exerted here
What numerous blessings to our country flow!
    Whales on our shores have run aground,
    Sturgeons are in our rivers found;
Nay--ships have on the Delaware sail'd,
    A sight most new!
    Wheat has been sown--
    Harvests have grown--
On coaches, now, gay coats of arm are bore
By some, who hardly had a coat before--
    Silk gowns, instead of homespun, now are seen,
    Instead of native *straw*, the Leghorn hat:
        And Sir, 'tis true
        (Twixt me and you,)
    That some have grown prodigious fat
    That were--prodigious lean!

Poems (1795), 402.

National Gazette   January 19, 1793

(Poem follows a lengthy prose piece entitled "Reflections on Balloons," a plea for public support for the new science of aeronautics. Freneau condemns the conventional prejudices that thwart discovery and progress in all sciences, and in this case, the argument that the aeronaut is going beyond his natural element. To the contrary, he argues that it would be worthwhile to determine, by a few experiments, whether human nature, "generated into higher regions of the atmosphere," might become more exalted and virtuous. He concludes by acknowledging the public's debt to M. Blanchard for gratifying their curiosity in his recent balloon ascension.)

BY science taught, on silken wings
Beyond our groveling race you rise,
And soaring from terrestrial things
Explore a passage to the skies--
    O, could I thus exalted sail,
    And rise with you beyond the jail!

Who'er shall thus presume to fly
While downward with disdain they look,
Shall own this journey through the sky
The dearest jaunt they ever took,
    And choose, next time, without reproach
    A humbler seat in Inskeep's coach--

Ah! when you rose, impell'd by fear
Each bosom swell'd its thousand sighs;
To you each lady lent a tear,
And held the kerchief to her eyes;
    All hearts still follow'd as you flew,
    All eyes admir'd a sight so new.

The birds that cleave th'expanse of air
Admiring, view your globe full-blown,
And chattering round the painted car
Complain your flight outdoes their own:
    Beyond their track you proudly swim
    Nor fear the loss of life or limb.

How vast the height! how grand the scene
That your enraptured eye surveys,
When towering in your gay machine
You leave th'astonish'd world to gaze,
  And wandering in the etherial blue
  Our eyes in vain your course pursue.

The *orb of day*! how dazzling bright!
In glittering radiance gleams the *moon;*
And *terra,* whence you took your flight,
Appears to you--a mere balloon,
  Its noisy crew no longer heard,
  Towns, cities, forests, disappear'd.

Yet travelling thro' the azure road,
Soar not too high for *Reason's* ken;
Reflect, our humble safe abode
Is all that *nature* meant for men:
  Take in your sails before you freeze
  And sink again among the trees.--

Poems (1795), 446-47.

Time-Piece May 15, 1797

Stanzas writtin some years since on Mr. Blanchard's 45th ascension, from the jail yard in Philadelphia-- January 9, 1793.

Substantively identical to the *1795* text, except for the following variants:

Stanza 1, line 6: And steer, with you, beyond the jail.

Stanza 2, line 1: Yes! when you rose--impell'd by fear,
     line 2: To you each lady lent a tear

Stanza 4, line 3: And, chattering round the pendent car,
     line 6: And fear no loss of life or limb.

Stanza 5:   The *Geese* that from *Arcadia* fly
               To seek some southern, warm abode
               Ask what new brother of the sky
               Pursues, with them, the airy road—
               Altho' they gabble, toil, and strain,--
               To catch you--they shall toil in vain.

Stanza 6:   Fifth stanza of the 1795 version.

Stanza 7:   Sixth stanza of the 1795 version.

Stanza 8:   Seventh stanza of the 1795 version

National Gazette   February 2, 1793

Text follows these comments:

> On Tuesday evening last, the weather suddenly changed from warm and moderate (as had uninterruptedly been the case since the beginning of the month) to a severe snow storm at north-east, which continued the whole of the succeeding day. This has for the present put an end to the expectations of our shad-epicures--That the *February salmon-eaters* in New York, will also be disappointed, at least for the first half of the month, is more than probable.

Where now are all our January shad
And salmon--eke--that came before their time--
Alas! they're fled to some less rigorous clime,
Where suns, that never *squint*, shall make them glad--
    Ladies, no more for salmon set your caps--
    Some weeks too (fish girls say) must now elapse
    'Till shad once more shall be so void of brains,
    As to be captured in our seins--
    Then pray don't sob and pout--
        If absent from our stream,
        There's only *one* to blame,
Winter, that *antifederal* knave--'tis--keeps them out.

Poems (1795), 360.

National Gazette   May 29, 1793[1]

ODE TO LIBERTY.
[See the original in our last]
"*O toi, dont l'auguste lumiere,*" &c.

THOU splendid light, that clouds obscur'd
So long from Gallic lands,
Goddess, in ancient days ador'd
    By Gallia's conquering bands:
Thou *Liberty*! whom savage kings
Have plac'd among forbidden things,
Tho' still averse that men be free
Secret, they bow to Liberty;
O, to my accents lend an ear,
Blest object of each tyrant's fear,
While I to modern days recall
The Lyric muse of ancient Gaul.

Ere yet my willing voice obeys
    The transports of the heart,
The goddess to my view displays
A temple rear'd in ancient days,
    Fit subject of the muse's art.
Now, round the world I cast my eye,
With pain, its ruins I descry.
This temple once to freedom rais'd
Thermoplyœ! in thy fam'd strait—
I see it to the dust debas'd,
And servile chains, its fate!

In those fair climes, where freedom reign'd,
Two thousand years degrade the Grecian name,

---

[1] The French original of this text was delivered at a dinner given by the French Benevolent Society for Ambassador Genet, on May 18, 1793. Freneau was asked to translate and publish the poem. The original text, which, according to Freneau's note in the 1795 collection, was penned by a M. Pichon, appeared in the *National Gazette* on May 25.

I see them still enslav'd, enchain'd;
But France from Rome and Athens caught the flame--
A temple now to heaven they raise
Where nations bound in ties of peace
With olive-boughs shall throng to praise
The gallant Gaul, that bade all discord cease.

Before this Pantheon fair and tall,
The piles of darker ages fall,
And freemen here no longer trace
The monuments of man's disgrace.
Before its porch, at freedom's tree
Exalt the *Cap of Liberty,*
The cap* that once Helvetia knew
(The terror of the tyrant crew)
And on our country's altar trace
The features of each honour'd face;
The men that strove for equal laws,
Or perish'd martyrs in their cause.

Ye gallant chiefs, above all praise,
Ye Brutus's of ancient days!
Tho' fortune long has strove to blast,
Your virtues are repaid at last.
Your heavenly feasts a while forbear
And deign to make my song your care:
My lyre a bolder note attains
And rivals old Tyrtœus' strains;
The ambient air returns the sound,
And kindles rapture all around.

With thee begins the lofty theme,
Eternal Being--power supreme,
Who planted *Freedom* in the mind,
The first great right of all mankind:

---

* Which owes its origin to William Tell, the famous deliverer of Switzerland.

Too long presumptuous folly dar'd
To veil our race from thy regard;
Tyrants on ignorance form'd their plan,
And made *their* crimes, the crimes of man.
Let victory but befriend our cause
And reason deign to dictate laws;
At once mankind their rights reclaim
And honours pay to thy great name.

But O! what cries our joys molest,
What discord drowns sweet music's feast!
What demon from perdition leads
Night, fire, and thunder o'er our heads!
In northern realms, prepar'd for fight
A thousand savage clans unite.--
To avenge a faithless Helen's doom
All Europe's slaves, determin'd, come
Freedom's fair fabric to destroy
And wrap in flames another Troy!

These, these are they--the murdering bands,
Whose blood, of old, distain'd our lands.
By our forefathers chac'd and slain,
The monuments of death remain.
Hungarians, wet with human blood,
Ye saxons fierce, so oft subdued
By ancient Gauls on Gallic plains,
Dread, dread the race, that still remains:
Return, and seek your dark abodes,
Your dens and caves in northern woods,
Nor stay to tell each kindred ghost
What thousands from your tribes are lost.

A fiend* from hell, of murderous brood,
Stain'd with a hapless husband's blood,

---

* Catherine the 2d, present empress of Russia, who deposed her husband Peter 3d, and deprived him of life in July 1762, while under confinement in prison.

Unites with Danube* and the Spree,*
Who arm to make the French their prey.
To check their hosts and chill with fear,
Frenchmen, advance to your frontier,
There dig the *eternal tomb* of kings,
Or *Poland's* fate each monster brings,
Mows millions down, your cause defeats,
And *Ismael's horrid scene*+ repeats.

Ye nations brave, so long rever'd,
Whom Rome, in all her glory, fear'd:
Whose stubborn mind no tyrant broke
To bow the neck to Cesar's yoke–
Scythian! whom Romans never chain'd;
Germans! that unsubdued remain'd
Ah! see your sons, a sordid race
With despots leagu'd, to their disgrace
And the base cause that you abhor,
And hurl on France the storm of war.

Our bold attempts shake modern Rome,
She bids her kindred despots come;
From Italy her forces draws
To waste their blood in *Tarquin's cause.*
A hundred hordes of foes advance,
Embodying on the verge of France;
'Mongst these, to guide the flame of war,
I see *Porsenna's*,** just a score,
While from the soil, by thousands spring
Scevola's++ to destroy each king.

---

* Two great rivers of Germany; here metaphorically designating the Austrian and Russian powers.

+ The Turkish fortress of Ismael, in 1789 stormed by the Russian army. After carrying it by assault, upwards of 30,000 persons, men, women, and children were slaughtered by the Russian barbarians, in less than three hours.

** An ancient king of Etruria who took Tarquin's part against the Romans.

++ *Scevola*, who attempted the life of Porsenna in his own camp, but failed.

O Rome! what glory you consign
To those who court your ancient fame!
Frenchmen, like Romans now shall shine,
And copying them, their ancient honours claim.
O France, my native clime, my country dear,
While youth remains may I behold you free,
Each tyrant crush'd, no threatening despot near
    To endanger Liberty!
By you unfetter'd be all human kind,
    No slaves on earth be known
And man be blest, in friendship join'd,
    From Tyber to the Amazon!

Poems (1795), 439-45.

Federal Gazette   June 3, 1793[1]

(Text follows an account of a testimonial dinner held in honor of Genet at Oeller's Hotel on Saturday, June 1. The account includes a list of toasts offered on the occasion as well as the texts of several songs composed and sung for the event.)

SONG.
By Major STAGG.

God save the Rights of Man!
Give us a heart to scan
    Blessings so dear!
Let them be spread around
Wherever man is found,
And with the welcome sound,
    Ravish his ear.

---

[1] The newspaper history of this text is rather complex. The first appearance of a text containing any of the stanzas of the 1795 collected version was in the *Baltimore Daily Repository* on April 20, 1793. This text contains one full stanza and six other lines which, with minor revisions, become the first two stanzas of the text in Freneau's 1795 collection. The rest of the seven stanza poem did not appear in Freneau's collected version. That this earlier version was not originally Freneau's poem is suggested by the introductory note in the Baltimore paper:

> The following Song has been transmitted to us by one of our Correspondents in London, which, he informs us, is in high Repute among the Friends to Liberty in that City:

The song contains no specific reference to America; rather, it reflects the sentiments of a pro-French Englishman. This earlier text was reprinted in the *New York Journal* on May 11, 1793, the text which Leary records as the first newspaper appearance of Freneau's poem. It also was printed, with one stanza deleted and other minor variants (a reference to France altered to refer to America) in Freneau's *Jersey Chronicle* on July 11, 1795, under the title "Hymn to Liberty." Here it is included in an account of a Fourth

Let us with France agree
And bid the world be free
   --While tyrants fall--
Let the rude savage host
In their vast numbers boast--
Freedom's almighty trust
   Laughs at them all.

Tho' hosts of slaves conspire
To quench fair Gallia's fire,
   Still shall they fail;
Tho' traitors round her raise,
Leagu'd with her enemies,
To war each patriot flies
   And will prevail.

---

of July celebration at Middletown Point, as the song sun for the occasion. This text was widely reprinted in other papers during the 1790's, and several of the reprints of Freneau's poem recorded in Leary's bibliography are actually reprints of this text.

    The first appearance of a text including every stanza, with minor variants, of the 1795 collected version, was in the *Federal Gazette,* June 3, 1793, where it is attributed to "Major Stagg." As noted above, it is included as a song composed for the occasion. The text was reprinted in several Philadelphia and New York papers that covered the dinner, sometimes attributed to Stagg and sometimes unatrributed. On June 5, it appeared in the *National Gazette,* with no introduction or attribution, but dated June 1, the day of the dinner, and with a new stanza added--one which also appears in the 1795 text. It was reprinted later that year in the *Daily Advertiser* on the occasion of the celebration of the evacuation of New York. All of the variants cited here are variants of this text. It should not be confused with reprints of the earlier text, which even Freneau printed in the *Jersey Chronicle,* but for which we have no evidence of his authorship, only evidence against in the *Baltimore Daily Repository* introduction. Also, it should not be confused with the many other imitations of "God Save the King" which appeared in papers between 1786 and 1800, but which have no lines in common with Freneau's collected text. It appears that, in composing a song for the Genet dinner, he simply borrowed twelve lines from the earlier text, added four new stanzas of his own, and then added another one when printing the poem, four days later, in the *National Gazette.*

The world at last will join
To aid thy great design
    Dear liberty!
To Russia's frozen lands,
The generous flame expands;
On Asia's burning sands
    Shall man be free.

In this our western world
Be Freedom's flag unfurl'd
    Through all our shores,
May no destructive blast
Our heav'n with clouds o'er cast,
May Freedom's fabric last
    While earth endures.

If e'er her cause should fail,
Ambition's fiends assail,
    Slaves to a throne;
May no proud despot daunt--
Should he his standard plant,
Freedom will never want
    Her Washington!--

General Advertiser   June 4, 1793

Text also included in an account of the Genet dinner:

After the 7th toast the following

SONG.
(Unattributed.)

Stanza 3, line 4: Tho' traitors round her rise,

National Gazette   June 5, 1793

NEW ODE--
To a popular tune.

Stanza 2, line 5: Of their vast numbers boast--
Stanza 3, line 4: Tho' traitors round her rise
Stanza 4:   No more is valour's flame
            Devoted to a name;
              Taught to adore--
            Soldiers of liberty
            Disdain to bow the knee;
            But teach *Equality*
              To every shore.
Stanza 5:   Fourth stanza of the *Federal Gazette* text.
Stanza 6:   Fifth stanza of the *Federal Gazette* text, with the following variants:
            line 5:   Our skies with clouds o'ercast,
            line 7:   While time endures!
Stanza 7:   Last stanza of the *Federal Gazette* text.

Daily Advertiser   November 26, 1793

Text follows a list of toasts at a dinner for militia officers, on November 25, 1793, in celebration of the anniversary of the evacuation of New York by British troops.

> The following ODE, written for the Day, was sung by Capt. *Van Zanot.*
> ODE.

Substantively identical to the *Federal Gazette* text, except for the following variants:

Stanza 1:   Lines 5 and 6 of the *Federal Gazette* text reversed.
Stanza 4, line 2: To aid thy grand design

New York *Weekly Museum*   November 30, 1793

Identical to the *Daily Advertiser* text, including the introduction, except for the following variants:

Stanza 1: Lines 5 and 6 appear as in the *Federal Gazette* text.

Poems (1795), 445-46.

National Gazette   July 6, 1793

REFLECTIONS on the death of a Country *Printer.*
(*By his Successor.*)

LIKE Sybils' leaves, his *sheets* he spread
To keep in awe the well-born few:
   Stock jobbers fainted while they read--
Each hidden scheme expos'd to view--
   Who could such doctrines spread abroad
   So long--and be not clapper claw'd?

   Content with slow, uncertain gains,
With hand and heart prepar'd he stood
   To gather pence from distant plains
And hills beyond th'Ohio flood--
   And, since he had no time to lose,
   Preach'd whiggish lectures with his news.

   Now Death, (that sly designing beast)
At whose command ev'n CAPETS go,
   Converts his savings all to waste,
And melts his hopes, like April snow--
   No pence he left, to ring the bell,
   Or pay the passage boat of hell.

   What shall be done in such a case?--
Shall I, because one brother fails,
   Call in his bull-dogs from the chace
To loll their tongues, and drop their tails?
   No faith!--th'aristocratic crew
   No longer fly--than we pursue.--

Poems (1795), 434-35.

Time-Piece   September 22, 1797

ON THE DEATH OF A COUNTRY PRINTER.

Substantively identical to the *1793* text, except for the following variants:

Stanza 3, line 2: At whose command ev'n monarchs go,
Stanza 4, line 3: Call in my bull-dogs from the chace,
line 5: No faith!--the sceptre-loving crew

National Gazette   July 17, 1793

PATRIOTIC STANZAS
On the Anniversary of the Storming of the
Bastille, At Paris, July 14th, 1789.

THE chiefs that bow to Capet's reign,
In mourning now their weeds display:
   But we, that scorn a monarch's chain,
Combine to celebrate the day
      To Freedom's birth that put the seal,
      And laid in dust the proud Bastille.

To Gallia's rich and splendid crown,
This mighty *day* gave such a blow,
   As Time's recording hand shall own,
No former *age* had power to do:
      No single gem some Brutus stole,
      But instant ruin seiz'd the whole.

Now tyrants rise, once more to bind
In royal chains, a nation freed--
   Vain hope! for they, to death consign'd,
Shall soon, like perjur'd Louis bleed:
      O'er every king, o'er every queen
      Fate hangs the sword, the guillotine.

"Plung'd in a gulf of deep distress,
France turns her back--(so traitors say)
Kings, priests, and nobles, round her press,
Resolv'd to sieze their destin'd prey:
  Thus Europe swears (in arms combin'd)
  To Poland's doom is France consign'd."

Yet those, who now are thought so low,
From conquests that were *basely* gain'd.
 Shall rise tremendous from the blow.
And free *two Worlds,* that still are chain'd,
  Restrict the Briton to his isle,
  And Freedom plant in every soil.

Ye sons of this degenerate clime,
Haste, arm the barque, expand the sail;
 Assist to speed that golden time,
When Freedom rules, and monarchs fail;
  All left to France--*new powers* may join,
  And help to crush the cause divine.

Ah! while I write, dear France *ally'd,*
My ardent wish I scarce restrain,
 To throw these Sybil leaves aside,
And fly to join you on the main:
  Pray heaven, your guns may never fail,
  Nor George reward me with a jail.

Poems (1795), 438-39.

National Gazette   July 31, 1793[1]

TO JUSTICE,*
An abusive Scribbler.
Quid facient domini, audent cam talia fures.   VIRG.

THE man that doth an elephant pursue
   Whose capture gains a noble price,
Amid the chace heeds not the barking crew
   Or lesser game of rats and mice.

On ocean's waste who chace the *royal flag*,
   Stop not to take the privateer:
Who aims to seize the steed, neglects the nag;
   No squirrel hunt will catch a deer.

---

* See Gazette of the United States of July 24.

[1] This poem and "To Justice (A writer in the Gazette of the United States)," *National Gazette,* August 7, 1793, were probably written in direct response to a letter in the *Gazette of the United States* on July 24, signed "Justice." In the letter, Justice attacks Freneau for publishing letters critical of Washington and, specifically, of the neutrality proclamation. He concludes by defending the president and scolding Freneau:

> Who then is the Editor of the "*National Gazette,*" that takes the liberty . . . not to examine with candor and decency into the conduct of our first magistrate, but to cast at him the most illiberal and unwarrantable abuse . . . Is he a great politician, and has he assisted the counsels of your cabinet . . .? . . . No!–but he can *describe* a more sublime battle than Washington ever fought.

Justice concludes by accusing Freneau of pursuing, after unsuccessful attempts to gain an honest living, a career as a professed slanderer of good men and good government, prostituting his talents by a degrading dependence on the vices of others.

A blockhead's venom ever spits in vain:
    To honour's coat no drop adheres--
Go wretch--to white-wash'd squires disclose your pain,
    Your tiny gods, and godling peers.

The little *apes,* that strut in courtly guise,
    May vile abuse thro' *you* impart;
But I--that on no Treasury lean, despise
    Your clumsy quill, and canker'd heart.

Mark'd for her prey, with vision quick and keen
    The gallic genius shall pursue,
Consign your weazon to the guillotine,
    And give the dogs their due.

Gazette of the United States   August 3, 1793

The *National Gazette* text appears, unaltered, on page 3 of the paper. On the first page, "Justice" provides a mock serious critical evaluation of the poem, complaining of an overabundance of metaphor. He refers to Lord Kames' definition of wit--joining things by distant and fanciful relations, surprising because unexpected--and argues that Freneau has improved upon the art by joining things with no relation at all. He complains that the meter is not accurate, but assumes that Freneau must be seeking Pope's "grace beyond the reach of art," again improving the technique by taking it beyond all human comprehension.

Poems (1795), 425-26.

National Gazette   August 3, 1793

A DIALOGUE between *Whacum* and *Whiffle.*

WHACUM! said Whiffle (eager to reproach)
Why ride you in that ancient crazy coach!
Hark, how it creaks!--freighted with you and Madam--
Many suppose it once belong'd to Adam;
So loose, so weak, your coachman makes report
You risque each hour a tumble in the dirt."

"WHIFFLE (said Whacum) tho' it be a wreck,
And threatens much the structure of my neck,
Yet, to the last this coach I swear I'll ride in
Which forty years my grandsire did confide in--
'Twill also prove--(pray, take it in good part--)
I had this coach, when you had scarce--a cart."

July 31.

Poems (1795), 362-63.

National Gazette   August 7, 1793[1]

TO JUSTICE,
(A writer in the *Gazette of the United States*.)

BECAUSE some pumpkin shells and lobster-claws
    (Thrown o'er his garden walls by *Braintree's* DUKE)
Have chanc'd to fall within your meagre jaws,
    A dose, at which all honest men would puke:

---

[1] For the provocation of this poem, see note to "To Justice, An Abusive Scribbler," *National Gazette,* July 31, 1793. See also the reprint of that poem in the *Gazette of the United States* on August 3, 1793.

Because some treasury-luncheons you have gnaw'd
    Like rats that prey upon the public store,
Must you for that, your crude stuff belch abroad
    And vomit lies on all that pass your door?

To modern bards, wherever bards are found,
    If sullen JUSTICE does not *give their due,*
Spruce tho' you be, your heels may drum the ground
    And make fine pastime for the sportive crew.

Why all these hints of menace—dark and sad?
    What is my crime that thus 'squire JUSTICE raves?--
No secret-service-money have I had
    For waging two years' war with fools & knaves.

Abus'd at courts--unwelcome to the GREAT,
    This page of ours no *well-born* aspect wears:
On honest yeomen we repose its fate:
    Clodhopper's dollar is as good as THEIRS.

Why would you then with *hangman-hand* destroy
    A wight that wastes his ink in freedom's cause;
Who, to the last, his arrows will employ
    To publish freedom's rights, and guard her laws

O Thou! that has a heart so flinty hard
    Thus oft, too oft, a poet to rebuke
From those that rhyme you ne'er shall meet regard,
    Of Braintree's dutchy you shall be no duke.

                                                            JUSTITIA FIAT.

Poems (1795), 403.

National Gazette   August 17, 1793

On a late memorable naval engagement.

RESOLV'D for a chace all the Frenchmen to face,
Bold Boston from Halifax sail'd,
With a full flowing sheet the pride of the fleet,
No vessel she saw but she hail'd:
With Courtney, commander, who never did fear,
Nor return'd from a fight with a flea in his ear.

As they steer'd for the Hook, each swore by his book
No prayers should their vengeance retard,
They would plunder and burn, "they would never return
Unattended by Captain Bompard!!!"
No Gaul can withstand us; when once we arouse–
We'll drown the monsieurs in the wash of our bows!

A sail now appear'd, when tow'rd her they steer'd,
Each crown'd with his liberty-cap;
Under colours of France did they boldly advance
And a small privateer did entrap–
(The time may have been when their nation was brave
But now they prefer to cajole and deceive.)

Arriv'd at the spot where they thought to dispute,
Thus Courtney observ'd, in a heat,
"Since fighting's our trade, then their bold Ambuscade
Must sink, or be forc'd to retreat:
Tell the captain Bompard, if his stomach's for war
To advance from his port and engage a true tar."

Bold captain Bompard, when this challange was heard,
Tho' his sails were unbent from the yards,
His topmasts struck down, and his men half in town:
Yet sent back his *humble regards*–
The challenge accepted–all hands, warn'd on board,
Bent their sails, swore revenge, and the frigate unmoor'd.

The Boston, at sea, being under her lee,
For windward manœuvred in vain,
'Till night coming on, both lay by till dawn

Then met on the watery plain;
The wind at north-east, and a beautiful day,
And the hearts of the Frenchmen in trim for the fray.
  [*The remainder in our next.*]

Poems (1795), 450-51.

National Gazette   August 24, 1793

   On a late memorable *Naval Engagement*.
   [*Concluded from No.* 188.]

   THEN to it they went, with a bloody intent
The fate of the day to decide,
   By the virtues of powder--(no argument louder
Was e'er to a subject apply'd)
   A Gaul with a Briton in battle contends,
   Let them stand to their guns, and we'll see how it ends.

   As the Frenchman shot past, Boston gave him a blast,
Glass bottles, case knives, and old nails,
   A score of round shot, and the devil knows what,
To cripple his masts and his sails--
   Madam Boston suppos'd it the best of her play,
   To prevent him from cheating--if she ran away.

   The Frenchman most cool, not a hot headed fool,
Return'd the broad-side in a trice,
   So keen was his logic, he brought down their cro'jick,
And gave them some rigging to splice,
   Some holes for to plug, where the bulldogs had gone,
   Some splinters to draw--and some heads to put on.

   Three glasses and more, their cannons did roar,
Shot flying in horrible squads;
   'Midst torrents of smoke the Republican spoke,
And frighten'd the Anglican gods--
   Their frigate so maul'd, they no longer defend her,
   And Courtney shot down, they bawl'd out for surrender.

O damn their French thunder, said captain O'Blunder,
I think with the devil he deals,
But since we dislike to surrender or strike,
Let us try the success of our heels:
    We may save the king's frigate by running away--
    The Frenchman will have us--all hands--if we stay.

So, squaring their yards--on all captain *Bompards*
A volley of curses they shed;
Having got their discharge, they bore away large,
While the Frenchman pursu'd as they fled:
But vain was his haste, and vain was his speed,
He ended the fray in a chace,
    The Gaul got the best of the fight, 'tis agreed,
The Briton--the best of the race.

Poems (1795), 451-52.

National Gazette   September 4, 1793

ORLANDO'S FLIGHT.

ON prancing steed, with spunge at nose,
From town behold Orlando fly;
    Camphor and Tar where'er he goes
Th'infested shafts of death defy--
        Safe in an atmosphere of stink,
        No doctor gets Orlando's chink.

'Twas right to fly! for well I ween
In Stygian worlds, by Jove's decree,
    No blushing blossom e'er was seen,
Or running brook, or budding tree:
        No splendid meats, no flowing bowls
        Smile o'er the meagre feast of souls.

No sprightly songs, to banish grief,
No balls, the *Stygian* beaus prepare,
   And he that fed on rounds of beef,
On onion shells shall fatten *there*--
      Monarchs are there of little note,
      And Caesar wears a ragged coat.

   Chloes on earth, of air and shape,
Whose eyes destroy'd poor love-lorn wights,
   There lower their topsails to the cap,
Rig in their booms and furl their kites:--
      Where Cupid's bow was never bent,
      What lover asks a maid's consent?

   All this, and more, Orlando knew,
(In Lucian is the story told)
   Took horse--clapp'd spurs--and off he flew
In no d----d doctor's list enroll'd--
      Blame not Orlando if he fled,--
So little's got by being dead.

August 31.

Poems (1795), 448.

National Gazette   September 18, 1793

ELEGY
On the Death of a BLACKSMITH.

   WITH the nerves of a Sampson this son of the sledge,
By the anvil his livelihood got:
   With the skill of old Vulcan could temper an edge;
And struck--while his iron was hot.

   By *forging* he liv'd, yet never was tried,
Or condemn'd by the laws of the land;
   But still it is certain, and can't be denied,
He often was *burnt in the hand.*

With the sons of St. Crispin no kindred he claim'd,
With the *last* he had nothing to do;
    He handled no awl, and yet in his time
Made many an excellent shoe.

    He blew up no coals of sedition, but still
His bellows was always in blast;
    And I will acknowledge (deny it who will)
That one *Vice,* and but *one,* he possess'd.

    No actor was he, or concern'd with the stage,
No audience to awe him appear'd;
    Yet oft in his shop (like a crowd in a rage)
The voice of a *hissing* was heard.

    Tho' *steeling* of axes was part of his cares,
In thieving he never was found;
    And, tho' he was constantly *beating on bars,*
No vessel he e'er ran aground.

    Alas and alack! and what more can I say
Of Vulcan's unfortunate son?--
    The priest and the sexton have bore him away,
And the sound of his hammer is done!

September 14.

Poems (1795), 449-50.

New York *Weekly Museum*   February 5, 1803

ON THE DEATH OF A BLACKSMITH.

Substantively identical to the 1793 text, except for the following variants:

In each stanza, lines 2 and 4 indented, lines 1 and 3 at margin.

Stanza 1, line 1: WITH the nerves of a Sampson this son of a sledge,
         line 4: And struck while his iron was red-hot.

Stanza 2, line 1: By *forging* he liv'd, yet he never was tried,

Stanza 5, line 3: Yet oft in the shop (like a crowd in a rage)

Stanza 7: Deleted.

Savannah *Republican*   June 10, 1809

Substantively identical to the 1793 text, except for the following variants:

In each stanza, lines 2 and 4 indented; lines 1 and 3 at margin.

Stanza 1, line 4: And struck--while the iron was hot.

Stanza 7, line 3: The Priest and the Sexton have borne him away.

National Gazette   September 25, 1793

LINES ADDRESSED
To a very Little Man, *who was fond of walking with a very large* CANE.

NATURE, in all her works, observes
    A fit proportion, just and true:
Man only from her great example swerves;
    In this we instance *you.*

Who bade you bear the huge Cyclopean beam,
    (Yourself an insect at its foot)
Which, if it fell, would end your mortal dream,
    And put your day-light out!

Rival to oaks, no hedge way shrub we see;
    No dwarf-like bush with pines is class'd;
No branch grows greater than the mother tree;
    No shallop wants an admiral's mast.

Goliah's self (that huge unwieldy beast)
    With such a staff had shunn'd his fate--:
This Cane might be your Liberty-Pole, at least,
    And streamers wear, on *days of state.*

Thus at *Honduras,* frequent I have seen
    Monkies *attach'd* to *Cedars* tall:
There chac'd, they climb, to shun the hostile train--
    What use to you, who ne'er could climb at all?

A staff like this (from hickory forests come)
    'Mongst cudgelling lads might rule the roast;
Might swing the main-gate of the *Federal Dome,*
    Potowmack's future--royal--boast!

Ah, take advice: this lofty stick forgo--
    With copper's hoop-pole rather choose to range;
Or, if your pride should deem *such* canes too low,
    Advance!--and take my pipe-stem in exchange.

Philadelphia, September 18.

Poems (1795), 365-66.

National Gazette   September 28, 1793

QUINTILIAN to LYCIDAS.

WHILE little lads their books forsake,
    Or sigh to meet the hour of play,
You, Lycidas, no leisure take,
    But still thro' learned pages stray--
    With years so few, ah why so grave,
    Why every hour to books a slave?

Hence, Lycidas, I pray retire:
    Go with your mates and take your play,
Not him I prize, or much admire

Who, curious, hangs on all I say;
The lad that's wise before his time
Will be a coxcomb in his prime.

Stay not too close in wisdom's shop--;
Till time a riper mind prepares
The *ball,* the *marble,* and the *top*
Are books that should divide your cares;--
The boys that life's gay morn enjoy,
I love to see them act the boy.

I hate the pert, I hate the bold,
Who proud of years, but half a score,
With none, but men, would converse hold
And things beyond their reach explore;
Like the fam'd Cretan, soaring high
To melt their waxen wings--and die!

Philadelphia, September 25.

Poems (1795), 87-88.

Jersey Chronicle   May 16, 1795

On the
APPROACHING DISSOLUTION
Of Transatlantic Jurisdiction in America.

FROM Britain's grasp forever freed,
Columbia glories in the deed:
From her rich soil, each tyrant flown,
She finds this fair estate her own.

But still o'er tracts of vast extent
European sway she must resent:
Whence came their right--what do they here
But force old laws, to tyrants dear?

How small a part of that domain
Is yet unbound from Europe's chain!
Peru beneath a monarch sighs,
And *Mexico* in fetters lies!

Throughout the wide *Canadian* waste
(In British bondage still embrac'd)
The native finds his vigour broke,
And bends beneath the galling yoke.--

To abridge the sway of foreign lands,
Time, with his years, leads up new bands:
To annul the power of Europe's kings,
To life, once more, some *Warren* springs!
Once more, *to arms!*--Fate's herald cries--
And other *Washingtons* shall rise.

Poems (1795), 437-38. (Since the 1795 collection was first advertised in April, this is probably a reprint of the text which first was published there; it contains no variants from that text.)

Jersey Chronicle   May 23, 1795[1]

The *Republican Genius* of Europe.

EMPERORS and kings! in vain you strive
    Your torments to conceal--
The age is come that shakes your thrones,
Tramples to dust despotic crowns,
    And bids the sceptre fall.

---

[1] This poem was reprinted without revision in the *Time-Piece,* July 3, 1797. It does not reappear until the 1815 collection, where it is lengthened and almost completely rewritten. Although several of the lines and all of the ideas expressed in this text appear somewhere in the 1815 version, since most of the lines here never reappear in this form in any of Freneau's collections, a complete edition of the poet might present this text separately.

In western worlds the flame began:
        From thence to France it flew--
Through Europe, now, it takes its way,
Beams an insufferable day,
        And lays all tyrants low.

Genius of France! pursue the chace
        Till *reason's* laws restore
Man to be *man*, in every clime;--
That *Being*, active, great, sublime
        Debas'd in dust no more.

In dreadful pomp he takes his way
O'er ruin'd crowns, demolish'd thrones--
Pale tyrants shrink before his blaze--
Round him terrific lightnings play--
With eyes of fire, he looks them through,
Crushes the vile despotic crew,
        And Pride in ruin lays.

Poems (1815), I, 108-09.

Jersey Chronicle   May 30, 1795

The *Rival Suitors* for *America*.

LIKE some fair girl in beauty's bloom,
To court her, see what suitors come!
An heiress, she, to large estate,
What rivals for her favours wait!

At haste to clasp her in their arms,
Each sees in her a thousand charms--
The *gems* that on her bosom glow
Attract where love was cold--'till now.

Freed from a cruel parent's care,
This maid so wealthy and so fair

Of each that for possession sues
Can hardly tell which beau to choose.

    Proud of his vast extended reign,
(His fancied empire o'er the main)
The Briton came, with haughty stride,
Preferr'd his suit--but was denied.

She thought his style, by much, too rude,
By ruffians she would not be woo'd;
From *man* she wish'd to choose a mate,
But not in such a savage state.

A Dane, a Dutchman, and a Swede
All hop'd to enjoy the charming maid:
The Russian, bred in frost and snow,
Made love to her that said--no, no.

The Spaniard grave, with cloak and sword,
Some favour from the nymph implor'd--
Vain were his tears and coaxing art--
She could not bear a jealous heart.

The Turk himself, to engage her love,
From Asia's coasts began to move;
While faded lay his Tartar crown
He sigh'd to make this girl his own.

In vain they paid the fond address--
No Pope, no Sultan would she bless--
No monarch, tho' allur'd with art,
Could gain her wealth, or touch her heart.

The Frenchman comes--salutes the fair--
She likes his gallant, martial air!--
With eager eye, around her waist
He clasp'd his arms, and her embrac'd:

Smit with the lofty, generous mien,
She admires the *Gaul,* as soon as seen,
Grants him her *commerce*--yields her charms,
And takes a hero to her arms!

Time-Piece   March 20, 1797

THE RIVAL CANDIDATES FOR THE FAVOURS OF AMERICA

Substantively identical to the *Jersey Chronicle* text, except for the following variants:

Stanza 1, line 1:   (Indented) A Wealthy girl in beauty's bloom,
           line 2:   To court her, lo! what suitors come;
           line 3:   An heiress, she, to vast estate,

Stanza 2, line 1:   All hope to clasp her in their arms

Stanza 3, line 1:   Freed from a foreign parent's care,
           line 4:   Could hardly tell which beau to choose.

Stanza 4, line 2:   His floating empire on the main,
           line 3:   The Briton for her favour sued
           line 4:   And spoke in words she understood.

Stanza 5, line 1:   She thought his style by much too coarse,
           line 2:   She would not yield her heart to force--
           line 3:   Give me (said she) my ships again,
           line 4:   And I'll admit you in my train.

Stanza 6, line 1:   The Dane, the Dutchman, and the Swede
           line 2:   At distance, eyed the charming maid;
           line 4:   Felt in his breast new ardours glow.

Stanza 7, line 2:   Some favours from the nymph implor'd.
           line 3:   Vain were his tears, and courting art;

Stanza 8, line 4:   He wish'd to make her wealth his own.

Stanza 9:   The Frenchman came, with leering eye,
          And from his breast hove many a sigh--
          Talk'd much and loud of favours past,
          And swore his love would always last:

Stanza 10:   That how from ruin, once, he sav'd,
           And many a danger for her brav'd,--

>   She dropt some tears at what he said,
>   But thought it was no time to wed:
>
> Stanza 11: Then thus to all her suitors cry'd,
>   I wish not yet to be a bride--
>   Who e'er would in my eye, excell,
>   The secret is,--*to treat me well,*--
>
> Stanza 12: If you would in my bosom find
>   The *treasure,* that enslaves mankind.
>   Take not my ships--seize not my men,
>   As some have done--and you know when.

Pennsylvania Democrat   September 15, 1809[1]

THE POLITICAL COURTSHIP.
By Philip Freneau.

When to the verge of warfare brought,
Who would not take a happy thought,
Conclude our foes, half way, to meet,
Prepare to fight them--or to *treat?*

All Europe hopes Columbia's aid;
Columbia in their scale is weighed!
Our favourite system they would mend,
Or bid our vast Republic end.

This Western World, a wealthy maid,
In Nature's richest garb arrayed,
Beholds a host of lovers wait,
All gaping for her vast estate.

For this bright nymph, in beauty's bloom,
Observe the selfish suitors come;

---

[1] This text contains variants from both earlier texts, as well as added portions. Consequently, the entire text is reproduced here.

Observe them, waiting in her train,
Of even the meanest favour vain.

Each smile, and every glance she lent,
Were all interpreted--consent;
Each thought he had her love possessed
And each his ardent vows professed.

They strove to clasp her in their arms,
They saw in her a thousand charms;
The gems that near her bosom glow,
Attracted love so cold till now.

Freed from a foreign parent's care
This dame, so wealthy and so fair,
Of each that for possession sues,
Can hardly tell which swain to choose.

Proud of his vast extended reign,
His floating empire on the main,
With anger to affection turned,
The Briton for her commerce burned.

With what a grip he seized her hand,
And bellowed--Yield to my command;*
Although I hug you black and blue,
Let us our ancient loves renew.

She thought his style by much too coarse,
She would not yield her heart to force.
Give me, said she, my ships again,
And you may dangle in my train.

The Dane, the Dutchman, and the Swede,
At distance viewed the handsome maid;
The Russian, bred in frost and snow,
Felt in his breast strange fervours glow?

---

* Attack on the Chesapeake.

So cold in these did passion move,
She said, They do not merit love;
These, heavy, formal, and demure,
I scarce esteem, but may endure.

The Spaniard grave, with cloak and sword
Some notice from the nymph implored.
Vain were his tears, and vain his art,
She could not bear a jealous heart.

Oh no!–she said–it will not do,
I feel averse to such as you;
Exclusive love I yield to none;
I keep my distance from the throne.

The Frenchman came, with leering eye,
And from his breast hove many a sigh;
Talked much and loud of favours past,
And swore his love would always last:

That once from ruin he had saved,
And many a danger for her brav'd–
She dropped some tears at what he said,
But thought it was no time to wed.

And thus to every suitor cried,
I wish not yet to be a bride;
Whoe'er would, in my view, excel,
The secret is–to *treat* me well.

Let those who in my heart would find
The treasure that enslaves mankind;
Let them return my ships and men,
And act on Honour's rules again.

The days, perhaps, at last may come,
When I may show my frowns to some;
When I with peace and love must part,
Resent your wrongs, and steel my heart,
Say to the world, Be all my friends,
Or meet the vengeance that impends.

Poems (1815), I, 46-54.

Jersey Chronicle   June 6, 1795

Lines written several years ago, and intended to have been engraved on a Tomb Stone under an Oak Tree, where a Despairing Lover had hanged himself.–
[*The Dead-man Speaking.*]

UNDERneath this lofty oak
Rests one who Nature's debt has paid:
What sent me hence?–a serious joke–
Love, and the rigour of a maid!
Conceive my pains, then mourn ye swains,
    And say he lov'd sincerely;
But still forebear to unbraid the fair;
    Tho' dead, I love her dearly.

Ye swains, whose lives no cares have known,
Forgive me now for what I've done:–
Oppress'd with care for Julia fair,
Love gave the stroke, that caus'd despair!

Here with a grace, and solemn face,
Come–see the effects of Love:
Adieu, ye plains, ye nymphs and swains,
'Till we shall meet above.

Ye nymphs and swains who love no more,
Assemble round my plaintive ghost!
Here contemplate the works of fate,
And drink me in your toasts–
And drink me in your toasts!–

Time-Piece   March 15, 1797

STANZAS supposed to have been written by a despairing Lover, who actually hanged himself, on a rejection of his addresses to a favourite Fair One.

    Stanza 1:   Line 5 of the 1795 text appears as two lines:
                    Conceive my pains,/Then mourn, ye swains
                    (Both short lines indented)

Line 6 of the 1795 text begins at the margin.

Line 7 of the 1795 text appears as two lines:
But still forbear/To upbraid the fair;
(Both short lines indented)

Stanza 2: Line 3 of the 1795 text appears as two lines:
Oppressed with care/For Julia fair
(Both short lines indented)

Stanza 3: Line 1 of the 1795 text appears as two lines:
Here, with a grace,/And solemn face,
(Both short lines indented)

Line 3 of the 1795 text appears as two lines:
Adieu, ye plains,/Ye nymphs and swains,
(Both short lines indented)

Stanza 4: Line 3 of the 1795 text appears as two lines:
Here contemplate/The works of fate,
(Both short lines indented)

Line 5 of the 1795 text deleted.

Poems (1809), I, 61.

Time-Piece   March 13, 1797

POETICAL ADDRESS.

WHEREVER our pages may chance to be read
For the feast of good humour a table we spread—
Let each bring his dish, and whoever may eat
Shall have no just cause to complain of the treat.

If the best on the market can't always be had
We'll mend what is middling, and better the bad;
To sense and to reason a place ne'er refuse
And give the due substance and sum of the *News*.

Embark'd on this ocean, and wishing no fray,
We'll strive for a chance with the prints of the day;
The news of all nations import from all climes,
And carefully copy *the cast of* THE TIMES.

The guest whom the arrows of satire may hit,
In political squib or poetical wit;
If a gust of vexation be-ruffles his mind
He's equally free *to return it in kind*.

In the service of *Freedom* for ever prepar'd
We'll join our endeavours this goddess to guard,
This idol that freemen should only adore,
And banish'd from Britain--to dwell on our shore.

In a country like this that has rose into fame,
The TRADE *of the* PRESS an importance may claim
That tyrants would never permit it to find,
Whose views are to chain and be-darken the mind.

Ye sons of Columbia! its efforts befriend,
And to *this* all the tyrants of Europe shall bend--
'Tis *this* that will throw a new light on the ball,
And man from his state of debasement recall.

Republics of old, that have sunk in the dust,
Could once--like ourselves--of their *Liberties* boast;
Both *Virtue* and *Wisdom* in Athens appear'd,
Each eye saw their charms, and each bosom rever'd.

But as *Virtue* and *Morals* fell into disgrace,
Pride, Splendor, and *Folly* stept into their place:
Where *Virtues domestic* no longer were known,
Simplicity lost, and *Frugality* flown,

Then tyrants and slaves--the worst plagues of this Earth--
From the change of old manners, were brought into birth;
And soon the base maxim all popular grew,
And allowed, *That the Many were made for the Few.*

From the fate of *Republics,* or Athens, or Rome,
'Tis *Time* we should learn a sad lesson at home--

From their faults and their errors a warning receive,
And steer from the shoals where they both found a grave.

Columbians! forever may Freedom remain,
And *Virtue* forever your Freedom retain;
To these--all attracting--all views should submit,
All labours of learning, all essays of wit.

'Tis time a new system of things was embrac'd
To encircle a world that has long been debas'd--
As *here,* with our Freedom, that system began,
Here, at least keep it pure--*for the honor of man.*

Poems *(1815),* I, 55-57.

Time-Piece   March 24, 1797

ON THE TOO REMOTE EXTENSION OF AMERICAN
COMMERCE

TO every clime, through every sea,
The bold adventurer steers;
In bounding barque, through such degree,
His country's produce bears.--
How far more blest to stay at home
Than thus on Neptune's waste to roam,
When fervours melt, or frosts congeal--
Ah! ye with toil and hardship worn,
Condemn'd to face the briny foam;
Ah! from such fatal projects turn
The wave-dividing keel.--

The product of yon' fertile plain
Transferr'd to foreign shores,
To pamper pride and please the vain,
Some fatal change restores:
Hence, every vice, the sail imports,
The glare of kings, the pomp of courts;

And man—design'd to till the ground—
Is sent to dwell on yonder wave—
Is made the cruel billow's sport,
Since commerce first to avarice gave
To sail old ocean round.

How far less wise than China's train,
Who ne'er remotely stray,
But leave the world to risque the main,
And safer tribute pay.
Thus, treasure to their country flows—
Freed from the danger and the woes
Of distant seas and dreary shores,
They see the eager stranger come
(Ah! too regardless of respose)
To waft superfluous riches home
That avarice there explores.

Americans! why half neglect
The culture of your soil?
From foreign traffic why expect
Sure payment for your toil?—
At home, a safer harvest springs
From mutual intercourse of things,
Domestic duties to fulfil—
Vast seas *within* your realm abound
Where commerce soon shall spread her sail,
Nor Europe's wrangling race be found
To bend you to their will.—

Poems (1815), I, 66-68.

Time-Piece   March 29, 1797

TO THE AMERICANS.

THE cause that rests on Virtue's ground
Shall potent through the world be found:
Mankind will bow to that decree
Which humbles vice and tyranny.

O'er this wide globe what darkness broods--
What misery, murders, wars, and feuds,
Must yon' fair lamps forever light
Man, to perform the deeds of night?

When to the gates of modern Rome
We see the Gallic legions come,
Their triumphs o'er that foe will be
To make them great, and make them free.

In those new wars, new views we trace;
Not slavery for the human race:
And France!--where'er you spread your blaze,
Lo! Superstition's reign decays.

But ah, behold! what nations join
This vast reform to undermine--
What labour, death, and deep-laid schemes
To quench the Sun--And Reason's beams.

Shall these succeed?--and will that sun
Continue yet his race to run
O'er scenes that he must blush to view,
Disorder and distraction too.

Must tyrants, still, of monstrous birth,
Enslave mankind, lay waste this earth?--
No--to the question answers Fate--
Their efforts came an age too late.

With such confederates to combine,
Columbia, can that part be thine?

Could e'er the thought possess your heart,
To take that vile, ungrateful part.

From Britain's yoke so lately freed,
Wouldst thou, new legions basely lead,
To crush that power, whose valour gain'd,
And once your sinking cause sustain'd.

From each true heart be banish'd far
The thought of so profane a war--
A curse would on your arms attend,
And with that war your honours end.

Fortune no more your toils would bless--
All woe, disorder, and distress--!
No gallant men your flags would rear,
No *Green's,* no *Washington's* appear;

No chiefs that check'd the pride of kings
On Monmouth plains, --at Eutaw springs;--
But blundering troops, not brave or warm,
With broken heart and nerveless arm

Would march to attack your Gallic foe.--
Would strive, in vain, a cause to o'erthrow,
Which gives to Europe endless fame
When all her Kings are--but a name.

Poems (1815), I, 60-62.

Time-Piece   April 3, 1797

WARNING *to the* WESTERN FIDDLING GENERAL.

GREAT Fiddler of the West! Whose vast design
Aims our New States with Spaniards to combine,
How couldst thou hope, with fiddle and with bow
(Such feeble arms) to work domestic woe;

How could'st thou hope our empires to divide
With not even sword or sabre at your side?
Such hopes, alas! on cat-gut who would place,
On treble, tenor, counter, or the base?
Who could--who did, that heavenly horse-hair spin,
Or lodge such virtue in your violin--
Methinks I see thee thrumming on thy strings,
Playing *C'ira*--by turns--then cursing kings--
I see thee now, like peddlar and his pack,
With that poor Fiddle swung across thy back,
(Like Reynard from the hen-roost hurrying home
With shoulder'd poultry, for the feast to come)
Trudging the woods, on vast atchievements bent,
Without a knapsack, coverlid, or tent,
To vile rebellion our new States to call;--
The attempt how mighty--and the means how small!

Amphion once, as ancient stories say,
When on his fiddle he began to play,
So soft, so sweet, so melting were his tunes
That even the stupid trees danc'd rigadoons--
Quitting the spot, where many a year they grew,
Quick round the Fiddler throng'd the leafy crew,
Form'd o'er his pate a sun-repelling bower,
And bent their savage heads to music's power.

Amphion's fiddle, your's by far exceeds--
Not *Trees* alone, but *Colonies* it leads:
All *Allegheny* dances to the sound,
And westward moves, to meet the *Iberian* bound.
Kentucky hears the soul-exalting notes
And on the fiddler and his music dotes;
Tip-toe for flight stands every hut and tree
From *Knoxville's* groves to savage *Tenessee:*
Arthur St. Clair* will soon its influence feel,
And 'gainst your fiddle point his vengeful steel,
Cut every string; the bridge and sound board seize;

---

* *Governor of the Territory North West of the Ohio.*

By your own cat-gut hang you to the trees,
And bid you learn--too late--it is no jest,
To play such dangerous music to the west.

Columbian Centinel   April 12, 1797[1]

Above text is reprinted, with the following introductory comments:

> The allusion is well kept up in it;--and originated in the assertion, that the French General mentioned by *Mr. Wilcox,* as having been sent by *Fauchet,* or some other ET, to spread insurgency in the western regions, was no other than an itinerant Fiddler. The truth of the assertion we doubt; as we have the name of the officer sent; though we know not his mission.

Poems (1815), I, 81-84.

---

[1] In the preceding issue, the *Centinel* had quoted an epigram, which it erroneously attributed to Freneau, to exemplify his "acumen in epigram." In a note which appeared with these lines, it was remarked that the *Centinal* admired the poet's talents and fancy, and even though it detested the politics of his *Gazette,* it still hoped "to enrich the *Centinel* with native gems from his rich cabinet." In the April 12 issue, the *Centinel* acknowledged its error in the former attribution, but offered this poem as indubitably Freneau's.

Time-Piece   April 7, 1797

On a young lady who wore in her cap, iron wire conductors, on the plan of Dr. Brydone, to guard against the effects of lightning.

HOW bold this project, to defy,
And brave the artillery of the sky--
Round YOU the lightning harmless plays,
That bids *us* perish in the blaze.

The fluid fire, in deafening peals,
Along the warm conductor steals;
And thence directed to the ground
It glances off, but leaves no wound

Thus guarded, you despise yon' cloud
That, bursting, wings the thunder loud;
And Jove's red bolts unheeded fall
Near you, that learns to scorn them all.

The *beaver* on your lovely scull
(Secure as salamander's wool)
Will help repel from your dress'd head
What strikes us, timid wretches, dead.

Why should *You* fear the electric fire
Who thus advance, a moving spire,
With Cupid's darts,--so fair and tall,
Not to be kill'd--but kill us all--?

April 3.

Poems (1809), II, 27.

Time-Piece   April 10, 1797

THETIS: *or the* HEROINE;
A Character.

THETIS a husband early took
Not for his virtues, or his look;
Whose business was, the seas to roam--
She could not bear a spouse at home.

This creature of amphibious kind,
This consort, suited to her mind,
Though sailing for her many a mile,
Returning, rarely met a smile.

When at her feet his gains he threw,
Madam receiv'd the tribute due;--
Wonder'd the anchor was not weigh'd,
And fretted at the stay he made.

His China ware, or India lace
Could hardly purchase one embrace;
Those sattinetts and diamond rings--
"*You should have brought me better things!*"

While he was silent as a mouse
She loudly curs'd the custom-house;
Did little else than scold and pout
Because they had not *clear'd him out.*

Though he in port rode commodore,
She tweak'd his nose when he came on shore--
Though he at sea discharg'd great guns,
She made him strike to squibs and puns.

When he at pride began to fret
And swore 'twould be his ruin yet--
When he reprov'd her freaks and whims--
She wish'd him swampt in southern clim's.

When he some fault was wont to find,
And said "*as how*," *that love was blind,*

With poison'd joys, embitter'd sweets--
She bade him mind his tacks and sheets.

Ah Thetis! why so hard a fate--
Such cruel conduct to your mate--
Like *Carey's chickens* would you have
Him always rambling on the wave?

Wild geese, themselves, that sail the wind,
Returning, meet their madams--kind--
Returning from some future cruise,
For God's sake--make him not a Goose.

Poems (1809), II, 28-29.

Time-Piece   April 12, 1797

    Reflections on Dr. Perkin's metallic rods.

    THE world grows old--but here one comfort lies,
The older it becomes, it grows more wise;
To this dull clod of dust no more confin'd,
'Tis common, now, to mount and sail the wind,
O'er different regions steer our airy course,
Fearless of sky-men, storms, or thunder's force.

    No less below, our anxious scheming race
On science bent, all Nature's movements trace,
In all her sports behold some wise design,
Her vengeance soften, or her smile refine--
Her pains, her plagues, her worst inflictions cure,
And death itself with patience scarce endure.

    Perkins! what verse is equal to your praise
What hocus-pocus from sick beds can raise!--
Pains in the head, or palsies in the joints
Henceforth shall yield to your *Metallic Points*:
Ricketts and rheums shall at your pretense fly

Like Satan's self, when holy water's nigh;
No more with drugs our stomachs shall be loaded;
Doctors: behold your system quite exploded!--
By one poor iron rod, and one of brass
Boerhaave himself is prov'd to have been an ass.--

Hereafter sick, all potion, drug, or pill
We'll shun, and trust to your *enchanting* skill:
Even mental ills shall cease at your approach,
Pride, Vanity, and Longings for a coach.
If rightly *paw'd,* some girls, that I might name,
Who, shopping, pilfer without fear or shame,
Shall, when your influence they are made to feel,
Be cured of their propensity to steal--
Touch'd by your magnet, dead men shall revive,
Old Bachelors for Humen's blessings strive--
Maidens, averse to men, be taught to love,
And wives--long barren--now prolific prove.

Poems (1815), I, 84-87.

Time-Piece   April 17, 1797

Stanzas written, several years since, on the first American ship (Empress of China, Capt. Greene) that explored the route to the East Indies and China, after the
REVOLUTION

WITH clearance from Bellona won
She spreads her wings to meet the Sun,
Those ancient regions to explore
Where *George* forbade to sail before.

Thus grown to strength, the bird of Jove
Impatient, quits his native grove,
With eyes of fire and lightning's force
Through the blue ether holds his course.

No foreign *tars* are here allow'd
To mingle with her chosen crowd.
Who, when return'd, might boasting say
They shew'd our native oak the way.

To that old track no more confin'd
By Britain's jealous court assign'd
She round the stormy Cape* shall sail
And, eastward, catch the odorous gale.

To countries plac'd in torrid climes
And islands of remotest times,
She now her eager course explores,
And soon shall greet Chinesian shores:

From thence their fragrant teas to bring
Without the aid of Britain's king,
And porcelain ware, enchas'd in gold,
The product of that finer mould.

Thus, commerce to our world conveys
All that the varying taste can please:
For us, the Indian looms are free,
And *Java* strips her spicy tree.

Proceed, great pile! and o'er the brine
May every prosperous gale be thine,
Till freighted deep with eastern gems
You seek again your native streams.

Poems (1795), 291. (No version of this poem has been located in any newspaper before its appearance in the 1795 *Poems.* This text demonstrates minor substantive variants from the 1795 collected text.)

---

* Cabo Tormentosa (the Cape of Storms) so called by the earliest Portuguese navigators to india--now the Cape of Good-Hope.

Time-Piece   April 26, 1797

ON THE PROGRESS OF THE FRENCH ARMIES IN ITALY.

LO! to the gates of once tremendous Rome,
Active as flame, the Gallic legions come,
While, smit with fear, to his despotic skies
On shorten'd wing the Austrian eagle flies.

Where, consecrated to the barren *God*
The silent Vestal *his* dark temples trod;
Where *Nero* once in cruel grandeur reign'd,
And Vandals conquer'd what from Goths remain'd;
Or where, triumphant in a later age,
The mitred Pontiff aw'd Religion's stage,
There march the heroic bands, that bring defeat,
And vengeance hurl on superstition's seat.

Oh! may their toils to Virtue's purpose tend,
May each new conquest Freedom's cause defend;
Still may those hosts some generous aim pursue
And not vile gold, but honour keep in view,
Thus arm'd--and still propitious heaven their trust--
Priests, Popes, and Kings shall tumble to the dust;
No more St. Peter shall their cause regard,
Lost are his keys, and every portal barr'd;
No sacred reliques from some saintly grave,
No Saint Antonio shall from ruin save--
All, all must sink before the invading dart
Of reasoning, conquering, pitying *Buonaparte,*
Who led by fate to Rome's disastrous walls
Loud, and more loud, for his last triumph calls;
While superstition--dull, deluding hag--
Looks up--and bows to the tri-colour'd flag,
And Nations, wakening, round the standard throng,
Exult, and wonder why they slept so long.

Poems (1815), I, 106-07.

Time-Piece   May 1, 1797

(Untitled poem follows a prose account, *Equestrian Exercises of Mr. Rickett's Circus*, which urges public support for the circus, and praises Rickett's company for their ingenuity in taming the animal, not merely to make it useful, but to provide an object for public amusement.)

Amidst the high affairs of state
Profound harangues and learn'd debate,
Amidst the noisy hum of things,
Declining popes and falling kings,
Where some must go, and some have gone;
May we not ask our men of mirth,
(Whose views lie nearer to the earth)
Not ask, amidst such great affairs
From morn to night that stun our ears,
How drives the circus on?

The Greeks of old their coursers train'd
To warlike toils--and led the band
Of gallant steeds to war's alarms--
They wing'd the car, or till'd the farms!
Olympia, at her festive games
Of Grecian youths, and Grecian dames,
Beheld assembled thousands meet
Of prancing steeds, with nimble feet
To rush across the plain.--
Almost instructed how to fly,
The multitude, in wild amaze
Pronounc'd such feats above all praise,
And wonder'd how these mortal steeds
Were taught, though bred in fields and meads.

But *Ricketts*, thy superior art
Can to the Horse new life impart,
A different soul inspires his frame:
He leaps, he bounds with other force
Than ever nerv'd the Grecian Horse.
From precepts that your skill explains
He human attitudes attains,
And moves through all the varying scene

With eye of fire and feeling keen;—
See, how majestic, how refin'd
The ideas in a brutal mind—

But RICKETTS! *Pray forbear!*
If we, the ruling human race,
    Must not on higher beings press,
    Make not the Horse, by precepts rare,
    A rival to mankind.

Poems (1809), II, 143-44.

Time-Piece   May 10, 1797

Lines written on a passage from New-York to the Island of
MADEIRA, *addressed to* CALISTA *on shore.*

IF I escape the dangers of the main
And heaven restores me to your arms again
No thought ambitious to increase my store
Should tempt me to petition God for more.

    But, peaceful, seated in some quiet shade,
No storms to vex me and no foes to dread,
A decent house, on humble model plann'd,
In order kept by good Maria's hand,
A thrifty garden, next, should be my care,
A barn well garnish'd, and an orchard fair,
Some books improving to our thoughtless kind
(Books may be called provision for the mind)
My private room should handsomely adorn,
And study purchase science every morn—
Justly, indeed, may they be counted sage,
Who knowledge gather from fair wisdom's page.

    A stock of wine, the heart of man to cheer,
I still would keep—with cyder sound and clear,
Jamaica's best, and Lispenard's joyous beer.

Nor should these blessings indiscreetly flow
Which, meanly used, become the greatest foe:
But when the neighbouring parson or the squire
On visits came to smoke beside my fire,
Or when the sun's more cheering rays invite
And shady trees, and western winds delight,
In sweet retreat, and social converse warm,
An extra bottle could not do us harm:
And such are the resistless charms of wit
Where reason guides and friendly tempers hit,
'Tis not bright Bacchus tempts to a delay,
But wit--enchanting wit--prolongs our stay.--

    When from Madeira's isle return'd once more
I meet the pilot near the Americ' shore,
Soon shall your swain to woodland scenes retire
And the sweet music of the groves admire,
Early, in summer, tread the morning dew,
And be supremely blest--if blest with you.

    To rural haunts retir'd, ah! how shall I
The ruder labours of a rustic try?--
How could I, tender to the fleecy kind,
In murdering them a selfish interest find?
The stately ox, intended for the plough,
Shall his bold front to me, his murderer bow?
And give we this reward for all his pain,
Who turn'd the clod and multiplied the grain--
Ah man ungrateful! that the weapon rears,
Confess thy shame, and give a vent to tears.
O man ungenerous! where's thy reason fled--
Is pity vanish'd--or compassion dead,--?
Far be from me and mine these scenes of blood,
To seize from nature such unlicenc'd food:--
The fleecy kind, that keep the body warm,
All innocent--who mean or know no harm;
The wakeful bird that hails the approach of day,
All, all to luxury must fall a prey.

    That rural life, which I so distant view,
With how much rapture does my soul pursue--
Lur'd by the music of the feather'd kind

What wild ideas rush upon my mind!--
Far from the arms of all that's dear and fair,
On barren seas I pine away with care:
No blossoms here their grateful odours shed,
Here trees are masts, and leaves to sails are spread,
No shrubs--no flowers--in blushing bloom dispense
Their charming fragrance on my ravish'd sense.
Nature, indeed, in aweful grandeur here
Is nature still--but still awakens fear:
Wise are her works and prudent every plan;
But, sure, she made not these abodes for *man*--
Who courting danger, born to be unbless'd,
Disdains the sod, or soars beyond his nest,
And slave to avarice, seeks amidst all ill
Wealth, still attractive, tho' destructive still.--

[Lat. 34, 50–Lon. 27, W.]

Poems (1815), I, 87-91.

Time-Piece   May 17, 1797

ON HEARING A REMARKABLY DULL DISCOURSE, OF NEAR TWO HOURS IN LENGTH, FROM A RAMBLING LAY PREACHER IN THE BACK WOODS OF NORTH CAROLINA
[*By the Singing Clerk of the Parish*]

SOUND without sense, and words devoid of force,
Through which no art could find a clue;
And poor, and shackling was the whole discourse,
That kept me, Julia, long from you!--

Heads of discourse, to heads less general split,
Seem'd like a small lath cleft from some heavy *log*:
Ideas cold, that could no object hit,
Clos'd every eye--all vapour, smoke, or fog.--

Grunts, and long groans, and periods of a mile
Were from the pulpit battery tumbled down:
'Twas thus from forts contriv'd in ancient style;
(From Troy's high walls, that shot no balls)
    The folks within
    Thought it no sin
By way of lessening their beseigers' number,
    To tumble on their heads
    Beans, roofing-tyles, and leads,
Cow's horns, stones, rubbish, chamber pots, and lumber.--

Ah Preacher!--with artillery like your own,
Hard will it be your *sleepers* to awake!
Trust me--although you fret, and scold, and frown,
    You may beseige
    But ne'er will take
    Old Satan's town.--

Poems (1809), II, 197-98.

Time-Piece   June 7, 1797

ON THE PROPOSED AMERICAN NEGOTIATION WITH THE FRENCH REPUBLIC.

THUS to the verge of warfare brought,
Our Congress takes a happy thought,
Agrees half way the Gaul to meet,
Prepar'd to fight him--or to treat.

But should this *triple mission* fail
And *we* be thrown in Britain's scale,
Will that retard her destin'd fall
Or humble them that humble all?

No fancied balances of power,
No projects can delay that hour
Which brings the regal sceptre low,
And bids mankind new systems know:

Fatigu'd with long *oppression's* reign
'Tis time the world should break its chain;
One gem *we* ravish'd from her crest,
And France, it seems, will seize the rest.

The revolutions of this age
That do our jarring race engage,
Are but old prospects drawing near,
The outset of a new career.

What *Plato* saw, in ages fled,
What *Solon* to the Grecians said,
Or what, *Montesquieu* did engage,
(The *Solon* of a modern age)

Is now unfolding to our view,
A system godlike, great, and new,
That from enlighten'd reason springs
And bodes a better course of things.

And will these States, at ocean's ends,
On whose resolve so much depends—
Will these, whose *Washington,* or *Greene*
Gave motion to the vast machine,

Will these, alas! be careless found
To help the mighty wheel go round,--?
These! who began the immortal strife,
And Liberty preferr'd to life.--

If not *the cause of France* we aid,
O never may the words be said,
That we, to royal factions prone,
Made not the cause of man our own.

Should Britain here renew her sway,
And *we* a servile homage pay,
Once more, the coming age would rise
And her invading force despise,

See some *Cornwallis,* yet unborn,
The triumphs of the south adorn,

And *him*--to war and slaughter bred--
Burgoyne, once more in fetters led.

But, muse! forbear so vast a theme--
Perhaps it may be all a dream,
And we, like Athens, pass'd her prime;
Grow dotards with the lapse of time.--

Poems (1815), I, 103-04.

Time-Piece   June 26, 1797

EPITAPH
On a sea captain that shot himself.

THE Shipwright, Nature, laid the keel
And gave proportions just and true;
She built him strong, and shaped him well
To pass life's stormy ocean through:
    A while he sailed that rugged sea
    With currents fair and breezes free:

At length, he met a sudden blast
That weaker vessels might have stood:
He saw the firmament o'ercast,
And sigh'd to view the shaded flood--
    "The port far off for which we steer,
    " 'Tis best (he said) to founder here."

Regardless of a feeble crew
Dependent on his care and skill,
He bored his planks and sheathing through,
And ocean did his vessel fill:
    So, down he went amidst that main
    From whence he cannot come again.

Poems (1809), II, 88.

ODE
FOR THE FOURTH OF JULY

To be sung on Tuesday next at the New Dutch-Church, by the *Uranian Society.*

ONCE more our annual debt to pay
We meet on this auspicious day
That shall through every coming age
The feelings of mankind engage;
Red war will soon be chang'd for peace,
All human woe for human bliss,
And nations that embrace again
Enjoy a long pacific reign.

chorus.

Thou source of every pure delight,
Fair peace! extend thy sway,
While to thy standard we invite
All nations on this day.

O dire effects of tyrant power,
How have ye darkened every hour,
And bade those years embitter'd flow,
That nature meant for bliss below!
With sceptred pride and looks of awe
Oppression gave the world her law;
And Man, that should such laws disdain,
Has bow'd to her malignant reign.

chorus.
Thou source, &c.

Here, on our quiet native coast
No more we dread the warlike host
That once alarm'd, when Britons rose,
And made *Columbia's* sons their foes.--
Parent of every cruel art
That strains the soul, that steels the heart,
Dire War! with all thy bleeding band
Molest no more this happy land!

chorus.
But source, &c.

May now all Despots disappear
And man to man be less severe--
The ties of love more firmly bind
Than fetters that enchain mankind.--
But *Virtue* must her Rights maintain,
Or short, too short, is *Freedom's* reign;
And when her precepts we despise
Tyrants and kings again will rise.

chorus.
O *Virtue!* source of pure delight,
Extend thy happy sway, &c.

No more a plundering, pageant race,
Man shall in every clime embrace;
And we, on this secluded shore,
Involv'd in horrid wars no more,
On this returning annual day,
To heaven our grateful tribute pay,
That here the happy times began
That made mankind the friends of man.

chorus.
Thou source, &c.

Aurora   July 7, 1809

In an article under "Philadelphia news" the poem is introduced as follows:

> Tuesday last being the birth day of American independence, the 6th company of artillery, commanded by capt. John Boyd, celebrated the day, at Mr. Sampson Crosby's tavern. The declaration of independence and the following address, written for the occasion were read.

FOR THE 4th OF JULY.

Stanza 1:   First four lines of the 1797 text, with the following

variants:
line 3: That will through every coming age,
line 4: Columbia's true born sons engage.

Stanza 2: From this fair day we date the birth
Of reason's reign restor'd to earth:
And millions learn, though long deprav'd
How to be govern'd, not enslav'd.

Stanza 3: First four line chrous of the 1797 text, with the following variants:
Word "chorus" deleted.
All lines begin at margin.
line 3: Whilst to thy standard we invite

Stanza 4: First four lines of the second stanza of the 1797 text, with the following variants:
line 1: not indented
line 2: How has it darken'd every hour,

Stanza 5: Last four lines of the second stanza of the 1797 text, with the following variants:
line 1: With sceptr'd pride and brow of awe,
line 3: And man, who should such laws disdain,
line 4: Bow'd down to her malignant reign.

Stanza 6: First four lines of the third stanza of the 1797 text, with the following variants:
line 1: (not indented) Here on our happy native coast;
line 2: No more we dread some warring host
line 4: And made Columbia's sons her foes.

Stanza 7: Last four lines of the third stanza of the 1797 text, with the following variants:
line 4: Molest no more this injured land.

Stanza 8: May your loud din be chang'd for peace,
All human woe for human bliss,
And nations sheathe the sword again
To find a long pacific reign

Stanza 9: First four lines of the fourth stanza of the 1797 text, with

the following variants:
line 1: (not indented) Soon may all despots disappear,
line 4: Not fetters to enchain the mind.

Stanza 10: Last four lines of the fourth stanza of the 1797 text, with the following variants:
line 1: But *virtue* must her force maintain
line 2: And if her precepts we despise,

Stanza 11: First four lines of the fifth stanza of the 1797 text, with the following variants:
line 1: (not indented) No more, an angry plundering race,
line 2: May man in every clime embrace;
line 4: Involv'd in bloody wars no more.

Stanza 12: Last four lines of the fifth stanza of the 1797 text, with the following variants:
line 2: May we to heaven our homage pay
line 3: Thankful that *here* the time began,
line 4: That made mankind the friend of man.

Poems (1815), I, 110-12.

Time-Piece   July 19, 1797

ON A VERY SMALL GARDEN BELONGING TO A CITIZEN OF N.Y.

A LITTLE garden, six foot square,
A little parsly planted there,
A cabbage that shall have no head,
Nine inches long, a spinnage bed;
Some little shrubs, a little tree.
Four little sprigs of rosemary,
A little sage, a little rue,
Some heads of sallad, very few;
Three bean hills, ranging in a line,

Five little tulips--very fine:
A carrot head with scarce a root,
A gooseberry bush that bears no fruit;
All these are planted in the shade,
And in a little time shall fade–
All these do in this garden grow,
And little more we want to know
Except, that they who here would eat
Shall have a very–little--treat.--

Poems (1809), II, 10-11.

Time-Piece   July 24, 1797

Stanzas occasioned by some illiberal reflections in Fenno's Gazette of the United States of the 18th ult. on the *Feast of Reason,* given by upwards of one hundred of the patriotic citizens of New-York, to citizen MUNROE, in testimony of their esteem for his character, public as well as private.

As late, at a feast that she gave to *Monroe,*
    Fair *Liberty* gather'd her train
The glasses and bumpers did merrily flow
    To honour her favorite swain.

Good humour, and pleasure, and friendship did join,
    And *reason,* above all the rest;
And the *hero* that conquer'd the British *Burgoyne*
    Presided–and honour'd the feast.

On a broom-stick from hell, with a pen in his hand,
    Old *Fenno* came riding the air;
He look'd–and he saw that among the whole band
    Not a single apostate was there.

Disappointed, he sigh'd–but still hover'd about
    'Till the *Toasts,* with a vengeance, begun;

He heard the *first four*--when the *next** they gave out,
    In a moment *Jack Fenno*--was gone.

In Liberty's Temple the petulant cur
    Could see not a man but he hates;
He fear'd he might prickle his hand with her BURR,
    And fled back to hell from her GATES.

Poems (1815), I, 121-22.

Time-Piece   September 1, 1797

The AMERICAN WAR-HAWK.

WEARY of peace, and hot for war
I saw him mount his crazy car:
To paper wars I saw him come
With pop-gun wads and sheep skin drum.

    Who'll bear the brunt, he never minds
While he a royal salary finds--
I saw him draw his rusty sword
A present from an English lord--
The sword return'd within its sheathe
Unfit to act the works of Death.
The point was blunt, the edge was dull,
Averse to cleave a Gallic skull.--

    What next will villainy contrive
To bid the days of war arrive?--
Is there no chance to pick a quarrel
And crown Pomposo's brows with laurel?

---

* The Fifth Toast was (See Time Piece of July 14)-- "Public Censure, armed with spear of Ithuriel! May it discover the demons of tyranny, wherever they lurk, and pursue them with its whip of scorpions to their native Hell."

> To those that deal in state affairs
> The world comes easy, and its cares:
> To those that wish for crown and king,
> A *Quarrel* is a lovely thing;
> It is for this that knaves anoint 'em;—
> Pray God, the Devil may disappoint 'em.--

Poems (1815), I, 124-27.

Time-Piece   September 6, 1797

ON A BEE
DRINKING FROM A GLASS OF WINE.

> THOU born to sip the lake or spring,
> Or quaff the waters of the stream,
> Why came you here on pleasure's wing
> Thus from my glass a share to claim.
>
> Did grief torment, or woes perplex,
> Did wasps or hornets cause you fear,
> Did wars distress, or labour vex--?
> Then drink oblivion to all care.
>
> Welcome, thrice welcome to my glass,
> If bliss therein you find;
> So shall the moments joyous pass
> Nor leave one care behind.
>
> No matter what the cause may be,
> If pain or folly draws,
> Enjoy your glass and be, like me,
> A martyr to the cause.
>
> If, chance, you take too deep a drink
> And in this ocean fall,
> Expire, and to the bottom sink
> In drunken funeral;

Fate never did for man provide
A tomb so rich as thine;—
In earth or ocean we shall hide,
But never in good wine.

Poems (1809), II, 97-98.

Time-Piece   September 13, 1797

ADDRESS to the REPUBLICANS OF AMERICA

SAY--shall we pause, and here conclude our page,
Or waft it onward to the coming age?--
--Just as YOU say, whose efforts shook his throne,
And pluckt the brightest gem from hearts of steel
Have through these stormy times toil'd for the common weal;
Nor quit that standard thousands have deserted,
By British arts, or gold, or titles re-converted.

If *you,* propitious to the press and pen,
Gave Vigour to the cause that rous'd up men
When slavery's sons approach'd with Britain's fleet,
Still we demand your aid--for Britain hates you yet;
Not with the sword and gun she now contends
But wages silent war, and by corruption bends,
Foe to the system that enlightens man
Here, thrones she would erect, and frustrate Freedom's plan.

Here, on this virgin earth, the soil unstain'd,
Where yet no tyrant has his purpose gained,
Keep bright that flame which every bosom fir'd
When Hessian hirelings from these lands retired,
When, worn and wasted, all that murdering crew
And Britains squadrons from the Hudson flew
When, leagued with France, you darts of vengeance hurl'd
And bade defiance to the despot world.

Ye heirs and owners of the future age
Who soon will shove old actors from the stage,
To you the care of Liberty they trust
When *Washington* and *Gates* are laid in dust,--
When *Jefferson*, with *Greene*, in long repose
Shall sleep, unconscious of your bliss or woes,
Seeming to say, Be wise, be free my sons
Nor let one tyrant trample on our bones--

Poems (1809), I, 280.

Time-Piece   September 15, 1797

Melancholy Reflections on passing by a burying ground in the neighbourhood of Philadelphia.

Pensive, on these green sods I cast my eye,
But why torment myself, and grieve and sigh,
Because, perhaps, beneath some scoundrel lie?

Who knows if these, who here so soundly sleep,
Alive, would not have stolen my flock of sheep,
Or, sailing, plung'd me headlong in the deep?

Perhaps below this turf in silence rests
Those, who when living were of man the pests,
Patrons of titles, ribbons, crowns, and crests.

What though made sacred by the parson's whine,
Why sorrowing on these *tombs* should I recline,
Sheltering some *Fenno* or some *Porcupine*:

Wretches, who breathing, poison'd freedom's air,
Brethren in villainy--a goodly pair*--
But now are gone to print--the Lord knows where.

       * *Par nobile fratrum.*   Virg.

Poems (1815), I, 137-38.

Time-Piece   September 25, 1797

(Untitled poem appears as part of an editorial repudiating the charge that Democratic printers and editors of the country have been bribed by French gold.)

Yes! they are brib'd—that's clear;
And paid French millions by the year;
And prov'd, most plainly, by the coats they wear:--
They are the lads that live in houses grand,
And own vast tracts of fertile land;
With so much self-denial in their natures
(They are such good, obliging creatures),
That shunning pleasure and the glare of wealth,
They for the public good waste time and health;
    Sit up all night,
    Compile and write;
One day a shilling from Kentucky get--
Then stay a week to starve and fret.
Why, Mr. Fenno, if this be French gold,
No wonder that you federalists look as bold.

Poems (1809), II, 274-76.

Time-Piece   September 25, 1797

REFLECTIONS ON THE GENERAL DEBASED CONDITION OF MANKIND.

Is there on earth—or do we dream?
Is there on earth one power supreme
    That acts a nation's mind?
No—still oppos'd to human bliss,
All other views they blend in this,
    That robs and cheats mankind.

Thou, tyrant! false to virtue's cause,
Whom pride, or rage, or folly draws
    To trample on the *right;*
Resign that base, perfidious plan,
Let Reason plead the cause of man,
    And Virtue spread her light.

What is this world, this sun, these skies,
If heaven's bright lamp on *man* must rise
    Dejected and distress'd?--
Why blazes round the mid-day beam?
Why, reason, art thou call'd supreme,
    Where virtue sinks oppress'd?--

What are the views of Nature's laws--
What is the deep, unfathom'd cause
    That does her plagues prolong?
Nature, on earth, confus'd appears;
On little things she wastes her cares,
    The great she models wrong.

                        Z.

City Gazette   December 24, 1800[1]

On False Systems of Government, and the generally debased condition of Mankind.

NO monarch lives, nor do I deem
There will exist one crown supreme,
    To act a Nation's mind;
Whose first great view will be to place
In their true scale the human race,
    The rank by Heaven design'd.

---

[1] The entire text appears in italics, except for the words underscored here, which appear in large caps.

How can we call that system just,
Which makes the *few* the high, the first,
    The lords of all that's good;
While millions, robb'd of all that's dear,
In silence drop the ceaseless tear,
    And leeches suck their blood?

Great Sun, that on our planet shines,
Whose power both light and heat combines,
    You should the model be,
To man the pattern now to reign
With equal sway, and how maintain
    The human dignity.

Impartially to all below,
The solar beams unstinted flow,
    On all is shed the ray;
No clime is left, where man is found,
Where Suns refuse to cheer the ground,
    And pour the blaze of day.

But kings not so--with selfish views
They partially their bliss diffuse,
    Their minions feel them kind:
And, still oppos'd to human bliss,
All other views they bend to this,
    To rob and cheat mankind.

Second stanza of the 1797 text, with the following variants:
line 1:   Thou, tyrant, false to Nature's cause,
line 4:   Forgo that base, perfidious plan,
line 5:   Let Honor plead the cause of man,
line 6:   Let Reason spread her light.

Third stanza of the 1797 text, with the following variants:
line 1:   What is this World, that Sun, those Skies,
line 2:   If all we see, on man must rise

Last stanza of the 1797 text, with the following variants:
line 1:   What are the ends of Nature's laws,
line 3:   That will her plagues prolong?
line 4:   Nature, *to us,* confus'd appears,
line 6:   The great *seem* often wrong.

December 23, 1800.

New York *Weekly Museum*   October 16, 1802

ON FALSE SYSTEMS OF GOVERNMENT
And the generally debased condition of Mankind.
[Said to be written by P. *Freneau*, of New-Jersey]

   Does there exist, or will there come
   An age, with wisdom to assume
      The rights by Heaven design'd;
   The rights which man was born to claim,
   From Nature's God which freely came
      To aid and bless our kind.

First stanza of the 1800 text, with the following variants:
line 2:   There will exist one power supreme
line 3:   The world in peace to sway,
line 5:   On their true scale the human race,
line 6:   And Discord's rage allay.

   Republics, must the task be your's
   To frame the *code* which life secures,
      And *right,* from man to man?
   Are you, in Time's declining age,
   Form'd only fit to tread the stage
      Where tyranny began?

Second stanza of the 1800 text, with the following variants:
line 1:   How can we call those systems just,
line 2:   Which bid the few, the high, the first,
line 3:   Possess all earthly good;
line 5:   In silence shed the ceaseless tear,

Third stanza of the 1800 text, with the following variants:
line 1:   Great orb, that on our planet shines,
line 6:   True human dignity.

Fourth stanza of the 1800 text, with the following variants:
line 3:   On all is pour'd the ray,
line 4:   Which warms, which cheers, which clothes the ground
line 5:   In robes of green, or breathes around
line 6:   Life, to enjoy the day.

Fifth stanza of the 1800 text, with the following variants:
line 1: But crowns not so—with selfish views
line 3: Their votaries feel them kind;
line 4: And still oppos'd to human right
line 5: Their plans, their views in this unite,
line 6: To embroil and curse mankind.

Ye tyrants, false to *him,* who gave
Life, and the virtues of the brave,
    All worth we own or know—
Who made you great, the lords of man,
To waste with wars, with blood to stain
    The maker's works below!

You have no iron race to rule;
Instruct them well in Reason's school,
    Inform our active race;—
True honor to the mind impart;
With Virtue's precepts warm the heart,
    Not urge it to be base.

Let laws revive, by Heaven design'd
To tame the tyger in the mind,
    And drive from human hearts
The love of wealth, that love of sway
Which leads the world and you astray,
    Which points envenom'd darts:

And men will rise from what they are
Superior, and sublimer far
    Than *Solon* guess'd, or *Plato* saw:
All will be just, all will be good,
That "harmony not understood"
    Will reign unerring law.

For, in our race, derang'd, bereft,
The parting God some vestige left
    Of worth before possess'd,
Which full, which fair, which perfect shone,
Which love and peace, in concord sown,
    Rul'd and inspir'd each breast.

Hence the small good, which yet we find,
In *shades* of that prevailing mind
    Which sways the worlds around:
Let *these* depart, once disappear,
The Earth would all the horrors wear
    In Hell's dominions found.

Just as yon tree, which bending grows,
To chance, not fate, its fortune owes;
    So man, from some rude shock,
Some slighted power, some hostile hand,
Has miss'd the state by nature plann'd,
    Has split on Passion's rock.

Yet shall that tree, when hew'd away,
(As human woes have had their day)
    A new creation find;
The infant-shoot in time will swell
Erect and tall, from that which fell,
    To all that Heaven design'd.

Third stanza of the 1797 text, with the following variants:
line 1:   What is this Earth, that Sun, these Skies,
line 2:   If all we see on man must rise
line 3:   Forsaken and oppress'd?
line 4:   Why blazes round the eternal beam,
line 6:   Where nations find no rest?

What are the splendours of this ball,
When life is clos'd, what are they all;—
    When dust to dust returns,
Does power or wealth attend the dead,
Are captives from the contest led,
    Is homage paid to urns?

Last stanza of the 1797 text, with the following variants:
line 1   What are the ends of nature's laws?
line 2:   What folly prompts, what madness draws
line 3:   Mankind in chains too strong?
line 4:   Nature *to us* confus'd appears;
line 6:   The great *seem* sometimes wrong.

Poems (1809), I, 253-56.

Time-Piece   September 29, 1797

> Untitled text follows prose account of the reasons why the Frigate *Constitution* failed to launch, noting the regrettable disappointment of the crowds who had gathered to see it.

Some with their airs aristocratic
And some with honours diplomatic,
    All came to see the show--
This frigate, Constitution call'd
In vain the builders pull and hawl'd,
    Alas! she would not go--! ! !

Each antifederal, with a smile
Survey'd this gallant glorious pile,
    As if he meant to say,
Builder! no doubt you know your trade,
A *Constitution* you have made,
    But should her *ways* have better laid.

Well--now to heave the ship afloat,
And move from this *unsettled* spot,
Take our advice, and give her soon
(What should have long ago been done)
Amendments--You know what.

Poems (1815), I, 141-42.

Time-Piece   September 29, 1797

Untitled poem concludes a prose piece condemning greed and those Americans who make wealth the *primum mobile* of all their actions.

"O Satan! I thy aid implore,
That thou wouldst yet increase my store,
For much does always covet more.

Thou first inventor of all coin,
Of *Banks* who plann'd the great design,
Give me but gold, and I am thine.

I crave no blessings parsons prate on,
My bags are what I most debate on,
Then fill them up--and take me, Satan."

Poems (1809), II, 57-58.

Time-Piece   September 29, 1797

THE ORDER OF THE DAY.
Occasioned by a Lady shedding tears on reading "A brief account of the Battles of the present Century."

IF on this sad distressing book
With curious eye you often look,
And there in dreary record find
The murder'd millions of mankind
Grieve not too much--reflect and say
'Tis but "The order of the day."

The crimes of kings, and men as base
That rear them up to crush our race,
Have all this dismal havock bred
And heaven's best works in ruin laid:
I sigh for this, as well as you,

And tears at times sincerely flow,
To see mankind by war decay
For the mere *order of the day.*

When first Britannia's squadrons came
And scattered here their fire and flame,
All saw *the order* drawing near;--
Some thought the order too severe,
Some said, "this royal British throng
Have had the order much too long,
Come now, suppose fair play we shew,
And take our turn "to order" too?"

So to the field, fierce legions led,
With various fortune fought and bled;
For eight long years that cause sustain'd
On which the heaven of Freedom lean'd,
And often vanquish'd knight or peer
That came to give their orders here,
And though their armies wish'd to stay
At length we ordered them away.

When France began her vast career,
Then every tyrant quak'd with fear,
And arm'd his legions far and wide
To keep supreme the royal side:
King Frederick led his gloomy host,
And Brunswick made his lofty boast
That Paris should in flames ascend
Ere Louis did to freedom bend--
Aye, he would shew them royal play,
And give *his* order of the day.

    Now monarchs are degraded low,
Their pride is gone where they must go--
In debt for navies, armies, wars,
The people cry, Pay up your scores--
Discouraged, worn, and famish'd down,
They curse all kings, and curse the crown,
And thus to George or Frederick say,
We wish you would *our orders pay.*

Now bad success to all that host,
Whose souls are stone, whose hearts are frost,
Whom science never yet could bind,
On Reason's plan, to rule mankind;
Whose schemes and views are to enslave,
And make of man both fool and knave,
A murderer, or a mere machine,
And born to serve a king or queen--
May such, opposed to reason's light,
    For time to come,
    Receive this doom,
To hell's dark shadows to sink outright,
And serve the *orders of the night.*

Poems (1815), I, 138-41.

Time-Piece   October 2, 1797

Untitled poem follows a prose piece condemning those leaders of the Revolutionary cause who have grown rich and lost their republican principles. The essay develops the argument that men of great wealth are incapable of possessing, for any length of time, a uniform principle in favor of human rights; the lower and middle classes are the guardians of this principle. The great are constantly fluctuating, while the low possess stability.

Thus, on yond' steeple towering high,
Where clouds and storms at random fly
    The weathercock is plac'd,
Which only while the gale does blow
Is to one point of compass true,
    Then veers with every blast.

But things are so appointed here
That weathercocks on high appear,
    On pinnacle display'd,
While sense, and worth, and preaching wights,
And clerk, that tunes grave Music's flights,
    Sit humble in the shade.

Poems (1809), II, 121-22.;

Time-Piece   October 23, 1797

THE BOOK OF ODES.

"He that first put a real mark upon the forehead of the *Beast* was the inventor of Printing. This mark was impressed deeply, and becomes deeper from day to day.
Erasmus.

NO. IV.
TO *PEST*-ELI-HALI,
A Democratic Printer, *on the western banks of the Hudson.*

NO common task your press assumes,
    That would on *Freedom's* basis stand,
And scatter through nocturnal glooms
    The blaze of *Reason* o'er our land:
        Each *empty bellows* will, no doubt,
        Rise, and aspire to put it out.

"*Pest,*" as you are! pursue your way;
    Night evermore precedes a sun:
Whate'er the angry *federals* say,
    Freedom's a game that must be won;
        And *human rights* the sacred prize
        That yet at stake with tyrants lies.

When first the wealthy, scheming *few*
    Their fatal drugs by *Herald* spread,
Your spirits o'er those regions flew,
    And smote the poisonous monster dead:
        With simple herb from *Ulster's* plains,
        You damn'd all *Webster's* shop contains.

Now narrow views, and low design
    Are busy to annoy your page,
Controul its strength, its fires confine,
    And war with Reason's precepts wage:
        Thus, by frail mists are moons undone,
        Thus, clouds attempt to quench the sun.

Who looks at kings, a court, a queen,
  With all their pomp, their crowns, their fame,
But wonders from what genius mean
  That system of disorder came?--
    No roots on tops of forests grow,
    No branches hide in depths below.

Poems (1809), II, 11-12.

Time-Piece   October 27, 1797

THE BOOK OF ODES.
"Let but a dancing bear arrive,
"A pig that counts you four or five,
"And Cato, with his moral strain,
"Shall strive to mend the town--in vain."

NO. VI.
TO THE LEARNED PIG.

O Thou! mark'd out by fate from common swine,
Amongst the learned of our age to shine;
    Bold, scientific pig
    Who, without gown or wig,
Canst force thy way through learning's endless maze;
    How many sages in the days of old,
    (That Fame has on her page enroll'd)
Starv'd by their sense! (on them the world look'd cold)
But you, on better ages fall'n, although a swine,
Can by your wit on pies and puddings dine.
    "When house and land are gone and spent,
    "Then learning is most excellent,"
So says a proverb, through the world well known,
    You that were pigg'd to grovel in a stye
    Have chang'd it well for education high:
    Wealth flows apace to scholars, such as you,
    Who knowing what is best, true wit pursue,
To be well fed on whate'er hog-stye thrown.

Now if one had the chance to choose his fate,
Before dismiss'd to this world's dark estate,
Who would not wish to have his little brains
> Lodg'd in the head of learned pig
> Than be a man, and toil, and sweat, and dig,
For all the sense the human skull contains.

What next will be the *science* you attain?
> She that to you has open'd all her store!
Already have you in your wonderous brain,
> More than most aldermen--and knowledge more
> Than some that capers cut on Congress floor.

May we not hope in this improving age
Of human things; to see on life's grand stage
Hogs take the lead of men--and grow so wise,
That they may to the highest honours rise,
> Preach, sing, plead law,
> Even William Cobbett's blood with lancet draw.
And lodge him in their styes.

Poems (1809), II, 99-100.

Time-Piece   November 1, 1797

THE BOOK OF ODES.
"And Alexander built a solid mole from the coast, even unto the isle of Tyre, through the deep waters of the channel between: and people said it would be everlasting; And yet at this day it is overwhelmed, and few vestiges left thereof."

Modern Travels.

NO. VIII.
TO THOS. SWAWGUM, A WHARF BUILDER.

WHERE Hudson once in angry pride,
> In surges burst upon the shore,
You plant amidst his boiling tide

Piles that defy his loudest roar;
    And princely mansions rise where late,
All Europe might discharge her freight.

From northern woods and wastes of snow
    This Hudson takes his distant rise,
From whose vast source to rivers grow
    The streams that Nature's breast supplies,
        And, join'd the *Mohawk* in their course,
        Come foaming on with headlong force.

Then cease! nor with too daring aim,
    Encroach upon this giant flood;
No rights, reserv'd by Nature, claim,
    Nor on his ancient bed intrude--
        The River may in rage awake,
        And Time return him all you take.

His sister, too *Eastona** raves
    At those who would her peace molest;
A city built upon her waves,
    The weight of mountains on her breast--
        As on her bed new fabrics gain,
        With quickened step she seeks the main.

Bold streams! and may our ode demand,
    Is there not coast for many a mile?
And soils, as form'd by Nature's hand,
    Arrang'd through *Manhattan's* isle?
        Then why these mounds does avarice raise,
        Where pale disease on nature preys?

But through this misty scene of things,
    A time we clearly may descry,
When fate again your triumph brings,
    When commerce shall in ruin lie,
        Her ships the death of traffic mourn,
        And Indians to their woods return!

Poems (1815), I, 147-48.

---

* That part of the sound opposite New York, commonly called the East River.

Time-Piece   November 10, 1797

THE BOOK OF ODES.

"And yet that Being you address,
"Who shap'd old chaos into form,
"May speak--and with a word suppress,
"The tyrant and the storm."

NO. X.

TO SANTONE SAMUEL, THE MILLENNIAL PROPHET, ON HIS SYSTEM OF UNIVERSAL PACIFICATION.

WITH language wild, in lofty strain,
  You bring the mighty period near
When tyranny shall close her reign,
  And wars and warriors disappear;
 When lambs with social lions meet
 To quaff the spring, or share the treat.

Alas! with superficial view
  You look on nature's mighty plan;
She endless modes of being drew
  Between the insect and a man,
 And form'd them all, with wise design--
 Distinguish'd each, and drew the line.

Observe the lion's aspect bold,
  His vengeful tooth, his cruel claw;
Each feature form'd in Anger's mould,
  The strength of Sampson in his paw--
 Was he design'd with lambs to stray,
 Or graze along the flowery way?

Since first his race on earth began,
  War was his trade, and war will be;
And when he quits that ancient plan,
  He, *lion* will no longer be,
 But change to something strange and new,
 Not to his former nature true.

One system see! through all this frame
        A seeming discord still prevails;
The Forest yields to active flame,
        The sea grows rough with stormy gales--
    No season did the God decree
    When these in friendship should agree.

And can you think that human kind
        Escapes this universal law,
Whose passions constitute their mind,
        Who action from disorder draw,
    Ere discord shall from man depart
    He must assume a different heart.

Yet, in the slow advance of things,
        A time may come when man may rise
By Reason's aid to stretch his wings,
        And see the world with other eyes,
    And when his midnight gloom is o'er,
    To brighter scenes his way explore.

The sun himself (so fates ordain)
        Irregularly loves to stray,
Keeps not the equatorial plane,
        But 'cross it takes his crooked way,
    And lessens yearly (sophists prove)
    His angle in the voids above.

When moving in its ancient line,
        Returning to a real sphere,
With *some new influence* he may shine;
        But you and I will not be here
    To see the lion shed his teeth,
    Or man forgo the works of death.

Poems (1815), I, 32-34.

Time-Piece   November 13, 1797

THE BOOK OF ODES.

"And the angel Michael disputed with the Devil about the
    "body of Moses."   *Ancient History.*
"To bleed or not to bleed--that is the question!
"Whether 'tis better in our beds to suffer
"The slights and snufflings of outrageous doctors,
"Or, by the *Lancet*--quit them."

TO THE PHILADELPHIA DOCTORS.
NO. XI.

      IN ancient days divines, in dismal humour,
With disputation kept the presses going;
Wrangled about some wondrous mighty things
    The difference "twixt" a *shadow* and a *shade*,"
And scribbled much of "way of man with maid."
      At length, as fades the *crown*
      Their bludgeons they lay down;
    And you, wise doctors, take the wrangle up,
    Each cursing all who will not drink his cup.

    Ah, Philadelphians! still to knaves a prey,
      Take your old philosophic way;
When from the *native spring* you seiz'd your draught,
    Health bloom'd on every face, and all was gay--
Dejection was remote--and Nature laugh'd.
      A question now, of *mighty weight* is put,
      Whether *to bleed a man is best, or not,*
    When scarce three drops (or not one drop) remains
In the poor devil's veins!--

    Well! *you* decide, who are in GALEN read--
Take *Boorhaave's*, if you please--whatever system--
(*Why are men such that doctors can enlist 'em?*)
Whether your methods be the *right* or *wrong,*
And man's existence shorten or prolong,
      We feverish fellows, must be--*put to bed.*

A secret has leak'd out--be cautious, doctors
(The whole shall be disclos'd *in room with lock'd doors*)
OLD WOMEN, with their *simple herbs and teas*
(And asking hardly two-pence for their fees)
Disarm the dreadful epidemic fever;
    Make it as tame and innocent,
        (Whether home-bred or from West-India sent)
As *Continental soldier, turn'd to weaver.*

[To be continued.]

Poems (1815), I, 146-47.

Time-Piece   November 15, 1797

THE BOOK OF ODES.
And he said unto him, Physician, *Heal thyself.*

NO. XII.
TO THE PHILADELPHIA DOCTORS

If *Florio* on his bed complains
Of feverish pulse, and boiling veins,
And whims and fancies in his brains,

Then round him flocks a ghastly crew
Of doctors old and doctors new,
And doctor Numsculls--not a few.

Hoping that each had learnt his trade,
He waits with patience for their aid,
But scarce a word of *help* is said.

Each quotes some book, by way of sham,
Or reads dull stuff from *Sydenham*;
Which some approve--and others damn.

At once he hears a barbarous noise
Like that from troops of butchers' boys,
That every hope of life destroys.

He promises all fees to pay,
But they go on in angry fray,
Poor Florio Frets,--and well he may.

Each looks at each with angry eyes,
As if contending for a prize;
Or rob him, if the sick man dies.

One talks of cure by calomell;
But his wise brother, Sydrophel,
Swears 'tis the nearest road to hell.

While *this* the LANCET recommends,
Another for a *blister* sends,
And warmly each his whim defends.

Listening to all they have to say
At last the patient swoons away--
Poor Florio faints,--and well he may.

In Fancy's dreams, he thinks he roams
In realms, where doctor Devil foams,
With Sydrophels and *Curry-combs.*

Reviv'd at length--he begs release,
And whines, "Pray let your brawlings cease,
"Dear doctors! let me die in peace.

"Oh! had I sent for doctress Nan,
"She would have found some better plan
"To get me on my legs again.

"She, with her cooling tamarind tea,
"At lease would not have murdered me:
"Come! if you love me, do agree--

"Good heaven! you cannot all be right;
"You keep me in a wretched plight--
"Ah, doctors! doctors! do not *fight.*"

Here they begin still louder fray;
To him 'tis death--to them 'tis play--
Poor Florio dies, and well he may.

Poems (1809), II, 8-10.

Time-Piece November 29, 1797

Elegaic Verses on a Man that was killed by a Cow.

All must to death by some sad mischief yield,
    One falls from trees, one walks into a well;
This by some fatal cannon ball is killed,
    That smothered in the stormy ocean's swell,

Some to the dust by stroke of thunder go,
    Some tumble from the *Bank* and break their necks;
Some slipping from the topmast, fall below
    And breathe their dying groans on bloody decks.

Hard is their fate, but how much harder thine
    (All sympathetic people will allow)
Who while you wander'd through a wood of pine
    Were met, attack'd, and murder'd by a Cow.

Why had not Fates saw'd short each cruel horn
    Ere you by those destructive weapons bled;
Why did they not with equal care adorn,
    And fix as good a pair on your own head?

Then had you fought with vigour all your own,
    (Like Michael and the devil) and laid her low;
And future times on the recording stone,
    Had said, *Here lies the man that kill'd a Cow.*

Now, when the cow her mortal life doth yield,
    Whether by battle, want of hay, or bran,
I'll raise her tomb in yonder flowery field
    And write, *Here lies the Cow that kill'd a man.*

Poems (1809), I, 257.

Time-Piece December 4, 1797

"A soldier should be made of sterner stuff!"

ON DEBORAH GANNET,

The American heroine, who on Tuesday last presented a petition to Congress, for a pension in consideration of services rendered during the whole of the late war, in the character of a common soldier, in the regular armies of America.

Ye Congress-men, and men of weight,
    Who fill the public chairs,
Who many a favour have conferr'd,
    On men unknown to Mars--
        And ye, that on the lofty bench
    Decide by vote our great affairs,
        Ah, turn a calm attentive ear
        To *her*, who never war did fear--
           --Relieve this gallant wench.

With the same generous heat inspir'd
    As Joan of Arc, of old;
With zeal against the Briton fir'd,
    A spirit warm and bold,
She march'd to meet her country's foes.
        Disguis'd in man's attire--
    Where'er they fled, through field or town,
    With steady step she follow'd on,
    Resolv'd fair Freedom to maintain
    She met them on the embattled plain,
        And hurl'd the blasting fire.

Oh!--for such generous toils endur'd,
    So many dangers run,
In life's decline at length reward,
    This gallant Amazon,
Who for no splendid pension sues,
    She asks no proud triumphal car,
No pompous flattery of the muse,
    No pageantries of war,

But something in the wane of days
    To cheer her heart and keep her warm;
A cottage--such as I would raise,
    To guard her from the storm;
And whate'er else in Reason's view
    Your bounty may afford,
To her who did our foes pursue
    With bayonet, gun and sword.

Reflect--how many tender ties
    A woman must forego
Ere to the field of war she flies,
    To meet a savage foe--
How many bars has nature plac'd,
    And custom many more
That women never should be grac'd
    With honours won from war.
All these she nobly overcame,
    And taught by reason sage,
Check'd not her military flame,
    But scorn'd a censuring age,
And men that with contracted mind,
    All arrogant, condemn
And make disgrace in woman kind,
    What honour is in them.

South Carolina State Gazette   August 24, 1798

Last line: What honor is to men.

Poems (1815), I, 70-72.

Time-Piece   December 6, 1797

THE HIGH-MINDED APPRENTICE.
A Tale.

A WIDOW that some miles from London liv'd
    Far in a vale obscure, of little note,
With much ado a bare subsistence gain'd
    From spinning wheel--or making shirt--or mending coat.

One son she had, a rude mischievous wight,
    Who now fourteen years, and more, arriv'd,
Would neither dig, nor thresh, nor drive the plough,
    But still upon the poor old woman liv'd.

Joan thought 'twas time this lazy lounging wight
    Should learn a trade, since farmers work he hated,
Jerry, said she, to London you must go,
    And learn some trade--I'm sure you're not thick-pated.

While tarrying here you eat up all my kale,
    My turnips and my pigs devouring still--
And nothing earn--my wheel 'tis true, goes round,
    But time must come, my lad, when stop it will!

Jerry with tears receiv'd this good advice,
    So up to London town next week they went--
Now choose, said *Joan,* the trade you fancy best,
    For to some trade you must and shall be sent.

So round he gap'd through every street and alley--
    Saw black-smiths here, like Vulcan, wielding sledges;
There taylors sitting cross-legg'd, on a board,
    Next barbers whetting up their razor's edges:

Now saw a cobbler cobbling in his stall,
    Then weaver busy with his warp and woof,
Now mason raising high some mighty wall,
    Then carpenter engag'd on lofty roof--

He shook his head, as if he meant to say,
    All this is worse than threshing--learn a trade!

Something I want that's fine, genteel, and airy,
   For common work these hands were never made.

At last he chanc'd to stray where lives the king,
   Great George the Third, in all his pomp and glare--
Well now, said *Jerry,* here must live a man
   That has a trade would suit me to a hair.

There's little doing; all is brisk and gay,
   And dainty dishes go a begging here;
Some seem to work yet all their work is play;
   I will be bound at least for *fourteen year.*

So back he came where honest *Joan* was waiting--
   Well Jerry, tell me, what's the trade you pitch on?
Mother, said he, there is but one I like,
   Or, which a man is likely to get rich on.

"Ah, what is that?--one trade in London only
   "Suits--that is indeed a curious thing--
"Come, tell me what it is?" *Jerry* replied,
   Why, mamma! bind me 'prentice to the king.

Poems (1815), I, 30-32.

Time-Piece   December 8, 1797[1]

   On a Fly, Fluttering round a Candle.

ATTRACTED by the taper's rays,
   Thou busy, curious fly,
Come not too near this quivering blaze,

---

[1] This text has only one line, the first, in common with the 1815 collected version. Although the titles and basic ideas developed are quite similar, every line but the first, as well as the stanza form, were completely altered. As such, a complete edition of the poet might reproduce this text separately.

> For if you do, you die--
> > This little sun destruction brings,
> > Destroys your coat, consumes your wings.
>
> Thus man, like thee, ambitious still
> > Some dangerous course to run,
> Aspires to drive with fancied skill,
> > The chariot of the sun,
> > > And while to mount that seat he tries,
> > > Like Phaeton, he falls and dies.
>
> Away from hence, nor tempt too near,
> > This fierce devouring flame,
> Whose flashy heat alarms my fear,
> > And your respect may claim--
> > > A safer beam you may enjoy,
> > > The sun that warms, but don't destroy.

Poems (1815), I, 75-76.

Time-Piece   December 11, 1797

> *Of Thomas Swaugum, an Oneida Indian,*
> *and a Missionary Parson.*

> AN Indian that liv'd in *Oneida* remote
> > Was plagu'd by a parson to join his dear flock,
> To throw off his blanket and put on a coat,
> > And no longer at churches or parsons to mock.
>
> A long time the Indian resisted, be sure,
> > He preferr'd to their preaching his fishing & fowling:
> He could not the sight of a meeting endure,
> > And their singing, to him, was no better than howling.
>
> However, by teazing and constant harrassing,
> > Poor *Swaugum* was brought to attend in the church
> Where knowledge by preaching was ever amassing,
> > And the Devil, as usual, was left in the lurch.

One day as the parson was speaking of heaven,
    And describing the beautiful things of the place--
The Indian, in part of the *Talk* to be even,
    Stopp'd the minister short in the midst of his race.

--Said he, Mr. Parson, the *place* that you talk of,
    Pray what is it like--or what have they got?
Have they venison and rum--if so, I'll stalk off
    And fix myself down in some plentiful spot.

Pooh! you fool, said the Parson, no such things are there;
    Why heaven, poor creature, is just like our meeting--
There's nothing but singing, and preaching, and prayer--
    They've nothing to do with drinking and eating.

But the doors are lock'd up against folks that are wicked;
    Few Indians, dear Thomas, do ever get there;
A life of contrition must purchase the ticket,
    And few of you Indians can buy it, I fear.

Well then, said the Indian, good-by Mr. Doctor;
    In such way of living no pleasure I'd feel,
What nonsense it is to be keeping a lock'd door
    Where there's nothing to eat and there's nothing to steal.

Poems (1809), I, 252.

Time-Piece   December 13, 1797

A MODERN TALE.

A LAWYER once in a certain town resided,
    Whose eye-teeth had been cut--he well knew men--
Of paltry suits he ever had abundance,
    And still his fee was--*two pound ten*.

When neighbours quarrell'd--some about a pig
    Breaking through fence, and rooting up potatoes,
Law was the word--and each as angry seem'd
    As if the hungry pig had gnaw'd their great toes.

The lawyer saw, and saw with deep delight,
    That *wrangle* was the order of the day;
And took his measures, to ensure advantage
    From every quarrel, tavern broil, and fray.

As business hove in fast, he pasted up
    A caveat in his shop, to warn all men
That if they came to him to ask advice,
    In whate'er case, his fee was--*two pound ten*.

Sometimes a farmer's limits were disputed,
    Which *law* alone could hope to reconcile;
And many weighty arguments were urg'd
    Of fixing breadths two inches by the mile.

Then came a widow in a mighty fret--
    It seems a hen had peck'd some grains of rye
From neighbour Bumkin's hundred acre crop,
    And justice he would have--or he knew why.

Ah! (said the lawyer) these are happy times,
    Things now are getting right--I thought that men
Would sometime have *millenium*--Yes its come.
    I see it plain--it lies in two pound ten.

Thus things went on for many a pleasant year--
    The lawyer plead for all, and made them pay
His usual fee--At last grown very rich
    And hairs, as fate would have it, rather grey.

Disease attack'd--he made his will, and died--
    And when approaching to old Satan's den,
What is the admission ticket? said the guide--
    Why, quoth the devil, it is *two pound ten*.

Poems (1809), I, 222-23.

Time-Piece   December 18, 1797

A COLLEGE STORY.
(*Appertaining to Secret History*.)

A SON of a college, for science renown'd,
Who long had been reading, and reading, and reading
Huge volumes as dry as the desert of Zaara,
With abstinence much, and little good feeding;
At length become fond of a glass of Madeira,
Beer, brandy or porter--whatever was found.

One Saturday evening, when socially met
With friends to his liking, call'd Fellows of College,
Each drank of his toast in a bumper of wine
Till mirth had took place of the stiffness of knowledge;
They talk'd away cheerly 'till twelve of the clock
And their eyes like the eyes of old Moses did shine,
When he came from the mount, and the clefts of his rock
At the sins of the people to fume and to fret.

Now the bell striking one they agreed to adjourn
Each bound to his lodging by different roads;
But our son of the college by drinking too much
Lost his way, and got into the dead men's abodes,
Where Scotchmen and Irish and English and Dutch
Each peaceably lay with his head-stone, forlorn.

He stumbled, and tumbled, stubb'd toes, broke his shins
And now 'gainst a tomb stone disabled his head;
The night was as dark as in Egypt of old,
But at last he found out it 'twas the yard of the dead;
Then rolling away 'twixt a couple of tombs
An effort he made to get up--but in vain,
Old Bacchus has stow'd him so snug in his bed
That the church might as soon have been rais'd up again.
When thus the poor *Fellow* was heard with a groan,
To mutter (thro' rather profane in his jest)
As he lay with his head at the foot of a stone,
"Well-well--I suppose I shall rise with the rest."

Carey's U.S. Recorder   February 27, 1798

Stanza 1:   Lines 2 and 4 indented.
Stanza 2:   Lines 1, 3, 6, 8 indented.
Stanza 3:   Lines 1, 2, 4, 6 indented.
  Line 5: Where Spanish and Irish, French, English and Dutch,
Stanza 4:   Lines 2, 4, 8, 10, and 12 indented.
  Line 4: But at last he found out 'twas the place for the dead;

Poems (1809), 256-57.

New York *Argus*   June 15, 1798

ODE.
TO THE AMERICANS.
That the progress of liberty in the world, considering the present state of things, cannot be impeded, or its complete establishment prevented.

THEY who survey this human stage
With wisdom's eye through time's long age,
Will find whatever nature plann'd,
Came first, imperfect from her hand.

Yon stately trees, so fresh and fair,
That now such golden burthen bear,
Were first mean shrubs that far from view,
In desart wastes, neglected grew.

Men saw the seeds of something good,
In these rude children of the wood;
Applied the knife, and prun'd with care,
'Till time has made them what they are.

With curious eye, search wisdom's page,
And *Man* observe through every age;
At first a mere barbarian, he
Bore nothing good, like that wild tree.

At length, by reason's secret aid,
And genius piercing night's dark shade,
Improvements rose by slow advance,
Direction, not the work of chance.

Forsaking, young, the savage den,
And fellow beasts, less fierce than men,
New rules they fram'd, for war or power,
And sunk the ditch or rais'd the tower.

In course of years the human mind,
Tho' slow in growth, grew more refin'd;
Less brutal in external show,
But secret vice lay hid below.

Despots and kings began their part,
And millions fell by rules of art,
Or malice, rankling all the while,
Retir'd behind a treacherous smile.

Religion lodg'd her potent aid
With kings, their subjects to degrade;
And Priests, or history much deceives,
Turn'd aids-de-camp to sceptred thieves.

At length, that cherub from the skies,
That does our nature humanize;
And sways without a king or crown,
Philosophy, to man came down.

She, only she, for virtue warm,
Dissolv'd the spell, and broke the charm;
That bade mankind their hands imbrue
In blood, to glut the artful *few.*

The moment that she whirl'd her sling,
Each trembling War-Hawk dropp'd his wing;

They saw that reason's game was won,
They saw the trade of tyrants done.

But struggling now to quench her flame,
Britain's amphibious legions aim
To chill the blossom in the bud,
And retrograde to chains and blood.

The *People*--to be bought and sold,
Are still the prize kings wish to hold;
As peasants, soldiers, sailors, slaves,
The common stake of rogues and knaves,

Yet nature must her circuit run--
Can they arrest the rising Sun;
Prevent his warm reflecting ray,
Or make the shades of midnight stay?

In vain their navy spreads its sails,
The strength of tho't o'er force prevails;
And, Reason! thy prodigious power,
Has brought it to its closing hour.

Appeals to arms henceforth must cease,
And man will learn to breathe in peace,
No Kings with iron sceptre reign,
To cease old ocean's free domain.

Americans! could you unite
In putting out this growing light--
Could you, so late from fetters freed,
Join, party in so base a deed?

Would you dear Freedom sacrifice,
Bid natives on the ocean rise,
Submit to military laws,
And all, to aid a despot's cause?

Oh! No!--but should all shame forsake,
And *Gratitude* her exit make,
Could you, as thousands say you can,
Desert the common cause of man?

A curse would on your efforts wait,
Old British laws to reinstate—
No standing troops could force a crown,
Or keep the bold *Republic* down.

The rising race combin'd, once more
Would honor to these climes restore,
And in your doom and baseness seal
Such woes as wicked kings shall feel.

Oh Liberty!—seraphic name,
With whom from heaven fair virtue came;
From whom, through years of mis'ry toss'd,
One hundred thousand lives were lost.*

Still shall all gen'rous hearts to thee
Bend the head and bow the knee;
For thee this dream of life forego,
And quit the world when thou dost go.

Poems (1815), I, 39-44.

---

* The number of Americans computed to have perished in accomplishing the Revolution.

New York *Argus*   June 16 1798

THE REPUBLIC AND LIBERTY.

Americans! rouse at the rumours of war,
Which now are distracting the hearts of the nation,
A flame blowing up by a race you abhor--
That aided so lately Old England's invasion,
    When with heart and with hand,
    And a murdering band
Of vagrants, she plunder'd and ravag'd our land.
In LIBERTY's cause we are ever array'd,
But yield not her substance to feast on her shade.

Remember the cause that induc'd you to rise,
When oppression came here with her king-making host;
'Twas the good of mankind that bade you despise,
And drive to destruction all Britain's proud host,
    That with cannon and sword,
    Under men they ador'd,
Rush'd into each village and rifled each shade,
To murder the shepherd or ravish the maid.

What tho' you arose and resolv'd to be free,
With spirit to humble all Europe combining,
You had soon bit the dust or been drown'd in the sea,
By the slaves of a King and a Court all designing,
    Had not France lent her aid,
    And with vengeance repaid,
The myriads that came from a blood-thirsty isle,
Our groves, and our streams, and our beds to defile.

Our Churches disgrac'd by a merciless foe,
Or made the poor captive's distress'd habitation;
The prison-ship fraught with its cargo of woe,
Where the thousands were starved without shame or compassion;
    All these, and yet more,
    Were the insults we bore,
From the wretches who now would be reckon'd our friends,
And are charming our country--to gain British ends.

All true born *Americans*! join as of old--
For Freedom's defence be your bold resolution,
Whoever invades you by force, or *with gold*,
Alike is a foe to a free Constitution--
    Unite to pull down
    That bauble, a Crown--
All Tyranny's engines again are at work,
To make you as poor and as base as the Turk.

Look round the wide world, and behold with a sigh,
Wherever a monarch presides o'er a nation,
Sweet nature is seen with a tear in her eye,
And the shadows of death enshroud her creation;
    The ocean is chain'd,
    And all blessings restrain'd,
To royals and nobles, the guards of a throne,
And the slaves they have bribed--to make freedom their own.

All hail to the *Nation,* immortal and GREAT,
That, rising on bold philosophical pinion,
Reforms and enlightens--but fetters no state,
Nor places her bliss and extent of dominion;
    Yet, true to the plan
    On which she began,
Will the standard display that's to freedom assign'd,
'Till tyrants are chac'd from the view of mankind.

Oh *Rome!* that so long had in darkness been lost,
Since on your Republic bright freedom was shining,
The warmth of your spirit congeal'd in a frost,
Under tyrants and popes many centuries pining,
    At the close of the page,
    Revives in our age--
No more of your Nero's and Cesar's complain,
For *Brutus* and *Cato* shall bless you again.

Approaching!--at hand!--in the circle of time,
A century comes to begin its career,
When nature reviving, and man in his prime,
His rights will attest, and maintain, without fear
    Of that scheming sly race,
    Who our species disgrace,

And climb into office on villainous plan,
To plunder all substance and trample on man.

Let Reason, that sun whose unquenchable ray,
Progressive, has dawn'd on the night of the mind,
From the source of all good her effulgence display,
And man a more dignified character find--
    May order and peace,
    Thro' creation increase,
And murder, and plunder, and tyranny cease;
Nor Man so the blessings of Freedom degrade,
As to give up the substance--and feast on the shade.

Poems (1815), II, 9-13.

New York *Argus*   June 25, 1798

(Text concludes the following comments:)

DEMOCRACY.

Prejudiced foreigners who are daily and hourly landing in this country to seek or make their fortunes, and bring with them their little ideas of men and things, are continually barking and growling against Democracy, without even understanding the word. It is the subject of the greater part of their conversation; and from the venom they discover on these occasions, it is evident they would destroy, banish, or proscribe every man of democratic principles in the United States. What is Democracy? Is it any thing more than a nation choosing to govern itself upon the principles of reason, liberty, and equality, at as small expence as possible, and through a fair and just representation, changeable at certain short periods to prevent corruption? These praters against democracy are *generally* shallow fellows, who would sacrifice their country, wherever it might be, for a title or a ribbon; and provided they can have what they call "*The King, my Master*," and tyrranize a little over their fellow creatures, would become the most quiet animals or the greatest

despots in the universe. Let them take cares, for
"A two headed engine at the door,
Stands ready to strike once, and strike no more."

A race has come in from old Scratch'em knows where,
To chatter and curse democratic Republic,
Who first when they landed, were poor and as bare,
As Porcupine's self, that look'd very scrub-like;
'Till his patrons from Europe, and some that were here,
Combin'd to support his base sink of scurrility,
And gave him, 'tis said, Four Thousand a year,
To print a vile libel to please our Nobility;
They tho't, it is true,
A mere blockhead would do,
To support the designs of a king-making few,
Who have got on the saddle and there would remain,
To spur us, and gallop, and spur us again.

With Porcupine's gabble their hearts are delighted,
All your better born people his merits confess;
To the shores of Columbia this prig was invited,
To shew in perfection an Englishman's press,
All blackguard and puff,
Egotistical stuff,
When I, is the hero of all that is said,
I, Corporal Cobbett, the Knight of the Blade,
If his countrymen tho't,
That for nothing we fought,
And mean to regain by the aid of his press,
The country they lost, to their shame and disgrace,
Willy Pitt should have sent us some genius acute,
Not Peter–a blackguard and blockhead to boot.

Ye Cocknies from London, dear lads stay at home,
'Tis madness so far from your country to roam,
To preach and to print, with coxcomical phiz,
And tell what a nuisance Democracy is;
'Tis a lesson we learn'd,
When you were concern'd,
In aiding and making such vast preparations,
To conquer and pillage these *Royal Plantations*.

We Americans, far from your king-ridden isle,
Do humbly beseech you, all Democrat haters,
That you may not your souls or your bodies defile,
Pack off with your printers, your lies, and your satires;
The monarch you love is in want of assistance,
And how can you help him at such a great distance?
  'Tis an Englishman's creed,
  And they long have agreed,
That out of Old England there's nothing (they swear)
That can with what's English, true English, compare;
So away to Old England, or we'll send you there.

Poems (1815), I, 37-39.

New York *Argus* July 7, 1798

On the causes of Political Degeneracy.

Oh! fatal day, when to this peaceful shore,
European despots sent this doctrine o'er,
That man's vast race was born to lick the dust,
Feed on the winds, or toil thro' life accurst;
Poor and despis'd, that others might be great,
And swoln to Monarchs to devour the State.

Whence came these ills, or from what causes grew,
This vortex vast, that only spares the few;
Despotic sway, whose very plague combin'd,
Distracts, degrades, and swallows up mankind?
Accuse not nature for the dreadful scene
That glooms her stage, or hides her sky serene;
She, equal she, in all her varying ways,
Her equal blessings through the world displays:
The Suns that now on northern climates glow,
Will soon retire, to melt Antarctic Snow;
The seas she robb'd, to make her clouds and rain,
Return in rivers to their breast again;
But man, wrong'd man, borne down, deceiv'd and vext,

Groans on thro' life, bewilder'd and perplext,
Few suns on him but suns of slavery shine,
Now starv'd in camps, now grovelling in the mine,
Chain'd fetter'd, tortur'd, sent from earth a slave,
To seek rewards in worlds beyond the grave.

If in her general system just to all,
We nature, our impartial parent call,
Why did she not on man's whole race bestow,
Those fine sensations spirits only know,
That, born with reason's uncorruptive mind,
Their proper bliss in common blessings find,
Which, shed o'er all, would all our race pervade,
In streams not niggard by the tyrant made?

Leave this a secret in great Nature's breast;
Confess that all her works tend to the best,
Yet own that man's neglected reason here,
Breeds all the mischiefs that we feel or fear,
In all beside the skill to ride his race,
Man, wise and skillful, gives each part its place,
Each nice machine he plans, to reason true,
Adapting all things to the end in view;
But turn to this, the art himself to rule,
His sense is folly, and himself a fool.

Where the prime strength resides, there rests, 'tis plain,
The power mankind to govern and restrain--
Where lies this strength but in the social plan,
Design'd for all, the common good of man:
The power concentered by the general voice,
In honest men, an honest people's choice,
With constant change, to keep the patriot pure,
And vain from views of power the heart secure;
There lies the secret, hid from Rome and Greece,
That holds the world in awe, and holds in peace.

See through this earth, in ages now retir'd,
Man foe to man, as policy requir'd:
At some proud tyrant's nod what millions rose,
To crush mankind, or make the world their foes.
View Asia ravaged, Europe drench'd in blood,

From feuds, whose cause no nation understood--
The cause, alas! of so much misery sown,
Known at the helm of state, and truly known.
Left to themselves, where'er mankind is found,
In peace they wish to walk life's little round,
In peace to sleep, in peace to till the soil,
Nor gain subsistence from a brother's toil,
All but the base, designing, cunning few,
Who seize on nations with a robber's view.
With crowns and sceptres awe the dazzled eye,
And priests, that hold the artillery of the sky;
These, these with armies, navies, potent grown,
Impoverish man, and bid the nations groan;
These, with pretended balance of free States,
Keep worlds at variance, breed eternal hates,
Make man the poor base slave of low design,
Degrade his nature and his tribes disjoin,
Shed hell's foul plagues o'er his exalted race,
And filch the hard earned mite, to make them base.

Shall views like these involve our happy land,
Where embrio monarchs thirst for wide command;
Shall our young nation's strength and fair renown,
Be sacrificed to prop a falling throne,
That ages past the world's great curse has stood,
To thrive on rapine, and to feed on blood--
Americans! will you controul such views!
Speak--for you must--you have no time to lose.

Trenton *True American*   March 17, 1801

Stanza 3:   Begins with the fifth line of the second stanza of the 1798 text, and concludes with the end of that stanza. (Remaining stanzas as in the 1798 text.)

Poems (1815), I, 13-16.

Time-Piece   July 13, 1798[1]

TO AN ALIEN.

Remote, beneath a Southern sun,
When Mississippi loves the plain
If things go on as they have done
In tyranny's dark train.
Alien! 'tis best to take your way,
When freedom doth her flag display,
Luisiana fair;
When nature, yet, is sweet and young,
All things such as poets sung
Ere kings or despots were.

No *Tracy* there, with brazen throat,
Shall set a murdering herd afloat,
With aspect fierce and wild;
Shall hell's worst votaries employ
To ravage, torture, and destroy--
Kill--woman, man, and child.

Alas! what fatal error led
Your footsteps to these shores,
Where all is changed--the genius fled
That now no art restores.
In midnight dreams, I see you roam
To regions far remov'd:
Perhaps, without a house, a home,
Remote from all you lov'd;
Remote from her, whose breast must swell
With grief and boding care--
But how will you, who lov'd so well
The fiery trial bear!

---

[1] Although the title and the first two lines here appear in the 1815 text of this poem, the remainder was completely rewritten, and the stanza form was altered. In 1815 the poet is more specific about the alien, and though the later text includes more detail, it lacks the eloquence of the more generalized sense of despair in the earlier. As such, a complete edition of the poet might reproduce this text separately.

No stranger here, henceforth will find
An asylum secure;
Some flinty despot soon will bind,
Nor liberty endure--

Embark, embark--some other clime
May better prospects yield,
Where liberty is not a crime
Nor friendship's laws repeal'd.

Poems (1815), I, 100-02.

Time-Piece   July 16, 1798

BOTANY BAY.

Lines, occasioned by Federal threats to take up and send off certain Patriotic characters to Botany Bay.

Swell'd with good wine, and stuff'd with pigs,
    I heard proud *Bufo* say
"These Democrats we once call'd whigs,
    Must off to Botany Bay."

Alas, alas! who would have thought,
    That they who wrote, who toil'd, who fought,
For many a year, and nothing got,
    Defending liberty,

Must now away, as these upstarts say,
    To Botany Bay, to Botany Bay,--
    Huzza for Botany Bay!

This Bay of bays, that makes such noise
Is own'd we're told, by British Boys,
Who send their outcasts every year
The spawn of jails and dungeons there.

Last week we heard a Federal say
"Pray tell me, where is Botany Bay?
"There are (quoth he) a meddling few
"That shall go there--and I know who."

This Botany Bay is in an Isle,
Remov'd from Britain many a mile,
Where scoundrels may for crimes atone,
But not too large to hold *her own.*

And, yet, from sending honest men,
Like *Thomas Muir* to that d--'d den,
'Tis thought she means, in times to come,
To keep her scoundrels all at home.

Ye Britains here by rancour led,
Who curse the land that gives you bread,
Restrain your threats, or let me say,
You'll find the route to Botany Bay.

Some little prince, that England owns,
Pick'd from the herd of George's sons,
To govern with despotic sway
Wants some such place as Botany Bay.

Ye upstart crew, of brazen face,
Who do our western world disgrace,
Ye turn-coat tribe, who build your all
On soldier's wrongs and freedom's fall,

This have we seen, and well we know
Each friend of freedom is your foe,
And you would them forthwith convey
To places worse than Botany Bay:

Be cautious how you talk so loud,
Above your heads there hangs a cloud
That, bursting with explosion vast,
May thunder vengeance in its blast,
And send you all, on satan's dray,
A longer road than Botany Bay.

Poems (1815), I, 91-93.

Kentucky Gazette November 28, 1798

RETIREMENT.
By *Philip Freneau.*

First newspaper appearance of this poem, which first was published in the 1786 collection. It is substantively identical to the 1786 text, but the stanza form is altered. In each stanza, lines 1, 3, and 4 and indented, and lines 2 and 5 begin at the margin. This text also appeared in the *New Jersey Journal*, January 15, 1799.

Poems (1786), 59.

Aurora July 6, 1799

(Untitled.)

This past--another Anniversive day,
Has smiled upon our states with *union* blest,
Pale envy shrinking hides her blood-stained crest
And lurking slav'ry flies without delay,
And let her fly far from Columbia's coast,
Her power destroyed her influence lost,
Far from the world, with grief, & woe, and pain,
May she be hurled, ne'er to arise again.

Here long with iron hand she held her reign,
And tyrants' satelites her power upheld,
Till freedom's sons through many a well fought field,
Did *Independence* glorious birth-right gain,
And may they still preserve the gift divine,
Freedom thy wreathe with *Independence* twine,
Nor end your cause till all the world ye see,
Arouse, inform, inspire, and render *free*,

Hark! 'tis the voice of kings, the curse of men,
That from Siberia calls the savage host,

Suwarrow, wild to finer feelings lost,
Terrific war to wage and aid the plan.
But thou fair *freedom* shalt victorious rise,
The boasts of kings, and savage hosts despise,
Man shall be free, debased nor more a slave,
Tho' Emp'rors gnash their teeth and kings impotent rave.

Too long, alas! had vile tyrannic power,
Held men in bondage great, the cup of grief,
His daily draught, and groans and death relief
Alone produc'd, 'till glorious hour,
Columbia rose in godlike form,
She rul'd their rage, assuag'd the storm,
Of bold tyrannic sway, brought to submit,
And own her right divine and kneel before her feet.

Dear *Independence* ever be our boast,
Unanxious we will grasp thee to our heart,
Despotic power avaunt--we neer shall part,
Sooner our hearts best blood shall all be lost,
Aurora rise, proclaim to all we're free,
Created equal, equal still we'll be,
And to posterity without alloy,
Transmit a *right* which tyrants can't destroy,

MARTIAL jun.

Slender's Letters (1799), 71-72.

City Gazette   January 10, 1800

STANZAS,
Occasioned by the Death of GENERAL GEORGE WASHINGTON

THE *Man,* that freed these suffering lands
From George the Third's beseiging bands;
The *Hero* through all countries known,
The Guardian Genius of his own--

Is gone to that sequestered bourne,
From which no traveller does return;
Where Scipio, and where Trajan went;
And Heaven reclaims the soul it lent.

 Each heart with secret woe congeals;
Down the pale cheek soft sorrow steals;
And all the gentler passions join,
To mourn, remember--and resign.

 O ye, that carve the marble bust,
To celebrate poor human dust,
And from Death's silent, sleepy shore,
The faded form of man restore--
Vain are your aims, by force of art,
To impress his image on the heart;
It lives, it glows in every breast,
And tears of millions tell the rest.

 Indebted to his guardian care,
And great alike in peace and war,
The loss they feel, these States deplore
Their Chief, their Father is no more.

 What will they do to avow their grief?
No sighs, no tears, afford relief.
Dark mourning weeds but ill express
The poignant grief that all confess;
Nor will the monumental stone,
Assuage one tear, relieve one groan.

 O *Washington*! thy honoured dust,
To Parent Nature we entrust;
Convinc'd that thy exalted mind
Still lives, but soars beyond mankind;
Still acts in Virtue's sacred cause,
Nor asks from man his vain applause.

 In raptures with a theme so great,
While thy fam'd actions they relate,
Each future age from thee shall know,
All that is good and great below;

Shall glow with pride, to hand thee down
To latest time, to long renown,
The brightest name on *Freedom's* page,
And the First Honour of our age.

MYRTILLA

New York *Argus*   February 12, 1800

Stanza 5, line 1: What will they do to avoid their grief?

Poems (1815), I, 156-58.

City Gazette   January 15, 1800

TO THE MEMORY OF
General George WASHINGTON.

DEPARTING with the parted age,
    To virtue, worth, and freedom true,
The chief, the patriot, and the sage
    To *Vernon* bids his last adieu,
        To reap, in some superior state,
        Rewards that crown the good and great.

Thou, *Washington*! by Heaven design'd
    To act a part in human things,
That few have known among mankind,
    And far beyond the lot of kings--
        We hail thee, now, to heaven receiv'd,
        Your mighty task in life atchiev'd.

While Sculpture, and her sister arts,
    For thee, their towering works prepare,
Fond Gratitude her share imparts,
    And begs thy corpse for burial there,
        Where, near *Virginia's* northern bound,
        Swells the vast pile* on federal ground.

---

* The Capitol.

I'll call from their obscure abodes
    Each Roman chief, each Grecian sage,
The kings, the heroes, and the Gods,
    That flourish'd in Time's earlier age–
        No one shall hold a rank with you,
        And none such objects did pursue.

Those fiery souls of vulgar mould,
    Blood their delight, and war their trade;
Their oaths prophan'd, their country sold,
    And trembling nations prostrate laid–
        Dare those, like you, assert their claim
        To honor, and immortal fame?

These monarchs, proud of trophied spoils,
    With nations fetter'd in their train,
Returning from their desperate toils,
    With aspect lofty, fierce, or vain–
        In all they did, no traits are known,
        Like those which mark'd our *Washington*.

Who now will guard our shores from harms,
    (To him a task so long assigned)
Who now will rouse the world to arms,
    And blaze conviction on mankind,
        That all is wrong, where vice prevails,
        Or Justice holds *unequal* scales?

Ah, gone!–and none your place supply,
    Nor will your equal soon appear–
But that *great name* alone can die,
    When Memory lives no longer here,
        And *man*, (for come the time it must)
        Dissolves into unconscious dust.

                SYLVIUS.

Orangeburgh, January 8, 1800.

Poems (1815), I, 154-56.

City Gazette   January 30, 1800

ELEGAIC STANZAS,
To the Memory of EDWARD RUTLEDGE, *Esq. late Governor of the State of South-Carolina.*

REMOV'D from Life's uncertain stage,
    In virtue firm, in honor clear,
One of the worthies of our age,
    Rutledge, resigns his station here.

Alike in arts of war and peace,
    And form'd by nature to excel,
From early Rome and ancient Greece,
    He modell'd all his actions well.

When Britons came with chains to bind,
    Or ravage these devoted lands,
He our firm league of freedom sign'd,
    And counsell'd how to break their bands.

To the great cause of honour true,
    He forward stept, with manly pride;
His spirit o'er these regions flew,
    The Patriot's and the Soldier's guide.

That task perform'd, in warlike scenes,
    Amongst our brightest stars he mov'd--
The Lees, the Moultries, Sunters, Greenes,
    By all admir'd, by all belov'd.

A Patriot of superior mould,
    He dar'd such foreign force oppose,
'Till from such mingled efforts bold
    The mighty Pile of *Freedom* rose.

In process of succeeding days,
    When *Peace* resum'd her joyous reign,
With laurel wreathes and twining bays,
    He sought less active life again.

There, warm to plead the Orphan's cause,
    From Misery's eye to dry the tear,
He stood, where justice guards the laws,
    At once humane, at once severe.

'Twas not his firm, enlighten'd mind,
    So ardent in affairs of state;
'Twas not, that he in armies shin'd,
    That made him so completely great:

Persuasion dwelt upon his tongue;
    He spoke–all hush'd, and all were aw'd—
From every word conviction sprung,
    And crowds were eager to applaud.

Thus long esteem'd, thus early lov'd,
    The tender husband, friend sincere,
The parent, patriot, sage approv'd,
    Had now surpass'd his fiftieth year;

Had now the highest honour met
    That *Carolina* can bestow,
Presiding o'er that potent state,
    Where streams of wealth and plenty flow;

Where Labour spreads his rural reign,
    To Western regions, bold and free,
And Commerce o'er the Atlantic main
    Wafts her rich stores of Industry:

Then left this scene of human things,
    To shine in a sublimer sphere,
Where Time to one assemblage brings
    All virtuous minds, all hearts sincere.

January 27, 1800.

Poems (1815), I, 26-28.

City Gazette   December 18, 1800

LINES *on the* FEDERAL CITY.

ALL human things must have their rise;
And Rome increas'd from pigmy size,
Till future ages saw her grown,
The mistress of the world then known.

So, bounding on Potawmac's flood,
Where forest-trees so lately stood,
An infant city grows apace,
Intended for a royal race.

Here Capitols of awful height,
Already burst upon the sight;
And palaces, for embrio kings,
Display their fronts and spread their wings.

This city bodes no common fate—
All other towns, as books relate,
With huts at first were thinly spread,
With hovel mean, the humble shed.

Not so are matters here design'd;
Here, palaces we only find;
And late must *common people* come,
In such a place to find a home:

Where Royalty, with vile grimace,
In *Louis* shews its scoundrel face;
And *Antoinette* a smile affords,
To Senators and would-be Lords.

Meantime, it will be fair and just,
Nor will our grandees fret, we trust,
If, while the poor at distance lurk,
Themselves do their own dirty work.

Rome's earliest citizens, they say,
Submitted to delusive sway,
In Romulus, who suck'd a bear,
Then went to Heaven, a royal star.

Pray Heaven, the case may be revers'd:
May they, who here inhabit first,
By some *reforms* that must be made,
And shaking off the *royal trade,*
Incline the late historian's pen,
To write, that *"Here were honest men."*

December 17th, 1800.

Poems (1815), I, 34-35.

City Gazette   December 20, 1800

On a View of the Planet JUPITER *and his* MOONS,
through a large Telescope.

ASTONISH'D at a sight so new,
Can I suppose this vision true--
A world on yonder azure ground,
That no less real worlds surround!
Proud Planet! Are my eyes deceiv'd?
Who has not seen has not believ'd,
That in the ethereal vaulted waste,
Spheres like our own, and worlds are plac'd,
Of size stupendous, mightier far
Than this our earth, a meaner star;
And Reason's eye another race
Of Nature's children there may trace.

Each mountain and each sunny plain
Were surely not design'd in vain:
Who knows but different *men* are there,
Joys of their own, or griefs to share?

This tell-tale tube to me displays
Vast rolling oceans, boundless seas,
That on yon ponderous planet, *Jove,*
To other Moons obedient move.

These Moons, in various orbs that stray,
To serve by night the want of day,
Are not like our's, which in her wane
Leaves us to grope in shades again.

May not this train of splendid guards,
Be part of Virtue's great rewards?
Be on a happier race bestow'd,
The natives of yon grand abode;
A race in rank that higher stand,
In Nature's happier humour plann'd,
And favor'd more, and more caress'd
Than Man, discordant and unblest?

But while I dwell on things like these,
Where fancy finds so much to please,
I see, while art thus brings him down,
The formidable Planet frown;
I hear him say, (in Reason's ear)
"What business have you prying here--
What treach'rous, or what slumb'ring god
Intrudes you on my bright abode?
I cannot bear that human eyes,
Should view my moons, my belts, my skies;
Search not, for Nature thus commands,
Search not my oceans or my lands:
If man were once admitted here,
What madness would distract my sphere;
He would perplex, intrigue, ensnare,
And every shape of mischief wear;
He would torment, unhinge, derange,
And half my lovely system change,
And make my globe, to wars unknown,
The horrid image of his own!
Reform, correct your wicked ways,
Nor longer walk in Folly's maze;
Learn to be good, be men of worth,
And then perhaps your little earth,
(Tho' not to be expected soon)
In time may have–another Moon."

December 18, 1800.

New York *Weekly Museum*   October 3, 1801

LINES,
Occasioned by a Telescopic View of the Planet JUPITER
and his MOONS.

Single space between stanzas.

Stanza 1:   First stanza of the 1800 text, with the following variants:
    line 2:   Who would suppose the vision true;
    line 6:   Who has not seen has scarce believ'd
    line 8:   Spheres like our own, and earths are plac'd,
    line 10: Than this our globe, a meaner star;
    line 11: And Reason's eye another kind
    line 12: Of nature's children there may find.

Stanza 2:   Second stanza of the 1800 text, with the following variants:
    line 2:   Were, surely, not contriv'd in vain,--

Stanza 3:   Third stanza of the 1800 text, with the following variants:
    line 2:   Vast shady regions, boundless seas,
    line 6:   To serve by night the loss of day,
    Four lines added:
    line 9:   *Those* shine by turns thro' every night,
    line 10: And nymphs and shepherds may invite
    line 11: In happy fields or shades to rove,
    line 12: And steal the kiss or talk of love.

Stanza 4:   Fourth stanza of the 1800 text, with the following variants:
    line 2:   Be part of Virtue's bright rewards,

Stanza 5:   Fifth stanza of the 1800 text, revised and lengthened.
    Entire stanza as follows:
        But while I dwell on things like these,
    (Where Fancy finds so much to please)
    I see, while art thus brings him down,
    The formidable Planet frown;
    The Genius of the star began,
    And thus I heard him speak to *man,*
    I heard him say (in Reason's ear)

"What business have you prying here,
"What treacherous or what slumbering God
"Intrudes you on my bright abode?
"I cannot bear that human eyes
"Should view my moons, my belts, my skies:
"Search not, for Nature thus commands,
"Search not my oceans or my lands.
"Who knows but some contriving brain
"A passage to my orb might gain;
"And introduce a host of woes,
"And arts, to break our sweet repose?
"If man were once admitted here
"His madness would distract my sphere,
"He would perplex, intrigue, ensnare,
"And every shape of mischief wear,
"And I should stretch my bended bow
"To pierce him deep, and hurl him low!
"This creature, call'd aspiring man,
"Would soon his schemes of ruin plan,
"He would torment, disturb, derange,
"And half my lovely system change,
"And make my globe, to wars unknown,
"The horrid image of his own!

Stanza 6:   Last six lines of the fifth stanza of the 1800 text.
            line 1:   indented.

September, 1801.
Signature: F.

Poems (1809), I, 221-22.

New York *Weekly Museum*   April 25, 1801

LINES,

Addressed to the inhabitants of a village, in one of the Southern States, some of whom, in nocturnal revel, gouged out the eyes of an itinerant Fiddler.

    WAS this the act of men of worth,
Or any but the scum of earth,
On Music's tuneful son to fall,
And sightless make each visual ball?

    Who first such savage warfare taught,
His heart was out of marble wrought,
He suck'd a bear, or tygers join'd
To turn him loose upon mankind.

    Henceforth this wretch his way must grope
Alone and eyeless, void of hope,
That time or art will sight restore,
Which he enjoy'd, like us, before.

    All nature is to him a shade,
And all the world is darkness made;
He sees no sun, no moon, no star,
Nor object near, nor object far,--
And, shine that sun however bright,
No ray illumines his long night,
The azure of the vaulted skies
Is shade to him who owns no eyes,
A chaos all, and all a gloom,
A next-door neighbor to the tomb.

    Why do I hold so dull a pen
To stigmatize ferocious men,
Why is it not inspired with force
To work despair, regret, remorse,
And make them conscious-smitten, sore
Lament the loss they can't restore!

From him, whom you have eyeless made
Forgiveness never can be had—
Resentment in his breast will rave
'Till Time has lodg'd him in the grave:—
'Tis true, he will the fiddle play,
(Alike to him, if night or day)
He for his skill may get a fee
But never will a shilling *see:*
A puppy, to his girdle tied,
For time to come must be his guide
To lead him through this dreary waste
Of nature, mangled and disgraced.

But you, possessors of this town,
(Who gain from gouging your renown,)
I heard him call you wrangling dogs,
I heard him curse this town of logs—
For vengeance he put up a prayer
And thus, and thus I heard him swear,
That, such an outrage to repay,
He ne'er again would come this way,
He never would an elbow shake,
Nor music for your maidens make,
Nor money spread for bread or beer,
Or brandy that is vended here—
He hoped that fevers might impend,
Or agues freeze you without end
He swore he would not come again
To please one nymph, or cheer one swain,
Nor tune his strings for Belial's sons
While forests grow, or water runs.—P.F.

Poems (1809), II, 98-99.

New York *Weekly Museum*   August 1, 1801

STANZAS ON SOUTH CAROLINA.
Said to be written by P. *Freneau*.

THE prosperous winds present once more
The gay and ever-pleasing shore,
Which every pleasure will restore
    To those who come again:
You, Carolina, from the seas
Emerging, claim all power to please,
Emerge with elegance and ease
    From Neptune's briny main.

To find in you a happier home,
Retirement for the days to come,
From northern coasts I wish'd to roam,
    While brilliant fancy mov'd;
I came, and in your fragrant woods,
Your verdant isles and gay abodes,
In rural haunts, by passing floods,
    Review'd the scenes I lov'd–

When sailing oft, from year to year,
And leaving all I counted dear,
I found the happy country here
    Where manly hearts abound,
Where Friendship's kind extended hand,
All social, leads a generous band;
Where heroes who redeem'd the land
    Still live to be renown'd;

Who live to fill the trump of fame,
Or, dying, left the honor'd name
Which Athens had been proud to claim
    From her historian's page . . . .
These with invading thousands strove,
These bade the foe their prowess prove,
And from their old possessions drove
    The tyrants of the age.

Long, long may every good be thine,
Sweet country, named from Caroline,
Once seen in Britain's court to shine
    The fairest of the fair:
Still may the wanderer find a home
Where'er the varied forests bloom,
And peace and pleasure with him come
    To take their station here.

Here Ashley with his brother stream,
By Charleston gliding, all may claim
That ever grac'd a poet's dream,
    And magic's aspect wears:
She, seated near her forests blue,
Which Winter's rigor never knew,
With half an ocean in her view,
    Her happy turrets tears.

Here stately oaks of living green,
Along the extended waste are seen,
That rise beneath a heaven serene,
    Unfading through the year....
In groves the tall Palmette grows,
Its shades inviting to repose,
The fairest, loveliest, scenes disclose....
    All nature charms us here.

Dark wilds are thine, the yellow field,
And rivers, by no frost congeal'd,
And, Ceres, all that you can yield
    To deck the festive board;
The snow white fleece, from pods that grows,
And every seed that Flora sows,
Here, on forsaken man, bestows
    A Paradise restored.

    [To be continued in our next.]

Poems (1815), I, 22-24.

New York *Weekly Museum*　　August 8, 1801

STANZAS ON SOUTH CAROLINA.
Said to be written by P. *Freneau*.
[*concluded.*]

HERE, rural love, to bless the swains,
In the bright eye of beauty reigns,
And brings a heaven upon the plains,
　　From some dear *Emma's* charms,
From *Circe* fair, that haunts the mead,
Some *Helen,* whom the Graces lead,
Whose charms the charms of her exceed
　　That set all Greece in arms.

And, distant from the sullen roar
Of oceans, bursting on the shore,
A region rises, valued more
　　Than half that kings possess:
There, endless wastes tall woods display,
Placed in a climate ever gay,
From wars and commerce far away,
　　Sweet nature's wilderness.

The prospect from the height display'd,
The river, wandering thro' the shade,
All these the happiest scene have made
　　That ever held the sight--
There all that art has taught to bloom,
The springs that from the mountain foam,
Eutaw, and thine, which onward roam,
　　Impart supreme delight.

Those heavenly springs will cease to flow,
When those, who there a hunting go,
Forget the scene of wild Eutaw,
　　Where *Greene* his banners rais'd,
Gave to the winds his standard bold,
To kings a different story told
From all the page of time enroll'd,
　　From all that Fame has prais'd.

See, Congaree his terrors pours,
Saluda through the forest roars,
And wild Catawba laves his shores
    With waters from afar,
'Till mingled with the proud Santee
Their force united finds the sea,
Through many a plain, by many a tree,
    Then rush across the bar.

Yes--where such lovely scenes combine,
Were but a single acre mine,
Blest with the cypress and the pine,
    Contentment might be found;
For, leaving all that men admire,
The cares that vex and joys that fire,
Here I would live, and here expire
    On nature's favorite ground.

Poems (1815), I, 24-26.

New York *Weekly Museum*   October 24, 1801

THE THIRD EPISTLE OF THE FIRST BOOK OF
OVID's TRISTIA.
Translated from the original Latin.

> *Ovid*, one of the best, if not the first of Roman Poets, from some cause of resentment, not specified in history, was banished by the Emperor Augustus to Tomos, (a barbarian city of Scythia) in the sixtieth year of his age----During his continuance in that savage country, which was the last seven years of his life, he wrote a considerable number of poetical epistles to his friends in Italy.----The following is a new translation of one of them, in which the poet in a very affecting manner expatiates on the agonies of grief he experienced on his being condemned to perpetual exile. He particularizes the transactions of the last night he was suffered to remain in Rome, describing in a most exquisite style of melancholy the lamentations of his wife and domestics. He then proceeds to relate some incidents on his voyage to Pontus, and his meeting with a violent tempest in the Ionian sea, in which the mariners nearly gave themselves up for lost.
>
> [The following translation was done by P. *Freneau*]

WHEN to my soul recurs the woeful sight,
The sad remembrance of that parting night,
That night, the source of many a trickling tear,
That snatch'd me far from all my soul held dear;
When I review that night of varied woe,
Grief swells, reflexion wakes, and sorrows flow.

Now had the dawn of that sad morning come
When Caesar bade me leave regretted Rome,
Bid me from all my soul adored depart,
From dear Ausonia, that still holds my heart.

Crazed as I was with anguish and despair
Short time the mandate gave me to prepare;
My bosom heav'd, so urged, so forc'd away,
No moment spar'd me for a longer stay:
No slave, no fond domestic was allow'd,

No kind companion on the watery road;
No vesture fit for exil'd men like me,
Nor monied store, resource in misery.
Like one I stood astonish'd and aghast,
Whom all Jove's vengeance has conspir'd to blast,
Who scarce from death existence may retrieve,
And lively, hardly can that life perceive.

But soon respiring from this palsied state,
Grief came on grief and made my woes complete:
Once more to anguish and to sense restor'd,
I just at parting gave the farewell word,
To friends yet faithful made my last address,
The few that yet felt friendship for distress.

My spouse, my love, half frantic to me clung,
Griev'd as I griev'd and near my bosom hung,
Down her pale cheeks distill'd incessant tears,
Indignant sorrows for a loss like hers;
My daughter, absent on the Libyan coast,
Was yet unconscious of a father lost:
Where'er I look'd, where'er I mov'd or turn'd,
All, all was grief, and all around me mourn'd.
Dark funeral scenes, in all their shades of woe,
Scenes not ficticious were presented now.
About me flock'd a melancholy throng,
Men, females, boys, the aged and the young;
Frantic they came, and wept around my door
When told their Ovid should return no more.

Thus, if with small great things I may compare,
Did Troy, when ravag'd, such an aspect wear!

Now ceas'd the hateful noise of dogs and men,
And near the zenith drove the moon her wane;
I saw--and gazing on my old abode,
Where neighboring to the Capitol it stood,
I cried, Ye immortals, who protect these towers,
These domes and temples,--all ye guardian powers,--
Blest seats, fair domes, the favorites of the skies,
Decreed no more to meet these longing eyes!
Ye Gods, from whom all life all blessings come,

Ye powers, propitious to the fates of Rome,
Farewell forever!--take my last adieu,
The last prostration I can make to you:
Tho' late, too late, I at your shrines am found,
And take the shield when I have met the wound,
Yet pardon grant, and from great Cesar's heart,
When I am gone, let all resentment part:
Say to the heavenly man, forgive, relent,
Nor charge to malice what no malice meant:
What you have seen, who all things see below,
Let too the author of my exile know;
His heart once touch'd, to me it reconciles,
None can be wretched when Augustus smiles.

    In words like these to heavenly powers I pray'd;
In bursts of grief my dame besought their aid,
And, as the altar's sacred flame expires,
She kiss'd, with quiv'ring lips, the dying fires;
Jove she invok'd, but Jove refus'd to hear,
Nor answer'd with assent the fruitless prayer.

[To be continued in our next.]

Poems (1809), I, 5-7.

New York *Weekly Museum*   October 31, 1801

THE THIRD EPISTLE OF THE FIRST BOOK OF OVID's TRISTIA.
Translated from the original Latin.
By P. Freneau.
[Continued from our last.]

NOW, unperceived, the night declin'd away,
The night, refusing long or more delay;
To eastern skies the circling bear had turn'd,
And bleams of morning o'er the mountains burn'd;
What could I do?--the love of home detain'd,

But scarce an hour to linger now remain'd:
My stay how often did the guards unbraid—
"Why urge me thus, where must I go?" I said;
"Consider, friends, I leave my much-lov'd home,
The world's first beauty, and its mistress--Rome."
  How often did I dream some future day
Was fix'd, as fitter, to prolong my stay!
Thrice on the threshold I my step impress'd,
Thrice I return'd at omen'd ills distrest;
My step, obedient to my soul's desire,
Slow and reluctant, strove not to retire:
Oft did I bid farewell, my steps retrace,
And like one dying, give the last embrace;
Repeated charges I before had given,
Lost in distraction, or by madness driven,
And oft review'd, or to forget them strove,
The once dear objects of unhappy love.
  Why should I haste?--to Scythia must I stray--
Rome must I leave?--both might excuse delay;
My wife torn from me, widow'd will remain--
My house--my old, my lov'd domestic train,
Farewell forever! friends, whom faithful found,
More than fraternal friendship to me bound,
Whose hearts, link'd to me by affection true,
(Bound by a stronger tie than Theseus knew)
While yet I can, I will embrace once more,
Since time nor fortune will that bliss restore.
Each hour, each moment while I dare remain,
To me most precious, is a heaven of gain;--
O grant delay!--with words half lost in air,
Again embracing what I held most dear,
I wept,--all wept--meantime the morning star
Beam'd in the east, the day's sad harbinger;
Condemn'd to part, dull, comfortless, forlorn,
Half of myself seem'd from the other torn.
  Thus Priam wept when Jove and adverse fates
To treach'rous Greece unlock'd his Trojan gates.
  Now groans and wailings burst from all around,
They smite their breasts, or in distraction wound:
My dame close to me hung with grief oppress'd,
And, drown'd in tears, these killing words address'd:
  "You must not go--or I will share your fate,

A banish'd woman with her banish'd mate:
Where'er you go I'll constant, faithful prove,
Will follow to the world's last bounds my love;
You to relieve, I every load will bear,
And tend you on the deep with all love's care:
You from your country Cesar's rage expels,
Affection, me--here Cesar's mandate fails."

[To be concluded in our next.]

Poems (1809), I, 7-9.

New York *Weekly Museum*   November 7, 1801

THE THIRD EPISTLE OF THE FIRST BOOK OF OVID's TRISTIA.
Translated from the original Latin.
By P. Freneau.
[*concluded.*]

SHE spoke, and fondly would her suit renew,
Then scarce convinc'd, her rash resolve withdrew.
I *left her*!--here my living death began,
The dreary funeral of a banish'd man!
In garb of woe, my beard, entangled hair,
No longer claim'd their wretched owner's care.
O'erwhelm'd with woes, when morning beam'd its ray,
On the cold ground my weeping consort lay,
Her lovely locks, so long, so late her pride,
Disgrac'd with dust, neglected and untied,
Uncouth hung round her--from the dust she rose,
Deplor'd the widow'd house, bewail'd my woes;
On her lost *Ovid* call'd with frantic moans,
And wept not less with agonizing groans,
Than if her daughter, my Perilla dear,
Lay stretch'd beside me on a funeral bier:
Death she invok'd--in death she wish'd to drown
This rage of grief, these sorrows half her own;

For me alone consenting to survive,
For me, though absent, she might bear to live,
Might still remain, to hope some happier day
Relief would grant, and Cesar's wrath allay,
    Now had the guardian of the northern bear
In ocean dimm'd the radiance of his star--
Embark'd!--my country ne'er to see again,
Reluctant sail'd I on the Ionian main.
Rude was the season, wild, inclement, cold,
But fear of Cesar made the seamen bold.
    Ah me! what tempests sweep this billowy waste,
What sands, in whirlpools from their depths displac'd!
What rage of ocean our poor galley drives,
Through what mad seas the carv'd Apollo dives!
The bellowing winds no rest, no truce allow,
And half the Ionian roars against the prow.
To every shock the batter'd barque rebounds,
And all Jove's winter through the rigging sounds!
Her groaning frame, unus'd such shocks to bear,
Creak'd, sympathizing with my own despair.
Pale, at the helm the trembling pilot stood,
Confess'd his fears, invoked each guardian God,
Relax'd his nervous hand, and rul'd no more
The ship, so pliant to his will before.
    Like him, who by some fiery steed is borne,
Who knows no rule, or knows it but to scorn,
He yields to madness, or to strength the rein,
Nor checks that spirit he would check in vain;
So, at the mercy of the tempest toss'd,
The trembling galley, half in ocean lost,
Forlorn, self-guided, drifts the wat'ry way,
And, plunging, reels, disdaining to obey.
The adverse gales propell'd us to that shore,
The Italian country, I must tread no more;
Far to the left emerg'd the Illyrian waste,--
My eyes once more my native country trac'd,
But left forever!--cease ye winds to blow,
And homeward drive me, where I dare not go.
    Thus while I spoke, and hopeless of return,
The quivering barque by angry seas is torn:
Ye pitying powers, that rule the azure main!
Spare me, O! spare me, and be kind again.

Enough for me, that Jove, my foe declar'd,
Decrees my ruin, and denies regard;
Of life though weary, save me from the deep,
Waft me to Scythia, there to breathe and weep;
Save me, at least, to reach the Pontic coast,
If sav'd he can be who's already lost.

Poems (1809), I, 9-10.

New York *Weekly Museum*   April 16, 1803

REFLECTIONS,
On walking over the ground on Long-Island, near New-York, where many Americans were interred from the Prison Ships, during the war with Great-Britain.
Written July, 1802.

ALONG these banks, throughout this shore,
And underneath the river, more
    Regretted corpses rest,
More crowds, by cruelty consign'd
To death, than shall be told mankind,
    To pain the feeling breast:

More bones of those, who, dying here
In floating prisons, anchored near,
    A prey to fierce disease,
Than fame in her recording page
Shall tell some late, enquiring age,
    When telling things like these.

Ah me!--what ills, what sighs, what groans,
What spectre forms, what moving bones,
    What woes on woes were found!
When here oppress'd, insulted, cross'd,
The vigor of the soul was lost,
    Pale misery hovering round.

Our chief, of firm, undaunted mind,
To climate nor to coast confined,
    All danger taught to bear;
I saw him at the customs clear'd,
I saw him by misfortune steer'd
    To capture and to care.

His ship, that brought us all our woe,
Prepared to meet, not seek, a foe,
    Yet forced at last to yield,
Saw by distress her sickening crew
Half perish in despair--while you,
    Columbia! kept the field.

They sunk, desponding in their bloom--
I help'd to dig the shallow tomb
    Which scarce conceal'd the bones;--
For feeble was the nervous hand
That once could toil, or once command,
    The force of Neptune's sons.

In aid of that immortal cause
Which spurn'd at Europe's iron laws,
    These pass'd the troubled main;
They pass'd the seas she call'd her own,
To meet the minions of a throne,
    And honor's purpose gain.

Too generous!--while that power they prov'd,
To war our hardy rustics mov'd
    And seiz'd the sailor's art,
Met, on his own domain, the foe;
With native valor taught to glow,
    They play'd the warrior's part.

Though night and storms were round them cast,
They climb'd the well supported mast,
    And reef'd the fluttering sail;
Tho' thunders roar'd and lightnings glar'd,
They toil, nor death, nor danger fear'd,
    They brav'd the loudest gale.

Thou, *Independence*, vast design!
The sufferings of the brave were thine,
    When doubtful all and dark;
It was a chaos to explore,
It seem'd all sea without a shore,
    Nor on that sea an ark.

For you the young, the ardent, brave,
Too often met an early grave,
    Unnotic'd and unknown.
On naked shores were seen to lie,
In scorching heats were doom'd to die
    With agonizing groan.

By strength, or chance, if some surviv'd
The fate, which crowds of life depriv'd,
    That life they should devote,
To act in freedom's sacred cause,
To combat tyrants and their laws,
    So felt near this sad spot.

Yes—and the spirit which began
(I swear by all that's great in man)
    That spirit shall go on,
To brighten and illume the mind
'Till tyrants vanish from mankind,
    And tyranny is done.

Monmouth, (New Jersey)
    February 28, 1803.

New York *Public Advertiser*   May 9, 1808

STANZAS,

Written several years ago, on the Long Island shore, near the city of New York, where vast numbers of Americans were interred, or sunk in the river, from the prison and Hospital ships, during the revolutionary war with Great Britain.

Stanza 1: First stanza of the 1803 text, with the following variants:
    line 1: Beneath these hills, along this shore,
    line 2: And underneath the waters more
    line 3: Neglected victims rest;
    line 6: To chill the feeling breast.

Stanza 2: Second stanza of the 1803 text, with the following variants:
    line 2: In floating dungeons, anchored near,
    line 5: Shall tell some late enquiring age,

Stanza 3: Third stanza of the 1803 text, with the following variants:
    line 2: What Spectre forms, what moving moans,
    line 6: From miseries thick'ning sound.

Stanza 4: Fourth stanza of the 1803 text, with the following variants:
    line 1: The youths, of firm undaunted mind,
    line 3: All misery taught to bear--
    line 4: I saw them as the sail they spread–
    line 5: I saw them by misfortune led,

Stanza 5: Ninth stanza of the 1803 text, with the following variants:
    line 6: They brav'd the fiercest gale.

Stanza 6: Fifth stanza of the 1803 text, with the following variants:
    line 1: *Great cause*, that brought them all their woe!
    line 2: Thou, *Freedom*, bade their bosoms glow–
    line 3: But forc'd at last to yield;
    line 4: Died in despair, each sickening crew,
    line 5: They vanish'd from the world–but you,

Stanza 7: Sixth stanza of the 1803 text, with the following variants:
    line 1: They sunk, dejected, in their bloom;

Stanza 8: Seventh stanza of the 1803 text, with the following variants:
    line 2: Which spurn'd at Britain's iron laws,
    line 4: They dar'd those seas, she calls her own,

Stanza 9: Eighth stanza of the 1803 text, revised as follows:
    All gen'rous!--while that power was prov'd,

> To war the bold adventurers mov'd,
> And catch'd the seaman's art;
> Met on their own domain, the crew,
> Of foreign slaves, that never knew
> The independent heart.

Stanza 10: Tenth stanza of the 1803 text, with the following variants:
line 2:   The efforts of the brave were thine,

Stanza 11: Eleventh stanza of the 1803 text, with the following variants:
line 2:   The fate that hosts of life depriv'd,
line 4:   To aid in freedom's sacred cause,
line 6:   So fell near this sad spot!

Stanza 13: Last stanza of the 1803 text.
Signature: F.

Poems (1809), II, 300-02.

City Gazette   July 2, 1804

STANZAS

Written at the Island of Maderia in April last, on the fatal and unprecedented torrents of water which collected from the Mountains, on the 9th of October, 1803, destroyed a considerable part of the city of Funchal, and damaged, to a great amount, several plantations, towns and villages in that neighbourhood.

> THE rude attack, if none will tell,
> On Bacchus, in his favourite Isle;
> If none, in verse, describe it well,
> Or venture, in poetic style
> These devastations to display--
> Ah! listen--and, perhaps, I may.

To those who claim the feeling breast,
This tragic scene I would present,
    Not in romantic colours drest,
Nor merely for the Fancy meant--
        'Tis all a shade of anguish keen,
        With death abounding on the scene.

    From hills, beyond the clouds that soar,
The Vaults of Heaven their floods begun;
    And, rushing with resistless power,
Assail'd the Island of the Sun:--
        Fond Nature saw the blasted Vine,
        And seem'd to sicken and repine.

    As sky-ward stream'd the electric fire,
The Heavens emblazed, or wrapp'd in gloom:
    They now appear, they now retire,
And Bacchus fear'd the time was come
        When all his groves and every plain,
        Should sink to Neptune's shades again.

    The cheerful God, who loves to smile,
And gladness on the world bestows,
    Almost resolv'd to quit this isle;
Then in unusual passion rose,
        Sought his deep caves in sad dismay,
        And left the Fates to have their way.

    The whistling winds had ceas'd to blow:
Not one of all the Aerial train,
    No breath, that bade the waters flow,
Disturb'd the slumbers of the Main;
        In tufted groves they silence kept,
        On mountain tops they soundly slept.

    The bursting rains in seas descend--
Machico heard the distant roar,
    And Lightnings, while the heavens they rend,
Show'd ruin marching to the shore:
        Egyptian darkness intervenes
        To shroud the horror of such scenes.

   The heavens on fire, the floods broke loose,
Seiz'd forests, vineyards, herds, and men--
  Calyetta sighed, and *Santa Cruz*
Saw ancient chaos come again.
     Through *Fonchial* the deluge raves
     And half repell'd old Ocean's waves.

   Ill fated town!--What works of pride
In one short hour were swept away!
   Huge piles that long had time defy'd
In ruthless ruin scattered lay!
     Some buried in the adjacent deep--
     With crowds dismiss'd to endless sleep.

   From her fond arms the Daughter torn,
The Mother saw destruction near:
   Both on the whirling surge were borne,
Scarce time to weep the parting tear.
     Life hardly found, with feeble cries,
     The Mother dead--the Infant dies.

   Her dear delight, her darling Boy,
In morn of days and morning bloom;
   This opening bud of promis'd joy,
Too early found a watry tomb,
     Or floated on the briny waste,
     No more belov'd, no more embrac'd!

   From cliffs enhaz'd, with force unknown
Enormous rocks and mangled trees
   Were headlong hurl'd, and hurrying down,
Took a new station in the seas:
     On Neptune's stormy bosom cast,
     In rolling gulphs they fix'd at last.

   The saintly tribes, who guard the domes,
Where stern Religion loves to come,
   Forsook their Gods, or left their homes,
With consternation almost dumb:
     In silent awe aghast they stood,
     Or dreamt once more of Noah's flood.

And *Santa Clara's* gloomy walls,
Where pines through life the pious Nun,
(Whose aspect to the mind recalls
What superstition's power has done)--
      No conquest there the floods presum'd,
      So beauty stays to be entomb'd!

What seem'd beyond destruction's reach,
Was soon demolish'd or displac'd;
Not even *our Lady of the Beach,*
With all her Saints, this deluge fac'd.
      Some mouldering walls alone remain,
      Which Priests and Monks bewail in vain.

Hard was her fate!--More happy thou,
The *Lady of the Mountain tall*:
When desolation raged below,
She stood secure and scorn'd it all,
      Where *Gordon** for retirement chose,
      His Groves, his Gardens, and the Muse.

Who on the Valley's rugged bed
E'er plans a street or builds again,
Unthinking as the Brazen Head,
Builds to posterity a pain--
      A Church, a Dome, that soon or late
      Must share the same, or worse a fate.

Let some vast Bridge supply their place,
Like those the Romans rais'd of yore,
Of strength--as firm as Nature's base,
To vent the Deluge to the shore.
      Thus may the existing race engage
      The thanks of a succeeding age.

Pontinia long must wear the marks
Of this wide wasting source of woe,
Where, near the Loo, the Tar embarks,
And now less angry currents flow--
      Those ruins, Jack, shall Time repair;
      But you and I--will not be there.

---

* *William Gordon. Esq. of Madeira.*

GENERAL NOTE.

From the best accounts that could be procured at Madeira in April last, there perished in and near the city of Funchal, five hundred and fifty persons. The ravages were chiefly confined to the eastern parts of the town, where the loss was immense in bridges, houses, streets and other property, public as well as private--There was one magnificent church totally destroyed, standing near the sea, and called in the Portuguese tongue, Nossa Senyora da Caillou (Lady of the Beach) besides this, there were five handsome chapels carried away. Five very considerable streets with their immense stone buildings have entirely disappeared, or but some insignificant parts remaining. The water rose in a short space of time from 14 to 15 feet in the adjacent parts of the city, and bursting into the buildings, where it did not much injure the latter, it greatly damaged the mercantile property lodged therein. There were about two hundred persons supposed to be lost in other parts of the island, particularly in the villages, and small towns. The following circumstance, it was asserted, added not a little to the devastations occasioned by the accumulation of water in the vallies. The late Governor, with several other considerable landholders in the mountains, had, for several years back, been in the practice of erecting stone dams across the vast and spacious valley above the city, at different intervals of distance, for the purpose of watering the adjacent grounds, or leading off streams in a variety of directions--when the immense body of rain fell in October last, all this gave way, and carried death and destruction therewith.

Poems (1815), I, 171-76.

City Gazette   July 9, 1804

STANZAS
Written at *Oratava*, in view of the *Peak* of *Teneriffe*, 1804.

No mean, no vulgar artist laid
The base of this prodigious pile,
The towering *Peak*--but Nature said,
"Let this adorn *Tenaria's* isle;
    "Be this for years and centuries found
    "The Polar Star to islands round."

The spiry point, that meets the skies,
Indebted to Volcanic fire;
Thus from the ocean bid to rise,
To Heaven was suffer'd to aspire;
    But man, ambitious, did not dare
    To fix one habitation there:

For torrents from the mountain came,
What melted rocks were seen to flow!
What arrowy sheets of vivid flame,
To deluge all that lay below!
    These older than the historian's page,
    Once bellow'd forth vext Nature's rage.

In ages past (as may again)
Such Lavas from these heights have run,
And hastening to the astonish'd main,
Disclos'd earth's entrails to the sun;
    These, barren once, neglected, dead,
    Are now with groves and pastures spread.

That plastic power, the solar ray,
Descending showers, and evening dews,
Have form'd a soil from slow decay,
Whose herbage in profusion grows;
    The stately palm, the unequall'd pine,
    The dulcet cane, the generous vine.

Upon the gaily verdant lawn
The flowers a thousand sweets disperse,

And pictures, there by nature drawn,
Inspire some island poet's verse;
    While streams through every valley rove,
    To bless the garden and the grove.

To blast a scene above all praise,
Should fate at length be so severe,
May not this hap' in *Julia's* days,--
While *Barrey* dwells, all honor'd, here--
    While *Little* lives, of generous mind,
    Or *Armstrong,* social as refin'd.

New York *Weekly Museum*   August 25, 1804

Underneath title: (By P. *Freneau.*)

In each stanza, lines 1 and 3 begin at margin, lines 2 and 4 indented three spaces, and lines 5 and 6 indented five spaces.

Stanza 1, line 4: "Let this adorn *Tymaria's* isle;

Poems (1815), I, 177-78.

Port Folio   October 17, 1807   (Part of extended review)

First newspaper appearance of "An Author's Soliloquy," *Miscellaneous Works* (1788), 170-71; "The Author," *Poems* (1795), 326-27. Three stanzas of the 1795 text, untitled, are reprinted and introduced as follows:

> The poet, as well as the oratour, is to be encouraged in his race *clamore plausuque*; our authour, however, if we may judge from the following lines, appears to have anticipated little of either:

Stanza 1:   First stanza of the 1795 text.
Stanze 2:   Third stanza of the 1795 text, with the following variants:

line 5:   But those condemn'd to stand alone,
line 12: Which only help'd to swell his fame.
Stanza 3:   First six lines of the fourth stanza of the 1795 text.

New York *Public Advertiser*   March 3, 1809[1]

LINES

ADDRESSED TO MR. JEFFERSON,
On his approaching retirement from the presidency of the United States.

Presenti tibi maturos largimur honores.   HOR.

To you, great sir, our heart-felt praise we give,
And your ripe honours yield you--while you live.

AT length the year which marks his course expires,
And *Jefferson* from public life retires,
That year, the close of years which owns his claim,
And gives him all his merit, all his fame.
Far in the heaven of fame I see him fly,
Safe in the realms of immortality;
On *equal worth* his honor'd mantle falls,
Him, whom Columbia her joint patriot calls,
Him, whom we saw her codes of freedom plan,*
To none inferior in the ranks of man.

---

* It is generally understood, that the constitution of the United States, now in force, in most of the important particulars, was the draft of Mr. Madison's pen.

[1] Leary notes an earlier appearance of this poem in the Trenton *True American*, March 2, 1809. However, the paper was not printed on that day, and I could find the poem in no earlier issue.

When to the helm of state your country call'd,
No danger awed you and no fear appall'd:
Each bosom, faithful to its country's fame,
Hail'd Jefferson, that long applauded name
All then was dark, and wrongs on wrongs accru'd,
Our treasures lavish'd, and our strength subdu'd.
What eight long years of war and blood had gain'd,
Was lost, abandon'd, squander'd, or restrain'd;
Britannia's tools had schemed their *easier way*
To conquer, ruin, pillage, or betray;
Domestic traitors with exotic join'd,
To shackle this last refuge of mankind,
Wars were provok'd, and France was made our foe,
That George's race might govern all below,
O'er this wide world unchek'd, unbounded, reign,
Seize every clime and subjugate the main.

All this was seen, and rising in your might,
By genius aided, you reclaim'd our right,
That right, which conquest, arms, and valour gave
To this young country, not to live a slave.

And what but toil has your long service seen,
Dark tempests gathering o'er a sky serene?--
For wearied years no treasured gold can pay,
No fame, nor all the plaudits of that day
Which now returns you to your rural shade
The sages' heaven, for our chiefs and patriots made,
Who, like the *Romans,* in their country's cause,
Exert their valour, or enforce its laws,
And late retiring, every wrong redress'd,
Give their last days to solitude and rest.

This great reward a generous nation yields,
Regret attends you to your native fields,
Their grateful thanks for every service done,
And hope, your thorny race of care is done.

From your sage counsels what effects arise!
The angry Briton from our waters flies;
His thundering ships no more our coasts assail,
But seize the advantage of the western gale.

Though bold and bloody, warlike, proud, and fierce,
They shun your vengeance for a murder'd *Pearce*,
And starv'd, dejected, on some hungry shore,
Sigh for the country they shall rule no more.

    Long in the assemblies of your native land
We saw you firm, unchang'd, intrepid stand--
When the firm *Congress,* still too firm to yield,
Staid masters of the long contested field,
Your wisdom aided what their councils fram'd--
By you the murderous savages are tam'd--
That *Independence* we had sworn to gain,
By you asserted, (nor declar'd in vain,)
We seiz'd, indignant, from a tyrant's throne,
And Britain totter'd when the work was done.

    You, when an angry faction vex'd the age,
Rose to your place at once, and check'd their rage;
The envenom'd shafts of malice you defy'd,
And turn'd all projects of *Revolt* aside;
We saw you libell'd by the *worst of men*,
While hell's red lamp hung quiv'ring o'er his pen,
And fiends, congenial, every effort try
To blast that merit which shall never die.--
These had their hour, and traitors wing'd their flight
To aid the screechings of distracted night.--
Vain were their hopes--the poinson'd darts of hell
Glanced from your flinty shield, and harmless fell.

    All this you bore, beyond it all you rose,
Nor ask'd despotic laws to crush your foes;
Mild was your language, temperate, though severe,
And not less potent than *Ithuriel's* spear
To *touch* the infernals in their loathsome guise,
Confound their slanders and detect their lies.--

    All this you brav'd--and now what task remains
But silent walks on solitary plains,
To illume the statesmen of the time to come
With the firm spirit of primeval Rome;
To taste the joys your long try'd service brings
And look with pity on the care of kings;

To bid the vast luxuriant harvest grow,
The slave be happy and secure from woe--
Whether, with Newton, you the heavens explore
And trace through nature the creating power,
Or if with morals you reform the age,
(Alike, in all, the patriot and the sage,)
May peace and soft repose attend you still,
In the lone vale or on the cloud-cap'd hill,
While smiling plenty decks the abounding plain,
And hails *Astrea** to the world again.

Poems (1815), II, 24-27.

True American   April 24, 1809

> *The following Verses were handed to the Editor of this paper, in manuscript, written at Fundeal, in the island of Maderia, by Capt. P. Freneau, July, 1803.*

Arrived at *Madeira*, the island of vines
    Where mountains and vallies abound,
Where the sun the mild juice of the cluster refines,
    And gladdens the magical ground;

As I trifled and strayed in her elegant shade,
    Now resting, and now on the move,
Old *Bacchus* I met, with a crown on his head,
    In the darkest recess of a grove.

I met him with awe, but no feeling of fear
    As I roved by his mountains and springs;
When he said with a sneer, "how dare you come here,
    You hater of despots and kings?

---

* The goddess of justice, among the Romans.

"Do you know that a royal,* a regent renown'd
    Resides in this island of wine,
Whose fame on the earth has encircled its round,
    And spreads from the pole to the line?

"Haste away with your barque, on the foam of the main,
    To *Charleston* I bid you repair;
There drink your hot whiskey that maddens the brain,
    You shall have no *Madeira*, I swear!"

Dear Bacchus, I answered--ah, why so severe?
    Since your nectar abundantly flows,
Permit me one cargo--without it, I fear,
    Columbians will soon come to blows:

I left them in wrangles, disorder, and strife,
    (Political feuds were so high)
I was sick of the people, and sick of my life,
    And almost petitioned to die.

The Deity smiled, and said, "I relent,
    For the sake of your coming so far,
Here, drink of my goblet, go tell them repent,
    And cease their political war.

"With the cargo I send I surely intend
    To hush them to peace and repose:
With this present of wine, on the wings of the wind
    You shall travel--and tell them, here goes

"A health to old Bacchus, who sends them the best
    Of the liquor his island affords,
The soul of the feast and the joy of the guest,
    Too good for your monarchs or lords.

"No rival I own on this insular waste,
    Alone will I govern the isle,

---

    * The Prince-Royal of Portugal, then regent of the Kingdom; the Queen Mother being insane.

With a king at my feet, and a court to my taste,
    And all in a popular style:

"And somewhat there is *in the order of things,*
    (To me it is perfectly plain)
That determines the ruin of despots and kings,
    And that only king *Bacchus* remain."

Poems (1815), I, 169-71.

New York *Public Advertiser*   November 11, 1809

LINES

Occasioned by the late disaster of one of the Paulus Hook passage-boat's upsetting from which accident one of our citizens was drowned and the remainder on board narrowly escaped.

    I saw a barque on Hudson's wave that plies,
Yield to the blast that rends the autumnal skies;
From Cortlandt's wharf she took her vent'rous way
Rude gloom'd the sky, and blustering was the day.
The fatal blast too powerful prov'd for art,
With pain I saw the shivering sail depart:
In vain the helm by cautious hands was held,
One flaw upset her and the skies prevail'd;
One worthy man, I tell with grief sincere,
One worthy man* was doom'd to perish there--
Leave all behind that could attract his love,
Without one farewell at this last remove.
    All you who on this rugged *Hudson* stray,
To seek fair Jersey's coast, or Bergen Bay,
Let sense direct, let prudence reign supreme,

---

* *Mr. Delaplaine.*

Let every future voyage be by *steam*;
Let *Fulton's* art, unrivalled art, prevail,
Nor trust existence to the dangerous sail;
Bid him apply the powers that reason gave,
To waft you safely o'er the treacherous wave;
On his firm deck you may all safety find,
Nor dread the madness of the threatening wind.
See *Neptune's Car*, a floating palace move,
And fears no danger from the blasts above--
No tides delay her, and no gales alarm,
The power of *steam* can every blast disarm.
Be such your choice--on such a barque rely--
And every danger of the winds defy.

New York *Evening Post* November 11, 1809

An insertion of the following will oblige
A *Lady*.
(Title as above)

line 6: With tears I saw the shivering sail depart!
line 9: One worthy man--I say, with grief sincere,
line 13: Not indented.
line 24: And fear no danger from the blasts above--

New York *Journal* November 11, 1809

line 8: One flaw upset her and the wind prevail'd:

Poems (1815), II, 29-30.

Fredonia   August 11, 1814

THE VOLUNTEER'S MARCH.

Ye, whom *Washington* has led,
Ye, who in his footsteps tread,
Ye, who death nor danger dread
    Haste to glorious victory.

Now's the day, and now's the hour;
See the British navy lower,
See approach proud George's power,
    England! chains and slavery.

Who will be a traitor knave,
Who can fill a cowards grave,
Who so base to be a slave?
    Traitor, coward, turn and flee.

Meet the tyrants, one and all,
Freemen stand or freemen fall,
At *Columbia's* patriot call,
    At her mandate, march away!

By her sons in servile chains--
By oppression's woes and pains--
We will bleed from all our veins
    But they shall be--shall be free.

Lay the proud invaders low,
Tyrants fall in every foe,
Liberty's in every blow,
    Forward! let us do or die!

New York *Columbian*   September 7, 1814

THE VOLUNTEERS' MARCH.
*[A Parody from Burns--although published in the Fredonian,
and offered here, as original.]*

    Stanza 3, line 1: Who would be a traitor knave--
            line 2: Who would fill a coward's grave--

Stanza 5: Former times have seen them yield,
Seen them drove from every field,
Routed, ruin'd, or repell'd:
    Seize the spirit of those times!

Stanza 6: Fifth stanza of the *Fredonian* text, with the following variants:
line 1: By oppression's woes and pains--
line 2: By our sons in servile chains--

Stanza 7: O'er the standard of their power
Bid Columbia's eagle tower,
Give them hail in such a shower,
    As shall blast them, horse and man.

Stanza 8: Sixth stanza of the *Fredonian* text.

Poems (1815), II, 43-44.

New York *Columbian*   September 24, 1814

THE BATTLE OF STONINGTON.

Three gallant ships from England came,
Freighted deep with fire and flame,
And other things we need not name,
    To have a dash at Stonington.

Now safe arrived--their work begun--
They thought to make the Yankees run,
And have a mighty deal of fun,
    In stealing sheep at Stonington.

A Yankee, then, popp'd up his head,
And parson Jones's sermon read,
In which the reverand doctor said,
    That they must fight for Stonington.

The ships advancing several ways,
The Britons soon began to blaze,
And put the old women in amaze,
    Who fear'd the loss of Stonington!

The Yankees to their fort repaired,
And made as though they little cared,
For all their shot--though very hard
    They blazed away on Stonington.

The Ramilies began the attack,
And Nimrod made a mighty crack,
And none can tell what kept them back,
    From setting fire to Stonington.

The old razee, with red hot ball,
Soon made a farmer's barrack fall,
And did a cow-house sadly maul,
    That stood a mile from Stonington.

The bombs were thrown, the rockets flew,
But not a man of all their crew,
(Though every man was full in view)
    Could kill a man of Stonington.

They have their turn, they thought but fair--
The Yankees brought two guns to bear,
And, sir, it would have made you stare,
    To see the smoke at Stonington!

They bored the Nimrod through and through,
And killed and mangled half her crew,
When riddled, crippled, she withdrew,
    And cursed the boys of Stonington.

The Ramilies gave up the fray,
And with her comrades, sneak'd away--
Such was the valor, on that day,
    Of British tars at Stonington.

But some assert, on certain grounds,
Beside the damage and the wounds,
It cost their king ten thousand pounds,
    To have a dash at Stonington.

Poems (1815), II, 45-47.

New York *Columbian*   September 29, 1814

TO THE SQUADRONS ON THE LAKES.

The brilliant stage to you assign'd,
Claims every effort of the mind,
And every energy combined,
        To crush the foe.

Where'er they sail, you must be there,
Where'er they lurk you will not spare
The blast of death--but all things dare,
        To hurl them low.

Your country's wrongs are all your own,
And to the world the word has gone,
Our *Independence* must to none
        Be signed away.

Be to your country's standard true,
To Britain and to Europe shew,
That you can fight and conquer too,
        And prostrate lay

That bitter foe, whose thousands rise
No more can fight us *in disguise*,
But count our freedom for their prize,
        If valor fails.

Beneath your feet let fears be cast--
Remember deeds of valor past,
And nail your colors to the mast,
        And spread your sails:

In all the pride and pomp of war
Let thunders from your cannon roar,
And lightnings flash from shore to shore,
        To wing the ball;

Let *Huron* from his slumbers wake,
Bid *Champlain* to his centre shake,
'Till foundering, in *Ontario's* Lake,
        You swamp them all.

September 8.

Poems (1815), II, 51-52.

Fredonian   September 29, 1814

A DIALOGUE
AT WASHINGTON'S TOMB:
Between the Genius of Virginia, and Virginia.

Genius.----Who are those that, prowling, come,
   Washington, too near thy tomb?
   Are they those, who long before,
   Sail'd to subjugate the shore;
   Are they those whom he repell'd,
   Captur'd, or imprison'd held;
   Or the sons of those of old,
   Cast in Nature's iron mould;
   Bold Virginia! can it be?
   What a stain is laid on thee!

Virginia.----Such a stain as I do swear,
   Fills my swelling heart with care
   How to wash away that stain,
   How to be myself again.
   From my breast the hero rose,
   In my soil his bones repose--
   But this insult to thy shade,
   Washington, shall be repaid.

Genius.----Dear Virginia, tell me how?
   Tell me not, or tell me now--
   Can you wield the bolts of Jove,
   Call the lightnings from above;
   Tear the mountain from its base
   To confound that hated race,
   Who, with hostile step presume
   To approach the sacred tomb
   Of my bravest, noblest son--
   Of the Immortal Washington?

Virginia.----Not the artillery of the sky,
   Not the vengeance from on high
   Did I want, to guard my son--
   I have lightnings of my own--
   But I wanted--------------!!!

Genius.--------------Wanted what?--

Virginia.----Men in war's hard practice taught,
      Men of fire and men of thought;
      All their spirits in a glow,
      Ever ready for a foe;
      Fit to stand the hostile shock,
      Sturdy as the mountain oak,
      Prompt to act, and well prepared,
      Active, steady, on their guard:
      Such I wanted to repel
      Sons of Britain, sons of h-ll--
      These--I say it with regret--
      I wanted, and must want them yet.

Genius.----By the powers that guard this spot,
      Want them longer you shall not;
      I, the Genius of your land,
      I this hour will take command,
      And inspire in every breast,
      Thirst of vengeance for the past;
      Vengeance, that from shore to shore
      Shall dye your bay with English gore;
      And see them leave their thousands slain,
      If they dare to land again--
      This is all I have to say,
      Seize your armor--let's away!--

September 8.

Poems (1815), II, 76-78.

Fredonian   September 29, 1814

THE PRINCE REGENT'S RESOLVE.

The Regent Prince, enraged to find
The standard from his frigate's torn,
To a full court thus spoke his mind
With hand display'd and soul of scorn:
    "Since fate decreed Napoleon's fall,
    "Now is the time to conquer ALL.

"We, at the head of all that's great--
" 'Tis ours to keep the world in awe:
"Let Louis reign in regal state,
"And let his armies own his law;
    "Their tide of power 'tis our's to stem,
    "We'll govern those who govern them.

"A land there lies towards the West--
"There *must* our royal WILL be done!
"That land is an infernal nest
"Of reptiles, rul'd by *Madison*.
    "That nest I swear to humble down,
    "There plant a king, and there a crown!

"Depart my fleet, depart my slaves!
"Invade that nest! attack and burn!
"Wherever ocean rolls its waves
"Subdue--or dare not to return:
    "Subdue--and plunder all you can,
    "Who plunders most shall be--my man!

"To scatter death with fire and sword,
"To prostrate all where'er you go--
"That is the mandate, that the word,
"Though seas of blood around you flow!
    "No more!--go--aid the Indian yell,
    "Be conquerors--and--I'll feed you well."--

So spoke the Prince--but little knew
His minions were for slaughter fed;
Nor did he guess that vengeance too

Must fall on his devoted head;
    And all his plans and projects fail,
    And he be sent to--Satan's Jail.

September 1814.

Poems (1815), II, 53-54.

Fredonian   November 10, 1814

A ROYAL DIALOGUE, &c. &c.

    Says the *Goth* to the *Vandal* (the Prince to the King)
Let us do a *mad* action, to make the world ring;
With Wellington's army we now have the means.
A slap at the STATES, has been long my desire,
To waste, and destroy them by famine and fire,
My vengeance to carry thro' village and town,
And even to batter their *Capitol* down.

    The *Vandal* then answered, and said to the *Goth*,
Son George, with yourself, I am equally wroth:
Of Wellington's army dispose as you please,
It is best, I believe, they should go beyond seas,
For, would they come home, I can easily shew
The hangman would have much duty to do.

So, away came the *Britons*, and when they came here,
Some mischief they did, but excited no fear;
They came to "*correct*," and they came to "*chastise*,"
And do all the evil that h-ll could devise.

At Washington City they burnt and destroy'd
'Till among the big buildings they made a sad void,
Then back to their shipping they flew like the wind
But left many more than five hundred behind
Of wounded and dead (and, others say double)
And thus was the hangman excused from his trouble.

Alexandria beheld them in battle array–
Alexandria they plundered a night and a day;
Then away they retreated, with too little loss,
Their forces conducted by Cockburn and Ross.

At Baltimore, next, was their plan of attack,
But Baltimore drove them repeatedly back.
The forts were assailed by the strength of their fleet,
And the forts in disorder beheld them retreat,
Torn, shattered and crippled, so mangled and sore
That the tide of *Patapsco* was red with their gore.

Their legions by land no better succeeded,
In vain they manoevred, in vain they paraded,
Their hundreds on hundreds were strew'd on the ground;
Each shot from our Rifles brought death or a wound;
One shot, with the others, completed their loss,
And their columns were headed no longer by Ross.

Where they mean to go next, we can hardly surmise,
But home they would go, if their leaders were wise,
We have beat them before, and can beat them again
On the lakes of the west or the Lake of Champlain;
On the land or the water to face them we join
And soon will contend with their ships of the line.

September 12.

Poems (1815), II, 78-81.

True American   June 15, 1822[1]

LINES
On the loss of the ship Albion, CAPT. WILLIAMS, *Wrecked near Kinsale Harbor, in Ireland, on the 22d of April last.*

BY CAPTAIN FRENEAU.

As near the cliffs of old *Kinsale*
   The *Albion* ploughed her desperate way,
From southern skies a threatening gale
   Howled thro' the shrouds and sung dismay:
Though bursting seas her sides assail'd,
No spirit drooped or efforts failed.

In weathering this too fatal shore,
   The land a-lee predicted ills,
Presaging she should see no more
   Dear *Sandy Hook* or *Jersey Hills:*
No more *Manhattan's* isle review,
The port, from which *at first* she flew.

"Cheer up, my friends, the Captain said,
   "We yet may shun the dangers nigh;
"When morning dawn shall be displayed,
   "The gale may break, and clear the sky,
"And then we soon *Old England* greet,
"With cheery hearts, and flowing sheet!"

The word was given--the canvas braced--
   The bow lines hauled--she dashed away,
Well trimm'd, the high, black wave she faced
   In hopes to pass St. George's sea,*
Her well known harbor to attain,
And ride on Mersey's+ stream again.

---

* The Channel of Ireland.
+ The river Mersey, on which stands the city of Liverpool.
[1] This poem and "On National Prospects and Improvements" (*New York Statesman*, July 27, 1822) were the only two poems published after 1815 under the poet's full signature.

That moment from distracted skies,
    The gallant *Albion* felt a blast
That human skill, or strength defies,
    And made a wreck of every mast!
With what a force, no tongue can tell,
The sails were split--the cordage fell!

'Twas *then* the worthy *Williams* cried,
    "Dear comrades, I command no more!
"Our doom is fixed, the swelling tide
    "Impels our barque to yonder shore;
"And *there* with all her costly freight,
"My noble ship* must meet her fate.

"A floating mass, a hulk she lies--
    "She takes her last tremendous roll,
"And fortune every hope denies
    "To shun the reef, or clear the shoal:
"No help, no port, no safety nigh,
" 'Tis ours to yield, and ours to die!"

He spoke--she struck, with thund'ring sound;
    The shrieks were heard that rent the sky,
And total ruin stalked around--
    But soon was hushed each fearful cry,
When o'er them burst the last high wave,
To all, or most, a watry grave.+

June 8.

---

    * The Albion was built about three years since in New York, and justly reckoned one of the finest ships of the mercantile class ever constructed in America. She was upwards of 500 tons burthen.
    + Forty-eight perished out of fifty-six.

New York Statesman June 15, 1822

The poem is introduced as follows:

> [The following poetical effusion, on a subject which has awakened the melancholy tones of many a lyre, both in this country and Europe, is from the pen of the veteran bard whom we mentioned a few days since, and who is now in his seventy-second year.] [1]

On the loss of the packet ship ALBION, *Captain Williams.*

Substantively identical to the *True American* text, except for the following variants:

In each stanza, the first four lines begin at the margin, and lines 5 and 6 are indented.

Stanza 1, line 5: Though boisterous seas her sides assail'd,
          line 6: No courage droop'd nor efforts failed.

Stanza 2, line 1: On weathering this too fatal shore,

Stanza 3, line 6: With wind abaft and flowing sheet.

Stanza 4, line 4: In hopes to gain St. *George's* sea,
          line 5: Her well known station to attain,

Stanza 5, line 3: That human strength and skill defies,
          line 6: The sails were cleft, the cordage fell!

Stanza 6: Includes eight lines.
          lines 1-4: first four lines of the *True American* Stanza 6.
          line 5: And *there*–as none appears to save,
          line 6: My noble ship must find a grave!–

---

[1] On June 11, 1822, the *Statesman* had included a poem, "The Military Ground," which first appeared in the *True American*, signed "R." (See appendix of "Probable Atrributions," *True American*, June 8, 1822.) Although unsigned, the text is introduced by the editor as follows:

line 7: Yes!--there, will all her costly freight,
line 8: This gallant ship must meet her fate!
(lines 5-8 all indented.)

Stanza 7, line 3: Our fortune every hope denies,
        line 6: 'Tis ours to yield, 'tis ours to die!

(Last stanza and all footnotes of the *True American* text ommitted.)

Fredonian   June 27, 1822

On the loss of the Packet ship Albion, *Captain Williams,* of *New-York*.

Substantively identical to the *True American* text, except for the following variants:

In each stanza, the first four lines begin at the margin, and the remaining lines are indented.

Stanza 1, line 4: Howl'd through her shrouds, and sung dismay;
        line 5: Though boisterous seas her flanks assail'd

Stanza 2, line 1: On weathering this too fatal shore,

[The following effusion is from the pen of a poet and patriot of the revolution, who is now in his seventy-second year, but whose body and mind, owing to a life of temperance and exercise, are still vigorous. His poetry, like that of Humphrey, often nerved the arm of the revolutionary soldier; and it is not strange, that his muse still loves to dwell on themes, and to linger around scenes, associated with other times and other men. There are few instances, in which Fancy lives to the age of three score and ten.--Cumberland, we believe, was about seventy, when he wrote his Retrospection; but such efforts in the decline of life are rare. The venerable author of the following lines has our warmest wishes, that the pleasures of literature may smoothe the declivity of age, and that he may be blest with frequent visitations of the Muse.]   *Ed. Statesman.*

Stanza 3: The Heavens in black their stars with-held,
A morning carpet veil'd the sky,
The hovering clouds in mists conceal'd
The reefs so near, and rocks so high.
    What, now, was skill?--what skill could do,
    Was try'd, and strength, and vigour too.

Stanza 4: Third stanza of the *True American* text, with the following variants:
line 2: We yet may shun the dangers near,
line 4: The gale may break, the heavens may clear;
line 6: With wind abaft, and flowing sheet!"

Stanza 5: Fourth stanza of the *True American* text, with the following variants:
line 1: The word was given--the yards were braced,
line 4: In hopes to gain St. George's sea;
line 5: Her well known station to attain,

Stanza 6: Fifth stanza of the *True American* text, with the following variants:
line 1: That instant from distracted skies,
line 3: That human power or force defies,
line 5: With what a shock I grieve to tell,
line 6: Her spars were broke, her cordage fell!

Stanza 7: Sixth stanza of the *Statesman* text, with the following variants:
line 1: 'Twas then the worthy *Williams* said,
line 8: My gallant *Albion* meets her fate.

Stanza 8: Seventh stanza of the *True American* text, with the following variants:
line 3: Our Fortune every hope denies
line 5: No help, no friend, no safety nigh,

Stanza 9: Last stanza of the *True American* text.

(All footnotes to the *True American* text deleted.)

New York Statesman   July 27, 1822[1]

The poem is introduced as follows:

> [An incorrect copy of the following stanzas having appeared in several papers, Mr. Freneau, the author, has requested us to publish the following, as revised by himself.]

On National Prospects and Improvements.
BY P. FRENEAU.

In this wide world, where'er she sketch'd her plan,
Dame Nature left one arduous task to man;
If she created soils, and coasts, and climes,
In distant regions and in different times,
While all began in universal love,
To man she gave her mandate–to improve.

She said, "a world of wonders I display,
In winter blasted as in summer gay;
In spring producing--autumn ripening all,
Such is my process on this wandering ball,
While all the west, and all that live beside,
Hold the same order, with their wants supplied,
To man I gave the power, the art, the skill
To mould creation's surface, at his will,
Oceans to tame, rude forests to reduce,
Enjoy my toils and turn them to his use."

Here, rivers flow, while cataracts intervene,
There, mountains rise, to discompose the scene,
But all, subjected, yields to man's control;
His is the task to reign where oceans roll,
To level mountains, or exalt the plain,
To act, contrive, like nature's self again.

---

[1] The only other appearance of this poem that I found was in the *True American*, May 25, 1822, where it appeared unattributed. That text varies from this one only accidentally; it displays a number of typographical errors, incorrect use of the apostrophe, and confusing punctuation.

But, of the millions who inhabit here,
The tenants of this sublunary sphere,
Amongst the countless thousands of mankind
How few exist, of a discerning mind!
How few aspire on reason's scale to rise,
And soar above the dust, they should despise;
To look through Nature, trace her vast design,
And copy nature's author, all divine.

How much we owe to those in every age
Who search, with active thought, through Nature's page:
Who think, explore, compare, design, contrive,
And, agents from above, keep man alive.

Columbia, too, may boast her honored names,
And more then *one* her grateful tribute claims;
Patriots exist, that claim no common share
Of well-earn'd fame, which time shall ne'er impair,
Men, to whose worth, in ancient story told,
Greece might have rear'd her statues cast in gold,
And Rome, even Rome, in her most virtuous days,
Rome might have built her monuments of praise.

In their own time shall they all hearts engage;
Or wait the honors of another age?
Wastes that for ages heard the savage yell
The force of Genius to mankind may tell.
Plains smile where rugged forests frowned before,
See cities rise on wild Ontario's shore;
See savage manners hastening to decay;
See commerce fix at bleak Sandusky's Bay;
See vast canals an infant world embrace,
And Art's great works improve wild Nature's face,
All, all subjected to the powers of man,
A world redeem'd from Nature's ruder plan.

To crown the whole, see Freedom's sons achieve
What few presumed and fewer would believe;
The wide Missouri spreads the social life,
And Christian love succeeds to Indian strife.
Hark! Asia's shores attend to freedom's sound,
And echoes from Kamschatka's cliffs rebound.

To thee, Columbia, once a monarch's slave,
Indulgent heaven the cheering prospect gave,
Of man renewed, and acting unconfined,
Lord of creation, with an upright mind.

She kings and despots from her soil has hurled,
And a bold front presents to either world,
Whether her *States* to western seas extend,
Or, bounded in the west, on mountains end,
Still, with her banners and her stars displayed,
Her great example will be well repaid;
And man be taught that all he owns or gains
Is due to genius that triumphant reigns,
While worlds remain, or man, to act his part,
Claims, or respects the merits of the heart.

INTRODUCTION TO THE APPENDIXES

As indicated earlier, in the comments on attribution in the general introduction, I have included the complete newspaper texts only of those poems which later appeared, however revised, in one of Freneau's collections and of those few uncollected poems that first appeared in newspapers under his full signature. However, previous scholars have attributed, with varying degrees of conviction, other poems to Freneau, some of which, I believe, are quite probably his contributions, and many more quite possibly. In these appendixes, I have cited every newspaper poem that has ever been attributed to Freneau by any Freneau scholar in any scholarly publication. I have also cited several other poems, heretofore unattributed, that I consider probably or possibly Freneau's. These appendixes exclude those poems uncollected by Freneau but attributed to him only by his contemporaries, primarily those newspaper editors who indiscriminately attributed to Freneau any poem extracted from papers which he edited.

The attributions have been divided into three appendixes, on the basis of the available evidence linking them to Freneau—probable, possible, and unlikely or erroneous attributions. In each appendix, the poems are listed chronologically, by earliest newspaper appearance. Under the title of the poem, I have cited the source of the attribution, indicating, by paraphrase, the basis of the ascription, as provided by the source, and the degree of certainty with which the ascription was made. Finally, a summary of all the evidence that I have accumulated for or against the attribution is provided for each poem.

All poems cited in these appendixes lack the one essential qualification for inclusion in the edition—they never appeared, in any published form, excluding unauthorized reprints, under the poet's full signature. The probable attributions are validated by all or most of the following criteria: in theme and manner, they are similar to other poems known to be Freneau's; they were first published in newspapers to which Freneau contributed during periods when poems known to be his were appearing; they seem to refer specifically to known facts about Freneau himself; specific parallels can be cited to other poems known to be Freneau's; they were signed with pseudonyms also attached to poems collected by Freneau. In some cases the attributions are so probable that the *only* basis for excluding them from the edition is that they never appeared under Freneau's full signature. But even in these cases, I believe, a reliable edition of the poet must exclude these texts, for the reasons provided in the comments on attribution in the general introduction. Because of the liberal newspaper practices of borrowing, imitating, extracting, paraphrasing, editorially revising, and joint authoring, and because of the ambiguous use of pseudonyms by editors and contributors of the period, the key point remains—we can never be absolutely certain an unsigned poem is Freneau's, either at all or in part.

The long list of possible attributions are supported by at least one of the criteria listed above, coupled with the lowest common editorial denominator I used—a lack of evidence that would clearly disqualify them. A survey of my "possible attributions" appendix indicates that some of these attributions are more convincing than others; my summaries of the evidence will reveal my own opinions respecting each "possible" ascription.

Finally, in the third appendix evidence is presented in support of my judgement that the attributions are all either unlikely or erroneous. I have cited earlier appearances than that recorded by the ascriber, in papers to which Freneau never was known to contribute, or I have provided evidence either that the poem was extracted by the editor from some other source, or that it was written by someone other than Freneau. In a few cases, I considered attributions so unlikely that, lacking hard evidence to disprove them, I nevertheless included them in this appendix. In each case, I have provided my reasons for rejecting the attribution.

My use of two major sources of proposed attributions requires explanation. In his *Freneau's Published Prose*, a chronological checklist of prose pieces probably or possibly written by Freneau, Philip Marsh records verses that appear with the prose selections. Occasionally he distinguishes between those stanzas appearing within quotation marks, presumably taken or adapted from some other source, and those which appear to be original by the notations "editorial with verse" and "editorial with original verse" respectively. In using this source I discovered that some of the verses described as original actually appeared within quotation marks. In these appendixes, I have included every poem that a student using *Freneau's Published Prose* might assume, on the basis of the description provided, was being ascribed to Freneau. I have not studied Freneau's prose to the same extent as his poetry and am not qualified to judge the validity of Marsh's possible or probable attributions. Consequently, all verses that appear to have been written by the author of the prose piece ascribed to Freneau are listed here under possible attributions.

Most of the poems included in Lewis Leary's *Last Poems of Philip Freneau* are listed in the appendix of Probable Attributions. Several, however, are listed as only possible or unlikely attributions, either because Leary misrecorded the signature, or because I found that they contained stanzas which probably were not Freneau's. The "initial" theory upon which Leary based these attributions is summarized in my comments on attribution in the general introduction. These attributions are probable, not only because they are signed with Freneau's initials but because portions from several were discovered in Freneau's handwriting. In some cases, editors publishing revised reprints claimed that the author was unquestionably Freneau; and some of the poems are similar in manner and pursue themes similar to those of some of his known poems. But the grounds for excluding them from this edition are the same as those for all other probable attributions. Since Freneau never acknowledged them as his own, as he did at least two poems published after 1815, there is no sure proof that they are authentic. In several instances, poems appearing under his initials in the *True American* and *Fredonian* in the 1820's contained stanzas probably or possibly not Freneau's originally (See Unlikely or Erroneous Attributions, *Freeman's Journal*, July 23, 1783, and Probable Attributions, *Freeman's Journal*, September 29, 1784.) Also, in at least one instance, it appears that stanzas discovered in Freneau's autograph were not originally his (see Unlikely or

Erroneous Attributions, *National Gazette*, October 2, 1793.)

Finally, as the appendixes indicate, my study of the *Fredonian* and *True American* after 1824, when Leary stops his attributions, proves that the initials are no longer a reliable basis of ascription, particularly for the years 1825-26. During 1827-28, however, a "pocket" of Freneau-like poems appeared signed exclusively "F." None of these was cited by Leary, yet among them are revised texts of poems included in the earlier 1821-24 group. During this later period, however, only the signature "F." appears to be reliable; other poems appeared under other letters of Freneau's last name that were definitely not his.

In citing the poems included in Leary's *Last Poems of Philip Freneau*, I refer the reader to the page where they appear in Leary's edition. Since the texts are available and since Leary explains his grounds for attribution, I have only added, where appropriate, evidence I have uncovered that supports or weakens Leary's attribution. I have listed these poems under the date and title of their first newspaper appearances; the location and titles of later appearances can be found either in Leary's notes to *Last Poems* or in the bibliography of *That Rascal Freneau*. I have noted all revised reprints that are not cited in those two texts.

In citing attributions of poems published after 1820, I have generally restricted myself to describing the poems. Specific parallels between unsigned newspaper texts and verses collected by Freneau are easier to cite among the earlier attributions, because so many of the same themes, and sometimes even the same lines, appear. Further, as one has five volumes of Freneau's known verse as a reference, one feels more confident in employing the phrase "in Freneau's manner." The later poems atrributed to Freneau generally appear to be more wordy, and more loosely constructed than his earlier verse, often "rambling" with a subject in no clear direction. Many are "chatty" and others sermonize. But one hesitates in excluding for consideration a poem that does not demonstrate this looser style on the grounds that it is not "in his manner," since, without a volume of collected verse as reference, his later "manner" is not really describable.

In fairness to those whose attributions I am assessing, I should note that many of the poems included in these appendixes were only casually ascribed, appearing in lists of poems described as "Freneau-like." In studying a particular paper which Freneau edited, or in discussing a particular phase of his career, scholars have cited a wide range of poems as "possibly Freneau's." They have made no attempt to mount evidence in defense of the attribution, or even to describe the poem, because, generally writing as biographers or critics, rather than as editors, this was not their purpose at the time. But in editing Freneau's newspaper verse, I considered it my job to examine seriously any newspaper poem that ever has been ascribed to Freneau, however casually, as well as any that possibly could be in the future. Most of the evidence presented in the appendixes supporting or undercutting each attribution is the product of my own study, supplementing the evidence originally provided by the ascriber in the source cited.

In conclusion, although my research convinced me that it was not safe to include the text of any newspaper poem in this edition unless it was acknowledged by Freneau's full signature, it also convinced me that Freneau contributed more verses to papers than he signed or collected. These appendixes, then, direct students of Freneau to a wide range of verses which he probably or possibly contributed to newspapers. All of the probable ascriptions will be of interest since they are verses he probably wrote yet for unknown reasons chose not to acknowledge. Conversely, the list of unlikely or erroneous attributions will suggest the danger of too casual an approach to ascription.

Because I refer repeatedly to several publications by Freneau scholars, I have employed several abbreviations to identify their works, as follows:

Leary--------------Leary, Lewis. *That Rascal Freneau A Study of Literary Failure.* 1941; rpt. New York: Octagon Books, 1971.

Leary, L.P.-------Leary, Lewis. *Last Poems of Philip Freneau.* New Brunswick: Rutgers University Press, 1945.

Marsh-------------Marsh, Philip. *Philip Freneau Poet and Journal-*

ist. Minneapolis: Dillon Press, 1967.

Marsh, W.P.F.---Marsh, Philip. *The Works of Philip Freneau*. Metuchen, New Jersey: Scarecrow Press, 1968.

Marsh, F.P.P.----Marsh, Philip. *Freneau's Published Prose: A Bibliography*. Metuchen, New Jersey: Scarecrow Press, 1970.

Marsh, F.S.-------Marsh, Philip. *A Freneau Sampler*. New York: Scarecrow Press, 1963.

Pattee--------------Pattee, Fred, L., ed. *The Poems of Philip Freneau*. 3 vols. Princeton: The University Library, 1902-07.

Appendix A

PROBABLE ATTRIBUTIONS

U.S. *Magazine*　　October, 1779

THE SEA VOYAGE

Pattee, I, 293-94:　　Unique to the October number of the magazine.

Leary, 79, 423:　　In October he contributed 'The Sea Voyage,' an account of his passage from Santa Cruz the year before. (Included in the Freneau bibliography.)

Pattee apparently ascribed these eight six-line stanzas (AABCBC) to Freneau because they appeared in the *U.S. Magazine* and treated a Freneau subject. Leary then asserted that the poem describes Freneau's voyage from Santa Cruz in 1778. The poem does describe a voyage "From a gay island, green and fair," past Puerto Rico, terminating in "Caesaria." However, the major portion of the poem describes a storm that welled, drove billows over the ship, tore the canvas, and then was quelled. Freneau's only record of the voyage from Santa Cruz, in his *Elements of Navigation*, mentions no storm, but does note that the ship was taken off the coast of Carolina. The only reference in this poem to another ship occurs near the end of the poem, after morning brought a calm: "A ship o'er took us on the way,/Her thousand sails were spread abroad/And flutter'd in the face of day." But as the reference ends there, it seems to mean that a ship merely *passed* them in the morning.

Although the subject is characteristic of Freneau, poems on sea voyages were popular in papers of the period; one of the more widely reprinted, "The Mariner," also dealt with a storm at sea. Others, including "The Shipwrecked Sailor," and "The Sailor, an Elegy," conclude, as does this poem, with the pleasures of returning to the charming ladies on shore. However, the geographical parallels to Freneau's voyage make the attribution probable.

Freeman's Journal   September 12, 1781

    Reflection of an American on the Above Lines.

Leary, 90:	Text quoted as Freneau's.
425:	Included in the Freneau Bibliography because it was marked in Freneau's file of the *Freeman's Journal*.

These are six couplets written in response to a quatrain of verse extracted from a London paper, on "Admiral Rodney's allowing the governor of St. Eustatius only one hour to consider of a surrender," praising Rodney for doing more in one hour than others had for years. This poem, printed under the extract, denounces as contemptible the plunder of a neutral and friendly land. The couplets sound like Freneau, branding the British "a degenerate pilfering race," and Rodney as "this fiend," "this plundering villain," and "this hodgepodge chief, composed of all that's base."

It is likely that Freneau would be penning editorial responses to material extracted for the paper, since he was playing his most active editorial role for the *Journal* during this period. His checking the poem in his personal file reinforces the attribution. But we have no proof that he ever single-handedly edited the *Freeman's Journal*, and, as Marsh has demonstrated, there are grounds for suspecting that some items checked in the personal file are not by Freneau (*Proceedings of the New Jersey Historical Society* LVII (1939), 163-70. He could have marked the poem because it suggested possible future applications. It is also possible that both the extract and the original verse were sent in by a contributor: it was common for correspondents to request that excerpts from other papers, as well as their own effusions, be printed by the editor.

Freeman's Journal   September 29, 1784

    From Bion.
(Reprints, at least, are probable Freneau contributions.)

Leary, 164:	Notes an appearance of this poem in the *Daily Advertiser*, December 16, 1789, but it actually appeared in the *City Gazette* on this date, and never in the *Daily Advertiser*.
369:	Notes an appearance in the *Fredonian*, signed "R." on November 28, 1822.
445:	Included in the Freneau Bibliography.
Leary, L.P., 107-08:	*Fredonian* text.
Marsh, P.F., 98:	Notes this *Freeman's Journal* text, and describes it as one of the works left with Bailey when Freneau set sail in June, 1784.
342:	Notes the *Fredonian* text.

Marsh, "Freneau and Bion," *Journal of the Rutgers University Library*, XIV (1951), 61-63: Notes five appearances of the poem—the *Freeman's Journal*, incorrect *Daily Advertiser*, and *Freedonian* texts cited above, plus *National Gazette*, October 16, 1793, and *True American*, November 23, 1822, signed "R." Compares the text to two other translations of the same passage from Bion. Notes that the five appearances in papers with which Freneau was associated, plus the signature "R." make it certainly Freneau's, even though he never collected it.

This is a two-stanza translation of a passage in which Bion argues that if there were an afterlife, it would make sense to lead a painful, hardworking life in order to accumulate rewards that could be enjoyed at that time. But since there is no life after death, he concludes, it is senseless to waste our little time here working for rewards we will never have a chance to enjoy. It is better to relax and enjoy what we can muster without much effort than to waste life in a vain struggle. The *Freeman's Journal* text follows the other prose and poetry translations of the same passage, quoted by Marsh, closely. A note is attached which explains that, although Bion personally believed that the soul and the body die together, he here admits that if he could have convinced himself that there is a life after death, he would have struggled diligently to attain it. As such, the fragment and note read like a recommendation of a life of diligence for all who believe in life after death, and, hence, have more to hope for than mediocre contentment in the pleasures of this life.

When the poem appeared in the *City Gazette* in 1789, the text was altered: the four lines in the second stanza that find consolation in the enjoyment of the little this life affords were deleted. (Marsh notes, in the *National Gazette* reprint of this text, that the vain pursuit of wealth, which agrees with the other translations, has been altered to the vain pursuit of joy, but this is not a major change. Both texts imply the vanity of sacrificing earthly pleasure, however limited, in the effort to earn a future life of infinite pleasure.) But there is no note with the *City Gazette* text offering a consoling moral to Christians. Instead, the poem argues bleakly that we neither have a promise of life after death nor get consolation from the little this life affords. This text was reprinted in the *National Gazette* with only minor changes and with a different note than that which had appeared in the *Freeman's Journal*. The note attacks the hypocrisy of Christians, who pretend to believe what Bion could not believe, yet fail to live their lives accordingly. Even a heathen saw that if one believed in life after death, the obvious course to take was one of self-sacrifice, in hopes of attaining eternal rewards. The note, then, implies that Christians do not really believe in eternal life, since if they did, they would live differently. Thus, the entire implication of the original fragment has been altered. The poet has turned the recommendation of a diligent life in view of the promise of eternal reward to an insinuation that no one really believes in eternal life, coupled with a denial of any other possible good life.

In the *True American* and *Fredonian* texts, which appeared much later under the signature "R.", we find the same two stanzas that originally were printed in the *Freeman's Journal*, with a new stanza added as introduction. This stanza is a translation of several of Bion's comments that must have preceded the statements originally translated in the earlier poem, as the other translations cited by Marsh include this passage as well. However, this version of that passage differs from the other translations. In the other translations, Bion notes that if his verses survive, he will have some sort of immortality. If they don't survive, then the effort it took to write them was wasted. In the *Fredonian* and *True American* texts, Bion argues that even if his verses do survive, he himself will be merely a mass of atoms. The note attached to this late version of the poem combines sentiments expressed in both of the previous notes, but it is closer in implication to the original *Freeman's Journal* note. The writer notes that Bion professed a disbelief in the afterlife, yet says he would have struggled to gain it, had he believed. "What a lesson to the professors of Christianity from a mere child of heathenism." He does not refer to Christians as hypocrites, as in the *National Gazette* note, but seems to be saying, "If you believe, take counsel from Bion, and act as if you did."

I believe that the *City Gazette, National Gazette* and later New Jersey appearances of this text were contributed and introduced by Freneau, and that he made all of the revisions noted in reprints of the earliest text. Since the earliest text so closely accords with other translations of this passage; since Freneau was contributing no known verse to the *Freeman's Journal* at this time; since the text was unsigned, introduced with a doctrinally unambiguous Christian comment, and was never collected by Freneau, we cannot be certain that the original *Freeman's Journal* text was penned or even contributed by Freneau. However, it is possible that he did write it, but deemed it so close a paraphrase of the original as to be unworthy of inclusion in his collections. But the changes made in the text in later appearances in papers to which he was contributing known verses, as well as the signature in the last published versions, convince me that he revised and contributed the text repeatedly throughout his career, modifying it to match his convictions at the time and introducing it accordingly. Other examples are cited in these appendixes of poems originally not Freneau's, but which he periodically revised and submitted to newspapers, or, as editor, published himself. See Appendix C, July 23, 1783, for an example of a text, definitely not his, which he also revised and printed in papers that he edited.

Columbian Herald   September 14, 1785

   To the Author of some Late Extraordinary Poetical Pieces.
                     Signed "K."

Columbian Herald   September 21, 1785   (only possible)

   Untitled attack on "K."
                      Signed "Satiricus."

Columbian Herald   September 30, 1785

To "Satiricus."
Signed "K."

Leary, 135-37	Attributes the two poems by "K." to Freneau.
437	Includes the two poems by "K." in the Freneau Bibliography.

Leary attributes the Septmber 14, poem to Freneau largely on the basis of the similarity between these lines, attacking the verses of another poet, and some poems that had appeared in the Philadelphia *Independent Gazeteer* three years earlier attacking Freneau himself. He hypothesises that Freneau actually wrote these poems, which could have circulated in manuscript, at that time, and finally published them, in a distant city, in order to have the last word in the quarrel. He also suggests that Freneau could have written the poetical defense of "K.'s" supposed victim, signed "Satiricus," which appeared on September 21, in keeping with an editorial promise that a response to "K." would be forthcoming. Finally, he attributes "K.'s" response to "Satiricus," appearing on September 30, to Freneau. "K." was the signature that Freneau used in Charleston consistently and exclusively for poems appearing in the *Columbian Herald*. All of the other poems that he contributed from January to July, 1786, were signed "K.," a signature that never appeared in the paper with any verses, except for these two, other than those later collected by Freneau.

The signature "K." first appearing in the *Columbian Herald* at this time, as well as the manner of the poems, strongly suggest the probability of Freneau's authorship. Both Leary and Marsh assume that he was in Charleston at this time because of the notes appearing in collected versions of his poem "The Invalid," where he explains that it was written in Charleston in 1785 and was occasioned by a visit to Pacolet Springs, in South Carolina. But the motive suggested by Leary seems unlikely. Would Freneau, however sensitive to criticism, revive a newspaper war after three years by publishing an attack merely to have the last word in a quarrel, long passed, in a paper that his original adversaries might not even read? The 1782 newspaper war between the *Freeman's Journal* and Oswald's *Independent Gazetteer* was rooted in a political controversy, having begun with Oswald's attacks on General Reed and the Constitutionalists. The September 14, poem in the *Columbian Herald,* however, is a completely literary attack, charging the author of late pieces only with dullness and technical ineptness. Had this poem actually been penned in 1782, it would have seemed an odd rejoinder in that contest. It is not improbable, that the language of those earlier poems, however, could have provided a source for later purely poetical attacks penned by the same poets.

It seems far more likely, then, that the poem actually was written, as the title indicates, to the author of recent poems in the *Columbian Herald.* Leary rejects this possibility because there could be no other victim of such an attack than the popular young Dr. Joseph Brown Ladd, whose harmless, lugubrious, sentimental, dull, technically flawed and immensely popular verses had begun to appear regularly in the *Columbian Herald,* under the signature "Arouet," in July of 1785. Ladd, who moved to Charleston from Rhode Island in 1784, and who died in a duel in the fall of 1786, began in 1785 to publish derivative verses—imitations of *Werther,* Ossian, *The Bristowe Tragedie,* poems on patriotic themes and popular virtues, moral fables, and sentimental love poems to "Amanda." He was the only regular contributor to the *Herald* during the fall of 1785. Although he was quite popular—over 284 subscriptions for a proposed volume of his verses sold between October of 1785 and August of 1786—he had other local critics besides Freneau. For instance, in a later poetry controversy in the *Charleston Evening Gazette* in August of 1786, between poets who identify themselves as "Cato" and "Crito," one of the subjects of debate is the value of "Arouet's" verses. Similarly, on January 12, 1786, the editor of the *Gazette of the State of Georgia* remarked that "Arouet's" poems were too highly touted—his verses, though sprightly, were incorrect. The writer of "To the Author of some Late Extraordinary Poetical Pieces" offers a similar criticism in the fourth stanza of his poem.

Leary furthermore rejects the possibility that Ladd could have been the object of Freneau's attack because Ladd praised the poetry of Freneau in an unfinished poem that appeared in his *Literary Remains,* published in 1832. The tribute probably was penned in response to the 1786 collection and could not have influenced Freneau in the fall of 1785. Freneau, having just arrived in Charleston, may not have been acquainted with Ladd at the time, or may not have known that he was the poet "Arouet."

It would be impossible to identify "Satiricus," who wrote the September 21 reply defending "K.'s" victim and attacking "K." The poem is introduced ironically by the editor as so beautiful and harmonious that "K." would have to confess himself inadequate to reply, but the couplets are shoddy and clumsy, accusing "K." of malice, jealousy, plagiarism and dullness. Leary again recalls in these attacks the charges against Freneau earlier in Philadelphia, and identifies the allusion to "L—" in the poem as Arthur Lee, with whom Freneau had been associated at that time. Again he suggests that Freneau could have written the attack against "K.," again reviving the old attacks on himself. But these are conventional poetic attacks; much of the poem simply directs at "K." the same insults "K." himself used in the first poem. It is not apparent that "L—" refers to Lee; throughout the rest of the poem, words with letters deleted are printed with as many hyphens as letters omitted—"D—" for "Devil" and "G--" for "God." In short, it seems as likely that an unskilled admirer of "K.'s" victim, whoever he was, wrote in his defense as that Freneau answered his own attack with charges that had been directed against himself three years before. Or, he could have written the lines simply in response to the editor's promise that a reply would be forthcoming, not in order to continue the old Philadelphia war, but simply to amuse himself by writing a clumsy poem in the voice of an imagined adversary in his attack on "The author of late pieces." It would not seem unusual that such a poem would echo earlier poetical assaults which he had written, or which had been written about him, as charges of jealousy, plagiarism, and dullness were the substance of poems in this vein.

The third poem, appearing on September 30—only four lines of verse--concludes the series, as the editor earlier had suggested that the exchange be terminated. It is addressed to "Satiricus," by "K.," and announces his farewell to the nonsense. The signature and the poem's place in the series make the attribution probable.

City Gazette   January 11, 1790   Rpt. *Daily Advertiser*, February 18, 1790

> Lines formerly addressed to Mr. Peter Markoe, the Philadelphia poet, upon hearing that he had got a new coat.
> Signed "M."

Leary, 84, 380   Tentative attribution.

A combination of factors makes this attribution probable. The poem first appeared in the *City Gazette* when Freneau was in Charleston, under a signature which he used occasionally for poems that he later collected. The poem was reprinted in the *Daily Advertiser* shortly after he returned to New York. Leary provides strong grounds for assuming that Freneau and Markoe were social acquaintances (121-22). The substance of the poem, a mild teasing of his friend for compromising his role as a poor poet by having a new coat, the playful implication that poverty and worn out clothes are touchstones of integrity, and a reference to the Dutch as unimaginative hoarders of wealth, all sound like Freneau.

Daily Advertiser   February 4, 1790

> A View of Rhode Island (Extracted from a new poem, entitled the Rising Empire, not yet published.)

Pattee, III, 7-8   Text included.
Leary, 446   Included in the Freneau Bibliography.

This poem is included in the Freneau Bibliography, even though it was never collected, because it was printed as part of the Rising Empire series, other poems of which appeared individually in Freneau's later collections. The poem demonstrates the typical characteristics of other poems in the series, each of which describes a particular state—a general survey of its typography, of its agricultural or commercial pursuits, and of the personality traits of its inhabitants. I find no grounds for skepticism with respect to this attribution, other than that it was never collected.

A possible explanation for Freneau's failure to collect this poem, and for his failure to complete the series, or to publish it as a complete work, appears in the revisions that were made in the original newspaper texts of the poems that were collected, or in one case, of a subsequent newspaper reprint of one of the poems in the series. In each case, lines that were sharply critical of the people were deleted. For instance, lines critical of the Quakers were deleted in the collected text of "Description of Pennsylvania," (*Daily Advertiser*, March 17, 1790). Even within the newspaper text of that poem, he interrupts the text to apologize—"Nor mean I hence to censure or condemn," as if uncomfortable about the picture he was painting. Similarly, his collected text of the sketch of Virginia excludes a number of lines, softening, though not deleting, the attack on slavery and deleting several disparaging comments about the haughtiness, dullness, and stupidity of the people. When his "Characteristic Sketch of the Long Island Dutch" (*City Gazette*, February 2, 1790) was reprinted in Matthew Carey's *American Museum* for June, 1790, lines 5-8, describing the selfishness of the Dutch, were deleted, either by Freneau or by the editor. Such a revision may have increased Freneau's qualms if it was not his own. In some poems, like those on Connecticut and Massachusetts, where he can demonstrate that certain character "flaws" actually have positive effects—avarice and ambition help to keep the world alive and moving—he does not alter the text in the collected version. In the poem on Rhode Island, what begins as a favorable sketch concludes with an attack on the litigious meanness that ruins the spirit of justice. The picture grows so painful to the poet that he is forced to quit the scene and move on to Connecticut. If Freneau had considered including this sketch in a collection, he would have had to rewrite practically the entire poem to exclude harshly critical comments. In short, there are grounds for suspecting that he failed to complete the Rising Empire series because he was too uncomfortable with his sketches. He may have feared that they would have the effect of reinforcing divisive prejudices and stereotypes about regional character.

Daily Advertiser   March 5, 1790

Lines Addressed to some Young Ladies, who were detected in attempting to cut to pieces an Old Great Coat of the Author's, that he might be under the necessity of buying a new and more genteel one.

Leary, 167-68	Text quoted as Freneau's.
384	Supplies grounds for the attribution summarized below.
446	Included in Freneau Bibliography.
Marsh, 116-17	Text quoted as Freneau's.

A reprint of this poem was found in an undated clipping from the *Monmouth Inquirer* attributed to the "Late Philip Freneau" and introduced with a note explaining that the poem was addressed to Fanny Ledyard and her brother-in-law's sister, Eleanor Foreman, who were caught cutting the author's coat shortly before his marriage. The paper from which this clipping was taken has not been located.

The author of the poem humorously begs that the "caitiffs" forebear their massacre of his "reverend" coat, which had protected him through many climes and at least seven years afloat. The poet promises to tempt the seas no more if they will let him keep the coat. I find no grounds for doubting this attribution other than that it was never collected.

Daily Advertiser   March 8, 1790

> The Boatman of Indian River

Leary, 169   Unqualified attribution to Freneau, although the poem is not included in the Freneau Bibliography.

Marsh, 124   Probably by Freneau.

This is a humorous sketch tracing the sad fate of a poor seaman who despises the land but knows every depth and shoal of all the local rivers. Remiss in maintaining his farm and family, he is forced to sell his land and to transport pitiful freights on an incresingly tattered barque. He drowns his troubles in drink, and eventually hangs himself from his mast. The poem reads like a playfully exaggerated self-portrait, written at the time when Freneau finally was deciding to settle permanently on shore, as if to suggest the sort of husband and provider he might turn out to be. Though unsigned and uncollected, I consider this attribution probable.

Daily Advertiser   July 5, 1790

> The River Delaware to the River Hudson

Leary, 172   Notes that the poem refers to the removal of Congress from New York to Philadelphia.

385   Included in a list of *Daily Advertiser* poems, not collected, but in his manner.

Marsh, 127   Notes that Freneau wrote it to emphasize the advantages of the new location.

This poem playfully argues the advantages of Philadelphia over New

Appendix A: Probable Attributions 703

York through the voice of the little Delaware River, who addresses her rival, the big and boisterous Hudson. The Delaware is depicted as an inland "small scale" river, slightly muddy because "unmingled with the ocean's brine," but ever fertile: "Like Nile, where're my waves o'er flow/I bid the golden harvests grow," and, since she is associated with art, she acts the "nobler part." The bolder and deeper Hudson, on the other hand, though she can boast of a superior size, is destructive rather than creative: "But you--when rising o'er your bounds--/You kill the verdure of the grounds." Unlike the more creative but less ambitious Delaware, the Hudson, "so anxious for renown/Can only grace a trading town." Here trade and commerce are viewed as mediocre rivals to art.

No one, I believe, but Freneau could have written this poem. We find precisely the same destruction by the Hudson of the life on her banks in a later poem, which he did collect—"To Thos. Swawcum, a Wharf Builder," *Time-Piece*, November 1, 1797. The contrast developed between art and commerce, and the parallel contrast between the Philadelphia-New Jersey and the New York city areas suggests tensions occasionally expressed by Freneau with respect to his own activity and his longing for retreat to a calmer atmosphere more conducive to the poet and thinker, where he might be "his own man," removed from the workaday world of ambition and money-making.

Daily Advertiser   March 10, 1791

To the Author of the Above.

Leary, 185-86	Quotes the poem and notes that it was written in response to a Philadelphia attack.
451	Included in Freneau Bibliography.
Marsh, 135-36	Notes that it was written in response to a Philadelphia attack.

This poem follows a stanza of verse reprinted from the Philadelphia *Independent Gazetteer*, asking Freneau ("Phil") why he had criticized a brother poet, noting that the poet's works sell while his sit on the shelf. The attack referred to here is Freneau's poem which had appeared in the *Daily Advertiser* on February 26, "The Useful Only in Vogue at Court," directed at poet David Humphreys, who had recently received a government appointment that Freneau attributed to his having dedicated his works prudently. The poem is a direct response to the questions raised by the writer of the *Independent Gazetteer* poem. In six lines, he denies jealousy, and asserts the popularity of his poems. There are no grounds for doubting this attribution except that it was never collected.

New York *Argus*   May 13, 1796

On the Federal City, and the projected Removal of the Supreme Legislature to the Banks of the Potowmack, in the year 1811.

Leary, 395   Much like Freneau.

This poem expresses doubts about the money and effort spent in building the new Federal town in Washington D.C. on the grounds that the elaborate plans will foster monarchs and aristocrats who will inhabit the "sky-topt towers" constructed by a race of slaves. The poet asserts that should the "British Plan" again be imposed on America, the plan would never endure. He warns citizens to take stock of things before they go that far—"Should wealth abound, just aims pursue,/Nor waste it on the aspiring few:".

Stanza four of this poem, with slight revisions, appeared within quotations, as the introductory epigram to Ode VII of "The Book of Odes," *Time-Piece,* October 31, 1797. That ode, never collected by Freneau, but also entitled "On the Federal City," develops a completely different theme and has nothing in common, except for the epigram, with this text. It is possible that the later ode was not Freneau's, but that the epigram was provided by the editor, extracted from his own earlier poem on the same subject.

In the *City Gazette*, on December 16, 1800, Freneau published another poem, "Lines on the Federal City," which he included in the 1815 collection, where it is dated "1797." It, however, has nothing in common with the 1797 *Time-Piece* ode, but instead is quite similar in content and development to this 1796 poem on the Federal City. In the 1800 text, Freneau again voices a fear that the city will be a haven for monarchs and aristocrats:

> Where Royalty, in vile grimace,
> In *Louis* shews its scoundrel face

> And *Antoinette* a smile affords,
> To senators and would-be Lords.

He mentions that it is meant for "embrio kings," and "intended for a ruling race." He repeats the fear that the splendid domes will be nourished by the poor who, at a distance, must do "the dirty work." As in the earlier poem, he concludes by urging those at the helm to shake off the "royal trade" and to achieve their ambitions with honest pursuits.

So many lines in the 1796 *Argus* text recall Freneau in general and echo the later text of a poem on the same subject, similarly developed, that I think it is probably an earlier version of the 1800 poem. Leary and Marsh both offer evidence that Freneau was connected with Greenleaf, editor of the *Argus,* after concluding the *Jersey Chronicle.*

New York *Weekly Museum*   August 10, 1816

> Stanzas Written in September 1811, on the great Comet, which had been passed its perhelion and was travelling rapidly to the southward.
> Signed "P.F."

Leary, L.P., 3-4

New York *Weekly Museum*   August 31, 1816

> On Madame Charity Careless. A Disconsolate Widow.
> Signed "P.F."

Leary, L.P., 5-6

The *True American* reprint of this poem (December 28, 1822) includes an introductory eight-line stanza, five lines of which were taken from Watts' "Indian Philosopher."

New York *Weekly Museum*   September 7, 1816

> Stanzas Written for a Boy about eight years of age, who, in walking with his parents through a forest of Pine Trees, very narrowly escaped being bitten by an uncommonly large and venomous Rattle Snake. The Snake, which was killed with some difficulty, measured more

than 13 feet long. Signed "P.F."

Leary, L.P., 7-8

New York *Weekly Museum* September 21, 1815

Stanzas addressed several years ago to Mr. Blanchard, the celebrated Aeronaut in America. Signed "P.F."

Leary, L.P., 8-10

It is interesting to compare this poem to Freneau's poem written after Blanchard's first ascent in America (*National Gazette,* January 19, 1793). The poem similarly describes the exciting vistas seen only by Blanchard but develops at greater length a point merely mentioned in the last stanza of the earlier poem: the aeronaut must not sever his ties to the earth altogether but must wait until death takes him to the etherial realms.

New York *Weekly Museum* September 28, 1816

The Fortunate Blacksmith. Signed "P.F."

Leary, L.P., 11-12

New York *Weekly Museum* October 5, 1816

Salutary Maxims, Derived for the old Cynic Philosophy.
Signed "F."

Leary, L.P., 13

New York *Weekly Museum* October 12, 1816

Stanzas Written in an ancient Burying Ground in Maryland, one corner of which was appropriated to the interment of Suicides, or self-murders. Signed "F."

Leary, L.P., 14

The verses which introduce this poem are a paraphrase from Martial.

A similar paraphrase, from which this deviates slightly, was one of the most widely reprinted poems in American newspapers in the last quarter of the eighteenth century. The earliest appearance that I found was in the *Pennsylvania Ledger*, December 9, 1775.

New York *Weekly Museum*   October 12, 1816

Epitaph upon a Spanish horse called Royal-Gift, sent over and presented to General Washington by the King of Spain in the year 1785.
Signed "F."

Lear, L.P., 15

New York *Weekly Museum*   October 19, 1716

The Tye-Wig. Lines of the old Dotard, who had cut away the blossoms of Sixty-Eight, and upwards, to put on a fashionable Tye-Wig.
Signed "F."

Leary, L.P., 16

New York *Weekly Museum*   November 9, 1816

A Dialogue between a News-Printer and his Cash-Collector.
Signed "F."

Leary, L.P., 19-20

Aurora   September 11, 1820

A Soldier of '76 to His Companions.

Marsh, 334   Freneauesque.

This poem employs the same stanza form and several of the same lines, with slight revisions, as Freneau's "Volunteer's March" (*Freedonian*, August 11, 1814), although the enemy against which the people are urged to take arms in this poem is corruption. The occasion was the fall election for governor of Pennsylvania, and the poem is apparently directed against the administration of Findley. Marsh notes several "Old Soldier" essays in the *Aurora* in September, ascribed to Freneau and supporting Heister over Findley. Although it is possible that another poet was imitating Freneau's "Volunteer's March," the title, form, theme and development are so like Freneau that I find the attribution probable.

True American   June 30, 1821

Stanzas written on the Grand Western Canal of the State of New York, contemplated to connect the Atlantic Ocean with the Interior Lakes of North America.
                    Revised reprint signed "F." *Fredonian*, August 8, 1822.

Leary, L.P., 21-24

True American   September 8, 1821

Address Presented to be spoken at the re-opening of the Park Theatre, in New-York, sometime since.

Leary, L.P., 25-27

Although not signed, this poem was tentatively attributed to Freneau by the editor of the *True American*, in which Freneau appears to have been publishing regularly ("Said to be written by P. Freneau of Monmouth, New Jersey.") This kind of attribution is usually more reliable than an editor's attribution of a poem reprinted from a paper where it originally appeared unsigned.

True American   September 29, 1821

Jersey City. Lines written in the Church-Yard on Bergen Heights, near the village of Hoboken, on the Hudson. (Draft of lines from this poem discovered in Freneau's autograph.)

Leary, L.P., 28-30

True American   October 6, 1821

                    The City Poet.
            (Draft discovered in Freneau's autograph.)

Leary, L.P., 31-32.

True American   April 13, 1822

      To a Young Friend with some Maple Sugar.
(Unsigned but the author is editorially identified, though not named, as Freneau.)

Leary, L.P., 52-53

True American   May 11, 1822

      The Youth of the Mind.
                               Signed "F."

Leary, L.P., 54

True American   May 18, 1822

Prologue to Kotzebue's Play, entitled 'The Stranger,' acted, for the celebrated Mrs. Baldwin's Benefit at Washington Hall, in New York, April 15, 1822.
(Not signed but tentatively attributed to Freneau by the editor: "Said to be written by P. Freneau, of New Jersey.")

Leary, L.P., 55-56

True American   June 8, 1822

Stanzas Written on a visit to a field called 'The Military Ground,' near Newburgh, in the State of New-York, where the American Army were disbanded by General Washington, almost forty years ago.
Revised reprint, *Fredonian*, July 18, 1822, signed "F."

In the New York *Statesman* reprint of this poem, June 11, 1822, the author is editorially described, though not named, as Freneau. The poem also was revised and reprinted in the *Fredonian*, August 15, 1827, under the title "Military Ground," signed "F."

Leary, L.P., 57-58

True American   July 6, 1822

    To a young Farmer, or Agriculturalist, being taken from the Plough, and sent to College.   Signed "R."

    Leary, L.P., 61-62.

New York *Statesman*   July 11, 1822

    Stanzas to the memory of General Lefevre Desnouettes.
    Revised reprints, *True American*, July 20, 1822, signed "R."
    Fredonian, July 25, 1822, signed "F."

    Leary, L. P., 67-68   (Leary notes the *True American* text appearing as the first.)

True American   July 13, 1822

    Stanzas Addressed to a Young Person of Condition, much addicted to the Gambling Table.   Signed "F."

    Leary, L.P., 53

Fredonian   July 18, 1822

        Philosophical Fortitude.
        Signed "F."

    Leary, L.P., 65-66

True American   July 20, 1822

    On the Civilization of the Western Aboriginal Country.
        Signed "A."

    Leary, L.P., 69-71

True American   August 24, 1822

    Lines written at Damarest's field, near Tappan, on the disinterment and transportation of Major Andre's Bones to England, in 1821.
    Signed "R."

    Leary, L.P., 72

True American   August 24, 1822

    Lines, written on leaving an elegant new mansion House, called Beaurepaire (pleasant retreat) not an hundred miles from Lake Cayuga.
                                                                                            Signed "N."

Leary, L.P., 73-75

Fredonian   August 29, 1822

    Verses on an Upper Street Physician who Deserted a Populous City on the Approach of Malignant Fever.
Revised reprint, *True American*, December 28, 1822
                                                                                            signed "R."

Leary, L.P., 76-78

True American   August 31, 1822

    Lines to a lady engaged in manufacturing an elegant superfine Carpet, intended to be forwarded, as a present to Nadir Shah, despot of Persia.   Signed "E."

Leary, L.P., 79-80

True American   September 7, 1822

    Lines written at an elegant and romantic Garden adjacent to Passaick River, in Essex county.   Signed "E."

Leary, L.P., 81-83

True American   September 14, 1822

    The following verses were written at the time the intelligence first arrived in America that Bonaparte, from the first consulship, had ascended the throne of France.   Signed "E."

Leary, L.P., 84-85

Fredonian   September 19, 1822

> A Midnight Storm in the Gulph Stream. Written on an outward bound voyage from Charleston to the Canary Islands.   Signed "E."

Leary, L.P., 86-87

True American   September 21, 1822

> Lines to a lady, remarkably fond of sleep, preparing for a voyage to Europe.   Signed "A."

Leary, L.P., 88-90

Fredonian   September 22, 1822

> The Arrival at Indian Sams (or, Wee-quali's) Wigwam.
>   Signed "E."

Leary, L.P., 91-95

True American   October 5, 1822

> Modern Greece
>   Signed "N.R."

Marsh, F.S., 145-46   Text quoted; attributed to Freneau on the basis of the signature.

Leary did not ascribe this signature to Freneau, but, on the basis of his theory, the signature would be valid for the *Fredonian*, at least, since one poem which appeared in the *True American* under the signature "R." was reprinted, with revisions, in the *Fredonian*, under the signature "N.R." The poem is much in the manner of other later verses ascribed to Freneau. In six stanzas, the poet links the decline of both ancient and modern Greece to the decline in public virtue and the failure to employ the "God given gift"—"The lamp of reason in the human breast." If Freneau's, it represents a modification of an earlier attitude, as here he associated "reason" more with the heart than with the stoically "noble mind."

Appendix A: Probable Attributions 713

True American   October 19, 1822

                         Circumnavigation.
                                                              Signed "E."

Leary, L.P., 96-98

This poem was reprinted with revisions in the *Fredonian*, September 15, 1827, signed "F." under the title "Female Circumnavigation."

True American   October 26, 1822

Ode Written from a remote perspective view of Princeton College (or Nassau Hall) from a remarkably woody eminence in Monmouth, commonly called Pine Hill.
                                                               Signed "R."

Leary, L.P., 99-102

True American   November 7, 1822

         Lines on a Transient View of Monticello, in Virginia.
                                                              Signed "E."

Leary, L.P., 103-04

True American   November 9, 1822

On the continuance of a Red-Streak apple on the Tree in the month of January.   Signed "A."

Leary, L.P., 105-06

Fredonian   December 5, 1822

Answer to a letter of despondency from an Invalid in the North.
                                                               Signed "F."

Leary, L.P., 109-11

True American January 4, 1823

> To a New England Poet.
> Signed "N."

Leary, L.P., 112-13

True American February 1, 1823

> On a widow Lady, (Very rich and very penurious.)
> Signed "R."

Leary, L.P., 114-15

True American February 1, 1823

> Lines written several years ago on the death of Robert Fulton.
> Signed "E."

Leary, L.P., 116-117

True American July 31, 1824

> General De La Fayette
> Revised reprint, *Fredonian*, August 18, 1824, signed "F."

Leary, L.P., 118-20

True American August 21, 1824

> Stanzas Made at the interment of a Sailor on the Island of Tortuga, near the north side of Hispaniola, or Hayti, as now called, (Written many years ago, but never published.)
> Revised reprint, *Fredonian*, September 8, 1824, signed "F."

Leary, L.P., 121-22

True American June 20, 1827

> Lines, (Anniversary forty-ninth,) on the battle of Monmouth, and subsequent retreat of Sir Henry Clinton—June 28th, 29th and 30th, 1778.
> Signed "F."

Appendix A: Probable Atrributions 715

Marsh, "Freneau's Last Published Poem," *American Literature*, XXX (1958), 103-06 Quotes and atrributes to Freneau.
Marsh, F.S., 146-49 Full text included as Freneau's.

This poem, in the manner of later verse ascribed to Freneau, recalls the events of the battle, praises the courage of Washington and La-Fayette, describes the blunder of Charles Lee, and pokes fun at Clinton. As Marsh notes, the subject would have been close to Freneau's home and heart, and, although Freneau's initials are not a reliable basis for probable attributions in the *True American* after 1824 (see comments on Possible Attribution, *Fredonian*, February 8, 1826), the combination of the signature, the subject and the manner makes this attribution probable.

Fredonian   July 11, 1827

Reflections on the Above.
Signed "F."

These seven couplets follow a poetical anecdote about a poor Irish farmer. They condemn the British treatment of Ireland, arguing that the poverty of the people is a necessary consequence of aristocrat and monarchal government. Although I have noted elsewhere that Freneau's initials are not a reliable basis for probable attributions in the New Jersey papers after 1824 (see Appendix of Possible Attributions, 1825-26), this poem is the first in a series of Freneau-like verses appearing in the *Fredonian* from July, 1827 to February, 1828, all signed "F." Among this series are revisions of earlier probable attributions ("Febale Circumnavigation," September 15, 1827—See Probable Attributions, *True American*, October 19, 1822; "Military Ground," August 15, 1827—See Probable Atrributions, June 8, 1822). All poems in this "pocket" of Freneau-like verses from July, 1827 to February, 1828, signed "F." and including earlier probable attributions, are also probable attributions.

Fredonian   August 22, 1827

The Body Inanimate.
Signed "F."

In ten stanzas the poet describes how, standing by a pond, he was inspired to build a miniature ship as soon as the breeze arose and stirred the waters. Untutored in the art, he built "a *something*" out of red cedar and newspaper, and launched it into the pond. But without a pilot to guide her, and without a "word of command," the ship upset. The poet concludes:

> Thus, fit *some men* as complete as you will,
>   If merely a *human machine,*
> On the lee-shores of life they are sure to be wreck'd
>   For *want of the God in the brain.*

Fredonian   August 22, 1827

The Brilliant Stranger, or Periodical Visitor: A comet, expected in 1833.   Signed "F."

In nine stanzas the poet discusses the anticipated appearance of the comet, providing the astronomical details about its speed, size, and period, as well as an imagined conversation between the comet and the astronomers who will study it when it arrives. It advised them to record all of its motions and to learn all they can, for it won't be back for seventy-eight years.

Fredonian   August 29, 1827

The Man of Sixty.

Signed "F."

The poet, speaking as if it were his sixtieth birthday, chastises those who lament and fear old age. He counsels them to follow Plutarch's advice about "how to be young when we are old." According to the poet, Plutarch advised the aging man to maintain a serene mind and clear conscience; to depend only upon himself; to remain temperate, although he should enjoy the comforts of wine; and to take walks every morning.

Fredonian   August 29, 1827

The Inchanted Mountain.

Signed "F."

In six stanzas the poet describes an ancient mountain in Tennessee where human footprints with six toes have been preserved in soft, flat rocks. In a long explanatory note appearing with the poem, the poet, citing the source of his information, precisely locates the spot, provides the size of the uncommonly large prints that appeared with horse tracks, also of unusual size, and speculates about the origin of this apparent *lusus naturae*.

Fredonian   January 2, 1828

>The Carrier's New-Years Address, to the Patrons of the *Fredonian*.

This address includes twenty-seven of the thirty-two lines of Freneau's autograph poem "Winter" (November 28, 1787). Freneau's original manuscript stanzas are broken up and dispersed throughout the first third of the poem, and several new lines have been added to fit the newsboys' occasion and the New Brusnwick setting. The latter two-thirds of the poem address the controversy arising from the presidential election of 1824 and the contest to be conducted in 1828. The poet begins by condemning party strife and party men, arguing that those who engage most fiercely in party struggle are motivated only by self interest: "The Scholar, Soldier, Patriot, Statesman lost!" The poet accuses Andrew Jackson and his supporters of engaging in such a struggle:

> Witness the desp'rate shifts, th'unholy leagues,
> The sland'rous falsehoods, and th'unblest intrigues,
> Which Andrew Jackson and his high compeers,
> Have had resort to for the past three years.

He accuses them of attempting to dim the fame of Clay, "And thereby with him, prostrate in the dust,/John Quincy Adams, of our Statesmen first," by claiming that Clay and Adams had bargained to defeat Jackson in 1824, a charge which, he says, was promptly met and refuted. He condemns Jackson supporter R.M. Johnson for threatening to employ any means "put down" the Adams Administration, and traces "plots" that actually were implemented, principally the charge of a bargain between Adams and Clay. The poet presents his own evidence to refute the claim, but notes that, for ignoble reasons, public support for Jackson continues to mount, despite the evidence of his treachery:

> Still Jackson, Jackson, is the constant cry

> Of those who seek for honor'd places high:
> They thirst for wealth, and practice every art--
> Touch but their pockets, and you touch their hearts.

Because Freneau's manuscript lines appear in the poem, the attribution would seem indubitable. However, the original manuscript lines have been broken up in the *Fredonian* text, and are employed merely as introduction to the rest of the poem, which focuses on the political issue. It is possible, that the editor of the paper, which was anti-Jackson in 1828, used Freneau's poem on winter for his own purposes, as introduction to a carriers' address penned by someone else. But as several lines in the latter portion of the poem are extracted from an earlier Freneau poem, he most probably wrote the entire text.

> Ne'er may she fail when Liberty implores,
> Nor want true valor to defend her shores,
> Till Europe, humbled, greets our western wave
> And owns an Equal whom she wished a slave.

(Last four lines of "On the American and French Revolutions," *Daily Advertiser*, March 6, 1790; "On the Prospect of a Revolution in France," *Poems* (1795), 323.)

Fredonian   February 13, 1828

> The Ruins of Topen-Amos: Formerly an Episcopal Church in Monmouth County, about twenty miles south of this city.   Signed "F."

The poet recalls the church during the period of the revolution, describing the various ministers who preached there, specifically the Reverend Samuel Cooke, who opposed the war. He discusses the pious behavior of youthful churchgoers in those times, which he contrasts to the irreverence of "modern devotion." The poem recalls Freneau's earlier "Ruins of a Country Inn," and "Modern Devotion," as well as a possible ascription "The Demolished Church" (See Possible Attributions, *City Gazette*, February 9, 1790).

Appendix B

POSSIBLE ATTRIBUTIONS

U.S. Magazine   June 3, 1779

    King George the Third's Speech to Lord North.

Marsh, 31   Not acknowledged by Freneau, but the poem is probably his.

In twelve couplets, George III reviews what he had hoped to gain by conquering and reducing lands and peoples from the Hudson to the Gulf of Mexico, as well as his original assumptions about the nature of the inhabitants. It is in the manner of "King George the Third's Soliloquy," (*U.S. Magazine*, May 1779) but the speech is less dramatic, less colloquial, and less varied in mood and intonation than the typical Freneau monologue. In the June "Notes to Correspondents," Brackenridge lists poems that have been contributed to the magazine by Freneau, including those in the present issue, and this poem is not among them. Paraphrases and parodies of royal speeches and proclamations, actual or imagined, were common in papers of the period.

U.S. Magazine   October, 1779

    The Forsaken Lover.

Marsh, 56   Perhaps written in the latter months at Santa Cruz.
WPF, 30   Probably his, but the poem was not acknowledged.

This is a nine stanza pastoral (AABCCB) in which shepherd Damon builds a bower and persuades shepherdess Clarinda to stay with him. But she leaves at dawn, and though she promises to return, she comes no more. It is in the manner of Freneau's conventional pastorals on the theme of lost love ("Prayer of Orpheus, "Female Frailty," "The Distrest Shepherdess," "The Misfortune of March," "Philander and Lavinia") but nothing particularly distinguishes it as his. I did, however, note a resemblance between two lines here and several lines in one of his later poems, "The Exile," *City Gazette*, February 2, 1788:

> Thrice happy they, too soon I said
> Who flee the sun to seek the shade
> ("The Forsaken Lover," Stanza 2, lines 1-2.)

> Think right--nor be the hour delay'd
> That flies the sun to seek the shade.
> ("The Exile," Stanza 8, lines 3-4.)

New Jersey Gazette   September 6, 1780

Untitled Satire against the British.

Signed "X."

(Rpt. *Pennsylvania Packet*, September 9, 1780)

Marsh, "Philip Freneau's Poetry in the *New Jersey Gazette*," *Proceedings of the New Jersey Historical Society*, 77 (1959), 40-43.

This is a long satirical tetrameter couplet poem in the guise of an "intercepted letter" from a flighty matron of New York to her sister Tabitha, detailing the arrival of an army of rebels and British cowardice in failing to meet them. The humor lies in her depiction of the British and in her hopelessly nonpartisan infatuation with officers. Marsh bases the attribution on the fact that Freneau was in nearby Monmouth at the time, was the author of another poem of the intercepted letter variety, was fond of satirizing the British, and was known to have used the signature "Z." on other occasions.

Freneau did write an intercepted letter poem (see the *Freeman's Journal*, September 5, 1783) and, later in his career, wrote two other epistolary satires in which we also are exposed to a feminine view of political events (See *Daily Advertiser*, July 1, 15, 1790). However, he used the signature "Z." on only one occasion, much later, for a newspaper version of a known poem (*Time-Piece*, September 25, 1797.)

Appendix B: Possible Attributions 721

On the other hand, none of Freneau's known poems ever appeared in the *New Jersey Gazette*, although several were reprinted there between 1782 and 1786. The "intercepted letter" format was fairly popular in newspapers of the period, and the combination of the epistolary form, a man-hungry matron, and the name "Tabitha" strongly suggests the influence of Smollett's popular *Humphry Clinker*, which could have provided a model for many other satirists besides Freneau. The signature "Z." was among the more widely used during the period. In short, it seems as likely that, being in the area, Freneau could have read this poem and imitated it in his later intercepted letter and feminine epistolary verses as that he wrote it himself. As the poem pokes mild, even playful, fun at the British, it seems foreign to the mood of *The British Prison Ship*, which he probably was revising at the time, and the other fierce anti-British satires published shortly after this time.

New Jersey Gazette   November 1, 1780

A Dialogue Between Satan and Arnold

(unsigned)

Marsh, W.P.F., 36   Linked with two poems by "Z." appearing on September 6 and November 15 as the work of Freneau.

This is a short, two-stanza dialogue in which Arnold vows to do the devil's work if Satan promises to let him die with his shoes on. Although this is similar in spirit to Freneau's later dialogues in the *Freeman's Journal* between Satan and James Rivington, the use of this format was common in political satire of the period. Repeatedly, the victims of political satire make deals with Satan and get rewards for their devilish conduct. The only grounds for that attribution, then, are that the poem appears between two other possible attributions and contains a motif later used by Freneau.

Pennsylvania Packet   November 14, 1780

Untitled Satire against the British.

Signed "Z."

Marsh, "Freneau's Poetry in the *New Jersey Gazette*," *Proceedings of the New Jersey Historical Society*, 77 (1959), 40-43.

A second "intercepted letter," which, according to the introductory note, was written by the same lady who penned the first (see *New Jersey Gazette*, September 6, 1780.) Marsh notes the later appearance of this poem in the *New Jersey Gazette* on November 15, but it actually first appeared in the *Packet* on the 14th. It continues the earlier satire of the social frustrations created by the war. This letter also includes an attack on un unnamed New York poet. The first published text of a later Freneau poem, "The Indian Student," appeared in the *Packet* on June 9, 1787.

Freeman's Journal   March 3, 1784

      The Tears of Melpomene.   Signed "L."

Marsh, "Philip Freneau and the Theatre," *Proceedings of the New Jersey Historical Society*, LXIV (1948), 96-105.

This poem was published in the midst of the debate surrounding the 1779 law passed by the Pennsylvania Legislature banning the performance of plays. In February and March of 1784, the *Journal* included arguments for and against the stage, among them two poetic pro-theatre arguments—this one and one on March 10. Nothing suggests that they were written by the same poet; rather, the latter refers to and appears to have been written in ironic response to the former, even while supplying additional fuel for the pro-stage side. This poem develops, in the mournful voice of Melpomene, a traditional defense of the stage—its power to mend and refine morals—as well as a conventional lament over the triumph of dullness that has banished the muse from the stage. We know that Freneau wrote a later poem on the same subject, developing the same traditional arguments when the theater was banned in Charleston (See *City Gazette* January 8, 1790), although there the points are developed didactically rather than dramatically in the voice of the banished muse.

None of Freneau's known poems were signed "L.," a fairly common signature of the period. In his article on Freneau's use of "L." (*Proceedings of the New Jersey Historical Society*, 88 (1965), 287-88), Marsh, for some reason, does not include this poem, but points out possible attributions among several prose pieces and poems that appeared many years later, under the signature "L." in papers to which Freneau was known to contribute. But he concludes that these all are speculative, since Freneau did not use the signature often. In short, there appears no evidence to suggest this is anything more than a possible Freneau attribution.

Freeman's Journal   March 10, 1784

> More Tears: or, the Tears of Thalia.   (Unsigned

Marsh, 96   Also probably by Freneau.

(See comments on preceding poem.) This defense of the stage argues from the opposite perspective. Audiences will be deprived not only of elevating models of virtue, but also of amusing examples of vice. Without comedy and the instruction it provides the libertine, the town will sink hopelessly into "dull virtue." Like the preceding poem, it could have been written by any amateur engaged in the debate.

Freeman's Journal   May 5, 1784

> Untitled tribute to Sterne
>
> Signed "Nerva."

Marsh, F.P.P., 104

Marsh attributes this poem to Freneau because the same signature appeared with an earlier essay defending Blair's lectures, which he also attributes to Freneau. The poem is written in response to an attack on Sterne. Although Freneau never used this signature for any known poems, this poem does recall Freneau in the stanzas which emphasize the bleakness of the realms beyond the grave, where Sterne now reclines—"Where pleasure shall invite no more . . . Where pensive ghosts in every grove/For joys neglected now repine."

Columbian Herald   September 26, 1785

> Ode Addressed to the Nymph of Pacolet Springs.
>
> Signed "Corydon."

Leary, 381   Perhaps Freneau's.

These are ten four-line stanzas celebrating the healing powers of waters. According to the 1809 text of his poem "The Invalid," Freneau visited Pacolet Springs for the recovery of his health. The first published text of the poem (*City Gazette*, February 9, 1788) is dated 1785, although there he refers not to Pacolet, but to "Pyrmont Springs." Its appearance in the *Columbian Herald* at this time, when Freneau probably was in Charleston, and his alleged visit to the springs during this year, make the attribution possible. But nothing distinguishes the text as Freneau's and the self-effacing conclusion is untypical:

> Not mine--be told the truth--not mine the lays;
> Unheard the favour of the *Nine* I sue:
> *Love* cull'd this chaplet of immortal praise,
> And grateful, sprinkled with *Castalian* dew.

Freneau never used this fairly common signature for any known poem.

City Gazette   February 9, 1790   (Reprint, *Daily Advertiser*, February 20, 1790, under the title "The Ruins of a Country Church.")

The Demolished Church

Leary, 384   Tentative attribution.

Marsh, W.P.F., 57   Partially quoted as Freneau's.

This poem first appeared in the *City Gazette* shortly before Freneau left Charleston and reappeared, with slight revisions, in the *Daily Advertiser* shortly after he returned to New York. It is similar to his "Deserted Farm House," developing the contrast between all that once happened here and the way the place looks now. But this is a conventional approach in poems on deserted places, common during the period, all echoing Gray's elegaic contrast between what was and might have been and Goldsmith's "Deserted Village." This poem employs the stanza of Gray's Elegy. Grounds for doubting the attribution include the fact that the title and several lines were slightly altered in the reprint, not in order to modify any ideas or statements, typically the case in Freneau's revisions of his own poems, but rather to improve rhyme and meter or make the statements more intelligible. For example, "The Demolished Church" is slightly misleading as a title since, according to the text, the church is still relatively intact. A new footnote appears in the reprint, clarifying an obscure reference, while an earlier footnote, which provided the exact location of the church, is deleted. These are the sorts of changes that sometimes appear in texts extracted from other sources when reprinted in papers edited by Freneau. As the Appendix of Erroneous Atrributions indicates, Freneau occasionally reprinted stanzas that appealed to him, often obscuring the source and perhaps making the minor changes that appear in the texts.

Daily Advertiser March 15, 1790 (rpt. *City Gazette*, April 13, 1790, "By Captain Freneau.")

Epistle to Peter Pindar Esq.

Pattee, Vol 3, 28	Text included as Freneau's; notes merely the source of the text and identifies Pindar.
Leary, 385	Not collected by Freneau, but the poem is in his manner. Notes *City Gazette* attribution.
446	Included in Freneau Bibliography.

This poem praises Pindar for exposing fools and deflating aristocratic pretention, suggesting that there would be many fit subjects for his pen on this "rebel coast." The *City Gazette* attribution is not compelling evidence, because we find several papers of the period attributing to Freneau any unsigned poem extracted from the papers which he was known to be editing. It is possible that Peter Freneau, editor of the *City Gazette*, attributed all poems "in Freneau's manner" and papers to his brother. John Wilcot, "Peter Pindar," was one of the most popular poets in America during this period. Scores of papers regularly reprinted the British poet's verses. Although his influence on Freneau has been noted by students of the poet, as well as by his contemporaries, this is not sufficient reason to assume that a poem praising him was Freneau's. The poem is really as much in the manner of Wilcot as of Freneau, and we find other poets of the period writing verses imitating Wilcot's. For instance, The Probationary Odes in the *National Gazette*, penned by "Jonathan Pindar," also were assumed to be Freneau's by his contemporaries, but we know that they were written by St. George Tucker, a Virginia judge.

Daily Advertiser   April 2, 1790

> A meditation among some old Books belonging to Capt. Peacock, at Sunbury in Georgia.

Leary, 385	Included in a list of *Daily Advertiser* poems, uncollected, but in his manner.
Marsh, 124	Probably by Freneau.

There are four stanzas describing the antiquity of Captain Peacock's books, dating them back before the flood and placing them on Noah's ark. Freneau probably had been in Sunbury, since his sloop Monmouth carried freight between that city and Charleston, and he occasionally expressed a preference for old and worn-out objects. But the poem is simple and childlike enough to be the work of any amateur. Freneau could have read the poem, or received it from someone who knew "Capt. Peacock," possibly providing the title himself.

Daily Advertiser   April 9, 1790

> A Rhode Island Meditation.

Marsh, 124   Probably by Freneau.

This poem, written in the voice of Rhode Island, is an apology for failing to ratify the Constitution. It develops Rhode Island's relation to the other twelve states, in part, by comparing a tiny and a bulky ship. The ship analogy, and the use of a youthful feminine persona, attempting, with varying degrees of success, to assert her independence (i.e. "The Bird at Sea," "The Rival Suitors for America") recall Freneau. Also, the suggestion of selfish, mercenary motives for refusing the ratification accords with his assessment of local character in "A View of Rhode Island" (Probable Attribution, *Daily Advertiser*, February 14, 1790.)

Daily Advertiser   May 28, 1790

> Description of H—— S——, the Paisley Poet, formerly of Princeton, New Jersey.

Appendix B: Possible Attributions

These are ten couplets describing a poor, eccentric poet, apparently unappreciated in his day. Several lines recall other poems by Freneau:

> Line 17: His shoes were often out at toes,

"The Newsmonger," *Columbian Herald,* February 20, 1786, stanza 10:

> Line 3: His boots were only out at toes.

> Lines 19-20: His tavern bill he could not pay--
> What wonder if he ran away?

"A Parody of Sappho's Ode" *City Gazette* January 28, 1788, Stanza 4:

> Lines 3,4: My Barber's bill I could not pay,
> I blunder'd--broke--and ran away.

Daily Advertiser   June 10, 1790

Lines inscribed to a Gentleman who was desirous that his passage to Flushing might be rendered conspicuous by some extraordinary commotion of the Elements.
                                Signed "Sargeant Major."

There are three mock serious stanzas in which the poet bids Boreas to blow his rudest blasts, so that he can prove to his love, waiting at the end of his voyage, how much he is willing to undergo for her. He assumes that the rougher and riskier his trip, the warmer his reception. The final lines suggest that the poem was written to smooth a minor "spat." This is a signature Freneau occasionally used for poems he later collected.

Daily Advertiser   June 12, 1790

Rhode Island Conversion

Leary, 385   Included in the list of *Daily Advertiser* poems, never collected, but in his manner.

This poem is very much in the manner of "A Rhode Island Meditation" (Possible Attributions, *Daily Advertiser*, April 9, 1790). It sets forth the argument that finally persuaded the "coy unwilling maid" of the first poem who was "so long averse to joining hands," to submit and enter the union. As in the earlier poem, Rhode Island is pictured as a stubborn little maid who here nevertheless is persuaded by the argument that she is too weak to resist the united strength of the other states. This poem also pursues the little ship analogy: "No longer now the ocean's sport/We'll moor her safe in freedom's port." It similarly suggests that her original motives for resisting were the mercenary aims of her scheming "little paws."

Daily Advertiser   June 15, 1790

   Line Addressed to a dull Country Parson.

Leary, 385	Included in the list of *Daily Advertiser* poems, uncollected, but "unmistakably in his manner."
Marsh, W.P.F., 58, 139	Partially quoted, probably by Freneau.

These are four stanzas attacking the inflated sermons of a vain and pompous preacher who takes advantage of his "patent to be dull." This poem is close in content and development, though it has no lines in common with, "On hearing a remarkably dull discourse . . . from a rambling lay preacher," *Time-Piece*, May 17, 1797.

Daily Advertiser   June 18, 1790

The following stanzas were written some Years ago, to a Lady going to live in the Western Country.

Leary, 385	Included in the list of *Daily Advertiser* poems, uncollected, but in his manner.

These six stanzas are similar to Freneau's "To Lydia" in advising the lady against following a rude lover to savage wastes in the west. Here, however, the poet warns her against quitting the safety of her native shore, just to please "a wandering wayward mind." In the earlier poem Freneau asks Lydia to sail the seas and wander with him. Here, the poet suggests that she be true, not to him, but to the "happier fields" of "sweet Jersey."

Daily Advertiser   June 23, 1790

On George's Square, a rural Walk between the State House and the New Jail, in Philadelphia.

Leary, 385   In his manner.

This is an interesting piece of social criticism developing the irony of planting a walk for belles in silks and love sick beaus between the haunts of two "harpies"—the jail where prisoners scream for bread and the state house, where "lawyers prate and judges nod." The writer suggests that the illusion of pastoral beauty provided by the walkway insulates the legislators from the reality of the jail, "checks the charitable hand," hardens the heart, and tutors us not to feel. The social indictment is reinforced in the conclusion, written from the perspective of a rural squire, who first snobbishly concludes that this is not the place for nymphs to play, "where half the swains are negro boys," and then he slinks away. The writer's critical stance is not maintained consistently, however: several lines suggest his ridicule of the prisoners and his sympathy with the squire. The poem recalls Freneau's ironic use of terms like "swains" and other pastoral images, social compassion, however inconsistently—or perhaps *because* inconsistently—expressed, and his phrasing, in certain lines:

   Line 1:   How strange a taste is here display'd

"Epistle to a gay young lady," *Poems*, 1795, 334, Stanza 2:

   Line 1:   How strange a taste is here display'd--

"The River Delaware to the River Hudson," Probable Atrribution, *Daily Advertiser*, July 5, 1790, stanza 3:

   Line 2:   How could they have so strange a taste.

Daily Advertiser   July 17, 1790

On the Prisoners in Albany Jail celebrating the Fourth of July.

Leary, 385   In his manner.

These are five couplets lamenting the plight of prisoners on the day which celebrates freedom and independence. The sentiments are parallel to those suggested in "On George's Square" (Possible Attribution, June 23, 1790), and the poem demonstrates a structure occasionally employed by Freneau—a series of rhetorical questions followed by a statement of the conclusion logically implied by the assumed responses.

Daily Advertiser   August 30, 1790

Lines occasioned by a visit to Federal Hall.

Leary, 174	Described as Freneau's last satirical poem on Congress.
385	In his manner.
Marsh, 128	Undoubtedly his work—indicates that he too lamented the loss of government in New York, particularly the degeneration of Federal Hall.

These four stanzas lament the loss of the canters who preached for pay and the "house that Folly raised so high." This is not a completely sarcastic lament, though, as the writer suggests that all their noise was better than "the dull blank," which is all that can be heard now.

Daily Advertiser   August 31, 1790

The City Lady to her Husband, fond of the Country.

Leary, 385   In his manner.

The City Lady prefers the life and activity of the city to the shady hills and purling rills that her husband enjoys. She speculates that perhaps rural life will suit her when she grows too old to enjoy herself. Addresses much in this manner, from people in the city to those in the country and vice versa, arguing the advantages of their respective lifestyles, were typical in papers of the period. Nothing particularly distinguishes this one as Freneau's.

Appendix B: Possible Attributions

Daily Advertiser   September 18, 1790

        The Happy Farmer.

Marsh, W.P.F., 59 — Partially quoted as one of the poems written by Freneau when New York must have seemed dull without the Federal government. Described as a sneer at cities.

This is a conventional poem praising life in the country over that in the city; nothing particularly distinguishes it as Freneau's.

Daily Advertiser   October 23, 1790

        A Farewell to New York.

Marsh, 131 — Notes that in October, Freneau may have been moving back to Monmouth and may have written this poem.

Marsh, W.P.F., 59 — Partially quoted; remarks that perhaps Freneau was at the point of leaving New York.

These are two stanzas wishing New York health, peace, and prosperity and recalling her past glories. It is a straightforward and conventional tribute the could have been written by anyone leaving town, particularly someone who had moved with the government to Philadelphia.

Daily Advertiser   November 16, 1790

        The Complaint of the Burling-slip Boatmen.

Leary, 385 — In his manner.

Marsh, 132 — Partially quoted; Freneauesque.

The poet complains about the dumping of trash in the East River from a wharf where boatmen must endure the stench. It appears to have been written from first hand experience.

Daily Advertiser   January 29, 1791

    Leary, 385   In his manner.

    Marsh, 134   Unauthorized Freneau poem.

This is a six stanza poem describing the despair of sailors in a sinking ship who sight a ship that refuses them aid. The poet concludes with a tribute to a Frenchman, unnamed in the text, who met such a ship and saved its crew. A note appearing with the poem explains that it was occasioned by the conduct of Monsieur Duroutois, who, at peril to his own crew, saved the survivors of a sinking schooner, for which he was choosen honorary member of the Marine Society of New York. The long explanation reads like Freneau in the precision of the nautical details, the parenthetical information supplied, and the numerous interjections in phrasing. The writer of the note does not specifically indicate that the poem, a mediocre effort, is his own.

Daily Advertiser   February 16, 1791

    On Leaving a Dutch House in the Western Parts of Pennsylvania.
            Written in 1776.)

    Leary, 386   In his manner.

    Marsh, 135   Unauthorized Freneau poem.

This four-stanza poem describes a dull, poor, inhospitable inn, with bawling brats and gloomy fires. The poet vows never to stop there again. It is close in choice of detail, mood and development to "Lines formerly written at a Tavern in Log-Town," *City Gazette*, December 8, 1789.

Daily Advertiser   March 5, 1791

    (Occasioned by the late Theatrical disturbances in Philadelphia.)

    Leary, 385   In his manner.

This poem condemns the unruly Philadelphia audiences. It describes the hazards and risks imposed upon actors and concludes that the vulgar age, intent upon building banks and pulling down kings, has no time for heroes of the stage. The poet invites the Philadelphia Company to New York, where their efforts would be appreciated. The text refers to an actor as "Mambrino," a name Freneau used in other poems at this time. In his "On the present situation of the theatre in Charleston," (*City Gazette*, January 8, 1790) he similarly attacks enemies of the theatre.

Daily Advertiser   April 16, 1791

The Potatoe Orator. Occasioned by hearing an Oration upon Potatoes, at a Public Commencement.

Leary, 385   In his manner.

These are four stanzas on an orator, who laments that all subjects of discourse and poetry have become hackneyed. It is typical of Freneau's colloquial manner and includes a complaint typical of speakers in his poems—that the age is inglorious, in this case because all compelling subjects of oration have been overworked.

Daily Advertiser   April 26, 1791

The Southern Jaunt.

Leary, 385   In his manner.

In two stanzas, this poem contrasts the man who earns a ride in a gilded coach by licking "Cesar's" boots to the man who walks on foot, at his own pace, "not dragg'd as others choose." It is typical of Freneau's attacks on sycophancy.

Daily Advertiser   April 27, 1791

The Morning Walker.

Leary, 385   In his manner.

Marsh, 136   Highly probably attribution; describes Freneau's morning walk.

This poem describes "Ascerbo's" morning walk from the battery to Greenwich point, during which he passes DeLancey's deserted mansion and Corlaer's Hook, and arrives home when everyone else is starting for work. There are many Freneau-like features in the poem, including references to the Dutch as hoarders and echoes of "The Deserted Farm House." The poet's suggestion that the walk is motivated by a desire to cheat the doctor—

> For they who early rise, and early walk
> Take the true step to shun his hateful potion:
> All nature's works, but man, enjoy good health,
> Since all but he, are constantly in motion—

recalls his comment to Seth Paine, "While I live I must be active. A sedentary, dull life has a strange effect on me. I must be in motion to be happy," (P.F. to Seth Paine, August 12, 1800, as quoted in Leary, p. 314.)

Daily Advertiser   May 5, 1791

The Sciota Indian's Complaint.

Leary, 385	In his manner.
Marsh, 134	Unauthorized poem; partially quoted as Freneau's.
Marsh, W.P.F., 63	Partially quoted as Freneau's; may indicate his changing concept of the Indian, which evolved in the Tomo Cheeki essays of 1795.

A Sciota Indian hails the sun "whose absence kills me, but whose presence cures" and asks him to dart red lightnings at the Frenchmen for offering no more than weak liquors. It is very like Freneau in the poet's ability to depict the Frenchman through Indian eyes. Also Freneau-like is the comic reference to the Indian's taste for strong drink, due to its power to kill one's cares.

Daily Advertiser   May 16, 1791   (Rpt. N. Y. *Diary*, November 9, 1797, "By Philip Freneau.")

The Origin of Lee Boards.

Leary, 171, 185, 453   Notes *Diary* attribution; in his manner;

Appendix B: Possible Attributions 735

included in Freneau Bibliography.

This is an anecdotal account of the invention of the lee board by an ancient Dutch woman, who, on a veering ship, seized a vast frying pan and forced it down on the leeward side. It recalls Freneau's depiction of the sturdy, resourceful, and commonsensical Dutch wife, who governs the helm while her husband sits back admiring her skill in Freneau's "Characteristic Sketch of the Long Island Dutch," *City Gazette,* February 2, 1790.

Daily Advertiser   June 9, 1791

To a young lady, who sent to the author, for "The Rights of Man."

Leary, 385   In his manner.

This poem asserts that Clara has no need to read *The Rights of Man* because, as she and everyone else knows, no matter how free men are politically they are slaves to the charms of women. There were a series of poems appearing in papers at this time (See the Philadelphia *American Daily Advertiser,* March to June, 1791) making light of feminine interest in the philosophy of Paine. All of them develop the same patronising argument that women have no need for "reason's plan" in asserting their rights because they already possess a natural ascendancy: "For though your arguments might fail/Your charms resistless must prevail!" ("To the Ladies, who so successfully have employed their pens in defense of the Rights of man," *American Daily Advertiser,* March 26, 1791.) Similar to other poems on this theme, this one has no special Freneauian characteristics.

Freeman's Journal   July 13, 1791

Verses on the arrival of the President.

Marsh, W.P.F., 69, 141   Appears to be Freneau's. Certainly Freneau's.

This is a conventional tribute to Washington apparently from the press: "Friend of the Press, the Press shall honor thee." The poem displays a fascination with the ceremonial aspects of the occasion that seems unlike Freneau: "Thus spoke the muse; the bells now charm my ears,/And *Washington* in virtue's pomp appears."

Freeman's Journal   August 24, 1791

> An Address to my old Hat.
>   Signed "Epaminodas."

Marsh, W.P.F., 68, 160   Partially quoted; apparently by Freneau; probably Freneau's.

The poet laments that his old hat has finally worn out, addressing it as an unfashionable but dependable friend. He describes the different styles in which he wore it—cocked, three cornered, and so on, and enumerates other kinds of less virtuous hats—a turk's turban, a king's crown, and so on. The poem recalls Freneau only in praising a dependable old garment (See Probable Attributions, *Daily Advertiser*, March 5, 1790.)

Freeman's Journal   September 7, 1791

> An Epistle from Peter Pindar Pennsylvanius, to the Right Honourable William Pitt, Exq. Chancellor of the Exechequer, &c. in Great Britain.

Marsh, W.P.F., 69, 141   Probably contributed by Freneau. Freneau imitating Peter Pindar.

These are ten irregular stanzas in the manner of Peter Pindar, attacking Pitt as a bully and an opportunist while praising his father. Imitations of Pindar were common in papers of the period, and nothing distinguishes this poem as Freneau's.

National Gazette   December 1, 1791

> Epigram.

This is an amusing anecdote, deriding the fop "Pomposo" for his inflated, lyrical approach to love making. Florio, more straightforward, overhears Pomposo complain that his poor taper shines but dimly next to the radiant beams of Miss Anna. Florio promptly volunteers to snuff Anna's fires that the fop will not suffer so by comparison. It recalls Freneau's impatience with rhetorical inflation and with foppery.

Appendix B: Possible Attributions

National Gazette March 29, 1792

Receipt to make an Echo Writer

Leary, 200-01	Quoted as Freneau's response to an attack in the *American Mercury*.
445	Included in the Freneau Bibliography.
Marsh, 153	Quoted as Freneau's.
Marsh, W.P.F., 70	Notes that Freneau was stirred by abuse in the *American Mercury* to retort in this poem.

On March 12, as part of "The Echo" series, the *American Mercury* ridiculed Freneau's verses. We know Freneau responded directly to the attack with "Ode to the Echo Writer" on April 2, but Leary and Marsh both attribute this poem to Freneau as an earlier response to the attack. Although this could be Freneau's poem, it contains no direct reference, as does the April 2 poem, to the "Echo's" attack. It is a conventional "receipt" (recipe) insult, typical of political/poetical abuse of the period. The writer lists a series of putrid or unsavory ingredients, the combination of which is supposed to produce the verses of the poet being ridiculed. Many readers and contributors to the *National Gazette* could have taken the occasion to attack the Hartford writers. For instance, the poem recalls the abusive verse of Brackenridge, who also was parodied in the same "Echo" number. (See edition, *National Gazette*, April 2, 1792, for a description of this "Echo" poem.)

National Gazette April 5, 1792

An Address to the Citizens of Holland, on considering the accounts of the Periodical Inundations, which have destroyed that country, agreeing with late accounts of the encroachment of the ocean there.

Leary, 388	Included in a list of *National Gazette* poems, uncollected, but which indicate his authorship.
Marsh, 141	Partially quoted as Freneau's.

Marsh, W.P.F., 71   Partially quoted as Freneau's.
141   Probably Freneau's.

In eleven couplets the poet warns Holland to heed Columbia, who is her friend, rather than the devastating flood of monarchal propaganda assaulting her shore. As the title suggests, the idea is developed by means of an analogy to ocean overwhelming land—in this case, a weak and defenseless shore which cannot hope to stem the flood with bulwarks built on sand. The analogy recalls similar imagery elsewhere in Freneau's poetry.

National Gazette   May 3, 1792

Untitled stanza on the funding system.

Leary, 388   Certainly Freneau's.

Marsh, 156   Freneau's poetic retort to an opposing view.

The controversial issue of maintaining a public debt inspired several "jingles" during the 1790's. Most parodied Hamilton's statement that a public debt was a public blessing, and this one was printed directly under a similar jingle which it parodies. The first jingle presents the Federalist view of the debt, and this verse, attributed to Freneau, twists that jingle to represent an opposing view. The rhyme that, according to Leary, particularly distinguishes the verse as Freneau's—"nothing worse is/public curses"—also was included in the verse being parodied. In short, these jingles, twisting the same phrases and rhymes to represent different sides of the issue, are too similar to be identified as the work of a particular poet.

National Gazette   May 14, 1792

The following lines were written on a back-country parson, whose custom it was to have his neighbours cows milked, whenever they broke into his pasture.

Leary, 383   Evidences his authorship because it treated just the kind of subject in which Freneau delighted.

Appendix B: Possible Attributions 739

Marsh, W.P.F., 71, 141   Partially quoted; probably Freneau's.

This poem sharply criticizes the parson for robbing the poor—"Celestial food to orphans he dispenses/And robs their cow--for jumping fences!" The poet argues that such an act invalidates everything he says in the pulpit. It is typical of Freneau's attacks on preachers and clerical hypocrisy in general.

National Gazette   May 31, 1792

                Editorial with verse.

Marsh, F.P.P., 335   Verse appearing with prose piece ascribed to Freneau.

These five stanzas are introduced by an essay, included under the heading "Foreign News," arguing that it is unreasonable to compare modern party leaders to the sages of antiquity because true classical virtues are not in vogue at present. The writer cites, as an example of this kind of comparison, the bust of Pitt recently placed by the Empress of Russia between those of Demosthenes and Cicero and concludes, "On this subject we will take the liberty to repeat a few lines."

The poet first praises the virtuous character and leadership of Demosthenes and then asks who deserves such praise in modern times. The ironic answer is "the tool confessed of foreign power/The Aeschines of modern days." The last three stanzas of this poem were reprinted in the *National Gazette*, within quotation marks, upon Pitt's resignation (January 16, 1793.) Several essays attacking and defending Pitt appeared in the *National Gazette* from May through July, 1792, most under the section entitled "London" and several extracted from British papers. The fact that the text is introduced as a poem "repeated" and that it appears elsewhere in the paper within quotations suggest that it may have been extracted from some other source.

National Gazette   September 22, 1792

                Untitled Satire against Freneau's enemies.

Leary, 214   Quotes the text as Freneau's.
      389   Identifies the allusions to the three

	enemies mentioned in the text.
Marsh, 169	Quoted without positive attribution.

These five derogatory couplets follow a paragraph describing the annoying "confederation of a high minded trio, to destroy the National Gazette," arguing that such an undertaking would require far "sterner stuff" than the "clubbing of their little abilities." The text of the poem denounces the efforts of these three "well fed lads"—"mutton fist" (John Fenno), "Breadth of belly" (John Adams), and "Length of nose" (Alexander Hamilton)—to denigrate the *National Gazette* as nothing more than impotent lies. Although Freneau could have written this poem, the battle between Freneau's and Fenno's papers and the charges against Freneau and Jefferson alleged by Hamilton were so well known to all readers that any friend of the *Gazette* could have been the author. Marsh, for instance, notes that Brackenridge was in town at this time, contributing other articles to the Gazette, and a poem like this is as much in his manner as in Freneau's.

National Gazette   October 17, 1792

Verse with Editorial.

Marsh, F.P.P., 386	Verse appearing with prose piece ascribed to Freneau.

These four lines of verse appear after an essay arguing that obscurity in money matters guarantees that the masses will not understand them and that the rich alone will benefit. But the fact that the quatrain, describing a flock of geese, is within quotation marks suggests that it was abstracted from some other source. It contains nothing explicit on the subject of the essay; an analogy between the geese and the favored few apparently was implied.

National Gazette   October 24, 1792

Verse with an editorial about Indains.

Marsh, F.P.P., 391	Verse appearing with prose piece ascribed to Freneau.

Appendix B: Possible Attributions 741

This verse follows an essay arguing that it would be more reasonable to try to civilize the Indians than to murder them and seize their lands. The seven lines of verse concluding the essay read as if penned by an enlightened Christian missionary: our object should be to introduce radiant beams into their dark brains, teach them the plan of the universe, and extend their hopes to immortal life—"More blest the task!" Neither the manner nor the content of the poem particularly recalls Freneau, whose precise views about the Indians are difficult to document from his poetry.

National Gazette   November 21, 1792

Untitled stanza on the removal of the Bust of Liberty from the Hall of Congress.

Marsh, 172   Second epigram quoted as Freneau's.

Marsh, W.P.F., 74   Notes that the attribution to correspondents was only to veil his authorship.
    141   Certainly Freneau's.

Two different stanzas, only the second of which is attributed to Freneau, follow an announcement of the removal of the Liberty bust from Congress Hall. According to the note, it was placed in a recess "hitherto appropriated to the reception of certain Queen's-ware vases--for the private accomodation of the honorable members." The note concludes, "On this occasion we have received from correspondents the two following epigrams:--"

The first, not attributed to Freneau, simply states that the Goddess of Liberty, once revered, is now kicked out of doors. The second describes the insult to the goddess with greater force and vulgarity. There is no reason to assume that Freneau wrote either. Though he was among the most forceful writers in papers of the period, he rarely employs vulgar language, insinuating "off-color" ideas instead.

National Gazette   January 12, 1793

                      Short Canes!
                                           Signed "Momus."

Leary, 226   Unqualified attribution to Freneau, but not included in bibliography.

Marsh, W.P.F., 75   Unqualified attribution to Freneau.

This is a brief anecdote mocking aristocratic beaus. It is very like Freneau in the double entendre suggested. An "off color" interpretation may have eluded the editors of the discreet *Port Folio*, however; it was reprinted there, unattributed, on December 8, 1804.

National Gazette   February 20, 1793

Verse with prose piece attacking Hartford "monarchists."

Marsh, F.P.P., 484

This stanza, appearing within quotations, concludes an essay attacking "the aristocratic, speculating faction at Hartford" for favoring monarchy and titular distinctions, describing them as coeval with the old Tories of 1775. However, the writer concludes that they will, like a useless part of the anatomy, eventually atrophy and fall off.

The six lines of verse concluding the essay pursue the anatomical analogy much in the manner of Sterne. The verse does not specifically refer to the political points developed in the essay. Since it appears within quotations, it may have been extracted from some other source.

National Gazette   September 4, 1793

A new way to tell an Old Lie.

Leary, 241   Partially quoted as Freneau's.

This poem is an unflattering slap at John Jay and Rufus King for affirming before the public that Ambassador Genet was planning to appeal directly to the American people on behalf of France. The poem depicts their actions as a conspiracy to circulate what they suspect is a lie in order to destroy American good will toward France and to ingratiate themselves with the public. The vulgar conclusion merely enlarges upon Jay's confession, paraphrased earlier in the poem, "if we stir, we shall stink." Written as a dialogue in the colloquial manner of Freneau, it is not masterful verse. It could have

Appendix B: Possible Attributions 743

been penned by any spirited republican engaged by this volatile issue.

National Gazette   October 12, 1793

Untitled stanza concluding an editorial condemning American neutrality in the affairs of Europe.

Marsh, F.P.P., 562

This quatrain clearly was written as part of the essay. It simply summarizes the essay's argument that it must "mortify your pride/To take the strict impartial side."

Jersey Chronicle   August 1, 1795

Lines, written by a Young Gentleman, during a tedious Consumption, of which he died in his twenty-second Year.--(Addressed to his fellow Collegians.)

Leary, 260   In Freneau's manner.

This is a long, labored piece in which the poet laments his illness, contemplates what he is missing, and rails against his fate. He protests his innocence of the kind of crime that might have earned him such bad luck. He laments the brevity of life and, in view of the precarious nature of health, the vanity of formulating plans for happiness. Finally he complains that none but a few cherished friends will miss him when he is gone. Although the brevity of life was a typical theme in Freneau, he seldom whined about it in this manner.

Jersey Chronicle   September 5, 1795

An Imitation of Spenser.

Leary, 260   In Freneau's manner.

These are two stanzas describing the absurdity of war, not much in the manner of Spenser or Freneau.

Jersey Chronicle September 12, 1795

    Mr, Jay's Treaty Disclosed by Stephens Thaddeus Mason.

    Pattee, Vol. 3, 132   Text included as Freneau's, on the basis of its appearance in his paper and of his anti-Treaty Treaty stance.

    Leary, 461   Included in the Freneau Bibliography, with reference to Pattee.

This poem has been attributed to Freneau because it appeared in the *Chronicle* and was critical of the treaty. Numerous articles attacking Jay's Treaty appeared during the summer and fall of 1795, many of them reprinted from the Philadelphia *Aurora*, where the original text of the treaty had been published, including the series "Features of Mr. Jay's Treaty" mistakenly attributed by Pattee to Freneau. This poem describes the Senate clandestinely discussing the treaty, fearing the opposition of the "rabble," until Mason, a freeman respectful of the *vox populi*, arises and delivers it to the people. It recalls Freneau in the reference to the Senate as "Sanhedrim," although he rarely employs a chorus repeated after each verse, as in this poem ("Ye are down, down, down, keep ye down.") The same chorus, however, ("Get you down, down, down, keep ye down") was included after each verse of a poem printed in the Philadelphia *Independent Gazetteer* on July 5, 1794. A British poem, it is an amusing travesty of Burke's *Reflections*, and could have inspired the writer of this poem, which closely resembles it. The note introducing the British poem explains that it is to be sung to the tune of a popular English song, "Derry down, Derry down." Since both "Mr Jay's Treaty" and this poem employ the same metrical pattern, it is likely that the former also was written to the tune of this song. Although Freneau occasionally wrote imitations of British poets, he rarely imitated popular British songs, which were widely imitated by other newspaper poets of the period.

Jersey Chronicle January 16, 1796

    A Simile--To a Young Lady.

    Leary, 260   In Freneau's manner.

This poem offers conventional moral advice to a virgin not to yield her charms. A lover's ardor is like a shepherd's thirst; once it is quenched, he moves on until thirsty again, at which point he frequents other streams. This poem was reprinted in the *Time-Piece* on April 5, 1797, under the title "Addressed to a Young Lady." The stanza form and individual lines were altered in the reprint. For instance, the original line describing the shepherd's response to the spring after his thirst is quenched read: "Then mark how with disdainful feet/He kicks her banks . . ." In the *Time-Piece* text, this scornful conduct is mitigated: "He quits her banks." Such a poem, seriously developing a single analogy on love for twenty-four lines really is not in the manner of Freneau. The minor revisions in the reprint, however, are like those Freneau occasionally made when extracting material from other sources.

Jersey Chronicle   April 16, 1796

Untitled stanza concluding an essay about British fears of a Revolution.

Marsh, F.P.P., 672

This six-line stanza, which appears to have been written for the essay, succinctly summarizes the main point: because of defensive and reactionary attitudes, despotism is more to be feared than insurrection in England.

Jersey Chronicle   April 23, 1796

Parody on the attempt to force the British Treat on the People of the United States.

Pattee, Vol. III, 133	Text included as Freneau's on the basis of its appearance in the *Chronicle* and Freneau's anti-Treaty stance.
Leary, 462	Included in Freneau Bibliography. Refers to its appearance in Pattee.
Marsh, W.P.F., 109, 146	Credits to Freneau; Refers to its appearance in the Leary Bibliography.

This three-stanza tetrameter couplet poem condemns Jay's treaty as the "sad result of base designs," formulated by traitors who sold thier country and made free Americans the pawns of Britain once again. Nothing positively marks it as Freneau's. Pattee notes that every issue of the paper during the period expressed dissatisfaction with the treaty and then erroneously ascribes the series of essays "Features of Mr. Jay's Treaty" to Freneau. Much of the Jay material was extracted.

Jersey Chronicle   April 30, 1796

Untitled stanzas against the Public Debt Program.

Leary, 267   Quoted as Freneau's.

Marsh, 278   Quoted as Freneau's.

Marsh, W.P.F., 109-10   Quoted as Freneau's.

This is another public debt jingle parodying Hamilton's statement that a public debt is a public blessing (see Possible Attributions, *National Gazette*, May 8, 1792, for the difficulty of identifying verses of this nature as the work of a particular poet.)

New York *Argus*   May 28, 1796

To The Swinish Multitude.

Marsh, 230   Partially quoted; probably Freneau's.

This poem, inspired by Burke's reference to the people as "a swinish multitude," in his *Reflections on the Revolution in France*, appears to be modeled after British travesties of the same speech, reprinted in several American papers (i.e. *Independent Gazetteer*, July 5, 1794). It focuses upon the reference to swine in its ironic argument, addressed to the masses, that nature has given appropriate attributes to all creatures; to man, freedom and the power to rule over beasts; to brutes, only servitude. Swine, then, have no natural right to oppose those who govern them. Except for the Republican sentiments, nothing in the poem particularly recalls Freneau; the accumulation of references to every brand of swine—hogs, sows, boars, barrows, sucklings, and pickled port—and to a wide variety of other beasts commonly associated with dirt is not typical of Freneau, who generally employs reference to dirt and animals more selectively, at key points in his satire, for more striking and intense effect. On the other hand, both Leary and Marsh provide evidence that Freneau was connected with Greenleaf, editor of the *Argus*, after concluding the Jersey Chronicle.

New York *Argus*   June 2, 1796

On a very Old Bachelor, who met with an angry Repulse on attempting to snatch a Kiss from a Young Lady.

Leary, 395   Much like Freneau.

This poem reprimands the old bachelor for imagining that he could appeal to a young girl. It employs analogies to the motions of stars, planets, and moons and to the natural laws of attraction and repulsion:

> She near her high meridian shines,
> Your planet to the dust reclines;
> You are a star eclips'd--and she,
> A sun in noon tide majesty.

The poet concludes that the old bachelor has lost his chance for love by having ignored her dictates when it was his time:

> When nature said *'Tis time to love*
> Why did you not that time improve,
> Not wait 'till years bade you deplore
> The feelings that are found no more?

It is very like Freneau and recalls his other poem on the unnatural relationship between an old man and a young woman—"To a Gay young Lady that was married to a doting old Deacon," *Poems* (1795), 334-35, although there the warning was offered on behalf of the lady. It also recalls his other warning to the bachelor to choose a wife before it is too late—"The Sea Faring Bachelor," *Poems* (1786), 83. His poem on the Planet Jupiter (*City Gazette*, December 20, 1800), as well as earlier poems and several later ones ascribed to him by Leary, express an interest in the motions of planets and their moons.

Aurora   February 6, 1797

    Untitled couplet satirizing effusive praise of Washington.

Marsh, F.P.P., 686

    This couplet appears at the end of an essay, within quotation marks. As it is a tribute to Washington, effusive, but not exaggerated enough to be obviously ironic, it possibly was quoted from a genuine specimen of the sort of poetry the essay criticizes.

Time-Piece   March 27, 1797

> On the Activity of the Mind
> (Rpt. *Time-Piece,* April 21, 1797 as "Action.")

    This long poem in couplets describes the wakeful activity of the human mind. It remains active even in sleep, when it is freed in dreams. It is described as a somewhat threatening presence; it "haunts" us and affords us no peace. The poet wonders about its substance— is it spirit or animal—and concludes that, though unconfined by time and space, it is still

> Incorporate with our dull and senseless clay,
> Through inert matter darts its active ray.

    Although this subject interested Freneau, the verbal patterns and diction do not particularly recall his work. Particularly Freneau-like, however, are the concluding five couplets, which follow the two lines just quoted. These ten lines abruptly push the discussion in a new direction. They could have been added by Freneau as a response to, or as the conclusion drawn from, this description of the mind, which may have agreed with his own view. They recommend physical activity and motion:

> And while subsists the union we are taught
> Motion to life is needful, as to thought—
> For all the several ills that men endure,
> In exercise is found the safest cure.
> With grief or gloom is the sad mind opprest,
> It is not thought, but action yields it rest;
> And every chronic ill that vexes Age,

> Like sin, is cancell'd by a pilgrimmage–
> To move unceasing is great Nature's will;
> Her life is Action, Death her standing still!

These lines recall Freneau's own statement about his need to remain physically active (see Possible Atrributions, *Daily Advertiser*, April 27, 1791) and read like a "doctor's orders" specifically directed as cure for the ailment suggested in the earlier portion of the poem. Although it is impossible to prove that he wrote merely the last ten lines, the title change in the otherwise unaltered reprint reinforces the suspicion. "Action" aptly titles only the last ten lines, since the rest of the poem only describes thought, albeit active thought. As editor, Freneau often penned poetic responses to material he printed in his columns, either from contributors or other sources.

Time-Piece   August 30, 1797   (Rpts. September 1, 4, 1797)

> Verse included in an advertisement.

Leary, 465   Included in Freneau Bibliography

This poem was included, within quotation marks, as part of an advertisement for a new volume, never actually published, entitled "The interesting travels of John Ledyard, with a summary of his life." On July 26, Freneau announced that he had obtained the manuscripts of John Ledyard, celebrated explorer who sailed around Cape Horn with Captain Cook and who died in Cairo. His letters, journals, and notes had been gathered by his cousin, Dr. Isaac Ledyard, the brother-in-law of Eleanor Forman Freneau's sister, Catharine. Freneau proposed to arrange the materials for a volume if enough subscriptions could be obtained to cover his expenses. On August 30, this poem was added to the announcement. It follows an account of how Ledyard had often encountered the finest examples of civilized conduct among those often termed "barbarians," while he had encountered barbarity itself in polished societies. . . . "To this circumstance, one of his panegyrists alludes in the subsequent graceful lines:"

The six stanza poem which is then quoted describes the independent soul of Ledyard, who scorned the power of tyrants, braved deserts, and, despising the "narrow reign," pursued a "liberal course o'er nature's wide domain." The poem does not specifically develop the "circumstance" alluded to in the introduction, as one might assume if the poem had been written for the advertisement to illustrate the point mentioned. Rather, it reads like a conventional tribute to a great explorer and aside from the admiration for manly independence it does not especially recall Freneau. Although he never collected it, the poem was attributed to Freneau in at least three reprints in other newspapers, probably because the advertisement had indicated that he would be the editor of the proposed volume. But if Freneau had access to all of the papers and notes on Ledyard, it is possible that a poem by a panegyrist was among them and that he is quoting another poet, as he indicates. Encouragement for the volume, once it was announced, was voiced in several other New York papers, all expressing a similar admiration for the explorer. The poem was not included in the ad until over a month after it first appeared in Freneau's paper, providing enough time for an admirer to contribute a panegyric, perhaps to help spur the sale of subscriptions.

Time-Piece September 13, 1797

Verse with prose piece attacking "Peter Porcupine."

Pattee, III, 156	Text included as Freneau's.
Leary, 287	Partially quoted a Freneau's response to attacks by Cobbett in *Porcupine's Gazette* on September 8.
465	Included in Freneau Bibliography.
Marsh, 244; W.P.F., 120	Partially quoted as Freneau's slap at Cobbett.

On September 8, William Cobbett published an attack in his *Porcupine's Gazette* against the *Time-Piece*, with which he says he has been plagued, and on Freneau personally. He offered a satirical and disparaging outline of Freneau's career, concluding with his present job of "grinding sedition" in New York. On the 13th, Freneau published an editorial referring to the attack, and announcing that he intended to continue plaguing Porcupine, just as he had plagued some of his brethren. The three stanza poem that follows associates Cobbett with the yellow fever in Philadelphia. Cobbett and Fenno are the two remaining "vipers" waiting to be carted away, Cobbett

Appendix B: Possible Attributions

is the "noisy whelp" of Pitt from the kennels of London; the poet exhorts him to be gone from the place once dignified by Franklin and Penn. The only basis for doubting the attribution is that the poem reads like a general attack on Cobbett; it does not refer specifically to the attack on Freneau. Cobbett had many enemies in Philadelphia, since he had been attacking brutally Bache's *Aurora* for months. The poem might have been penned by any of his journalistic enemies and used by Freneau for the occasion. Freneau printed other anti-Cobbett verses in the *Time-Piece* that were evidently not his own. On September 20, for instance, a long, disparaging narrative attacking Porcupine appeared under the signature "Patronella." Poems by "Patronella" had been appearing in the paper, primarily humorous anecdotes that have never been ascribed to Freneau.

Time-Piece September 15, 1797

Verse with prose attacking Henry VIII.

Marsh, F.P.P., 737

This prose piece, describing Henry as a beast and a royal brute, concludes, "The following lines, written by Henry, in the last years of his disastrous reign, on a pane of glass with a diamond, are still preserved." The four-line stanza describes the fate of each of his wives. After the stanza, the author of the prose piece comments on the shoddiness of the rhyme. Although the verse may not have been written by Henry VIII, there are few grounds for assuming that it was written by Freneau.

Time-Piece September 18, 1797

Poetry with a prose attack on Porcupine.

Leary, 288	Describes poem as Freneau's third reply to Porcupine's attack of September 8.
465	Included in Freneau Bibliography.

Frank Smith, "Philip Freneau and the *Time-Piece*," *American Literature* IV (1932), 270-87. Attributes to Freneau.

Marsh, F.P.P., 742

This is another stanza attacking Cobbett, arguing that, since he worships the king, he should have stayed at home. However, since he insists on being here, he should know that many are prepared to drive him to hell. Although quite possibly Freneau's, the grounds for doubting the attribution are the same as those raised with respect to the anti-Cobbett verses which appeared on September 13 (Possible Attributions, September 13, 1797.)

Time-Piece   September 25, 1797

       Verse included with prose attack on Fenno

Marsh, F.P.P., 745

This four-line stanza concludes a prose attack on Fenno's support of the ruined system of Royalty. It is introduced by a latin quotation which it allegedly translates. However, the stanza actually claims that "John" (Adams? Fenno?) is the American version of George III. Though not in quotation marks, the verse does not follow directly from the prose comments and could have been derived from some other source for the occasion.

Time-Piece   September 29, 1797

       On the Death of a Tea-Pot.

Marsh, 244   Certainly Freneau's.

These are two stanzas lamenting the fall of a tea pot which once stood with "graceful pride" while the tea cups around it stared in awe. A conventional lament on the loss of a favorite object, nothing particularly marks it as Freneau's.

Time-Piece   October 6, 1797

       Verse included with a prose attack on Fenno.

Leary, 294-95   Notes that the poem is a response to Fenno's son's denial of Freneau's charge (September 27) that it was

Appendix B: Possible Attributions 753

	Fenno to whom Trumball referred, in *M'Fingal*, as having been tarred and feathered.
446	Included in the Freneau Bibliography.

Frank Smith, "Philip Freneau and the *Time-Piece*," *American Literature* IV (1932), 280-87. Atrributes to Freneau.

Marsh, F.P.P., 758

On September 27, the *Time-Piece* had included at attack on Fenno which suggested that he had been tarred and feathered for Tory sympathies in 1775. This attack was prompted by an article in Fenno's *Gazette of the United States* on September 22 accusing Freneau of hypocrisy in claiming to revive the spirit of the revolution, when he in fact had done nothing during the war but write idle rhymes. Fenno's son defended his father's honor in the *Gazette* on September 29th, vigorously denying the tar and feather charge, but on the 6th of October the *Time-Piece* included a prose essay repeating the charge and asserting that the matter should be left open to investigation, concluding with ten lines of verse claiming that the "dark affair" would be dragged out to light. Although the prose piece and poem prolonging the issue were quite possibly Freneau's, the *Time-Piece* charges also were enthusiastically reported in the *Aurora*; this satiric demand that they be further investigated could have been contributed by any anti-Fenno friend of Freneau.

Time-Piece   October 13, 1797

> To the Lovers.
> Signed "Duncan Downright."

Leary, 274	Suspects that "Downright" is speaking for the editor.

This poem, allegedly written by a correspondent, complains about the dull love lyrics that had been appearing in the *Time-Piece*, requesting that the "duncified" scribblers desist, and concludes by asserting that, if the paper is really unbiased and free, these lines will appear in the next issue. The poem is editorially introduced with an announcement that the printer refuses to publish any more verses in the poetical controversy between "L.", one of the love scribblers, and his rivals: ". . . the following verses from a correspondent will set the reasons for discontinuance in a clear point of view." Although the poem could have been Freneau's, there would have been ample reason for any reader to be annoyed with the insipid lyrics that had been appearing; receiving such a poem might have prompted Freneau, who had been printing these poems without critical com=ment, to stop accepting them for fear of annoying readers.

Time-Piece   October 16, 18, 20, 25, 31, and November 6, 1797

Book of Odes, Nos. I, II, III, V, VII, and IX.

Pattee, III, 161-65; 167-69; 171-72; 174-75. Texts included.

Leary, 466-67   Included in Freneau Bibliography.

Marsh, 245-46;   Ascribes to Freneau.
    W.P.F., 122-23

Of the twelve odes that comprise the Book of Odes, appearing in the *Time-Piece* from October 16 through November 15, 1797, Freneau collected only six, but all editors and biographers of the poet have assumed that he wrote all twelve. All have described the poems as weak, facile verse, most interesting for their satirical comments on various aspects of contemporary life. The verses, appearing in rapid succession, may have been hastily written, and the "ode," as it was employed by newspaper poets of the period, was most conducive to rapid composition. Lacking any prescribed form, it enabled any poet to say exactly what he wanted, almost prosaically, saving the time it would take to concentrate on rhyme and meter. These same factors, however, make the attribution of odes quite difficult; since form or "manner" is relatively obscured, we can only rely on the "content" of the poems. We know, for instance, that the Probationary Odes, which appeared in the *National Gazette*, were ascribed erroneously to Freneau because they appeared in the *Gazette* and expressed ideas consistent with the bias of the paper. Since Freneau never collected half ot the *Time-Piece* odes, I believe it is risky casually to ascribe all of them to him.

It is possible to see differences between the poems that were and were not collected. Although this fact does not preclude the possibility that he wrote them all, since Freneau seems to have been able to write, in his popular or casual verse, on both sides of an issue, it does provide grounds for suspecting that he may not have written them all. For instance, neither of the two odes on the Frigate Constitution (II and IX) were collected, and both develop the point that it is better for the ship to stay peacefully on shore, avoiding dangers, risks and entanglement with foreign "blackguards." In the second ode on the Constitution, the poet refers to Richard Brothers' millenial prophecy of imminent peace on earth, and however lightly he regards it, he seems genuine in his appeal for pacifism:

> If Richard proves a prophet true
> Why may we not be quiet too,

as well as in his final faith that universal peace is a realistic possibility:

> The times approach when men of might
> And squadrons roving round the ball,
> Shall fight each other not at all.

Ode X, however, which was collected by Freneau, also addresses the subject of this millenial prophecy of peace, as if in response to the conclusion reached in the preceding poem. Freneau rejects the prophecy as inconsistent with the laws of human nature as they now operate:

> Ere discord shall from man depart
> He must assume a different heart.

Similarly, in Ode VII, "On the Federal City," also not collected, the main point of the satire is that this place, the new center of national life, is nothing but a dull country town. The writer bids Congress to defer no longer in moving from Philadelphia. Such a response to the new Capitol is different from that expressed in Freneau's poem on the Federal City (*City Gazette*, December 18, 1800) later collected in the 1815 *Poems*. There it is dated "1797" but is entirely different from this ode. The first version of the 1815 poem probably was published in 1796 (See Probable Atrributions, New York *Argus*, May 13, 1796). The 1796, 1800 and 1815 texts reflect grave doubts about bringing the Federal City to life—the poet suggests that the money and effort could be misdirected and abused and that the town's growth and development will be at the expense of those who will not profit from the aims of the leaders they have elevated.

On the other hand, there are grounds for believing that the entire series was penned by a single poet: several poems refer specifically to earlier ones, i.e. the opening lines of Ode VII refer to the subjects discussed in Odes V and VI, and, as noted above, Ode X pursues the reference to millenial philosophy which concludes Ode IX. However, due to the ease with which this type of poem could be written, and the possibility that the entire series may have been penned at some time prior to the dates of publication (the Constitution, for instance, was launched one month before the *Time-Piece* odes appeared), references to earlier odes do not preclude the possibility that more than one writer contributed to the project.

Time-Piece   December 1, 1797

Untitled Satire on Robert Harper

Marsh, 249   Partially quoted: Not acknowledged, but clearly Freneau's.

This poem, a three-stanza pun playing repeatedly on the name "Harper," satirizes the Federalist congressman, described as a "harpie," for his "harping" in Congress. Several lines recall Freneau, though he does not typically pursue a single pun this far.

Time-Piece   December 4, 1797

Verse included with a prose piece attacking royalty.

Leary, 298   Ascribed to Freneau.
468   Included in Freneau Bibliography.

Marsh, F.P.P., 798

These five couplets follow a prose piece on the deceptiveness of the pomp and pageantry of kings and courts, first instituted to convince the ignorant that those who govern are divine. The caustic couplets, very like Freneau, describe the manner in which divine pretension is infused into the new monarch at the moment of coronation. It clearly was penned by the writer of the editorial.

Time-Piece   July 18, 1798

The Political Parson, occasioned by a Clergyman's expressing his disapprobation of the French republicanizing in Italy.

Marsh, 254   Probably by Freneau.

This is a long and wordy account of a parson who for twenty years has prayed for the extinction of the pope but who is shocked when he hears that infidel "sans cullottes" have dethroned him. Now he prays that the pope will be restored, as "None but priests shall maul a brother priest." The poem recalls Freneau only in the anticlerical sentiments.

Aurora   October 31, 1799

Epitaph on Mrs. Rittenhouse
Signed "L."

Marsh, W.P.F., 134   Attributes to Freneau.

A conventional epitaph, these seven couplets praise Mrs. Rittenhouse for her superior mind, devotion to her husband, goodness, and sympathy. A common signature of the period, this initial never appeared with verses collected by Freneau.

Aurora   January 8, 1800

Verse appearing with prose piece.
Signed "Bob Buckskin."

Marsh, F.P.P., 886
         W.P.F., 134   Tentative attribution.

This six stanza poem appears with an essay critical of effusive elegies for Washington. The writer concludes by offering a little effusion of his own. Entitled "Elegy, or Dirge," the poem consists of a quick-paced dialogue between "Cato" and "Cesar" concerning the nature of truth. Cesar argues that one lives truly by looking out for one's own interests, and Cato, for the good of the whole. But when Cesar dies, Cato worships him and writes "Emperor" on his urn. The poem concludes by urging "sons of the Backwood" to remember that the people are kings. Only the objection to effusive rhetoric, expressed in the essay, distinctively recalls Freneau. If the "Cesar" of the poem is Washington, it would be hard to imagine Freneau penning such a caustic poem within weeks of his two sincerely respectful tributes occasioned by Washington's death (*City Gazette*, January 10, 15, 1800.)

Aurora   January 24, 1801

Jefferson and Liberty, A Patriotic Song, for the Glorious Fourth of March 1801. Tune: "Willy was a Wanton Wag."

Marsh, W.P.F., 137   Probably Freneau's.

These are fourteen stanzas with a chorus repeated after each hailing the end of tyranny and the Reign of Terror and the beginning of the reign of liberty with the anticipated election of Jefferson. The poet foresees, as the gifts of liberty, progress in industry and art. As the poem expresses Republican enthusiasm, and as Freneau still was contributing essays to the *Aurora* at this point, the attribution is possible, although, typical of many poems celebrating Jefferson's election, it does not especially recall Freneau's manner.

Aurora   February 20, 1801

Lines extempore on the spur of the occasion.

Marsh, 280; W.P.F., 138   Partially quoted; probably Freneau's.

This is a twenty-line stanza hailing the election of Jefferson as the victory of honesty over "fraud, chicane, and every art/That would be practic'd on the human heart," and bidding monarchists and "sychophantic feds" to hang their heads and slink home. It is typical of the many victory poems appearing in papers on this occasion.

Aurora   February 24, 28, and March 9, 1801

Marsh, 280   Partially quoted as Freneauesque satire.

Marsh, W.P.F., 138, 151   Certainly by Freneau.

This is a three-part satire, each part attacking members of Adams' cabinet but all three linked by an ironic attack on Duane, publisher of the *Aurora* and successor to Bache, for having so little discretion about whom he exposes: "Every paper produces a new consternation/ No creature escapes you, you reverence no station." Through the tongue in cheek criticism of his audacity for peeping "into all parties, their plots to unravel/Crawl into each caucus and there play the devil," Duane emerges as hero of the series, a portrait completed in the last part, which describes the power merely of his presence at an assembly meeting to intimidate the Federalist speaker. The series is effective satire and quite like Freneau, particularly in the tireless insistence that if Duane had "gone with the stream" and bent his knees to power, he could have been rewarded with fame and renown.

Aurora   March 3, 1801

Extempore. On his excellency the governor of Pennsylvania receiving by express the joyful news of Mr. Jefferson's election—as President of the United States.

Marsh, 280-81   Quoted as Freneau's.

Marsh, W.P.F., 138-51   Certainly Freneau's.

This poem announces the fall of the thirteen Federalist senators of Pennsylvania, bids them return to a land where despots wear crowns, and hails, by name, five leading Pennsylvania Republicans. Nothing particularly distinguishes it as Freneau's.

True American   February 28, 1803

Dialogue between his Satanic Majesty and the Connecticut youth who prints the Trenton Federalist.
                    Signed "One of the Swinish Multitude."

Marsh, F.P.P., 931

This poetic dialogue, satirizing the New Jersey Federalist press, is in the manner of Freneau's *Freeman's Journal* dialogues between Satan and James Rivington where Satan bids the printer to publish lies for a reward in hell. Freneau used this signature after Slender's name in the collection of *Slender's Letters*. However, "O.S.M." was a popular signature among Republicans, probably originating with versified travesties of Burke's *Reflections*, in which poets ironically referred to themselves and all their common breathren as "swines." Another poem, quite unlike and never attributed to Freneau, appeared under the same signature in the *True American* on January 31, 1803.

Aurora September 1, 1804

> Verse with editorial mocking Tench Coxe.

Marsh, 290-91   Tentatively attributed to Freneau.

Marsh, F.P.P., 941

In this eight-line stanza, Tench Coxe creates such faction in the middle of hell that hell vomits him up, restoring quiet. Following directly from the text, it appears to have been written by the author of the editorial. Marsh attributes the "Joe Bunker" letters, appearing in the *Aurora* at this time, to Freneau, indicating that he still was contributing to the Philadelphia paper.

Port Folio December 15, 1804

> To Miss Ann B----, of New-York, on her birthday.
>   Signed "P.F."

This two stanza poem, a conventional tribute wishing a young girl the best on her birthday, particularly recalls Freneau only in the introductory lines that announce the poet's intention to eschew flattery, "the venal lay," and studied praise, all inappropriate for "Ann B.," who is "nature's child." The poem appears with another, "For Anna," and both are editorially introduced as follows: " 'Two poets, in two different countries born,' offer the following for the Port-Folio." Leary bases post-1815 attributions on the signature "P.F." which Freneau occasionally employed for earlier newspaper verses that he collected. Its appearance here makes this attribution possible. If it was not Freneau's poem, it follows that the signature must have been used by some other poet of the period.

Aurora January 1, 1812

> Newsboy New Years Poem.

Appendix B: Possible Attributions

Marsh, W.P.F., 163   Partially quoted; attributed to Freneau.

A conventional newsboy poem, summarizing the events of the preceding year, it is difficult to distinguish anything that marks this as particularly Freneau's. The poem predicts the defeat of England, complains of British impressment and cargo seizure, attacks British government and character in general, refers to the treacheries of Indians, which the army bravely repelled, praises American fighters, and concludes by declaring that the nation is prosperous and contented. Marsh attributes to Freneau several essays by "Old Soldier" appearing in the *Aurora* in December and January, indicating that Freneau still was contributing to the paper when this poem was published.

True American   June 29, 1812

> The Voice of America.
> Signed "A Citizen of Monmouth."

Leary, 402-03   Much in Freneau's manner.

This is a "rally to war" poem composed of nine quatrains (AAAB), the same rhyme pattern used by Freneau for "Volunteer's March" and "The Battle of Stonington" (*Fredonian*, August 11, 1814; New York *Columbian*, September 24, 1814). Freneau notes in the 1815 text of "The Volunteer's March" that this stanza is modeled after Burns' rendition of Robert Bruce's address to his army before the Battle of Bannockburn. Although other war poems appearing in papers of the period also employed this stanza, the signature here and the fact that the poem is so similar to Freneau's 1814 war poems make this attribution possible.

True American   July 20, 1812

> To the Soldiers of America. Imitated from Cambell's Ode "Ye Mariners of England."
> Signed "A Citizen of Monmouth."

Leary, 402-03   Much in Freneau's manner.

Several other imitations of the Campbell Ode, originally addressed to mariners, appeared in the *True American* during this period, most of them following the idea of the original—that "Columbia needs no bulwark—her seamen are her walls." This poem differs from the other imitations in arguing, to the contrary, that

> Columbia needs no navies
> No bulwarks but the sea
> Her strength is in a million hearts
> Determined to be free.

The poet bids the soldiers of Columbia, who guard the sacred cause of freedom, to meet their ancient foe. Three years earlier, Freneau expressed the same conviction about the superiority of a strong and unified spirit over a strong navy in a speech delivered at the erection of a Liberty Pole in Middletown, New Jersey (*True American*, April 17, 24, 1809.) Both the substance of the poem, then, and the signature make the attribution possible.

Aurora   January 1, 1813

> Newsboy poem.

Marsh, W.P.F., 164-65   Partially quoted; attributed to Freneau.

In the conventional manner, this poem summarizes the events of the past year: America's declaration of war, prompted by British outrages to her honor; America's naval victories; and the conduct of the Indian war in the west. In describing the Indian war, the poet criticizes the army and its commanders for lack of discipline, excepting Harrison, who has done everything possible to reduce the Indians, here described as "engines of hell and fiends of perdition." Marsh notes that several other Freneau-like essays appeared in the *Aurora* in December of 1812 and throughout 1813, suggesting that Freneau still was contributing to the Philadelphia paper at the time this poem was published.

Aurora   June 1, 1813

> Lines on the Late General Pike, written immediately after hearing of the capture of York.

Marsh, 315   Apparently Freneau's.

Several poems appeared in the *Aurora* on the occasion of Pike's death, referring, like this one, to Collins' Ode ("How Sleep the Brave"), the conventional and most widely employed source for poems on the death of soldiers. This poem, echoing Collins, is no more or less like Freneau than the others written on Pike.

New York *Weekly Museum*   November 2, 1816

> Letitia; or, the Fortunate Spinning Girl.
> Signed "P."

Leary, L.P., 17-18   Text included as Freneau's.

Leary ascribes this poem to Freneau, mistakenly noting that it was signed "F." The only signatures that he accepts as Freneau's in the *Weekly Museum* are "F." and "P.F." Freneau never signed any poem which was later collected with the initial "P.," which was employed by other poets in New York papers during this decade. Other poems, quite unlike Freneau's, signed "P." appeared in the *Weekly Museum* in 1817. However, this poem, describing a blacksmith who scorned the love of a young girl until she won a lottery, at which point she scorned him, is in the manner of other later poems ascribed to Freneau. Although the similarity could be coincidental, it shares one line in common with Freneau's earlier "Elegy on the Death of a Blacksmith," *National Gazette*, September 19, 1793:

> Should have struck while the iron was hot! ("Letitia")
> And struck--while his iron was hot. ("Elegy")

Aurora   December 3, 1816

> The Battle of New Orleans.
> In imitation of Hohelinden--By Campbell
> Signed "R."

Marsh, "Freneau in Philadelphia, War of 1812," *Proceedings of the New Jersey Historical Society*, LXXVI (1958), 19-22.

> Attributes to Freneau.

This Freneau-like poem celebrating Jackson's victory at New Orleans employs the same stanza as "Volunteer's March," (*Fredonian*, August

11, 1814) although here the stanza is described as an imitation of Campbell, not Burns, as indicated in the 1815 collected text of "Volunteer's March." "R." is a signature ascribed to Freneau for later poems appearing in the *Fredonian* and *True American*. Marsh notes four essays contributed by Freneau to the *Aurora* in 1816. Other war poems, however, appearing in papers of the period also employed the stanza form of Freneau's "Volunteer's March."

New York *Evening Post*   March 8, 1820

Love's But a Lottery.

Signed "N.R."

These are six stanzas, the first of which explains that Cupid does not always grant a prize to all who take a ticket. The subsequent stanzas provide several examples of unlikely matches, primarily grotesque relationships based on financial interest rather than love. This was a signature employed in later poems attributed to Freneau by Leary ("Ode Written on a remote perspective of Princeton College," *True American*, October 31, 1822). This signature also appears with another possible attribution, also on the theme of marriage, in the *Monmouth Star*, March 22, 1820.

Monmouth Star   March 22, 1820

Celibacy

Signed "N.R."

This is a nine stanza poem about a fickle bachelor who talked of nothing but love but could not settle on a wife because his feelings for women continually vacillated between ecstasy and disgust. The poet hopes that he will be saved from such a fate and that if he once feels love's dart he either will absolutely resist it or else yield his heart completely. He concludes that "The best way to find out, however, is to try it." This is a signature appearing with later verses ascribed to Freneau by Leary. Among Freneau's collected poems are several on the bachelor and the deferment of marriage. See also Possible Attributions, March 8, 1820.

Aurora   November 6, 1820

Song for the celebration of the election of Joseph Heister, as governor, October, 1820. Sung at Spring Garden.

Marsh, 334   Probably by Freneau, partially quoted.

This six stanza song celebrates the victory of honesty, reason and reform and the defeat of oppression, corruption, slavery and falsehood in the victory of Heister. Freneau probably contributed an earlier poem to the *Aurora* indirectly favoring Heister (See Probable Attributions, September 11, 1820), but this poem is much less in his manner.

True American   July 28, 1821

> On the Cession of East and West Florida, from Spain to the United States

Leary, "Philip Freneau on the Cession of Florida," *Florida Historical Quarterly*, XXI (1942), 40-43.

    Quotes text; attributes to Freneau.

Leary, L.P., 125   Clearly in Freneau's manner.

Marsh, 339   Almost certainly his.

These are fifteen stanzas celebrating the acquisition of Florida. The poet praises the first patriots, Franklin and Washington, who designed the chain of states. He claims the acquisition as a victory for liberty, winning from "selfish Spain" a "golden link in freedom's chain." He describes the mild tropical climate and landscape and concludes by hailing Jackson and his victory at New Orleans. It is much in the manner of later poems ascribed to Freneau.

True American   August 14, September 1 and 15, 1821

> The Exile of St. Helena.

Leary, L.P., 125   In Freneau's manner.

In a three part soliloquy, Napoleon, at St. Helena, reviews his ambitions and hopes for France and for mankind. He laments the failure of his aims, longs for Louisa, and ponders the eternal nature of the soul and the mind. It is very much in the manner of Freneau.

True American   August 11, 1821

                 The Dotage of Royalty.

Leary, L.P., 125   In Freneau's manner.

The text of this poem is introduced by a quote from Machiavelli to the effect that war is necessary. The poem begins by rejecting this assumption on the grounds of mankind's lack of warlike features like horns, tusks, and claws:

     Human forms through all their structure prove
     That *man* was made for harmony and love.

But, he continues, war must be endured because there is in man an incurable envy of the wealth and fame of others. These angry passions must be checked or ambitious fiends will "seize and swallow all." War, then, is justified by both law and reason "to check the wolves and vultures of mankind." This poem reflects a pattern typical of him: in many poems he begins with an objectionable hypothesis, argues against it, and then, in the course of his argument, comes back to affirm, with a deeper understanding, the original assumption. A similar pattern is visible in several of his poems on Indians, natural goodness, human and political perfectibility, and the value of religious faith.

True American   October 13, November 3, December 1 and 15, 1821

         Elijah, the New England Emigrant.
                                                   (unsigned.)

Leary, 352-53	Describes and quotes the poem as Freneau's.
Leary, L.P., 33-52	Full text provided.

This long narrative about a Massachusetts farmer and his wife who plan to emigrate west against the wishes of her father has been ascribed to Freneau because of its appearance in the *True American* during the period when other poems signed with his initials were appearing and because it includes a character "Hesekiah Salem," a persona used by Freneau in a series of *Time-Piece* essays and in his 1809 collection. Although it was quite possibly his contribution, the name "Salem" would have been known to all friends and relatives of the poet: this long, discursive, simplistic tale could have been written by a far less experienced poet attempting to imitate Freneau's manner or revive his "Salem."

True American   June 8, 1822

>   The Allegheny Beer-House
>   Written several years ago.)
>   Addressed to a Man in Power.

Leary, L.P., 126   In Freneau's manner.

This poem, written in the voice of the Beer-House keeper, is addressed to one who "governs states." The speaker defends his choice of an obscure life in "Laurel Hill" beneath "Allegheny's sacred shade," where he can smoke his pipe and sell his beer. He speculates on possible fame, presumably for former accomplishments, but suspects that no one will remember him in his decline. He maintains that even celebrated men cannot know, in their own lifetime, whether their fame will endure. He concludes by lamenting his fate, noting that if fortune had smiled on him when he was younger, he would have been among the foremost of his time. But he finds consolation in the fact that he still can talk, smile, and help the traveller to a pint of beer. Bolstering the attribution is the fact that the first line of the poem "The hermit's wish, a cell be mine!" was also the first line of Freneau's "To Harriot," (*City Gazette*, November 28, 1789), but none of the other lines ever appeared in a poem known to be his.

True American   June 15, 1822

On the New York claims to the exclusive navigation and use of waters bounding the Eastern Coasts of New Jersey, as far as the high water mark.

Leary, L.P., 125   In Freneau's manner.

The poet describes New York's claims as a violation of the spirit of justice, which must consider the interests of all parties. The poet stresses the necessity of preserving good terms among the states in order to maintain the spirit of '76. In the manner of Freneau, the poet attacks the evils of hoarded wealth and of asserting interest over right. He refers to Napoleon as an example of one who, conquering much, always wanted more.

True American   June 29, 1822

    The Promenade; or the Walks of Art and Nature.

    Leary, L.P., 125   In Freneau's manner.

Cynthia wishes to transplant wild dogwood to her domestic garden, eventually for display in her dining room. When Florio warns her that rude and wild plants should not be domesticated, she ignores his advice, transplants the dogwood and kills it. The poet draws the analogy to a rural lass transplanted to the city: flattered by attentive beaus, she "obeys the call," only to mourn her fate "when sad repentence comes too late."

True American   June 29, 1822

    The Female Astrologer (A New England Story)

    Leary, L.P., 125   In Freneau's manner.

Rebecca, tired of female toys and aspiring to "masculine" knowledge, buys a book on astrology and convinces herself that an astrological calamity is imminent. A Deacon, however, persuades her to trust nature's plan, to keep her spinning wheel moving, and to read and study less.

True American   July 13, 1822

    Stanzas following an Account of Eleuthra in the Bahamas.

    Leary, L.P., 125   In Freneau's manner.

The prose piece describes a mohogany monument in a cavern, with melancholy stanzas to a young boy who died in 1640. "The subsequent stanzas were written on the aforementioned spot in 1786, but have not appeared in print."

In five stanzas, the poet discusses the folly of placing a monument where so few would ever see it, notes that even great men must die, and concludes by addressing poor sailors—should they perish on the nearby reef, perhaps a friend will mark their graves to tell the world that they have lived.

True American   July 27, 1822

>Margery and Patty. A Boston Dialogue.

Leary, 53	Attributes to Freneau.
420	Included in the Freneau Bibliography for the year 1773.

This poem was included within the essay entitled "Recollections of Past Times and Events, No. II," appearing under the signature "U." The essay describes the Boston Tea Party, the subsequent scarcity of tea, and efforts to find a substitute. The writer then notes that the following dialogue was printed in a "New York Half sheet weekly paper of those days called *The American Whig*," a paper which is not known to have been printed during the years 1773-74.

The poem is a dialogue between Margery and Patty, the former lamenting the lack of tea, the latter persuading her to make the best of things for the good of the cause. The writer of the essay does not claim that the poem was his—he says the paper in which it was printed was "lately recovered in a bundle of old transcripts." However, following naturally from the introduction, it is likely that the poem was written at the time of the essay rather than fifty years earlier. The poem is much in the manner of other later poems ascribed to Freneau (See Possible Attributions, *True American*, October 1, 1824.)

True American   August 10, 1822

>Verse with prose essay.

Marsh, W.P.F., 175	Attributes to Freneau.
Marsh, F.S., 139-40	Text included as Freneau's.
165	Speculates that it may have been written to Frances Bruere, daughter of Bermuda governor, with whom Freneau may have been in love.

This poem appears in the essay "Recollections of Past Times and Events, No. III," signed "F." The essay is an account of Bermuda during the American Revolution, when parties in that country also sought independence from Britain. The writer explains that the following poem, "written, circulated and addressed to a democratic lady of the Island, violent in Republican politics and detesting even the shadow of Royalty," was founded on the tradition that Bermuda was the scene of Shakespear's *Tempest*.

The poem, dated September, 1778, explains that Shakespeare's Miranda stlll lives in this democratic lady, who wishes to see Bermuda made a state. The poet discourages her hopes, until Sycorax appears and predicts that brilliant changes are at hand.

The writer of the essay does not indicate that the poem was his own.

True American   August 17, 1822

>   The New Liberty Pole.--Take Care!

| Leary, 54-55 | Text partially quoted. |
| 420-21 | Included in Freneau Bibliography for the year 1775. |

This poem is included in the essay "Recollections of Past Times and Events, No. IV," signed "R." The essay describes a 1775 Tory attack on a Liberty Pole in New York and the erection of a new one. The verses that follow, according to the author, were read to the crowds when the new pole was dedicated and then were printed on a handbill and circulated throughout the city. The poem consists of a series of threats at whomever might try to strike down the new pole. The author of the essay does not present the poem as his own; following naturally from the prose introduction, the poem appears to have been written with the essay rather than fifty years before.

Fredonian   January 30, 1823

>   The Dying Prophecy of Tecumseh.

| Leary, L.P., 125 | In Freneau's manner. |
| Marsh, 346 | In his style. |

This is a long, rambling speech by the dying Tecumseh, who describes his murderous participation in the War of 1812, when he was bribed by the British to destroy frontier settlements. He predicts the devastation of the British in the war, detailing the victory of Jackson at New Orleans.

True American   January 3, 1824

True-American News-Boys' Annual Address.

Marsh, W.P.F., 174   Apparently by Freneau.

This poem is a typical news carrier's address; nothing distinguishes it as particularly Freneau's.

True American   August 28, 1824

On the Reign of Peace, and improvements in Arts and Sciences, with some lines commemorative of Gen. James J. Wilson, deceased.

Leary, L.P., 125   In Freneau's manner.

This poem begins by condemning those who canonize the dead, heaping more honors on them than they could claim in life. Such "vain show" is insulting to the truly honorable man who has a heart that feels for others and who is content to enjoy his portion and to share the rest with mankind. The remainder of the poem is a tribute to James J. Wilson, here described as one who used the press for its most noble purpose—"to illume the mind." He also is praised as an outstanding senator, shunning rash extremes, and as a soldier.

True American   September 4, 1824

On Signiora Crachami, the Sicilian dwarf Lady, about eighteen and one quarter inches in height; and for several years, past, exhibited as a curiosity, or *lusus naturae*, in London—(The London papers say she died in the Month of May last.)

Leary, L.P., 125   In Freneau's manner.

This is a clever little poem, recalling Swift in its depiction of the world through the eyes of a Lilliputian, "perfect in form and feature," loved like a plaything or fairy. The poet skillfully accounts for her prejudices, derived from her physical distinction. He particularly notes her aversion to men, especially the doctors who have examined her too closely. It reads like a feminine version of Gulliver in Brobdingnag.

True American   September 11, 1824

Submarine Taxation. A Voice from the Sea-Coasts of New-Jersey.

Leary, L.P., 125   In Freneau's manner.

The poet, addressing "men of assemblies," speaks for the desperate oyster and clam harvesters, bidding the legislators to come and see what it is like to be poor, and claiming that the tax will "knock us down dead." He concludes by urging men along the shore to resist the tax.

True American   September 25, 1824

Extract of a Letter from Cadet George to his Cousin Jonathan. West Point, August 28, 1824. (Reprint, *Fredonian*, October 20, 1824)

Leary, L.P., 125   In Freneau's manner.

The cadet writes to his cousin about the anticipated arrival of Marquis de la Fayette, who is expected to take the back way down the Hudson and pass through West Point. George also describes his favorite haunts along the Hudson, which he frequents when he is tired of studying. He describes a hugh rock that for years had rested precariously on the top of a summit, until a bold Yankee Captain, seeing it totter, determined to knock it down with his "engines of art." He managed to complete the task successfully, although the forest was demolished along the rock's course. George regards the incident as proof of the truism that Yankees carry through whatever project they undertake. He concludes by describing the manner in which hordes of women received la Fayette in Manhattan, slightly disappointed because, expecting an angel, they saw a mere man.

Fredonian   September 29, 1824

Lines to the Memory of John Nathan Hutchins, the well known

Appendix B: Possible Attributions 773

Astronomer, who formerly, for about fifty years, Published an Almanack in the middle States (then provinces,) and who died several years ago at a very advanced age, and in very indigent circumstances.

Leary, L.P., 125   In Freneau's manner.

This poem praises Hutchins for his interest in astronomy—for tirelessly marking the movements of moons and planets—and for his commitment to extra-terrestial, unworldly pursuits. The poet concludes by noting the man's proverty, remarking that had he been content to grovel on the ground, he might have been a rich and famous man. The verses specifically echo two of Freneau's earlier poems—"The Almanack Maker," and "Lines on the failure of Mr. Churchman's scheme of going to Baffin's Bay to ascertain the truth of his Variation Chart."

True American   October 1, 1824   (Reprint, *Fredonian*, October 6, 1824)

A Village Dialogue, Between Madame Fly-About and Dorothy Doolittle, her Female Companion.

Leary, L.P., 126   In Freneau's manner.

In this dialogue, on the eve of La Fayette's arrival, Madame Fly-About stews over the rainy weather, fearful that all the fun will be spoiled because she will look like a drowned rat when the Marquis arrives. Dorothy attempts to shake her from the dumps by arguing that La Fayette, a man of good sense, would not be pleased with such peevish complaints. This is very much in the manner of "Margery and Patty.", Possible Attributions, *True American*, July 27, 1822.

True American   October 16, 1824

The Portrait Painter,--On several ill drawn Pictures of men celebrated in American, suspended on the walls of a certain County Hotel, or Tavern.

Leary, L.P., 126   In Freneau's manner.

The poet laments that the portraits are poor likenesses, lacking flesh, blood and soul. He bids the innkeeper to remove them, and to replace them with a new, more lifelike set. One of the old pictures, however, should remain " . . . to give information/That--rotation of Rulers is *Freedom's Salvation.*"

True American   October 30, 1824

    On General De La Fayette's approach at York, in Virginia.

Leary, L.P., 126   In Freneau's manner.

This poem discusses the necessity of war, noting that reason compels the brave man to take arms only in self-defense but that passion commands others to fill the world with woe. The poet praises the bravery of La Fayette and concludes with a stanza suggesting that there is a hidden force which directs and controls events:

    Something *unseen* that guides the game,
    Beyond our utmost skill to name,
    That holds the scales it did create
    And reads alone the Book of Fate.

True American   November 13, 1824

Stanzas, written at a Small House in Chester Street, Philadelphia, occupied some years ago, as a tavern or Beer House; and erected by the famous William Penn about the year 1679, being the first House built on the spot where Philadelphia now stands. (Sept. 20, 1809)

Leary, L.P., 126   In Freneau's manner.

The poet explains that he loves this house erected by Penn because it represents a time for him that can come no more—a time when nations lived as nature meant; when Indians still were innocent; when no city separated the Schuylkill from its native wood. The contrast between that time and the present makes the poet wish that Penn, with his clear conscience and upright mind, were here again.

Fredonian   January 5, 1825

                    New-Year Address
                                      Signed "Printer's Devil."

Appendix B: Possible Attributions 775

Marsh, 347 Partially quoted as a typical Freneau New Years Address.

Nothing distinguishes this address, announcing the apparent victory of Jackson in the 1824 election, as distinctively Freneau's.

True American February 5, 1825

Contemplations, from a view of Saturn's Ring, or the immense material circle that surrounds that Planet at the distance of twenty-one thousand miles from his body.

Reprinted: *Fredonian*, June 13, 1827, entitled "Stanzas on the Solar and Planetary Heavens. "An undevout astronomer is mad."

Marsh, W.P.F., 176-77 Notes only the *True American* text; certainly Freneau's.

A view of Saturn's ring inspires in the poet a strong desire to see more. In nine stanzas he expresses a wish for some direct view of the great Artist who stands forever concealed "Behind the fabrics of his hand!" He finds that every natural object points out some letter of his name—there is not one spot in the heavens where the Creator has not trod "And left the footsteps of a God.--" But, he asks, are his footsteps all that we can see or know? "Should not the Author of its frame/Unveil his face, pronounce his name?" He bids the mists and clouds to disperse if they conceal the throne, but then wonders if God is diffused abroad: "--unseen, unheard, yet ever near." He wonders, then, if there might be some "mysterious art" by which man can "gain His presence to the heart. . . . To hear his whispers soft and kind/In sacred silence of the mind." He commands his thoughts to rest, "--no longer roam,/For God is near, and heaven at home." But still he wishes to feel "his beams of warmest love!/Are they confined to worlds above!" He concludes by asking for a wing to waft him beyond the Evening Star: "Fain would I trace the etherial way/That leads to scenes of endless day."

Fredonian January 4, 1826

The News-Carriers' Address, to the Patrons of the *Fredonian*.

Marsh, 334 Like Freneau; partially quoted.

In this summary of the events of 1825, the poet includes a tribute to the former presidents still living; pleads to Christians to help Greece preserve liberty, without which men are beasts; hopes that the time will come when the Hudson and Delaware Rivers are joined by a canal, enabling people to sail by Princeton; and concludes by hoping that the new year will bring a millenium when fraud and persecution disappear and jails are cleared.

Fredonian   January 25, 1826

To Women.

Marsh, 348   Like Freneau; a translation from A-nacreon.

I could not find this issue of the *Fredonian*; however, it may be in the New Jersey State Library at Trenton.

Fredonian   February 8, 1826; Reprinted, *True American*, March 11, 1826

Macdonough.

Signed "R."

Marsh, 348-49   Partially quoted; can be added to the canon of his known work, according to the initial theory.

This is a three stanza poem developing the contrast between the warrior "nerved in fight" who inspired noble deeds and "waved high the battle brand," and the cold and powerless corpse. The final stanza affirms the immortality of his spirit. For a number of reasons, Freneau's initials in the *Fredonian* and *True American* cannot be trusted as a sole basis for probable attribution after 1824. A close study of both papers for the years 1825 and 1826 reveals his initial appearing with poems that, according to the introductory comments, were written by someone else, or were reprinted from other papers. (See *True American*, November 5, 1825—"Sonnet" by Guido, signed "F."; "From the *Baltimore Patriot*," "Sonnet to Sorrow," signed "F." Also see *Fredonian*, March 15, 1826—"From the New York Commercial Advertiser," "The Rainy Week," Signed "E.") Although possibly Freneau's this poem is not in the manner of later verse ascribed to him. It is brief, condensed, tight, pithy, and strong.

The rhyme pattern is more complex than that employed in the later poetry ascribed to Freneau. Further, in the *True American* reprint, a month later, not one word has been altered, which would make it an exception to every later poem ascribed to Freneau that appeared in both papers. I think it probable either that "R." does not refer to Freneau or that Freneau liked the poem and contributed it to both papers under his initial.

Fredonian   January 31, 1827

>The Monticello Vendue. A Vision.

Marsh, 349   Partially quoted; probably Freneau's.

This long poem in the form of a dream vision ironically describes the auction of Jefferson's property. Objects of priceless historical value are sold off to "dolts and drones," like "throwing pearl to swine."

Fredonian   February 14, 1827

>Peter's Ride to the Wedding.

Marsh, "Freneau's Last Published Poem," *American Literature*, XXX (1958), 103-06.

This is an anecdote about a horse who refused to stir when both Peter and his wife mounted him to go to a wedding. But when Peter pricks him both in the front and rear, the horse arrives in good time—without his load.

Fredonian   April 25, 1827

>The Cricket.
>   Signed "L."

Marsh, 349   Probably a Freneau poem; "L." was a Freneau pseudonym.

A cricket, who first complains about her obscurity and plainness, is reconciled to her fate when she sees some playful boys catch the more colorful butterfly and tear her apart. "L." is not a reliable signature for identifying Freneau's later poems. It never appeared in the *Fredonian* or *True American* between 1821 and 1824, when the majority of probable attributions were published. Other writers apparently were publishing under this signature in the New Jersey papers after 1824. For instance, a long series of poems signed "L.", foreign to the manner of later poems ascribed to Freneau, appeared in the *True American* between February and April, 1825. "The Cricket" might have been penned by the same poet "L." "To a Handsome Young Lady Beset by Flatterers" (March 5, 1825) develops much the same theme as "The Cricket." Both are signed "L." but neither particularly recalls Freneau. Similarly, a poet "L." contributed verses to the *Fredonian* in May of 1827 and June of 1828; Both are long blank verse sentimental effusions, alien to the manner of any poem every penned by or ascribed to Freneau.

Fredonian　　April 25, 1827

Upon Love

Signed "Anacreon."

Marsh, 349　　　　　　　　Probably a Freneau poem; translation of Anacreon.

This poem, possibly a translation, tells of a bee sting suffered by Cupid. Venus consoles him by comparing this minor pain to that suffered by the victims of Cupid's own arrows. Nothing particularly marks the poem as Freneau's.

Fredonian　　May 9, 1827

Moving Day.

In four stanzas, much in the manner of late poems ascribed to Freneau, the poet describes the confusion and vexation of moving day, worse than towns ransacked in wars, or spires wracked by earthquakes. At such a time "Female power usurps the sway/As if it were a nation." The poet hopes that he never again "Shall be compell'd to feel the pain,/The agony of moving." Freneau moved for the last time from his old homestead in Monmouth to a farmhouse eight miles away in 1826.

Fredonian   September 24, 1828

> Hans Petition for the Purchase of An Old Chestnut Tree.

The poet explains that he refuses to sell his dying chestnut tree because it and he have grown old together: "In the spot where I now am reclined in the shade,/In the days of George (Second) I frolick'd & played." He explains that, unlike other, more ambitious men, he is not one to sell either his tree or his soul. The poem distinctively recalls Freneau both in subject and manner.

Monmouth Enquirer   July 7, 1829

> The Vale of Obscurity.

John F. Collins, "Two Last Poems of Philip Freneau," *Early American Literature*, 7 (1972), 111-19.

> Text included, attributes to Freneau.

This poem, much in the manner of later verse ascribed to Freneau, recommends contentment with an obscure life as the noblest virtue. An active public life is admirable only when it is committed to the good of the country, "with others' benefit in view," not when it is motivated by a desire to spread one's name through the pages of history. The poet praises Washington, who quit the public scene as soon as his work was complete, and concludes with several lines describing the various beauties of the rural scene.

Appendix C

UNLIKELY OR ERRONEOUS ATTRIBUTIONS

New Jersey Gazette   December 13, 1780

> Verses to the Memory of Captain Nicholas Biddle, of the Randolph Frigate 32 guns, blown up in an engagement with Yarmouth, a British man of war of 64 guns.
>
> Signed "W.S."

Leary, 75, 85, 424   Mistaken for Freneau's poem on Biddle; included in the Freneau Bibliography.

Leary confused this poem on Biddle with Freneau's poem "On the Death of Captain N. Biddle, who was blown up in the Randolph Frigate," which first appeared with the 1781 *British Prison Ship*. Biddle's biographer, William B. Clark, attributes the *New Jersey Gazette* poem on Biddle to Biddle's cousin, William Scull, (*Captain Dauntless*, Baton Rouge, 1949, 251-52.) Although obviously similar in subject matter, the two poems are completely different in their treatment of it. However, there are clear parallels between the first two lines of each and between several lines that appear later in the poems, which may ssuggest that the poem by "W.S.", published in December of 1780, inspired Freneau's composition, which first appeared in March, 1781:

> What dread explosion rends the distant skies!
> What sulph'rous flames in spiral volumes rise!
> (W.S.'s poem, lines 1-2)

> What distant thunders rend the skies,
> What clouds of smoke in columns rise,
> (Freneau's poem, lines 1-2)

Near the end of W.S.'s poem appears an image of Biddle's ascension:

> Mounting in air amidst his warlike crew,
> To Heav'n's blest seats heroick *Biddle* flew;

Freneau includes a similar image, similarly phrased, in stanzas X and XIII of the 1781 text:

> Let her brave lads demand thy care,
> To Heaven's blest seats bid them repair,--
>
> But Mars his flaming arrow threw--
> To heaven triumphant Biddle flew, ...

Freeman's Journal   July 23, 1783

To the Memory of Charles Lee, who died in America, having served more Nations than Britain.

Marsh, W.P.F., 109	Notes *Jersey Chronicle* text; Probably by Freneau.
Leary, 406	Atrribution implied—attributes poems signed "F." in the *Fredonian* to Freneau.

Marsh attributed this mildly cynical yet sympathetic poem on the character of Charles Lee to Freneau on the basis of its later appearance in the *Jersey Chronicle*, April 16, 1796. However, it first appeared in the *Freeman's Journal* in 1783, shortly after Lee died. An introductory note explains that it was extracted from the London *St. James's Chronicle*, and a later appearance in the *Massachusetts Centinel* also is printed under the heading "From a London Paper." I have not seen the *St. James's Chronicle* for 1783, but the title appearing with the *Freeman's Journal* text—"who died in America, having served more nations than Britain,"—tends to confirm the British source, as does the fact that Lee was born and raised in England. These lines, apparently not Freneau's originally, must have appealed to him, since he reprinted them in the *Jersey Chronicle* under the title "Lines written some years ago to the memory of general Charles Lee, an officer well known in the history of the American Revolution, and in whom posterity will, perhaps, pronounce a different sentence from that of his contemporaries" and in the *Time-Piece* under the titled "Lines Written after the Death of General Charles Lee." Finally, they were later contributed to the

Fredonian on February 6, 1828, under the signature "F.", and titled "Lines on General Charles Lee, a character well known in the American Revolution." In the *Fredonian*, the poem appears as the latter half of a longer poem on Lee, to which introductory verses, more in Freneau's manner, have been added. This is a significant example of the possible dangers of ascribing to Freneau and editing as his poems that were signed with his initials, but that he never collected as his own. He appears not to have regarded the pseudonym as a declaration of complete originality.

State Gazette of South Carolina   January 28, 1788

On the New Constitution

Louie M. Miner, *Our Rude Forefathers*, Cedar Rapids, 1937, p. 203.

Tentative attribution.

Leary, 383   Cites source of the attribution.

Referring to this poem, which was reprinted in several northern papers, Miner notes that a voice "very like Freneau's" spoke out in Charleston in opposition to the new federal constitution. Leary remarks that the poem is in Freneau's manner and that Freneau was in Charleston at the time, but he is skeptical of the attribution because the poem never was collected and because none of Freneau's known poems ever appeared in this paper.

Freneau was contributing known verse exclusively to the *City Gazette* in 1788, and none of his verses during this period has any direct bearing on political affairs. The writer of this poem was engaged deeply in the debate over the Constitution and assumes a rigid anti-Federalist view of the situation:

> When *13* states are moulded into *one*
> Your rights are vanish'd and your honors gone.

I think it unlikely that, at this busy point in his nautical career, Freneau could have formulated such a strong partisan position on the Constitution issue. Further, I doubt that he ever would have voiced such a dogmatic position against a strong federal union. Though he would find occasion to lash out at particular federalists for "monarchal tendencies," much of his later writing indicates that he never lost faith in the value of a strong federal union, first inspired by the revolutionary struggle.

American Museum   January, 1787

The Death Song of a Cherokee Indian.

Pattee, II, 313   Ascribed to Freneau on the basis of Matthew Carey's attribution in the *American Museum*. Full text edited as Freneau's.

This poem was not attributed to Freneau in the first and second editions of the *American Museum*, Vol. I, January-June, 1787, both of which I have seen. The attribution to Freneau apparently appeared in the third edition, the preface of which was dated July 20, 1790, but which I have not seen (See F.E. Farley in *Anniversary Papers by the Colleagues and Pupils of George Lyman Kittredge*, Boston, 1913, 251-60.) In his note to the poem, Pattee remarks that it appeared among the verses of Mrs. John Hunter in 1806, yet still attributes the poem to Freneau. However, I found it, unattributed, in papers to which Freneau never was known to contribute as early as 1785. It appeared in the *Charleston Evening Gazette* on September 20, 1785, under the title "Death Song of a Cherokee Chief" and under the same title in the *Massachusetts Spy* on September 22, 1785. It also appeared in the *Boston Gazette* on February 26, 1787 under the title "The Indian Chief."

Daily Advertiser   April 12, 1790

Fidelity.

Marsh, 124   Probably by Freneau.

This poem praises the sailor's loyalty to his native land. When captive to a foreign prince, he refuses to bend to the tyrant, but remains true, in his heart at least, to his native prince. The only possible reason for linking this poem with Freneau is that it is about a sailor, but it has little in common with any of his other poems on seamen, one of the more popular themes in newspaper verse of the period. Almost always, Freneau's sailors are disassociated, in some manner, from the land—either comically, by their distaste for the responsibilities of settled life, or, seriously, by their exposure to perils unknown to those on land. Such a view is foreign to the theme of pious patriotism described in this poem as the sailor's supreme virtue.

Daily Advertiser   February 15, 1791

The Physician and his Patient
(Translated from the French.)

Leary, 385   In his manner.

This is a two stanza dialogue in which a patient, forbidden love, wine, and friends by his doctor, says he would prefer to die. Leary bases the attribution on the poem's appearance in the *Daily Advertiser* at this time, when Freneau still was contributing heavily to the paper, but the poem can be found nearly four years earlier in the *Pennsylvania Evening Herald*, August 6, 1787, a paper to which Freneau never was known to contribute.

Freeman's Journal   August 31, 1791

An Heroic Tale
Translated from the French of Monsieur la Fontaine, the Younger.

Marsh, W.P.F., 68, 141   Much like Freneau.

This is a playful and irreverent account of the French King and Queen's attempt to leave France. The poem is quite unlike anything penned by Freneau or any other American poet of the period. The verse pattern is extremely elaborate and intricate, and the tone of assured and super-sophisticated suavity is unlike that of any native writer.

National Gazette   March 29, 1792

Occasioned by the Debate this day, in the House of Representatives, On the Amendment proposed by Mr. Key to the Bill for establishing a Mint, which originated in the Senate.

Leary, 202   Quoted as Freneau's.

Marsh, 155; W.P.F., 71   Unqualified attribution to Freneau.

When this poem, which attacks the amendment to print the likeness of Washington on federal coins as monarchal, appeared in Matthew Carey's *American Museum* for June of 1792, under the title "Lines occasioned by a debate in the house of representatives of the United States, on the subject of having the likeness of the president impressed upon federal coins," it was attributed to "a member of Congress from one of the southern states." Although Carey's attributions were not always correct—he attributed at least one poem to Freneau that was not his—all of Freneau's poems that appeared in the *Museum* were either unattributed or correctly attributed; none ever was attributed to anyone else. The poem could have been written by any anti-federalist poet. Conventional phrases—references to Liberty as "celestial maid"—as well as the low-keyed and unaggressively sincere tone, are somewhat foreign to the manner of Freneau's satire, which typically bites harder.

National Gazette   April 19, 1792

An Old Story New Dressed.

Signed "A.B."

Leary, 388   Indicates his authorship.

This six-line anecdote about a hen-pecked husband who thoroughly enjoyed the funeral of his wife was reprinted in other papers of the period under a variety of pseudonyms. The signature "A.B." was employed by Freneau on several occasions, but it is one that he shared with other contributors of the period. (See Marsh's article, "The Francis Hopkinson Quarrel," *Proceedings of the New Jersey Historical Society*, LXXIV (1956), 304-14, for evidence that Hopkinson was using this signature during the period.) "A.B." had contributed an earlier poem to the *National Gazette*, on January 23, 1792, entitled "A Kind of Epigram," with a covering note asking Freneau to insert it. A simple and pointless analogy between the creation myth in Genesis and the working pace of Congress, this earlier poem by "A.B." has never been ascribed to Freneau.

Appendix C: Unlikely or Erroneous Attributions

National Gazette   May 8, 1793

       Extempore.
            Signed "C."

Leary, 260   Notes appearance in the *Jersey Chronicle*, August 15, 1795; In Freneau's manner.

Although reprinted in the *Jersey Chronicle* under the title "The History of Monarchy," this poem, describing how Satan sent monarchs to plague mankind until France rose to revenge and sent them home, first appeared in the *National Gazette*. The earlier text never has been ascribed to Freneau. He never used the signature "C." for any known poem, but it was among the more widely used in the period. The text, however, was revised somewhat when reprinted in the *Chronicle*: the title was changed to indicate the precise subject of the poem; the one long, irregular stanza with sporadically indented lines was broken up into regular quatrains; a few words in the original text were changed; and four additional lines (one whole quatrain) were inserted in the middle of the text. As this stanza merely repeats what was said, in different words, immediately before and after it in the original text, it might well have been added by the editor to fill up the column evenly. I suspect that this poem appealed to Freneau when it first was contributed to the *National Gazette* and that he used it again, with minor changes, in the *Chronicle*.

New York Journal   May 11, 1793

       A New Song.

Leary, 457   Included in the Freneau Bibliography as the earliest newspaper appearance of Freneau's "Ode," *Poems*, 1795, 445-56.

Marsh, W.P.F., 75   Describes the poem as the first newspaper appearance of "Ode."

(See Edition, *Federal Gazette*, June 3, 1793.)

This poem first appeared in the *Baltimore Daily Repository* on April 20, 1793, where it was attributed to a British source. One full stanza and six additional lines of this text appear in Freneau's "Ode," first printed in the *Federal Gazette* on June 3, 1793. The rest of the poem was never collected by Freneau. Leary and Marsh have confused this text, which was widely reprinted in the 1790's, with Freneau's "Ode," with which it has only several lines in common.

National Gazette   May 25, 1793

    Verse with Prose Piece.

Marsh, F.P.P., 484

This is not really a poem—just a prose epitaph, printed in a "tombstone meter."

National Gazette   July 17, 1793

    The Royalist and the Republican.

Marsh, W.P.F., 114   Notes a later appearance in the *Time-Piece*; probably Freneau's.

Marsh noted a later appearance of this poem in the *Time-Piece* on April 26, 1797, but it actually first appeared, under a different title, in the *North Carolina Journal* on July 3, 1793. There the poem was titled "The Lion and the Tarapen," and was signed " 'Columbus,' Halifax, July, 1793." The poem was reprinted two weeks later in the *National Gazette*, but the title was altered to "The Royalist and the Republican," lending a political implication to this mock heroic account of a battle between the kingly and lowly beasts. Also, several colorful lines were added to the original text, and several other lines were slightly revised. A survey of poems reprinted from other sources in the *National Gazette* and other papers edited by Freneau suggests that he frequently may have been inspired to "touch up" poems in this manner.

National Gazette   October 2, 1793

    Untitled pro-French ode, appearing with an editorial.

Marsh, 147   Notes later appearance in the *Time-*

Appendix C: Unlikely or Erroneous Attributions

Marsh, W.P.F., 114-15
Marsh, F.P.P., 696

Piece; Probably by Freneau.
Text quoted as Freneau's.

Marsh noted an appearance of this pro-French poem in the *Time-Piece* on April 26, 1797, but it appeared earlier in the *National Gazette* on this date, within quotation marks, and with a note stating that it was extracted from the *Virginia Chronicle*, where it first appeared as "ODE," on September 21, 1793. It is interesting to note how the original Virginia text was altered when it appeared two weeks later in the *National Gazette*. The stanza form was completely altered, a repetitious chorus was deleted, several lines were slightly revised, and two grammar errors were corrected. The poem appears in the *Time-Piece* at the conclusion of a pro-French editorial "from a correspondent." The text reflects the *National Gazette* substantive revisions, but the stanza form is different from both earlier texts.

National Gazette   October 2, 1793

Poem on the death of General Moreau.

Charles Batten, "A Newly Discovered Poem by Philip Freneau on the Death of General Moreau," *American Literature*, 44 (1972), 457-59.

In this article Batten ascribes to Freneau a two-stanza poem discovered in his autograph in his copy of *Brydone's Tour through Sicily and Malta*. The poem appears under a note about the death of General Moreau (1813), and Batten dates the poem at about 1815. However, the second of these two stanzas appeared twenty-one years earlier in the *National Gazette*, within quotations, under the heading "Extract," where, along with another stanza, it concludes an essay on death. The same stanza also appeared in the *Time-Piece* on March 31, 1797 in a longer poem, entitled "On the Folly of War and Heroism," attributed to "The Late King of Prussia." This poem contains the other stanza that had appeared in the *National Gazette* extract, and is probably the poem from which that extract originally was taken. Translations of poems attributed to Frederick II were popular in newspapers of the period, usually extracted from British periodicals. Thus as least one stanza, the second, discovered by Batten in Freneau's autograph appears to have been derivative. The first stanza, since it refers specifically to Moreau, or to some fighter drawn repeatedly back to war, may have been composed on the occasion of his death as I have not found it earlier. Freneau may then have recalled the other stanza, which discusses the vanity of ambition, and which had been printed twice before in papers he had edited, as particularly suitable to the occasion. Both the *Time-Piece* and autograph texts of the stanza vary slightly from the original *National Gazette* text; in the earliest text, the vainly ambitious man is bound by "pleasure's flowery wreaths; in the *Time-Piece*, by "Victory's golden chain;" and in the autograph, by "Wild Ambition's power." Not only did Freneau reprint this stanza twice, but he almost directly paraphrased it in one of his original poems, "On the Tomb of Patriots" (*Poems*, 1815, 31-37.) Stanza three of this poem is an extended paraphrase, in entirely original lines, of this same stanza, and the other stanza that was printed with it in the original *National Gazette* extract.

Jersey Chronicle   December 5, 1795

        Epitaph on Dr. Monsey.

Leary, 260   In Freneau's manner.

This is a mildly cynical epitaph, in which the speaker, now dead, denies any interest in another life, since he has had enough in this one. It appeared and was reprinted widely in papers before 1795. Usually it was attributed to "Peter Pindar" (British poet, John Wilcot). See, for instance, *New York Daily Gazette*, September 11, 1789. Freneau printed it again in the *Time-Piece* on July 7, 1797.

Jersey Chronicle   December 19, 1795

        An Epitaph on a Hermit.

Leary, 260   In Freneau's manner.

This light epitaph on a hermit about whom little was known appeared in several newspapers, to which Freneau never was known to contribute, before it was printed in the *Chronicle*. See the *Richmond and Manchester Advertiser*, September 10, 1795; Philadelphia *Minerva*, September 12, 1795; and the *Connecticut Courant*, November 23, 1795.

Appendix C: Unlikely or Erroneous Attributions 791

Jersey Chronicle   March 26, 1796

Stanzas Written some years ago to the Memory of Miss Field, a young lady of North Carolina."

Leary, 260   In Freneau's manner.

In these four stanzas the poet expresses his "ecstasy of speechless joy" in his assurance of the afterlife, and plays in each stanza on the name "Field." Though death has robbed him of his Field, it cannot destroy the happy Field of heaven. This is quite unlike Freneau, both in its Christian tone and its overworked pun. It was reprinted, however, in the *Time-Piece* on March 27, 1797.

Time-Piece   June 2, 1797

To Matilda.
Signed "The Slave."

Marsh, 214   Almost acknowledged by an editorial direction—a reply to a letter defending Washington's ownership of slaves.

Marsh, W.P.F., 115   Probably Freneau's.

This poem is part of a series of poems appearing in the *Time-Piece* in May and June of 1797. The series began on May 24 with a poem entitled "The Vindication," signed "Matilda," a long and rambling poem in couplets defending Washington's ownership of slaves against recent attacks. Matilda laments the institution of slavery but argues that it is too dangerous to free slaves until they all are educated. The poem, appearing on June, 2, attacks Matilda for defending the perpetuation of slavery for any reason and reiterates the criticism of Washington. The long poem is not much in the manner of Freneau, and the main basis of Marsh's attribution, that it was written in reply to an earlier poem, is not compelling. As the *Time-Piece* appeared tri-weekly, there would have been adequate time between May 24 and June 2 for a correspondent to reply to the earlier poem. There are other examples of poetry dialogues conducted among correspondents to the *Time-Piece* on other themes. Marsh also bases the attribution on Freneau's lifelong disapproval of slavery. We recall Freneau's earlier poems and prose passages condemning the brutal treatment of slaves in the West Indies by the British, but he was not vocal on the institution in America. As slaves apparently were used to work the Freneau farm (Leary, 319), he would be guilty of rather blatant hypocrisy in blaming Washington for the same thing.

Time-Piece   June 2, 1797

Bermuda.

Marsh, W.P.F., 116	Partially quoted; clearly Freneau's.
147	Resembles "The Beauties of Santa Cruz."

This poem is extracted from Waller's "Battle of the Summer Islands."

Time-Piece   June 9, 1797

To Matilda.
Signed "Saparinc."

Marsh, W.P.F., 116	Another reply to Matilda, apparently by Freneau.
147	The reply is so prompt, it must have been the editor's.

These three stanzas are another response to Matilda's reservations with respect to immediate abolition, making the point that if slavery is wrong, as Matilda had acknowledged, then it is always wrong, and to defend it for any period of time is a disgrace. Marsh attributes this poem, dated June 8, to Freneau, assuming that it is a response to Matilda's second poem, which appeared on June 7 and which particularly argued for gradual abolition. No one, he argues, but the editor could have replied so rapidly. However, the same argument for gradual abolition also appeared in Matilda's May 24th poem. Since nothing in this poem specifically refers to the Matilda poem of June 7, it easily could have been another reply, by a third correspondent, to the May 24th poem. As there is no evidence that Freneau contributed to this exchange on the slavery issue, and as this poem takes an unambiguous stand for the immediate abolition of slavery in America, a position we find expressed nowhere in his known writings, I consider the attribution unlikely.

Appendix C: Unlikely or Erroneous Attributions   793

Time-Piece   June 12, 1797

                       To Matilda.
                       Signed "The Slave."

Marsh, W.P.F., 116   Attributed to Freneau by the signature, also used in the June 2 poem attributed to Freneau.

This long anti-slave poem concludes the series as a final retort to Matilda. It argues that slavery is a repudiation of all the values defended in the American fight for freedom. It is most unlike Freneau in manner, commencing with an allusion to the inspired voices of Old Testament prophets and an appeal to the muses for the same power to utter fiery truths.

Time-Piece   September 15, 1797

               Verse appearing with an editorial.

Marsh, 243   Partially quoted as evidence of Freneau's disapproval of monasteries; might be called "The Lost Louisa."

Marsh, W.P.F., 13   Among the dozen or so of Freneau's lyrics worth preserving; ranks with the best in American poetry.
121   Demonstrates that Freneau found time for tenderness; might be called "The Lost Louisa."

Marsh, F.S., 120-21   Includes text as Freneau's, contributing the title "The Lost Louisa."
162   Notes appearance in the *Time-Piece* and describes content of editorial in which it appeared.

Marsh, F.P.P., 738

This poem appears at the conclusion of an editorial hailing the dissolution of monasteries and the unnatural incarceration of young women. The essay concludes, "The following lines were written some years ago, on a beautiful young woman, who by the tyranny of her father was shut up in the monastery of Santa Clara, in the island of Madeira; and affords a striking example of a convent." Actually, these lines first were published in 1792 in a novel entitled *Vancenza, or the Dangers of Cruelty* (Dublin, 1792, 206-07) by Mrs. Mary Robinson. The poems of Mary Robinson, British actress, novelist, and poet, were reprinted widely in America, and excerpts from this novel, including the chapter containing this poem, appeared in several newspapers of the period. (See New York *Weekly Museum*, July 12, 1794 and February 26, 1814; *New Jersey Journal*, August 9, 1797, under the title "The Tears of a Nun, or A Picture of a Convent"—this could have been Freneau's source, since he remarks that the poem affords "a striking picture of a convent;" and Philadelphia *Minerva*, August 19, 1979.) The novel was set in Avignon, not Madeira, and this poem was recited by a wandering pilgrim who fell in love with the nun.

Time-Piece   September 20, 1797

      Untitled Poem against Cobbett.
                                      Signed "Patronella."

Marsh, W.P.F., 121   Apparently Freneau's.

This is an eleven stanza narrative describing the pitiful return of the beaten British troops after the revolution. "Discord," furious at the indignity, commands them to find the most uncouth and venomous youth, to school him in scurility and to send him to Columbia to set up a press and shamelessly assault virtue. After a long search, Plutus finds the boy in obscurity's den and sends him to America. This long narrative is both more elaborate and more low-keyed than any of Freneau's attacks on Fenno or Cobbett. "Patronella" had already contributed light anecdotes to the *Time-Piece* that have never been attributed to Freneau.

Time-Piece   December 22, 1797

      Address to the New Invented Eagle
                                        Signed "Jonathan."

Marsh, F.P.P., 804   Certainly Freneau's.
Marsh, W.P.F., 128, 149

Appendix C: Unlikely or Erroneous Attributions

This long, seven stanza ode is included in a letter addressed to "Messrs. Freneau and Davis," describing a painting of an eagle and Washington. The poet proposes to praise it in his ode, hoping that the poem will conduct him to the heaven of immortal fame along with the eagle. The poem is quite unlike any penned by Freneau, and since it is included in a letter to the editors, there seems to be little reason for attributing it to him.

Aurora   February 23, 1801   (Reprint, March 3, 1801)

    A Song--Tune, Anacreon in Heaven.

Marsh, 281   Notes only the March 3, 1801 reprint of this poem and attributes it to Freneau along with another poem in the same issue.

Marsh noted the second *Aurora* reprint of this song, celebrating the election of Jefferson as the triumph of freedom. But when it first appeared on February 23, the introductory note states that it was composed for and sung at the celebration of Jefferson's election in Petersburgh, Virginia.

Aurora   March 6, 1801

    The People's Friend.

Marsh, W.P.F., 138-39, 151   Quoted as Freneau's.

These five stanzas and chorus are a song which, according to the introductory note, was sung at a service in the German Reformed Church in Philadelphia in celebration of Jefferson's inauguration. They celebrate the commencement of hope and joy and the advancement of art and science with the inauguration of Jefferson. A conventional victory song, nothing about it recalls Freneau.

Aurora   August 30, 1804

    Verse with prose.

Marsh, F.P.P., 937

This four-line epigram included in a "Joe Bunker" essay appears within quotation marks. A cynical definition of "Friendship," it probably was extracted or adapted from another source.

Aurora   February 15, 1810

>Verse with prose piece by Strophel Funk."

Marsh, F.P.P., 1035

This essay, ironically praising Governor Snyder, includes two lines of verse within quotation marks, introduced as if derived or adapted from another source ("in the language of *Rogers* . . .")

True American   November 23, 1812

>The Navy.
>   dated "Monmouth, November 15, 1812."

Leary, 403   In Freneau's manner.

This is a ballad recalling American naval victories and describing them through the voice of a lofty bard who will inscribe them in the annals of fame. Naval heroes and their victories are cited by name as part of the bard's splendid story. The bard's song is intended to inspire in the souls of patriots the "warmth and fire of prophecy," lifting the eternal veil, revealing Columbia in distant days as "mistress of the ocean." A number of naval tributes appeared in the *True American* during this period. Despite the fact that this one is from Monmouth, the loose ballad form and the "bardic" stance are most unlike Freneau.

Aurora   October 9, 1815

>A Congratulatory Ode to the Impenetrable Idol of Corruption.
>   Signed "Sam Short."

Marsh, W.P.F., 167, 169   Partially quoted; "probably Freneau's.

These are three stanzas accusing Governor Snyder of covert corruption. They are not in the manner of Freneau or of any practiced poet, due to the unusual and forced contractions employed to main-

Appendix C: Unlikely or Erroneous Attributions 797

tain the meter.

True American   October 15, 1825

The German to his Sword.
Signed "R."

Leary did not include this poem in his Freneau Bibliography, because his *True American* attributions stop in 1824, but according to his theory of signatures for later poems, this one should be ascribed to Freneau. However, as noted elsewhere (see Possible Attributions, February 8, 1826), Freneau's initials are not a reliable basis for probable attributions after 1824 in the two New Jersey papers. This poem, in which a German bids his gory sword rest until the fatherland again is threatened, bears little resemblance to any of the later poems ascribed to Freneau.

Fredonian   February 1, 1826

Grecian Liberty
Signed "P."

Marsh, 248   Like Freneau.

This poem was reprinted in the *Fredonian* from the *U.S. Literary Gazette*, a paper to which Freneau never was known to contribute. He never used the signature "P." for any known poem, but it appears to have been used by other contributors of the period. The poem is quite unlike any of Freneau's collected verses and any of the later poetry attributed to him. Highly metaphoric, the stanzas employ a complex rhyme scheme and many run on lines. It is a more "literary" and "high brow" effort than anything attributed to Freneau during these years.

Fredonian   November 7, 1827

Hebrew Melody.
Signed "R."

Although not noted by Leary, who discontinues his *Fredonian* attributions in 1824, this poem, signed "R.", would be a probable ascription on the basis of his attribution theory. As I have noted elsewhere, (See Possible Attributions, 1825-26) Freneau's initials are not a reliable basis for making attributions after 1824, except for the series of poems appearing from July, 1827 to February, 1828, all signed exclusively "F." (See Probable Attributions, July 11, 1827.) This poem, an imitation of Byron's "Hebrew Melodies," describes the incorruptible soul of an exotically beautiful Jewish woman sold into Assyrian slavery. It is alien in concept and development to later poetry ascribed to Freneau.

Bibliography of Newspapers Cited in the Edition and Appendixes

The following list, containing all newspapers cited in the edition and appendixes, including footnotes, is provided for any reader who wishes to check the original of any text duplicated or mentioned in this edition. I have provided the locations where I found the original, photostat, or microform of all issues of each newspaper cited in this edition. The libraries cited may not have the complete holdings of the newspapers, but they have at least all of the issues cited in this edition. In many cases, the papers can be located in other libraries as well. The newspapers are listed alphabetically, by the titles under which they are cited in this edition. If the town or city of publication is part of the title—the name of the city or town is italicized in the edition—it will be alphabetized by the name of the city. If it is not a part of the newspaper title, I have provided the name of the city or town of publication in parentheses after the newspaper title.

American Mercury (Hartford, Connecticut): Library of Congress.

American Museum (Philadelphia) 1787: University of Maryland, McKeldin Library; 1787-1792: Library of Congress.

Argus (New York): Library of Congress.

Aurora (Philadelphia): Library of Congress.

Bailey's Pocket Almanack (Philadelphia): University of Maryland, McKeldin Library; 1784: New York Historical Society.

Baltimore Daily Repository: Maryland Historical Society.

Boston Gazette: Library of Congress

Carey's Daily Advertiser (Philadelphia): Library Company of Philadelphia.

Carey's U. S. Recorder (Philadelphia): Library of Congress.

Centinel of Freedom (Newark): Library of Congress.

Charleston Evening Gazette: Charleston Library Society.

City Gazette (Charleston): Charleston Library Society; 1789: New York Public Library.

Columbian (New York): Library of Congress.

Columbian Centinel (Boston): Library of Congress.

Columbian Herald (Charleston): Charleston Library Society.

Columbian Repository (Washington D.C.): Harvard University.

Connecticut Courant (Hartford): Library of Congress.

Constitutional Gazette (New York): New York Historical Society.

Daily Advertiser (New York): Library of Congress.

Daily Advertiser (Philadelphia): Library Company of Philadelphia.

Evening Post (New York): Library of Congress.

Federal Gazette (Philadelphia): Library of Congress.

Fredonian (New Brunswick) 1811-1820's: Rutgers (New Brunswick); 1821-1828: Library of Congress.

Freeman's Journal (Philadelphia): Library of Congress; January, 1789 and January, 1790: American Antiquarian Society.

Gazette of the United States (New York and Philadelphia): Library of Congress.

General Advertiser (Philadelphia): Library of Congress.

Independent Chronicle (Boston): Library of Congress.

Independent Gazetteer (Philadelphia): Library of Congress.

Independent Ledger (Boston): Library of Congress.

Jersey Chronicle (Mount Pleasant): Library of Congress; July 11, 1795: Monmouth County Historical Association.

Kentucky Gazette (Lexington): Library of Congress.

Maryland Gazette (Baltimore): Maryland Historical Society.

Maryland Journal (Baltimore): Library of Congress.

Massachusetts Centinel (Baltimore): Library of Congress.

Massachusetts Spy (Worcester): University of Maryland, McKeldin Library.

Minerva (Philadelphia): Library of Congress.

Monmouth Enquirer (Freehold, New Jersey): Monmouth County Historical Association.

Monmouth Star (Freehold, New Jersey): New Jersey Historical Society.

National Gazette (Philadelphia): Library of Congress.

New Hampshire Journal (Walpole): Library of Congress.

New Jersey Gazette (Trenton): Library of Congress.

New Jersey Journal (Elizabeth): New Jersey Historical Society.

New York Daily Gazette: New York Historical Society.

New York Gazetteer: Library of Congress.

New York Journal: Library of Congress; 1809: New York Historical Society.

New York Statesman: Library of Congress.

Norfolk and Portsmouth Journal (Norfolk): Library of Congress.

North Carolina Journal (Halifax): Library of Congress.

Packet (New York): Library of Congress.

Pennsylvania Democrat (Philadelphia): Library of Congress.

Pennsylvania Evening Herald (Philadelphia): Library of Congress.

Pennsylvania Packet (Philadelphia): Library of Congress.

Port Folio (Philadelphia, New York): Library of Congress.

Public Advertiser (New York): Library of Congress; May, 1809 and 1812: New York Historical Society.

Republican (Savannah): Library of Congress.

Richmond and Manchester Advertiser (Richmond): Library of Congress.

Royal Gazette (New York): University of Maryland, McKeldin Library.

South Carolina State Gazette (Charleston): Charleston Library Society.

State Gazette of South Carolina (Charleston): Charleston Library Society.

Time-Piece (New York): Library of Congress.

True American (Trenton): 1801-1820's: New Jersey State Library; 1820-1828: Library of Congress.

U.S. Magazine (Philadelphia): Library of Congress.

Virginia Chronicle (Norfolk): Library of Congress.

Weekly Museum (New York): Library of Congress; August, 1801: New York Historical Society; October 1801: American Antiquarian Society.

Weekly Visitor (New York): Library of Congress.

Bibliography of All Newspapers Examined

The newspapers are listed alphabetically, by state, city, and the title under which they are cited in Brigham's *Bibliography of American Newspapers, 1690-1820*, and *The Union List of Newspapers*. I have not indicated changes that occurred in newspaper titles during the period of my survey. All of these are listed in the two bibliographies just cited; I have used the main title under which the papers are listed in those bibliographies. Each title is followed by the years for which I examined the paper. In a few cases, when a paper published little or no poetry, or when complete holdings were not accessible, my survey of the years listed was scattered.

Connecticut

    Danbury

    Farmer's Journal 1790-1793

    Fairfield

    Fairfield Gazette 1786-1789

    Hartford

    American Mercury 1784-1812
    Connecticut Courant 1777-1815

    New London

    Bee 1797-1800

Delaware

    Wilmington

    Delaware and Eastern Shore Advertiser 1794-1799

Georgia

    Augusta

    Augusta Chronicle 1789-1809

    Savannah

    Columbian Museum 1796-1809
    Gazette of the State of Georgia 1783-1788
    Georgia Gazette 1788-1802
    Georgia Republican 1802-1809
    Savannah Daily Republican 1803-1810

Kentucky

    Lexington

    Kentucky Gazette 1787-1800

Maryland

    Baltimore

    American and Commercial Advertiser 1808-1810
    Baltimore Daily Repository 1791-1793
    Baltimore Evening Post 1806, 1808-1810
    Baltimore Telegraph 1805
    Federal Gazette 1796-1810
    Federal Republican 1808-1810
    Maryland Gazette 1784-1790
    Maryland Journal 1786-1794
    North American and Mercantile Advertiser 1808-1809
    Republican, or Anti-Democrat 1802

Massachusetts

    Boston

    American Apollo 1792-1794
    American Herald 1784-1788
    Argus 1791-1793

Boston Gazette 1778-1798
Boston Gazette 1784-1790
Columbian Centinel 1790-1815
Continental Journal 1784-1786
Exchange Advertiser 1785
Herald of Freedom 1788-1791
Independent Chronicle 1782-1809
Independent Ledger 1778-1786
Massachusetts Centinel 1784-1790
Massachusetts Gazette 1785-1788

Charleston

American Recorder and Charleston Advertiser 1785-1787

Worcester

Massachusetts Spy 1791-1809

New Hampshire

Walpole

Farmer's Weekly Museum 1797-1810
New Hampshire Journal 1793-1797

New Jersey

Bridgetown

Plain Dealer 1775-1776

Burlington

Burlington Advertiser 1790-1791
New Jersey Gazette 1777-1778
The Rural Visitor 1810-1811

Elizabeth

New Jersey Journal 1779-1815

Freehold

Monmouth Inquirer 1829
Monmouth Star 1819-1820

Morristown

Genius of Liberty 1798-1811
Morris County Gazette 1797-1798
Palladium of Liberty 1798-1811

Mount Holly

New Jersey Mirror 1820-1824

Mount Pleasant

Jersey Chronicle 1795-1796

Newark

Centinel of Freedom 1796-1820
Modern Spectator 1807-1808
Newark Gazette 1797-1804
New Jersey Telescopy 1808-1809
New York Gazette 1776

New Brunswick

Brunswick Gazette 1787-1792
Fredonian 1811-1828
Guardian 1792-1807
Political Intelligencer 1783-1786

Trenton

Miscellany 1805
New Jersey Gazette 1778-1786
New Jersey State Gazette 1792-1798
New Jersey State Gazette 1799-1800
State Gazette and New Jersey Advertiser 1796-1799
Trenton Federalist 1798-1815

True American 1801-1828

New York

New York

American Citizen 1801-1810
American Minerva 1793-1796
Argus 1795-1800
Catskill Packet 1792-1794
Chronicle Express 1802-1804
Columbian 1809-1821
Columbian Gazetteer 1793-1794
Commercial Advertiser 1797-1815
Constitutional Gazette 1775-1776
Daily Advertiser 1785-1804
Daily Advertiser 1808-1809
Diary 1792-1798
Evening Post 1801-1820
Forlorn Hope 1800
Impartial Gazetteer 1788
Independent Gazette 1784
Independent Journal 1783-1788
Mercantile Advertiser 1798-1815
Military Monitor 1812-1813
Minerva 1796-1797
The National Advocate 1813-1815
New York Corrector 1804
New York Daily Gazette 1788-1795
New York Evening Post 1794-1795
New York Gazette and General Advertiser 1795-1815
New York Gazette and Weekly Mercury 1775-1783
New York Gazetteer 1783-1787
New York Herald 1794-1797
New York Herald 1802-1817
New York Journal 1784-1800; 1809-1811
New York Morning Chronicle 1802-1807
New York Morning Post 1783-1788
New York Morning Post 1810-1812
New York Packet 1783-1792
New York Remembrancer 1805
New York Spy 1806-1807

New York Statesman 1822-1826
New York Weekly Chronicle 1795
New York Weekly Inspector 1806-1807
Observer 1809-1811
Olio 1813-1814
L'Oracle 1808
The People's Friend 1806-1807
Port Folio 1801-1827
Public Advertiser 1807-1813
Royal Gazette 1777-1783
Shamrock 1810-1815
Spectator 1797-1815
Standard of Union 1813-1814
Temple of Reason 1800-1801
Time-Piece 1797-1798
The War 1812-1814; 1917
Weekly Museum 1788-1817
Weekly Visitor 1817-1822
Weekly Visitor or Ladies Miscellany 1802-1807

Poughkeepsie

American Farmer 1798-1800

North Carolina

Edentown

State Gazette of North Carolina 1788-1799

Halifax

North Carolina Journal 1792-1799

New Bern

North Caroline Gazette 1787-1798

Pennsylvania

Philadelphia

Bibliography of All Newspapers Examined

American Daily Advertiser (Dunlap's) 1791-1795
American Museum 1787-1792
Aurora 1794-1830
Bailey's Pocket Almanack 1784-1800
Bureau 1812
Carey's Daily Advertiser 1797
Carey's U.S. Recorder 1798
Complete Counting House Companion 1785-1788
Constitutional Diary 1799-1800
Democratic Press 1807-1815
Evening Chronicle 1787
Federal Gazette 1788-1793
Findlay's American Naval and Commercial Register 1795-1798
Freeman's Journal 1781-1792
Freeman's Journal 1804-1815
Gazette of the United States 1789-1804
General Advertiser 1790-1794
Independent Gazetteer 1782-1796
Level of Europe 1794-1795
Mail, or, Claypoole's Daily Advertiser 1791-1793
Merchant's Daily Advertiser 1797-1798
National Gazette 1791-1793
The New World 1796-1797
Pennsylvania Democrat 1809-1810
Pennsylvania Evenine Herald 1785-1788
Pennsylvania Evening Post 1775-1784
Pennsylvania Gazette 1775-1815
Pennsylvania Ledger 1775-1778
Pennsylvania Journal 1775-1789
Pennsylvania Mercury 1775
Pennsylvania Mercury 1784-1792
Pennsylvania Packet 1778-1790
Philadelphia Evening Post 1804
Philadelphia Gazette 1794-1808
Philadelphia Minerva 1795-1798
Philadelphia Repository and Weekly Register 1800-1806
Philadelphia True American 1798-1815
Political and Commercial Register 1804-1815
Porcupine's Gazette 1797-1799
Poulson's American Daily Advertiser 1800-1815
Relf's Philadelphia Gazette 1803-1815
Spirit of the Press 1808

Temple of Reason 1801-1803
Tickler 1807-1813
U.S. Gazette 1804-1809
U.S. Magazine 1779
Universal Gazette 1797-1800
Weekly Monitor 1804
Whig Chronicle 1812

South Carolina

Charleston

Carolina Gazette 1801-1811
Charleston Courier 1803-1810
Charleston Evening Gazette 1785-1786
Charleston Morning Post 1786-1787
Charleston Times 1800-1809
City Gazette 1787-1809
Columbian Herald 1784-1796
Gazette of the State of South Carolina 1783-1784
Investigator 1812-1814
South Carolina Gazette and General Advertiser 1783-1784
South Carolina State Gazette 1794-1802
South Carolina Weekly Gazette 1783-1786
State Gazette of South Carolina 1785-1793

Virginia

Fredericksburg

Virginia Herald 1788-1790; 1800-1810
Norfolk Herald 1801-1803
Norfolk and Portsmouth Journal 1787-1789
Virginia Chronicle 1792-1794

Richmond

Enquirer 1804-1810
Examiner 1801-1803
Richmond and Manchester Advertiser 1795
Spirit of 76 1808-1809
Virginia Argus 1801-1810

Virginia Gazette 1799-1810
Virginia Gazette and General Advertiser 1790-1799
Virginia Gazette and Richmond and Manchester Advertiser 1793-1795
Virginia Gazette, or, the American Advertiser 1782-1786
Virginia Independent Chronicle 1787-1790
Virginia Patriot 1809-1810

INDEX OF POEMS

Poems the full texts of which are included in the edition are listed by the title of the earliest newspaper texts. Untitled poems are listed under the first collected title, with a notation that they originally appeared untitled.

Address to Misfortune, 304-305
Address of the Republicans of America, 583-584
The Almanack Maker, 289-291
The American Soldier (A Picture from the Life), 414-415
The American War-Hawk, 581-582
The Author and the Critic, 281-283
An Author's Soliloquy (Untitled), 661-662

A Bacchanalian Dialogue. Written in 1803 (Untitled), 665-667
The Battle of Stonington, 670-671
The Beauties of Santa Cruz (Untitled), 41-47
Bedlow Island, 415-416
The Bergen Planter, 400-402
The Bird at Sea (Untitled), 352-254
The Blessings of the Poppy, 412
The Book of Odes
    No. IV.   To Pest-Eli-Hali, A democratic Printer, on the western banks of the Hudson, 595-596
    No. VI.   To the Learned Pig, 596-597
    No. VIII.   To Thos. Swawcum, a Wharf Builder, 597-598
    No. X.   To Santone Samuel, the Millenial Prophet, on his System of Universal Pacification, 599-600
    No. XI.   To the Philadelphia Doctors, 601-602
    No. XII.   To the Philadelphia Doctors, 602-604
Botony Bay. Lines occasioned by Federal threats to take up and send off certain Patriotic characters to Botony Bay, 625-626
The British Prison Ship, 78

A characteristic sketch of the Long Island Dutch (From the Rising Empire, a poem), 363-365
Charity A-La-Mode, 444-446
A College Story (Appertaining to Secret History), 612-613
A Columbian Dialogue. Supposed to have been written by Capt. Freneau, 365-366
Columbus to Ferdinand, 50-51
Constantia (Untitled), 387-389
Copy of an intercepted Letter from a New-York Tory, to his Friend in this city, 85
The Country Printer, 477-482
A Curious Dialogue (Occasioned by the Emblematical Devices on a certain Travelling-Coach.), 507-508

Democracy, 619-621
The Departure (Written at Leaving Sandy-Hook on a voyage to the West Indies), 297-299
Description of Connecticut, 390-391
A Description of Pennsylvania, 380-381
A Descriptive Sketch of Maryland, 372-373
A Descriptive Sketch of Virginia, 393-395
The Deserted Farm House, 250-252
The Desolate Academy, 284
A Dialogue at Hyde-Park Corner, 126-127
A Dialogue at Washington's Tomb. Between the Genius of Virginia and Virginia, 673-674
A Dialogue between his Britannic Majesty and Mr. Fox. Supposed to have passed about the time of the approach of the combined Fleets of France and Spain to the British Coasts, about 1779, 70-77
A Dialogue between Lords Donmore and Mansfield, 86
A Dialogue between Whaacum and Whiffle, 537
The Drunkard's Apology, 461-462
The Drunken Soldier, 274
The Dying Elm. An irregular Ode., 49
The Dying Indian; or the Last Words of Shalum, 205-208

Elegaic stanzas to the Memory of Edward Tutledge, Esq. late Governor of the State of South-Carolina, 632-633
Elegaic Verses on the Death of a favourite Dog, 237-239
Elegaic Verses on a Man that was killed by a Cow, 604

Elegy on the Death of a Blacksmith, 542-544
The English Quixote of 1778; or, Modern Idolatry, 137-139
Epigram occasioned by the title of Rivington's Royal Gazette being scarcely legible, 107-108
An Epistle from Lord Cornwallis to Sir Henry Clinton, 88-89
Epitaph intended for the tombstone of Patrick Bay, an Irish Soldier and Inn-holder, killed by an ignorant physician, 248-249
Epitaph on Frederick the second, late king of Prussia (Untitled), 476
Epitaph on a Sea Captain that Shot Himself, 575
The Exile, 319-322

The Fair Buckle-Thief, 490-491
Farmer Dobbin's Complaint, 360-361
Federal Hall, 373-375
The Five Ages, 241-243
The Flagellators, 150-151
The following lines are addressed to the Foe of Tyrants, in the Independent Gazetteer of Saturday by a Foe to Malice, 156
The following lines were addressed to a gay young Lady that was courted by a grave religious Lover, and far advanced in years, 413-414
Fourth of July–An Ode (Untitled), 627-628

The High-Minded Apprentice, A Tale, 607-608
Horace, Lib. II. Ode 16. Imitated and addressed to Governor Parr, 307-309
The House of Night; Or, Six Hours Lodging with Death. A Vision, 55-68
Hugh Gaine's Life, 174-181
Humanity and Ingratitude; A Common Case (Translated from the Mercure de France), 211-214

Independence, 497
The Indian Student, or Force of Nature, 301-303
The Insolvent's Release, or Miseries of a Country Jail, 294-296
The Invalid, Written in 1785, 322-323
The Island Field Negro, 421-423
The Island Savage, 438-439

The Jug of Rum, 430-434

Kay-Grove, 443
King George the Third's Soliloquy, 47-49

The Landlord's Soliloquy, 458-560
Lines, Addressed to the inhabitants of a village, in one of the Southern States, some of whom, in a nocturnal revel, gouged out the eyes of an itinerant Fiddler, 639-640
Lines Addressed to Mr. Jefferson, On his Approaching Retirement from the Presidency of the United States, 662-665
Lines Addressed To a very little Man, who was fond of walking with a very large Cane, 544-545
Lines formerly written in a tavern in Log-Town, a small place in the Pine Barrens of North Carolina, 343-351
Lines intended for Mr. Peale's Exhibition, May 10, 1784, 208-211
Lines occasioned by the Death of General Joseph Reed–March 5, 1785 (Untitled), 240-241
Lines occasioned by The Death of Mr. Robert Bell, the celebrated humourist, and truly philanthropic Bookseller, formerly of Philadelphia, 293-294
Lines occasioned by General Robertson's Proclamation, New-York, June 22, 1782 (Untitled), 143-144
Lines Occasioned by the late disaster of one of the Paulas Hook passage-boat's upsetting from which accident one of our citizens was drowned and the remainder on board narrowly escaped, 667-668
Lines occaseioned by Mr. Rivington's new titular Types to his Royal Gazette, 113-114
Lines Occasioned by reading Mr. Paine's Rights of Man, 456-457
Lines Occasioned by the Skeletons dug up in Fort George, 395-396
Lines occasioned by a visit to an old Indian burying ground, 311-314
Lines on the failure of Mr. Churchman's scheme of going to Baffin's Bay to ascertain the truth of his Variation Chart, 423-425
Lines on the Federal City, 634-635
Lines on the loss of the ship Albion, Capt. Williams, Wrecked near Kinsale Harbor, in Ireland, on the 22d of April Last, 678-682
Lines written at the Pallisades, near Port-Royal, in the Island of Jamaica–September, 1784, 261-262
Lines Writtes at Sea. Addressed to Miss ---, New Jersey, 332-335
Lines Written for Mr. Ricketts, on the Exhibitions at his Equestran Circus (Untitled), 569-570
Lines Written in a severe February on a Shad, &c. caught in a mild January (Untitled), 522

Lines written on a passage from New-York to the island of Madeira, addressed to Calista on shore, 570-572
Lines written several years ago, and intended to have been engraved on a Tomb Stone under an Oak Tree, where a despairing Lover had hanged himself, 554-555
Lines written some years ago on the death of a Fiddler. Addressed to Mrs. ---, 449-450
Literary Importation, 259-260
The Literary Plunderers, 233-236
Lord Dunmore's Petition to the Legislature of Virginia, 105-107
The Lost Adventurer, 270-271
The Loyalists, 52-54

The Man of Ninety: or, a Visit to the Oak, 367
The Market Maid, 419-420
Marriage A-la-Mode, 439-440
May to April, 300
Melancholy reflections in passing by a burying ground in the neighbourhood of Philadelphia, 584
Minerva's Advice, 464-466
A Mistake Rectified, 471-473
Modern Devotion, 324-325
A Modern Tale, 610-611
The Monument of Phaon, 253-256
A Moral Thought, 89

Nabby, the New York House-Maid, to Nanny, her friend in Philadelphia, 402-403
Nanny, the Philadelphia House Maid, to Nabby, her friend in New York, 399-400
The Newsmonger, 265-270
New-York, 189-191
A New-York Tory's Epistle to one of his Friends in Pennsylvania--Written previous to his departure for Nova Scotia, 185-188

Ode for the Fourth of July. To be Sung Tuesday next at the New Dutch Church, by the Uranian Society, 576-579
Odes on Various Subjects
    Ode I.   On the Fourteenth of July, 498-499

Index of Poems 817

Ode II. Addressed to Crispin O'Connor, Esq. a backwoods planter, 500-501
Ode III. 504-505
Ode IV. To the National Gazette, 505-506
Ode. To the Americans. That the progress of liberty in the world, considering the present state of things, cannot be impeded, or its complete establishment prevented, 613-616
Ode to the Echo Writer, 483-484
Ode to Liberty, 523-527
Of Thomas Swaugum, an Oneida Indian, and a Missionary Parson, 609-610
An Old Heathen Story Adapted to Modern Times, 508-509
On the American and French Revolution, 367-369
On the Approaching Dissolution of Transatlantic Jurisdiction in America, 546-547
On a Bee Drinking from a Glass of Wine, 582-583
On the Causes of Political Degeneracy, 621-623
On City Burying Places (Untitled), 166
On the Crew of a certain Vessel, several of whom happened to be of the same name with celebrated clergymen, 454-456
On Deborah Gannet, The American Heroine, who on Tuesday last presented a petition to Congress, for a pension in consideration of services rendered during the whole of the late war, in the character of a common soldier, in the regular armies of America, 605-606
On the Demolition of Dartmouth College, 383-385
On the fall of general earl Cornwallis, who, with above eight thousand men, surrendered themselves prisoners of war to the renowned and illustrious general George Washington, commander in chief of the allied armies of France and America, on the memorable 19th of October, 1781, 90-95
On a Fly, fluttering round a Candle, 608-609
On the French Republicans (Untitled), 514
On hearing a remarkably dull discourse, of near two hours in length, from a rambling lay-preacher in the back woods of North-Carolina, 572-573
On the Honourable Emanuel Swedenborg's Universal Theology, 278-280
On a Lady's Singing Bird, a native of the Canary Islands, confined in a very small cage: Written in Bermuda, 1778, 141-142
On a late memorable naval engagement, 539-541
On the late royal sloop of war Gen. Monk (formerly the Washington) mounting six quarter deck wooden guns, 127-128
On the Launching of the Frigate Constitution (Untitled), 591
On Mr. Rivington's new engraved King's Arms to his Royal Gazette, 114
On National Prospects and Improvements, 683-685

On a Painter, who was endeavouring to recover from memory the features & portrait of a Lady, who died at sea. Written 1788, 466-467
On the present state of the theatre in Charleston, 357-360
On the present state of Rivers, 482-483
On the Progress of the French Armies in Italy, 568
On prohibiting the sale of Dr. David Ramsay's History of the Revolution of South-Carolina, in London, 280-281
On the prohibition of Spiritous Liquors in the New-York and Albany Jails, 442
On the proposed American Negotiation with the French Republic, 573-575
On the proposed demolition of Fort George, in this city, 369-371
On the proposed taxation of News-Papers, 434-435
On Putting a Dog ashore at the island of Sapola for Stealing: written 1778, 441
On the Royal Portraits, in the Senate Chamber, 518
On Sir Henry Clinton's Recall, 131-134
On the Sleep of Plants (A curious new discovery), 381-382
On the too Remote Extension of American Commerce, 557-558
On a very Small Garden Belonging to a Citizen of N.Y., 579-580
On a View of the Planet Jupiter and his Moons through a large telescope, 635-638
On a young lady who wore in her cap, iron wire conductors, on the plan of Dr. Brydone, to guard against the effects of lightning, 563
The Orator of the Woods (Occasioned by hearing a very elegant discourse preached in a mean Building, by the Parson of an obscure Parish, 397-398
The Order of the Day. (Occasioned by a Lady shedding tears on reading "A brief account of the Battles of the present century,"), 592-594
Orlando's Flight, 541-542

Palemon to Lavinia (Untitled), 410-411
A Parody of Sappho's Ode: Blest as the immortal Gods is he, &c. Addressed to Old England, 314-316
The Parting Glass, Written at an Inn, 467-469
Patriotic Stanzas on the Anniversary of the Storming of the Bastille, at Paris, July 14th, 1789, 533-534
Pewter Platter Alley: A Poem, 239-240
Philosophical Reflections, 146-148
Philosophical Sketch of America, 375-376
The Pilot of Hatteras, 336-340
Plato the Philosopher to his friend Theon, 97-99

A Poem on the memorable victory obtained by the gallant capt. Paul Jones, of the Good Man Richard, over the Seraphis, &c. under the command of capt. Pearson, 79-82
The Poetaster, 257-259
Poetical Address, 555-557
Poetical Address to the Public of the United States, 470-471
The Political Balance; or, the Fates of Britain and America compared. A Tale, 116-123
The Political Weathercock (Untitled), 594
Pamposo and his Printer, 462-464
The Prayer of Orpheus, 323
Present View of France and her Combined Enemies, 514-517
The Prince Regent's Resolve, 675-676
Prince William Henry's Soliloquy, 148-150
The Prisoner, 263-264
The Procession to Columbia, 354-355
The progress of Balloons, 220-224
The Projectors, 140-141
Prologue. Written to a Theatrical Entertainment in Philadelphia, 100-101
A Prophecy (Untitled), 115
The Prophecy of King Tammany, 162-164
The Prudent Philosopher (Occasioned by the conduct of some gentlemen at the conflagration of a certain Southern Court-House, during the sessions), 473-475
Psal. cxxxvii. Imitated, 68-69
The Pyramid of the Fifteen American States (Untitled), 513-514

Quintilian to Lycidas, 545-546

Reflections on Credit, 327-330
Reflections on the Death of a Country Printer: (By his Partner and Successor), 532-533
Reflections on Dr. Perkins Metallic Rods, 565
Reflections on Gage's Letter to General Washington, of Aug. 13, 39-40
Reflections on the General Debased Condition of Mankind, 585-590
Reflections, on walking over the ground on Long-Island, near New-York, where many Americans were interred from the Prison Ships, during the war with Great-Britain, Written July, 1802, 561-655
The Refugees Petition to Sir Guy Carleton, 154
The Removal, 404-405

The Republic and Liberty, 617-619
The Republican Genius of Europe, 547-548
Retirement, 627
The Rival Suitors for America, 548-553
Rivington's Confession Addressed to the Whigs of New York, 197-204
Rivington's Last Will and Testament, (A true copy from the Records), 110-113
Rivington's Reflections, 160-162; 168-170
The Roguish Shoemaker, In Imitation of Watt's Indian Philosopher, 275-278
The Royal Adventurer, 103-104
A Royal Dialogue, 676-677
The Rural Bachelor. A Real Character, 451-452

The Sabbath-Day Chace (Untitled), 377-379
St. Preux to Eloisa, 296-297
Satan's Remonstrance. (Occasioned by Mr. Rivington's late Apology for Lying), 152-153
Scandinavian War Song (Untitled), 136-137
The Scornful Lady, 305-306
The Sea-faring Bachelor, 319
The Seasons Moralized, 232-233
The Shelbourne Threat (A true Story), 428-429
Sir Guy Carleton's Address to the Americans, 134-136
Sir Guy's Answer, 155
Sir Harry's Call, 124-125
Sketches of America History, 215-219, 224-229
Song, 528-532
Song on Captain Barney's victory over the ship General Monk (Untitled), 128-131
The Speculator, 509-510
A Speech that should have been spoken by the king of the island of Britain to his Parliament, 108-110
Stanzas Occasioned by the Death of Dr. Franklin, 387
Stanzas Occasioned by the Death of General George Washington, 628-630
Stanzas occasioned by the departure of the British from Charlestown, 181-183
Stanzas, occasioned by the King's speech, recommending Peace with the American States--March, 1783 (Untitled), 184-185
Stanzas occasioned by the ruins of a country Inn, unroofed and blown down in a storm, 102-103

Stanzas occasioned by some illiberal reflections in Fenno's Gazette of the United States of the 18th ult of the Feast of Reason, given by upwards of one hundred patriotic citizens of New-York, to Citizen Monroe, in testimony of their esteem of his character, public as well as private, 580-581
Stanzas on the Emmigration to America, and peopling the Western Country, 230-232
Stanzas on South Carolina, 641-644
Stanzas on a Young Lady in a Consumption, 287-289
Stanzas to the memory of Mrs. Gertrude Burnet, who died at Newark, in Essex County, New-Jersey on the 4th of May, 1791, 452-453
Stanzas to the Memory of two young persons (twin brothers) Robert Sevier and William Sevier, who were killed by the Savages on Cumberland River, in North-Carolina, in attempting to assist a new settler, who was then passing the river with a numerous family (Untitled), 501-503
Stanzas written at Baltimore in Maryland, January, 1789. By Capt. P. Freneau, To Cynthia, 362-363
Stanzas Written at the Island of Madeira in April last, on the fatal and unprecedented torrents of water which collected from the Mountains, on the 9th of October, 1803, destroyed a considerable part of the city of Funchal, and damaged, to a great amount, several plantations, towns, and villages in that neighbourhood, 655-659
Stanzas written at Oratava, in view of the Peak of Teneriffe, 1804, 660-661
Stanzas written at St. Catherine's, an island upon the coast of Georgia, Nov. 1789, 355-356
Stanzas written In a blank leaf of Burke's History of the West India Islands (Untitled), 284-286
Stanzas Written on the Hills of Neverskink, near Sandy Hook, 1790, 417-419
Stanzas written, several years since, on the first American ship (Empress of China, Capt. Greene) that explored the route to the East Indies and China, after the Revolution, 566-567
The Student's Complaint, 272

The Tea-Drinker, 426-427
The tenth Ode of Horace's Book of Epodes, imitated. Written in December, 1781, upon the departure of gen. Arnold from New York, 145-146
Thetis: or the Heroine; a Character, 564-565
The Third Epistle of the First Book of Ovid's Tristia. Translated from the

original Latin, 645-651
Thomas and Susan. An Irish-town dialogue.--(Suitable to the times), 291-293
To the Americans, 559-560
To an Alien, 624-625
To an Angry Zealot: (In Answer to Sundry Virulent Charges) (Untitled), 511
To the Democratic Editors, on a Charge of Bribery (Untitled), 585
To the Foe to Tyrants, 157
To the Foe to Tyrants on his Farewell in the Independent Gazetteer of the 7th inst., 158
To the Great--the Warlike--the Independent Americans, 243-246
To Harriot, 342
To his Excellency General Washington, 82-84
To John Dickinson, Esq., 331-332
To Justice. An abusive Scribbler, 535-536
To Justice (A Writer in the Gazette of the United States), 537-538
To the Keeper of the King's Water-Works, near Rock-Fort, in Jamaica; on being refused a Puncheon of Fresh Water, Written, August 1784, 446-447
To the Ladies, 408-409
To Lord Cornwallis, 87
To Lydia (Untitled), 316-318
To the Memory of the Brave, Accomplished and Patriotic Col. John Laurens, Who, in the 27th year of his age, was killed in an engagement with a detachment of the British from Charleston, near the river Cambahee, in South Carolina, August, 1782 (Untitled), 310-311
To the memory of the brave Americans, under general Greene, who fell in the action of September 8, 1781, 96
To the Memory of General George Washington, 630-631
To Mr. Blanchard; the Celebrated Aeronaut, on his ascent in a Balloon, from the jail-yard in Philadelphia: 1793 (Untitled), 520-522
To a Noisy Politician (Untitled), 519
To the Squadrons on the Lakes, 672
To Sylvius. On his preparing to leave the town (Untitled), 437-438
To those whom it may Concern, 159
To Those Whom It May Concern (Untitled), 167
Tormentina's Complaint. Written at Cape Hatteras, June 1789, 406-407

The Useful only in Vogue at Court, 435-436
A Usurer's Prayer (Untitled), 592

Verses From the other World, by Dr. Fr--k--n, 391-392
Verses, made at Sea, in a Heavy Gale, 246-248
Verses occasioned by General Washington's arrival in this city, on his way to his Seat in Virginia, 191-197
A View of Columbia, 340-341
A View of Massachusetts, 385-386
The Village of Merchant, 485-489; 492-496
The Virtue of Tobacco, 325-327
The Volunteer's March, 669-670

Warning to the Western Fiddling General, 560-562
The Wild Honey Suckle, 273
Written on a Beau drowned in a Mill Road, 447-448

LIBRARY OF DAVIDSON

Books on regular loan may be checked
must be presented at the Circulati

A fine is charged after da

Special